AF691783

FINRA SIE PrepPro

SIE Exam Preparation Guide

Mastering FINRA SIE: Your Comprehensive Exam Prep Guide with 3000+ Questions Bank & Detailed Answer Explanations for the Securities Industry Essentials (SIE) Exam

P. Anshu
BFSI Domain Trainer
MFP, CFP, CAM, FIII, FINRA 6/7/24/66, NLP, Six-Sigma
Trainer for All FINRA Certification Exams

It's the Power of Network, Not Net-Worth! – P. Anshu

Copyright © 2023 by P. Anshu

All rights reserved. No part of this book may be used or reproduced in any form whatsoever without written permission except in the case of brief quotations in critical articles or reviews.
For more information, or to book an event, contact:
http://www.GurukulOnRoad.com

Book design by P. Anshu
Cover Design & Edited by Shivi & Kriti

ISBN - Paperback: Awaiting
1st Edition: December 2023

2X POWERS TO YOU IN THIS BOOK

FINRA SIE Exam Preparation Guide - FINRA SIE PrepPro designed as an "Interactive Learning: Questions and Answers for SIE exam" This book is your comprehensive self-paced guide to mastering the intricacies of SIE exam through an engaging question-answer format. Designed to cater to different learning styles, this resource allows learners to enhance their knowledge and test their understanding without the need for additional study materials. Each section presents a series of thought-provoking questions followed by helpful hints, allowing you to hone your critical thinking skills and reinforce key concepts. After attempting each question, review the correct answers and detailed explanations, providing valuable insights and enhancing your comprehension. This interactive approach ensures a dynamic learning experience, combining the benefits of simulated quizzes with the depth of study materials. This book is your go-to resource for effective and engaging learning. Get ready to challenge yourself, learn from mistakes, and deepen your understanding of concepts & test objectives of SIE exam in an interactive and stimulating manner. Wish you a great success for your exam in 2024.

POWER 1: HINTS: Unlock the power of hints!

Each question in this book comes with a "HINTS". Hints are strategically crafted to gently guide you in the right direction, nudging your thought process without giving away the solution entirely. Think of them as friendly nudges from a mentor, providing valuable insights to help you navigate the problem. Embrace the hints and let them illuminate the path to understanding. They're not just clues; they're your allies in conquering complexity and mastering the art of problem-solving. Happy hinting! When you encounter a question with hints, consider it your secret weapon for overcoming challenges.

POWER 2. EXPLANATIONS: Double Power for Your Success!!

Apart from HINTS, another tool is given to you for your success in **FINRA SIE Exam** is Explanations along with correct answers for all tests. After each test the correct answer sheet is given along with Explanations, which are crucial for learners for several reasons:

- **Understanding the Concept:** Explanations provide a deeper understanding of the underlying concept or principle for each test objective of **FINRA SIE Exam**. Learners can grasp not just the answer but the reasoning and logic behind it.

- **Clarification of Doubts:** Learners may have misconceptions or doubts about certain Learning Outcome required to achieve through **FINRA SIE Exam**. Explanations help address these doubts, ensuring that learners have a clear and accurate understanding.

- **Application of Knowledge:** Explanations show how the learned concept is applied in a particular context in **FINRA SIE Exam** This helps learners see the practical relevance of the knowledge and how it can be used in real-world situations.

- **Critical Thinking**: By providing explanations, learners are encouraged to think critically about the subject matter for **FINRA SIE Exam**. They can analyze the information, connect it to other concepts, and develop a more comprehensive understanding.

- **Most Imp. Retention and Memory:** Understanding the 'why' behind an answer enhances memory retention. Learners are more likely to remember information when they understand the reasons and logic behind it, rather than memorizing isolated facts. This will surely be an advantage for **FINRA SIE Exam**.

- **Building Confidence:** Clear explanations build confidence in learners before they go for final **FINRA SIE Exam**. When they understand the material thoroughly, they feel more confident in their ability to apply their knowledge in different situations.

Explanations play a vital role in the learning process by providing clarity, fostering understanding, and empowering learners to apply their knowledge effectively for sure success in real **FINRA SIE Exam**. They transform learning from a memorization task into a meaningful and engaging exploration of concepts.

ABOUT THIS BOOK

Unlock your success in the Securities Industry Essentials (SIE) Exam with the **"FINRA SIE Exam Preparation Guide: 3000+ Questions Bank."** This comprehensive resource is your ultimate interactive learning companion, offering a vast array of questions and answers to master the intricacies of the financial world. With over 3000+ questions, meticulously crafted to cover each learning outcome, this guide ensures a thorough understanding of the exam content. Divided into four units, it navigates through the essential domains: Knowledge of Capital Market, Understanding Products and Their Risks, Trading, Customer Accounts, & Prohibited Activities, and Overview of the Regulatory Framework.

Authored by P. Anshu, a qualified finance professional and seasoned BFSI Domain Trainer holding credentials such as MFP, CFP, CAM, FIII, and multiple FINRA certifications (6/7/24/66), this guide reflects the expertise needed to succeed. The author's extensive experience as a trainer for all FINRA Certification Exams adds a practical edge, ensuring that the content is not only comprehensive but also tailored for effective exam preparation. Each learning outcome features a minimum of 15 and a maximum of 100 questions, allowing learners to test their knowledge progressively.

Whether you're a candidate preparing for the SIE exam or a financial professional seeking a robust review, this guide is your go-to resource for interactive learning. Dive into a wealth of questions, review detailed answer explanations, and embark on a journey to mastering the FINRA SIE exam.

This publication, dated December 2023, represents the concepts covered as per content outline available on FINRA website accessed dated 1st Nov 2023.

Upcoming Mastery Test Series:

Dear learners, I am happy to inform you that by the time you finished this QnA mode study guide for FINRA SIE exam, I will be presenting you a mastery test series in February 2024. The Mastery test series is consisting of 25+ Mastery assessment test simulating the real exam, each covering the whole test objective of FINRA SIE exam. So be ready and happy learning.

ABOUT THE AUTHOR

Anshu, a passionate Six-Sigma Certified corporate trainer, qualified financial planner, driven by an objective to achieve & empower financial inclusion through quality education with a fundamental principle of "Earn living hood by serving". Equipped with over a decades of national & international financial industry experience specialized in area of operation, training & Content development.

Numerous contributions have been made by him in the field, being associated with world renowned organizations, NGOs, Educational Institute & Consultants. Also serving as visiting Faculty to various financial academic institution & Global Advisor: American Academy of Financial Management® Presidential Board, AAFM® Board of Standards.

He is a passionate traveller, travelled all Indian states & union territories as road trip, covering around 5lkh+ kilometres. His travel story on road begins with a quote "Design rather than default", was the great saying which somehow shaken him since childhood. It's been told to him that; he was born on road… Yes true! Since the time of birth, he got his graduation as BBA (Born Before Arrival at the hospital). Probably it was the 1st unconditional decision taken by him to come out into this world. The Love for ROAD & Travel is inherited from the creation itself.

It was not well known to all that ROADs would have a major role to play in later stage of his life. Life moved on the way it was supposed to as everyone moves, with imposed conditionings. It's always been told to him "You cannot always choose how, when and even where?". But for him Its **Journey is the Destination**.

ACKNOWLEDGMENTS

I would like to express my heartfelt gratitude to all those who contributed to the creation of this book. Your support, encouragement, and expertise have been invaluable throughout this journey. I am deeply thankful to my family & friends for their unwavering support and understanding during the long hours and late nights spent writing and researching. Your patience and belief in me kept me motivated.

I extend my appreciation to my friends and colleagues who provided valuable insights, feedback, and inspiration. Your diverse perspectives enriched the content of this book. A special thank you to my sweet twin partner in creativity **Shivi & Kriti** for editing & designing a beautiful cover.

Finally, I express my gratitude to the learners, students and readers. Your interest and engagement with this book make all the effort worthwhile. I wish you a great success in your upcoming FINRA SIE Exam.

FREE RESOURCES

@TabarKiKhushi : A new age YouTube channel helping learners in publishing good quality exam related quiz, hence we have given them 2000+ additional question bank for each FINRA SIE Exam and they are publishing those in form of quiz video. We recommend you go through those free quizzes to increase your chances of passing the exam in first attempt.

Channel Link: https://www.youtube.com/@TabarkiKhushi
Instagram Link: https://www.instagram.com/tabarkhushi/

Gurukul On Road:
www.GurukulOnRoad.com This is my website going live in beginning 2024 and will be publishing Practice Test, Mock Test on through this website.

OTHER REGULATORY EXAM PREPARATION BOOKS BY AUTHOR

1. NISM Exam Preparation Guide | NISM Series V A Mutual Fund Distributors Exam | Practice & Mock Test | 500+ Question Bank: Mastering the NISM-Series-V-A: Mutual Fund Distributors Certification Exam
2. NISM Exam Preparation Guide for NISM-Series-VIII: Equity Derivatives Certification Exam Practice & Mock Test: Mastering the NISM Exam with 600+ Questions
3. NISM Exam Preparation Guide for NISM-Series-XXI-A: Portfolio Management Services (PMS) Distributors Certification Examination
4. NISM Exam Preparation Guide for NISM-Series-X-A-Investment Adviser
5. III Licentiate Exam Preparation Guide | IC 01 PRINCIPLES OF INSURANCE for Insurance Institute of India Exams
6. All Indian Financial Market Regulator NISM Certification Exams
7. FINRA Series 6, 7, & 24 Exam Preparation Guide

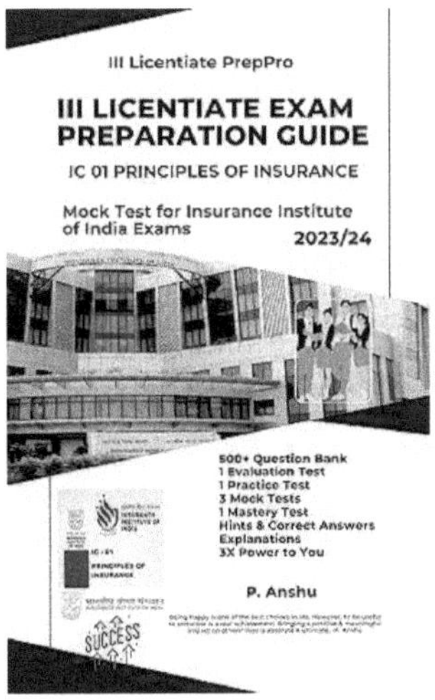

TABALE OF CONTENT

TEST OBJECTIVES & LEARNING OUTCOMES COVERED
3000+ QUESTIONS

UNIT 1 Knowledge of Capital Market (750+ Questions)

This UNIT is designed to provide learners with a comprehensive understanding of the primary and secondary financial markets, the key participants involved, and the regulatory frameworks governing the securities industry. Additionally, the module covers essential economic indicators and their impact on financial markets. The whole module is designed as study guide in QnA mode using 750+ MCQs. Hence you can start topic with QnA which will also solve the purpose of reading materials. The following test objectives are covered under UNIT 1

1. Understand the role and significance of primary markets in the issuance of securities.
2. Explore various types of primary market offerings, including initial public offerings (IPOs) and seasoned equity offerings (SEOs).
3. Identify and comprehend the roles of different stakeholders in the primary market.
4. Examine the steps involved in offering a nonexempt security issue.
5. Define shelf offerings and green shoe offerings and their relevance in the securities market.
6. Explore exemptions in the issuance process and the entities that qualify for such exemptions.
7. Understand the importance and variations of disclosure documents in the securities issuance process.
8. Comprehend the functions and importance of secondary markets in the trading of existing securities.
9. Identify key participants in secondary markets and their roles.
10. Differentiate between exchanges and over-the-counter (OTC) markets and understand their dynamics.
11. Explore the regulatory role and authority of the SEC in the securities industry.
12. Name the branches of the Treasury with regulatory oversight over the securities industry.
13. Understand the role of the Federal Reserve Bank in monetary policy and financial stability.
14. Determine the protections offered by the Federal Deposit Insurance Corporation (FDIC).
15. Define state administrators and their association (NASAA) in the regulation of securities at the state level.
16. Understand the scope of authority of FINRA in regulating securities firms and professionals.
17. Recognize the Municipal Securities Rulemaking Board's authority and enforcement capabilities.
18. Understand the regulatory authority of exchanges in overseeing market activities.
19. Define and understand Gross Domestic Product (GDP), Consumer Price Index (CPI), and Gross National Product (GNP) as key economic indicators.
20. Explore leading, coincident, and lagging indicators and their role in forecasting economic trends.
21. Define and distinguish between different economic conditions: inflation, deflation, stagnation, and hyperinflation.
22. Put the five phases of the business cycle in proper chronological order.
23. Define recession and depression and understand their implications for the economy.
24. Understand the role and objectives of the Federal Reserve in monetary policy.
25. Define and explain different measures of money supply and their significance.
26. Explore the tools and mechanisms employed by the Federal Reserve to influence monetary policy.
27. Identify and understand the significance of four key interest rates in the financial system.
28. Define the purpose and objectives of fiscal policy in economic management.
29. Differentiate between demand-side and supply-side economic theories.
30. Analyze the influence of exchange rates on international trade and prices.
31. Classify industries into cyclical, noncyclical, countercyclical, and growth categories.
32. Recognize how the business cycle affects different industries.
33. Understand the components and applications of balance sheets and income statements.

UNIT 2 Understanding Products and Their Risks (1150+ Questions)

This UNIT aims to provide participants with a comprehensive understanding of various securities and investment instruments. It covers the characteristics of common stocks, bonds, options, mutual funds, and other financial products. Learners will gain insights into the benefits, risks, and practical considerations associated with different investment vehicles. The whole module is designed as study guide in QnA mode using 1150+ MCQs. Hence you can start each topic with QnA which will also solve the purpose of reading materials. The following test objectives are covered under UNIT 2

1. Explore the fundamental features and ownership characteristics of common stock.
2. Establish a clear understanding of what constitutes a security in the context of financial markets.
3. Learn about dividends, a key source of income for common stockholders.
4. Understand the advantages and potential benefits of holding common stock in an investment portfolio.
5. Explore the concepts of rights and warrants, along with an understanding of Rule 144 regarding restricted stock and control persons.
6. Examine the features and benefits of American Depositary Receipts.
7. Understand the unique features and benefits of preferred stock compared to common stock.
8. Explore the fundamental characteristics of bonds as debt securities.

9. Understand the relationship between bond yields and interest rates.
10. Learn about bond ratings and their implications for safety and volatility.
11. Explore the features of zero-coupon bonds and other types of corporate debt.
12. Understand the hierarchy and order of liquidation for different types of corporate debt.
13. Evaluate the benefits and risks associated with investing in debt securities.
14. Differentiate between general obligation and revenue bonds, and understand the tax aspects of bond investments.
15. Explore the characteristics of Treasury STRIPS and TIPS.
16. Understand the features of certificates issued by government-sponsored entities.
17. Gain insights into money market instruments and their role in short-term financing.
18. Explore the characteristics of mortgage-backed and asset-backed securities.
19. Define derivatives and the concept of premium in financial instruments.
20. Understand the components of option pricing, including intrinsic and time value.
21. Explore the distinctions between equity, currency, and index options.
22. Learn practical calculations associated with options trading.
23. Determine how to use long options to hedge against market risk.
24. Understand the correct steps for incorporating options trading into a brokerage account.
25. Explore strategies for generating income through the sale of options.
26. Understand the role and functions of the Options Clearing Corporation in options trading.
27. Differentiate between various types of investment companies.
28. Understand the structures and characteristics of open-end and closed-end investment companies.
29. Explore the features and benefits of variable annuity contracts.
30. Understand the characteristics and implications of different mutual fund share classes.
31. Learn about the mechanics of forward pricing, calculating Net Asset Value (NAV), and understanding expense ratios.
32. Identify and understand the contents of different types of mutual fund prospectuses.
33. Understand the distinctions between 529 college savings plans and prepaid tuition plans.
34. Explore the purpose and utilization of local government investment plans.
35. Understand the organizational structure and characteristics of a general partnership.
36. Explore the various types of limited partnerships and their characteristics.
37. Understand the suitability and tax implications of Direct Participation Programs (DPPs).
38. Identify and understand the characteristics of Real Estate Investment Trusts (REITs).
39. Explore the suitability and risks associated with hedge fund investments.
40. Understand the concepts of Exchange-Traded Funds (ETFs) and Exchange-Traded Notes (ETNs).
41. Evaluate the advantages, disadvantages, and risks associated with ETFs and ETNs.
42. Understand the concept of systematic risk in financial markets.
43. Understand the concept of nonsystematic risk and its implications for investors.
44. Explore strategies for mitigating both systematic and nonsystematic risks in investment portfolios.

UNIT 3 Trading, Customer Accounts, & Prohibited Activities (1050+ Questions)

This UNIT 3 is designed to equip learners with the essential knowledge and skills required for effective securities trading, compliance with regulations, and client service in the financial industry. The unit covers a range of topics from trading strategies and market orders to regulatory compliance and ethical considerations when handling client accounts. The whole module is designed as study guide in QnA mode using 1050+ MCQs. Hence you can start each topic with QnA which will also solve the purpose of reading materials. The following test objectives are covered under UNIT 3

1. Understand the concepts of bullish and bearish sentiments in financial markets.
2. Learn the distinctions between market and limit orders and their implications for trading execution.
3. Understand the purpose and mechanics of a stop order in managing investment risk.
4. Differentiate between specialized, day, and Good 'til Cancelled (GTC) order instructions.
5. Understand the key terms bid, ask, and size in the context of securities trading.
6. Gain insights into the processes and considerations associated with buying and selling securities on a long position.
7. Distinguish between solicited and unsolicited trades and their implications for compliance.
8. Understand the settlement and delivery processes in securities transactions.
9. Explore the distinctions between cash dividends from stocks and mutual funds.
10. Understand the tax implications of different types of income generated from investments.
11. Learn about common security benchmarks and indices used to measure market performance.
12. Understand how to calculate cost basis and share price adjustments in the context of stock dividends and splits.
13. Explore the concepts of mergers and acquisitions, spin-offs, buybacks, and tender offers.
14. Understand the tax implications and notification requirements associated with corporate actions.
15. Understand the role and process of proxy voting in corporate governance.
16. Understand the differences between individual and joint registrations for securities accounts.
17. Explore the use and implications of transfer on death and power of attorney instructions.
18. Learn about various types of business accounts and their characteristics.
19. Understand the distinctions between living, revocable, and irrevocable trusts.

20. Explore the features and purposes of custodial accounts.
21. Understand the differences between Education Savings Accounts (ESAs) and 529 plans.
22. Learn about the contribution and distribution rules for Traditional and Roth IRA accounts.
23. Understand the characteristics and differences between defined benefit and defined contribution retirement plans.
24. Explore the features and implications of cash accounts, fee-based accounts, and margin accounts.
25. Understand the necessary forms and documentation for opening and managing a margin account.
26. Learn how to calculate the initial deposit requirements for margin accounts.
27. Understand the concept of money laundering and its implications for financial institutions.
28. Understand the responsibilities and requirements for an Anti-Money Laundering (AML) Officer under the Bank Secrecy Act (BSA).
29. Understand the importance and implications of the Know Your Customer (KYC) rule.
30. Explore guidelines and considerations for making investment recommendations.
31. Understand the general rules governing communication with the public in the financial industry.
32. Learn about the rules and regulations governing cold calls under the Telephone Consumer Protection Act of 1991.
33. Understand the privacy expectations and requirements under Regulation S-P.
34. Explore the records that financial firms are required to keep throughout their existence.
35. Understand the concept of insider trading and its legal implications.
36. Explore various forms of market manipulation and their impact on fair market practices.
37. Identify individuals and entities considered restricted under Rule 5130.
38. Understand the concept of the improper use of customer assets and the associated risks.
39. Learn about the unique considerations and expectations when serving senior clients.
40. Understand the rules and best practices for handling documents in the financial industry.

UNIT 4: Overview of the Regulatory Framework (150+ Questions)

This UNIT 4 is designed to provide participants with a deep understanding of key regulatory aspects related to securities registration, compliance, and professional conduct. The unit addresses critical topics such as registration information, limitations on nonregistered personnel, Form U-5, continuing education requirements, and rules governing professional conduct in areas like political contributions. The whole module is designed as study guide in QnA mode using 150+ MCQs. Hence you can start each topic with QnA which will also solve the purpose of reading materials. The following test objectives are covered under UNIT 4

1. Understand the significance of U4 information, including the purpose and importance of Form U4 in the securities industry.
2. Learn about the restrictions and limitations applicable to nonregistered personnel within a securities firm.
3. Gain insights into the content and implications of Form U-5, which is used for terminating the registration of individuals in the securities industry.
4. Understand the requirements and importance of continuing education in the securities industry to ensure ongoing professional development and regulatory compliance.
5. Define and comprehend the concept of "selling away" in the context of securities regulations.
6. Learn about the restrictions, limitations, and regulatory rules governing political contributions within the securities industry.

UNIT 1 - Knowledge of Capital Market

The Securities Act of 1933 and the Primary Markets

Q1_LO1: What is the primary purpose of the primary market?
a. Securities trading between investors
b. Issuer transactions for selling securities to the public.
c. Secondary market transactions
d. Capital market investments

HINTS: Focus on the primary function of the primary market in relation to issuer transactions.

Q2_LO1: In which market do securities trade between investors?
a. Primary market
b. Capital market
c. Secondary market
d. Issuer market

HINTS: Consider the market where securities trade between investors.

Q3_LO1: What allows corporations to raise capital quickly in the primary market?
a. Secondary market transactions
b. Capital market investments
c. Issuer transactions
d. Trading between investors

HINTS: Focus on the mechanism that enables corporations to raise capital in the primary market.

Q4_LO1: How does the primary market contribute to job creation in the economy?
a. By facilitating secondary market transactions.
b. By enabling corporations to raise capital for expansion.
c. By encouraging capital market investments.
d. By promoting trading between investors.

HINTS: Consider the role of the primary market in supporting economic growth and job creation.

Q5_LO1: What is another term for the primary and secondary markets collectively?
a. Trading markets
b. Issuer markets
c. Capital markets
d. Investor markets

HINTS: Focus on the collective term used for both primary and secondary markets.

Q6_LO1: How does the primary market benefit investors in a modern economy?
a. By promoting speculative trading.
b. By facilitating quick sales of securities.
c. By allowing investors to grow assets alongside the economy.
d. By encouraging short-term investments.

HINTS: Consider the benefit that the primary market provides to investors in a modern economy.

Q7_LO1: What role do governments play in the primary market?
a. Selling securities to the public.
b. Funding infrastructure projects and public programs
c. Encouraging secondary market transactions.
d. Facilitating capital market investments.

HINTS: Focus on the involvement of governments in the primary market.

Q8_LO1: How do investors benefit from owning mutual fund shares in the primary market?
a. They earn higher returns on short-term investments.
b. They gain voting rights in corporations.

c. They earn returns alongside the economy's growth.
d. They receive guaranteed fixed income.

HINTS: Consider the benefit that mutual fund shares provide to investors in the primary market.

Q9_LO1: What is the significance of the High Water Mark Principle in the primary market?
a. It determines entry fees for investors
b. It links fees to fund performance
c. It regulates issuer transactions
d. It sets a maximum fee cap

HINTS: Consider the role of the High Water Mark Principle in the primary market.

Q10_LO1: As a representative in the securities industry, what important role do you play in the primary market?
a. Promoting speculative trading
b. Facilitating secondary market transactions
c. Providing capital needed for economic growth
d. Encouraging short-term investments

HINTS: Focus on the role of representatives in the securities industry in the primary market.

Q11_LO2: What is the primary purpose of the Securities Act of 1933?
a. Encouraging speculative trading
b. Requiring full and fair disclosure in public securities offerings
c. Limiting investor access to prospectuses
d. Exempting new issues from SEC registration

HINTS: Focus on the primary purpose of the Securities Act of 1933.

Q12_LO2: What is the term for the first time an issuer distributes securities to the public?
a. Follow-on offering
b. Secondary offering
c. Initial public offering (IPO)
d. Additional public offering (APO)

HINTS: Focus on the term used for the first-time distribution of securities to the public.

Q13_LO2: When do follow-on offerings typically occur in the capital markets?
a. Before IPOs
b. Simultaneously with IPOs
c. After IPOs
d. Without any relation to IPOs

HINTS: Consider the timing of follow-on offerings in relation to IPOs.

Q14_LO2: What is the purpose of the High Water Mark Principle in IPO rules?
a. Determine entry fees for investors
b. Link fees to fund performance
c. Regulate secondary market transactions
d. Set a maximum fee cap

HINTS: Focus on the role of the High Water Mark Principle in IPO rules.

Q15_LO2: Who is considered a restricted person in IPO rules?
a. Public investors
b. Investment bankers
c. Portfolio managers
d. All of the above

HINTS: Consider the categories of restricted persons in IPO rules.

Q16_LO2: What is the de minimis exemption in IPO rules?
a. A maximum fee cap for restricted persons
b. An exemption for small IPOs

c. An exemption for restricted persons with less than 10% interest
d. A restriction on immediate family members

HINTS: Focus on the concept of the de minimis exemption in IPO rules.

Q17_LO2: When does a corporation engage in an initial public offering (IPO)?
a. After a follow-on offering
b. Simultaneously with a follow-on offering
c. Before any public offerings
d. Only once in its corporate lifetime

HINTS: Consider the timing of an initial public offering (IPO) in a corporation's lifecycle.

Q18_LO2: What is the term for subsequent money raises after an IPO?
a. Follow-on offerings
b. Secondary offerings
c. Initial public offerings
d. Additional public offerings

HINTS: Focus on the term used for subsequent money raises after an IPO.
Q19_LO2: What is the significance of the Securities Act of 1933 for public offerings?
a. It limits advertising for public offerings.
b. It regulates public offering prices.
c. It requires full and fair disclosure in public offerings.
d. It exempts public offerings from SEC registration.

HINTS: Focus on the primary purpose of the Securities Act of 1933 for public offerings.

Q20_LO2: Who ensures a bona fide public offering in IPOs?
a. Restricted persons
b. public investors
c. Investment bankers
d. SEC examiners

HINTS: Focus on the role of investment bankers in ensuring a bona fide public offering.

Q21_LO2: What is the primary purpose of a primary offering in the securities market?
a. Facilitating secondary market transactions
b. Distributing securities to the public
c. Providing capital to investors
d. Regulating underwriters

HINTS: Focus on the primary purpose of a primary offering.

Q22_LO2: Under which regulation are public offerings of securities regulated?
a. Securities Exchange Act of 1934
b. Securities Act of 1933
c. Dodd-Frank Wall Street Reform and Consumer Protection Act
d. Investment Company Act of 1940

HINTS: Consider the regulation that governs public offerings of securities.

Q23_LO2: What is the term for the first time an issuer distributes securities to the public?
a. Secondary offering
b. Follow-on offering
c. Subsequent offering
d. Initial public offering (IPO)

HINTS: Focus on the term used for the first-time distribution of securities to the public.

Q24_LO2: What is the primary purpose of the Securities Act of 1933?
a. Regulating secondary market transactions
b. Ensuring full and fair disclosure in public offerings
c. Governing investment company activities

d. Facilitating underwriter transactions

HINTS: Focus on the primary purpose of the Securities Act of 1933.

Q25_LO2: What are subsequent money raises known as after an IPO?
a. Additional public offerings (APOs)
b. Secondary offerings
c. Follow-on offerings
d. Both A and C

HINTS: Consider the terms used for additional money raises after an IPO.

Q26_LO2: What do IPO rules and regulations primarily aim to protect in the public offering process?
a. Protecting secondary market transactions.
b. Ensuring underwriters' profitability.
c. Safeguarding public offering integrity and investor interests
d. Facilitating private securities offerings.

HINTS: Focus on the primary aim of IPO rules and regulations.

Q27_LO2: Who are considered restricted persons in the context of IPO rules?
a. General public investors
b. Employees of the issuer
c. Portfolio managers
d. Both B and C

HINTS: Consider the categories of individuals listed as restricted persons.

Q28_LO2: What is the de minimis exemption in IPO rules?
a. It limits the number of shares offered in an IPO
b. It exempts small companies from IPO regulations
c. It allows restricted persons to have an interest in an account up to 10%
d. It regulates underwriter compensation

HINTS: Focus on the purpose of the de minimis exemption in IPO rules.

Q29_LO2: What is the term for subsequent primary offerings after an IPO?
a. Additional public offerings (APOs)
b. Secondary offerings
c. Follow-on offerings
d. Both B and C

HINTS: Consider the terms used for subsequent primary offerings after an IPO.

Q30_LO2: What is the primary objective of IPO rules regarding the sale of new issues to accounts with restricted persons?
a. Maximizing underwriter profits
b. Ensuring a fair distribution to the general public
c. Limiting the number of shares sold in an IPO
d. Facilitating secondary market liquidity

HINTS: Focus on the primary objective of IPO rules in selling new issues to accounts with restricted persons.

Q31_LO2: What is the primary purpose of the Securities Act of 1933?
a. Regulating secondary market transactions
b. Ensuring full and fair disclosure in public offerings
c. Restricting private securities offerings
d. Governing underwriting practices

HINTS: Focus on the primary purpose of the Securities Act of 1933.

Q32_LO2: What is the term for the first time an issuer distributes securities to the public?
a. Subsequent public offering
b. Follow-on offering

c. Additional public offering
d. Initial public offering

HINTS: Consider the term for the first-time distribution of securities to the public.

Q33_LO2: What is the term for subsequent offerings after the initial public offering (IPO)?
a. Initial public offering (IPO)
b. Secondary public offering
c. Follow-on offering
d. Primary market offering

HINTS: Focus on the term for subsequent offerings after the IPO.

Q34_LO2: What are the defining characteristics of follow-on offerings (APOs)?
a. Secondary offerings with proceeds going to the issuer
b. Primary offerings with proceeds going to the issuer
c. Tertiary offerings with proceeds going to the issuer
d. Private offerings with restricted access

HINTS: Focus on the defining characteristics of follow-on offerings.

Q35_LO2: What is the primary market offering where the issuer receives the entire deal proceeds?
a. Follow-on offering
b. Secondary offering
c. Initial public offering (IPO)
d. Private placement

HINTS: Focus on the primary market offering where the issuer receives the entire deal proceeds.

Q36_LO2: What regulatory act governs public offerings of securities?
a. Securities Exchange Act of 1934
b. Securities Act of 1933
c. Investment Company Act of 1940
d. Investment Advisers Act of 1940

HINTS: Consider the regulatory act that specifically governs public offerings.

Q37_LO2: Who facilitates public offerings by using the services of underwriters?
a. Investment bankers and BDs
b. Retail investors
c. Market makers
d. Securities analysts

HINTS: Focus on the entities that facilitate public offerings.

Q38_LO2: What is the purpose of IPO rules and regulations?
a. To restrict public access to IPOs
b. To protect the integrity of the public offering process
c. To encourage speculative trading in IPOs
d. To minimize disclosure requirements

HINTS: Consider the purpose of rules and regulations related to IPOs.

Q39_LO2: Who are considered restricted persons in the context of IPOs?
a. All investors participating in IPOs
b. Employees of the issuing corporation
c. Immediate family members of industry insiders
d. Any person owning less than 10% of a member firm

HINTS: Focus on the definition of restricted persons in the context of IPOs.

Q40_LO2: What is the de minimis exemption in IPOs?
a. Exemption for small-sized IPOs
b. Exemption for restricted persons with less than 10% ownership

c. Exemption for large-sized IPOs
d. Exemption for underwriters

HINTS: Consider the purpose of the de minimis exemption in the context of IPOs.

Q41_LO3: Who are the participants that work with an issuer to bring its securities to the market and sell them to the investing public?
a. Investors
b. Municipal advisors
c. Underwriters
d. Syndicates

HINTS: Focus on entities that assist in bringing securities to the market.

Q42_LO3: What is the term for underwriting where the underwriters act as agents, not committing to purchase the shares themselves and collecting client funds into an escrow account?
a. Firm commitment underwriting
b. Mini-max underwriting
c. Best efforts underwriting
d. All-or-none underwriting

HINTS: Consider underwriting where underwriters act as agents and do not commit to purchasing the shares themselves.

Q43_LO3: In an All-or-None (AON) underwriting, what must the underwriter do if all the shares cannot be sold?
a. Keep the shares in inventory
b. Cancel the underwriting
c. Sell the shares at a discount
d. Hold a private placement

HINTS: Focus on the outcome of an AON underwriting if all shares cannot be sold.

Q44_LO3: What is the purpose of a Mini-max underwriting in determining floor and ceiling amounts?
a. To maximize underwriter profits
b. To minimize issuer risk
c. To set a minimum and maximum issuance requirement
d. To expedite the underwriting process

HINTS: Focus on the purpose of a Mini-max underwriting in setting floor and ceiling amounts.

Q45_LO3: In a Firm Commitment underwriting, who is at risk for any unsold shares?
a. Investors
b. Issuers
c. Underwriters
d. Syndicates

HINTS: Consider the party at risk for unsold shares in a Firm Commitment underwriting.

Q46_LO3: What is the role of the managing underwriter in a syndicate?
a. Sell securities to the public
b. Provide significant resources and take on a lead role
c. Act as an agent for the issuer
d. Form a selling group

HINTS: Focus on the role of the managing underwriter in a syndicate.

Q47_LO3: Who are considered institutional investors?
a. Individual investors
b. Banks, insurance companies, and mutual funds
c. Retail investors
d. Accredited investors

HINTS: Identify the entities included in the category of institutional investors.

Q48_LO3: What financial criteria must be met by retail investors to be classified as accredited investors?
a. Minimum annual income of $100,000

b. Minimum net worth of $500,000
c. Minimum net worth of $1,000,000
d. Minimum annual income of $200,000

HINTS: Focus on the financial criteria for retail investors to be classified as accredited investors.

Q49_LO3: What do municipal advisors assist municipalities with in the primary market?
a. Selling municipal securities
b. Underwriting municipal offerings
c. Providing investment advice to retail investors
d. Advising on debt structure and bond features

HINTS: Focus on the role of municipal advisors in assisting municipalities.

Q50_LO3: What is the largest issuer of debt in the United States?
a. Municipalities
b. Corporations
c. Underwriters
d. Treasury Department

HINTS: Identify the largest issuer of debt in the context of the United States.

Q51_LO3: Who are the participants involved in bringing securities to the market and selling them to the public?
a. Retail investors
b. Underwriters
c. Institutional investors
d. Municipal advisors

HINTS: Focus on the entities that work with issuers to bring securities to the market.

Q52_LO3: In a best efforts underwriting, what role does the underwriter play?
a. Principal
b. Agent
c. Syndicate member
d. Lead underwriter

HINTS: Consider the underwriter's commitment and risk in a best efforts underwriting.

Q53_LO3: What is the primary purpose of a firm commitment underwriting?
a. To minimize disclosure requirements
b. To act as an agent for the issuer
c. To buy securities from the issuer and resell them to the public
d. To form syndicates with other underwriters

HINTS: Focus on the nature of firm commitment underwriting and the role of underwriters.

Q54_LO3: What is the role of a syndicate in a large firm commitment underwriting?
a. Lead underwriter
b. Selling group
c. Managing underwriter
d. Underwriting commitments

HINTS: Consider the structure and roles within a syndicate in a large firm commitment underwriting.

Q55_LO3: In an all-or-none (AON) underwriting, what condition must be met for the underwriting to be successful?
a. All shares must be sold
b. Only a minimum floor must be reached
c. A maximum ceiling must be reached
d. No condition needs to be met

HINTS: Focus on the specific condition outlined in an all-or-none underwriting.

Q56_LO3: What is the purpose of a mini-max underwriting?
a. To set a minimum and maximum price for securities

b. To determine the underwriter's spread
c. To establish the floor and ceiling for the number of securities to be sold
d. To limit the liability of the issuer

HINTS: Focus on the function of a mini-max underwriting in setting issuance limits.

Q57_LO3: What category includes banks, insurance companies, pensions, hedge funds, and mutual funds?
a. Retail investors
b. Accredited investors
c. Institutional investors
d. Syndicate members

HINTS: Identify the category that includes entities pooling money to purchase securities.

Q58_LO3: What criteria must retail investors meet to be considered accredited investors?
a. Net worth of $500,000
b. Income of $100,000 or more
c. Net worth of $1,000,000 or more
d. Income of $200,000 or more

HINTS: Focus on the financial criteria for retail investors to be classified as accredited investors.

Q59_LO3: What type of investor generally owns and invests a minimum of $100 million in securities on a discretionary basis?
a. Retail investor
b. Institutional investor
c. Accredited investor
d. Syndicate member

HINTS: Identify the investor type that pools money and invests a significant amount in securities.

Q60_LO3: What role do municipal advisors play in the primary market?
a. Selling securities to the public
b. Advising municipalities on debt issuance
c. Forming syndicates with underwriters
d. Acting as lead underwriters

HINTS: Focus on the advisory role of municipal advisors in the primary market.

Q61_LO3: Who are the participants that work with an issuer to bring its securities to the market and sell them to the investing public?
a. Investors
b. Underwriters
c. Municipalities
d. Corporations

HINTS: Focus on entities facilitating the issuance and sale of securities.

Q62_LO3: What type of underwriting calls for the underwriters to act as agents, not principals, and not commit to purchasing the shares themselves?
a. Firm commitment underwriting
b. Best efforts underwriting
c. Mini-max underwriting
d. All-or-none underwriting

HINTS: Consider the underwriting type where underwriters act as agents.

Q63_LO3: In a mini-max underwriting, what is the minimum issuance requirement called?
a. Floor
b. Ceiling
c. Syndicate
d. Spread

HINTS: Focus on the term for the minimum amount the issuer needs to raise.

Q64_LO3: What is the term for a group of BDs forming a joint venture to share both the risk and profits from a large firm commitment underwriting?
a. Syndicate
b. Selling group
c. Accredited investors
d. Municipal advisors

HINTS: Focus on the term for a joint venture formed by BDs.

Q65_LO3: What is the term for institutional investors that own and invest a minimum of $100 million in securities on a discretionary basis?
a. Qualified institutional buyers (QIBs)
b. Retail investors
c. Accredited investors
d. Municipal advisors

HINTS: Focus on the term for institutional investors meeting specific criteria.

Q66_LO3: Who are considered accredited investors among retail investors?
a. Insiders of the security's issuer
b. Investors with a net worth of $500,000
c. Investors with an income of $150,000
d. Investors with a net worth of $1,000,000

HINTS: Focus on the criteria for accredited investors among retail investors.

Q67_LO3: What do municipal advisors assist municipalities with in the primary market?
a. Selling securities
b. Underwriting functions
c. Providing investment advice
d. Structuring capital raises

HINTS: Focus on the role of municipal advisors in the primary market.

Q68_LO3: What is the primary market offering where underwriters act as principals, committing to purchasing any unsold shares for the syndicate account?
a. Best efforts underwriting
b. Mini-max underwriting
c. Firm commitment underwriting
d. All-or-none underwriting

HINTS: Focus on the type of underwriting where underwriters act as principals.

Q69_LO3: What is the term for the difference between the price at which underwriters buy securities from the issuer and the price at which they sell them to the public?
a. Spread
b. Ceiling
c. Floor
d. Syndicate

HINTS: Focus on the term for the price differential earned by underwriters.

Q70_LO3: What is the primary purpose of the Securities Act of 1933?
a. Regulating secondary market transactions
b. Ensuring full and fair disclosure in public offerings
c. Restricting private securities offerings
d. Governing underwriting practices

HINTS: Focus on the primary purpose of the Securities Act of 1933.

Q71_LO4: What is the primary purpose of the Securities Act of 1933 concerning new securities in the primary market?
a. Ensure secondary market stability
b. Protect investors in new issues
c. Facilitate short selling
d. Regulate corporate governance

HINTS: Focus on the primary goal of the Securities Act of 1933.

Q72_LO4: During the cooling-off period, which activity is allowed for advertising a new issue with minimal information?
a. Delivering a final prospectus
b. Running tombstone advertisements
c. Soliciting sales of the securities
d. Offering shares to investors

HINTS: Focus on the allowed form of advertising during the cooling-off period.

Q73_LO4: What is the document used as a prospecting tool during the cooling-off period to gather indications of interest?
a. Final prospectus
b. Registration statement
c. Preliminary prospectus (red herring)
d. Cooling-off notice

HINTS: Consider the document used for prospecting and gathering investor interest.

Q74_LO4: What is the minimum duration of the cooling-off period for a nonexempt issue?
a. 15 calendar days
b. 20 calendar days
c. 25 calendar days
d. 30 calendar days

HINTS: Recall the minimum duration of the cooling-off period.

Q75_LO4: What does the registration statement (S-1) filed with the SEC include?
a. Final prospectus
b. Tombstone advertisement
c. Preliminary prospectus (red herring)
d. Material information about the issue

HINTS: Focus on the content of the registration statement.

Q76_LO4: During the cooling-off period, what is the purpose of delivering a preliminary prospectus (red herring) to customers?
a. Finalize the offering price
b. Gauge investor interest
c. Solicit sales of the securities
d. Begin secondary market trading

HINTS: Consider the purpose of the preliminary prospectus during the cooling-off period.

Q77_LO4: What term refers to an investor's declaration of potential interest in purchasing the issue after it comes out of registration?
a. Firm commitment
b. Indication of interest
c. Underwriting commitment
d. Cooling-off commitment

HINTS: Focus on the term for an investor's declaration of potential interest.

Q78_LO4: What takes place during the cooling-off period to examine the issue's suitability for different customers?
a. Sales solicitation
b. Due diligence
c. Final prospectus delivery
d. State registration (blue sky filing)

HINTS: Focus on the activity involving the examination of the issue.

Q79_LO4: Which activity allows the issuer to announce a new issue with minimal information during the cooling-off period?
a. Delivering a final prospectus
b. Placing tombstone advertisements
c. Gathering indications of interest
d. Running a full-fledged advertisement

HINTS: Consider the activity allowed for announcing a new issue with minimal information.

Q80_LO4: What term refers to the process of coordinating federal and state registrations for a new issue?
a. Cooling-off period
b. Blue sky filing
c. Red herring period
d. Offering coordination

HINTS: Recall the term for coordinating federal and state registrations.

Q81_LO4: What is the term for the date when the SEC allows the security to be offered to investors, starting the sale period?
a. Registration date
b. Cooling-off date
c. Release date
d. Offering date

HINTS: Focus on the term for the date when the SEC allows the security to be offered.

Q82_LO4: What must precede or accompany all sales confirmations during the offering of a new security?
a. Tombstone advertisement
b. Cooling-off notice
c. Preliminary prospectus
d. Final prospectus

HINTS: Consider the document required to precede or accompany sales confirmations.

Q83_LO4: What disclaimer does the SEC include in its statements regarding new offerings?
a. Approval disclaimer
b. Endorsement disclaimer
c. Accuracy disclaimer
d. SEC disclaimer

HINTS: Focus on the standard disclaimer included in SEC statements.

Q84_LO4: What is an additional primary offering of stock to the public for a company that has already completed an IPO?
a. Initial Public Offering (IPO)
b. Secondary Offering
c. Hybrid Offering
d. Combination Offering

HINTS: Recall the term for a subsequent offering after the IPO.

Q85_LO4: If the issuer is receiving the funds from an offering, what type of market transaction is it?
a. Secondary market transaction
b. Tertiary market transaction
c. Primary market transaction
d. Hybrid market transaction

HINTS: Focus on the type of market transaction when the issuer receives the funds.

Q86_LO4: What is the main purpose of the Securities Act of 1933 concerning new issues?
a. Facilitating secondary market trading
b. Protecting investors in the primary market
c. Regulating underwriting practices
d. Governing securities exchanges

HINTS: Focus on the purpose of the Securities Act of 1933 in the primary market.

Q87_LO4: What document must an issuer file with the SEC when selling a nonexempt security?
a. Final prospectus
b. Preliminary prospectus
c. Registration statement (S-1)
d. Tombstone advertisement

HINTS: Identify the initial filing required for nonexempt securities.

Q88_LO4: During the cooling-off period, what type of advertisements is permitted to announce a new issue?
a. Full disclosure ads
b. Preliminary prospectus ads
c. Tombstone ads
d. Final prospectus ads

HINTS: Recognize the permissible form of advertising during the cooling-off period.

Q89_LO4: What is the purpose of a preliminary prospectus, also known as a red herring?
a. To finalize the offering price
b. To gather indications of interest
c. To solicit sales during the cooling-off period
d. To announce the effective date

HINTS: Understand the purpose of the preliminary prospectus during the cooling-off period.

Q90_LO4: What is an indication of interest during the offering process?
a. A commitment to buy from the investor
b. A promise to sell by the underwriter
c. A nonbinding declaration of potential interest
d. An agreement to purchase securities

HINTS: Recognize the nature of an indication of interest during the offering process.

Q91_LO4: What takes place during the due diligence phase of the offering process?
a. The effective date determination
b. Examination of the issue's suitability for customers
c. SEC disclaimer preparation
d. Tombstone advertisement placement

HINTS: Identify the purpose of the due diligence phase.

Q92_LO4: What is the process called for coordinating federal and state registrations?
a. Cooling-off period
b. Blue sky filings
c. Final prospectus delivery
d. Indications of interest gathering

HINTS: Recognize the term for coordinating federal and state registrations.

Q93_LO4: What marks the beginning of the period during which investors may purchase the new issue?
a. Cooling-off period
b. Final prospectus
c. Effective date
d. Preliminary prospectus

HINTS: Identify the event marking the start of the period for purchasing the new issue.

Q94_LO4: What does the final prospectus include in addition to the preliminary prospectus?
a. SEC disclaimer
b. Offering price
c. Cooling-off period duration
d. Issuer's business description

HINTS: Recognize the additional information included in the final prospectus.

Q95_LO4: What is the term for selling additional shares to the public after the initial public offering (IPO)?
a. Primary market offering
b. Secondary market offering
c. Hybrid offering
d. Follow-on offering

HINTS: Identify the term for selling additional shares after the IPO.

Q96_LO4: If an investor expresses interest in the securities during the cooling-off period, what must be made available to them?
a. Final prospectus
b. SEC disclaimer
c. Preliminary prospectus
d. Tombstone advertisement

HINTS: Recognize the document that must be made available to an investor expressing interest.

Q97_LO4: During the cooling-off period, what activity is prohibited?
a. Tombstone advertisement
b. Delivery of a preliminary prospectus
c. Indications of interest gathering
d. Soliciting sales of securities

HINTS: Identify the prohibited activity during the cooling-off period.

Q98_LO4: What does the tombstone advertisement include?
a. Full disclosure of the offering
b. Details of the effective date
c. A minimal amount of information
d. A commitment to purchase

HINTS: Understand the content of tombstone advertisements.

Q99_LO4: What does the SEC's standard disclaimer state about the securities being offered?
a. Approved by the SEC
b. Accuracy of the information
c. Adequacy of the information
d. Endorsement by the SEC

HINTS: Identify the content of the standard SEC disclaimer.

Q100_LO4: What term is used for a primary offering where existing shareholders sell their shares along with the new issued shares?
a. Hybrid offering
b. Secondary market offering
c. Rights offering
d. Follow-on offering

HINTS: Recognize the term for an offering involving both new and existing shares.

Q101_LO4: What is the main purpose of the Securities Act of 1933?
a. Facilitate secondary market transactions
b. Ensure full and fair disclosure in primary market offerings
c. Regulate stock exchanges
d. Prevent insider trading

HINTS: Focus on the primary purpose of the Securities Act of 1933.

Q102_LO4: What document must an issuer file with the SEC when it desires to sell a nonexempt security?
a. Tombstone ad
b. Indication of interest
c. Registration statement (S-1)
d. Preliminary prospectus

HINTS: Consider the filing required when an issuer wants to sell a non-exempt security.

Q103_LO4: During the cooling-off period, what activity is allowed that provides a bare-bones announcement of the securities to be offered?
a. Preliminary prospectus delivery
b. Tombstone advertisement
c. Gathering indications of interest
d. Due diligence meetings

HINTS: Focus on the allowed activity during the cooling-off period that announces the new issue.

Q104_LO4: What is the purpose of a preliminary prospectus (red herring) during the cooling-off period?
a. Finalizes the offering price
b. Announces the release date
c. Gauges investor interest
d. Provides a legal opinion

HINTS: Focus on the purpose of the preliminary prospectus during the cooling-off period.

Q105_LO4: What does an indication of interest represent during the cooling-off period?
a. A commitment to buy from the investor
b. A promise to sell by the underwriter
c. A nonbinding declaration of potential interest
d. A legally binding contract

HINTS: Focus on the nature of an indication of interest during the cooling-off period.

Q106_LO4: What occurs during due diligence meetings in the primary market offering process?
a. Actual sales of the securities
b. Examination of the issue's suitability for customers
c. Issuer's submission of corrected registration statement
d. SEC's review and approval of the offering

HINTS: Focus on the purpose of due diligence meetings in the primary market offering process.

Q107_LO4: What is the process of coordinating federal and state registrations called?
a. Cooling-off period
b. Release date
c. Due diligence
d. Blue sky filings

HINTS: Focus on the term for coordinating federal and state registrations.

Q108_LO4: When does the SEC allow the security to be offered to investors in the primary market?
a. Upon final prospectus delivery
b. At the start of the cooling-off period
c. After the effective date
d. After a deficiency letter is issued

HINTS: Focus on the point when the SEC allows the security to be offered to investors.

Q109_LO4: What must precede or accompany all sales confirmations in the primary market offering process?
a. Cooling-off period
b. Tombstone advertisement
c. Final prospectus
d. Preliminary prospectus

HINTS: Focus on the document that must precede or accompany sales confirmations.

Q110_LO4: What does the spread represent in the context of the primary market offering process?
a. Offering price range
b. Selling discounts
c. Management history
d. SEC disclaimer

HINTS: Focus on the term representing the price differential earned by underwriters.

Q111_LO4: What is an additional primary offering (APO) in the primary market?
a. First-time sale of securities to the public
b. Subsequent sale of more shares after an IPO
c. Offering by municipal advisors
d. Blue sky filings

HINTS: Consider the definition of an additional primary offering (APO).

Q112_LO4: If the issuer is receiving funds from an offering, what type of market transaction is it?
a. Secondary market transaction
b. Hybrid offering
c. Private securities offering
d. Primary market transaction

HINTS: Focus on the type of market transaction when the issuer receives funds.

Q113_LO4: What is the term for coordinating federal and state securities registrations?
a. Cooling-off period
b. Blue sky filings
c. Final prospectus
d. Release date

HINTS: Focus on the term for coordinating federal and state registrations.

Q114_LO4: What is the standard SEC disclaimer in the final prospectus?
a. "These securities have been approved by the SEC."
b. "The SEC endorses this offering."
c. "SEC disclaims responsibility for thc offering."
d. "These securities have not been approved or disapproved by the SEC."

HINTS: Focus on the standard disclaimer in the final prospectus.

Q115_LO4: What is the term for a hybrid offering where both new shares and existing shares are sold to the public?
a. Additional primary offering (APO)
b. Initial public offering (IPO)
c. Blue sky offering
d. Hybrid combination offering

HINTS: Focus on the term for an offering where both new and existing shares are sold.

Q116_LO5: What is the primary advantage of a shelf offering for an issuer?
a. Immediate sale of all registered shares
b. Ability to sell portions over a two-year period
c. Exemption from Securities Act regulations
d. Unlimited shelf life for the registration

HINTS: Focus on the key advantage for issuers with a shelf offering.

Q117_LO5: How long is a shelf offering registration valid once filed with the SEC?
a. One year
b. Two years
c. Three years
d. Indefinite

HINTS: Recall the duration of validity for a shelf offering registration.

Q118_LO5: What criteria must an issuer meet to qualify as a well-known seasoned issuer (WKSI)?
a. Minimum two-year existence
b. Listing on a major exchange
c. Heavy demand for securities
d. Compliance with state blue sky laws

HINTS: Consider the criteria for a well-known seasoned issuer (WKSI).

Q119_LO5: What is required before each sale of securities offered via a shelf registration?
a. SEC approval
b. Final prospectus filing
c. Supplemental prospectus filing
d. Blue sky filings

HINTS: Focus on the requirement for securities offered via a shelf registration.

Q120_LO5: What is the purpose of the greenshoe option in a stock offering?
a. Allow unlimited oversubscription
b. Increase the number of offered shares by up to 15%
c. Extend the offering period
d. Provide a price stabilization mechanism

HINTS: Focus on the purpose for the greenshoe option in a stock offering.

Q121_LO5: In what circumstance might an issuer extend the shelf offering to three years?
a. High market volatility
b. Well-known seasoned issuer (WKSI) status
c. Economic recession
d. Increased competition

HINTS: Focus on the circumstance for extending a shelf offering to three years.

Q122_LO5: What is the formal name for the greenshoe option?
a. Over-subscription option
b. Over-allotment option
c. Extended offering option
d. Supplemental offering option

HINTS: Recall the formal name for the greenshoe option.

Q123_LO5: What regulatory act governs the shelf offering and greenshoe option?
a. Securities Act of 1933
b. Securities Exchange Act of 1934
c. Investment Company Act of 1940
d. Sarbanes-Oxley Act of 2002

HINTS: Focus on the regulatory act for the shelf offering and greenshoe option.

Q124_LO5: How does a shelf offering benefit an issuer during market fluctuations?
a. Eliminates market risks
b. Allows for immediate sales
c. Provides flexibility to sell when conditions are favorable
d. Grants immunity from SEC regulations

HINTS: Focus on the benefit for an issuer during market fluctuations.

Q125_LO5: What is the significance of a supplemental prospectus in the shelf offering process?
a. Gains SEC approval for the shelf offering
b. Finalizes the offering price
c. Updates material information before each sale
d. Initiates the greenshoe option

HINTS: Consider the purpose of a supplemental prospectus in the shelf offering process.

Q126_LO5: What does the greenshoe option protect against in a stock offering?
a. Market volatility
b. Underpricing of shares
c. SEC investigations
d. Over-subscription by investors

HINTS: Focus on the purpose for the greenshoe option in a stock offering.

Q127_LO5: What is the primary purpose of a greenshoe option in a stock offering?
a. Stabilize the offering price
b. Prevent oversubscription by investors
c. Extend the offering period
d. Eliminate underwriters' risks

HINTS: Focus on the primary purpose for a greenshoe option in a stock offering.

Q128_LO5: What does the shelf offering registration allow an issuer to do over a two-year period?
a. Sell all registered shares immediately
b. Re-register the security multiple times
c. Sell portions of the registered shares at intervals
d. Extend the shelf life indefinitely

HINTS: Recall the benefit for an issuer with a shelf offering registration.

Q129_LO5: What is the Greenshoe option's maximum increase in the number of offered shares?
a. 5%
b. 10%
c. 15%
d. 20%

HINTS: Consider the maximum percentage increase for the Greenshoe option.

Q130_LO5: In what situation might a greenshoe option be particularly useful for underwriters?
a. Low market demand
b. High market demand
c. Economic stability
d. Long shelf offering duration

HINTS: Focus on the circumstance where a greenshoe option might be useful for underwriters.

Q131_LO6: Which of the following is NOT an exempt issuer under the Securities Act of 1933?
a. Federal government
b. Municipal government
c. Publicly traded company
d. National bank

HINTS: Identify the exempt issuers in the Securities Act of 1933.

Q132_LO6: What is the maximum offering amount for Tier 2 under Regulation A+ in a 12-month period?
a. $5 million
b. $20 million
c. $50 million
d. Unlimited

HINTS: Recall the maximum offering amounts for Tier 2 under Regulation A+.

Q133_LO6: Under Rule 147, when are securities offerings exempt from registration requirements?
a. If the issuer is a bank
b. If the issuer is a well-known seasoned issuer
c. If the offering takes place entirely in one state
d. If the offering has SEC approval

HINTS: Focus on the conditions for securities offerings to be exempt under Rule 147.

Q134_LO6: How long must securities sold under Rule 147 be held before resale to nonresidents is allowed?
a. 3 months
b. 6 months
c. 9 months
d. 12 months

HINTS: Consider the restriction for resale of securities sold under Rule 147.

Q135_LO6: What is the primary purpose of Regulation D with regard to exempt transactions?
a. Limit the number of accredited investors
b. Allow unlimited capital raising
c. Ensure SEC approval for private placements
d. Impose restrictions on advertising

HINTS: Focus on the primary purpose for Regulation D in exempt transactions.

Q136_LO6: How does Regulation D define an accredited investor?
a. High net worth or income
b. Participation in multiple offerings
c. Previous investment experience
d. SEC registration status

HINTS: Identify the criteria for an accredited investor under Regulation D.

Q137_LO6: What is the primary requirement for private placements to solicit or advertise under Regulation D?
a. All purchasers must be nonaccredited investors
b. All purchasers must be accredited investors
c. No advertising allowed
d. Must be a Tier 1 offering

HINTS: Focus on the requirement for soliciting or advertising private placements under Regulation D.

Q138_LO6: What is the maximum percentage of an investor's net worth or income allowed for Tier 2 Regulation A+ offerings?
a. 5%
b. 10%
c. 15%
d. 20%

HINTS: Recall the maximum percentage for Tier 2 Regulation A+ offerings.

Q139_LO6: Which term is synonymous with private placement stock that is held for a six-month period?
a. Registered stock
b. Letter stock
c. Legend stock
d. Unrestricted stock

HINTS: Recognize the synonymous term for private placement stock held for a six-month period.

Q140_LO6: What is the key distinction between Tier 1 and Tier 2 offerings under Regulation A+?
a. Offering size
b. SEC review level
c. Investment limits
d. Accredited investor status

HINTS: Focus on the distinction between Tier 1 and Tier 2 offerings under Regulation A+.

Q141_LO6: What does the SEC require companies to file under Regulation D for nonpublic offerings?
a. Full prospectus
b. Form D
c. Offering circular
d. Registration statement

HINTS: Identify the filing requirement for companies raising capital in a nonpublic offering under Regulation D.

Q142_LO6: What must private placement investors sign to indicate their intent to hold the stock for investment purposes?
a. Offering circular
b. Letter of intent
c. Investment letter
d. Registration statement

HINTS: Recognize the document that private placement investors must sign.

Q143_LO6: What is the primary condition for securities sold under Rule 147 to be exempt from registration?
a. Majority of employees must work in the state
b. At least 80% of offering proceeds used within the state
c. SEC approval of the issuer
d. Broker-dealer must be based in the state

HINTS: Focus on the condition for securities sold under Rule 147 to be exempt from registration.

Q144_LO6: What is the primary purpose of Rule 147 in intrastate offerings?
a. Encourage interstate commerce
b. Facilitate SEC oversight
c. Promote local investment
d. Impose federal regulations

HINTS: Identify the primary purpose for Rule 147 in intrastate offerings.

Q145_LO6: What information is provided to investors in a Regulation A+ offering instead of a full prospectus?
a. Offering circular
b. Letter of intent
c. SEC approval document
d. Full prospectus

HINTS: Recall the document that is provided to investors in a Regulation A+ offering.

Q146_LO6: Which of the following securities is NOT exempt from the registration and prospectus requirements of the Securities Act of 1933?
a. U.S. government securities
b. Municipal securities
c. Securities with maturities of 270 days or less
d. Variable annuities

HINTS: Focus on the type of securities exempt from registration.

Q147_LO6: What is the maximum duration of validity for a shelf offering registration once filed with the SEC?
a. One year
b. Two years
c. Three years
d. Indefinite

HINTS: Recall the duration of validity for a shelf offering registration.

Q148_LO6: Which securities are exempt from registration due to the issuer's level of creditworthiness?
a. Municipal securities
b. Commercial paper with maturities of 270 days or less
c. Insurance policies
d. Variable annuity contracts

HINTS: Focus on securities exempt due to the issuer's creditworthiness.

Q149_LO6: What criterion must a company meet to be eligible for Tier 2 offerings under Regulation A+?
a. No coordination with individual states
b. Offering up to $20 million
c. Selling up to $6 million on behalf of existing shareholders
d. Subject to rigorous disclosure requirements to the SEC

HINTS: Focus on the criteria for Tier 2 offerings under Regulation A+.
Q150_LO6: Under Rule 147, when are securities exempt from registration?
a. When offered by a federal agency
b. When sold to nonresidents of the state
c. When the issuer has its principal office in the state
d. When securities have a maturity of 270 days or less

HINTS: Focus on the conditions under Rule 147 for exemption.

Q151_LO6: What is the primary purpose of Regulation D in the context of exempt transactions?
a. Allow unlimited solicitation
b. Exempt securities with unlimited nonaccredited investors
c. Exempt transactions with no disclosure requirements
d. Exempt transactions with up to 35 nonaccredited investors

HINTS: Focus on the purpose of Regulation D in exempt transactions.

Q152_LO6: What is the significance of a legend on a stock certificate in a private placement?
a. Allows unlimited transferability
b. Indicates accreditation status of the investor
c. Prohibits transfer without registration or exemption
d. Exempts the stock from SEC filings

HINTS: Focus on the significance of a legend in private placement stock.

Q153_LO6: What is the key requirement for businesses intending to solicit or advertise private securities offerings under Regulation D?
a. All purchasers must be nonaccredited investors
b. All purchasers must be accredited investors
c. Securities must be offered publicly
d. No verification of investor status required

HINTS: Focus on the key requirement for soliciting or advertising under Regulation D.

Q154_LO6: What is the primary purpose of the greenshoe option in a stock offering?
a. Stabilize the offering price
b. Prevent oversubscription by investors
c. Extend the offering period
d. Eliminate underwriters' risks

HINTS: Focus on the primary purpose for the greenshoe option.

Q155_LO6: Which securities are exempt under Rule 147?
a. Securities with maturities of 270 days or less
b. Securities offered by federal agencies
c. Securities sold to nonresidents of the state
d. Securities sold entirely in one state

HINTS: Focus on the conditions under Rule 147 for exemption.

Q156_LO6: What is the purpose of the Intrastate Offering Rule (Rule 147)?
a. Exempt securities with unlimited nonaccredited investors
b. Facilitate offerings up to $50 million
c. Exempt securities sold entirely in one state
d. Regulate securities with maturities of 270 days or less

HINTS: Focus on the purpose for the Intrastate Offering Rule.

Q157_LO6: What does a company need to file electronically via the internet under Regulation D?
a. Full prospectus
b. Form D
c. Offering circular
d. Investment letter

HINTS: Focus on what a company must file electronically under Regulation D.

Q158_LO6: What is the primary advantage of Regulation A+ Tier 2 over Tier 1 for small- and medium-sized companies?
a. No investment limits for Tier 2
b. Coordination with individual states for Tier 2
c. Subject to SEC review only for Tier 2
d. No disclosure requirements for Tier 2

HINTS: Focus on the advantage for Regulation A+ Tier 2 over Tier 1.

Q159_LO6: Under Regulation D, what type of information must purchasers have access to in a private placement?
a. Minimal information
b. No information required
c. Same type as in a registered offering
d. Only financial information

HINTS: Focus on the information requirement under Regulation D for private placements.

Q160_LO6: What is the primary criterion for an offering to be exempt under Rule 147?
a. No broker-dealer involvement
b. Securities offered by federal agencies
c. All purchasers must be residents of the state
d. Issuer's principal office must be in the state

HINTS:

Q161_LO6: Which of the following securities is exempt from registration due to the issuer's creditworthiness?
a. Municipal securities
b. Commercial paper with a maturity of 270 days
c. Variable annuities
d. Bank securities

HINTS: Focus on exempt securities based on the issuer's creditworthiness.

Q162_LO6: What type of securities are included in the bank exemption from registration?
a. Bank holding company securities
b. Municipal securities
c. Fixed annuity contracts
d. Variable annuities

HINTS: Recognize the specific securities included in the bank exemption.

Q163_LO6: Which securities fall under the Regulation A+ Tier 2 offering?
a. Up to $6 million with state and SEC review
b. Up to $20 million with state and SEC review
c. Up to $15 million with SEC review only
d. Unlimited offering with SEC review only

HINTS: Focus on the specifics of the Tier 2 offering under Regulation A+.

Q164_LO6: Under Rule 147, what criterion must a company meet for an intrastate offering to be exempt from registration?
a. 60% of assets located within the state
b. 80% of offering proceeds used within the state
c. Majority of employees working in the state
d. 90% of income received in the state

HINTS: Consider the criteria for Rule 147 intrastate offerings.

Q165_LO6: What distinguishes Tier 2 investors in a Regulation A+ offering?
a. No investment limits
b. Accredited investor status
c. Self-certification of net worth
d. Limited to 5% of net worth

HINTS: Focus on the qualification criteria for Tier 2 investors in Regulation A+.

Q166_LO6: How does Regulation D differ from Rule 147 in terms of investor accreditation?
a. No accreditation required for Regulation D
b. All investors must be accredited in Regulation D
c. No specific requirements in Rule 147
d. Accreditation required only for Tier 2 in Regulation D

HINTS: Recognize the accreditation requirement difference between Regulation D and Rule 147.

Q167_LO6: What is the primary purpose of Form D in private placements?
a. SEC approval for the private placement
b. Limit the number of nonaccredited investors
c. Electronic filing of offering information
d. Secure accreditation status for investors

HINTS: Focus on the purpose for Form D in private placements.

Q168_LO6: What condition must be met for a business to solicit or advertise private securities offerings?
a. All purchasers must be nonaccredited investors
b. Majority of purchasers must be accredited investors
c. Securities offered under Regulation D exemption
d. Meeting Regulation A+ Tier 2 requirements

HINTS: Consider the condition for soliciting or advertising private securities offerings.

Q169_LO6: What term is synonymous with private placement stock that must be held for a six-month period?
a. Unregistered stock
b. Letter stock
c. Restricted stock
d. Legend stock

HINTS: Recognize the synonymous term for private placement stock with a holding period.

Q170_LO6: How does Rule 147 prevent the resale of securities to nonresidents after the initial purchase?
a. Six-month holding period
b. SEC approval for resale
c. State-level restrictions
d. Mandatory legend on the certificate

HINTS: Focus on the mechanism for preventing resale to nonresidents under Rule 147.

Q171_LO6: What distinguishes Regulation A+ from Regulation D in terms of advertising?
a. Advertising allowed in Regulation A+
b. No advertising allowed in Regulation A+
c. Advertising restricted in Regulation D
d. Both allow unrestricted advertising

HINTS: Focus on the advertising allowance in Regulation A+.

Q172_LO6: How is the investor qualification different between Tier 1 and Tier 2 in Regulation A+?
a. Tier 1 has no investment limits
b. Tier 2 requires self-certification
c. Tier 2 allows unlimited investment
d. Tier 1 requires accredited investor status

HINTS: Focus on the investment limits for Tier 1 in Regulation A+.

Q173_LO6: What requirement does Regulation D impose on private placement investors regarding the holding of stock?
a. Six-month holding period
b. Annual reporting requirement
c. Mandatory resale after one year
d. No specific holding requirement

HINTS: Recognize the holding period requirement for private placement stock under Regulation D.

Q174_LO6: In a private placement, what is the significance of a legend on the stock certificate?
a. Allows resale without restrictions
b. Indicates accredited investor status
c. Prevents transfer without registration or exemption
d. Grants SEC approval for resale

HINTS: Focus on the purpose of the legend on the stock certificate in private placements.

Q175_LO6: What is the key difference in SEC filing requirements between Regulation A+ and private placements under Regulation D?
a. Full prospectus filing for Regulation A+
b. Electronic Form D filing for Regulation D
c. No filing requirement for Regulation A+
d. SEC approval needed for Regulation D

HINTS: Recognize the filing requirement difference for Regulation A+ and Regulation D.

Q176_LO7: What document is amended when the registration statement becomes effective, adding information such as the final offering price?
a. Preliminary prospectus
b. Final prospectus
c. Full prospectus
d. Summary prospectus

HINTS: Think about the document that is updated when the registration is complete.

Q177_LO7: Which information is not required on the cover page of a summary prospectus?
a. Fund's name and class of shares
b. Exchange ticker symbol
c. Toll-free number for prospectus delivery
d. Historical performance over 10 years

HINTS: Consider the necessary information for the cover page of a summary prospectus.

Q178_LO7: What does the SEC disclaimer state regarding the approval of securities offerings?
a. SEC approves all offerings
b. SEC endorses approved offerings
c. SEC releases offerings for sale
d. SEC evaluates the adequacy of information

HINTS: Reflect on the role of the SEC in the disclaimer.

Q179_LO7: Which disclosure document provides key information in a standardized order, including investment policies and performance histories?
a. Preliminary prospectus
b. Full (statutory) prospectus
c. Summary prospectus
d. Statement of additional information

HINTS: Think about the comprehensive document providing detailed information.

Q180_LO7: What is the primary purpose of a summary prospectus?
a. Detailed disclosure for investors
b. Comprehensive financial statements
c. Providing historical performance
d. Offering a brief overview of key information

HINTS: Consider the purpose of a summary prospectus in relation to detailed disclosure.

Q181_LO7: Which document is useful to investors seeking additional information beyond the prospectus but is not mandatory for an informed decision?
a. Omitting prospectus
b. Summary prospectus
c. Full (statutory) prospectus
d. Statement of additional information (SAI)

HINTS: Consider the purpose and content of the document .

Q182_LO7: How often is a mutual fund prospectus updated, and what is the period for which it may be used for sales solicitations?
a. Updated annually, 12 months
b. Updated quarterly, 16 months
c. Updated biannually, 18 months
d. Updated monthly, 14 months

HINTS: Think about the frequency of updates and the duration for sales solicitations.

Q183_LO7: What is the official term for an advertisement for a mutual fund that omits most information needed for an investing decision?
a. Preliminary prospectus
b. Final prospectus

c. Omitting prospectus
d. Full (statutory) prospectus

HINTS: Recall the name for an advertisement that lacks essential information.

Q184_LO7: What disclosure document is required for municipal securities and is similar to a prospectus?
a. Preliminary prospectus
b. Full (statutory) prospectus
c. Offering circular
d. Summary prospectus

HINTS: Consider the disclosure document used for municipal securities.

Q185_LO7: What must a mutual fund provide to investors within three business days of a request, offering expanded discussions on history and policies?
a. Full (statutory) prospectus
b. Summary prospectus
c. Preliminary prospectus
d. Statement of additional information (SAI)

HINTS: Think about the document that offers expanded discussions and additional details.

Q186_LO7: In what circumstances is access to a prospectus on the SEC website considered sufficient for meeting delivery requirements?
a. Only for NMS securities
b. Only for non-NMS securities
c. For both NMS and non-NMS securities
d. Only for IPOs

HINTS: Consider the circumstances under which access to the SEC website is sufficient.

Q187_LO7: What is the timeline for an investor to be entitled to the final prospectus after buying a new security in the secondary market for IPOs of NMS securities?
a. 25 days
b. 90 days
c. Zero days
d. 40 days

HINTS: Think about the timeline for entitlement after buying a new security in the secondary market.

Q188_LO7: What information is required on the cover page of a summary prospectus?
a. Investment objectives and strategies
b. Exchange ticker symbol
c. Toll-free number for prospectus delivery
d. Historical performance over 10 years

HINTS: Consider the necessary information for the cover page of a summary prospectus.

Q189_LO7: What does the term "full and fair disclosure document" refer to in the context of mutual funds?
a. Preliminary prospectus
b. Final prospectus
c. Ongoing prospectus
d. Summary prospectus

HINTS: Think about the document providing continuous disclosure for mutual funds.

Q190_LO7: What key information must a mutual fund prospectus contain in a standardized order on the front page?
a. Investment policies and performance
b. Exchange ticker symbol
c. Historical performance over 10 years
d. Balance sheet and income statement

HINTS: Reflect on the key information required on the front page of a mutual fund prospectus.

Q191_LO7: What document provides a prospective investor with the material information needed to make a fully informed investment decision?
a. Preliminary prospectus
b. Final prospectus
c. Full (statutory) prospectus
d. Summary prospectus

HINTS: Focus on the comprehensive disclosure document for informed investment decisions.

Q192_LO7: When can registered representatives take orders from customers who indicated interest in buying during the cooling-off period?
a. During the preliminary prospectus
b. After the cooling-off period
c. Before the registration statement becomes effective
d. After the final prospectus is issued

HINTS: Consider the timing for taking orders from interested customers.

Q193_LO7: What information must precede or accompany all sales confirmations according to SEC requirements?
a. Description of the offering
b. Offering price
c. SEC disclaimer
d. Use of the proceeds

HINTS: Focus on the information mandated by the SEC to precede or accompany sales confirmations.

Q194_LO7: What does the SEC disclaimer state regarding securities offerings?
a. Approval of the offering
b. Endorsement of the offering
c. Clearance for sale
d. No representation about accuracy or adequacy

HINTS: Recognize the nature of the statement in the SEC disclaimer.

Q195_LO7: Which document must be distributed to an investor before or during the solicitation if used to solicit a sale?
a. Preliminary prospectus
b. Final prospectus
c. Full (statutory) prospectus
d. Summary prospectus

HINTS: Focus on the document required for distribution during solicitation.

Q196_LO7: What is the purpose of an ongoing prospectus in a mutual fund?
a. Annual performance histories
b. Standardized order of information
c. Required for sales solicitations
d. Availability for new share purchases

HINTS: Consider the role of an ongoing prospectus in mutual funds.

Q197_LO7: What is the annual update period for a mutual fund prospectus?
a. 6 months
b. 12 months
c. 16 months
d. 24 months

HINTS: Recall the duration for which a mutual fund prospectus is updated annually.

Q198_LO7: Which prospectus is an abbreviated summary of key information in a fund's full prospectus?
a. Preliminary prospectus
b. Final prospectus
c. Full (statutory) prospectus
d. Summary prospectus

HINTS: Recognize the purpose of a prospectus providing a summary of key information.

Q199_LO7: What must be included on the cover page of a summary prospectus according to specific requirements?
a. Portfolio holdings
b. Ticker symbol
c. Legend about full prospectus
d. Financial highlights

HINTS: Focus on the required elements on the cover page of a summary prospectus.

Q200_LO7: What document is required for mutual funds and closed-end funds, providing expanded discussions on the fund's history and policies?
a. Preliminary prospectus
b. Final prospectus
c. Summary prospectus
d. Statement of additional information (SAI)

HINTS: Focus on the document that allows expanded discussions on fund history and policies.

Q201_LO7: What is the official name for an advertisement for a mutual fund, omitting most information required for investment decisions?
a. Preliminary prospectus
b. Final prospectus
c. Omitting prospectus
d. Summary prospectus

HINTS: Recognize the official name for an advertisement that omits most information.

Q202_LO7: What is the primary disclosure document for municipal securities?
a. Preliminary prospectus
b. Final prospectus
c. Official statement
d. Omitting prospectus

HINTS: Focus on the disclosure document specific to municipal securities.

Q203_LO7: What term is commonly used for the disclosure document for exempt securities like private placements and Regulation A+?
a. Offering circular
b. Preliminary prospectus
c. Final prospectus
d. Summary prospectus

HINTS: Recognize the common term for the disclosure document for exempt securities.

Q204_LO7: What SEC rule mandates prospectus delivery timelines for secondary market investors?
a. Rule 144
b. Rule 482
c. Rule 147
d. Rule 506

HINTS: Focus on the SEC rule related to prospectus delivery for secondary market investors.

Q205_LO7: What is the timeline requirement for providing the final prospectus to an investor purchasing IPO shares of NMS securities?
a. 25 days
b. 40 days
c. 60 days
d. 90 days

HINTS: Consider the timeline requirement for providing the final prospectus for IPO shares of NMS securities.

Q206_LO7: What document provides material information needed for a fully informed investment decision and is amended when the registration statement becomes effective?
a. Preliminary prospectus
b. Final prospectus
c. Full prospectus
d. Summary prospectus

HINTS: Focus on the document amended when the registration becomes effective.

Q207_LO7: What information must be included in the final prospectus?
a. Investment strategies
b. Exchange ticker symbol
c. Summary of risks
d. Toll-free number for paper delivery

HINTS: Identify the key information for inclusion in the final prospectus.

Q208_LO7: What is the SEC disclaimer's purpose in the prospectus?
a. Endorsement of the offering
b. Approval of the securities
c. Clearance for sale
d. Guarantee of accuracy

HINTS: Recognize the purpose of the SEC disclaimer in the prospectus.
Q209_LO7: Which type of prospectus must always be available for open-end managed investment companies?
a. Preliminary prospectus
b. Full prospectus
c. Summary prospectus
d. Ongoing prospectus

HINTS: Consider the specific requirement for open-end managed investment companies.

Q210_LO7: How often is a mutual fund prospectus updated?
a. Quarterly
b. Semi-annually
c. Annually
d. Biennially

HINTS: Recall the update frequency for mutual fund prospectuses.

Q211_LO7: What is the maximum period a summary prospectus may be used for sales solicitations from the date of publication?
a. 6 months
b. 12 months
c. 16 months
d. 24 months

HINTS: Identify the specified period for using a summary prospectus for sales solicitations.

Q212_LO7: What must be included on the cover page of a summary prospectus?
a. Portfolio holdings
b. Toll-free number for paper delivery
c. Legal opinion disclaimer
d. Investment objectives

HINTS: Focus on the specific requirements for the cover page of a summary prospectus.

Q213_LO7: What additional information is found in the Statement of Additional Information (SAI)?
a. Final offering price
b. Balance sheet
c. Offering date
d. SEC disclaimer

HINTS: Recognize the additional information typically found in the SAI.

Q214_LO7: What is the official name for an advertisement for a mutual fund that omits most information needed for an investment decision?
a. Final prospectus
b. Omitting prospectus
c. Summary prospectus
d. Preliminary prospectus

HINTS: Identify the official name for an advertisement omitting crucial information.

Q215_LO7: What is the primary disclosure document for municipal securities?
a. Summary prospectus
b. Omitting prospectus
c. Offering circular
d. Full prospectus

HINTS: Recognize the primary disclosure document for municipal securities.

Q216_LO7: What are the prospectus delivery requirements for an investor buying new securities in the secondary market?
a. Always entitled to a final prospectus
b. 30 days for NMS securities
c. 60 days for non-NMS securities
d. Depends on the IPO type

HINTS: Consider the timelines for prospectus delivery to investors in the secondary market.

Q217_LO7: For IPOs of non-NMS securities, within how many days is an investor entitled to the final prospectus?
a. 20 days
b. 30 days
c. 60 days
d. 90 days

HINTS: Focus on the specific timeline for IPOs of non-NMS securities.

Q218_LO7: What is the purpose of an omitting prospectus for a mutual fund?
a. Comprehensive information for investment decisions
b. Advertisement for new fund launches
c. Meeting prospectus delivery requirements
d. Providing detailed historical performance

HINTS: Recognize the purpose of an omitting prospectus for a mutual fund.

Q219_LO7: What type of disclosure document is commonly used for exempt securities like Regulation A+ offerings?
a. Full prospectus
b. Preliminary prospectus
c. Offering circular
d. Summary prospectus

HINTS: Identify the common term for the disclosure document for exempt securities like Regulation A+ offerings.

Q220_LO7: Which document provides material information to make an informed investment decision and is distributed to an investor before or during solicitation?
a. Ongoing prospectus
b. Final prospectus
c. Preliminary prospectus
d. Summary prospectus

HINTS: Focus on the document used for solicitation that must be distributed to an investor.

Correct Answers & Explanations
The Securities Act of 1933 and the Primary Markets

Q1_LO1: Correct Answer: b. Issuer transactions for selling securities to the public EXPLANATIONS: b, as the primary market is where securities are sold to the public through issuer transactions.

Q2_LO1: Correct Answer: c. Secondary market EXPLANATIONS: c, as the secondary market is where securities trade between investors.

Q3_LO1: Correct Answer: c. Issuer transactions EXPLANATIONS: c, as issuer transactions in the primary market allow corporations to raise capital quickly.

Q4_LO1: Correct Answer: b. By enabling corporations to raise capital for expansion EXPLANATIONS: b, as the primary market enables corporations to raise capital for expansion, contributing to job creation.

Q5_LO1: Correct Answer: c. Capital markets EXPLANATIONS: c, as another term for the primary and secondary markets collectively is the capital markets.

Q6_LO1: Correct Answer: c. By allowing investors to grow assets alongside the economy EXPLANATIONS: c, as the primary market allows investors to grow their assets alongside the economy.

Q7_LO1: Correct Answer: b. Funding infrastructure projects and public programs EXPLANATIONS: b, as governments use the primary market to raise money for infrastructure projects and public programs.

Q8_LO1: Correct Answer: c. They earn returns alongside the economy's growth EXPLANATIONS: c, as investors earn returns alongside the economy's growth by owning mutual fund shares.

Q9_LO1: Correct Answer: c. It links fees to fund performance EXPLANATIONS: b, as the High Water Mark Principle links fees to the performance of funds in the primary market.

Q10_LO1: Correct Answer: c. Providing capital needed for economic growth EXPLANATIONS: c, as representatives in the securities industry play an important role in providing the capital needed for economic growth in the primary market.

Q11_LO2: Correct Answer: b. Requiring full and fair disclosure in public securities offerings EXPLANATIONS: b, as the act requires full and fair disclosure in connection with the sale of securities to the public.

Q12_LO2: Correct Answer: c. Initial public offering (IPO) EXPLANATIONS: c, as the first time an issuer distributes securities to the public is called an Initial Public Offering (IPO).

Q13_LO2: Correct Answer: c. After IPOs EXPLANATIONS: c, as follow-on offerings typically occur after the initial public offering (IPO).

Q14_LO2: Correct Answer: b. Link fees to fund performance EXPLANATIONS: b, as the High Water Mark Principle links fees to the performance of funds in IPOs.

Q15_LO2: Correct Answer: d. All of the above EXPLANATIONS: d, as restricted persons include member firms, employees, finders, fiduciaries, portfolio managers, and immediate family members of certain individuals.

Q16_LO2: Correct Answer: c. An exemption for restricted persons with less than 10% interest EXPLANATIONS: c, as it allows restricted persons with less than 10% interest to participate in new equity issues.

Q17_LO2: Correct Answer: c. Before any public offerings EXPLANATIONS: c, as an IPO is the first time a corporation distributes securities to the public.

Q18_LO2: Correct Answer: a. Follow-on offerings EXPLANATIONS: a, as subsequent money raises after an IPO are known as follow-on offerings.

Q19_LO2: Correct Answer: c. It requires full and fair disclosure in public offerings EXPLANATIONS: c, as the act requires full and fair disclosure in connection with the sale of securities to the public.

Q20_LO2: Correct Answer: c. Investment bankers EXPLANATIONS: c, as investment bankers play a role in ensuring a bona fide public offering of securities at the public offering price (POP) in IPOs

Q21_LO2: Correct Answer: b. Distributing securities to the public EXPLANATIONS: b, as a primary offering involves distributing securities to the public to raise capital for the issuing corporation.

Q22_LO2: Correct Answer: b. Securities Act of 1933 EXPLANATIONS: b, as public offerings of securities are regulated under the Securities Act of 1933.

Q23_LO2: Correct Answer: d. Initial public offering (IPO) EXPLANATIONS: d, as the first-time distribution of securities to the public is called an Initial Public Offering (IPO).

Q24_LO2: Correct Answer: b. Ensuring full and fair disclosure in public offerings EXPLANATIONS: b, as the Securities Act of 1933 aims to ensure full and fair disclosure in connection with the sale of securities to the public.

Q25_LO2: Correct Answer: d. Both A and C EXPLANATIONS: d, as subsequent money raises after an IPO are known as Additional Public Offerings (APOs) or Follow-on Offerings.

Q26_LO2: Correct Answer: c. Safeguarding public offering integrity and investor interests EXPLANATIONS: c, as IPO rules and regulations primarily aim to safeguard the integrity of the public offering process and protect investor interests.

Q27_LO2: Correct Answer: d. Both B and C EXPLANATIONS: d, as restricted persons include employees of member firms, portfolio managers, and other specified individuals.

Q28_LO2: Correct Answer: c. It allows restricted persons to have an interest in an account up to 10% EXPLANATIONS: c, as the de minimis exemption allows restricted persons to have an interest in an account up to 10% without restricting the account from purchasing new equity issues.

Q29_LO2: Correct Answer: d. Both B and C EXPLANATIONS: d, as subsequent primary offerings after an IPO can be referred to as both Additional Public Offerings (APOs) and Follow-on Offerings.

Q30_LO2: Correct Answer: b. Ensuring a fair distribution to the general public EXPLANATIONS: b, as the primary objective is to ensure a fair distribution of new issues to the general public.

Q31_LO2: Correct Answer: b. Ensuring full and fair disclosure in public offerings EXPLANATIONS: The correct option is b, as the act requires full and fair disclosure in connection with the sale of securities to the public.

Q32_LO2: Correct Answer: d. Initial public offering EXPLANATIONS: The correct option is d, as the first time an issuer distributes securities to the public is called an initial public offering (IPO).

Q33_LO2: Correct Answer: c. Follow-on offering EXPLANATIONS: The correct option is c, as subsequent offerings after the IPO are known as follow-on offerings or additional public offerings (APOs).

Q34_LO2: Correct Answer: b. Primary offerings with proceeds going to the issuer EXPLANATIONS: The correct option is b, as follow-on offerings are primary market transactions with proceeds going to the issuer.

Q35_LO2: Correct Answer: c. Initial public offering (IPO) EXPLANATIONS: The correct option is c, as the first time an issuer distributes securities to the public (IPO) is where the issuer receives the entire deal proceeds.

Q36_LO2: Correct Answer: b. Securities Act of 1933 EXPLANATIONS: The correct option is b, as public offerings of securities are regulated under the Securities Act of 1933.

Q37_LO2: Correct Answer: a. Investment bankers and BDs EXPLANATIONS: The correct option is a, as investment bankers and BDs (underwriters) facilitate public offerings of securities.

Q38_LO2: Correct Answer: b. To protect the integrity of the public offering process EXPLANATIONS: The correct option is b, as IPO rules and regulations aim to protect the integrity of the public offering process.

Q39_LO2: Correct Answer: c. Immediate family members of industry insiders EXPLANATIONS: The correct option is c, as immediate family members of industry insiders are considered restricted persons.

Q40_LO2: Correct Answer: b. Exemption for restricted persons with less than 10% ownership EXPLANATIONS: The correct option is b, as the de minimis exemption allows restricted persons to have an interest in an account purchasing new equity issues if their ownership does not exceed 10%

Q41_LO3: Correct Answer: c. Underwriters EXPLANATIONS: The correct option is c, as underwriters work with an issuer to bring its securities to the market and sell them to the investing public.

Q42_LO3: Correct Answer: c. Best efforts underwriting EXPLANATIONS: The correct option is c, as best efforts underwriting involves underwriters acting as agents and collecting client funds into an escrow account.

Q43_LO3: Correct Answer: b. Cancel the underwriting EXPLANATIONS: The correct option is b, as in an AON underwriting, the underwriter must either sell all the shares or cancel the underwriting.

Q44_LO3: Correct Answer: c. To set a minimum and maximum issuance requirement EXPLANATIONS: The correct option is c, as a Mini-max underwriting sets a floor and ceiling on the dollar amount of securities the issuer is willing to sell.

Q45_LO3: Correct Answer: c. Underwriters EXPLANATIONS: The correct option is c, as in a Firm Commitment underwriting, underwriters are at risk for any unsold shares.

Q46_LO3: Correct Answer: b. Provide significant resources and take on a lead role EXPLANATIONS: The correct option is b, as the managing underwriter provides significant resources and takes on a lead role in a syndicate.

Q47_LO3: Correct Answer: b. Banks, insurance companies, and mutual funds EXPLANATIONS: The correct option is b, as institutional investors include entities like banks, insurance companies, and mutual funds.

Q48_LO3: Correct Answer: c. Minimum net worth of $1,000,000 EXPLANATIONS: The correct option is c, as accredited investors must have a minimum net worth of $1,000,000 (excluding primary residence) or meet specific income criteria.

Q49_LO3: Correct Answer: d. Advising on debt structure and bond features EXPLANATIONS: The correct option is d, as municipal advisors assist municipalities with issues like debt structure and bond features.

Q50_LO3: Correct Answer: d. Treasury Department EXPLANATIONS: The correct option is d, as the Treasury Department is the largest issuer of debt in the United States.

Q51_LO3: Correct Answer: b. Underwriters EXPLANATIONS: Underwriters, specifically broker-dealers or investment bankers, play a key role in bringing securities to the market and selling them to the investing public.

Q52_LO3: Correct Answer: b. Agent EXPLANATIONS: In a best efforts underwriting, the underwriter acts as an agent, not committing to purchase the shares but facilitating the sale to the public.

Q53_LO3: Correct Answer: c. To buy securities from the issuer and resell them to the public EXPLANATIONS: In a firm commitment underwriting, underwriters buy securities from the issuer and resell them to the public at a higher price.

Q54_LO3: Correct Answer: c. Managing underwriter EXPLANATIONS: The managing underwriter plays a lead role in a syndicate, providing significant resources to the venture.

Q55_LO3: Correct Answer: a. All shares must be sold EXPLANATIONS: In an all-or-none underwriting, the condition for success is that all shares must be sold, or the underwriting is canceled.

Q56_LO3: Correct Answer: c. To establish the floor and ceiling for the number of securities to be sold EXPLANATIONS: A mini-max underwriting sets a floor (minimum) and a ceiling (maximum) on the number of securities to be sold.

Q57_LO3: Correct Answer: c. Institutional investors EXPLANATIONS: Institutional investors include entities like banks, insurance companies, pensions, hedge funds, and mutual funds.

Q58_LO3: Correct Answer: c. Net worth of $1,000,000 or more EXPLANATIONS: Retail investors can be accredited if they have a net worth of $1,000,000 or more, excluding equity in the primary residence.

Q59_LO3: Correct Answer: b. Institutional investor EXPLANATIONS: Institutional investors, especially qualified institutional buyers (QIBs), generally invest a minimum of $100 million in securities.

Q60_LO3: Correct Answer: b. Advising municipalities on debt issuance EXPLANATIONS: Municipal advisors provide advice to municipalities on debt issuance and related matters but do not participate in underwriting.

Q61_LO3: Correct Answer: b. Underwriters EXPLANATIONS: Underwriters, such as broker-dealers and investment bankers, work with issuers to bring securities to the market.

Q62_LO3: Correct Answer: b. Best efforts underwriting EXPLANATIONS: Best efforts underwriting involves underwriters acting as agents, not committing to purchasing shares themselves.

Q63_LO3: Correct Answer: a. Floor EXPLANATIONS: The minimum issuance requirement in a mini-max underwriting is called the floor.

Q64_LO3: Correct Answer: a. Syndicate EXPLANATIONS: A syndicate is a joint venture formed by BDs to share the risk and profits of a large firm commitment underwriting.

Q65_LO3: Correct Answer: a. Qualified institutional buyers (QIBs) EXPLANATIONS: Qualified institutional buyers (QIBs) own and invest a minimum of $100 million in securities on a discretionary basis.

Q66_LO3: Correct Answer: d. Investors with a net worth of $1,000,000 EXPLANATIONS: Accredited retail investors have a net worth of $1,000,000 or more (excluding primary residence equity) or meet specific income criteria.

Q67_LO3: Correct Answer: d. Structuring capital raises EXPLANATIONS: Municipal advisors assist municipalities in structuring capital raises and providing advice on debt and securities issuance.

Q68_LO3: Correct Answer: c. Firm commitment underwriting EXPLANATIONS: Firm commitment underwriting involves underwriters committing to purchasing unsold shares for the syndicate account.

Q69_LO3: Correct Answer: a. Spread EXPLANATIONS: The spread is the difference between the price at which underwriters buy securities from the issuer and sell them to the public.

Q70_LO3: Correct Answer: b. Ensuring full and fair disclosure in public offerings EXPLANATIONS: The Securities Act of 1933 aims to ensure full and fair disclosure in connection with the sale of securities to the public.

Q71_LO4: Correct Answer: b. Protect investors in new issues EXPLANATIONS: The Securities Act of 1933 aims to protect investors in new issues by requiring registration and ensuring full disclosure.

Q72_LO4: Correct Answer: b. Running tombstone advertisements EXPLANATIONS: Tombstone ads are permitted during the cooling-off period, providing minimal information about the new issue.

Q73_LO4: Correct Answer: c. Preliminary prospectus (red herring) EXPLANATIONS: The preliminary prospectus, or red herring, is used as a prospecting tool during the cooling-off period.

Q74_LO4: Correct Answer: b. 20 calendar days EXPLANATIONS: The cooling-off period for a nonexempt issue lasts for a minimum of 20 calendar days.

Q75_LO4: Correct Answer: d. Material information about the issue EXPLANATIONS: The registration statement includes material information about the new issue.

Q76_LO4: Correct Answer: b. Gauge investor interest EXPLANATIONS: The preliminary prospectus is used to gauge investor interest during the cooling-off period.

Q77_LO4: Correct Answer: b. Indication of interest EXPLANATIONS: An indication of interest is an investor's declaration of potential interest in purchasing the issue.

Q78_LO4: Correct Answer: b. Due diligence EXPLANATIONS: Due diligence takes place during the cooling-off period to examine the issue's suitability for different customers.

Q79_LO4: Correct Answer: b. Placing tombstone advertisements EXPLANATIONS: Tombstone ads are allowed during the cooling-off period for announcing a new issue with minimal information.

Q80_LO4: Correct Answer: b. Blue sky filing EXPLANATIONS: The process of coordinating federal and state registrations is called "blue sky filing."

Q81_LO4: Correct Answer: c. Release date EXPLANATIONS: The date when the SEC allows the security to be offered is called the "release date."

Q82_LO4: Correct Answer: d. Final prospectus EXPLANATIONS: The final prospectus must precede or accompany all sales confirmations during the offering of a new security.

Q83_LO4: Correct Answer: d. SEC disclaimer EXPLANATIONS: The standard SEC disclaimer reads, "These securities have not been approved or disapproved by the SEC nor have any representations been made about the accuracy or the adequacy of the information."

Q84_LO4: Correct Answer: b. Secondary Offering EXPLANATIONS: An additional primary offering for a company that has completed an IPO is called a "Secondary Offering."

Q85_LO4: Correct Answer: c. Primary market transaction EXPLANATIONS: If the issuer is receiving the funds from an offering, it is a primary market transaction.

Q86_LO4: Correct Answer: b. Protecting investors in the primary market EXPLANATIONS: The main purpose is to protect investors in the primary market by ensuring full disclosure and regulating new issues.

Q87_LO4: Correct Answer: c. Registration statement (S-1) EXPLANATIONS: The registration statement (S-1) is filed with the SEC when an issuer plans to sell a nonexempt security.

Q88_LO4: Correct Answer: c. Tombstone ads EXPLANATIONS: Tombstone ads, providing minimal information, are allowed during the cooling-off period.

Q89_LO4: Correct Answer: b. To gather indications of interest EXPLANATIONS: The preliminary prospectus is used to gather indications of interest and gauge investor interest.

Q90_LO4: Correct Answer: c. A nonbinding declaration of potential interest EXPLANATIONS: An indication of interest is a nonbinding declaration of potential interest to purchase securities.

Q91_LO4: Correct Answer: b. Examination of the issue's suitability for customers EXPLANATIONS: During due diligence, underwriters examine the issue to determine its suitability for customers.

Q92_LO4: Correct Answer: b. Blue sky filings EXPLANATIONS: The process of coordinating federal and state registrations is known as "blue sky filings."

Q93_LO4: Correct Answer: c. Effective date EXPLANATIONS: The effective date marks the beginning of the period when investors can purchase the new issue.

Q94_LO4: Correct Answer: b. Offering price EXPLANATIONS: The final prospectus includes the offering price in addition to the information found in the preliminary prospectus.

Q95_LO4: Correct Answer: d. Follow-on offering EXPLANATIONS: Selling additional shares to the public after the IPO is known as a follow-on offering.

Q96_LO4: Correct Answer: c. Preliminary prospectus EXPLANATIONS: The preliminary prospectus must be made available to any customer who expresses interest during the cooling-off period.

Q97_LO4: Correct Answer: d. Soliciting sales of securities EXPLANATIONS: Soliciting sales of securities is prohibited during the cooling-off period.

Q98_LO4: Correct Answer: c. A minimal amount of information EXPLANATIONS: Tombstone ads contain a minimal amount of information about the offering.

Q99_LO4: Correct Answer: c. Adequacy of the information EXPLANATIONS: The standard SEC disclaimer states that the securities have not been approved or disapproved by the SEC, nor have representations been made about the adequacy of the information.

Q100_LO4: Correct Answer: a. Hybrid offering EXPLANATIONS: A primary offering with both new and existing shares is termed a hybrid offering.

Q101_LO4: Correct Answer: b. Ensure full and fair disclosure in primary market offerings EXPLANATIONS: The Securities Act of 1933 aims to ensure full and fair disclosure in primary market offerings.

Q102_LO4: Correct Answer: c. Registration statement (S-1) EXPLANATIONS: An issuer must file a registration statement (S-1) with the SEC when selling a nonexempt security.

Q103_LO4: Correct Answer: b. Tombstone advertisement EXPLANATIONS: Tombstone ads, providing minimal information, are allowed during the cooling-off period.

Q104_LO4: Correct Answer: c. Gauges investor interest EXPLANATIONS: The preliminary prospectus is used to gauge investor interest and gather indications of interest.

Q105_LO4: Correct Answer: c. A nonbinding declaration of potential interest EXPLANATIONS: An indication of interest is a nonbinding declaration of potential interest from an investor.

Q106_LO4: Correct Answer: b. Examination of the issue's suitability for customers EXPLANATIONS: Due diligence meetings involve examining the issue's suitability for customers.

Q107_LO4: Correct Answer: d. Blue sky filings EXPLANATIONS: The process of coordinating federal and state registrations is called "blue sky filings."

Q108_LO4: Correct Answer: c. After the effective date EXPLANATIONS: The SEC allows the security to be offered to investors after the effective date.

Q109_LO4: Correct Answer: c. Final prospectus EXPLANATIONS: The final prospectus must precede or accompany all sales confirmations.

Q110_LO4: Correct Answer: b. Selling discounts EXPLANATIONS: The spread represents the selling discounts earned by underwriters.

Q111_LO4: Correct Answer: b. Subsequent sale of more shares after an IPO EXPLANATIONS: An APO is a subsequent sale of more shares by a corporation after an IPO.

Q112_LO4: Correct Answer: d. Primary market transaction EXPLANATIONS: If the issuer is receiving funds, it is a primary market transaction.

Q113_LO4: Correct Answer: b. Blue sky filings EXPLANATIONS: Coordinating federal and state securities registrations is termed "blue sky filings."

Q114_LO4: Correct Answer: d. "These securities have not been approved or disapproved by the SEC." EXPLANATIONS: The standard SEC disclaimer in the final prospectus states: "These securities have not been approved or disapproved by the SEC."

Q115_LO4: Correct Answer: d. Hybrid combination offering EXPLANATIONS: A hybrid combination offering involves selling both new and existing shares to the public.

Q116_LO5: Correct Answer: b. Ability to sell portions over a two-year period EXPLANATIONS: A shelf offering allows the issuer to sell portions over a two-year period without re-registering.

Q117_LO5: Correct Answer: b. Two years EXPLANATIONS: A shelf offering registration is valid for two years after filing with the SEC.

Q118_LO5: Correct Answer: b. Listing on a major exchange EXPLANATIONS: A WKSI is generally an issuer listed on a major exchange.

Q119_LO5: Correct Answer: c. Supplemental prospectus filing EXPLANATIONS: A supplemental prospectus must be filed with the SEC before each sale in a shelf registration.

Q120_LO5: Correct Answer: b. Increase the number of offered shares by up to 15% EXPLANATIONS: The greenshoe option allows underwriters to increase offered shares by up to 15% based on demand.

Q121_LO5: Correct Answer: b. Well-known seasoned issuer (WKSI) status EXPLANATIONS: A WKSI may extend a shelf offering to three years based on its status.

Q122_LO5: Correct Answer: b. Over-allotment option EXPLANATIONS: The greenshoe option is formally known as an over-allotment option.

Q123_LO5: Correct Answer: a. Securities Act of 1933 EXPLANATIONS: The shelf offering and greenshoe option are governed by the Securities Act of 1933.

Q124_LO5: Correct Answer: c. Provides flexibility to sell when conditions are favorable EXPLANATIONS: A shelf offering provides flexibility for the issuer to sell when market conditions are favorable.

Q125_LO5: Correct Answer: c. Updates material information before each sale EXPLANATIONS: A supplemental prospectus updates material information before each sale in a shelf offering.

Q126_LO5: Correct Answer: b. Underpricing of shares EXPLANATIONS: The greenshoe option helps protect against the underpricing of shares by providing flexibility to increase offered shares.

Q127_LO5: Correct Answer: a. Stabilize the offering price EXPLANATIONS: The primary purpose of a greenshoe option is to stabilize the offering price.

Q128_LO5: Correct Answer: c. Sell portions of the registered shares at intervals EXPLANATIONS: A shelf offering allows an issuer to sell portions of registered shares over a two-year period.

Q129_LO5: Correct Answer: c. 15% EXPLANATIONS: The Greenshoe option allows underwriters to increase the number of offered shares by up to 15%.

Q130_LO5: Correct Answer: b. High market demand EXPLANATIONS: A greenshoe option is particularly useful for underwriters in situations of high market demand.

Q131_LO6: Correct Answer: c. Publicly traded company EXPLANATIONS: Exempt issuers include the federal government, municipal government, and certain regulatory agencies, not publicly traded companies.

Q132_LO6: Correct Answer: c. $50 million EXPLANATIONS: Tier 2 under Regulation A+ allows securities offerings up to $50 million in a 12-month period.

Q133_LO6: Correct Answer: c. If the offering takes place entirely in one state EXPLANATIONS: Securities offerings are exempt under Rule 147 if they take place entirely in one state.

Q134_LO6: Correct Answer: b. 6 months EXPLANATIONS: Securities sold under Rule 147 may not be resold to nonresidents for six months after the initial purchase.

Q135_LO6: Correct Answer: b. Allow unlimited capital raising EXPLANATIONS: Regulation D allows unlimited capital raising without SEC registration for private placements.

Q136_LO6: Correct Answer: a. High net worth or income EXPLANATIONS: An accredited investor under Regulation D is generally defined by high net worth or income.

Q137_LO6: Correct Answer: b. All purchasers must be accredited investors EXPLANATIONS: For soliciting or advertising private placements, all purchasers must be accredited investors.

Q138_LO6: Correct Answer: b. 10% EXPLANATIONS: For Tier 2 Regulation A+ offerings, investors must limit the investment to the greater of 10% of net worth or 10% of net income.

Q139_LO6: Correct Answer: b. Letter stock EXPLANATIONS: Private placement stock held for a six-month period is also known as letter stock.

Q140_LO6: Correct Answer: b. SEC review level EXPLANATIONS: Tier 1 offerings are subject to state and SEC review, while Tier 2 offerings are subject only to SEC review.

Q141_LO6: Correct Answer: b. Form D EXPLANATIONS: Companies must file information on Form D electronically for nonpublic offerings under Regulation D.

Q142_LO6: Correct Answer: c. Investment letter EXPLANATIONS: Private placement investors must sign an investment letter indicating their intent to hold the stock for investment purposes.

Q143_LO6: Correct Answer: a. Majority of employees must work in the state EXPLANATIONS: Securities sold under Rule 147 must have the majority of employees working in the state.

Q144_LO6: Correct Answer: c. Promote local investment EXPLANATIONS: Rule 147 is designed to promote local investment by exempting intrastate offerings from federal registration requirements.

Q145_LO6: Correct Answer: a. Offering circular EXPLANATIONS: In a Regulation A+ offering, investors are provided with an abbreviated notice of sale, known as an offering circular, rather than a full prospectus.

Q146_LO6: Correct Answer: d. Variable annuities EXPLANATIONS: Variable annuities are not exempt and must be registered as securities with the SEC.

Q147_LO6: Correct Answer: b. Two years EXPLANATIONS: A shelf offering registration is valid for two years after filing with the SEC.

Q148_LO6: Correct Answer: b. Commercial paper with maturities of 270 days or less EXPLANATIONS: Commercial paper with maturities of 270 days or less is exempt based on creditworthiness.

Q149_LO6: Correct Answer: d. Subject to rigorous disclosure requirements to the SEC EXPLANATIONS: Tier 2 offerings are subject to rigorous disclosure requirements to the SEC.

Q150_LO6: Correct Answer: c. When the issuer has its principal office in the state EXPLANATIONS: Securities are exempt under Rule 147 when the issuer has its principal office in the state.

Q151_LO6: Correct Answer: d. Exempt transactions with up to 35 nonaccredited investors EXPLANATIONS: Regulation D exempts transactions with up to 35 nonaccredited investors.

Q152_LO6: Correct Answer: c. Prohibits transfer without registration or exemption EXPLANATIONS: A legend indicates restricted transfer and prohibits transfer without registration or exemption.

Q153_LO6: Correct Answer: b. All purchasers must be accredited investors EXPLANATIONS: For soliciting or advertising under Regulation D, all purchasers must be accredited investors.

Q154_LO6: Correct Answer: a. Stabilize the offering price EXPLANATIONS: The primary purpose of a greenshoe option is to stabilize the offering price.

Q155_LO6: Correct Answer: d. Securities sold entirely in one state EXPLANATIONS: Securities are exempt under Rule 147 when sold entirely in one state.

Q156_LO6: Correct Answer: c. Exempt securities sold entirely in one state EXPLANATIONS: Rule 147 exempts securities sold entirely in one state from registration.

Q157_LO6: Correct Answer: b. Form D EXPLANATIONS: A company must file Form D electronically via the internet under Regulation D.

Q158_LO6: Correct Answer: c. Subject to SEC review only for Tier 2 EXPLANATIONS: Tier 2 offerings are subject to SEC review only, not at the state level.

Q159_LO6: Correct Answer: c. Same type as in a registered offering EXPLANATIONS: Purchasers must have access to the same type of information as in a registered offering under Reg D.

Q160_LO6: Correct Answer: c. All purchasers must be residents of the state

Q161_LO6: Correct Answer: b. Commercial paper with a maturity of 270 days EXPLANATIONS: Commercial paper with a maturity of 270 days is exempt due to creditworthiness.

Q162_LO6: Correct Answer: a. Bank holding company securities EXPLANATIONS: The bank exemption applies only to securities of banks, not bank holding companies.

Q163_LO6: Correct Answer: c. Up to $15 million with SEC review only EXPLANATIONS: Regulation A+ Tier 2 allows offerings up to $50 million with SEC review only.

Q164_LO6: Correct Answer: b. 80% of offering proceeds used within the state EXPLANATIONS: Rule 147 requires at least 80% of offering proceeds to be used within the state.

Q165_LO6: Correct Answer: b. Accredited investor status EXPLANATIONS: Tier 2 investors must be accredited investors under specified criteria.

Q166_LO6: Correct Answer: b. All investors must be accredited in Regulation D EXPLANATIONS: Regulation D requires all investors to be accredited.

Q167_LO6: Correct Answer: c. Electronic filing of offering information EXPLANATIONS: Form D is used for electronic filing of offering information for private placements.

Q168_LO6: Correct Answer: b. Majority of purchasers must be accredited investors EXPLANATIONS: All purchasers must be accredited investors for solicitation or advertising.

Q169_LO6: Correct Answer: c. Restricted stock EXPLANATIONS: Restricted stock must be held for a six-month period in private placements.

Q170_LO6: Correct Answer: a. Six-month holding period EXPLANATIONS: Rule 147 imposes a six-month holding period before resale to nonresidents.

Q171_LO6: Correct Answer: a. Advertising allowed in Regulation A+ EXPLANATIONS: Advertising is permitted for both Tier 1 and Tier 2 in Regulation A+.

Q172_LO6: Correct Answer: a. Tier 1 has no investment limits EXPLANATIONS: Tier 1 in Regulation A+ has no investment limits.

Q173_LO6: Correct Answer: a. Six-month holding period EXPLANATIONS: Regulation D imposes a six-month holding period for private placement stock.

Q174_LO6: Correct Answer: c. Prevents transfer without registration or exemption EXPLANATIONS: A legend indicates restricted transfer, preventing transfer without registration or exemption.

Q175_LO6: Correct Answer: b. Electronic Form D filing for Regulation D EXPLANATIONS: Regulation D private placements require electronic Form D filing.

Q176_LO7: Correct Answer: b. Final prospectus EXPLANATIONS: The final prospectus is amended to include details like the final offering price.

Q177_LO7: Correct Answer: d. Historical performance over 10 years EXPLANATIONS: Historical performance over 10 years is not required on the cover page of a summary prospectus.

Q178_LO7: Correct Answer: c. SEC releases offerings for sale EXPLANATIONS: The SEC releases offerings for sale but does not approve or endorse them.

Q179_LO7: Correct Answer: b. Full (statutory) prospectus EXPLANATIONS: The full (statutory) prospectus provides key information in a standardized order.

Q180_LO7: Correct Answer: d. Offering a brief overview of key information EXPLANATIONS: A summary prospectus offers a brief overview of key information from the full prospectus.

Q181_LO7: Correct Answer: d. Statement of additional information (SAI) EXPLANATIONS: The SAI provides additional information but is not mandatory for an informed decision.

Q182_LO7: Correct Answer: a. Updated annually, 12 months EXPLANATIONS: A mutual fund prospectus is updated annually and can be used for sales solicitations for 16 months.

Q183_LO7: Correct Answer: c. Omitting prospectus EXPLANATIONS: An omitting prospectus is the official name for an advertisement lacking critical information.

Q184_LO7: Correct Answer: c. Offering circular EXPLANATIONS: The offering circular is the disclosure document for municipal securities.

Q185_LO7: Correct Answer: d. Statement of additional information (SAI) EXPLANATIONS: The SAI provides expanded discussions on history and policies, among other details.

Q186_LO7: Correct Answer: c. For both NMS and non-NMS securities EXPLANATIONS: Access to a prospectus on the SEC website is sufficient for both NMS and non-NMS securities.

Q187_LO7: Correct Answer: a. 25 days EXPLANATIONS: For IPOs of NMS securities, an investor is entitled to the final prospectus within 25 days.

Q188_LO7: Correct Answer: c. Toll-free number for prospectus delivery EXPLANATIONS: The cover page of a summary prospectus must include a toll-free number for prospectus delivery.

Q189_LO7: Correct Answer: c. Ongoing prospectus EXPLANATIONS: The full and fair disclosure document for mutual funds is the ongoing prospectus.

Q190_LO7: Correct Answer: a. Investment policies and performance EXPLANATIONS: The front page must contain key information, including investment policies and performance, in a standardized order.

Q191_LO7: Correct Answer: c. Full (statutory) prospectus EXPLANATIONS: The full (statutory) prospectus provides material information for fully informed decisions.

Q192_LO7: Correct Answer: d. After the final prospectus is issued EXPLANATIONS: Orders can be taken after the final prospectus is issued.

Q193_LO7: Correct Answer: c. SEC disclaimer EXPLANATIONS: The SEC requires the SEC disclaimer to precede or accompany all sales confirmations.

Q194_LO7: Correct Answer: d. No representation about accuracy or adequacy EXPLANATIONS: The SEC disclaimer states no representations about accuracy or adequacy.

Q195_LO7: Correct Answer: c. Full (statutory) prospectus EXPLANATIONS: The full (statutory) prospectus must be distributed during solicitation.

Q196_LO7: Correct Answer: d. Availability for new share purchases EXPLANATIONS: An ongoing prospectus is necessary for new share purchases in a mutual fund.

Q197_LO7: Correct Answer: c. 16 months EXPLANATIONS: A mutual fund prospectus is updated annually for a period of 16 months.

Q198_LO7: Correct Answer: d. Summary prospectus EXPLANATIONS: The summary prospectus is an abbreviated summary of key information in a fund's full prospectus.

Q199_LO7: Correct Answer: c. Legend about full prospectus EXPLANATIONS: The cover must include a legend about the availability of the full (statutory) prospectus.

Q200_LO7: Correct Answer: d. Statement of additional information (SAI) EXPLANATIONS: The Statement of Additional Information (SAI) provides expanded discussions on fund matters.

Q201_LO7: Correct Answer: c. Omitting prospectus EXPLANATIONS: The omitting prospectus is the official name for a mutual fund advertisement lacking essential information.

Q202_LO7: Correct Answer: c. Official statement EXPLANATIONS: The official statement is the primary disclosure document for municipal securities.

Q203_LO7: Correct Answer: a. Offering circular EXPLANATIONS: The offering circular is commonly used for exempt securities like private placements and Regulation A+.

Q204_LO7: Correct Answer: b. Rule 482 EXPLANATIONS: Rule 482 mandates prospectus delivery timelines for secondary market investors.

Q205_LO7: Correct Answer: a. 25 days EXPLANATIONS: For IPOs of NMS securities, the timeline for providing the final prospectus is 25 days.

Q206_LO7: Correct Answer: b. Final prospectus EXPLANATIONS: The final prospectus is amended with information, including the final offering price.

Q207_LO7: Correct Answer: a. Investment strategies EXPLANATIONS: The final prospectus must include information such as investment strategies.

Q208_LO7: Correct Answer: c. Clearance for sale EXPLANATIONS: The SEC disclaimer indicates clearance for sale, not endorsement or approval.

Q209_LO7: Correct Answer: d. Ongoing prospectus EXPLANATIONS: Ongoing prospectus is required for open-end managed investment companies.

Q210_LO7: Correct Answer: c. Annually EXPLANATIONS: A mutual fund prospectus is updated annually.

Q211_LO7: Correct Answer: c. 16 months EXPLANATIONS: A summary prospectus may be used for 16 months from the date of publication.

Q212_LO7: Correct Answer: b. Toll-free number for paper delivery EXPLANATIONS: The cover page must include a toll-free number for paper delivery.

Q213_LO7: Correct Answer: b. Balance sheet
EXPLANATIONS: The SAI typically includes the fund's consolidated financial statements, including the balance sheet.

Q214_LO7. Correct Answer: b. Omitting prospectus EXPLANATIONS: The omitting prospectus is the official name for an advertisement for a mutual fund.

Q215_LO7: Correct Answer: c. Offering circular EXPLANATIONS: The offering circular is the primary disclosure document for municipal securities.

Q216_LO7: Correct Answer: a. Always entitled to a final prospectus EXPLANATIONS: An investor buying new securities in the secondary market is always entitled to a final prospectus.

Q217_LO7: Correct Answer: c. 60 days EXPLANATIONS: For IPOs of non-NMS securities, an investor is entitled to the final prospectus within 60 days.

Q218_LO7: Correct Answer: b. Advertisement for new fund launches EXPLANATIONS: Omitting prospectuses are advertisements, often for new fund launches, lacking comprehensive information.

Q219_LO7: Correct Answer: c. Offering circular EXPLANATIONS: The common term is the offering circular for exempt securities like Regulation A+ offerings.

Q220_LO7: Correct Answer: d. Summary prospectus EXPLANATIONS: A summary prospectus is distributed to an investor before or during solicitation for informed decision-making.

The Securities Exchange Act of 1934 and the Secondary Markets

Q221_LO8: Why do secondary markets play a crucial role in supporting the primary markets?
a. Enhance stock prices
b. Boost economic expansion
c. Increase liquidity risk
d. Facilitate illiquid securities

HINTS: Consider the role of secondary markets in supporting the primary markets.

Q222_LO8: What term is used to describe the ability to buy or sell a security easily?
a. Market centers
b. Liquidity
c. Illiquidity risk
d. Primary markets

HINTS: Recognize the term associated with the ease of buying or selling a security.

Q223_LO8: Which market type operates as a double-auction market with central marketplaces and trading floor facilities?
a. Over-the-counter market
b. Third market
c. Fourth market
d. Exchanges

HINTS: Identify the market type with central marketplaces and trading floors operating as double-auction markets.

Q224_LO8: Where does trading take place in the over-the-counter (OTC) market?
a. Trading floors
b. Computer networks
c. Central marketplaces
d. Trading rooms

HINTS: Focus on the location of trading in the over-the-counter (OTC) market.

Q225_LO8: What distinguishes the third market (Nasdaq Intermarket) from other markets?
a. Central marketplaces
b. ECN trading
c. OTC trading of exchange-listed securities
d. Negotiated market

HINTS: Recognize the distinctive feature of the third market involving exchange-listed securities.

Q226_LO8: In the fourth market, where do large blocks of stock trade, unassisted by broker-dealers?
a. Dark pools
b. ECNs
c. Trading floors
d. Central marketplaces

HINTS: Identify the market where large blocks of stock trade without broker-dealer assistance.

Q227_LO8: What is a characteristic of dark pools of liquidity?
a. High market transparency
b. Publicly available trading volume
c. Anonymous order placement
d. Immediate impact on public quotes

HINTS: Focus on the characteristic related to order placement in dark pools.

Q228_LO8: During what hours does the NYSE typically trade each business day?
a. 8:00 am - 3:00 pm ET
b. 9:30 am - 4:00 pm ET
c. 10:00 am - 5:00 pm ET
d. 11:30 am - 6:30 pm ET

HINTS: Recall the typical trading hours of the NYSE.

Q229_LO8: What is the primary function of the over-the-counter (OTC) market?
a. Facilitate auction trading
b. Support exchange-listed securities
c. Allow anonymous order placement
d. Provide liquidity to investors

HINTS: Identify the primary function of the over-the-counter (OTC) market.

Q230_LO8: How do exchanges like the NYSE operate in terms of pricing?
a. Interdealer network
b. Negotiated market
c. Double-auction market
d. Electronic communications networks

HINTS: Recognize the pricing mechanism of exchanges like the NYSE.

Q231_LO8: What criterion is common for both exchanges and OTC markets regarding listed securities?
a. Physical location
b. Central marketplaces
c. Quality of issues
d. Negotiated market

HINTS: Consider the common criterion for both exchanges and OTC markets regarding listed securities.

Q232_LO8: Which market operates as a negotiated market through an interdealer network?
a. Exchanges
b. Dark pools
c. OTC market
d. Fourth market

HINTS: Identify the market operating through an interdealer network as a negotiated market.

Q233_LO8: What distinguishes the dark pools of liquidity in terms of transparency?
a. Open availability to the public
b. Immediate impact on public quotes
c. Limited market participants
d. High market transparency

HINTS: Focus on the characteristic related to transparency in dark pools.

Q234_LO8: Why is the after-hours market less liquid compared to regular trading hours?
a. Limited order flow
b. Wider bid-ask spreads
c. Increased market transparency
d. Higher price volatility

HINTS: Consider the factor contributing to lower liquidity in the after-hours market.

Q235_LO8: What is the primary concern regarding dark pools and market transparency?
a. Limited anonymity
b. Impact on public quotes
c. Increased order flow
d. Disadvantage for some participants

HINTS: Recognize the primary concern related to dark pools and market transparency.

Q236_LO8: Why do secondary markets play a crucial role in supporting the primary markets?
a. To increase liquidity
b. To connect buyers and sellers
c. To regulate securities
d. To issue new securities

HINTS: Think about the role secondary markets play in relation to the primary markets.

Q237_LO8: What term is used to describe the ability to easily buy or sell a security, and why is it important?
a. Stability
b. Liquidity
c. Volatility
d. Flexibility

HINTS: Consider the term used for the ease of buying or selling a security.

Q238_LO8: Which market operates as a double-auction market, where floor participants compete to execute trades at favorable prices?
a. Over-the-counter market
b. Third market
c. Fourth market
d. Exchanges

HINTS: Recall the characteristics of an exchange market.

Q239_LO8: Where does trading take place in the over-the-counter (OTC) market?
a. Central marketplace
b. Trading floor facilities
c. Electronic communications networks
d. Over the phone and computer networks

HINTS: Focus on the location of OTC trading.

Q240_LO8: What characterizes the third market, or Nasdaq Intermarket, in terms of the securities traded?
a. Unlisted securities only
b. Exchange-listed securities in OTC market
c. Institutional investors only
d. Dark pool trading

HINTS: Think about the nature of securities traded in the third market.

Q241_LO8: In the fourth market, how do large blocks of stock trade, and what facilitates these transactions?
a. On exchanges with broker-dealer assistance
b. In dark pools with complete transparency
c. Through electronic communications networks (ECNs)
d. On the Nasdaq Intermarket

HINTS: Consider the characteristics of the fourth market.

Q242_LO8: What is the primary feature of dark pools in terms of trading volume and transparency?
a. High transparency
b. Low trading volume
c. Openly available to the public
d. Volume not openly available to the public

HINTS: Focus on the nature of trading volume in dark pools.

Q243_LO8: During what hours does the NYSE typically trade, and what happens to liquidity in after-hours trading?
a. 8:00 am to 3:30 pm; Higher liquidity
b. 9:30 am to 4:00 pm; Lower liquidity
c. 10:00 am to 4:30 pm; Same liquidity
d. 9:00 am to 5:00 pm; Greater price volatility

HINTS: Consider the standard trading hours for the NYSE and the impact on liquidity in after-hours trading.

Q244_LO8: Why are institutional trading desks interested in using dark pools for large block orders?
a. Greater market transparency
b. Lower trading volume
c. No impact on public quotes
d. Complete price transparency

HINTS: Think about the advantage of using dark pools for institutional trading desks.

Q245_LO8: How do market centers like exchanges support the secondary markets?
a. By providing liquidity to investors
b. By issuing new securities
c. By regulating securities
d. By connecting buyers and sellers

HINTS: Reflect on the role of market centers in supporting the secondary markets.

Q246_LO8: What differentiates the pricing system of listed markets (exchanges) from the OTC market?
a. Centralized pricing
b. Negotiated pricing
c. Interdealer network pricing
d. Dark pool pricing

HINTS: Focus on the pricing system characteristic of listed markets.

Q247_LO8: In the OTC market, how do registered market makers determine bid and ask prices?
a. Negotiation with investors
b. Competitive bidding among market makers
c. Interdealer network competition
d. Dark pool facilitation

HINTS: Consider how bid and ask prices are determined in the OTC market.

Q248_LO8: What commonality exists between exchanges and the third market in terms of securities traded?
a. Exchanges trade unlisted securities
b. Third market trades exchange-listed securities
c. Both trade institutional securities
d. Both operate as dark pools

HINTS: Identify the commonality between exchanges and the third market.

Q249_LO8: How do ECNs differ from traditional broker-dealer-assisted transactions in the fourth market?
a. ECNs operate in dark pools
b. ECNs trade only unlisted securities
c. ECNs are open 24 hours
d. ECNs facilitate unassisted transactions

HINTS: Reflect on the role of ECNs in the fourth market.

Q250_LO8: Why is the NYSE considered an auction market, and what does this imply for trade execution?
a. Centralized floor auction; Transparent prices
b. Decentralized floor auction; Limited competition
c. Interdealer network auction; Anonymous trading
d. Double-auction system; Floor participants compete

HINTS: Understand the characteristics of the NYSE as an auction market.

Q251_LO8: Why are secondary markets essential for the economy?
a. To complicate stock transactions
b. To limit stock ownership
c. To provide liquidity
d. To hinder economic growth

HINTS: Consider the role of secondary markets in supporting the primary markets and overall economic growth.

Q252_LO8: What term describes the ability to buy or sell a security easily?
a. Volatility
b. Liquidity
c. Solvency
d. Stability

HINTS: Focus on the term used to describe the ease of buying or selling a security.

Q253_LO8: Which market type operates as a double-auction market with central marketplaces and trading floor facilities?
a. OTC market
b. Third market
c. Fourth market
d. Exchange market

HINTS: Identify the market type characterized by central marketplaces and trading floor facilities.

Q254_LO8: Where does trading occur in the over-the-counter (OTC) market?
a. Physical trading floors
b. Electronic communications networks
c. Dark pools
d. Central marketplaces

HINTS: Recognize the location where OTC trading takes place.

Q255_LO8: What distinguishes the third market (Nasdaq Intermarket) from other markets?
a. It operates 24 hours a day
b. It exclusively trades unlisted securities
c. It requires physical trading floors
d. It trades exchange-listed securities in the OTC market

HINTS: Identify the distinctive feature of the third market.

Q256_LO8: In which market do institutional investors trade large blocks of stock through electronic communications networks (ECNs)?
a. Over-the-counter market
b. Exchange market
c. Dark pools
d. Fourth market

HINTS: Recognize the market where institutional investors trade large blocks of stock unassisted by broker-dealers.

Q257_LO8: What is the primary characteristic of dark pools?
a. Publicly available trading volume
b. Anonymity and limited transparency
c. Small-volume transactions
d. Exclusive trading hours

HINTS: Identify the key characteristic of dark pools.

Q258_LO8: When does the NYSE conduct its normal trading hours?
a. 8:00 am - 2:00 pm ET
b. 9:00 am - 3:30 pm ET
c. 9:30 am - 4:00 pm ET
d. 10:00 am - 4:30 pm ET

HINTS: Recall the normal trading hours of the New York Stock Exchange (NYSE).

Q259_LO8: What is the concern with dark pools in terms of market participants?
a. Lack of liquidity
b. Lack of anonymity
c. Impact on public quotes
d. Transparent trading

HINTS: Consider the concern associated with dark pools and market transparency.

Q260_LO8: Which market center operates as an auction market and has central marketplaces?
a. Over-the-counter market
b. Third market
c. Fourth market
d. Exchange market

HINTS: Identify the market center characterized by an auction market with central marketplaces.

Q261_LO8: What distinguishes the over-the-counter (OTC) market from exchanges?
a. Central marketplaces
b. Auction-style trading
c. Negotiated market
d. Centralized pricing system

HINTS: Recognize the key characteristic of the over-the-counter (OTC) market.

Q262_LO8: What criteria must a company meet to be traded on the over-the-counter (OTC) market?
a. Strict location requirements
b. Strict pricing system
c. High-quality listed issues
d. Historical trading floors

HINTS: Identify the criteria a company must meet to be traded on the OTC market.

Q263_LO8: What is the role of broker-dealers in the fourth market?
a. Facilitate transactions with central marketplaces
b. Operate as OTC market makers
c. Execute large block orders unassisted
d. Compete on the floor of the NYSE

HINTS: Recognize the role of broker-dealers in the fourth market.

Q264_LO8: What distinguishes the fourth market from other markets?
a. Electronic communications networks (ECNs)
b. Limited trading hours
c. Central marketplaces
d. Institutional trading

HINTS: Identify the distinctive feature of the fourth market.

Q265_LO8: In which market do institutional traders engage in large-volume transactions away from exchange markets?
a. Third market
b. Over-the-counter market
c. Dark pools
d. Fourth market

HINTS: Recognize the market where institutional traders engage in large-volume transactions away from exchange markets.

Q266_LO9: Who are the participants in the secondary markets?
a. Only retail investors
b. Only institutional investors
c. Both investors and facilitators
d. Only accredited investors

HINTS: Recall the two broad categories of participants in the secondary markets.

Q267_LO9: What is the primary source of revenue for broker-dealers?
a. Asset management fees
b. Transaction fees like commissions
c. Interest income
d. Customer service charges

HINTS: Identify the main revenue source for broker-dealers.

Q268_LO9: Who is responsible for ensuring securities are issued in the correct owner's name?
a. Clearing agencies
b. Transfer agents
c. Institutional investors
d. Registrars

HINTS: Identify the role responsible for ensuring correct ownership in securities.

Q269_LO9: What distinguishes a fully disclosed (introducing) firm from other broker-dealers?
a. Proprietary trading
b. Lower net capital requirements
c. Securities lending
d. Acts as its own clearing firm

HINTS: Recognize the characteristic that distinguishes fully disclosed firms.

Q270_LO9: What is the role of a custodian in the securities industry?
a. Execute trades for customers
b. Hold assets in a qualified retirement account
c. Oversee a trust
d. Act as a fiduciary

HINTS: Identify the role of a custodian in the securities industry.

Q271_LO9: When does a day trader typically close the day?
a. With open positions
b. With all positions closed
c. At noon
d. When market conditions are favorable

HINTS: Recall the typical practice of day traders.

Q272_LO9: What is a prime broker's key advantage in a prime brokerage account?
a. Multiple executing brokers
b. Centralized master account
c. Specialized services
d. Securities lending

HINTS: Identify the key advantage of a prime brokerage account.

Q273_LO9: Who are fiduciaries in the securities industry?
a. Investment advisers
b. Retail investors
c. Market makers
d. Institutional investors

HINTS: Recognize the role that always acts as a fiduciary.

Q274_LO9: What is the primary function of a clearing agency in securities transactions?
a. Execute trades
b. Guarantee option contracts
c. Hold custody of funds and securities
d. Facilitate payments and securities delivery

HINTS: Identify the primary function of a clearing agency.

Q275_LO9: Which type of investor is often a pension fund or insurance company?
a. Retail investor
b. Accredited investor
c. Institutional investor
d. Day trader

HINTS: Identify the type of investor often associated with pension funds and insurance companies.

Q276_LO9: What distinguishes a carrying firm from a fully disclosed (introducing) firm?
a. Acts as its own clearing firm
b. Carries customer accounts and accepts funds
c. Lower net capital requirements
d. Executes trades for customers

HINTS: Recognize the distinguishing feature of a carrying firm.

Q277_LO9: In which market are securities traded in the OTC market but reported to the Consolidated Tape?
a. Third market
b. Fourth market
c. Dark pools
d. Exchange market

HINTS: Identify the market where exchange-listed securities are traded in the OTC market.

Q278_LO9: What is the main function of a trustee in the securities industry?
a. Execute trades for customers
b. Oversee a living trust
c. Provide investment advice
d. Act as a fiduciary for customers

HINTS: Identify the main function of a trustee.

Q279_LO9: What is the primary responsibility of a registrar?
a. Facilitate securities lending
b. Hold custody of funds and securities
c. Audit and oversee transfer agents
d. Execute trades for customers

HINTS: Recognize the primary responsibility of a registrar.

Q280_LO9: What role does the Options Clearing Corporation (OCC) play in the securities industry?
a. Securities lending
b. Clearing agent for listed options contracts
c. Facilitates dark pools
d. Acts as a fiduciary

HINTS: Identify the role of the Options Clearing Corporation (OCC).

Q281_LO9: Who are the participants engaged in the secondary markets?
a. Facilitators and investors
b. Brokers and issuers
c. Regulators and traders
d. Underwriters and dealers

HINTS: Consider the two broad categories of participants in the secondary markets.

Q282_LO9: What distinguishes retail investors from day traders?
a. Trading frequency
b. Wealth level
c. Professional status
d. Investment objectives

HINTS: Identify the characteristic that distinguishes day traders from retail investors.

Q283_LO9: What is the primary role of institutional investors in the secondary markets?
a. Rapid trading
b. Managing retail accounts
c. Custody and fiduciary services
d. Issuing securities

HINTS: Focus on the primary role of institutional investors in the secondary markets.

Q284_LO9: What is the common obligation of fiduciaries in the securities industry?
a. Trading securities for profit
b. Managing assets in the best interest of beneficiaries
c. Providing investment advice
d. Proprietary trading

HINTS: Recall the definition of a fiduciary and its obligation.

Q285_LO9: What distinguishes a custodian from a trustee?
a. Professional status
b. Management of living trusts
c. Role in managing minor's accounts
d. Oversight of pension trusts

HINTS: Focus on the specific roles for custodians and trustees.

Q286_LO9: When is a representative considered "dually registered" in the securities industry?
a. When registered as an investment adviser
b. When acting as a fiduciary
c. When managing institutional accounts
d. When endorsed by a regulator

HINTS: Consider the conditions under which a representative is considered "dually registered."

Q287_LO9: What is the primary source of revenue for broker-dealers?
a. Transaction fees
b. Advisory fees
c. Account maintenance fees
d. Interest from margin accounts

HINTS: Identify the primary source of revenue for broker-dealers.

Q288_LO9: Which type of broker-dealer may execute trades but relies on a carrying firm for clearing and settlement?
a. Carrying firm
b. Fully disclosed firm
c. Prime broker
d. Market maker

HINTS: Recognize the type of broker-dealer that relies on a carrying firm for clearing and settlement.
Q289_LO9: What key advantage does a prime brokerage account offer to clients?
a. Lower transaction fees
b. Centralized master account
c. Access to proprietary trading
d. Reduced margin requirements

HINTS: Identify the key advantage for clients with a prime brokerage account.

Q290_LO9: What is the primary responsibility of a transfer agent for a corporation?
a. Execute trades on behalf of customers
b. Facilitate securities lending
c. Ensure correct ownership on stock certificates
d. Act as a clearing agency

HINTS: Recognize the primary responsibility of a transfer agent for a corporation.

Q291_LO9: What does a registrar provide oversight services for in the securities industry?
a. Broker-dealers
b. Clearing agencies
c. Issuers and transfer agents
d. Institutional investors

HINTS: Identify the entities for which a registrar provides oversight services.

Q292_LO9: What function does a clearing agency perform in the securities industry?
a. Managing margin accounts
b. Providing investment advice
c. Standardizing and guaranteeing option contracts
d. Handling lost securities certificates

HINTS: Recognize the function performed by a clearing agency.

Q293_LO9: Which organization is considered the world's largest securities depository?
a. Options Clearing Corporation (OCC)
b. Federal Reserve System
c. Depository Trust & Clearing Corporation (DTCC)
d. Securities and Exchange Commission (SEC)

HINTS: Identify the organization as the world's largest securities depository.

Q294_LO9: What is the primary role of the Options Clearing Corporation (OCC)?
a. Providing custody services
b. Clearing listed options contracts
c. Facilitating securities lending
d. Managing pension trusts

HINTS: Focus on the specific function for the Options Clearing Corporation (OCC).

Q295_LO9: What is the purpose of a clearing agency in the securities industry?
a. Facilitating trades for institutional investors
b. Ensuring compliance with trading rules
c. Standardizing and guaranteeing option contracts
d. Providing investment advice

HINTS: Identify the primary purpose for a clearing agency in the securities industry.

Q296_LO9: Who are the participants in the secondary markets?
a. Traders and Brokers
b. Investors and Facilitators
c. Retailers and Wholesalers
d. Buyers and Sellers
HINTS: Identify the two broad categories of participants in the secondary markets.

Q297_LO9: What distinguishes retail investors from day traders?
a. Frequency of trading
b. Wealth status
c. Professionalism
d. Investment objectives

HINTS: Consider the characteristic that typically defines day traders.

Q298_LO9: Who falls under the category of institutional investors?
a. Retail investors
b. Accredited investors
c. Mutual funds
d. Day traders

HINTS: Identify the large investors among the options.

Q299_LO9: What is the common characteristic of custodians and trustees?
a. Professionalism
b. Fiduciary roles
c. Retail focus
d. Proprietary trading

HINTS: Focus on the shared responsibility of custodians and trustees.

Q300_LO9: What distinguishes a fully disclosed (introducing) firm from other broker-dealers?
a. Proprietary trading
b. Lower net capital requirements
c. Exclusive focus on institutional investors
d. Independent trade execution

HINTS: Identify the distinguishing feature of fully disclosed (introducing) firms.

Q301_LO9: What is the key advantage of a prime brokerage account?

a. Higher trading fees
b. Centralized master account
c. Limited executing broker outlets
d. Exclusively for retail clients

HINTS: Focus on the primary advantage provided by a prime brokerage account.

Q302_LO9: What function does a transfer agent perform for a corporation?
a. Securities lending
b. Trade processing
c. Registration of stock certificates
d. Margin financing

HINTS: Identify the specific function performed by a transfer agent for a corporation.

Q303_LO9: Who provides audit and oversight services for transfer agents?
a. Custodians
b. Registrars
c. Clearing agencies
d. Prime brokers

HINTS: Recognize the role of entities providing audit and oversight services for transfer agents.

Q304_LO9: What is the primary function of clearing agencies in securities transactions?
a. Securities lending
b. Trade execution
c. Custody of funds
d. Intermediary between buy and sell sides

HINTS: Identify the primary role of clearing agencies in securities transactions.

Q305_LO9: What does the Depository Trust & Clearing Corporation (DTCC) provide?
a. Retail banking services
b. Securities custody services
c. Margin financing
d. Securities lending

HINTS: Recognize the services provided by the DTCC.

Q306_LO9: Who determines the contract specifications for listed options contracts?
a. Broker-dealers
b. Securities depositories
c. Clearing agencies
d. Options Clearing Corporation (OCC)

HINTS: Identify the entity responsible for determining contract specifications for listed options.

Q307_LO9: What is a fiduciary's legal and moral obligation?
a. Profit maximization
b. Compliance with regulations
c. Beneficiary's best interest
d. Client satisfaction

HINTS: Focus on the fundamental obligation of a fiduciary.

Q308_LO9: When is the role of a prime broker advantageous?
a. Only for retail clients
b. Infrequent trading activities
c. Active trading clients with multiple brokerage houses
d. Limited executing broker outlets

HINTS: Recognize the circumstances under which a prime brokerage account is beneficial.

Q309_LO9: What is the primary source of revenue for broker-dealers?

a. Asset management fees
b. Transaction fees (commissions and loads)
c. Securities lending
d. Custodial fees

HINTS: Identify the main source of revenue for broker-dealers.

Q310_LO9: In what capacity does an investment adviser act when providing advice?
a. Broker-dealer
b. Market maker
c. Fiduciary
d. Proprietary trader

HINTS: Recognize the role an investment adviser takes when providing advice.

Q311_LO10: Where does trading in the secondary markets take place for OTC-traded companies tracked by the Nasdaq system?
a. Exchanges
b. Online platforms
c. OTC market
d. Physical locations

HINTS: Focus on the market where Nasdaq-tracked OTC companies trade.
Q312_LO10: What is a defining characteristic of exchanges that distinguishes them from the OTC market?
a. Physical location
b. Electronic trading
c. Centralized clearing
d. Market makers

HINTS: Identify a key characteristic of exchanges that sets them apart from the OTC market.

Q313_LO10: Who guarantees liquidity and acts as the dealer for a specific security on the floor of an exchange?
a. Floor broker
b. Two-dollar broker
c. Designated market maker
d. Floor trader

HINTS: Focus on the member responsible for maintaining liquidity on the exchange.

Q314_LO10: In the OTC market, how does the bid-ask spread represent the market maker's income?
a. It reflects market volatility
b. It indicates liquidity
c. It represents the difference between buying and selling prices
d. It shows the volume of trades

HINTS: Consider the role of the bid-ask spread in the market maker's income.

Q315_LO10: When a customer sells a security in the OTC market, who is the customer selling to?
a. Market maker
b. Floor broker
c. Designated market maker
d. Two-dollar broker

HINTS: Focus on the participant involved when a customer sells a security in the OTC market.

Q316_LO10: What is a key similarity between the DMM on exchanges and market makers in the OTC market?
a. Physical location
b. Guaranteeing liquidity
c. Floor representation
d. Handling customer orders

HINTS: Identify the common function between the DMM on exchanges and market makers in the OTC market.

Q317_LO10: How do floor brokers handle trades on an exchange?
a. Directly execute trades

b. Enlist the services of $2 brokers
c. Represent their firms on the floor
d. Maintain an inventory of securities

HINTS: Consider the role of floor brokers in the exchange market.

Q318_LO10: What does the bid-ask spread in the OTC market represent?
a. Market volatility
b. Market maker's income
c. Volume of trades
d. Liquidity

HINTS: Focus on the significance of the bid-ask spread in the OTC market.

Q319_LO10: In the OTC market, what does the broker do when a customer places an order to purchase a security?
a. Chooses a market maker
b. Directly executes the trade
c. Enlists the services of $2 brokers
d. Guarantees liquidity

HINTS: Identify the broker's role when a customer places an order to purchase a security in the OTC market.

Q320_LO10: Which entity is responsible for standardizing and specifying options contract features for listed options contracts?
a. Floor broker
b. Designated market maker
c. Options Clearing Corporation (OCC)
d. Two-dollar broker

HINTS: Identify the organization responsible for options contract standardization.

Q321_LO10: What distinguishes Nasdaq-traded securities from those traded in the OTC market?
a. Physical location
b. Market maker involvement
c. Floor representation
d. Considered listed

HINTS: Focus on the status of securities traded on Nasdaq.

Q322_LO10: Which term is used for members that buy and sell on the floor for their firm's accounts in an exchange?
a. Floor brokers
b. Designated market makers
c. Two-dollar brokers
d. Floor traders

HINTS: Identify the specific term for members trading for their firm's accounts on the exchange floor.

Q323_LO10: What distinguishes a fully disclosed (introducing) firm from a prime broker?
a. Centralized master account
b. Lower net capital requirements
c. Exclusive focus on institutional clients
d. Custodial services

HINTS: Recognize the distinguishing feature of fully disclosed (introducing) firms.

Q324_LO10: How do floor brokers handle trades on the exchange?
a. Enlist the services of $2 brokers
b. Directly execute trades
c. Represent their firms on the floor
d. Guarantee liquidity

HINTS: Focus on the role of floor brokers on the exchange floor.

Q325_LO10: What function does the Options Clearing Corporation (OCC) perform for listed options contracts?
a. Market making

b. Standardization of features
c. Floor representation
d. Guaranteeing liquidity

HINTS: Identify the primary function of the OCC for listed options contracts.

Q326_LO10: Where does trading take place for the largest OTC-traded companies tracked by Nasdaq?
a. NYSE
b. OTC market
c. AMEX
d. CME

HINTS: Focus on the venue for trading OTC-traded companies tracked by Nasdaq.

Q327_LO10: What is a defining characteristic of exchanges that differentiates them from the OTC market?
a. Double-auction system
b. Physical location (floor)
c. Electronic trading
d. Decentralized market

HINTS: Identify the characteristic distinguishing exchanges from the OTC market.

Q328_LO10: Who is responsible for maintaining a "fair and orderly" market in a specific security on the exchange floor?
a. Two-dollar broker
b. Floor trader
c. Designated market maker (DMM)
d. Floor broker

HINTS: Recognize the role responsible for maintaining order on the exchange floor.

Q329_LO10: What role do floor brokers play on the exchange floor?
a. Execute trades for their firm's accounts
b. Maintain inventory of securities
c. Enlist the services of two-dollar brokers
d. Guarantee liquidity

HINTS: Identify the primary function of floor brokers on the exchange floor.

Q330_LO10: How is the best bid established in the exchange market?
a. By floor traders
b. By selling broker-dealers
c. Initiating a bid at least $0.01 higher
d. By floor brokers

HINTS: Focus on the process of establishing the best bid on the exchange.

Q331_LO10: In the OTC market, what does the difference between the bid and ask prices represent?
a. Market maker's income
b. Broker's fee
c. Customer's profit
d. Spread

HINTS: Identify the term representing the difference between the bid and ask prices in the OTC market.

Q332_LO10: How do quotes in the OTC market represent bid and ask prices?
a. Average bid and ask
b. Highest bid and lowest ask
c. Midpoint bid and ask
d. Closing bid and ask

HINTS: Recognize how quotes in the OTC market represent bid and ask prices.

Q333_LO10: Where does OTC trading occur between market makers?
a. On the exchange floor

b. In a centralized electronic market
c. On the OTC market floor
d. In a decentralized electronic market

HINTS: Focus on the location of OTC trading between market makers.

Q334_LO10: When a customer sells a security in the OTC market, who is the customer selling to?
a. Market maker
b. Floor broker
c. Floor trader
d. Designated market maker

HINTS: Recognize the party to whom a customer sells a security in the OTC market.

Q335_LO10: What function does a two-dollar broker perform in the exchange market?
a. Execute trades for floor traders
b. Enlist the services of floor brokers
c. Place trades for floor brokers
d. Execute trades for floor brokers

HINTS: Identify the role of a two-dollar broker on the exchange floor.

Q336_LO10: What role do floor traders play on the exchange floor?
a. Execute trades for customers
b. Guarantee liquidity
c. Enlist the services of two-dollar brokers
d. Execute trades for floor brokers' accounts

HINTS: Recognize the primary responsibility of floor traders on the exchange floor.

Q337_LO10: What does the OTC market lack in comparison to exchanges?
a. Bid and ask prices
b. Physical location (floor)
c. Market makers
d. Decentralization

HINTS: Identify the characteristic that the OTC market lacks in comparison to exchanges.

Q338_LO10: How do exchanges conduct trades?
a. Between market makers
b. Between broker-dealers
c. Between floor traders
d. Between members (not employees)

HINTS: Identify how exchanges conduct trades.

Q339_LO10: What is a market maker's function in the OTC market?
a. Guarantee liquidity
b. Execute trades for customers
c. Maintain an inventory
d. Enlist the services of floor brokers

HINTS: Recognize the role of a market maker in the OTC market.

Q340_LO10: What is one similarity between exchanges and the OTC market?
a. Physical location
b. Double-auction system
c. Floor brokers
d. Decentralized trading

HINTS: Identify a common characteristic between exchanges and the OTC market.

Q341_LO10: Where does trading in the secondary markets take place?
a. Exchanges only

b. OTC market only
c. Both exchanges and OTC market
d. None of the above

HINTS: Consider the venues for secondary market trading.

Q342_LO10: What is a defining characteristic of exchanges?
a. No physical location
b. Centralized electronic market
c. Floor for transactions
d. Decentralized market makers

HINTS: Focus on the unique feature of exchanges.

Q343_LO10: Who acts as the dealer on the floor for a specific security on an exchange?
a. Floor broker
b. Designated market maker
c. Two-dollar broker
d. Floor trader

HINTS: Identify the member responsible for maintaining liquidity on the exchange floor.

Q344_LO10: How do floor brokers handle trades on the exchange floor?
a. As market makers
b. As intermediaries for customers
c. By placing trades for floor traders
d. By maintaining inventory

HINTS: Consider the role of floor brokers in exchange transactions.

Q345_LO10: In the OTC market, what is the function of a market maker?
a. Represent clients on the floor
b. Guarantee liquidity on the floor
c. Maintain an inventory and facilitate trades
d. Enlist the services of $2 brokers

HINTS: Focus on the role of market makers in the OTC market.

Q346_LO10: What is the primary similarity between DMMs on exchanges and market makers in the OTC market?
a. Physical location
b. Guaranteeing liquidity
c. Floor transactions
d. Multiple market makers

HINTS: Identify the common function of both DMMs and market makers.

Q347_LO10: How does a customer sell a security in the OTC market?
a. To a floor broker
b. To a market maker at the bid price
c. To a dealer at the ask price
d. To an exchange specialist

HINTS: Focus on the selling process in the OTC market.

Q348_LO10: What is the spread in the OTC market?
a. Difference between bid and ask
b. Difference between floor and ceiling
c. Difference between high and low price
d. Difference between market and limit order

HINTS: Recognize the term representing the market maker's income.

Q349_LO10: What do quotes in the OTC market represent?
a. Highest bid and lowest ask

b. Opening and closing prices
c. Market maker's income
d. Floor transactions

HINTS: Identify the information conveyed by quotes in the OTC market.

Q350_LO10: How is the Nasdaq system involved in the OTC market?
a. Tracks and provides trading for OTC-traded companies
b. Guarantees liquidity on the OTC floor
c. Acts as a floor for OTC transactions
d. Represents OTC market makers

HINTS: Focus on the role of the Nasdaq system in the OTC market.

Q351_LO10: What initiates the establishment of the best bid on an exchange?
a. Highest bid
b. Floor broker's decision
c. Buying broker-dealer's bid
d. Current best bid plus $0.01

HINTS: Consider the conditions for initiating the best bid on an exchange.

Q352_LO10: What is the main role of floor traders on the exchange floor?
a. Guarantee liquidity
b. Represent their firms
c. Execute trades for customers
d. Maintain inventory

HINTS: Focus on the primary responsibility of floor traders.

Q353_LO10: What happens when a customer buys a security in the OTC market?
a. Buys from a floor trader
b. Buys from a dealer at the bid price
c. Buys from a market maker at the ask price
d. Buys from a floor broker

HINTS: Recognize the buying process in the OTC market.

Q354_LO10: What is the key difference in the trading process between exchanges and the OTC market?
a. Floor transactions vs. electronic market
b. Guaranteeing vs. competing for orders
c. Bid and ask vs. highest and lowest
d. DMMs vs. market makers

HINTS: Identify the contrasting elements in the trading processes.

Q355_LO10: Which market trades most bonds, including municipals and treasury debt?
a. NYSE
b. OTC market
c. Nasdaq
d. AMEX

HINTS: Recognize the market trading unlisted stocks and most bonds.

Correct Answers & Explanations
The Securities Exchange Act of 1934 and the Secondary Markets

Q221_LO8: Correct Answer: b. Boost economic expansion EXPLANATIONS: Secondary markets support the primary markets, fostering economic expansion and job growth.

Q222_LO8: Correct Answer: b. Liquidity EXPLANATIONS: Liquidity refers to the ability to buy or sell a security easily.

Q223_LO8: Correct Answer: d. Exchanges EXPLANATIONS: Exchanges, such as the NYSE, operate as double-auction markets.

Q224_LO8: Correct Answer: b. Computer networks EXPLANATIONS: OTC trading takes place over the phone, computer networks, and in trading rooms.

Q225_LO8: Correct Answer: c. OTC trading of exchange-listed securities EXPLANATIONS: The third market involves OTC trading of exchange-listed securities.

Q226_LO8: Correct Answer: b. ECNs EXPLANATIONS: The fourth market involves large block trades through electronic communications networks (ECNs).

Q227_LO8: Correct Answer: c. Anonymous order placement EXPLANATIONS: Dark pools allow anonymous order placement, concealing the entity's identity and strategy.

Q228_LO8: Correct Answer: b. 9:30 am - 4:00 pm ET EXPLANATIONS: The NYSE trades between 9:30 am and 4:00 pm ET each business day.

Q229_LO8: Correct Answer: d. Provide liquidity to investors EXPLANATIONS: The OTC market provides liquidity to investors.

Q230_LO8: Correct Answer: c. Double-auction market EXPLANATIONS: Exchanges, like the NYSE, operate as double-auction markets.

Q231_LO8: Correct Answer: c. Quality of issues EXPLANATIONS: Both exchanges and OTC markets have criteria related to the quality of issues-traded.

Q232_LO8: Correct Answer: c. OTC market EXPLANATIONS: The OTC market operates as a negotiated market through an interdealer network.

Q233_LO8: Correct Answer: c. Limited market participants EXPLANATIONS: Dark pools have limited market participants, reducing transparency for some market participants.

Q234_LO8: Correct Answer: b. Wider bid-ask spreads EXPLANATIONS: The after-hours market is less liquid with wider bid-ask spreads due to limited order flow.

Q235_LO8: Correct Answer: d. Disadvantage for some participants EXPLANATIONS: Some market participants may be disadvantaged due to the lack of visibility into trades, volume, and prices in dark pools.

Q236_LO8: Correct Answer: b. To connect buyers and sellers EXPLANATIONS: Secondary markets provide a place for buyers and sellers to connect and transact business, supporting the primary markets.

Q237_LO8: Correct Answer: b. Liquidity EXPLANATIONS: Liquidity is the ability to easily buy or sell a security, and it's important for market functioning.

Q238_LO8: Correct Answer: d. Exchanges EXPLANATIONS: Exchanges, like the NYSE, operate as double-auction markets with floor participants competing for favorable prices.

Q239_LO8: Correct Answer: d. Over the phone and computer networks EXPLANATIONS: OTC trading takes place over the phone, computer networks, and trading rooms.

Q240_LO8: Correct Answer: b. Exchange-listed securities in OTC market EXPLANATIONS: The third market involves trading exchange-listed securities in the OTC market.

Q241_LO8: Correct Answer: c. Through electronic communications networks (ECNs) EXPLANATIONS: Large blocks of stock trade through ECNs in the fourth market.

Q242_LO8: Correct Answer: d. Volume not openly available to the public EXPLANATIONS: Dark pools involve trading volume not openly available to the public.

Q243_LO8: Correct Answer: b. 9:30 am to 4:00 pm; Lower liquidity EXPLANATIONS: NYSE trades from 9:30 am to 4:00 pm, and after-hours trading is less liquid with wider spreads.

Q244_LO8: Correct Answer: c. No impact on public quotes EXPLANATIONS: Dark pools allow large block orders without impacting public quotes or prices.

Q245_LO8: Correct Answer: a. By providing liquidity to investors EXPLANATIONS: Market centers, like exchanges, provide liquidity to investors in the secondary markets.

Q246_LO8: Correct Answer: a. Centralized pricing EXPLANATIONS: Listed markets operate with centralized or double-auction pricing systems.

Q247_LO8: Correct Answer: c. Interdealer network competition EXPLANATIONS: Registered market makers compete in an interdealer network to determine bid and ask prices.

Q248_LO8: Correct Answer: b. Third market trades exchange-listed securities EXPLANATIONS: The third market involves trading exchange-listed securities, similar to exchanges.

Q249_LO8: Correct Answer: d. ECNs facilitate unassisted transactions EXPLANATIONS: ECNs facilitate unassisted transactions without broker-dealer assistance.

Q250_LO8: Correct Answer: d. Double-auction system; Floor participants compete EXPLANATIONS: The NYSE operates as a double-auction system with floor participants competing for trade execution at favorable prices.

Q251_LO8: Correct Answer: c. To provide liquidity EXPLANATIONS: Secondary markets provide liquidity, making it easier to buy or sell securities.

Q252_LO8: Correct Answer: b. Liquidity EXPLANATIONS: Liquidity refers to the ease of buying or selling a security.

Q253_LO8: Correct Answer: d. Exchange market EXPLANATIONS: The exchange market operates as a double-auction market with central facilities.

Q254_LO8: Correct Answer: b. Electronic communications networks EXPLANATIONS: OTC trading occurs over the phone, over computer networks, and in trading rooms.

Q255_LO8: Correct Answer: d. It trades exchange-listed securities in the OTC market EXPLANATIONS: The third market trades exchange-listed securities in the OTC market.

Q256_LO8: Correct Answer: d. Fourth market EXPLANATIONS: The fourth market involves large-block trading through electronic communications networks (ECNs).

Q257_LO8: Correct Answer: b. Anonymity and limited transparency EXPLANATIONS: Dark pools offer anonymity and limited transparency in trading.

Q258_LO8: Correct Answer: c. 9:30 am - 4:00 pm ET EXPLANATIONS: The NYSE trades between 9:30 am and 4:00 pm ET each business day.

Q259_LO8: Correct Answer: c. Impact on public quotes EXPLANATIONS: Dark pools can impact public quotes and price transparency for some market participants.

Q260_LO8: Correct Answer: d. Exchange market EXPLANATIONS: The exchange market operates as an auction market with central facilities.

Q261_LO8: Correct Answer: c. Negotiated market EXPLANATIONS: The OTC market operates as a negotiated market.

Q262_LO8: Correct Answer: c. High-quality listed issues EXPLANATIONS: OTC markets require companies to meet criteria similar to exchanges for quality listed issues.

Q263_LO8: Correct Answer: c. Execute large block orders unassisted EXPLANATIONS: Broker-dealers in the fourth market execute large block orders unassisted.

Q264_LO8: Correct Answer: a. Electronic communications networks (ECNs) EXPLANATIONS: The fourth market involves trading through electronic communications networks (ECNs).

Q265_LO8: Correct Answer: c. Dark pools EXPLANATIONS: Dark pools facilitate large-volume transactions away from exchange markets.

Q266_LO9: Correct Answer: c. Both investors and facilitators EXPLANATIONS: Both investors (buying and selling securities) and facilitators are participants in the secondary markets.

Q267_LO9: Correct Answer: b. Transaction fees like commissions EXPLANATIONS: Broker-dealers generate revenue primarily from transaction fees like commissions.

Q268_LO9: Correct Answer: b. Transfer agents EXPLANATIONS: Transfer agents are responsible for ensuring securities are issued in the correct owner's name.

Q269_LO9: Correct Answer: b. Lower net capital requirements EXPLANATIONS: Fully disclosed firms have lower net capital requirements than self-clearing or carrying BDs.

Q270_LO9: Correct Answer: b. Hold assets in a qualified retirement account EXPLANATIONS: A custodian holds assets in a qualified retirement account or on a minor's account under UTMA or UGMA.

Q271_LO9: Correct Answer: b. With all positions closed EXPLANATIONS: Day traders typically close the day with all positions closed.

Q272_LO9: Correct Answer: b. Centralized master account EXPLANATIONS: A prime brokerage account provides a centralized master account for cash and securities.

Q273_LO9: Correct Answer: a. Investment advisers EXPLANATIONS: Investment advisers always act as fiduciaries when giving investment advice.

Q274_LO9: Correct Answer: d. Facilitate payments and securities delivery EXPLANATIONS: A clearing agency facilitates payments and securities delivery in securities transactions.

Q275_LO9: Correct Answer: c. Institutional investor EXPLANATIONS: Institutional investors, such as pension funds and insurance companies, are large investors.

Q276_LO9: Correct Answer: b. Carries customer accounts and accepts funds EXPLANATIONS: Carrying firms carry customer accounts and accept funds and securities.

Q277_LO9: Correct Answer: a. Third market EXPLANATIONS: The third market involves OTC trading of exchange-listed securities.

Q278_LO9: Correct Answer: b. Oversee a living trust EXPLANATIONS: A trustee oversees a trust, which could be a living trust, pension trust, or any other trust type.

Q279_LO9: Correct Answer: c. Audit and oversee transfer agents EXPLANATIONS: Registrars provide audit and oversight services for transfer agents.

Q280_LO9: Correct Answer: b. Clearing agent for listed options contracts EXPLANATIONS: The OCC is the clearing agent for listed options contracts, guaranteeing their performance.

Q281_LO9: Correct Answer: a. Facilitators and investors EXPLANATIONS: Participants in the secondary markets include investors and facilitators.

Q282_LO9: Correct Answer: a. Trading frequency EXPLANATIONS: Day traders are characterized by rapid trading in and out of positions.

Q283_LO9: Correct Answer: c. Custody and fiduciary services EXPLANATIONS: Institutional investors often provide custody and fiduciary services.

Q284_LO9: Correct Answer: b. Managing assets in the best interest of beneficiaries EXPLANATIONS: Fiduciaries have a legal and moral obligation to manage assets in the best interest of beneficiaries.

Q285_LO9: Correct Answer: c. Role in managing minor's accounts EXPLANATIONS: Custodians often manage minor's accounts under UTMA or UGMA.

Q286_LO9: Correct Answer: a. When registered as an investment adviser EXPLANATIONS: Dually registered representatives are registered as both investment advisers and registered representatives (RRs).

Q287_LO9: Correct Answer: a. Transaction fees EXPLANATIONS: Broker-dealers earn revenue from transaction fees like commissions and loads.

Q288_LO9: Correct Answer: b. Fully disclosed firm EXPLANATIONS: Fully disclosed (introducing) firms rely on clearing firms for clearing and settlement.

Q289_LO9: Correct Answer: b. Centralized master account EXPLANATIONS: A prime brokerage account provides a centralized master account for clients with multiple executing broker outlets.

Q290_LO9: Correct Answer: c. Ensure correct ownership on stock certificates EXPLANATIONS: Transfer agents ensure that securities are issued in the correct owner's name.

Q291_LO9: Correct Answer: c. Issuers and transfer agents EXPLANATIONS: Registrars provide oversight services for issuers and transfer agents.

Q292_LO9: Correct Answer: c. Standardizing and guaranteeing option contracts EXPLANATIONS: Clearing agencies standardize, guarantee, and issue option contracts.

Q293_LO9: Correct Answer: c. Depository Trust & Clearing Corporation (DTCC) EXPLANATIONS: The DTCC is the world's largest securities depository.

Q294_LO9: Correct Answer: b. Clearing listed options contracts EXPLANATIONS: The OCC is the clearing agent for listed options contracts.

Q295_LO9: Correct Answer: b. Ensuring compliance with trading rules EXPLANATIONS: Clearing agencies ensure compliance with trading rules between buy and sell sides.

Q296_LO9: Correct Answer: b. Investors and Facilitators EXPLANATIONS: Participants in the secondary markets include investors (buying and selling) and facilitators.

Q297_LO9: Correct Answer: a. Frequency of trading EXPLANATIONS: Day traders engage in rapid, frequent trading, closing positions daily.

Q298_LO9: Correct Answer: c. Mutual funds EXPLANATIONS: Institutional investors include mutual funds, pension funds, banks, and other financial organizations.

Q299_LO9: Correct Answer: b. Fiduciary roles EXPLANATIONS: Both custodians and trustees serve as fiduciaries, managing assets in the best interest of the beneficiary.

Q300_LO9: Correct Answer: b. Lower net capital requirements EXPLANATIONS: These firms have lower net capital requirements compared to self-clearing or carrying BDs.

Q301_LO9: Correct Answer: b. Centralized master account EXPLANATIONS: A prime brokerage account offers the ability to trade with multiple brokerage houses while maintaining a centralized master account.

Q302_LO9: Correct Answer: c. Registration of stock certificates EXPLANATIONS: Transfer agents handle the issuance and maintenance of correct ownership on stock certificates.

Q303_LO9: Correct Answer: b. Registrars EXPLANATIONS: Registrars offer audit and oversight services for transfer agents.

Q304_LO9: Correct Answer: d. Intermediary between buy and sell sides EXPLANATIONS: Clearing agencies act as intermediaries, facilitating payments and securities delivery between buyers and sellers.

Q305_LO9: Correct Answer: b. Securities custody services EXPLANATIONS: The DTCC provides custody services for a wide range of securities globally.

Q306_LO9: Correct Answer: d. Options Clearing Corporation (OCC) EXPLANATIONS: The OCC is responsible for standardizing and specifying options contract features.

Q307_LO9: Correct Answer: c. Beneficiary's best interest EXPLANATIONS: A fiduciary is obligated to act in the best interest of the beneficiary.

Q308_LO9: Correct Answer: c. Active trading clients with multiple brokerage houses EXPLANATIONS: Prime brokers are advantageous for active trading clients with multiple executing broker outlets.

Q309_LO9: Correct Answer: b. Transaction fees (commissions and loads) EXPLANATIONS: Broker-dealers generate revenue primarily from transaction fees, such as commissions and loads.

Q310_LO9: Correct Answer: c. Fiduciary EXPLANATIONS: When providing advice, an investment adviser acts as a fiduciary, placing the customer's interest first.

Q311_LO10: Correct Answer: c. OTC market EXPLANATIONS: Securities traded on Nasdaq are considered listed and trade in the OTC market.

Q312_LO10: Correct Answer: a. Physical location EXPLANATIONS: Exchanges have a physical location, often called a floor.

Q313_LO10: Correct Answer: c. Designated market maker EXPLANATIONS: The DMM (designated market maker) acts as the dealer on the floor for a specific security.

Q314_LO10: Correct Answer: c. It represents the difference between buying and selling prices EXPLANATIONS: The spread is the difference between the bid and ask prices, representing the market maker's income.

Q315_LO10: Correct Answer: a. Market maker EXPLANATIONS: The customer sells to a market maker at the bid price.

Q316_LO10: Correct Answer: b. Guaranteeing liquidity EXPLANATIONS: Both guarantee liquidity in their respective markets.

Q317_LO10: Correct Answer: c. Represent their firms on the floor EXPLANATIONS: Floor brokers represent their firms and clients on the floor of the exchange.

Q318_LO10: Correct Answer: b. Market maker's income EXPLANATIONS: The spread in the OTC market represents the market maker's income.

Q319_LO10: Correct Answer: a. Chooses a market maker EXPLANATIONS: The broker chooses a market maker to complete the trade.

Q320_LO10: Correct Answer: c. Options Clearing Corporation (OCC) EXPLANATIONS: The OCC standardizes and specifies features for listed options contracts.

Q321_LO10: Correct Answer: d. Considered listed EXPLANATIONS: Nasdaq-traded securities are considered listed.

Q322_LO10: Correct Answer: d. Floor traders EXPLANATIONS: Floor traders buy and sell on the floor for their firm's accounts.

Q323_LO10: Correct Answer: a. Centralized master account EXPLANATIONS: Fully disclosed firms offer a centralized master account for clients.

Q324_LO10: Correct Answer: c. Represent their firms on the floor EXPLANATIONS: Floor brokers represent their firms and clients on the floor of the exchange.

Q325_LO10: Correct Answer: b. Standardization of features EXPLANATIONS: The OCC performs the standardization and specification of features for listed options contracts.

Q326_LO10: Correct Answer: b. OTC market EXPLANATIONS: Nasdaq provides trading for the largest OTC-traded companies.

Q327_LO10: Correct Answer: b. Physical location (floor) EXPLANATIONS: Exchanges have a physical location, often referred to as a floor.

Q328_LO10: Correct Answer: c. Designated market maker (DMM) EXPLANATIONS: The DMM (specialist) ensures a "fair and orderly" market for a specific security.

Q329_LO10: Correct Answer: a. Execute trades for their firm's accounts EXPLANATIONS: Floor brokers execute trades for their firm's accounts on the exchange floor.

Q330_LO10: Correct Answer: c. Initiating a bid at least $0.01 higher EXPLANATIONS: To establish the best bid, a buying broker-dealer must initiate a bid at least $0.01 higher than the current best bid.

Q331_LO10: Correct Answer: d. Spread EXPLANATIONS: The difference between the bid and the ask is the spread in the OTC market.

Q332_LO10: Correct Answer: b. Highest bid and lowest ask EXPLANATIONS: Quotes in the OTC market represent the highest bid and lowest ask posted in the system.

Q333_LO10: Correct Answer: d. In a decentralized electronic market EXPLANATIONS: OTC trading occurs between market makers in a decentralized electronic market.

Q334_LO10: Correct Answer: a. Market maker EXPLANATIONS: A customer sells to a market maker at the bid price in the OTC market.

Q335_LO10: Correct Answer: b. Enlist the services of floor brokers EXPLANATIONS: Two-dollar brokers assist floor brokers by placing trades for them.

Q336_LO10: Correct Answer: d. Execute trades for floor brokers' accounts EXPLANATIONS: Floor traders buy and sell on the floor for their firm's accounts.

Q337_LO10: Correct Answer: b. Physical location (floor) EXPLANATIONS: The OTC market lacks a physical location or floor.

Q338_LO10: Correct Answer: d. Between members (not employees) EXPLANATIONS: Trades on exchanges happen between members, not employees.

Q339_LO10: Correct Answer: c. Maintain an inventory EXPLANATIONS: A market maker in the OTC market maintains an inventory in a given security.

Q340_LO10: Correct Answer: b. Double-auction system EXPLANATIONS: Both exchanges and the OTC market are sometimes referred to as double-auction markets.

Q341_LO10: Correct Answer: c. Both exchanges and OTC market EXPLANATIONS: Trading occurs on exchanges (listed) and in the OTC market (nonlisted).

Q342_LO10: Correct Answer: c. Floor for transactions EXPLANATIONS: Exchanges, unlike the OTC market, often have a physical floor for trading.

Q343_LO10: Correct Answer: b. Designated market maker EXPLANATIONS: The designated market maker (DMM) acts as the dealer for a specific security.

Q344_LO10: Correct Answer: b. As intermediaries for customers EXPLANATIONS: Floor brokers represent their firms and clients on the exchange floor.

Q345_LO10: Correct Answer: c. Maintain an inventory and facilitate trades EXPLANATIONS: OTC market makers maintain an inventory and facilitate buying and selling throughout the day.

Q346_LO10: Correct Answer: b. Guaranteeing liquidity EXPLANATIONS: Both DMMs and OTC market makers guarantee liquidity for specific securities.

Q347_LO10: Correct Answer: c. To a dealer at the ask price EXPLANATIONS: Customers selling in the OTC market sell to a dealer at the bid price.

Q348_LO10: Correct Answer: a. Difference between bid and ask EXPLANATIONS: The spread in the OTC market is the difference between the bid and ask prices.

Q349_LO10: Correct Answer: a. Highest bid and lowest ask EXPLANATIONS: Quotes represent the highest bid and lowest ask prices in the system.

Q350_LO10: Correct Answer: a. Tracks and provides trading for OTC-traded companies EXPLANATIONS: Nasdaq tracks and facilitates trading for the largest OTC-traded companies.

Q351_LO10: Correct Answer: d. Current best bid plus $0.01 EXPLANATIONS: To establish the best bid, a buying broker-dealer must bid at least $0.01 higher than the current best bid.

Q352_LO10: Correct Answer: c. Execute trades for customers EXPLANATIONS: Floor traders execute trades for their firm's accounts on the exchange floor.

Q353_LO10: Correct Answer: c. Buys from a market maker at the ask price EXPLANATIONS: Customers buying in the OTC market buy from a market maker at the ask price.

Q354_LO10: Correct Answer: a. Floor transactions vs. electronic market EXPLANATIONS: Exchanges often involve floor transactions, while the OTC market is a decentralized electronic market.

Q355_LO10: Correct Answer: b. OTC market EXPLANATIONS: The OTC market trades unlisted stocks and most bonds, including municipals and treasury debt.

The Government Regulators

Q356_LO11: What is the primary regulatory body for the securities industry?
a. FINRA
b. SEC
c. IRS
d. OCC

HINTS: Consider the entity created under the Securities Exchange Act of 1934.

Q357_LO11: What action can the SEC take against a BD that does not comply with its rules?
a. Censure
b. Fine
c. Registration suspension
d. All of the above

HINTS: Recognize the potential consequences for non-compliance.

Q358_LO11: Under the Securities Exchange Act of 1934, what areas does the act cover?
a. Primary market transactions
b. Insider transactions
c. Financial responsibility of BDs
d. All of the above

HINTS: Identify the areas covered by the act.

Q359_LO11: What is the purpose of the Financial Crimes Enforcement Network (FinCEN)?
a. Enforce tax laws
b. Combat money laundering
c. Regulate exchanges
d. Oversee national banks

HINTS: Focus on FinCEN's mission.

Q360_LO11: Which branch of the Treasury is the primary tax enforcement agency?
a. FinCEN
b. IRS
c. OCC
d. SEC

HINTS: Consider the role related to tax enforcement.

Q361_LO11: What is the mission of the Office of the Comptroller of the Currency (OCC)?
a. Combat money laundering
b. Supervise national banks
c. Ensure fair access to financial services
d. Analyze financial intelligence

HINTS: Identify the primary mission of the OCC.

Q362_LO11: According to the SEC, can a BD claim SEC approval based on registration?
a. Yes, always
b. Yes, if financial standing is strong
c. No, never
d. Only for certain types of BDs

HINTS: Pay attention to the limitations on claims.

Q363_LO11: In the event of a BD's bankruptcy, what does the Securities Investor Protection Act of 1970 (SIPA) cover?
a. Insider transactions
b. Protection thresholds for customers
c. Financial responsibility of BDs
d. Reporting requirements for issuers

HINTS: Focus on the coverage area of SIPA.

Q364_LO11: What legislative act governs the new issuance (primary) market?
a. Securities Exchange Act of 1934
b. Investment Company Act of 1940
c. Securities Act of 1933
d. USA PATRIOT Act

HINTS: Identify the act related to the new issuance market.

Q365_LO11: Which act defines penalties for the misuse of material, nonpublic information?
a. Investment Advisers Act of 1940
b. Securities Investor Protection Act of 1970
c. Insider Trading and Securities Fraud Enforcement Act of 1988
d. The USA PATRIOT Act

HINTS: Recognize the act related to penalties for insider trading.

Q366_LO11: What is the focus of the Investment Advisers Act of 1940?
a. Regulation of client accounts
b. Reporting requirements for issuers
c. Governs trading markets
d. Covers anti-money laundering

HINTS: Identify the primary focus of the act.

Q367_LO11: Which act covers anti-money laundering (AML) policies and procedures?
a. Securities Investor Protection Act of 1970
b. The USA PATRIOT Act
c. Investment Advisers Act of 1940
d. Securities Exchange Act of 1934

HINTS: Recognize the act related to AML policies and procedures.

Q368_LO11: According to the Securities Exchange Act of 1934, what does the act regulate?
a. Primary market transactions
b. Trading markets for existing securities
c. Registration of investment companies
d. Financial crimes enforcement

HINTS: Focus on the areas regulated by the act.

Q369_LO11: What is the primary mission of the Financial Crimes Enforcement Network (FinCEN)?
a. Ensure fair access to financial services
b. Combat money laundering
c. Supervise national banks
d. Regulate exchanges

HINTS: Focus on FinCEN's mission.

Q370_LO11: Which act governs packaged products such as mutual funds and closed-end funds?
a. Securities Act of 1933
b. Investment Company Act of 1940
c. Securities Exchange Act of 1934
d. Insider Trading and Securities Fraud Enforcement Act of 1988

HINTS: Identify the act governing packaged investment products.

Q371_LO11: What is the primary regulatory body for the securities industry?
a. FINRA
b. SEC
c. IRS
d. FinCEN

HINTS: Identify the regulatory body established under the Securities Exchange Act of 1934.

Q372_LO11: What consequences may a BD face for non-compliance with SEC rules?
a. Increased registration fees
b. Fine and suspension of registration
c. Mandatory training sessions
d. Public commendation

HINTS: Recognize the potential repercussions for BDs violating SEC rules.

Q373_LO11: Which act is concerned with providing a fair marketplace for all investors?
a. Securities Act of 1933
b. Securities Exchange Act of 1934
c. Investment Company Act of 1940
d. USA PATRIOT Act

HINTS: Focus on the act designed to ensure a fair market for investors.

Q374_LO11: Who has regulatory authority over licensing of securities representatives?
a. SEC
b. IRS
c. FINRA
d. FinCEN

HINTS: Identify the organization delegated with regulatory authority over licensing.

Q375_LO11: What is the mission of the Financial Crimes Enforcement Network (FinCEN)?
a. Regulating securities exchanges
b. Promoting national security
c. Ensuring fair access to financial services
d. Safeguarding the financial system from illicit use

HINTS: Understand the mission of FinCEN.

Q376_LO11: Which branch of the Treasury is the primary tax enforcement agency?
a. FinCEN
b. IRS
c. SEC
d. OCC

HINTS: Identify the primary tax enforcement agency among the Treasury branches.

Q377_LO11: What information must financial services companies provide to the IRS as part of licensing?
a. Trading strategies
b. Customer and firm information
c. Marketing plans
d. Internal communications

HINTS: Recognize the information required by financial services companies.

Q378_LO11: Which legislative act governs the new issuance (primary) market?
a. Securities Act of 1933
b. Securities Exchange Act of 1934
c. Investment Company Act of 1940
d. USA PATRIOT Act

HINTS: Identify the act governing the primary market and new issuances.

Q379_LO11: What does the Securities Investor Protection Act of 1970 (SIPA) cover?
a. Licensing requirements
b. Reporting requirements for issuers
c. Protection thresholds for customers in BD bankruptcy
d. Regulation of insider transactions

HINTS: Understand the coverage of SIPA.

Q380_LO11: Which act defines penalties for the misuse of material, nonpublic information?
a. Insider Trading and Securities Fraud Enforcement Act of 1988
b. Investment Advisers Act of 1940
c. Securities Exchange Act of 1934
d. Securities Act of 1933

HINTS: Identify the act addressing the misuse of nonpublic information.

Q381_LO11: What is the mission of the Office of the Comptroller of the Currency (OCC)?
a. Regulating securities exchanges
b. Ensuring safe and sound operations of national banks
c. Safeguarding the financial system
d. Promoting national security

HINTS: Understand the mission of the OCC.

Q382_LO11: Which organization safeguards the financial system from illicit use?
a. SEC
b. IRS
c. FinCEN
d. OCC

HINTS: Recognize the organization focused on preventing illicit use of the financial system.

Q383_LO11: What role does the Securities Act of 1933 play in the securities industry?
a. Governs trading markets
b. Governs the new issuance market
c. Regulates investment advisers
d. Covers anti-money laundering policies

HINTS: Identify the specific market governed by the Securities Act of 1933.

Q384_LO11: What does the Investment Advisers Act of 1940 regulate?
a. Trading markets
b. New issuances
c. Investment advisers
d. Client accounts

HINTS: Identify the entities regulated by the Investment Advisers Act of 1940.

Q385_LO11: What does the USA PATRIOT Act primarily cover?
a. Securities trading
b. Anti-money laundering policies
c. Reporting requirements for issuers
d. Tax enforcement

HINTS: Recognize the primary focus of the USA PATRIOT Act.

Q386_LO11: What is the primary regulatory body for the securities industry?
a. IRS
b. FinCEN
c. SEC
d. OCC

HINTS: Identify the organization responsible for securities industry regulation.

Q387_LO11: What consequence may a BD face for non-compliance with SEC rules?
a. Fine only
b. Revocation of registration
c. Limits on operations
d. Censure

HINTS: Recognize the potential outcomes for non-compliance with SEC rules.

Q388_LO11: According to the Securities Exchange Act of 1934, what is a primary focus for ensuring a fair market?
a. Reporting requirements for issuers
b. Regulation of client accounts
c. Net capital rule
d. Insider transactions regulation

HINTS: Identify a key area covered by the Securities Exchange Act of 1934.

Q389_LO11: What does the Financial Crimes Enforcement Network (FinCEN) aim to combat?
a. Securities fraud
b. Insider trading
c. Money laundering
d. Market manipulation

HINTS: Understand the mission of FinCEN.

Q390_LO11: Which branch of the U.S. Treasury serves as the primary tax enforcement agency?
a. IRS
b. OCC
c. FinCEN
d. SEC

HINTS: Recognize the branch responsible for tax enforcement.

Q391_LO11: What does the Office of the Comptroller of the Currency (OCC) supervise?
a. Mutual funds
b. National banks
c. Investment advisers
d. Securities exchanges

HINTS: Identify the entities supervised by the OCC.

Q392_LO11: What is the primary role of the Comptroller?
a. Ensure fair access to financial services
b. Enforce tax laws
c. Supervise securities exchanges
d. Oversee safety and soundness of banks

HINTS: Recognize the primary role of the Comptroller.

Q393_LO11: In the event of a BD's bankruptcy, what does the Securities Investor Protection Act of 1970 (SIPA) cover?
a. Insider trading penalties
b. Anti-money laundering policies
c. Customer protection thresholds
d. Reporting requirements for issuers

HINTS: Identify the area covered by SIPA.
Q394_LO11: Which legislative act focuses on regulating firms providing investment advice?
a. Securities Act of 1933
b. Investment Company Act of 1940
c. Investment Advisers Act of 1940
d. USA PATRIOT Act

HINTS: Recognize the act governing firms providing investment advice.

Q395_LO11: What does the USA PATRIOT Act primarily cover for financial firms?
a. Net capital rule
b. Anti-money laundering policies
c. Client accounts regulation
d. Insider trading penalties

HINTS: Understand the focus of the USA PATRIOT Act.

Q396_LO11: Which act defines penalties for the misuse of material, nonpublic information?
a. Securities Act of 1933
b. Insider Trading and Securities Fraud Enforcement Act of 1988
c. Securities Exchange Act of 1934
d. Investment Company Act of 1940

HINTS: Identify the act addressing penalties for insider trading.

Q397_LO11: According to the Securities Act of 1933, what does it govern?
a. Existing securities trading
b. Tax enforcement
c. New issuance (primary) market
d. Insider transactions

HINTS: Recognize the focus of the Securities Act of 1933.

Q398_LO11: Which act covers the regulation of packaged products like mutual funds?
a. Investment Advisers Act of 1940
b. Securities Exchange Act of 1934
c. Investment Company Act of 1940
d. Securities Investor Protection Act of 1970

HINTS: Identify the act regulating packaged products such as mutual funds.

Q399_LO11: What is the primary purpose of the Securities Act of 1933?
a. Regulate client accounts
b. Enforce tax laws
c. Govern the new issuance market
d. Combat money laundering

HINTS: Recognize the primary purpose of the Securities Act of 1933.

Q400_LO11: Which act covers the protection thresholds for customers in the event of a BD's bankruptcy?
a. Securities Exchange Act of 1934
b. Securities Investor Protection Act of 1970 (SIPA)
c. Investment Advisers Act of 1940
d. USA PATRIOT Act

HINTS: Identify the act covering customer protection in bankruptcy.

Q401_LO12: Which branch of the U.S. Treasury focuses on safeguarding the financial system from illicit use and combating money laundering?
a. Internal Revenue Service (IRS)
b. Financial Crimes Enforcement Network (FinCEN)
c. Office of the Comptroller of the Currency
d. Federal Deposit Insurance Corporation

HINTS: Think about the agency responsible for preventing illicit financial activities.

Q402_LO12: What is the primary role of the Internal Revenue Service (IRS) concerning financial services companies?
a. Tax law creation
b. Investigation of potential tax evasion
c. Licensing financial services companies
d. Regulation of trading markets

HINTS: Consider the IRS's primary function in relation to financial services companies.

Q403_LO12: The Office of the Comptroller of the Currency supervises and ensures the safe and sound operation of:
a. Credit unions
b. National banks and federal savings associations
c. State-chartered banks
d. Securities exchanges

HINTS: Think about the entities that the Comptroller supervises.

Q404_LO12: Which Act governs the regulation of packaged products such as mutual funds, closed-end funds, and unit investment trusts?
a. Securities Act of 1933
b. Securities Exchange Act of 1934
c. Investment Company Act of 1940
d. Investment Advisers Act of 1940

HINTS: Focus on the purpose of the Act related to packaged investment products.

Q405_LO12: The Securities Investor Protection Act of 1970 (SIPA) is designed to:
a. Regulate trading markets
b. Govern the issuance market
c. Cover protection thresholds for customers in BD bankruptcy
d. Define penalties for insider trading

HINTS: Consider the purpose of SIPA in the context of customer protection.

Q406_LO12: What does the 1988 Insider Trading and Securities Fraud Enforcement Act define penalties for?
a. Violating AML policies
b. Securities fraud enforcement
c. Misuse of material, nonpublic information
d. Insider trading by individuals

HINTS: Think about the focus area of this Act.

Q407_LO12: The USA PATRIOT Act primarily focuses on:
a. Governing trading markets
b. Regulating investment advisers
c. Covering AML policies and procedures
d. Defining penalties for securities fraud

HINTS: Consider the purpose of the USA PATRIOT Act.

Q408_LO12: In 1933, the Securities Act of 1933 was enacted to govern the:
a. Issuance (primary) market
b. Existing securities market
c. Regulation of packaged products
d. Protection thresholds for customers

HINTS: Focus on the specific market regulated by this Act.

Q409_LO12: Which branch of the Treasury is responsible for supervising national banks, federal savings associations, and federal branches/agencies of foreign banks?
a. Financial Crimes Enforcement Network (FinCEN)
b. Internal Revenue Service (IRS)
c. Office of the Comptroller of the Currency
d. Securities and Exchange Commission (SEC)

HINTS: Consider the supervisory responsibilities of different Treasury branches.

Q410_LO12: The Financial Crimes Enforcement Network (FinCEN) requires most financial services companies to report:
a. Tax evasion cases
b. Customer and firm information to the SEC
c. Suspicious or unusual activity
d. Material, nonpublic information

HINTS: Think about FinCEN's mission and reporting requirements.

Q411_LO12: What is the main purpose of the Securities Exchange Act of 1934?
a. Regulating packaged products
b. Governing issuance market
c. Governing trading markets for existing securities
d. Defining penalties for securities fraud

HINTS: Focus on the specific market and securities covered by this Act.

Q412_LO12: The primary mission of the Financial Crimes Enforcement Network is to:
a. Combat money laundering
b. Regulate securities exchanges
c. Investigate tax evasion
d. Define penalties for insider trading

HINTS: Consider the primary focus area of FinCEN's mission.

Q413_LO12: What does the Investment Advisers Act of 1940 govern the regulation of?
a. Securities issuance market
b. Packaged products like mutual funds
c. Firms providing investment advice
d. Trading markets for existing securities

HINTS: Think about the entities regulated by this Act.

Q414_LO12: The Securities Investor Protection Act of 1970 (SIPA) covers protection thresholds for customers in the event of:
a. Insider trading
b. A BD's bankruptcy
c. Securities fraud
d. Violation of AML policies

HINTS: Focus on the purpose related to customer protection in financial distress.

Q415_LO12: What is the purpose of the 2001 USA PATRIOT Act?
a. Regulate trading markets
b. Cover AML policies and procedures
c. Define penalties for securities fraud
d. Govern the issuance market

HINTS: Consider the focus area related to national security.

Q416_LO13: What legislation established the Federal Reserve System as the central bank of the United States?
a. Securities Investor Protection Act of 1970
b. Federal Reserve Act of 1913
c. Securities Act of 1933
d. Securities Exchange Act of 1934

HINTS: Think about the historical event that created the Federal Reserve System.

Q417_LO13: How many regional Federal Reserve Banks are there in the Federal Reserve System?
a. 6
b. 8
c. 10
d. 12

HINTS: Consider the structure of the Federal Reserve System.

Q418_LO13: What is the primary responsibility of the Federal Reserve Board (FRB)?
a. Setting tax policies
b. Determining monetary policy
c. Enforcing securities regulations
d. Regulating banking mergers

HINTS: Focus on the key function of the Federal Reserve Board.

Q419_LO13: In the context of the Federal Reserve, what aspect of the U.S. economy do the FRB decisions significantly impact?
a. Real estate market
b. Stock market
c. Technology sector
d. Agricultural production

HINTS: Consider the consequences of FRB decisions on economic elements.

Q420_LO13: Under the Securities Investor Protection Corporation (SIPC), what determines if an account represents a separate customer for coverage purposes?
a. Account balance
b. Account type
c. Account title
d. Account location

HINTS: Think about the factor that determines separate customer status.

Q421_LO13: What is the maximum coverage limit per separate account under SIPC?
a. $100,000
b. $250,000
c. $500,000
d. $1,000,000

HINTS: Consider the maximum coverage limit provided by SIPC.

Q422_LO13: Regarding SIPC coverage, what portion is covered in cash within the $500,000 limit?
a. $100,000
b. $150,000
c. $250,000
d. $300,000

HINTS: Focus on the specific coverage limit for cash under SIPC.

Q423_LO13: What happens if a customer has claims exceeding the SIPC coverage limits when a BD fails?
a. Claims are fully covered by SIPC
b. The customer becomes a general creditor for the uncovered amount
c. SIPC increases coverage for the customer
d. Claims are transferred to another BD

HINTS: Consider the status of claims beyond SIPC coverage limits.

Q424_LO13: What types of accounts are combined for the purposes of determining SIPC coverage?
a. Cash and margin accounts
b. Individual and joint accounts
c. Retirement and non-retirement accounts
d. Corporate and partnership accounts

HINTS: Focus on the combination of accounts for coverage determination.

Q425_LO13: What is NOT covered by SIPC in the case of BD failure?
a. Commodities
b. Futures contracts related to currencies
c. Securities
d. Cash

HINTS: Consider the specific items excluded from SIPC coverage.

Q426_LO13: When must BDs disclose their SIPC membership to customers?
a. Only at account closure
b. At least once each year
c. Only to new customers
d. Only during market downturns

HINTS: Think about the timing of SIPC disclosure to customers.

Q427_LO13: In SIPC disclosures, what must member firms include in their advertising regarding coverage?
a. SIPC coverage is unlimited
b. SIPC benefits are unique to the specific BD
c. SIPC coverage is less than it actually is
d. SIPC coverage is not

HINTS: Focus on the requirement for accurate disclosure in advertising.

Q428_LO13: What action may SIPC take if it determines that a BD is in imminent danger of failing?
a. Directly liquidate the firm
b. Notify the SEC for investigation
c. Increase SIPC coverage for the BD
d. Provide a bailout package

HINTS: Consider the protective actions SIPC may take when a BD is in financial difficulty.

Q429_LO13: What is a customer, according to SIPC?
a. Only an account holder
b. Only a person with a margin account
c. Anyone with cash or securities in BD possession
d. Only individuals, not entities

HINTS: Think about the broad definition of a customer under SIPC.

Q430_LO13: If a BD fails, what is the status of the member firm once a trustee has been appointed?
a. Continues business as usual
b. Prohibited from engaging in business as a BD
c. Allowed to conceal assets temporarily
d. Can alter securities records

HINTS: Focus on the restrictions placed on the member firm after a trustee's appointment.

Q431_LO14: Why was the FDIC created during the Great Depression?
a. To regulate banks
b. To insure bank deposits
c. To provide loans to banks
d. To invest in the stock market

HINTS: Think about the historical context and purpose of FDIC.

Q432_LO14: How does the FDIC preserve public confidence in the banking system?
a. By regulating interest rates
b. By insuring deposits
c. By investing in the stock market
d. By providing loans to individuals

HINTS: Consider the primary function of the FDIC.

Q433_LO14: In the event of a financial institution's failure, what does the FDIC usually do with customer deposits and loans?
a. Refund them in full
b. Sell them to another institution
c. Invest them in government securities
d. Distribute them among the shareholders

HINTS: Focus on the typical action taken by the FDIC in case of failure.

Q434_LO14: What is the maximum amount of deposit insurance provided by the FDIC for each deposit ownership category in each insured bank?
a. $100,000
b. $250,000
c. $500,000
d. $1,000,000

HINTS: Consider the limit set by the FDIC for deposit insurance.

Q435_LO14: Which of the following accounts is covered by FDIC deposit insurance?
a. Mutual funds
b. Annuities
c. Self-directed IRA accounts
d. Stocks and bonds

HINTS: Focus on the types of accounts covered by FDIC insurance.

Q436_LO14: What types of investment products are NOT covered by FDIC deposit insurance?
a. Certificates of deposit
b. Annuities
c. Money market deposit accounts
d. Mutual funds

HINTS: Think about the nature of the products that FDIC does not cover.

Q437_LO14: How does FDIC coverage differ from SIPC coverage regarding joint accounts?
a. FDIC covers per separate account
b. SIPC covers per separate account
c. FDIC covers per owner per account
d. SIPC covers per owner per account

HINTS: Compare the coverage criteria for joint accounts under FDIC and SIPC.

Q438_LO14: In an individual account, a joint account, and an IRA, how much coverage does SIPC provide collectively?
a. $250,000
b. $500,000
c. $750,000
d. $1,000,000

HINTS: Consider how SIPC provides coverage for accounts with differing registrations.

Q439_LO14: What happens to accounts with differing registrations under FDIC coverage?
a. Each account is covered up to $500,000
b. Coverage is combined for all accounts
c. FDIC does not cover accounts with differing registrations
d. Each account is covered separately

HINTS: Focus on how FDIC treats accounts with different registrations.

Q440_LO14: In FDIC terminology, what is considered a separate ownership category?
a. Different account types
b. Different account balances
c. Different account holders
d. Different account locations

HINTS: Think about what defines a separate ownership category under FDIC.

Q441_LO14: If a bank fails, what does FDIC coverage guarantee regarding a depositor's accounts?
a. Full repayment of all deposits
b. Immediate transfer to another bank
c. Safety of deposits up to $250,000
d. Priority access to the bank's assets

HINTS: Consider the guarantee provided by FDIC coverage in case of a bank failure.

Q442_LO14: What is the source of funds for the FDIC, similar to a private insurance company?
a. Government grants
b. Taxpayer money
c. Premiums paid by participating institutions
d. Federal Reserve loans

HINTS: Think about how the FDIC funds its operations.

Q443_LO14: What is the primary function of the FDIC in the event of a member financial institution's failure?
a. Liquidate the institution
b. Provide bailout funds
c. Sell deposits and loans to another institution
d. Increase coverage limits

HINTS: Focus on the typical action taken by the FDIC during a financial institution's failure.

Q444_LO14: Why was the FDIC created during the Great Depression?
a. To insure deposits
b. To regulate banks
c. To provide loans to individuals
d. To invest in the stock market

HINTS: Consider the historical context and primary purpose of creating the FDIC.

Q445_LO14: What is the primary goal of FDIC deposit insurance?
a. Guaranteeing high interest rates
b. Protecting depositors by insuring accounts
c. Facilitating stock market investments
d. Regulating financial markets

HINTS: Focus on the primary goal and function of FDIC deposit insurance.

Q446_LO15: What is the Uniform Securities Act (1956) used for by the states?
a. To create federal securities laws
b. As a template for state securities laws
c. To regulate international securities markets
d. To enforce broker-dealer regulations

HINTS: Think about the purpose of the Uniform Securities Act.

Q447_LO15: In the Uniform Securities Act, what provision mandates the appointment of state securities administrators?
a. Section on broker-dealer regulations
b. Requirement for investment adviser registration
c. Provision on state regulatory authority
d. Method of selection for state administrators

HINTS: Consider the specific provision related to state securities administrators.

Q448_LO15: What authority is granted to state administrators according to the Uniform Securities Act?
a. Authority to create federal laws
b. Authority to regulate international securities
c. Significant authority within their states
d. Authority to override federal regulations

HINTS: Focus on the powers granted to state administrators.

Q449_LO15: How do states typically select their state securities administrators?
a. Federal appointment
b. NASAA recommendation
c. Appointment or election method
d. Direct federal assignment

HINTS: Consider the flexibility provided to states in selecting administrators.

Q450_LO15: What is the primary role of state securities administrators?
a. Enforce federal securities laws
b. Regulate international securities markets
c. Enforce state securities laws
d. Oversee broker-dealer mergers

HINTS: Think about the primary responsibility of state securities administrators.

Q451_LO15: Which organization represents state and provincial securities regulators in North America?
a. SEC
b. FINRA
c. CFTC
d. NASAA

HINTS: Focus on the organization representing state securities regulators.

Q452_LO15: What does NASAA stand for?
a. National Association of Securities Agents and Administrators
b. North American Securities Administrators Association
c. Securities Regulatory Council
d. State Administrators Alliance
HINTS: Consider the correct acronym for the organization.

Q453_LO15: What is the regulatory authority of NASAA?
a. Specific regulatory authority over states
b. Authority to override state regulations
c. No specific regulatory authority
d. Authority only over federal regulations
HINTS: Focus on NASAA's regulatory role.

Q454_LO15: What role does NASAA play in state securities regulations?
a. Direct enforcement of regulations
b. Producing guidelines for state administrators
c. Overriding state regulations
d. Acting as a federal regulatory body
HINTS: Consider the supportive role of NASAA in state securities regulations.

Q455_LO15: What is the significance of NASAA's guidelines for state administrators?
a. Mandatory regulations for all states
b. Suggested best practices for enforcement
c. Federal laws for uniformity
d. Guidelines for international cooperation
HINTS: Focus on the purpose of NASAA's guidelines.

Q456_LO15: What geographic region does NASAA cover in its representation?
a. United States only
b. North America
c. Europe and Asia
d. Worldwide
HINTS: Think about the areas covered by NASAA's representation.

Q457_LO15: Which entity uses the Uniform Securities Act as a template for state securities laws?
a. SEC
b. FINRA
c. State administrators
d. NASAA
HINTS: Consider the users of the Uniform Securities Act.

Q458_LO15: What is the official title of the state securities administrator in each state?
a. Securities Commissioner
b. Chief Financial Officer
c. Chief Compliance Officer
d. Chief Executive Officer
HINTS: Focus on the official title given to state securities administrators.

Q459_LO15: In the context of state securities administrators, what is left to the states to decide?
a. Regulatory authority
b. Method of selection
c. Specific enforcement powers
d. Appointment by the federal government

HINTS: Consider the flexibility provided to states in selecting administrators.

Q460_LO15: What is the primary function of NASAA members from Canada and Mexico?
a. Enforce U.S. federal laws
b. Produce guidelines for international cooperation
c. Represent their respective countries in NASAA
d. Override state regulations
HINTS: Think about the role of NASAA members from Canada and Mexico.

Correct Answers & Explanations
The Government Regulators

Q356_LO11: Correct Answer: b. SEC EXPLANATIONS: The Securities and Exchange Commission (SEC) is the primary regulatory body for the securities industry.

Q357_LO11: Correct Answer: d. All of the above EXPLANATIONS: The SEC can take various actions, including censure, fine, and registration suspension, against a non-compliant BD.

Q358_LO11: Correct Answer: d. All of the above EXPLANATIONS: The act covers insider transactions, financial responsibility, and more.

Q359_LO11: Correct Answer: b. Combat money laundering EXPLANATIONS: FinCEN's mission is to combat money laundering and safeguard the financial system.

Q360_LO11: Correct Answer: b. IRS EXPLANATIONS: The IRS is the primary tax enforcement agency of the federal government.

Q361_LO11: Correct Answer: b. Supervise national banks EXPLANATIONS: The OCC supervises national banks to ensure safe and sound operations.

Q362_LO11: Correct Answer: c. No, never EXPLANATIONS: A BD cannot claim SEC approval based on registration; any such claim is misrepresentation.

Q363_LO11: Correct Answer: b. Protection thresholds for customers EXPLANATIONS: SIPA covers protection thresholds for customers in the event of a BD's bankruptcy.

Q364_LO11: Correct Answer: c. Securities Act of 1933 EXPLANATIONS: The Securities Act of 1933 governs the new issuance (primary) market.

Q365_LO11: Correct Answer: c. Insider Trading and Securities Fraud Enforcement Act of 1988 EXPLANATIONS: The Insider Trading and Securities Fraud Enforcement Act of 1988 defines penalties for the misuse of material, nonpublic information.

Q366_LO11: Correct Answer: a. Regulation of client accounts EXPLANATIONS: The Investment Advisers Act of 1940 governs the regulation of firms providing investment advice.

Q367_LO11: Correct Answer: b. The USA PATRIOT Act EXPLANATIONS: The USA PATRIOT Act covers anti-money laundering (AML) policies and procedures.

Q368_LO11: Correct Answer: b. Trading markets for existing securities EXPLANATIONS: The Securities Exchange Act of 1934 regulates trading markets for existing securities.

Q369_LO11: Correct Answer: b. Combat money laundering EXPLANATIONS: FinCEN's mission is to combat money laundering and safeguard the financial system.

Q370_LO11: Correct Answer: b. Investment Company Act of 1940 EXPLANATIONS: The Investment Company Act of 1940 governs packaged products such as mutual funds and closed-end funds.

Q371_LO11: Correct Answer: b. SEC EXPLANATIONS: The SEC is the primary regulatory body for the securities industry.

Q372_LO11: Correct Answer: b. Fine and suspension of registration EXPLANATIONS: Non-compliance may result in fines, suspension of registration, and other penalties.

Q373_LO11: Correct Answer: b. Securities Exchange Act of 1934 EXPLANATIONS: The Securities Exchange Act of 1934 aims to provide a fair marketplace for all investors.

Q374_LO11: Correct Answer: c. FINRA EXPLANATIONS: FINRA has regulatory authority over licensing of securities representatives.

Q375_LO11: Correct Answer: d. Safeguarding the financial system from illicit use EXPLANATIONS: FinCEN's mission is to safeguard the financial system from illicit use.

Q376_LO11: Correct Answer: b. IRS EXPLANATIONS: The IRS is the primary tax enforcement agency of the federal government.

Q377_LO11: Correct Answer: b. Customer and firm information EXPLANATIONS: Financial services companies must provide customer and firm information to the IRS upon demand.

Q378_LO11: Correct Answer: a. Securities Act of 1933 EXPLANATIONS: The Securities Act of 1933 governs the new issuance (primary) market.

Q379_LO11: Correct Answer: c. Protection thresholds for customers in BD bankruptcy EXPLANATIONS: SIPA covers protection thresholds for customers in the event of a BD's bankruptcy.

Q380_LO11: Correct Answer: a. Insider Trading and Securities Fraud Enforcement Act of 1988 EXPLANATIONS: The Insider Trading and Securities Fraud Enforcement Act of 1988 defines penalties for misuse of information.

Q381_LO11: Correct Answer: b. Ensuring safe and sound operations of national banks EXPLANATIONS: The OCC's mission is to ensure safe and sound operations of national banks.

Q382_LO11: Correct Answer: c. FinCEN EXPLANATIONS: FinCEN safeguards the financial system from illicit use.

Q383_LO11: Correct Answer: b. Governs the new issuance market EXPLANATIONS: The Securities Act of 1933 governs the new issuance (primary) market.

Q384_LO11: Correct Answer: c. Investment advisers EXPLANATIONS: The act governs the regulation of firms that provide investment advice.

Q385_LO11: Correct Answer: b. Anti-money laundering policies EXPLANATIONS: The USA PATRIOT Act primarily covers anti-money laundering (AML) policies and procedures.

Q386_LO11: Correct Answer: c. SEC EXPLANATIONS: The SEC, created under the Securities Exchange Act of 1934, is the primary regulatory body for the securities industry.

Q387_LO11: Correct Answer: b. Revocation of registration EXPLANATIONS: Non-compliance with SEC rules may lead to consequences such as revocation of registration.

Q388_LO11: Correct Answer: a. Reporting requirements for issuers EXPLANATIONS: The act focuses on ensuring a fair market, including reporting requirements for issuers.

Q389_LO11: Correct Answer: c. Money laundering EXPLANATIONS: FinCEN's mission is to safeguard the financial system from illicit use, combat money laundering, and promote national security.

Q390_LO11: Correct Answer: a. IRS EXPLANATIONS: The Internal Revenue Service (IRS) serves as the primary tax enforcement agency.

Q391_LO11: Correct Answer: b. National banks EXPLANATIONS: The OCC supervises national banks, federal savings associations, and federal branches/agencies of foreign banks.

Q392_LO11: Correct Answer: d. Oversee safety and soundness of banks EXPLANATIONS: The Comptroller oversees the safety and soundness of national banks and federal savings associations.

Q393_LO11: Correct Answer: c. Customer protection thresholds EXPLANATIONS: SIPA covers protection thresholds for customers in the event of a BD's bankruptcy.

Q394_LO11: Correct Answer: c. Investment Advisers Act of 1940 EXPLANATIONS: The Investment Advisers Act of 1940 regulates firms that provide investment advice.

Q395_LO11: Correct Answer: b. Anti-money laundering policies EXPLANATIONS: The USA PATRIOT Act primarily covers anti-money laundering (AML) policies for financial firms.

Q396_LO11: Correct Answer: b. Insider Trading and Securities Fraud Enforcement Act of 1988 EXPLANATIONS: The Insider Trading and Securities Fraud Enforcement Act of 1988 defines penalties for the misuse of nonpublic information.

Q397_LO11: Correct Answer: c. New issuance (primary) market EXPLANATIONS: The Securities Act of 1933 governs the new issuance (primary) market, involving money-raising activities.

Q398_LO11: Correct Answer: c. Investment Company Act of 1940 EXPLANATIONS: The Investment Company Act of 1940 covers the regulation of packaged products like mutual funds.

Q399_LO11: Correct Answer: c. Govern the new issuance market EXPLANATIONS: The act governs the new issuance (primary) market, involving the money-raising activities of issuers.

Q400_LO11: Correct Answer: b. Securities Investor Protection Act of 1970 (SIPA) EXPLANATIONS: SIPA covers protection thresholds for customers in the event of a BD's bankruptcy.

Q401_LO12: Correct Answer: b EXPLANATIONS: FinCEN's mission is to safeguard the financial system from illicit use and combat money laundering.

Q402_LO12: Correct Answer: b EXPLANATIONS: The IRS primarily investigates potential tax evasion among financial services companies.

Q403_LO12: Correct Answer: b EXPLANATIONS: The Comptroller supervises national banks, federal savings associations, and federal branches/agencies of foreign banks.

Q404_LO12: Correct Answer: c EXPLANATIONS: The Investment Company Act of 1940 regulates packaged products like mutual funds, closed-end funds, and unit investment trusts.

Q405_LO12: Correct Answer: c EXPLANATIONS: SIPA covers protection thresholds for customers in the event of a BD's bankruptcy.

Q406_LO12: Correct Answer: c EXPLANATIONS: The 1988 Act defines penalties for the misuse of material, nonpublic information by both firms and individuals.

Q407_LO12: Correct Answer: c EXPLANATIONS: The USA PATRIOT Act primarily covers anti-money laundering (AML) policies and procedures.

Q408_LO12: Correct Answer: a EXPLANATIONS: The Securities Act of 1933 governs the issuance (primary) market.

Q409_LO12: Correct Answer: c EXPLANATIONS: The Office of the Comptroller of the Currency supervises national banks and federal savings associations.

Q410_LO12: Correct Answer: c EXPLANATIONS: FinCEN requires reporting of suspicious or unusual activity by financial services companies.

Q411_LO12: Correct Answer: c EXPLANATIONS: The Securities Exchange Act of 1934 governs trading markets for existing securities.

Q412_LO12: Correct Answer: a EXPLANATIONS: FinCEN's primary mission is to combat money laundering.

Q413_LO12: Correct Answer: c EXPLANATIONS: The Investment Advisers Act of 1940 governs the regulation of firms that provide investment advice.

Q414_LO12: Correct Answer: b EXPLANATIONS: SIPA covers protection thresholds for customers in the event of a BD's bankruptcy.

Q415_LO12: Correct Answer: b EXPLANATIONS: The USA PATRIOT Act primarily covers anti-money laundering (AML) policies and procedures.

Q416_LO13: Correct Answer: b EXPLANATIONS: The Federal Reserve Act of 1913 established the Federal Reserve System as the central bank of the United States.

Q417_LO13: Correct Answer: d EXPLANATIONS: The Federal Reserve System consists of 12 regional Federal Reserve Banks.

Q418_LO13: Correct Answer: b EXPLANATIONS: The FRB's primary responsibility is determining monetary policy.

Q419_LO13: Correct Answer: b EXPLANATIONS: FRB decisions significantly impact the stock market and overall economic conditions.

Q420_LO13: Correct Answer: c EXPLANATIONS: How an account is titled determines if it represents a separate customer under SIPC.

Q421_LO13: Correct Answer: c EXPLANATIONS: The basic coverage under SIPC is no more than $500,000 per separate account.

Q422_LO13: Correct Answer: c EXPLANATIONS: SIPC covers no more than $250,000 in cash within the $500,000 limit.

Q423_LO13: Correct Answer: b EXPLANATIONS: Customers with claims exceeding SIPC coverage become general creditors for the uncovered amount.

Q424_LO13: Correct Answer: a EXPLANATIONS: Cash and margin accounts for the same customer are combined for SIPC coverage.

Q425_LO13: Correct Answer: b EXPLANATIONS: Futures contracts related to currencies are not covered by SIPC.

Q426_LO13: Correct Answer: b EXPLANATIONS: BDs must disclose their SIPC membership to all customers at least once each year.

Q427_LO13: Correct Answer: c EXPLANATIONS: BDs must not imply that SIPC coverage is more than it actually is.

Q428_LO13: Correct Answer: a EXPLANATIONS: SIPC may petition a federal court to appoint a trustee for the liquidation of the BD.

Q429_LO13: Correct Answer: c EXPLANATIONS: A customer is broadly defined as anyone with cash or securities in the possession of a BD.

Q430_LO13: Correct Answer: b EXPLANATIONS: Once a trustee is appointed, the member firm is prohibited from engaging in business as a BD.

Q431_LO14: Correct Answer: b EXPLANATIONS: The FDIC was created to insure bank deposits and restore confidence during the Great Depression.

Q432_LO14: Correct Answer: b EXPLANATIONS: The FDIC preserves confidence by insuring deposits and ensuring the safety of bank accounts.

Q433_LO14: Correct Answer: b EXPLANATIONS: Usually, the FDIC sells customer deposits and loans to another institution.

Q434_LO14: Correct Answer: b EXPLANATIONS: The FDIC provides deposit insurance up to $250,000 for each deposit ownership category.

Q435_LO14: Correct Answer: c EXPLANATIONS: FDIC covers self-directed IRA accounts along with other traditional bank deposit accounts.

Q436_LO14: Correct Answer: d EXPLANATIONS: FDIC does not cover non-deposit investment products such as mutual funds.

Q437_LO14: Correct Answer: c EXPLANATIONS: FDIC covers joint accounts based on per owner per account, not per separate account.

Q438_LO14: Correct Answer: b EXPLANATIONS: SIPC provides coverage up to $500,000 for accounts with differing registrations.

Q439_LO14: Correct Answer: d EXPLANATIONS: Each account with differing registrations is covered separately up to the specified limit.

Q440_LO14: Correct Answer: c EXPLANATIONS: Different account holders represent separate ownership categories under FDIC.

Q441_LO14: Correct Answer: c EXPLANATIONS: FDIC coverage guarantees the safety of deposits up to $250,000 per ownership category.

Q442_LO14: Correct Answer: c EXPLANATIONS: The FDIC funds its operations through premiums paid by participating institutions.

Q443_LO14: Correct Answer: c EXPLANATIONS: The FDIC typically sells deposits and loans to another institution.

Q444_LO14: Correct Answer: a EXPLANATIONS: The FDIC was created to insure deposits during the Great Depression.

Q445_LO14: Correct Answer: b EXPLANATIONS: The primary goal of FDIC deposit insurance is to protect depositors by insuring their accounts.

Q446_LO15: Correct Answer: b EXPLANATIONS: The Uniform Securities Act is a template for state securities laws.

Q447_LO15: Correct Answer: d EXPLANATIONS: The Uniform Securities Act mandates the appointment of state securities administrators; the method of selection is left to the states.

Q448_LO15: Correct Answer: c EXPLANATIONS: State administrators have significant authority within their states regarding securities registration and regulations.

Q449_LO15: Correct Answer: c EXPLANATIONS: The method of selection for state securities administrators is left to the states, whether by appointment or election.

Q450_LO15: Correct Answer: c EXPLANATIONS: State securities administrators primarily enforce state securities laws.

Q451_LO15: Correct Answer: d EXPLANATIONS: NASAA represents state and provincial securities regulators in North America.

Q452_LO15: Correct Answer: b EXPLANATIONS: NASAA stands for North American Securities Administrators Association.

Q453_LO15: Correct Answer: c EXPLANATIONS: NASAA has no specific regulatory authority but is influential in state securities regulations.

Q454_LO15: Correct Answer: b EXPLANATIONS: NASAA often produces guidelines that state administrators use in enforcing state regulations.

Q455_LO15: Correct Answer: b EXPLANATIONS: NASAA's guidelines often serve as best practices for state administrators in enforcing state regulations.

Q456_LO15: Correct Answer: b EXPLANATIONS: NASAA represents state and provincial securities regulators in the United States, Canada, and Mexico, covering North America.

Q457_LO15: Correct Answer: c EXPLANATIONS: State administrators use the Uniform Securities Act as a template for state securities laws.

Q458_LO15: Correct Answer: a EXPLANATIONS: The state securities administrator is often known as the Securities Commissioner.

Q459_LO15: Correct Answer: b EXPLANATIONS: The method of selection for state securities administrators is left to the states.

Q460_LO15: Correct Answer: c EXPLANATIONS: NASAA members from Canada and Mexico represent their respective countries within NASAA.

The Self-Regulatory Organizations

Q461_LO16: What areas does FINRA regulate?
a. International trade
b. Securities underwriting
c. Agricultural commodities
d. Real estate investments

HINTS: Focus on the specific areas in the passage.

Q462_LO16: What is one of FINRA's objectives regarding commercial honor?
a. Promoting unfair practices
b. Encouraging violation of laws
c. Promoting high standards of commercial honor
d. Discouraging communication between members

HINTS: Consider FINRA's objectives related to commercial honor.

Q463_LO16: What is the purpose of FINRA's Code of Procedure (COP)?
a. Promotion of self-discipline
b. Enforcement of FINRA rules
c. Prevention of fraudulent practices
d. Communication among members

HINTS: Focus on the role and purpose of FINRA's Code of Procedure.

Q464_LO16: What may FINRA do upon finding a violation of its rules by a member firm?
a. Arrest the individuals involved
b. Impose fines and censure
c. Override the SEC's decision
d. Investigate without any action

HINTS: Think about the consequences for member firms found in violation.

Q465_LO16: Which FINRA division may handle appeals of Code of Procedure (COP) decisions?
a. Department of Enforcement (DOE)
b. National Adjudicatory Council
c. Uniform Practice Code (UPC)
d. Code of Arbitration (COA)

HINTS: Consider the structure of FINRA and its divisions.

Q466_LO16: What do the Uniform Practice Code (UPC) rules cover?
a. Technical aspects of trading
b. Enforcement procedures
c. Arbitration processes
d. Communication guidelines

HINTS: Focus on the specific areas covered by the UPC rules.

Q467_LO16: What is the goal of FINRA's Code of Arbitration (COA)?
a. Legal prosecution of members
b. Fast and cost-effective dispute resolution
c. Regulation of securities markets
d. Prevention of fraudulent practices

HINTS: Think about the purpose and objectives of the Code of Arbitration.

Q468_LO16: When is a customer required to agree to arbitration for a monetary dispute with a BD?
a. After the incident
b. During the traditional court process
c. Before the incident (prospectively)
d. If the BD is a FINRA member

HINTS: Consider the timing and conditions for arbitration agreements.

Q469_LO16: Who agrees to FINRA rules when applying for membership?
a. Department of Enforcement
b. Associates
c. SEC
d. Member firms

HINTS: Think about the entities that agree to abide by FINRA rules.

Q470_LO16: What is a common exception for a FINRA member firm doing business with another FINRA member firm?
a. Foreign firm with no FINRA equivalent
b. A bank in the underwriting of a municipal issue
c. A firm dealing exclusively in U.S. government securities
d. A firm dealing exclusively in mutual funds

HINTS: Consider the exceptions for FINRA member firms doing business.

Q471_LO16: What authority has FINRA been delegated by the SEC?
a. Authority to arrest individuals
b. Authority to override state securities laws
c. Authority to administer qualification tests
d. Authority to enforce federal laws

HINTS: Focus on the specific authority delegated to FINRA by the SEC.

Q472_LO16: What is the primary role of FINRA's Department of Enforcement (DOE)?
a. Communication among members
b. Investigation of suspected violations
c. Code of Arbitration administration
d. Regulation of technical aspects of trading

HINTS: Think about the primary function of the DOE within FINRA.

Q473_LO16: What is the primary function of the Uniform Practice Code (UPC) rules?
a. Prevention of fraudulent practices
b. Regulation of communication
c. Administration of arbitration processes
d. Cover technical aspects of trading

HINTS: Focus on the purpose and function of the UPC rules.

Q474_LO16: What is the status of Code of Arbitration (COA) decisions?
a. Non-binding
b. Final and binding
c. Subject to SEC approval
d. Appealable to federal courts

HINTS: Consider the finality of decisions made through the Code of Arbitration.

Q475_LO16: What do broker-dealer associates agree to when working for FINRA firms?
a. SEC regulations
b. FINRA's guidelines
c. Department of Enforcement decisions
d. Uniform Practice Code rules

HINTS: Think about the rules and guidelines associates agree to when working for FINRA firms.

Q476_LO16: What areas does FINRA regulate, as per its scope of authority?
a. Banking and insurance
b. Real estate and commodities
c. Securities underwriting and OTC trading
d. Retail and hospitality

HINTS: Focus on the specific areas in the scope of FINRA's authority.

Q477_LO16: What are FINRA's objectives regarding federal and state securities laws?
a. Override federal laws
b. Encourage violations of state laws
c. Promote and observe federal and state securities laws
d. Propose amendments to federal laws

HINTS: Consider FINRA's purpose and objectives related to securities laws.

Q478_LO16: What is the primary purpose of the Conduct Rules established by FINRA?
a. Enforce trading procedures
b. Establish relationships between firms and customers
c. Regulate securities underwriting
d. Administer financial audits

HINTS: Think about the focus of the Conduct Rules in FINRA.

Q479_LO16: What does the Code of Procedure (COP) cover in FINRA?
a. Technical aspects of trading
b. Enforcement of FINRA rules and punishment for violations
c. Dispute resolution processes
d. Good delivery of securities

HINTS: Focus on the coverage of the Code of Procedure (COP) in FINRA.

Q480_LO16: In a FINRA audit, what might trigger an investigation by the Department of Enforcement (DOE)?
a. Routine compliance checks
b. Employee salary adjustments
c. Customer complaints
d. Marketing strategy updates

HINTS: Consider common triggers for investigations by the Department of Enforcement.

Q481_LO16: What actions can FINRA take upon finding a violation, according to the Code of Procedure (COP)?
a. Impose taxes
b. Suspend, expel, or bar from membership
c. Grant amnesty
d. Provide financial rewards

HINTS: Think about the potential consequences for a member firm or associated person found in violation.

Q482_LO16: What does the Uniform Practice Code (UPC) in FINRA cover?
a. Conduct of member firms
b. Technical aspects of trading and payment for securities transactions
c. Code of Arbitration (COA) procedures
d. Banking and insurance regulations

HINTS: Focus on the technical aspects covered by the Uniform Practice Code.

Q483_LO16: What is the primary goal of the Code of Arbitration (COA) in FINRA?
a. Enforce federal laws
b. Settle monetary disputes through a faster and cheaper process
c. Override state regulations
d. Investigate violations of Conduct Rules

HINTS: Consider the purpose of the Code of Arbitration in FINRA.

Q484_LO16: When is a customer required to agree to arbitration for monetary disputes with a broker-dealer (BD)?
a. Only after the incident
b. Only during a FINRA audit
c. Only if mandated by state law
d. Prospectively, before the incident

HINTS: Think about the timing and agreement for arbitration in monetary disputes.

Q485_LO16: What is a member firm in FINRA?
a. A financial institution not affiliated with FINRA
b. A firm that trades commodities
c. A firm that applies for membership to FINRA and abides by its rules
d. A firm that only does business with other FINRA member firms

HINTS: Consider the definition and characteristics of a member firm in FINRA.

Q486_LO16: What are associates in FINRA?
a. Individuals who work for FINRA without abiding by its rules
b. Individuals who work for FINRA member firms and agree to FINRA rules
c. Independent consultants not bound by FINRA regulations
d. Individuals with arrest powers in FINRA

HINTS: Focus on the definition and characteristics of associates in FINRA.

Q487_LO16: Under what circumstances may a FINRA member firm do business with a non-FINRA member firm?
a. Only if it's a foreign firm dealing exclusively in U.S. government securities
b. Only if it's a bank in the underwriting of a municipal issue
c. Only if it's a financial institution not affiliated with FINRA
d. Only if it's a foreign firm dealing exclusively in commodities

HINTS: Consider the exceptions allowing a FINRA member firm to do business with a non-FINRA member firm.

Q488_LO16: What authority has FINRA been delegated by the SEC?
a. Authority to override federal laws
b. Authority to create federal laws
c. Authority to administer qualification tests for associates
d. Authority to enforce state securities laws

HINTS: Focus on the specific authority delegated to FINRA by the SEC.

Q489_LO16: Where can decisions made by FINRA's Department of Enforcement (DOE) be appealed?
a. SEC and then to appellate courts
b. Only to the National Adjudicatory Council
c. Only to the SEC
d. Only to the appellate courts

HINTS: Think about the appeal process for decisions made by FINRA's Department of Enforcement.

Q490_LO16: What is the final and binding nature of decisions made through the Code of Arbitration (COA)?
a. Final, but not binding
b. Neither final nor binding
c. Final and binding
d. Final, but subject to SEC review

HINTS: Consider the nature of decisions made through the Code of Arbitration in FINRA.

Q491_LO17: What is the primary focus of the Municipal Securities Rulemaking Board (MSRB)?
a. Insurance regulations
b. Underwriting and trading of state and municipal securities
c. Trading of commodities
d. Securities fraud investigation

HINTS: Consider the main responsibilities of the MSRB in the municipal securities market.

Q492_LO17: Who enforces MSRB rules on the banking industry?
a. SEC
b. Comptroller of the Currency, The Federal Reserve, and FDIC
c. CFTC
d. FINRA

HINTS: Identify the primary regulators responsible for enforcing MSRB rules on the banking industry.

Q493_LO17: What types of securities does MSRB create rules for?
a. Municipal debt only
b. Municipal securities and commodities
c. Corporate bonds only
d. Federal securities

HINTS: Focus on the scope of MSRB rules regarding the types of securities.

Q494_LO17: Which organization has regulatory power over municipalities issuing municipal securities?
a. MSRB
b. SEC
c. FINRA
d. Comptroller of the Currency

HINTS: Consider the regulatory authority over municipalities issuing municipal securities.

Q495_LO17: How are MSRB rules on securities firms primarily enforced?
a. SEC and CFTC
b. SEC and FINRA
c. CFTC and NFA
d. FINRA and NFA

HINTS: Identify the primary regulators responsible for enforcing MSRB rules on securities firms.

Q496_LO17: What is the role of MSRB in securities rulemaking?
a. Enforcement of rules
b. Writing rules with enforcement powers
c. Investigating securities fraud
d. Issuing licenses to securities firms

HINTS: Consider the role of MSRB in the creation of rules.

Q497_LO17: In the context of MSRB, what is the role of the Comptroller of the Currency?
a. Rule creation
b. Enforcement of MSRB rules on banking industry
c. Enforcement of MSRB rules on securities firms
d. Investigating municipal securities fraud

HINTS: Focus on the role of the Comptroller of the Currency in the enforcement of MSRB rules.

Q498_LO17: What powers does MSRB have in terms of enforcement?
a. Full enforcement powers
b. Advisory powers only
c. No enforcement powers
d. Powers delegated by the SEC

HINTS: Consider the enforcement powers of MSRB.

Q499_LO17: Who has the regulatory authority over MSRB itself?
a. SEC
b. CFTC
c. FINRA
d. NFA

HINTS: Identify the regulatory authority overseeing MSRB.

Q500_LO17: What is the significance of the MSRB in the regulation of 529 plans?
a. No relevance to 529 plans
b. Writes rules for 529 plans
c. Enforces rules for 529 plans
d. Collaborates with state administrators on 529 plans

HINTS: Consider the role of MSRB in the regulation of 529 plans.

Q501_LO17: In the absence of MSRB enforcement, who handles violations of MSRB rules by securities firms?
a. SEC
b. CFTC
c. FINRA
d. NFA

HINTS: Consider the regulatory authority responsible for handling violations by securities firms.

Q502_LO17: How do MSRB rules affect securities fraud investigation?
a. MSRB conducts investigations
b. MSRB collaborates with SEC on investigations
c. MSRB rules have no impact on securities fraud investigation
d. MSRB defers investigations to FINRA

HINTS: Focus on the impact of MSRB rules on securities fraud investigation.

Q503_LO17: What is the significance of MSRB rules in promoting fair practices?
a. MSRB has no role in fair practices
b. MSRB writes rules but does not enforce them
c. MSRB rules establish fair practices in securities markets
d. MSRB only enforces fair practices for banking institutions

HINTS: Consider the role of MSRB rules in promoting fair practices in securities markets.

Q504_LO17: What types of securities are not covered by MSRB deposit insurance?
a. Municipal securities
b. Corporate bonds
c. Mutual funds
d. Securities issued by the federal government

HINTS: Identify the types of securities not covered by MSRB deposit insurance.

Q505_LO17: How do MSRB rules influence state securities regulations?
a. MSRB overrides state regulations
b. MSRB provides guidelines for state administrators
c. MSRB has no impact on state regulations
d. MSRB enforces state securities laws

HINTS: Consider the relationship between MSRB rules and state securities regulations.

Q506_LO18: What is one of the roles of exchanges besides serving as market centers?
a. Tax collection
b. Regulatory authority
c. Currency issuance
d. Legislative drafting

HINTS: Consider the additional responsibilities of exchanges.

Q507_LO18: In the context of exchanges, what does delisting refer to?
a. Listing a new security
b. Suspending trading on a listed security
c. Removing a listed security
d. Regulating market makers

HINTS: Focus on the term "delisting" in the context of exchanges.

Q508_LO18: What power do exchanges have in relation to a listed security that is not meeting standards?
a. Power to increase the stock price
b. Power to lower trading fees
c. Power to suspend trading on the security
d. Power to issue dividends

HINTS: Consider the authority of exchanges when a listed security is not meeting standards.

Q509_LO18: Which exchange is as a model with regulatory authority?
a. NASDAQ
b. NYSE
c. London Stock Exchange
d. Tokyo Stock Exchange

HINTS: Identify the exchange as a model with regulatory authority.

Q510_LO18: What action can exchanges take if there are irregularities in trading activity on the exchange?
a. Issue new securities
b. Investigate and suspend trading
c. Lower transaction costs
d. Increase the number of market makers

HINTS: Focus on the authority of exchanges in response to irregularities in trading activity.

Q511_LO18: How do exchanges contribute to market integrity?
a. By increasing volatility
b. By encouraging market manipulation
c. By regulating trading activity
d. By promoting insider trading

HINTS: Consider the role of exchanges in maintaining market integrity.

Q512_LO18: What is the significance of exchanges having authority over listed securities?
a. Exchanges can set interest rates
b. Exchanges can create new securities
c. Exchanges can delist securities
d. Exchanges can influence tax policies

HINTS: Focus on the authority of exchanges over listed securities.

Q513_LO18: In what circumstances might an exchange suspend trading on a listed security?
a. Routine market activity
b. High trading volume
c. Non-compliance with listing standards
d. Frequent dividend payouts

HINTS: Consider the conditions under which an exchange might suspend trading on a listed security.

Q514_LO18: What distinguishes exchanges from other market participants in terms of regulatory authority?
a. Ability to issue regulations
b. Authority over market makers only
c. Authority over listed securities
d. Control over investor portfolios

HINTS: Identify the distinguishing factor regarding regulatory authority for exchanges.

Q515_LO18: Why is the NYSE as a model for regulatory authority?
a. It has the highest trading volume
b. It is the oldest exchange
c. It has comprehensive regulatory measures
d. It excludes small-cap securities

HINTS: Consider the reason the NYSE is as a model for regulatory authority.

Q516_LO18: What role do exchanges play in overseeing issuers of listed securities?
a. Issuing securities on behalf of issuers
b. Setting interest rates for issuers
c. Investigating issuer financials
d. Regulating issuers and their compliance

HINTS: Focus on the role of exchanges in overseeing issuers of listed securities.

Q517_LO18: How does the authority to delist a security contribute to market stability?
a. By increasing volatility
b. By removing underperforming securities
c. By creating uncertainty
d. By encouraging speculative trading

HINTS: Consider the impact of the authority to delist securities on market stability.

Q518_LO18: What distinguishes exchanges from regulatory bodies like the SEC?
a. Exchanges focus on market makers only
b. Exchanges regulate trading activity and listed securities
c. Exchanges have legislative powers
d. Exchanges have the authority to issue fines

HINTS: Identify the distinguishing factor regarding regulatory authority for exchanges.

Q519_LO18: In what way can exchanges influence the behavior of market participants?
a. By setting interest rates
b. By regulating trading activity
c. By issuing new securities
d. By controlling tax policies

HINTS: Consider the means by which exchanges can influence the behavior of market participants.

Q520_LO18: What role do exchanges play in maintaining fair and orderly markets?
a. By promoting market manipulation
b. By increasing transaction costs
c. By regulating trading activity
d. By encouraging speculative trading

HINTS: Focus on the role of exchanges in maintaining fair and orderly markets.

Correct Answers & Explanations
The Self-Regulatory Organizations

Q461_LO16: Correct Answer: b EXPLANATIONS: FINRA regulates investment banking (securities underwriting), trading in the OTC market, and trading in exchange-listed securities.

Q462_LO16: Correct Answer: c EXPLANATIONS: One of FINRA's objectives is to promote high standards of commercial honor.

Q463_LO16: Correct Answer: b EXPLANATIONS: The COP covers the enforcement of FINRA rules and details the punishment of members who violate the Conduct Rules.

Q464_LO16: Correct Answer: b EXPLANATIONS: FINRA may impose fines, censure, and take other appropriate actions upon finding a violation.

Q465_LO16: Correct Answer: b EXPLANATIONS: Appeals of COP decisions may go to the National Adjudicatory Council (a FINRA division).

Q466_LO16: Correct Answer: a EXPLANATIONS: UPC rules cover technical aspects of trading and payment for securities transactions.

Q467_LO16: Correct Answer: b EXPLANATIONS: The COA aims to provide a faster and cheaper resolution for monetary disputes.

Q468_LO16: Correct Answer: c EXPLANATIONS: Customers must agree to arbitration, often prospectively (before the incident) in new account forms.

Q469_LO16: Correct Answer: d EXPLANATIONS: Broker-dealer firms apply for membership to FINRA and agree to abide by FINRA's rules and regulations.

Q470_LO16: Correct Answer: b EXPLANATIONS: A bank in the underwriting of a municipal issue is one of the common exceptions.

Q471_LO16: Correct Answer: c EXPLANATIONS: FINRA has been delegated authority by the SEC to administer qualification tests for associates of member firms and investment advisers.

Q472_LO16: Correct Answer: b EXPLANATIONS: The DOE investigates suspected violations, often arising from audits or customer complaints.

Q473_LO16: Correct Answer: d EXPLANATIONS: UPC rules cover technical aspects of trading and payment for securities transactions.

Q474_LO16: Correct Answer: b EXPLANATIONS: COA decisions are final and binding, providing a faster and cheaper resolution.

Q475_LO16: Correct Answer: b EXPLANATIONS: Associates working for FINRA firms agree to abide by FINRA rules and regulations, often called associates.

Q476_LO16: Correct Answer: c EXPLANATIONS: FINRA regulates investment banking, securities underwriting, OTC trading, and conduct of member firms.

Q477_LO16: Correct Answer: c EXPLANATIONS: FINRA's objectives include promoting and observing federal and state securities laws.

Q478_LO16: Correct Answer: b EXPLANATIONS: Conduct Rules establish the relationship between firms and their customers.

Q479_LO16: Correct Answer: b EXPLANATIONS: The COP covers the enforcement of FINRA rules and details the punishment for violations.

Q480_LO16: Correct Answer: c EXPLANATIONS: Investigations by DOE often arise from customer complaints during a FINRA audit.

Q481_LO16: Correct Answer: b EXPLANATIONS: FINRA, through the COP, can suspend, expel, bar, impose fines, censure, or take other appropriate actions.

Q482_LO16: Correct Answer: b EXPLANATIONS: UPC rules cover technical aspects of trading and payment for securities transactions.

Q483_LO16: Correct Answer: b EXPLANATIONS: The primary goal of the COA is to settle monetary disputes through a faster and cheaper process.

Q484_LO16: Correct Answer: d EXPLANATIONS: Customers must agree to arbitration prospectively, often before the incident, as stated in new account forms.

Q485_LO16: Correct Answer: c EXPLANATIONS: A member firm in FINRA is one that applies for membership and agrees to abide by FINRA's rules.

Q486_LO16: Correct Answer: b EXPLANATIONS: Associates are individuals who work for FINRA member firms and agree to FINRA rules.

Q487_LO16: Correct Answer: a EXPLANATIONS: One exception is if it's a foreign firm dealing exclusively in U.S. government securities.

Q488_LO16: Correct Answer: c EXPLANATIONS: FINRA has been delegated authority by the SEC to administer qualification tests for associates.

Q489_LO16: Correct Answer: a EXPLANATIONS: Decisions may be appealable to the National Adjudicatory Council (NAC), then to the SEC, and from there to the appellate courts.

Q490_LO16: Correct Answer: c EXPLANATIONS: COA decisions are final and binding.

Q491_LO17: Correct Answer: b EXPLANATIONS: The MSRB is the primary industry regulator for the underwriting and trading of state and municipal securities.

Q492_LO17: Correct Answer: b EXPLANATIONS: MSRB rules on the banking industry are enforced primarily by the Comptroller of the Currency, The Federal Reserve, and FDIC.

Q493_LO17: Correct Answer: a EXPLANATIONS: MSRB creates rules for municipal securities, not just municipal debt.

Q494_LO17: Correct Answer: a EXPLANATIONS: MSRB has no regulatory power over municipalities issuing municipal securities.

Q495_LO17: Correct Answer: b EXPLANATIONS: MSRB rules on securities firms are enforced primarily by the SEC and FINRA.

Q496_LO17: Correct Answer: b EXPLANATIONS: MSRB writes the rules but does not have enforcement powers.

Q497_LO17: Correct Answer: b EXPLANATIONS: The Comptroller of the Currency enforces MSRB rules on the banking industry.

Q498_LO17: Correct Answer: c EXPLANATIONS: MSRB does not have enforcement powers; it relies on other regulators for enforcement.

Q499_LO17: Correct Answer: a EXPLANATIONS: MSRB is overseen by the SEC.

Q500_LO17: Correct Answer: a EXPLANATIONS: MSRB rules are not specifically related to 529 plans.

Q501_LO17: Correct Answer: a EXPLANATIONS: Violations of MSRB rules by securities firms are handled primarily by the SEC.

Q502_LO17: Correct Answer: c EXPLANATIONS: MSRB rules do not grant investigative powers; they depend on other regulators for enforcement.

Q503_LO17: Correct Answer: c EXPLANATIONS: MSRB rules contribute to establishing fair practices in the securities market.

Q504_LO17: Correct Answer: c EXPLANATIONS: MSRB rules do not cover deposit insurance for mutual funds.

Q505_LO17: Correct Answer: b EXPLANATIONS: MSRB provides guidelines that state administrators use in the enforcement of state regulations.

Q506_LO18: Correct Answer: b EXPLANATIONS: Exchanges serve as market centers and also have regulatory authority over trading activity and listed securities.

Q507_LO18: Correct Answer: c EXPLANATIONS: Delisting refers to the removal of a listed security from the exchange.

Q508_LO18: Correct Answer: c EXPLANATIONS: Exchanges have the power to suspend trading on a listed security that fails to meet standards.

Q509_LO18: Correct Answer: b EXPLANATIONS: The NYSE is as the model used with regulatory authority.

Q510_LO18: Correct Answer: b EXPLANATIONS: Exchanges can investigate and suspend trading in the case of irregularities.

Q511_LO18: Correct Answer: c EXPLANATIONS: Exchanges contribute to market integrity by regulating trading activity.

Q512_LO18: Correct Answer: c EXPLANATIONS: Exchanges have the power to delist securities that do not meet standards.

Q513_LO18: Correct Answer: c EXPLANATIONS: Exchanges may suspend trading if a listed security does not comply with listing standards.

Q514_LO18: Correct Answer: c EXPLANATIONS: Exchanges have regulatory authority over both trading activity and listed securities.

Q515_LO18: Correct Answer: c EXPLANATIONS: The NYSE is as a model due to its comprehensive regulatory measures.

Q516_LO18: Correct Answer: d EXPLANATIONS: Exchanges have authority over issuers of listed securities, regulating them and ensuring compliance.

Q517_LO18: Correct Answer: b EXPLANATIONS: The authority to delist allows exchanges to remove underperforming securities, contributing to market stability.

Q518_LO18: Correct Answer: b EXPLANATIONS: Exchanges have authority over both trading activity and listed securities, differentiating them from regulatory bodies like the SEC.

Q519_LO18: Correct Answer: b EXPLANATIONS: Exchanges influence behavior by regulating trading activity.

Q520_LO18: Correct Answer: c EXPLANATIONS: Exchanges contribute to fair and orderly markets by regulating trading activity.

The Economic Indicators

Q521_LO19: What does GDP measure for a nation?
a. Goods production only
b. Annual economic output
c. Foreign investment
d. Stock market performance

HINTS: Consider the definition of GDP.

Q522_LO19: How often are GDP figures typically released by the Commerce Department in the United States?
a. Monthly
b. Annually
c. Quarterly
d. Biennially

HINTS: Think about the frequency of GDP data releases.

Q523_LO19: What is the significance of a positive GDP figure?
a. The economy is contracting
b. Inflation is high
c. The economy is stagnant
d. The economy is growing

HINTS: Focus on the interpretation of GDP figures.

Q524_LO19: What does the Consumer Price Index (CPI) primarily measure?
a. Interest rates
b. General price changes
c. Unemployment rates
d. Foreign investments

HINTS: Consider the primary focus of the Consumer Price Index (CPI).

Q525_LO19: Why is real GDP considered a constant dollar measurement?
a. It adjusts for changes in the costs of goods
b. It remains fixed over time
c. It includes inflation data
d. It represents current market values

HINTS: Focus on the term "constant dollar measurement" in relation to real GDP.

Q526_LO19: In economic comparisons, what does real GDP reflect?
a. Nominal GDP
b. Actual growth
c. Current market values
d. Seasonal variations

HINTS: Consider the purpose of using real GDP in economic comparisons.

Q527_LO19: What is the basis for calculating Gross National Product (GNP)?
a. Foreign investment only
b. Activity within the country
c. Stock market performance
d. Activity of citizens and entities wherever it occurs

HINTS: Think about the basis for calculating GNP.

Q528_LO19: How often is Gross National Product (GNP) published by the Commerce Department?
a. Monthly
b. Annually
c. Biennially
d. Quarterly

HINTS: Consider the frequency of GNP data releases.

Q529_LO19: In what aspect is GNP similar to GDP?
a. In measuring only goods production
b. In including foreign investment
c. In reflecting actual growth
d. In being published annually

HINTS: Focus on the similarities between GNP and GDP.

Q530_LO19: How does GNP differ from GDP in terms of the basis for calculation?
a. GNP includes only foreign activity
b. GNP is based on current market values
c. GNP includes citizens' activity wherever it occurs
d. GNP is calculated annually

HINTS: Consider the key difference in the basis for calculating GNP compared to GDP.

Q531_LO19: What does the term "real GDP" mean in economic contexts?
a. The latest GDP figure
b. GDP adjusted for inflation
c. GDP in constant dollars
d. Nominal GDP

HINTS: Focus on the meaning of "real GDP" in economic contexts.

Q532_LO19: When comparing economic periods, why is real GDP used instead of nominal GDP?
a. Real GDP includes current market values
b. Real GDP accounts for seasonal variations
c. Real GDP reflects actual growth
d. Nominal GDP includes inflation data

HINTS: Consider the reason for using real GDP in economic comparisons.

Q533_LO19: What factor does the Consumer Price Index (CPI) help adjust for in economic comparisons?
a. Seasonal variations
b. Changes in interest rates
c. Inflation or deflation
d. Currency exchange rates

HINTS: Focus on the purpose of using the Consumer Price Index (CPI) in economic comparisons.

Q534_LO19: How does the GDP figure change if it is negative?
a. The economy is contracting
b. The economy is stagnant
c. Inflation is high
d. Interest rates are low

HINTS: Consider the interpretation of a negative GDP figure.

Q535_LO19: What does GNP measure that GDP does not?
a. Foreign investment
b. Government spending
c. Gross private investment
d. Activity of citizens and entities wherever it may occur

HINTS: Focus on the aspect measured by GNP that is distinct from GDP.

Q536_LO19: Which indicator tends to change direction ahead of the overall economy?
a. GDP
b. Number of hours worked
c. Money supply (M2)
d. Industrial production

HINTS: Consider indicators that change direction ahead of the economy.

Q537_LO19: What is a coincident economic indicator?
a. Changes direction ahead of the economy
b. Changes direction along with the economy
c. Confirms a new trend
d. Serves as a long-term trend indicator

HINTS: Focus on indicators that change direction along with the economy.

Q538_LO19: How does the average work week in manufacturing relate to economic indicators?
a. Leading indicator
b. Coincident indicator
c. Lagging indicator
d. Both a and b

HINTS: Consider the nature of the average work week in manufacturing in relation to the economy.

Q539_LO19: What does the ratio of inventories to sales indicate?
a. Leading economic trend
b. Coincident economic trend
c. Lagging economic trend
d. Overall economic stability

HINTS: Think about indicators that confirm a new trend.

Q540_LO19: Which indicator is often considered a confirmation tool for leading indicators?
a. Personal income
b. Industrial production
c. Building permits
d. GDP

HINTS: Focus on indicators that confirm leading indicators.

Q541_LO19: In what way do lagging indicators help analysts?
a. Identify short-term reversals
b. Confirm new trends
c. Predict economic downturns
d. Act as early warning signs

HINTS: Consider the role of lagging indicators in helping analysts.

Q542_LO19: Which factor is a lagging economic indicator?
a. New orders for consumer goods
b. Corporate profits
c. Money supply (M2)
d. Changes in sensitive materials prices

HINTS: Focus on indicators that change after the economy has begun a new trend.

Q543_LO19: What is the primary role of coincident indicators?
a. Lead the economy
b. Confirm new trends
c. Predict economic changes
d. Identify long-term trends
HINTS: Consider the primary role of coincident indicators.

Q544_LO19: Why are leading indicators considered reliable?
a. They confirm new trends
b. They predict economic changes
c. They change direction with the economy
d. They have a short time frame

HINTS: Focus on the reliability of leading indicators.

Q545_LO19: What does the ratio of consumer installment credit to personal income indicate?
a. Leading economic trend
b. Coincident economic trend
c. Lagging economic trend
d. Overall economic stability

HINTS: Think about the nature of the ratio of consumer installment credit to personal income.

Q546_LO19: Which indicator reflects the rate of unemployment?
a. Personal income
b. Employment levels
c. Machine tool orders
d. Money supply (M2)

HINTS: Consider the indicator related to the rate of unemployment.

Q547_LO19: How do changes in sensitive materials prices relate to economic indicators?
a. Leading indicator
b. Coincident indicator
c. Lagging indicator
d. Both a and c

HINTS: Focus on the nature of changes in sensitive materials prices.

Q548_LO19: What does the average duration of unemployment measure?
a. Short-term trends
b. Long-term trends
c. Confirming new trends
d. Serves as an early warning sign

HINTS: Consider the nature of the average duration of unemployment.

Q549_LO19: Which economic indicator is related to the number of hours worked?
a. GDP
b. Changes in business and consumer borrowing
c. Nonagricultural employment
d. Money supply (M2)

HINTS: Think about the indicator related to the number of hours worked.

Q550_LO19: What role do lagging indicators play in differentiating trends?
a. Identify short-term reversals
b. Confirm new trends
c. Predict economic downturns
d. Indicate overall economic stability

HINTS: Focus on the role of lagging indicators in trend analysis.

Q551_LO20: What is inflation?
a. General decline in prices
b. Prolonged slow economic growth
c. General increase in prices
d. Unemployment accompanied by rising prices

HINTS: Focus on the definition of inflation.

Q552_LO20: When does deflation typically occur?
a. During economic growth
b. During hyperinflation
c. During severe recessions
d. During periods of stagflation

HINTS: Consider the economic conditions associated with deflation.

Q553_LO20: What characterizes economic stagnation?
a. General decline in prices
b. High unemployment
c. Accelerating inflation
d. Prolonged slow economic growth

HINTS: Focus on the characteristics of economic stagnation.

Q554_LO20: What is hyperinflation?
a. Gradual increase in prices
b. Accelerating inflation
c. Prolonged slow economic growth
d. General decline in prices

HINTS: Pay attention to the intensity of inflation.

Q555_LO20: How does deflation impact a dollar's buying power?
a. Strengthens the dollar
b. Reduces the dollar's buying power
c. Has no impact on the dollar
d. Stabilizes the dollar

HINTS: Consider the impact of deflation on the purchasing power of a currency.

Q556_LO20: What is stagflation?
a. Rise in prices with high unemployment
b. General decline in prices
c. Gradual increase in prices
d. Prolonged slow economic growth

HINTS: Focus on the combination of economic factors in stagflation.

Q557_LO20: When does hyperinflation severely erode the purchasing power of a currency?
a. During economic growth
b. During stagflation
c. When inflation is moderate
d. When the pace of inflation is extremely high

HINTS: Pay attention to the conditions leading to the severe erosion of purchasing power.

Q558_LO20: How does mild inflation impact economic growth?
a. Stimulates business investments
b. Causes hyperinflation
c. Leads to deflation
d. Causes stagnation

HINTS: Consider the impact of mild inflation on economic growth.

Q559_LO20: What is the primary impact of deflation on the economy?
a. Accelerates economic growth
b. Reduces unemployment
c. Decline in overall prices
d. Stimulates business investments

HINTS: Focus on the primary impact of deflation.

Q560_LO20: In what conditions does stagflation occur?
a. High economic growth
b. Lack of consumer demand
c. Periods of hyperinflation
d. Prolonged economic stagnation

HINTS: Focus on the conditions leading to stagflation.

Q561_LO20: What is the key characteristic of hyperinflation?
a. Gradual increase in prices
b. Decline in overall prices
c. Extremely high and accelerating inflation
d. Economic stagnation

HINTS: Pay attention to the intensity and speed of inflation.

Q562_LO20: When is deflation likely to happen?
a. During periods of economic growth
b. During stagflation
c. During periods of hyperinflation
d. During severe recessions

HINTS: Consider the economic conditions associated with deflation.

Q563_LO20: What is the rarity of hyperinflation?
a. Common occurrence
b. Uncommon occurrence
c. Regular economic cycle
d. Frequent economic phenomenon

HINTS: Think about the frequency of hyperinflation.

Q564_LO20: What does stagflation indicate about the economy?
a. Growing economy
b. High unemployment and rising prices
c. Declining inflation
d. Stable economic conditions

HINTS: Focus on the combination of factors in stagflation.

Q565_LO20: How does inflation impact a nation's economy in the short term?
a. Stimulates business investments
b. Reduces purchasing power
c. Accelerates economic growth
d. Leads to deflation

HINTS: Consider the short-term impact of inflation.

Correct Answers & Explanations
The Economic Indicators

Q521_LO19: Correct Answer: b EXPLANATIONS: GDP measures a nation's annual economic output, including goods and services produced within the nation.

Q522_LO19: Correct Answer: c EXPLANATIONS: GDP figures are typically released quarterly by the Commerce Department.

Q523_LO19: Correct Answer: d EXPLANATIONS: A positive GDP figure indicates that the economy is growing.

Q524_LO19: Correct Answer: b EXPLANATIONS: The CPI primarily measures general price changes in a broad range of consumer goods and services.

Q525_LO19: Correct Answer: a EXPLANATIONS: Real GDP is a constant dollar measurement because it adjusts for changes in the costs of goods, providing an inflation-adjusted figure.

Q526_LO19: Correct Answer: b EXPLANATIONS: Real GDP reflects actual growth in economic comparisons.

Q527_LO19: Correct Answer: d EXPLANATIONS: GNP is based on the activity of the citizens and entities of the nation, wherever it may occur.

Q528_LO19: Correct Answer: d EXPLANATIONS: GNP figures are published by the Commerce Department on a quarterly basis.

Q529_LO19: Correct Answer: c EXPLANATIONS: GNP, like GDP, reflects actual growth in economic output.

Q530_LO19: Correct Answer: c EXPLANATIONS: GNP is based on the activity of citizens and entities wherever it may occur.

Q531_LO19: Correct Answer: b EXPLANATIONS: Real GDP refers to GDP adjusted for inflation, providing a constant dollar measurement.

Q532_LO19: Correct Answer: d EXPLANATIONS: Real GDP is used to compare economic periods as it adjusts for changes in the costs of goods, providing an inflation-adjusted figure.

Q533_LO19: Correct Answer: c EXPLANATIONS: The CPI helps adjust for inflation or deflation in economic comparisons.

Q534_LO19: Correct Answer: a EXPLANATIONS: A negative GDP figure indicates that the economy is contracting.

Q535_LO19: Correct Answer: d EXPLANATIONS: GNP measures the activity of citizens and entities wherever it may occur, not limited to within the country's boundaries.

Q536_LO19: Correct Answer: c EXPLANATIONS: Leading indicators, such as money supply (M2), tend to change direction ahead of the overall economy.

Q537_LO19: Correct Answer: b EXPLANATIONS: Coincident indicators change direction along with the overall economy.

Q538_LO19: Correct Answer: b EXPLANATIONS: The average work week in manufacturing is a coincident economic indicator.

Q539_LO19: Correct Answer: c EXPLANATIONS: The ratio of inventories to sales is a lagging economic indicator, confirming a new trend after it has started.

Q540_LO19: Correct Answer: b EXPLANATIONS: Industrial production is a coincident indicator and is often considered a confirmation tool for leading indicators.

Q541_LO19: Correct Answer: b EXPLANATIONS: Lagging indicators help analysts differentiate long-term trends from short-term reversals, confirming new trends.

Q542_LO19: Correct Answer: b EXPLANATIONS: Corporate profits are lagging economic indicators.

Q543_LO19: Correct Answer: b EXPLANATIONS: Coincident indicators primarily confirm new trends in the overall economy.

Q544_LO19: Correct Answer: c EXPLANATIONS: Leading indicators are considered reliable because they tend to change direction ahead of the overall economy.

Q545_LO19: Correct Answer: c EXPLANATIONS: This ratio is a lagging economic indicator, indicating trends after they have started.

Q546_LO19: Correct Answer: b EXPLANATIONS: Employment levels, a coincident indicator, reflect the rate of unemployment.

Q547_LO19: Correct Answer: a EXPLANATIONS: Changes in sensitive materials prices are leading indicators in the overall economy.

Q548_LO19: Correct Answer: b EXPLANATIONS: The average duration of unemployment is a lagging indicator, measuring long-term trends.

Q549_LO19: Correct Answer: c EXPLANATIONS: Nonagricultural employment, a coincident indicator, is related to the number of hours worked.

Q550_LO19: Correct Answer: b EXPLANATIONS: Lagging indicators help analysts differentiate long-term trends from short-term reversals, confirming new trends.

Q551_LO20: Correct Answer: c EXPLANATIONS: Inflation is a general increase in prices.

Q552_LO20: Correct Answer: c EXPLANATIONS: Deflation typically occurs during severe recessions when unemployment is on the rise.

Q553_LO20: Correct Answer: d EXPLANATIONS: Economic stagnation refers to prolonged periods of slow or little economic growth, accompanied by high unemployment.

Q554_LO20: Correct Answer: b EXPLANATIONS: Hyperinflation is the pace of inflation being extremely high and accelerating.

Q555_LO20: Correct Answer: b EXPLANATIONS: Deflation reduces a dollar's buying power.

Q556_LO20: Correct Answer: a EXPLANATIONS: Stagflation is the combination of inflation (a rise in prices) and high unemployment.

Q557_LO20: Correct Answer: d EXPLANATIONS: Hyperinflation severely erodes the purchasing power when the pace of inflation is extremely high.

Q558_LO20: Correct Answer: a EXPLANATIONS: Mild inflation can encourage economic growth because gradually increasing prices tend to stimulate business investments.

Q559_LO20: Correct Answer: c EXPLANATIONS: Deflation is a general decline in prices.

Q560_LO20: Correct Answer: b EXPLANATIONS: Stagflation occurs when there is a lack of consumer demand and business activity, but prices for goods are still rising.

Q561_LO20: Correct Answer: c EXPLANATIONS: Hyperinflation is characterized by extremely high and accelerating inflation.

Q562_LO20: Correct Answer: d EXPLANATIONS: Deflation is likely to happen during severe recessions.

Q563_LO20: Correct Answer: b EXPLANATIONS: Hyperinflation is a very rare occurrence.

Q564_LO20: Correct Answer: b EXPLANATIONS: Stagflation indicates high unemployment and rising prices.

Q565_LO20: Correct Answer: a EXPLANATIONS: In the short term, mild inflation can stimulate business investments.

The Business Cycle

Q566_LO21: What characterizes the expansion phase of the business cycle?
a. Low unemployment
b. Decreasing GDP
c. Falling stock prices
d. Decreasing consumer demand

HINTS: Focus on the characteristics of the expansion phase.

Q567_LO21: When does the contraction phase occur in the business cycle?
a. After a trough
b. After a peak
c. During expansion
d. During the recovery phase

HINTS: Consider the sequence of phases in the business cycle.

Q568_LO21: What is a characteristic of the peak or prosperity phase?
a. Rising stock prices
b. Low unemployment
c. Steady consumer demand
d. Decreasing GDP

HINTS: Focus on the characteristics of the peak phase.

Q569_LO21: What is a sign of the trough in the business cycle?
a. Rising inventories
b. Decreasing GDP
c. High unemployment
d. Low inflation

HINTS: Consider the characteristics associated with the trough.

Q570_LO21: When does the recovery phase occur in the business cycle?
a. After a peak
b. After a trough
c. During expansion
d. During the contraction phase

HINTS: Pay attention to the sequence of phases in the business cycle.

Q571_LO21: What is a feature of the peak phase in the business cycle?
a. Rising industrial production
b. Steady GDP growth
c. Slowdown in inflation
d. Decreasing stock prices

HINTS: Focus on the features associated with the peak or prosperity phase.

Q572_LO21: Which phase is characterized by rising numbers of bankruptcies and bond defaults?
a. Expansion
b. Peak
c. Contraction
d. Trough

HINTS: Consider the characteristics associated with the contraction phase.

Q573_LO21: What is a typical sign of the expansion phase in the business cycle?
a. Decreasing consumer demand
b. Falling stock prices
c. Rising property values
d. Decreasing GDP

HINTS: Focus on the characteristics of the expansion phase.

Q574_LO21: When does the trough phase occur in the business cycle?
a. After a peak
b. After a trough
c. During expansion
d. During the contraction phase

HINTS: Pay attention to the sequence of phases in the business cycle.

Q575_LO21: What is a characteristic of the trough phase?
a. Steady GDP
b. High unemployment
c. Falling stock prices
d. Decreasing consumer demand

HINTS: Focus on the characteristics associated with the trough.

Q576_LO21: What occurs during the recovery phase of the business cycle?
a. Increasing GDP
b. Falling stock prices
c. Decreasing consumer demand
d. Rising numbers of bankruptcies

HINTS: Consider the outcomes of the recovery phase.

Q577_LO21: What is a feature of the contraction phase in the business cycle?
a. Steady consumer demand
b. Decreasing GDP
c. Rising stock prices
d. Falling property values

HINTS: Focus on the characteristics associated with the contraction phase.

Q578_LO21: What does the peak phase signify in terms of inflation?
a. Acceleration in inflation
b. Slowdown in inflation
c. Hyperinflation
d. No impact on inflation

HINTS: Focus on the impact of the peak phase on inflation.

Q579_LO21: What happens to GDP during the contraction phase of the business cycle?
a. Steady growth
b. Decreases
c. Increases rapidly
d. Remains unchanged

HINTS: Consider the impact on GDP during the contraction phase.

Q580_LO21: What is a characteristic of the expansion phase's effect on industrial production?
a. Decreases
b. Increases
c. Remains unchanged
d. Has no impact

HINTS: Focus on the effect of the expansion phase on industrial production.

Q581_LO22: What defines a recession in economic terms?
a. Contraction lasting 3 months
b. Contraction lasting 6 months or longer
c. Expansion lasting 12 months
d. Recovery lasting 9 months

HINTS: Focus on the duration of economic contraction.

Q582_LO22: When does a contraction become classified as a depression?
a. After 12 months
b. After 15 months
c. After 18 months
d. After 24 months

HINTS: Consider the duration for a downturn to be labeled as a depression.

Q583_LO22: What characterizes a severe recession?
a. Contraction lasting 3 months
b. Contraction lasting 6 months or longer
c. Contraction with high inflation
d. Contraction with deflation

HINTS: Focus on the duration and severity of a recession.

Q584_LO22: How rare is a depression in economic cycles?
a. Very common
b. Rare
c. Always occurs after a recession
d. Predictable

HINTS: Consider the frequency of severe downturns in economic cycles.

Q585_LO22: In which economic phase is inflation likely to be very low or deflationary?
a. Expansion
b. Contraction
c. Peak
d. Trough

HINTS: Focus on the association of inflation with economic phases.

Q586_LO22: When does inflation tend to increase more seriously?
a. During a contraction
b. During an expansion
c. At the trough
d. At the peak

HINTS: Focus on the relationship between inflation and economic phases.

Q587_LO22: What is a characteristic of inflation during an expansion?
a. Very low or deflation
b. Moderate and stable
c. High and accelerating
d. Unpredictable

HINTS: Consider the nature of inflation during economic expansion.

Q588_LO22: Why does inflation rise during an economic expansion?
a. Excess production capacity
b. Decreased demand
c. Difficulty meeting increased demand
d. Low consumer spending

HINTS: Focus on the reasons behind inflation during expansion.

Q589_LO22: What is the typical duration of a recession?
a. 3 months
b. 6 months
c. 12 months
d. 18 months

HINTS: Focus on the duration of a recession.

Q590_LO22: In which scenario does inflation stay mild during an expansion?
a. Excess production capacity
b. Decreased demand
c. Increased demand
d. High unemployment

HINTS: Consider the factors that contribute to mild inflation during an expansion.

Q591_LO22: What is the primary factor contributing to high inflation during an expansion?
a. Excess production capacity
b. Increased demand
c. Decreased consumer spending
d. Low unemployment

HINTS: Focus on the key factor driving high inflation during an expansion.

Q592_LO22: What is the significance of the 18-month duration in economic cycles?
a. Marks the end of a contraction
b. Defines a depression
c. Marks the peak phase
d. Marks the beginning of an expansion

HINTS: Consider the economic phase associated with the 18-month duration.

Q593_LO22: What is a common characteristic of a depression?
a. High unemployment
b. Low inflation
c. Rapid economic growth
d. Excess production capacity

HINTS: Focus on the characteristic associated with severe economic downturns.

Q594_LO22: During which economic phase is the economy growing?
a. Contraction
b. Trough
c. Peak
d. Expansion

HINTS: Consider the economic phase associated with overall growth.

Q595_LO22: What happens to inflation during a contraction phase?
a. Accelerates
b. Stays mild
c. Decreases
d. Becomes unpredictable

HINTS: Focus on the impact of a contraction on inflation.

Correct Answers & Explanations
The Business Cycle

Q566_LO21: Correct Answer: a EXPLANATIONS: The expansion phase is characterized by increased consumer demand, rising stock prices, and increasing GDP, which results in low unemployment.

Q567_LO21: Correct Answer: b EXPLANATIONS: The contraction phase occurs after a peak in the business cycle.

Q568_LO21: Correct Answer: b EXPLANATIONS: The peak phase is characterized by very low unemployment, a slowdown in inflation, and steady consumer demand.

Q569_LO21: Correct Answer: c EXPLANATIONS: The trough is characterized by high unemployment and low, but not decreasing, consumer demand.

Q570_LO21: Correct Answer: b EXPLANATIONS: The recovery phase occurs after a trough in the business cycle.

Q571_LO21: Correct Answer: c EXPLANATIONS: The peak phase is characterized by a slowdown in inflation.

Q572_LO21: Correct Answer: c EXPLANATIONS: Downturns (contractions) are characterized by rising numbers of bankruptcies and bond defaults.

Q573_LO21: Correct Answer: c EXPLANATIONS: The expansion phase is characterized by increased consumer demand, rising stock prices, and rising property values.

Q574_LO21: Correct Answer: d EXPLANATIONS: The trough phase occurs during the contraction phase.

Q575_LO21: Correct Answer: b EXPLANATIONS: A trough is characterized by high unemployment.

Q576_LO21: Correct Answer: a EXPLANATIONS: The recovery phase is characterized by increasing GDP.

Q577_LO21: Correct Answer: b EXPLANATIONS: Contractions are characterized by decreasing GDP.

Q578_LO21: Correct Answer: b EXPLANATIONS: The peak phase is characterized by a slowdown in inflation.

Q579_LO21: Correct Answer: b EXPLANATIONS: GDP decreases during the contraction phase.

Q580_LO21: Correct Answer: b EXPLANATIONS: Expansion is characterized by increases in industrial production.

Q581_LO22: Correct Answer: b EXPLANATIONS: A recession is defined as an extended period of contraction lasting six months or longer.

Q582_LO22: Correct Answer: c EXPLANATIONS: A contraction becomes a depression if it continues for 18 months or longer.

Q583_LO22: Correct Answer: b EXPLANATIONS: A severe recession is characterized by a contraction lasting six months or longer.

Q584_LO22: Correct Answer: b EXPLANATIONS: Depressions are thankfully rare and occur if a contraction lasts for 18 months.

Q585_LO22: Correct Answer: b EXPLANATIONS: In normal cycles, inflation is low or deflationary during contractions.

Q586_LO22: Correct Answer: b EXPLANATIONS: Inflation tends to increase more seriously during the expansion phase of the economy.

Q587_LO22: Correct Answer: c EXPLANATIONS: Inflation during an expansion is typically high and accelerating.

Q588_LO22: Correct Answer: c EXPLANATIONS: Inflation rises during expansion because existing production capacity struggles to meet increased demand.

Q589_LO22: Correct Answer: b EXPLANATIONS: A recession typically lasts for six months or longer.

Q590_LO22: Correct Answer: a EXPLANATIONS: Inflation stays mild during an expansion when there is excess production capacity.

Q591_LO22: Correct Answer: b EXPLANATIONS: High inflation during an expansion is primarily driven by increased demand.

Q592_LO22: Correct Answer: b EXPLANATIONS: The 18-month duration defines a contraction as a depression.

Q593_LO22: Correct Answer: a EXPLANATIONS: High unemployment is a common characteristic of a depression.

Q594_LO22: Correct Answer: d EXPLANATIONS: The economy is growing during the expansion phase.

Q595_LO22: Correct Answer: c EXPLANATIONS: Inflation tends to decrease or stay mild during a contraction phase.

The Federal Reserve Fiscal Policy, Trade, Currency Rate & the Balance of Trade

Q596_LO23: What is the primary purpose of the Federal Reserve System?
a. Promoting international trade
b. Conducting monetary policy
c. Regulating stock markets
d. Managing fiscal policy

HINTS: Focus on the core functions of the Federal Reserve.

Q597_LO23: What is the common acronym used for the Federal Reserve Board?
a. FED
b. FRS
c. FRB
d. FSB

HINTS: Consider the abbreviation commonly associated with the Federal Reserve Board.

Q598_LO23: Who directs the Federal Reserve System?
a. President of the United States
b. Federal Reserve Board
c. Secretary of the Treasury
d. Congress

HINTS: Focus on the entity responsible for directing the Federal Reserve System.

Q599_LO23: What is the main goal of the Federal Reserve's monetary policy?
a. Maximizing government revenue
b. Promoting maximum employment
c. Controlling fiscal deficits
d. Managing trade balances

HINTS: Focus on the primary goal associated with the Federal Reserve's monetary policy.

Q600_LO23: How does the Federal Reserve promote a stable price environment?
a. Controlling fiscal policy
b. Managing stock markets
c. Conducting monetary policy
d. Regulating international trade

HINTS: Consider the specific action taken by the Federal Reserve to achieve a stable price environment.

Q601_LO23: What is the impact of increasing the money supply according to the Federal Reserve?
a. Economic contraction
b. Job creation and economic expansion
c. Currency devaluation
d. Stagnant economic growth

HINTS: Focus on the consequence of increasing the money supply as managed by the Federal Reserve.

Q602_LO23: Why does the Federal Reserve aim to keep inflation under control?
a. To promote international trade
b. To protect consumers from price fluctuations
c. To maximize government revenue
d. To encourage borrowing and lending

HINTS: Consider the rationale behind the Federal Reserve's goal of controlling inflation.

Q603_LO23: What is the term for the tools used by the Federal Reserve to directly impact the economy?
a. Diagnostic tools
b. Analytical tools
c. Prescriptive tools
d. Active tools

HINTS: Focus on the category of tools used for directly impacting the economy.

Q604_LO23: Which metaphor is used to describe diagnostic tools of the Federal Reserve?
a. Wrench
b. Ruler or level
c. Screwdriver
d. Hammer

HINTS: Consider the comparison made to describe diagnostic tools.

Q605_LO23: What is the potential consequence if the economy expands too quickly according to the Federal Reserve?
a. High levels of unemployment
b. Stable price environment
c. Currency appreciation
d. High levels of inflation

HINTS: Focus on the consequence associated with a rapid expansion of the economy.

Q606_LO23: How are diagnostic tools different from active tools of the Federal Reserve?
a. Diagnostic tools directly impact the economy
b. Active tools read the economy
c. Diagnostic tools measure the economy
d. Active tools are used for analysis

HINTS: Consider the role of diagnostic tools in relation to the economy.

Q607_LO23: Which tool is metaphorically described as a wrench by the Federal Reserve?
a. Diagnostic tools
b. Active tools
c. Analytical tools
d. Prescriptive tools

HINTS: Focus on the metaphor used to describe a specific category of tools.

Q608_LO23: What is the potential impact of high inflation on consumers according to the Federal Reserve?
a. Economic contraction
b. Increased purchasing power
c. Economic growth
d. Hurt the same people a healthy economy helps

HINTS: Focus on the consequence of high inflation by the Federal Reserve.

Q609_LO23: How does the Federal Reserve manage the money supply?
a. By controlling fiscal policy
b. By regulating international trade
c. Through monetary policy
d. By managing stock markets

HINTS: Consider the specific policy used by the Federal Reserve to manage the money supply.

Q610_LO23: What is the term for the amount of cash available within the U.S. economy?
a. Currency supply
b. Liquidity volume
c. Money circulation
d. Money supply

HINTS: Focus on the term used for the amount of cash within the economy.

Q611_LO24: What are the primary measures of money supply used by the Federal Reserve?
a. M1, M2, M4
b. M1, M3, M5
c. M1, M2, M3
d. M2, M3, M4

HINTS: Focus on the measures specifically in the context of the Federal Reserve.

Q612_LO24: What does M1 include in the measures of money supply?
a. Savings accounts
b. Cash and coinage, and money in demand deposit accounts
c. Jumbo CDs
d. Multiday repurchase agreements

HINTS: Consider the components included in M1.

Q613_LO24: Which measure is considered the most readily available money for spending?
a. M2
b. M3
c. M1
d. M4

HINTS: Focus on the measure that represents the most immediately spendable money.

Q614_LO24: What does M2 consist of in addition to M1?
a. Jumbo CDs
b. Consumer savings deposits, including savings accounts
c. Actual cash
d. Negotiable CDs

HINTS: Consider the components added in M2 beyond those in M1.

Q615_LO24: What is included in M3 in addition to M2?
a. Retail CDs
b. Large time deposits, including negotiable (jumbo) CDs
c. Money market funds
d. Overnight repurchase agreements

HINTS: Focus on the components added in M3 beyond those in M2.

Q616_LO24: Which measure includes assets that are a bit harder to move into a demand deposit account (DDA)?
a. M1
b. M2
c. M3
d. M4

HINTS: Consider the description of assets in M3.

Q617_LO24: If a measure of money supply is part of another measure, what can be inferred?
a. They are unrelated
b. They have similar components
c. They have opposing goals
d. They are interchangeable

HINTS: Consider the relationship between different measures of money supply.

Q618_LO24: Which component is common to both M2 and M3?
a. Money market funds
b. Overnight repurchase agreements
c. Retail CDs
d. M1

HINTS: Focus on the shared component between M2 and M3.

Q619_LO24: Why is M1 considered the money closest to being spent and turned into economic activity?
a. It includes savings accounts
b. It consists of large time deposits
c. It includes cash and coinage, and money in demand deposit accounts
d. It includes jumbo CDs

HINTS: Focus on the components of M1 and their immediacy for spending.

Q620_LO24: Which measure includes savings accounts and retail (non-negotiable) CDs?
a. M1
b. M2
c. M3
d. M4

HINTS: Consider the components added in M2.

Q621_LO24: What distinguishes "large time deposits" included in M3?
a. They are easily moved to a DDA
b. They are part of M1
c. They are harder to move into a DDA
d. They are part of M2

HINTS: Focus on the characteristic of "large time deposits" in M3.

Q622_LO24: If an asset is included in M2, is it also part of M1?
a. Yes
b. No

HINTS: Focus on the relationship between M1 and M2.

Q623_LO24: Which measure encompasses the broadest range of assets?
a. M1
b. M2
c. M3
d. M4

HINTS: Consider the components added in M3.

Q624_LO24: What is the term for assets that are easily moved to a DDA and spent?
a. Consumer savings deposits
b. Large time deposits
c. Retail CDs
d. Overnight repurchase agreements

HINTS: Focus on the category of assets included in M2.

Q625_LO24: If a measure includes assets that are a bit harder to move into a DDA, which measure is it likely to be?
a. M1
b. M2
c. M3
d. M4

HINTS: Consider the characteristic of assets in M3.

Q626_LO25: What is the primary function of Federal open-market operations?
a. Influencing interest rates
b. Managing inflation
c. Controlling stock prices
d. Regulating banks

HINTS: Focus on the primary purpose of open-market operations.

Q627_LO25: How does the Federal Reserve influence the money supply when it wants to expand it?
a. Sells securities to banks
b. Sets higher Regulation T requirements
c. Buys securities from banks
d. Raises the discount rate

HINTS: Consider the action taken by the Fed to expand the money supply.

Q628_LO25: What is the role of the Federal Open Market Committee (FOMC) in open-market operations?
a. Deciding on Regulation T requirements
b. Directing the government's open-market operations
c. Setting the discount rate
d. Managing the reserve requirement

HINTS: Focus on the responsibility of the FOMC in open-market operations.

Q629_LO25: How does the Federal Reserve tighten the money supply through open-market operations?
a. Sets lower Regulation T requirements
b. Buys securities from banks
c. Sells securities to banks
d. Lowers the discount rate

HINTS: Consider the action taken by the Fed to contract the money supply.

Q630_LO25: What is the purpose of Regulation T set by the Federal Reserve?
a. Controlling inflation
b. Influencing stock prices
c. Regulating the reserve requirement
d. Managing investor credit when buying securities

HINTS: Focus on the purpose of Regulation T in the context of investor credit.

Q631_LO25: How does a decrease in the initial deposit requirement under Regulation T impact the economy?
a. Slows down the economy
b. Increases stock prices
c. Limits credit
d. Contracts the money supply

HINTS: Focus on the impact of a lower initial deposit requirement.

Q632_LO25: What does the discount rate represent in the context of the Federal Reserve?
a. The base rate for the nation
b. Interest rates for consumers
c. Rates for interbank transactions
d. The inflation rate

HINTS: Consider the role of the discount rate and its significance.

Q633_LO25: How does raising the discount rate affect interest rates throughout the economy?
a. Lowers interest rates
b. Has no impact on interest rates
c. Causes rates to drop
d. Expands the economy

HINTS: Focus on the impact of raising the discount rate on interest rates.
Q634_LO25: What is the primary purpose of the reserve requirement set by the Federal Reserve?
a. Influencing inflation
b. Regulating banks
c. Expanding the economy
d. Controlling stock prices

HINTS: Focus on the primary function of the reserve requirement.

Q635_LO25: How does lowering the reserve requirement impact the economy?
a. Expands the economy
b. Raises interest rates
c. Contracts the money supply
d. Increases borrowing

HINTS: Consider the impact of lowering the reserve requirement.

Q636_LO25: When does the Federal Reserve rarely change the reserve requirement?

a. During economic expansions
b. In response to inflation
c. When banks face bankruptcy
d. Because of dramatic impacts throughout the banking system

HINTS: Focus on the considerations for changing the reserve requirement.

Q637_LO25: What does a decrease in the reserve requirement indicate?
a. A need for more cash at banks
b. An impending economic recession
c. A potential increase in stock prices
d. Banks may have insufficient cash

HINTS: Consider the implications of a decrease in the reserve requirement.

Q638_LO25: Which measure is used by the Federal Reserve when banks need additional capital to meet reserve requirements?
a. Discount rate
b. Regulation T
c. Reserve requirement
d. Open-market operations

HINTS: Focus on the tool used for banks needing additional capital.

Q639_LO25: What is the significance of the discount rate in news stories about the Federal Reserve?
a. Base rate for the nation
b. Consumer interest rates
c. Interbank borrowing rates
d. Inflation rate

HINTS: Consider the context in which the discount rate is often in news stories.

Q640_LO25: What does the Federal Reserve use in a repurchase agreement as collateral for a short-term loan to a bank?
a. Cash reserves
b. Government securities
c. Consumer savings deposits
d. Reserve requirements

HINTS: Focus on the collateral used by the Fed in repurchase agreements.

Q641_LO26: What does the federal funds rate represent in the economy?
a. Rate charged by the Federal Reserve
b. Rate for overnight loans between commercial banks
c. Prime rate for corporate borrowers
d. Interest rate for broker call loans

HINTS: Consider the nature and purpose of the federal funds rate.

Q642_LO26: Which benchmark rate is considered a barometer of short-term interest rates?
a. Prime rate
b. Broker call loan rate
c. Discount rate
d. Federal funds rate

HINTS: Focus on the benchmark rate indicative of short-term interest rates.

Q643_LO26: What is the prime rate used for in the banking industry?
a. Overnight loans between banks
b. Unsecured loans to creditworthy corporate borrowers
c. Loans for margin account customers
d. Short-term loans to member banks

HINTS: Consider the purpose and borrowers associated with the prime rate.

Q644_LO26: What is another name for the broker call loan rate?

a. Prime rate
b. Federal funds rate
c. Call money rate
d. Discount rate

HINTS: Focus on the alternative name for the broker call loan rate.

Q645_LO26: How do banks adjust their prime rates in response to Federal Reserve actions?
a. Lower prime rates when the Fed tightens the money supply
b. Raise prime rates when the Fed eases the money supply
c. Keep prime rates constant regardless of Fed actions
d. Determine prime rates independently of Fed policy

HINTS: Consider the relationship between prime rates and Federal Reserve actions.

Q646_LO26: What does the broker call loan rate apply to?
a. Loans between commercial banks
b. Unsecured loans to corporate borrowers
c. Loans for margin account customers
d. Short-term loans to member banks

HINTS: Focus on the borrowers and purpose associated with the broker call loan rate.

Q647_LO26: What does the discount rate represent in Federal Reserve policy tactics?
a. Rate for overnight loans between banks
b. Rate for unsecured loans to corporate borrowers
c. Rate charged by the Federal Reserve for short-term loans to member banks
d. Rate for margin account customers

HINTS: Consider the role of the discount rate in Federal Reserve policy.

Q648_LO26: In which situation does the Federal Reserve adopt an easy money policy?
a. To slow economic expansion
b. To prevent inflation
c. During a recession to stimulate the economy
d. To tighten credit

HINTS: Consider the economic conditions associated with an easy money policy.

Q649_LO26: What action does the Federal Reserve take during an easy money policy to expand credit?
a. Sell U.S. government securities
b. Raise the discount rate
c. Lower reserve requirements
d. Buy U.S. government securities

HINTS: Focus on the actions associated with an easy money policy.

Q650_LO26: What is the purpose of a tight money policy adopted by the Federal Reserve?
a. To stimulate a slow economy
b. To prevent inflation
c. To lower interest rates
d. To expand credit during a recession

HINTS: Consider the purpose of a tight money policy in the context of the economy.

Q651_LO26: Which action does the Federal Reserve take during a tight money policy to tighten credit?
a. Sell U.S. government securities
b. Lower the discount rate
c. Lower reserve requirements
d. Buy U.S. government securities

HINTS: Focus on the actions associated with a tight money policy.

Q652_LO26: What happens to interest rates when the Federal Reserve raises the discount rate?

a. Interest rates drop
b. No impact on interest rates
c. Causes rates to rise
d. Expands the economy

HINTS: Consider the impact of raising the discount rate on interest rates.

Q653_LO26: How does the Federal Reserve influence interest rates in open-market operations?
a. Buying U.S. government securities
b. Lowering the discount rate
c. Lowering reserve requirements
d. Selling U.S. government securities

HINTS: Focus on the action that influences interest rates in open-market operations.

Q654_LO26: What benchmark rate is influenced by the supply and demand of money?
a. Federal funds rate
b. Prime rate
c. Broker call loan rate
d. Discount rate

HINTS: Consider the relationship between the supply and demand of money and benchmark rates.

Q655_LO26: What does an increase in demand for money relative to supply lead to?
a. Falling interest rates
b. Rising interest rates
c. No impact on interest rates
d. Expansion of credit

HINTS: Focus on the impact of increased demand for money relative to supply.

Q656_LO27: What is the primary focus of fiscal policy?
a. Regulating interest rates
b. Controlling the money supply
c. Influencing government spending and taxation
d. Adjusting the money supply through open-market operations

HINTS: Consider the tools and objectives of fiscal policy.

Q657_LO27: How does fiscal policy differ from monetary policy in managing the money supply?
a. Uses open-market operations
b. Relies on taxation and federal spending
c. Controls interest rates
d. Adjusts reserve requirements

HINTS: Focus on the specific tools used by fiscal policy.

Q658_LO27: Why is fiscal policy considered less efficient for solving short-term economic problems?
a. Limited government control
b. Relies on monetary tools
c. Political process and implementation time
d. Lack of impact on overall demand

HINTS: Consider the factors that contribute to the efficiency of fiscal policy.

Q659_LO27: Which economic forces can fiscal policy influence by adjusting overall demand?
a. Interest rates
b. Inflation levels
c. Reserve requirements
d. Stock market fluctuations

HINTS: Focus on the outcomes that fiscal policy aims to impact.

Q660_LO27: What distinguishes fiscal policy from monetary policy in terms of tools?

a. Use of open-market operations
b. Dependence on interest rates
c. Reliance on taxation and government spending
d. Adjustment of reserve requirements

HINTS: Focus on the specific tools associated with fiscal policy.

Q661_LO27: How does fiscal policy manage the money supply through encouraging or discouraging spending?
a. By controlling reserve ratios
b. Through open-market operations
c. By adjusting interest rates
d. Via taxation and federal spending

HINTS: Consider the mechanisms through which fiscal policy impacts spending.

Q662_LO27: What role does the political process play in the implementation of fiscal policy?
a. Accelerates policy decisions
b. Has no impact on policy implementation
c. Introduces delays and complexities
d. Streamlines decision-making

HINTS: Consider the factors that contribute to the timing of fiscal policy decisions.

Q663_LO27: Which economic theories are explored in the context of fiscal policy?
a. Keynesian and supply-side
b. Monetarist and classical
c. Keynesian and monetarist
d. Supply-side and classical

HINTS: Focus on the two prominent fiscal theories .

Q664_LO27: What does fiscal policy aim to control through influencing spending and taxation?
a. Money supply
b. Inflation
c. Interest rates
d. Reserve requirements

HINTS: Consider the outcome that fiscal policy seeks to influence.

Q665_LO27: How does fiscal policy impact overall demand for goods and services?
a. By lowering interest rates
b. Through changes in reserve requirements
c. Via adjustments in taxation and government spending
d. By conducting open-market operations

HINTS: Focus on the mechanisms through which fiscal policy influences demand.

Q666_LO27: Why is trade considered an important part of a healthy economy?
a. Limits exposure to international markets
b. Reduces economic activity
c. Enhances diversity and strengths through trading
d. Causes currency devaluation

HINTS: Consider the benefits associated with international trade.

Q667_LO27: What directly affects international trade in terms of a nation's currency?
a. Fiscal policy
b. Inflation levels
c. Interest rates
d. Relative value of the currency

HINTS: Focus on the factor that directly impacts international trade.

Q668_LO27: In fiscal policy, what does the government seek to control to influence economic conditions?

a. Interest rates
b. Stock market fluctuations
c. Money supply
d. Overall demand for goods and services

HINTS: Focus on the aspect of the economy that fiscal policy aims to influence.

Q669_LO27: How does fiscal policy impact unemployment levels?
a. Directly by controlling interest rates
b. Indirectly through open-market operations
c. By adjusting government spending and taxation
d. Via changes in reserve requirements

HINTS: Consider the mechanisms through which fiscal policy influences unemployment.

Q670_LO27: What distinguishes fiscal policy from monetary policy in terms of time efficiency?
a. Fiscal policy is more efficient
b. No significant difference in efficiency
c. Monetary policy is more efficient
d. Both are equally efficient

HINTS: Consider the time considerations associated with fiscal and monetary policy.

Q671_LO28: Who is associated with Keynesian (demand-side) theory?
a. Adam Smith
b. Karl Marx
c. John Maynard Keynes
d. Milton Friedman

HINTS: Focus on the economist linked to Keynesian theory.

Q672_LO28: What does Keynesian theory emphasize as vital for the health and stability of a nation's economy?
a. Limited government involvement
b. Active government involvement
c. Market forces determining prices
d. Reduction of government spending

HINTS: Consider the key emphasis of Keynesian theory.

Q673_LO28: According to Keynesians, what controls employment and prices in an economy?
a. Market forces
b. Government spending
c. Supply and demand
d. Inflation and deflation

HINTS: Focus on the key factor according to Keynesian theory.

Q674_LO28: How does insufficient demand for goods impact the economy according to Keynesian theory?
a. Causes inflation
b. Increases unemployment
c. Reduces government spending
d. Encourages business growth

HINTS: Consider the consequence of insufficient demand according to Keynesian theory.

Q675_LO28: In Keynesian theory, how does the government intervene to manipulate the economy?
a. By adjusting interest rates
b. By reducing taxes
c. Through market forces
d. By changing levels of spending and taxation

HINTS: Focus on the actions attributed to the government in Keynesian theory.

Q676_LO28: What does Keynesian theory suggest about government's role in creating prosperity?

a. Limited intervention
b. Active force in creating prosperity
c. Absence of government involvement
d. Sole reliance on market forces

HINTS: Consider the view of Keynesian theory on government's role.

Q677_LO28: How does government influence individual levels of spending and saving in Keynesian theory?
a. By increasing taxes
b. By decreasing government spending
c. Through market forces
d. By adjusting taxes

HINTS: Focus on the mechanism through which government influences spending and saving.

Q678_LO28: What is another name for Keynesian theory?
a. Supply-side theory
b. Classical theory
c. Monetarist theory
d. Demand-side theory
HINTS: Consider the alternative name given to Keynesian theory.

Q679_LO28: What does supply-side economics suggest regarding government's role in market forces?
a. Government should control all prices
b. Government should reduce spending and taxes
c. Government should increase regulations
d. Government should determine demand

HINTS: Focus on the role that supply-side economics assigns to government.

Q680_LO28: What is the primary focus of supply-side theory?
a. Encouraging consumer spending
b. Allowing market forces to determine prices
c. Increasing government spending
d. Regulating businesses

HINTS: Consider the main emphasis of supply-side theory.

Q681_LO28: What does supply-side theory believe will lead to a strong and steady demand for labor?
a. Decreasing taxes
b. Increasing government debt
c. Expanding government regulations
d. Reducing business growth
HINTS: Focus on the factor that supply-side theory believes leads to a strong demand for labor.

Q682_LO28: How does supply-side theory view government debt in relation to economic activity?
a. As an efficient approach
b. As an inefficient and temporary approach
c. As irrelevant to economic activity
d. As a sustainable long-term approach

HINTS: Consider the view of supply-side theory on government debt.

Q683_LO28: In which theory does government spending focus on the consumer for economic stimulus?
a. Monetarist theory
b. Keynesian theory
c. Classical theory
d. Supply-side theory

HINTS: Focus on the theory that emphasizes stimulus on the consumer.

Q684_LO28: What does supply-side theory believe is a more sustainable long-term approach for economic expansion?
a. Increasing government debt
b. Encouraging business success and expansion

c. Relying on market forces
d. Expanding government regulations

HINTS: Focus on the approach that supply-side theory considers more sustainable.

Q685_LO28: What is a shared belief between demand- and supply-side theories regarding taxes?
a. Decreasing taxes encourages economic activity
b. Increasing taxes encourages economic activity
c. Taxes have no impact on economic activity
d. Taxes should be eliminated

HINTS: Consider the shared belief between the two theories regarding taxes.

Q686_LO29: What is the exchange rate defined as?
a. Balance of trade
b. Interest rate
c. Value of one currency against another
d. Balance of payments

HINTS: Focus on the definition of the exchange rate.

Q687_LO29: How does a decline in the value of the U.S. dollar impact U.S. exports and imports?
a. Exports increase, imports decrease
b. Exports decrease, imports increase
c. Both exports and imports increase
d. Both exports and imports decrease
HINTS: Consider the impact of a weaker U.S. dollar on trade.

Q688_LO29: When the U.S. dollar strengthens, what happens to the prices of U.S. products in terms of foreign currency?
a. Prices decrease
b. Prices increase
c. Prices remain unchanged
d. Prices fluctuate randomly

HINTS: Focus on the impact of a stronger U.S. dollar on the prices of U.S. products.

Q689_LO29: Define the balance of payments.
a. The exchange rate
b. The flow of money between the U.S. and other countries
c. The balance of trade
d. The balance between exports and imports

HINTS: Consider the broader concept related to the flow of money between countries.

Q690_LO29: What does a deficit in the balance of payments indicate?
a. More money flowing into the U.S. than out
b. More money flowing out of the U.S. than in
c. An equal flow of money in and out
d. A surplus of exports over imports
HINTS: Focus on the meaning of a deficit in the balance of payments.

Q691_LO29: Which of the following is the largest component of the balance of payments?
a. Interest rate
b. Balance of trade
c. Balance of payments
d. Balance of foreign aid

HINTS: Focus on the primary element contributing to the balance of payments.

Q692_LO29: What contributes to the U.S. credit side in the balance of payments?
a. U.S. imports
b. U.S. investments abroad
c. Foreign spending in the U.S.
d. U.S. bank loans abroad

HINTS: Consider the items that contribute positively to the U.S. balance of payments.

Q693_LO29: Which of the following is a debit item in the balance of payments?
a. Exports
b. Foreign spending in the U.S.
c. U.S. investments abroad
d. U.S. exports
HINTS: Focus on the items that lead to money flowing out of the U.S.

Q694_LO29: What causes a surplus in the balance of payments?
a. Debits exceeding credits
b. Credits exceeding debits
c. Equal flow of credits and debits
d. An increase in U.S. imports

HINTS: Focus on the condition for a surplus in the balance of payments.
Q695_LO29: What does a deficit in the balance of payments indicate about interest rates in another country?
a. High interest rates
b. Low interest rates
c. Unrelated to interest rates
d. Fluctuating interest rates

HINTS: Consider the relationship between a deficit and interest rates in another country.

Q696_LO29: In the context of the balance of payments, what are credit items?
a. Imports
b. Exports
c. U.S. investments abroad
d. U.S. foreign aid

HINTS: Focus on items contributing positively to the U.S. balance of payments.

Q697_LO29: What contributes to the U.S. debit side in the balance of payments?
a. Foreign spending in the U.S.
b. U.S. imports
c. U.S. bank loans abroad
d. U.S. investments abroad

HINTS: Consider the items that contribute negatively to the U.S. balance of payments.

Q698_LO29: What is a debit item associated with the balance of payments?
a. U.S. investments abroad
b. Foreign spending in the U.S.
c. U.S. imports
d. Exports

HINTS: Focus on items leading to money flowing out of the U.S.

Q699_LO29: What is the primary focus of the balance of trade?
a. U.S. investments abroad
b. Balance of payments
c. Exports and imports of merchandise
d. Foreign spending in the U.S.

HINTS: Consider the main components of the balance of trade.

Q700_LO29: What happens when debits exceed credits in the balance of payments?
a. A surplus occurs
b. A deficit occurs
c. Interest rates decrease
d. Interest rates increase
HINTS: Focus on the result of debits exceeding credits in the balance of payments.

Correct Answers & Explanations
The Federal Reserve Fiscal Policy, Trade, Currency Rate & the Balance of Trade

Q596_LO23: Correct Answer: b EXPLANATIONS: The primary purpose of the Federal Reserve is to conduct the nation's monetary policy.

Q597_LO23: Correct Answer: c EXPLANATIONS: The common acronym for the Federal Reserve Board is FRB.

Q598_LO23: Correct Answer: b EXPLANATIONS: The Federal Reserve System is directed by the Federal Reserve Board.

Q599_LO23: Correct Answer: b EXPLANATIONS: The main goal is to promote maximum employment.

Q600_LO23: Correct Answer: c EXPLANATIONS: The Federal Reserve promotes a stable price environment by conducting monetary policy.

Q601_LO23: Correct Answer: b EXPLANATIONS: Increasing the money supply is aimed at creating jobs and expanding the economy.

Q602_LO23: Correct Answer: b EXPLANATIONS: Controlling inflation helps protect consumers from the negative impact of price fluctuations.

Q603_LO23: Correct Answer: d EXPLANATIONS: The tools used by the Federal Reserve to directly impact the economy are referred to as active tools.

Q604_LO23: Correct Answer: b EXPLANATIONS: Diagnostic tools are metaphorically described as a ruler or a level, used to measure the economy.

Q605_LO23: Correct Answer: d EXPLANATIONS: An overly quick expansion may lead to high levels of inflation.

Q606_LO23: Correct Answer: c EXPLANATIONS: Diagnostic tools are used to measure or "read" the economy.

Q607_LO23: Correct Answer: b EXPLANATIONS: Active tools are metaphorically described as a wrench, used to loosen or tighten the money supply.

Q608_LO23: Correct Answer: d EXPLANATIONS: High inflation hurts consumers, particularly the same people a healthy economy aims to help.

Q609_LO23: Correct Answer: c EXPLANATIONS: The Federal Reserve manages the money supply through monetary policy.

Q610_LO23: Correct Answer: d EXPLANATIONS: The amount of cash available within the U.S. economy is referred to as the money supply.

Q611_LO24: Correct Answer: c EXPLANATIONS: The primary measures of money supply used by the Federal Reserve are M1, M2, and M3.

Q612_LO24: Correct Answer: b EXPLANATIONS: M1 includes cash, coinage, and money in demand deposit accounts (DDAs).

Q613_LO24: Correct Answer: c EXPLANATIONS: M1 is the measure of the most readily available money for spending.

Q614_LO24: Correct Answer: b EXPLANATIONS: M2 consists of M1 plus "consumer savings deposits," including savings accounts.

Q615_LO24: Correct Answer: b EXPLANATIONS: M3 consists of M2 plus "large time deposits," including negotiable (jumbo) CDs.
Q616_LO24: Correct Answer: c EXPLANATIONS: M3 includes assets that are a bit harder to move into a DDA.

Q617_LO24: Correct Answer: b EXPLANATIONS: If a measure is part of another, they share similar components.

Q618_LO24: Correct Answer: d EXPLANATIONS: M1 is common to both M2 and M3.

Q619_LO24: Correct Answer: c EXPLANATIONS: M1 includes cash, coinage, and money in demand deposit accounts (DDAs), making it the closest to being spent.

Q620_LO24: Correct Answer: b EXPLANATIONS: M2 includes savings accounts and retail (non-negotiable) CDs.

Q621_LO24: Correct Answer: c EXPLANATIONS: Large time deposits in M3 are assets that are a bit harder to move into a DDA.

Q622_LO24: Correct Answer: a EXPLANATIONS: Yes, M2 includes M1 as one of its components.

Q623_LO24: Correct Answer: c EXPLANATIONS: M3 encompasses the broadest range of assets, including large time deposits.
Q624_LO24: Correct Answer: a EXPLANATIONS: Assets that are easily moved to a DDA and spent are termed "consumer savings deposits" in M2.

Q625_LO24: Correct Answer: c EXPLANATIONS: If assets are a bit harder to move into a DDA, they are likely part of M3.

Q626_LO25: Correct Answer: a EXPLANATIONS: The primary function of open-market operations is to influence interest rates.

Q627_LO25: Correct Answer: c EXPLANATIONS: The Fed buys securities from banks to expand the money supply.

Q628_LO25: Correct Answer: b EXPLANATIONS: The FOMC directs the government's open-market operations.

Q629_LO25: Correct Answer: c EXPLANATIONS: The Fed sells securities to banks to tighten the money supply.

Q630_LO25: Correct Answer: d EXPLANATIONS: Regulation T sets the minimum amount an investor must deposit when using credit to buy a security.

Q631_LO25: Correct Answer: b EXPLANATIONS: A lower initial deposit requirement under Regulation T would likely raise stock prices.

Q632_LO25: Correct Answer: a EXPLANATIONS: The discount rate is seen as the base rate for the nation.

Q633_LO25: Correct Answer: c EXPLANATIONS: Raising the discount rate tends to cause interest rates to drop throughout the economy.

Q634_LO25: Correct Answer: b EXPLANATIONS: The reserve requirement is set to regulate banks and ensure they maintain sufficient cash.

Q635_LO25: Correct Answer: a EXPLANATIONS: Lowering the reserve requirement frees up cash at banks, expanding the economy.

Q636_LO25: Correct Answer: d EXPLANATIONS: The Fed rarely changes the reserve requirement due to its dramatic impact throughout the banking system.

Q637_LO25: Correct Answer: a EXPLANATIONS: A decrease in the reserve requirement indicates a need for more cash at banks.

Q638_LO25: Correct Answer: a EXPLANATIONS: Banks borrow money from the Federal Reserve through repurchase agreements, involving the discount rate.

Q639_LO25: Correct Answer: a EXPLANATIONS: The discount rate is often referred to as the base rate for the nation.

Q640_LO25: Correct Answer: b EXPLANATIONS: The Fed uses government securities as collateral for short-term loans to banks in a repurchase agreement.

Q641_LO26: Correct Answer: b EXPLANATIONS: The federal funds rate represents the rate for overnight loans between commercial banks.

Q642_LO26: Correct Answer: d EXPLANATIONS: The federal funds rate is considered a barometer of short-term interest rates.

Q643_LO26: Correct Answer: b EXPLANATIONS: The prime rate is the interest rate for unsecured loans to creditworthy corporate borrowers.

Q644_LO26: Correct Answer: c EXPLANATIONS: The broker call loan rate is also known as the call money rate.

Q645_LO26: Correct Answer: b EXPLANATIONS: Banks raise prime rates when the Fed contracts the money supply.

Q646_LO26: Correct Answer: c EXPLANATIONS: The broker call loan rate applies to loans for margin account customers.

Q647_LO26: Correct Answer: c EXPLANATIONS: The discount rate represents the rate charged by the Federal Reserve for short-term loans to member banks.

Q648_LO26: Correct Answer: c EXPLANATIONS: An easy money policy is adopted during a recession to stimulate the economy.

Q649_LO26: Correct Answer: d EXPLANATIONS: During an easy money policy, the Fed buys U.S. government securities to expand credit.

Q650_LO26: Correct Answer: b EXPLANATIONS: A tight money policy is adopted to prevent inflation.

Q651_LO26: Correct Answer: a EXPLANATIONS: During a tight money policy, the Fed sells U.S. government securities to tighten credit.

Q652_LO26: Correct Answer: c EXPLANATIONS: Raising the discount rate tends to cause interest rates to rise.

Q653_LO26: Correct Answer: a EXPLANATIONS: The Fed influences interest rates by buying U.S. government securities in open-market operations.

Q654_LO26: Correct Answer: a EXPLANATIONS: The federal funds rate is influenced by the supply and demand of money.
Q655_LO26: Correct Answer: b EXPLANATIONS: An increase in demand for money relative to supply tends to lead to rising interest rates.

Q656_LO27: Correct Answer: c EXPLANATIONS: Fiscal policy focuses on influencing government spending and taxation.

Q657_LO27: Correct Answer: b EXPLANATIONS: Fiscal policy relies on taxation and federal spending to manage the money supply.

Q658_LO27: Correct Answer: c EXPLANATIONS: Fiscal policy takes time due to the political process and implementation time.
Q659_LO27: Correct Answer: b EXPLANATIONS: Fiscal policy can influence inflation levels by adjusting overall demand.

Q660_LO27: Correct Answer: c EXPLANATIONS: Fiscal policy relies on taxation and government spending as its primary tools.

Q661_LO27: Correct Answer: d EXPLANATIONS: Fiscal policy manages the money supply by adjusting spending through taxation and federal spending.

Q662_LO27: Correct Answer: c EXPLANATIONS: The political process introduces delays and complexities in the implementation of fiscal policy.

Q663_LO27: Correct Answer: a EXPLANATIONS: The prominent fiscal theories explored are Keynesian and supply-side.

Q664_LO27: Correct Answer: b EXPLANATIONS: Fiscal policy aims to control inflation through influencing spending and taxation.

Q665_LO27: Correct Answer: c EXPLANATIONS: Fiscal policy impacts overall demand by adjusting taxation and government spending.

Q666_LO27: Correct Answer: c EXPLANATIONS: Trade enhances diversity and strengths through trading with other nations.

Q667_LO27: Correct Answer: d EXPLANATIONS: The relative value of a nation's currency directly affects international trade.

Q668_LO27: Correct Answer: d EXPLANATIONS: Fiscal policy seeks to control overall demand for goods and services.

Q669_LO27: Correct Answer: c EXPLANATIONS: Fiscal policy impacts unemployment by adjusting government spending and taxation.

Q670_LO27: Correct Answer: c EXPLANATIONS: Monetary policy is generally considered more efficient in addressing short-term economic problems.

Q671_LO28: Correct Answer: c EXPLANATIONS: John Maynard Keynes is associated with Keynesian (demand-side) theory.

Q672_LO28: Correct Answer: b EXPLANATIONS: Keynesian theory emphasizes active government involvement in the economy.

Q673_LO28: Correct Answer: c EXPLANATIONS: Keynesians believe that demand for goods controls employment and prices.

Q674_LO28: Correct Answer: b EXPLANATIONS: Insufficient demand for goods, according to Keynes, causes unemployment.

Q675_LO28: Correct Answer: d EXPLANATIONS: According to Keynesian theory, the government manipulates the economy by changing its levels of spending and taxation.

Q676_LO28: Correct Answer: b EXPLANATIONS: Keynesian theory sees the government as an active force in creating prosperity.

Q677_LO28: Correct Answer: d EXPLANATIONS: Government influences individual levels of spending and saving in Keynesian theory by adjusting taxes.
Q678_LO28: Correct Answer: d EXPLANATIONS: Keynesian theory is also called demand-side theory.

Q679_LO28: Correct Answer: b EXPLANATIONS: Supply-side economics suggests that government should reduce spending and taxes.

Q680_LO28: Correct Answer: b EXPLANATIONS: Supply-side theory focuses on allowing market forces to determine prices.

Q681_LO28: Correct Answer: a EXPLANATIONS: Supply-side theory believes that decreasing taxes will lead to a strong and steady demand for labor.
Q682_LO28: Correct Answer: b EXPLANATIONS: Supply-side theory sees government debt as an inefficient and temporary approach to economic activity.

Q683_LO28: Correct Answer: b EXPLANATIONS: Keynesian theory, or demand-side theory, focuses stimulus on the consumer.

Q684_LO28: Correct Answer: b EXPLANATIONS: Supply-side theory believes that encouraging business success and expansion is a more sustainable long-term approach.

Q685_LO28: Correct Answer: a EXPLANATIONS: Both theories believe that decreasing taxes encourages economic activity.

Q686_LO29: Correct Answer: c EXPLANATIONS: The exchange rate is defined as the value of one currency against another.

Q687_LO29: Correct Answer: a EXPLANATIONS: A weaker U.S. dollar makes U.S. products cheaper in terms of foreign currency, leading to increased exports and decreased imports.

Q688_LO29: Correct Answer: b EXPLANATIONS: A stronger U.S. dollar increases the prices of U.S. products in terms of foreign currency.
Q689_LO29: Correct Answer: b EXPLANATIONS: The balance of payments refers to the flow of money between the U.S. and other countries.

Q690_LO29: Correct Answer: b EXPLANATIONS: A deficit occurs when more money flows out of the U.S. than in.

Q691_LO29: Correct Answer: b EXPLANATIONS: The largest component of the balance of payments is the balance of trade.

Q692_LO29: Correct Answer: c EXPLANATIONS: Foreign spending in the U.S. contributes to the U.S. credit side.

Q693_LO29: Correct Answer: c EXPLANATIONS: U.S. investments abroad are debit items in the balance of payments.

Q694_LO29: Correct Answer: b EXPLANATIONS: A surplus occurs when credits exceed debits.

Q695_LO29: Correct Answer: a EXPLANATIONS: A deficit may occur when interest rates in another country are high.

Q696_LO29: Correct Answer: b EXPLANATIONS: Credit items in the balance of payments include exports and U.S. foreign aid.

Q697_LO29: Correct Answer: b EXPLANATIONS: U.S. imports contribute to the U.S. debit side in the balance of payments.

Q698_LO29: Correct Answer: c EXPLANATIONS: U.S. imports are debit items in the balance of payments.

Q699_LO29: Correct Answer: c EXPLANATIONS: The balance of trade focuses on the export and import of merchandise.

Q700_LO29: Correct Answer: b EXPLANATIONS: A deficit occurs when debits exceed credits in the balance of payments.

Industries and Companies

Q701_LO30: What is the primary focus of fundamental analysis?
a. Individual companies
b. Economic indicators
c. Industry classification
d. Political factors

HINTS: Focus on the primary objective of fundamental analysis.

Q702_LO30: Why is fundamental analysis sometimes called top-down analysis?
a. It starts from the bottom (companies)
b. It starts from the middle (industries)
c. It starts from the top (the economy)
d. It doesn't have a specific starting point

HINTS: Consider the direction of analysis in fundamental analysis.

Q703_LO30: Which class of industries is highly sensitive to business cycles and inflation trends?
a. Noncyclical
b. Countercyclical
c. Growth
d. Cyclical

HINTS: Focus on the characteristics of cyclical industries.

Q704_LO30: What types of goods do most cyclical industries produce?
a. Nondurable goods
b. Capital goods
c. Consumables
d. Raw materials

HINTS: Consider the products associated with cyclical industries.

Q705_LO30: Which industry tends to decline during recessions due to decreased demand for its products?
a. Noncyclical
b. Countercyclical
c. Growth
d. Cyclical

HINTS: Focus on the impact of recessions on specific industries.

Q706_LO30: What is a characteristic of noncyclical industries during bear markets?
a. Decline more than other industries
b. Advance less than other industries
c. Experience higher volatility
d. Exhibit higher risk

HINTS: Consider the behavior of noncyclical industries during bear markets.

Q707_LO30: What type of industry is characterized by products that are used once and consumed in the process?
a. Countercyclical
b. Growth
c. Cyclical
d. Noncyclical

HINTS: Focus on the characteristic of products in defensive industries.

Q708_LO30: Which industry is likely to turn down as the economy heats up and rise during economic downturns?
a. Growth
b. Countercyclical
c. Noncyclical
d. Cyclical

HINTS: Focus on the behavior of countercyclical industries.

Q709_LO30: What is a characteristic of countercyclical industries during economic downturns?
a. Decreased demand for safety
b. Increased demand for safety
c. Stable demand regardless of economic conditions
d. Fluctuating demand

HINTS: Consider the behavior of countercyclical industries during economic downturns.

Q710_LO30: What distinguishes a growth industry from other types of industries?
a. Connection to the business cycle
b. Disconnection from the business cycle
c. Stability in economic downturns
d. Focus on consumables

HINTS: Focus on the characteristic of growth industries.

Q711_LO30: In the context of a special situation, what does it apply to?
a. Specific companies
b. Individual stocks
c. The entire industry
d. Cultural shifts

HINTS: Consider the typical scope of a special situation.

Q712_LO30: What does a special situation in an industry or company refer to?
a. A cultural shift
b. A positive or negative condition
c. A connection to the business cycle
d. A cyclical trend

HINTS: Focus on the nature of a special situation.

Q713_LO30: Which type of industry is least affected by normal business cycles?
a. Cyclical
b. Noncyclical
c. Countercyclical
d. Growth

HINTS: Focus on the stability of noncyclical industries.

Q714_LO30: During recessions, which industry is likely to experience increased demand for its products?
a. Growth
b. Cyclical
c. Countercyclical
d. Noncyclical

HINTS: Consider the behavior of countercyclical industries during economic downturns.

Q715_LO30: What is the risk-return relationship often associated with investments in defensive industries?
a. High risk, high return
b. Low risk, low return
c. High risk, low return
d. Low risk, high return

HINTS: Consider the general risk level associated with defensive industries.

Q716_LO31: In which economic phase do cyclical industries tend to perform poorly?
a. Expansion
b. Contraction
c. Stagnation
d. Recession

HINTS: Focus on the performance of cyclical industries in different economic phases.

Q717_LO31: What is a characteristic of defensive industries during poor economies?
a. Significant growth
b. Stable sales
c. High volatility
d. Rapid expansion

HINTS: Consider how defensive industries behave during economic downturns.

Q718_LO31: When is the value of countercyclical industries likely to decrease?
a. During economic contractions
b. During economic expansions
c. In stagnant economies
d. In recessionary phases

HINTS: Focus on the behavior of countercyclical industries during economic phases.

Q719_LO31: What is a characteristic of growth industries in relation to the economy?
a. Sensitive to economic fluctuations
b. Tend to shrink during recessions
c. Continuously expanding
d. Perform well in contractions

HINTS: Focus on the nature of growth industries in relation to the business cycle.

Q720_LO31: Which type of industry is least impacted by the business cycle?
a. Cyclical
b. Defensive
c. Countercyclical
d. Growth

HINTS: Consider the characteristic of industries that are less impacted by economic fluctuations.

Q721_LO31: In which economic phase do defensive industries not drop as much as cyclical industries?
a. Expansion
b. Contraction
c. Stagnation
d. Recession

HINTS: Focus on the comparison between the performance of defensive and cyclical industries.

Q722_LO31: When do countercyclical industries tend to perform better?
a. During economic expansions
b. During economic contractions
c. In stagnant economies
d. In recessionary phases

HINTS: Focus on the behavior of countercyclical industries during economic phases.

Q723_LO31: What is a characteristic of special situations in industries?
a. Continuous growth
b. Stable performance
c. Situational influence
d. Consistent contraction

HINTS: Consider the nature of special situations in industries.

Q724_LO31: In which economic phase do growth industries tend to keep expanding?
a. Expansion
b. Contraction
c. Stagnation
d. Recession

HINTS: Focus on the behavior of growth industries in different economic phases.

Q725_LO31: When do cyclical industries tend to do well?
a. During economic expansions
b. During economic contractions
c. In stagnant economies
d. In recessionary phases

HINTS: Focus on the performance of cyclical industries in different economic phases.

Q726_LO31: What is a characteristic of cyclical industries during economic expansions?
a. Stable growth
b. Poor performance
c. Rapid contraction
d. Significant sales

HINTS: Consider the behavior of cyclical industries in expanding economies.

Q727_LO31: What is a key difference between defensive and cyclical industries in poor economies?
a. Both decline equally
b. Defensive industries decline more
c. Cyclical industries decline more
d. Neither declines

HINTS: Compare the decline patterns of defensive and cyclical industries in poor economies.

Q728_LO31: What is a likely outcome for countercyclical industries during economic contractions?
a. Increased value
b. Stable value
c. Decreased value
d. No impact on value

HINTS: Focus on the behavior of countercyclical industries during economic contractions.

Q729_LO31: When do defensive industries generally decline less than other industries?
a. In stagnant economies
b. During economic expansions
c. During economic contractions
d. In recessionary phases

HINTS: Focus on the behavior of defensive industries during economic contractions.

Q730_LO31: What is a characteristic of growth industries during recessions?
a. Significant decline
b. Continuous expansion
c. Stability in performance
d. No impact on growth

HINTS: Consider the behavior of growth industries during economic contractions.

Q731_LO32: What does a balance sheet provide?
a. Quarterly earnings
b. Snapshot of financial position
c. Marketing strategies
d. Employee salaries

HINTS: Focus on the primary purpose of a balance sheet.

Q732_LO32: What is the difference between assets and liabilities on a balance sheet?
a. Assets are what the company owes; liabilities are what it owns.
b. Assets represent ownership; liabilities represent debts.
c. Assets are debts; liabilities are ownership.
d. Assets and liabilities are the same.

HINTS: Understand the fundamental distinction between assets and liabilities.

Q733_LO32: What is the formula for working capital?
a. Current assets:current liabilities
b. Current liabilities:current assets
c. Current assets – current liabilities
d. Current liabilities – current assets

HINTS: Recall the formula for calculating working capital.

Q734_LO32: How is the current ratio calculated?
a. Current assets:current liabilities
b. Current liabilities:current assets
c. Current assets – current liabilities
d. Current liabilities – current assets

HINTS: Remember the formula for the current ratio.

Q735_LO32: What does the acid ratio test on a balance sheet?
a. Long-term solvency
b. Short-term liquidity in a crisis
c. Profitability
d. Employee satisfaction

HINTS: Consider the purpose of the acid ratio.

Q736_LO32: What is included in the category of fixed assets on a balance sheet?
a. Cash and equivalents
b. Real estate and equipment
c. Securities and inventory
d. Trademarks and copyrights

HINTS: Identify the assets classified as fixed assets.

Q737_LO32: Which liabilities are due within 12 months?
a. Long-term liabilities
b. Current liabilities
c. Notes and bonds
d. Net worth liabilities

HINTS: Distinguish between current and long-term liabilities.

Q738_LO32: What does the debt ratio measure?
a. Short-term liquidity
b. Long-term solvency
c. Profit margin
d. Inventory turnover

HINTS: Focus on the purpose of the debt ratio.

Q739_LO32: What is included in the net worth section of a balance sheet?
a. Current assets
b. Preferred stock
c. Current liabilities
d. Retained earnings

HINTS: Recognize the components of the net worth section.

Q740_LO32: How is the current ratio expressed?
a. As a percentage
b. As a ratio
c. In dollars
d. In shares

HINTS: Recall the expression of the current ratio.

Q741_LO32: What does a high debt ratio indicate?
a. Strong liquidity
b. Low leverage
c. High solvency
d. High leverage

HINTS: Interpret the implications of a high debt ratio.

Q742_LO32: What does the net worth of a corporation represent?
a. Short-term obligations
b. Long-term assets
c. Ownership interest
d. Inventory value

HINTS: Understand the nature of net worth on a balance sheet.

Q743_LO32: What is the primary focus of the acid ratio?
a. Profitability
b. Short-term liquidity
c. Long-term solvency
d. Asset valuation

HINTS: Recognize the primary concern addressed by the acid ratio.

Q744_LO32: When are long-term liabilities reflected in current liabilities?
a. Never
b. During economic expansions
c. In stagnant economies
d. When interest is due within 12 months

HINTS: Understand the relationship between long-term and current liabilities.

Q745_LO32: What is the purpose of the working capital figure?
a. Measure of profitability
b. Indicator of short-term liquidity
c. Calculation of long-term debt
d. Assessment of inventory turnover

HINTS: Identify the purpose served by the working capital figure.

Q746_LO33: What does the income statement summarize?
a. Balance sheet
b. Cash flow
c. Revenues and expenses
d. Long-term liabilities

HINTS: Identify the primary focus of the income statement.

Q747_LO33: What is another term for the income statement?
a. Statement of cash flows
b. Statement of retained earnings
c. Profit and loss (P&L)
d. Balance sheet

HINTS: Recall the alternative name for the income statement.

Q748_LO33: How is operating profit calculated on the income statement?
a. Net sales + nonoperating income
b. Net sales - operating costs
c. Operating income - interest expenses
d. Operating income + taxes

HINTS: Focus on the calculation of operating profit.

Q749_LO33: What does the PE ratio measure?
a. Profit efficiency
b. Market value compared to earnings
c. Operating income
d. Taxable income

HINTS: Recognize the purpose of the PE ratio.

Q750_LO33: What is the formula for calculating earnings per share (EPS)?
a. CMV / EPS
b. EPS / CMV
c. Net income / number of outstanding shares
d. Number of outstanding shares / net income

HINTS: Recall the correct formula for EPS calculation.

Q751_LO33: What does nonoperating income contribute to on the income statement?
a. Taxable income
b. Net income after taxes
c. Operating income
d. Earnings available to common

HINTS: Identify the impact of nonoperating income on the income statement.

Q752_LO33: What is subtracted to calculate taxable income on the income statement?
a. Operating costs
b. Taxes
c. Nonoperating income
d. Interest expenses

HINTS: Focus on the element subtracted to derive taxable income.

Q753_LO33: What does the PE ratio express as?
a. Percentage
b. Ratio
c. Dollars
d. Earnings

HINTS: Recall the expression used for the PE ratio.

Q754_LO33: What is retained earnings calculated as?
a. Net income after taxes - common dividends
b. Earnings available to common - common dividends
c. Operating income + nonoperating income
d. Taxable income - taxes

HINTS: Recognize the correct formula for retained earnings.

Q755_LO33: When is the PE ratio particularly useful?
a. In isolation
b. During recessions
c. For all industries
d. During expansions

HINTS: Consider the context in which the PE ratio is valuable.

Q756_LO33: What does EPS represent?
a. Market value
b. Net income
c. Earnings available to common
d. Earnings per share

HINTS: Identify the correct interpretation of EPS.

Q757_LO33: How is net income after taxes calculated?
a. Operating income - taxes
b. Taxable income - taxes
c. Net income / preferred dividends
d. Operating income + nonoperating income

HINTS: Focus on the calculation of net income after taxes.

Q758_LO33: What is subtracted to calculate net income after taxes?
a. Preferred dividends
b. Common dividends
c. Earnings available to common
d. Operating income

HINTS: Identify the element subtracted to derive net income after taxes.

Q759_LO33: When does a high PE ratio suggest overvaluation?
a. Always
b. During economic contractions
c. In mature industries
d. During economic expansions

HINTS: Recognize the condition when a high PE ratio may indicate overvaluation.

Q760_LO33: What is the purpose of calculating the PE ratio?
a. Assess liquidity
b. Measure profitability
c. Evaluate market value compared to earnings
d. Analyze current assets

HINTS: Understand the primary purpose of the PE ratio.

Correct Answers & Explanations
Industries and Companies

Q701_LO30: Correct Answer: c EXPLANATIONS: Fundamental analysis focuses on studying industries and companies.

Q702_LO30: Correct Answer: c EXPLANATIONS: Fundamental analysis starts at the top (the economy) and works down to the company.

Q703_LO30: Correct Answer: d EXPLANATIONS: Cyclical industries are highly sensitive to business cycles and inflation trends.

Q704_LO30: Correct Answer: b EXPLANATIONS: Most cyclical industries produce durable goods and raw materials, such as heavy machinery and steel.

Q705_LO30: Correct Answer: d EXPLANATIONS: Cyclical industries, such as autos and steel, tend to decline during recessions.

Q706_LO30: Correct Answer: b EXPLANATIONS: Noncyclical stocks generally decline less than stocks in other industries during bear markets.

Q707_LO30: Correct Answer: d EXPLANATIONS: Noncyclical industries, also known as defensive industries, produce consumables that are used once and consumed.

Q708_LO30: Correct Answer: b EXPLANATIONS: Countercyclical industries tend to turn down during economic expansions and rise during downturns.

Q709_LO30: Correct Answer: b EXPLANATIONS: Countercyclical industries, like gold mining, see increased demand when people seek safety.

Q710_LO30: Correct Answer: b EXPLANATIONS: A growth industry is one that seems disconnected from the business cycle.

Q711_LO30: Correct Answer: a EXPLANATIONS: A special situation is normally applied to a specific company.

Q712_LO30: Correct Answer: b EXPLANATIONS: A special situation may be a positive or negative condition, such as a hostile takeover or a cultural shift.

Q713_LO30: Correct Answer: b EXPLANATIONS: Noncyclical or defensive industries are least affected by normal business cycles.

Q714_LO30: Correct Answer: c EXPLANATIONS: Countercyclical industries, like gold mining, tend to experience increased demand during economic downturns.

Q715_LO30: Correct Answer: d EXPLANATIONS: Investments in defensive industries tend to involve less risk and lower investment returns.

Q716_LO31: Correct Answer: b EXPLANATIONS: Cyclical industries tend to do poorly in contractions.

Q717_LO31: Correct Answer: b EXPLANATIONS: Defensive industries maintain stable sales throughout the business cycle.

Q718_LO31: Correct Answer: b EXPLANATIONS: Countercyclical industries tend to lose value when the economy strengthens.

Q719_LO31: Correct Answer: c EXPLANATIONS: Growth industries keep growing, irrespective of the economy's condition.

Q720_LO31: Correct Answer: b EXPLANATIONS: Defensive industries tend to be less impacted by the business cycle.

Q721_LO31: Correct Answer: b EXPLANATIONS: Defensive industries do not drop as much as cyclical industries do in poor economies.

Q722_LO31: Correct Answer: b EXPLANATIONS: Countercyclical industries tend to perform better when the economy is weak.

Q723_LO31: Correct Answer: c EXPLANATIONS: Special situations are situational; some specific circumstance is affecting them.

Q724_LO31: Correct Answer: a EXPLANATIONS: Growth industries tend to keep expanding, especially during economic expansions.

Q725_LO31: Correct Answer: a EXPLANATIONS: Cyclical industries tend to do well in economic expansions.

Q726_LO31: Correct Answer: d EXPLANATIONS: Cyclical industries tend to have significant sales during economic expansions.

Q727_LO31: Correct Answer: c EXPLANATIONS: Cyclical industries decline more than defensive industries in poor economies.

Q728_LO31: Correct Answer: a EXPLANATIONS: Countercyclical industries tend to do better and may see increased value during economic contractions.

Q729_LO31: Correct Answer: c EXPLANATIONS: Defensive industries generally decline less than other industries during economic contractions.

Q730_LO31: Correct Answer: a EXPLANATIONS: Growth industries may experience a significant decline during recessions.

Q731_LO32: Correct Answer: b EXPLANATIONS: The balance sheet provides a snapshot of a company's financial position at a specific time.

Q732_LO32: Correct Answer: b EXPLANATIONS: Assets represent ownership, and liabilities represent debts.

Q733_LO32: Correct Answer: c EXPLANATIONS: Working capital = current assets – current liabilities

Q734_LO32: Correct Answer: a EXPLANATIONS: Current ratio = current assets / current liabilities

Q735_LO32: Correct Answer: b EXPLANATIONS: The acid ratio tests a company's liquidity if everything goes bad.

Q736_LO32: Correct Answer: b EXPLANATIONS: Fixed assets include real estate, furniture, and equipment.

Q737_LO32: Correct Answer: b EXPLANATIONS: Current liabilities are due now or in the near future (within 12 months).

Q738_LO32: Correct Answer: b EXPLANATIONS: The debt ratio measures long-term solvency.

Q739_LO32: Correct Answer: b EXPLANATIONS: Net worth includes preferred stock, common stock, capital in excess of par, and retained earnings.

Q740_LO32: Correct Answer: b EXPLANATIONS: Current ratio is expressed as a ratio (current assets:current liabilities).

Q741_LO32: Correct Answer: d EXPLANATIONS: A high debt ratio indicates that a corporation is highly leveraged.

Q742_LO32: Correct Answer: c EXPLANATIONS: Net worth represents the ownership interest of shareholders.

Q743_LO32: Correct Answer: b EXPLANATIONS: The acid ratio focuses on short-term liquidity, especially in crisis situations.

Q744_LO32: Correct Answer: d EXPLANATIONS: The interest due within the next 12 months is reflected in current liabilities.

Q745_LO32: Correct Answer: b EXPLANATIONS: Working capital is an indicator of short-term liquidity.

Q746_LO33: Correct Answer: c EXPLANATIONS: The income statement summarizes a corporation's revenues and expenses for a fiscal period.

Q747_LO33: Correct Answer: c EXPLANATIONS: The income statement is also called a profit and loss (P&L) statement.

Q748_LO33: Correct Answer: b EXPLANATIONS: Operating profit = Net sales - operating costs

Q749_LO33: Correct Answer: b EXPLANATIONS: The PE ratio measures the amount of earnings a company makes compared with its current market value.

Q750_LO33: Correct Answer: c EXPLANATIONS: EPS = Net income / Number of outstanding shares

Q751_LO33: Correct Answer: c EXPLANATIONS: Nonoperating income contributes to operating income.

Q752_LO33: Correct Answer: b EXPLANATIONS: Taxable income = Operating income - Taxes

Q753_LO33: Correct Answer: b EXPLANATIONS: The PE ratio is expressed as a ratio (CMV / EPS).

Q754_LO33: Correct Answer: b EXPLANATIONS: Retained earnings = Earnings available to common - common dividends

Q755_LO33: Correct Answer: d EXPLANATIONS: The PE ratio is particularly useful during expansions.

Q756_LO33: Correct Answer: d EXPLANATIONS: EPS stands for earnings per share.

Q757_LO33: Correct Answer: a EXPLANATIONS: Net income after taxes = Taxable income - taxes

Q758_LO33: Correct Answer: a EXPLANATIONS: Net income after taxes = Taxable income - taxes - preferred dividends

Q759_LO33: Correct Answer: d EXPLANATIONS: A high PE ratio may suggest overvaluation, particularly during economic expansions.

Q760_LO33: Correct Answer: c EXPLANATIONS: The PE ratio evaluates market value compared to earnings.

UNIT 2 Understanding Products and Their Risks
Individual Securities – Equities

Q1_LO34: According to the definition, what is a security?
a. Tangible financial asset
b. Physical asset
c. Intangible financial asset
d. Liquid asset

HINTS: Focus on the key characteristic of a security.

Q2_LO34: How is a security represented?
a. Physical certificate or electronic record
b. Tangible certificate only
c. Electronic record only
d. Cash transaction only

HINTS: Recall the forms in which a security can be represented.

Q3_LO34: What legal case led to the creation of the Howey Test?
a. SEC v. W.J. Howey Co.
b. SEC v. Smith & Co.
c. SEC v. Johnson Corp.
d. SEC v. Anderson Ltd.

HINTS: Identify the case that established the Howey Test.

Q4_LO34: What is the Howey Test used for?
a. Identifying fraud cases
b. Defining a security
c. Evaluating market trends
d. Assessing company profits

HINTS: Recognize the purpose of the Howey Test.

Q5_LO34: According to the Howey Test, which of the following is a requirement for a security?
a. A tangible form
b. A common enterprise
c. A direct sale to the public
d. A sole individual's effort

HINTS: Identify one of the elements of the Howey Test.

Q6_LO34: What is NOT considered a security?
a. Stocks
b. Fixed annuities
c. Mutual funds
d. Options

HINTS: Recognize the non-security item from the examples.

Q7_LO34: What does the Howey Test state about the expectation of profit?
a. Optional criterion
b. Not considered
c. Mandatory criterion
d. Irrelevant criterion

HINTS: Focus on the aspect of profit in the Howey Test.

Q8_LO34: Which of the following is an example of a debt security?
a. Stocks
b. Options
c. Mutual funds
d. Bonds

HINTS: Identify the type of security represented by bonds.

Q9_LO34: According to the Howey Test, what must be the source of profit for a security?
a. Individual investors
b. Common enterprise
c. Government
d. Market fluctuations

HINTS: Recognize the requirement for the source of profit in the Howey Test.

Q10_LO34: What is NOT considered a security?
a. Depositary receipts
b. Commodities
c. Jumbo CDs
d. Life insurance

HINTS: Identify the non-security item from the examples.

Q11_LO34: What is the primary focus of the Howey Test?
a. Tangibility of assets
b. Identifying potential fraud
c. Defining a security
d. Government regulations

HINTS: Recognize the central purpose of the Howey Test.

Q12_LO34: Which of the following is considered a basic security?
a. Mutual funds
b. Jumbo CDs
c. Bonds
d. Variable life annuities

HINTS: Identify one of the basic securities .

Q13_LO34: What is the primary function of the Howey Test's "expectation of profit" criterion?
a. Assess investor knowledge
b. Evaluate market conditions
c. Determine if an investment is speculative
d. Identify potential scams

HINTS: Focus on the purpose of the "expectation of profit" criterion.

Q14_LO34: According to the definition, what may be done with a security?
a. Loaned only
b. Sold, bought, or gifted
c. Consumed
d. Used as collateral

HINTS: Identify the permissible actions with a security.

Q15_LO34: What type of financial asset is a security?
a. Tangible
b. Intangible
c. Hybrid
d. Non-financial

HINTS: Recall the classification of a security as a financial asset.

Q16_LO34: How is a security defined in the context of this course?
a. Tangible financial asset
b. Intangible financial asset
c. Real estate property
d. Electronic record

HINTS: Recall the definition of a security.

Q17_LO34: What legal case established the Howey Test for defining a security?
a. SEC v. W.J. Howey Co.
b. SEC v. Smith Bros.
c. SEC v. Johnson Inc.
d. SEC v. XYZ Corporation

HINTS: Identify the landmark case associated with the establishment of the Howey Test.

Q18_LO34: According to the Howey Test, what is a security?
a. Any financial asset
b. An investment of money with the expectation of profit
c. A tangible asset
d. An asset held in electronic record

HINTS: Understand the key elements of the Howey Test.

Q19_LO34: What is the second criterion of the Howey Test?
a. Investment of money
b. Common enterprise
c. Expectation of profit
d. Efforts of a third party

HINTS: Focus on the four-part criteria of the Howey Test.

Q20_LO34: In the context of the Howey Test, what does "common enterprise" refer to?
a. Shared business goals
b. A publicly traded company
c. A partnership agreement
d. The pooling of investors' money

HINTS: Understand the concept represented by "common enterprise" in the Howey Test.

Q21_LO34: Which of the following is an example of a security?
a. Cash and currency
b. Fixed annuities
c. Life insurance
d. Mutual funds

HINTS: Identify the example that is considered a security.

Q22_LO34: What is NOT considered a security in the context of the exam?
a. Cash and currency
b. Life insurance
c. Fixed annuities
d. Jumbo CDs

HINTS: Recognize the example that is not considered a security.

Q23_LO34: What are the two basic securities in the text?
a. Commodities and futures contracts
b. Options and depositary receipts
c. Stocks and bonds
d. Units in an investment

HINTS: Recall the fundamental securities discussed in the text.

Q24_LO34: What term is often used interchangeably with equities?
a. Options
b. Commodities
c. Bonds
d. Stocks

HINTS: Identify the term often used interchangeably with equities.

Q25_LO34: What type of asset is NOT included in the list of securities seen on the SIE Exam?
a. Variable life insurance
b. Depositary receipts
c. Real estate
d. Jumbo CDs

HINTS: Identify the type of asset excluded from the list of securities seen on the SIE Exam.

Q26_LO34: According to the Howey Test, what does "efforts of a third party" refer to?
a. Professional services
b. Managerial or entrepreneurial efforts
c. Legal representation
d. Investment advisory services

HINTS: Understand the meaning of "efforts of a third party" in the Howey Test.

Q27_LO34: What did the SEC accuse W.J. Howey Co. of in the case SEC v. W.J. Howey Co.?
a. Selling oranges directly to the public
b. Violating federal law by not registering a security
c. Insider trading
d. False advertising

HINTS: Identify the accusation made by the SEC in the case SEC v. W.J. Howey Co.

Q28_LO34: In the context of the Howey Test, what does "interest in the profits" refer to?
a. Ownership of physical assets
b. Ownership of a common enterprise
c. Stake in financial returns
d. Control over management

HINTS: Understand the significance of "interest in the profits" in the Howey Test.

Q29_LO34: What does the Howey Test define as a security regarding the expectation of profit?
a. Guaranteed profit
b. Speculative profit
c. Assured profit
d. Expected profit

HINTS: Identify how the Howey Test characterizes the expectation of profit.

Q30_LO34: What is the primary takeaway from the SEC v. W.J. Howey Co. case?
a. The definition of oranges as securities
b. The establishment of the Howey Test
c. The promotion of federal law
d. The protection of orange groves

HINTS: Recognize the significant outcome of the SEC v. W.J. Howey Co. case.
Q31_LO34: What is the primary way individual investors benefit from purchasing common stock?
a. Guaranteed interest
b. Capital appreciation and dividends
c. Fixed returns
d. Bond interest

HINTS: Recall the benefits of owning common stock.

Q32_LO34: What is the legal term for individuals who buy shares of stock in a company?
a. Bondholders
b. Stockholders or shareholders
c. Debt holders
d. Preferred shareholders

HINTS: Identify the legal term for individuals who own shares of stock.

Q33_LO34: What is the purpose of a corporate charter in the context of issuing stock?
a. Electing board members
b. Specifying the number of authorized shares
c. Approving dividends
d. Selecting company officers

HINTS: Understand the role of a corporate charter in the issuance of stock.

Q34_LO34: What happens if a company wants to issue more shares than authorized in the corporate charter?
a. No action is required
b. Obtain shareholder approval
c. Increase the number of outstanding shares
d. Issue the shares without restrictions

HINTS: Identify the correct procedure when a company wants to issue more shares than authorized.

Q35_LO34: What is the term for authorized stock that has been sold to investors?
a. Unissued stock
b. Outstanding stock
c. Issued stock
d. Treasury stock

HINTS: Recognize the term for authorized stock that has been sold.

Q36_LO34: What does outstanding stock include?
a. Unissued shares
b. Shares in the hands of investors
c. Treasury stock
d. Authorized shares

HINTS: Understand the composition of outstanding stock.

Q37_LO34: What is treasury stock?
a. Stock that pays dividends
b. Stock reacquired by a corporation
c. Preferred stock
d. Stock issued for the first time

HINTS: Identify the definition of treasury stock.

Q38_LO34: What rights does treasury stock carry in terms of voting and dividends?
a. Full voting and dividend rights
b. No voting or dividend rights
c. Voting rights only
d. Dividend rights only

HINTS: Recognize the limited rights of treasury stock.

Q39_LO34: How is market capitalization (market cap) calculated?
a. Outstanding shares + Issued shares
b. Outstanding shares × Current market value (CMV)
c. Issued shares - Outstanding shares
d. Treasury shares × CMV

HINTS: Recall the formula for calculating market capitalization.

Q40_LO34: What are large-cap stocks known for, especially those with a history of steady dividend payments?
a. Rapid growth
b. Blue-chip stocks
c. Speculative nature
d. Volatility

HINTS: Identify the characteristic associated with large-cap stocks.

Q41_LO34: What is the defining characteristic of mid-cap stocks?
a. High volatility
b. Small size
c. Reflect characteristics of both small and large caps
d. Slow growth

HINTS: Understand the defining characteristic of mid-cap stocks.

Q42_LO34: What distinguishes small-cap stocks?
a. High dividends
b. High growth potential
c. Listing on national exchanges
d. Orientation toward growth with minimal dividends

HINTS: Recognize the distinguishing feature of small-cap stocks.

Q43_LO34: What is the price range for a penny stock?
a. $1 to $3 per share
b. $3 to $5 per share
c. Less than $1 per share
d. $5 to $10 per share

HINTS: Identify the price range defining a penny stock.

Q44_LO34: According to SEC rules, what must customers receive before their initial transaction in a penny stock?
a. Stock certificate
b. Risk disclosure document
c. Dividend payment schedule
d. Market capitalization report

HINTS: Understand the requirement for customers dealing with penny stocks.

Q45_LO34: What determines whether an established customer is exempt from the suitability statement requirement for penny stocks?
a. Length of account holding
b. Number of penny stock purchases
c. Customer's trading frequency
d. Market capitalization preferences

HINTS: Recognize the criteria for an established customer to be exempt from the suitability statement requirement.

Q46_LO34: What is the primary reason a company issues (sells) stock?
a. Generate profits
b. Distribute dividends
c. Raise capital
d. Expand operations

HINTS: Recall the main purpose of issuing stock as discussed in the text.

Q47_LO34: What term is used to describe individuals who purchase shares of stock in a company?
a. Shareholders
b. Investors
c. Stakeholders
d. Stockholders

HINTS: Identify the term used for individuals who buy shares of stock.

Q48_LO34: What does each share of common stock entitle its owner to?
a. Guaranteed dividends
b. A portion of the company's earnings and a vote in major decisions
c. Executive privileges
d. Unlimited voting power

HINTS: Understand the rights associated with each share of common stock.

Q49_LO34: What is the purpose of a Board of Directors (BOD) in a corporation?
a. Day-to-day operations
b. Overseeing the company's business
c. Stock issuance
d. Setting stock prices

HINTS: Recognize the role of a Board of Directors in a corporation.

Q50_LO34: What does "authorized stock" refer to in a corporate context?
a. Issued stock
b. Outstanding stock
c. The total number of shares a company can issue
d. Stock held in treasury

HINTS: Understand the concept of authorized stock as explained in the text.

Q51_LO34: What is "treasury stock," and how is it treated regarding common shares?
a. Unissued stock
b. Reacquired stock held by the corporation
c. Outstanding stock
d. Preferred stock

HINTS: Identify the definition of treasury stock and its treatment regarding common shares.

Q52_LO34: What is "market capitalization" (market cap) based on?
a. Earnings per share
b. Dividend yield
c. Number of outstanding shares multiplied by current market value
d. Book value

HINTS: Recall the basis for determining market capitalization.

Q53_LO34: What are "large-cap stocks" characterized by?
a. Rapid growth and small market share
b. Being small, high-risk companies
c. Being the largest companies with a long history of steady dividends
d. Speculative and highly volatile nature

HINTS: Identify the characteristics of large-cap stocks as described in the text.

Q54_LO34: What are "penny stocks," and how are they defined?
a. Stocks trading at less than $10 per share
b. Unlisted securities trading at less than $5 per share
c. Small-cap stocks
d. Highly valuable and secure securities

HINTS: Understand the definition and characteristics of penny stocks.

Q55_LO34: Why is a risk disclosure document required for penny stocks?
a. They are speculative and carry high risk
b. They guarantee profits
c. They are listed on U.S. stock exchanges
d. They are government-regulated

HINTS: Recognize the reason behind the requirement of a risk disclosure document for penny stocks.

Q56_LO34: What do SEC rules require when a BD's representative contacts a potential customer to purchase penny stocks?
a. A signed and dated acknowledgment from the customer
b. Market quotations only
c. Commission details only
d. A summary of the company's history

HINTS: Understand the SEC rules related to cold-calling for penny stocks.

Q57_LO34: What exemption applies to established customers regarding penny stocks?
a. Exemption from trading penny stocks
b. Exemption from suitability statement requirement
c. Exemption from monthly account statements
d. Exemption from SEC regulations

HINTS: Identify the exemption that applies to established customers regarding penny stocks.

Q58_LO34: What is the primary concern of analysts regarding stock?
a. Treasury stock
b. Outstanding shares
c. Issued stock
d. Authorized but unissued stock

HINTS: Recognize the primary focus of analysts when considering stock.

Q59_LO34: What does "mid-cap stocks" reflect in terms of size?
a. Small and high-risk companies
b. Huge and rapidly growing companies
c. Companies too large to be small cap but not large cap
d. Companies with an average market capitalization

HINTS: Understand the size classification represented by mid-cap stocks.

Q60_LO34: What are "blue-chip stocks," and what is a characteristic associated with them?
a. Highly volatile stocks
b. Stocks with a long history of steady dividend payments
c. Small-cap stocks
d. Penny stocks

HINTS: Identify the characteristic associated with blue-chip stocks.

Q61_LO35: What are dividends?
a. Investments in the stock market
b. Distributions of a company's profits to shareholders
c. Stock options for employees
d. Bond interest payments

HINTS: Recall the definition of dividends from the text.

Q62_LO35: How are cash dividends typically distributed?
a. By product samples
b. By issuing additional shares
c. By check or brokerage account deposit
d. By reinvesting in research and development

HINTS: Identify the typical method of distributing cash dividends.

Q63_LO35: What is a stock dividend, and how does it affect shareholders?
a. A dividend paid in stock options
b. A dividend paid in cash
c. Additional shares issued to current stockholders
d. A one-time bonus payment

HINTS: Understand the concept of a stock dividend and its impact on shareholders.

Q64_LO35: When is a stock dividend taxable for shareholders?
a. Always taxable at the ordinary income tax rate
b. Never taxable
c. Taxable when shares are sold, based on the adjusted cost per share
d. Taxable only for high-income investors

HINTS: Recognize the taxation aspect related to stock dividends.

Q65_LO35: What is a product dividend?
a. A dividend paid in products
b. A unique form of stock option
c. A dividend paid to employees
d. A rare dividend payment method

HINTS: Identify the definition of a product dividend.

Q66_LO35: How are cash dividends taxed, and what influences the tax rate?
a. Always taxed as qualified dividends
b. Taxed at the investor's ordinary income tax rate or as qualified
c. Never taxed
d. Taxed only for low-income investors

HINTS: Understand the taxation of cash dividends and the factors influencing the tax rate.

Q67_LO35: What are the four dates associated with the dividend disbursing process?
a. Issue, sell, redeem, buyback
b. Record, purchase, tax, declaration
c. Declaration, ex-dividend, record, payable
d. Buy, hold, sell, settle

HINTS: Recall the four key dates related to the dividend disbursing process.

Q68_LO35: What is the ex-dividend date, and why is it important for investors?
a. The date the dividend is paid
b. The date stock must be purchased to qualify for the dividend
c. The date the dividend is declared
d. The date the record is set for dividend distribution

HINTS: Understand the significance of the ex-dividend date for investors.

Q69_LO35: What happens if a stock is purchased on or after the ex-dividend date?
a. Entitled to receive the dividend
b. Entitled to a higher dividend
c. Not entitled to receive the dividend
d. Receives a bonus dividend

HINTS: Recognize the outcome if a stock is purchased on or after the ex-dividend date.

Q70_LO35: What do stockholders of record receive on the record date?
a. Stock options
b. Dividend checks
c. Tax statements
d. New shares

HINTS: Identify what stockholders of record receive on the record date.

Q71_LO35: On which date are investors taxed for the tax year the dividend is paid?
a. Declaration date
b. Ex-dividend date
c. Record date
d. Payable date

HINTS: Understand when investors are taxed for the tax year the dividend is paid.

Q72_LO35: Why is the ex-dividend date set one business day before the record date?
a. Administrative convenience
b. To prevent dividend trading abuses
c. To favor long-term investors
d. For tax calculation purposes

HINTS: Recognize the reason for setting the ex-dividend date before the record date.

Q73_LO35: What must a customer do to qualify for a dividend?
a. Sell stock on or after the ex-dividend date
b. Hold stock on the ex-dividend date
c. Purchase stock on or after the record date
d. Buy stock two business days before the ex-dividend date

HINTS: Understand the actions required for a customer to qualify for a dividend.

Q74_LO35: What does the term "ex" in ex-dividend date signify?
a. Exclusive
b. Extra
c. Exponential
d. Without

HINTS: Recognize the meaning of the term "ex" in ex-dividend date.

Q75_LO35: Why might a company issue a stock dividend instead of a cash dividend?
a. To increase shareholder taxes
b. To reward long-term investors
c. To reduce the number of outstanding shares
d. To avoid dividend distribution altogether

HINTS: Identify a potential reason for a company to issue a stock dividend.

Q76_LO36: What right do common stockholders have concerning corporate directors?
a. Right to sell shares
b. Right to vote for corporate directors
c. Right to issue additional shares
d. Right to declare dividends

HINTS: Remember the rights of common stockholders discussed.

Q77_LO36: How can a stockholder cast votes, and what is a proxy?
a. In-person voting; an additional share
b. Statutory voting; an absentee ballot
c. Cumulative voting; a board candidate
d. Online voting; a stock certificate

HINTS: Recall the methods of casting votes and the concept of a proxy.

Q78_LO36: What is the key feature that allows common stock to be freely transferable?
a. Statutory voting
b. Cumulative voting
c. Limited liability
d. Proxy voting

HINTS: Identify the feature that enables the transferability of common stock.

Q79_LO36: How is the number of votes calculated for a stockholder?
a. One vote per shareholder
b. One vote per share owned
c. One vote per dividend received
d. One vote per proxy submitted

HINTS: Understand the basis for calculating the number of votes for a stockholder.

Q80_LO36: What is the difference between statutory voting and cumulative voting?
a. One allows online voting, the other does not
b. One requires a majority vote, the other does not
c. One allows allocation of total votes, the other does not
d. One is for board candidates, the other for stock dividends

HINTS: Differentiate between statutory voting and cumulative voting.

Q81_LO36: What rights do common stockholders have concerning the corporation's books?
a. Limited access to financial statements
b. Right to receive only audited statements
c. Right to examine BOD minutes and stockholder lists
d. No right to examine any corporate records

HINTS: Recognize the rights of common stockholders regarding corporate records.

Q82_LO36: What is the preemptive right of common stockholders?
a. Right to declare dividends
b. Right to maintain proportionate ownership
c. Right to issue additional shares
d. Right to prioritize in liquidation

HINTS: Identify the nature of the preemptive right of common stockholders.

Q83_LO36: What is capital appreciation in the context of common stock?
a. Increase in dividend payments
b. Increase in stock market value
c. Increase in bond interest
d. Increase in shareholder voting rights

HINTS: Understand the concept of capital appreciation in relation to common stock.

Q84_LO36: What is the historical role of common stock in portfolios as a hedge?
a. Hedge against market risk
b. Hedge against inflation
c. Hedge against interest rate changes
d. Hedge against dividend income

HINTS: Recognize the historical role of common stock in portfolios.

Q85_LO36: What is the significance of dividends for investors?
a. They are always guaranteed
b. They are a source of income
c. They decrease with time
d. They are only paid in stock

HINTS: Identify the importance of dividends for investors.

Q86_LO36: How do issuers pay dividends other than in cash?
a. Stock dividends
b. Proxy dividends
c. Statutory dividends
d. Cumulative dividends

HINTS: Recognize the alternatives to cash dividends discussed.

Q87_LO36: What is limited liability in the context of common stock ownership?
a. No liability for stockholders
b. Limited liability for stockholders
c. Liability for the entire investment
d. Liability for business debts

HINTS: Understand the concept of limited liability for common stockholders.

Q88_LO36: In case of a corporation's bankruptcy, what are common stockholders personally at risk for?
a. The entire investment
b. Business debts
c. Personal assets
d. Additional shares

HINTS: Identify the extent of personal risk for common stockholders in bankruptcy.

Q89_LO36: Why would you include common stock in a client's portfolio?
a. To maximize income
b. To minimize market risk
c. For potential capital appreciation, income, and as a hedge against inflation
d. To prioritize in liquidation

HINTS: Summarize the reasons for including common stock in a client's portfolio.

Q90_LO36: What is the priority of common stockholders in case of dissolution?
a. Senior to bondholders
b. Equal to preferred shareholders
c. Priority over preferred shareholders
d. Most junior class of investors

HINTS: Recognize the priority of common stockholders in liquidation.

Q91_LO36: What is a proxy in the context of common stock?
a. An online trading platform
b. An absentee ballot for voting
c. A stock trading strategy
d. A dividend calculation method

HINTS: Remember the term used for voting in absentee.

Q92_LO36: How are common stockholders' votes calculated?
a. One vote per share, regardless
b. Statutory voting only
c. Cumulative voting only
d. Either statutory or cumulative voting

HINTS: Understand the two types of voting rights common stockholders may have.

Q93_LO36: What is the preemptive right of common stockholders?
a. Right to unlimited stock purchases
b. Right to buy additional shares to maintain ownership
c. Right to vote on all corporate decisions
d. Right to dissolve the corporation

HINTS: Identify the feature that allows common stockholders to maintain their proportionate ownership.

Q94_LO36: What is capital appreciation in the context of common stock?
a. Increase in the dividend payout
b. Increase in stock market volatility
c. Increase in market price of securities
d. Increase in voting power

HINTS: Recognize the term associated with the increase in the market price of securities.

Q95_LO36: What is a significant reason for investors to invest in common stock?
a. Guaranteed returns
b. Potential capital appreciation
c. Fixed dividend income
d. Low market risk

HINTS: Identify a key reason for investors to include common stock in their portfolios.

Q96_LO36: What do common stockholders have a right to examine?
a. Minutes of shareholder meetings only
b. Minutes of BOD meetings only
c. Minutes of both BOD and shareholder meetings
d. Financial statements only

HINTS: Understand the rights of common stockholders related to examination.

Q97_LO36: How is growth (capital gains) realized for common stockholders?
a. Through voting rights
b. Through dividends
c. Through stock price appreciation
d. Through preemptive rights

HINTS: Identify the method through which common stockholders achieve growth.

Q98_LO36: Why might common stockholders include common stock in a portfolio?
a. Fixed income from dividends
b. Speculative returns
c. Hedging against bankruptcy
d. Potential capital appreciation

HINTS: Recognize the reasons for including common stock in a portfolio.

Q99_LO36: What is limited liability in the context of common stock ownership?
a. Limited ownership rights
b. Limited voting power
c. Personal assets not at risk in case of bankruptcy
d. Limited dividend income

HINTS: Understand the concept related to personal assets in case of bankruptcy.

Q100_LO36: In the event of bankruptcy, what is the maximum amount a common stockholder can lose?
a. Entire investment plus personal assets
b. Entire investment
c. Half of the investment
d. None of the investment

HINTS: Recognize the extent of potential loss for common stockholders in bankruptcy.

Q101_LO36: What is the risk associated with market risk in owning common stock?
a. Fluctuation in the stock's dividend
b. Fluctuation in the stock's price
c. Decrease in voting power
d. Decrease in market capitalization

HINTS: Identify the risk related to changes in the stock's price.

Q102_LO36: What determines whether common stockholders receive dividends?
a. Decision of the SEC
b. Decision of the bondholders
c. Decision of the BOD
d. Decision of the stock exchange

HINTS: Understand the authority responsible for determining dividend payments.

Q103_LO36: In the event of dissolution, who has priority over common stockholders?
a. Preferred stockholders
b. Bondholders
c. Both preferred stockholders and bondholders
d. Creditors

HINTS: Recognize the priority structure in the event of dissolution.

Q104_LO36: What is a common characteristic of common stockholders in a company?
a. Senior class of investors
b. Junior class of investors
c. Equal priority with bondholders
d. Exempt from liquidation rules

HINTS: Identify the class classification of common stockholders in a company.

Q105_LO36: What is a residual right in the context of common stockholders?
a. Right to unlimited dividends
b. Right to vote on all corporate decisions
c. Right to corporate assets upon dissolution
d. Right to issue new shares

HINTS: Recognize the right associated with corporate assets in case of dissolution.

Q106_LO37: What is the purpose of stock rights (preemptive rights)?
a. To increase voting power
b. To maintain proportionate ownership
c. To sell shares at a premium
d. To provide voting privileges

HINTS: Remember the term associated with maintaining ownership shares.

Q107_LO37: In a rights offering, how are rights valued?
a. They are valued based on voting power
b. They are valued below the market price
c. They are valued at a premium
d. They are not valued separately

HINTS: Identify the characteristic of rights valuation in a rights offering.

Q108_LO37: How many rights do existing shareholders receive per share owned?
a. One
b. Two
c. Three
d. Four

HINTS: Recall the number of rights received per share owned in a rights offering.

Q109_LO37: What determines the number of rights required to purchase a new share in a rights offering?
a. Total market capitalization
b. Number of outstanding shares and new shares offered
c. Stock price volatility
d. Dividend yield

HINTS: Understand the factors influencing the number of rights required.

Q110_LO37: What is one option for a stockholder who receives rights but doesn't wish to buy new shares?
a. Sell the rights in the secondary market
b. Exchange the rights for voting power
c. Hold the rights indefinitely
d. Convert the rights into warrants

HINTS: Recognize the alternative for stockholders not wishing to buy new shares.

Q111_LO37: What is a warrant in the context of securities?
a. A right to sell securities
b. A long-term certificate granting purchase rights
c. A voting privilege
d. A negotiable security

HINTS: Identify the characteristic of a warrant related to purchase rights.

Q112_LO37: How does the exercise price of a warrant compare to the market value at the time of issuance?
a. Lower than the market value
b. Equal to the market value
c. Higher than the market value
d. Unrelated to market value

HINTS: Understand the relationship between the exercise price of a warrant and the market value at issuance.

Q113_LO37: Why are warrants often offered along with other securities like bonds or preferred stock?
a. To decrease market volatility
b. To increase voting rights
c. To make the securities more attractive
d. To limit ownership concentration

HINTS: Recognize the purpose of offering warrants with other securities.

Q114_LO37: In what form are warrants commonly bundled with other securities?
a. Packages
b. Units
c. Bundles
d. Bundled securities

HINTS: Identify the common term used for the combination of warrants with other securities.

Q115_LO37: What is the typical time frame for exercising a warrant?
a. Short-term
b. Medium-term
c. Long-term
d. Unlimited

HINTS: Understand the usual time frame associated with warrant exercise.

Q116_LO37: What is the purpose of Rule 144 in securities regulation?
a. To restrict short-selling
b. To regulate stock rights offerings
c. To govern the resale of restricted securities
d. To determine dividend payments

HINTS: Recognize the area of securities regulation covered by Rule 144.

Q117_LO37: When can an investor resell restricted securities under Rule 144?
a. Anytime after purchase
b. Only during trading hours
c. After a specified holding period
d. Before the expiration date

HINTS: Identify the condition for the resale of restricted securities under Rule 144.

Q118_LO37: What is the holding period requirement for restricted securities under Rule 144?
a. 30 days
b. 60 days
c. 90 days
d. 120 days

HINTS: Recall the holding period specified by Rule 144 for restricted securities.

Q119_LO37: What information must be filed with the SEC for the resale of restricted securities under Rule 144?
a. Proxy statement
b. Form 144
c. Annual report
d. Financial statements

HINTS: Recognize the required filing related to the resale of restricted securities under Rule 144.

Q120_LO37: Why might an investor use Rule 144 when selling restricted securities?
a. To avoid market volatility
b. To speed up the resale process
c. To ensure a higher selling price
d. To comply with legal requirements

HINTS: Understand the purpose of using Rule 144 in selling restricted securities.

Q121_LO38: What does Rule 144 apply to?
a. All stock transactions
b. Standard stock offerings
c. Nonstandard offerings and restricted securities
d. Registered public offerings

HINTS: Recall the scope of Rule 144.

Q122_LO38: When are securities considered restricted?
a. When purchased in a public offering
b. When held for less than three months
c. When purchased in a private placement
d. When traded on an exchange

HINTS: Identify the condition for securities to be considered restricted.

Q123_LO38: How long must restricted stock be held fully paid before selling according to Rule 144?
a. Three months
b. Six months
c. Nine months
d. Twelve months

HINTS: Recall the holding period requirement for restricted stock under Rule 144.

Q124_LO38: What is a characteristic of restricted stock when issued?
a. No holding period restriction
b. No need for an issuer's release
c. Bears a restrictive legend
d. Immediate trading permission

HINTS: Recognize the feature associated with restricted stock when issued.

Q125_LO38: What must the issuer do before restricted stock can be sold freely?
a. Issue new stock certificates
b. Release the restriction
c. Sell additional shares
d. Notify the SEC

HINTS: Identify the action required by the issuer before restricted stock can be sold freely.

Q126_LO38: What does the phrase "the sale effectively registers the stock" mean?
a. The stock is registered with the SEC
b. The stock is unrestricted for resale
c. The sale is reported to FINRA
d. The sale requires shareholder approval

HINTS: Understand the meaning of the phrase related to the sale of restricted stock.

Q127_LO38: Who are considered control persons or affiliates under Rule 144?
a. Any large shareholder
b. Directors, officers, or 5% stockholders
c. All employees of the company
d. Any shareholder holding over 100 shares

HINTS: Identify the category of individuals classified as control persons or affiliates.

Q128_LO38: What must a control person complete when selling shares under Rule 144?
a. Form 10-K
b. Form 144
c. Form 8-K
d. Form S-1

HINTS: Recall the form used by control persons when selling shares under Rule 144.

Q129_LO38: How long is the period for which the volume limitations under Rule 144 are calculated?
a. 30 days
b. 60 days
c. 90 days
d. 120 days

HINTS: Recall the time frame for calculating volume limitations under Rule 144.

Q130_LO38: What are the volume limitations based on under Rule 144?
a. 1% of the issuer's outstanding shares
b. 5% of the issuer's outstanding shares
c. The average weekly trading volume
d. Total market capitalization

HINTS: Identify the factors used in calculating volume limitations under Rule 144.

Q131_LO38: What is the purpose of volume limitations under Rule 144?
a. To restrict control persons from selling shares
b. To control market volatility
c. To prevent insider trading
d. To balance supply and demand

HINTS: Recognize the regulatory objective achieved by volume limitations under Rule 144.

Q132_LO38: Why do families aggregate their positions when determining control ownership?
a. To reduce reporting requirements
b. To simplify voting procedures
c. To avoid restrictions on stock sales
d. To determine the percentage of ownership

HINTS: Understand the purpose of aggregating family positions in control ownership calculations.

Q133_LO38: In Rule 144, what happens if a control person wishes to sell more shares than the volume limitations allow?
a. They must wait for an SEC waiver
b. They can sell additional shares privately
c. They must file an amended Form 144
d. They are prohibited from selling additional shares

HINTS: Identify the action required if a control person wishes to sell more shares than the volume limitations allow.

Q134_LO38: What is the consequence if a control person fails to file Form 144?
a. Loss of voting rights
b. Temporary suspension from trading
c. Fine by the SEC
d. Prohibition from future stock sales

HINTS: Recognize the consequence of failing to file Form 144 for a control person.

Q135_LO38: Why is Rule 144 important in the context of securities regulation?
a. To promote speculative trading
b. To protect the interests of control persons
c. To ensure fair and transparent markets
d. To restrict public access to stock

HINTS: Understand the broader purpose of Rule 144 in securities regulation.

Correct Answers & Explanations
Individual Securities – Equities

Q1_LO34: Correct Answer: c EXPLANATIONS: A security is an intangible financial asset.

Q2_LO34: Correct Answer: a EXPLANATIONS: A security may be represented by a paper certificate or held in an electronic record.

Q3_LO34: Correct Answer: a EXPLANATIONS: The Howey Test originated from SEC v. W.J. Howey Co.

Q4_LO34: Correct Answer: b EXPLANATIONS: The Howey Test is used to define what constitutes a security.

Q5_LO34: Correct Answer: b EXPLANATIONS: A security requires a common enterprise.

Q6_LO34: Correct Answer: b EXPLANATIONS: Fixed annuities are not considered securities.

Q7_LO34: Correct Answer: c EXPLANATIONS: The Howey Test requires an expectation of profit.

Q8_LO34: Correct Answer: d EXPLANATIONS: Bonds are an example of debt securities.

Q9_LO34: Correct Answer: b EXPLANATIONS: Profit must be through the efforts of a common enterprise.

Q10_LO34: Correct Answer: d EXPLANATIONS: Life insurance is not considered a security.

Q11_LO34: Correct Answer: c EXPLANATIONS: The Howey Test is used to define what constitutes a security.

Q12_LO34: Correct Answer: c EXPLANATIONS: Bonds are considered basic securities.

Q13_LO34: Correct Answer: c EXPLANATIONS: The "expectation of profit" criterion helps determine if an investment is speculative.

Q14_LO34: Correct Answer: b EXPLANATIONS: A security may be bought, sold, or gifted between persons.

Q15_LO34: Correct Answer: b EXPLANATIONS: A security is classified as an intangible financial asset.

Q16_LO34: Correct Answer: b EXPLANATIONS: A security is an intangible financial asset that may be bought, sold, or gifted and may be represented by a paper certificate or held in an electronic record.

Q17_LO34: Correct Answer: a EXPLANATIONS: The Howey Test was established in the case SEC v. W.J. Howey Co.

Q18_LO34: Correct Answer: b EXPLANATIONS: A security, according to the Howey Test, is an investment of money with the expectation of profit.

Q19_LO34: Correct Answer: b EXPLANATIONS: The second criterion is a common enterprise.

Q20_LO34: Correct Answer: d EXPLANATIONS: Common enterprise in the Howey Test refers to the pooling of investors' money.

Q21_LO34: Correct Answer: d EXPLANATIONS: Mutual funds are considered securities.

Q22_LO34: Correct Answer: a EXPLANATIONS: Cash and currency are not considered securities in the context of the exam.

Q23_LO34: Correct Answer: c EXPLANATIONS: The two basic securities are stocks (equities) and bonds (debt).

Q24_LO34: Correct Answer: d EXPLANATIONS: Equities are often referred to as stocks.

Q25_LO34: Correct Answer: c EXPLANATIONS: Real estate is not typically considered a security in this context.

Q26_LO34: Correct Answer: b EXPLANATIONS: Efforts of a third party refer to managerial or entrepreneurial efforts.

Q27_LO34: Correct Answer: b EXPLANATIONS: The SEC accused W.J. Howey Co. of violating federal law by not registering a security.

Q28_LO34: Correct Answer: c EXPLANATIONS: Interest in the profits refers to a stake in financial returns.

Q29_LO34: Correct Answer: d EXPLANATIONS: A security is an investment with the expectation of profit.

Q30_LO34: Correct Answer: b EXPLANATIONS: The primary takeaway is the establishment of the Howey Test for defining securities.

Q31_LO34: Correct Answer: b EXPLANATIONS: Common stock allows investors to benefit from capital appreciation and dividends.

Q32_LO34: Correct Answer: b EXPLANATIONS: Individuals who buy shares of stock are called stockholders or shareholders.

Q33_LO34: Correct Answer: b EXPLANATIONS: The corporate charter specifies the number of authorized shares a company can issue.

Q34_LO34: Correct Answer: b EXPLANATIONS: Increasing the authorized shares requires shareholder approval.

Q35_LO34: Correct Answer: c EXPLANATIONS: Issued stock is authorized stock that has been sold to investors.

Q36_LO34: Correct Answer: b EXPLANATIONS: Outstanding stock includes shares that are in the hands of investors.

Q37_LO34: Correct Answer: b EXPLANATIONS: Treasury stock is stock that has been issued and subsequently reacquired by a corporation.

Q38_LO34: Correct Answer: b EXPLANATIONS: Treasury stock does not carry the rights of outstanding common shares, such as voting rights and the right to receive dividends.

Q39_LO34: Correct Answer: b EXPLANATIONS: Market cap is determined by multiplying outstanding shares by the current market value (CMV) per share.

Q40_LO34: Correct Answer: b EXPLANATIONS: Large-cap stocks, especially those with a history of steady dividend payments, are often called blue-chip stocks.

Q41_LO34: Correct Answer: c EXPLANATIONS: Mid-cap stocks tend to reflect characteristics of both small and large caps.

Q42_LO34: Correct Answer: d EXPLANATIONS: Small-cap stocks are oriented toward growth and produce minimal dividends.

Q43_LO34: Correct Answer: c EXPLANATIONS: A penny stock is an unlisted security trading at less than $5 per share.

Q44_LO34: Correct Answer: b EXPLANATIONS: SEC rules require customers to receive a risk disclosure document before their initial transaction in a penny stock.

Q45_LO34: Correct Answer: b EXPLANATIONS: An established customer is exempt if they have made at least three penny stock purchases of different issuers on different days.

Q46_LO34: Correct Answer: c EXPLANATIONS: A company issues stock primarily to raise capital.

Q47_LO34: Correct Answer: a EXPLANATIONS: Individuals who buy shares of stock are referred to as shareholders.

Q48_LO34: Correct Answer: b EXPLANATIONS: Each share entitles its owner to a portion of the company's earnings and a vote in major management decisions.

Q49_LO34: Correct Answer: b EXPLANATIONS: The BOD oversees the company's business, and stockholders elect individuals to the board.

Q50_LO34: Correct Answer: c EXPLANATIONS: Authorized stock refers to the total number of shares a company can issue as specified in its corporate charter.

Q51_LO34: Correct Answer: b EXPLANATIONS: Treasury stock is reacquired stock held by the corporation, and it does not carry the rights of outstanding common shares.

Q52_LO34: Correct Answer: c EXPLANATIONS: Market cap is determined by multiplying the number of outstanding shares by the current market value of a share.

Q53_LO34: Correct Answer: c EXPLANATIONS: Large-cap stocks are characterized by being the largest companies with a long history of steady dividends.

Q54_LO34: Correct Answer: b EXPLANATIONS: Penny stocks are unlisted securities trading at less than $5 per share.

Q55_LO34: Correct Answer: a EXPLANATIONS: Penny stocks are considered highly speculative and carry high risk.

Q56_LO34: Correct Answer: a EXPLANATIONS: SEC rules require a signed and dated acknowledgment from the customer before initial penny stock trades may be placed.

Q57_LO34: Correct Answer: b EXPLANATIONS: Established customers are exempt from the suitability statement requirement but not from the disclosure requirements.

Q58_LO34: Correct Answer: b EXPLANATIONS: Analysts are primarily concerned with outstanding shares when analyzing stock.

Q59_LO34: Correct Answer: c EXPLANATIONS: Mid-cap stocks reflect companies that are too large to be small cap but not large cap.

Q60_LO34: Correct Answer: b EXPLANATIONS: Blue-chip stocks are characterized by a long history of steady dividend payments.

Q61_LO35: Correct Answer: b EXPLANATIONS: Dividends are distributions of a company's profits to its shareholders.

Q62_LO35: Correct Answer: c EXPLANATIONS: Cash dividends are distributed by check or automatically deposited to a brokerage account.

Q63_LO35: Correct Answer: c EXPLANATIONS: A stock dividend involves issuing additional shares of common stock to current stockholders.

Q64_LO35: Correct Answer: c EXPLANATIONS: The stock dividend itself is not taxable, but the adjusted cost per share (new cost basis) impacts tax consequences when shares are sold.

Q65_LO35: Correct Answer: a EXPLANATIONS: Though rare, some companies pay a dividend by sending a sample of the company's product to shareholders.

Q66_LO35: Correct Answer: b EXPLANATIONS: Cash dividends may be taxed as either nonqualified or as qualified, and the tax rate depends on the investor's income tax bracket.

Q67_LO35: Correct Answer: c EXPLANATIONS: The four dates are declaration, ex-dividend, record, and payable.

Q68_LO35: Correct Answer: b EXPLANATIONS: The ex-dividend date is one business day before the record date, and investors must purchase stock by this date to qualify for the dividend.

Q69_LO35: Correct Answer: c EXPLANATIONS: If purchased on or after the ex-date, the new owner is not entitled to receive the dividend.

Q70_LO35: Correct Answer: b EXPLANATIONS: Stockholders of record receive dividend checks on the record date.

Q71_LO35: Correct Answer: d EXPLANATIONS: Investors are taxed based on the payable date.

Q72_LO35: Correct Answer: b EXPLANATIONS: The ex-dividend date is set one business day before the record date to prevent dividend trading abuses.

Q73_LO35: Correct Answer: d EXPLANATIONS: To qualify for a dividend, the stock must be purchased two business days before the ex-dividend date.

Q74_LO35: Correct Answer: d EXPLANATIONS: The term "ex" signifies without, indicating that the stock is purchased without the dividend on this date.

Q75_LO35: Correct Answer: b EXPLANATIONS: A company might issue a stock dividend to reinvest profits for business purposes, especially common among growth companies focused on research and development.

Q76_LO36: Correct Answer: b EXPLANATIONS: Common stockholders have the right to vote for corporate directors.

Q77_LO36: Correct Answer: b EXPLANATIONS: A proxy is an absentee ballot made available for stockholders who want to vote but can't attend the shareholder meeting.

Q78_LO36: Correct Answer: c EXPLANATIONS: Common stock is freely transferable without permission of the corporation, a key feature.

Q79_LO36: Correct Answer: b EXPLANATIONS: A stockholder can cast one vote per share owned.

Q80_LO36: Correct Answer: c EXPLANATIONS: Cumulative voting allows stockholders to allocate their total votes in any manner they choose.

Q81_LO36: Correct Answer: c EXPLANATIONS: Common stockholders have the right to examine BOD minutes and stockholder lists.

Q82_LO36: Correct Answer: b EXPLANATIONS: Common stockholders have the preemptive right to maintain their proportionate share of ownership.

Q83_LO36: Correct Answer: b EXPLANATIONS: Capital appreciation refers to an increase in the market price of securities, including common stock.

Q84_LO36: Correct Answer: b EXPLANATIONS: Common stock is included as a hedge against inflation in portfolios with a long-term investment horizon.

Q85_LO36: Correct Answer: b EXPLANATIONS: Dividends are a major reason many people invest in stocks as they provide a source of income.

Q86_LO36: Correct Answer: a EXPLANATIONS: Issuers may also pay stock dividends or property dividends.

Q87_LO36: Correct Answer: b EXPLANATIONS: Limited liability means a shareholder's personal assets are not at risk in the event of a corporation's bankruptcy.

Q88_LO36: Correct Answer: a EXPLANATIONS: Common stockholders are personally at risk only for the amount they invested.

Q89_LO36: Correct Answer: c EXPLANATIONS: Common stock is included for potential capital appreciation, income from dividends, and as a hedge against inflation.

Q90_LO36: Correct Answer: d EXPLANATIONS: Common stockholders are the most junior class of investors in a company.

Q91_LO36: Correct Answer: b EXPLANATIONS: A proxy is an absentee ballot made available for shareholders who want to vote but can't attend the meeting.

Q92_LO36: Correct Answer: d EXPLANATIONS: Common stockholders may have either statutory or cumulative voting rights.

Q93_LO36: Correct Answer: b EXPLANATIONS: The preemptive right allows common stockholders to buy additional shares to maintain their proportionate ownership.

Q94_LO36: Correct Answer: c EXPLANATIONS: Capital appreciation refers to the increase in the market price of securities.

Q95_LO36: Correct Answer: b
EXPLANATIONS: Potential capital appreciation is a major reason for investing in common stock.

Q96_LO36: Correct Answer: c EXPLANATIONS: Common stockholders have the right to examine the minutes of meetings of the BOD and the list of stockholders.

Q97_LO36: Correct Answer: c EXPLANATIONS: Growth or capital appreciation is realized through an increase in the market price of common stock.

Q98_LO36: Correct Answer: d EXPLANATIONS: Common stock might be included for potential capital appreciation, income from dividends, and as a hedge against inflation.

Q99_LO36: Correct Answer: c EXPLANATIONS: Limited liability means personal assets are not at risk in the event of a corporation's bankruptcy.

Q100_LO36: Correct Answer: b EXPLANATIONS: Common stockholders can lose the entire amount invested but are not forced to sell personal assets.

Q101_LO36: Correct Answer: b EXPLANATIONS: Market risk is the chance that a stock will decline in price.

Q102_LO36: Correct Answer: c EXPLANATIONS: The BOD decides whether to pay dividends to common stockholders.

Q103_LO36: Correct Answer: c EXPLANATIONS: Preferred stockholders and bondholders have priority over common stockholders in dissolution.

Q104_LO36: Correct Answer: b EXPLANATIONS: Common stockholders are considered the most junior class of investors.

Q105_LO36: Correct Answer: c EXPLANATIONS: Common stockholders have a residual right to corporate assets upon dissolution after debts and preferred stock are paid.

Q106_LO37: Correct Answer: b EXPLANATIONS: Stock rights, or preemptive rights, allow existing stockholders to maintain their proportionate ownership shares.

Q107_LO37: Correct Answer: b EXPLANATIONS: Rights in a rights offering are valued separately and are typically below the market price.

Q108_LO37: Correct Answer: a EXPLANATIONS: Existing shareholders receive one right per share owned.

Q109_LO37: Correct Answer: b EXPLANATIONS: The number of rights required depends on the number of outstanding shares and the number of new shares offered.

Q110_LO37: Correct Answer: a EXPLANATIONS: Stockholders can sell the rights in the secondary market for profit.

Q111_LO37: Correct Answer: b EXPLANATIONS: A warrant is a certificate granting its owner the right to purchase securities at a specified price in the future.

Q112_LO37: Correct Answer: c EXPLANATIONS: The exercise price of a warrant is usually higher than the market value at the time of issuance.

Q113_LO37: Correct Answer: c EXPLANATIONS: Warrants are offered as sweeteners to make other securities, like bonds or preferred stock, more attractive.

Q114_LO37: Correct Answer: b EXPLANATIONS: Warrants are often bundled with other securities as units.

Q115_LO37: Correct Answer: c EXPLANATIONS: Warrants are usually long-term instruments with the option to buy shares at a later date.

Q116_LO37: Correct Answer: c EXPLANATIONS: Rule 144 governs the resale of restricted securities.

Q117_LO37: Correct Answer: c EXPLANATIONS: An investor can resell restricted securities after a specified holding period.

Q118_LO37: Correct Answer: c EXPLANATIONS: Rule 144 typically requires a holding period of 90 days for restricted securities.

Q119_LO37: Correct Answer: b EXPLANATIONS: Investors must file Form 144 with the SEC for the resale of restricted securities.

Q120_LO37: Correct Answer: d EXPLANATIONS: Investors use Rule 144 to comply with legal requirements when selling restricted securities.

Q121_LO38: Correct Answer: c EXPLANATIONS: Rule 144 applies to nonstandard offerings and restricted securities.

Q122_LO38: Correct Answer: c EXPLANATIONS: Restricted securities are those acquired through means other than a registered public offering, such as a private placement.

Q123_LO38: Correct Answer: b EXPLANATIONS: Rule 144 requires holding restricted stock fully paid for six months before selling.

Q124_LO38: Correct Answer: c EXPLANATIONS: Restricted stock when issued bears a restrictive legend on the certificate indicating the holding period restriction.

Q125_LO38: Correct Answer: b EXPLANATIONS: The issuer must release (remove) the restriction before restricted stock can be sold freely.

Q126_LO38: Correct Answer: b EXPLANATIONS: The phrase means that the stock is unrestricted for resale after the sale.

Q127_LO38: Correct Answer: b EXPLANATIONS: Control persons or affiliates include directors, officers, or persons who own or control 10% or more of the issuer's voting stock.

Q128_LO38: Correct Answer: b EXPLANATIONS: Control persons must complete Form 144.

Q129_LO38: Correct Answer: c EXPLANATIONS: Volume limitations are calculated over a 90-day period under Rule 144.

Q130_LO38: Correct Answer: c EXPLANATIONS: The volume limitations are based on the greater of 1% of the outstanding shares or the average weekly trading volume over the most recent four weeks.

Q131_LO38: Correct Answer: c EXPLANATIONS: Volume limitations aim to regulate the resale of control stock and prevent market manipulation.

Q132_LO38: Correct Answer: d EXPLANATIONS: Families aggregate their positions to determine the percentage of ownership for control purposes.

Q133_LO38: Correct Answer: a EXPLANATIONS: The control person must wait for an SEC waiver to exceed volume limitations.

Q134_LO38: Correct Answer: d EXPLANATIONS: Failure to file Form 144 may result in a prohibition from future stock sales for the control person.

Q135_LO38: Correct Answer: c EXPLANATIONS: Rule 144 is important to ensure fair and transparent markets by regulating the resale of restricted securities and control stock.

Individual Securities – ADRs AND PREFERRED STOCK

Q136_LO39: What is the primary purpose of American depositary receipts (ADRs)?
a. Simplify foreign investing for non-U.S. investors
b. Facilitate currency conversion for U.S. investors
c. Diversify holdings for foreign companies
d. Simplify foreign investing for U.S. investors

HINTS: Identify the main purpose of ADRs.

Q137_LO39: How are ADRs created?
a. By purchasing shares in the U.S. market
b. By depositing foreign currency in a U.S. bank
c. By purchasing shares in the foreign company's home market
d. By converting U.S. dollars to foreign currency

HINTS: Recall the process of creating ADRs.

Q138_LO39: Where are ADRs typically listed for trading?
a. Only on foreign stock exchanges
b. Exclusively on over-the-counter (OTC) markets
c. Only on the New York Stock Exchange (NYSE) or Nasdaq
d. On any stock exchange globally

HINTS: Identify the common listing locations for ADRs.

Q139_LO39: How do ADRs trade and settle?
a. T+0 settlement
b. T+1 settlement
c. T+2 settlement
d. T+3 settlement

HINTS: Recall the settlement period for ADRs.

Q140_LO39: What is the benefit of ADRs trading in U.S. dollars for investors?
a. Lower transaction costs
b. Reduced currency conversion complications
c. Higher dividend payouts
d. Faster trade execution

HINTS: Recognize the advantage of ADRs trading in U.S. dollars.

Q141_LO39: How does ADR taxation work for U.S. investors?
a. Dividends are tax-exempt
b. Dividends are subject to a withholding tax
c. Capital gains are taxed by the home country
d. Capital gains are tax-exempt

HINTS: Understand the tax implications for U.S. investors holding ADRs.

Q142_LO39: What is the impact of currency exchange rate changes on ADR dividends?
a. No impact
b. Dividends increase
c. Dividends decrease
d. Dividends invariable

HINTS: Identify the effect of currency exchange rate changes on ADR dividends.

Q143_LO39: In what currency are ADR dividends paid?
a. Home currency of the ADR issuer
b. U.S. dollars
c. Foreign currency
d. Bitcoin

HINTS: Recognize the currency in which ADR dividends are paid.

Q144_LO39: What risk are ADRs specifically designed to eliminate?
a. Market risk
b. Currency risk
c. Interest rate risk
d. Political risk

HINTS: Identify the risk that ADRs aim to eliminate.

Q145_LO39: What is the consequence of the value of the ADR being influenced by currency swings?
a. Higher dividends
b. Lower dividends
c. Unchanged dividends
d. No impact on dividends

HINTS: Recognize the impact of currency swings on the value of ADRs.

Q146_LO39: Why do ADR issuers filing periodic reports with the SEC provide comfort to buyers?
a. To ensure tax-exempt status
b. To increase dividend payouts
c. To demonstrate regulatory compliance
d. To reduce listing fees

HINTS: Understand the reason ADR issuers filing reports with the SEC provides comfort.

Q147_LO39: What is the purpose of trading ADRs in a familiar, well-regulated setting?
a. To increase transaction costs
b. To attract foreign investors
c. To simplify tax reporting
d. To provide comfort to U.S. investors

HINTS: Identify the benefit of trading ADRs in a familiar, well-regulated setting.

Q148_LO39: What situation exposes investors holding ADRs to political risk?
a. Currency exchange rate changes
b. Dividend fluctuations
c. ADRs trading over the counter
d. ADR issuer based in an unstable country

HINTS: Recognize the condition that exposes ADR investors to political risk.

Q149_LO39: What happens if ADRs are traded over the counter (OTC)?
a. Lower liquidity
b. Higher transaction costs
c. Faster trade execution
d. Reduced investor confidence

HINTS: Identify a characteristic associated with trading ADRs over the counter.

Q150_LO39: How do ADRs contribute to foreign companies attracting a U.S. investor base?
a. By increasing dividend payouts
b. By simplifying tax reporting
c. By providing comfort through SEC filings
d. By reducing listing fees

HINTS: Recognize the factor that contributes to foreign companies attracting a U.S. investor base through ADRs.

Q151_LO40: What does the rate of return on preferred stock resemble?
a. Variable
b. Fixed
c. Fluctuating
d. Equity-based

HINTS: Recall the characteristic of the rate of return on preferred stock.

Q152_LO40: What is the typical par value assumed for preferred stock?
a. $50
b. $75
c. $100
d. $150

HINTS: Remember the standard par value for preferred stock.

Q153_LO40: Which group of shareholders generally has no voting rights in a corporation?
a. Common shareholders
b. Preferred shareholders
c. Cumulative shareholders
d. Callable shareholders

HINTS: Identify the shareholders with no voting rights.

Q154_LO40: When are owners of preferred shares paid dividends in relation to common shareholders?
a. After common shareholders
b. Simultaneously with common shareholders
c. Before common shareholders
d. Alongside cumulative shareholders

HINTS: Recognize the dividend preference order of preferred shareholders.

Q155_LO40: What risk involves the potential loss of purchasing power due to inflation?
a. Interest rate sensitivity
b. Decreased dividend income
c. Purchasing power risk
d. Priority at dissolution

HINTS: Identify the risk associated with loss of purchasing power.

Q156_LO40: In what scenario do preferred shareholders receive current dividends and accumulated dividends in arrears?
a. When dividends are reduced
b. During bankruptcy proceedings
c. When cumulative preferred stock is called
d. After resumption of dividend payments

HINTS: Understand the situation where accumulated dividends are paid.

Q157_LO40: What is the purpose of callable preferred stock for corporations?
a. To increase fixed-dividend obligations
b. To reduce the cost of money
c. To raise interest rates
d. To decrease refinancing options

HINTS: Recognize the purpose of issuing callable preferred stock.

Q158_LO40: What happens to dividend payments when a corporation calls a preferred stock?
a. Dividend payments increase
b. Dividend payments cease
c. Dividend payments become variable
d. Dividend payments double

HINTS: Understand the impact on dividend payments when a preferred stock is called.

Q159_LO40: Why might convertible preferred stock have a lower stated dividend rate?
a. Higher risk
b. Lower quality
c. Potential for capital gain
d. Increased volatility

HINTS: Identify the reason for a lower stated dividend rate on convertible preferred stock.

Q160_LO40: What is the characteristic of adjustable-rate preferred stock?
a. Fixed dividend rates
b. Variable dividend rates
c. No dividends
d. Cumulative dividends

HINTS: Recognize a key feature of adjustable-rate preferred stock.

Q161_LO40: In addition to fixed dividends, what do participating preferred stockholders receive?
a. Priority in dissolution
b. Voting rights
c. Share of corporate profits
d. Cumulative dividends

HINTS: Identify the additional benefit for participating preferred stockholders.

Q162_LO40: What is the purpose of issuing participating preferred stock?
a. To increase dividend payouts
b. To attract income-oriented investors
c. To share corporate profits
d. To reduce refinancing costs

HINTS: Recognize the purpose of issuing participating preferred stock.

Q163_LO40: What privilege does a callable preferred stock grant to a corporation?
a. Increased fixed-dividend obligations
b. Lower refinancing options
c. The right to buy back shares
d. Higher dividend payments

HINTS: Understand the privilege granted to a corporation by callable preferred stock.

Q164_LO40: What risk is associated with the potential decline in the value of preferred shares when interest rates rise?
a. Purchasing power risk
b. Interest rate sensitivity
c. Priority at dissolution
d. Decreased dividend income

HINTS: Identify the risk related to the decline in value with rising interest rates.

Q165_LO40: What is the dividend payment status for straight (noncumulative) preferred stock?
a. Dividends are paid in arrears
b. Dividends are cumulative
c. Dividends are variable
d. Missed dividends are not paid

HINTS: Recognize the dividend payment status for straight preferred stock.

Q166_LO40: What is a key attraction for income-oriented investors in preferred stock?
a. Voting rights
b. Fixed rate of return
c. Preemptive rights
d. Growth potential

HINTS: Identify a characteristic that is attractive to income-oriented investors.

Q167_LO40: What is the typical par value assumed for preferred stock unless stated otherwise?
a. $50
b. $75
c. $100
d. $150

HINTS: Recall the typical par value assumed for preferred stock.

Q168_LO40: Which characteristic is NOT shared by preferred stock with debt securities?
a. Fixed rate of return
b. Priority at dissolution over common stock
c. Voting rights
d. No preemptive rights

HINTS: Recognize a characteristic that is specific to preferred stock and not shared with debt securities.

Q169_LO40: When do owners of preferred shares have a priority claim over common shareholders at dissolution?
a. After paying off creditors
b. Before paying off creditors
c. Simultaneously with paying off creditors
d. Only in the absence of creditors

HINTS: Understand the priority of preferred stock over common stock at dissolution.

Q170_LO40: What is the potential risk associated with the fixed income produced by preferred stock due to inflation?
a. Interest rate sensitivity
b. Decreased dividend income
c. Purchasing power risk
d. Priority risk

HINTS: Recognize the risk related to the fixed income produced by preferred stock.

Q171_LO40: How does the value of preferred shares respond when interest rates rise?
a. Increases
b. Decreases
c. Remains unchanged
d. Depends on inflation

HINTS: Understand the relationship between the value of preferred shares and changes in interest rates.

Q172_LO40: What is the role of the Board of Directors (BOD) in deciding dividend payments for preferred stock?
a. Fixed percentage guaranteed
b. Subject to investor vote
c. Decision rests with the BOD
d. Guaranteed to be paid

HINTS: Recognize the authority responsible for deciding dividend payments for preferred stock.

Q173_LO40: In a bankruptcy scenario, when are preferred shareholders paid relative to common shareholders?
a. After common shareholders
b. Simultaneously with common shareholders
c. Before common shareholders
d. Only if there are no common shareholders

HINTS: Understand the priority of preferred shareholders in a bankruptcy scenario.
Q174_LO40: Why would you include preferred stock in a client's portfolio?
a. Potential capital appreciation
b. Fixed income from dividends
c. Convertibility for capital gain
d. Priority at dissolution over creditors

HINTS: Identify a reason for including preferred stock in a client's portfolio.

Q175_LO40: What is a characteristic of cumulative preferred stock?
a. Missed dividends are never paid
b. Dividends accrue on reduction or suspension
c. Dividends are variable
d. Callable by the issuing company

HINTS: Recognize a characteristic specific to cumulative preferred stock.

Q176_LO40: What is the purpose of callable preferred stock for issuing companies?
a. Increase fixed-dividend obligation
b. Lower fixed-dividend obligation
c. Enhance voting rights
d. Ensure dividend payments

HINTS: Understand the purpose of issuing callable preferred stock for companies.

Q177_LO40: When a corporation calls a preferred stock, what happens to dividend payments?
a. Dividend payments continue
b. Dividend payments cease
c. Dividend payments increase
d. Dividend payments become variable

HINTS: Recognize the impact on dividend payments when a corporation calls preferred stock.

Q178_LO40: What distinguishes convertible preferred stock from nonconvertible preferred stock?
a. Higher stated dividend rate
b. Lower stated dividend rate
c. No dividend payments
d. Guaranteed dividends

HINTS: Identify a characteristic that distinguishes convertible preferred stock from nonconvertible preferred stock.

Q179_LO40: What distinguishes adjustable-rate preferred stock from other types of preferred stock?
a. Fixed dividend rates
b. Variable dividend rates
c. Fixed conversion ratio
d. Participation in corporate profits

HINTS: Recognize a characteristic specific to adjustable-rate preferred stock.

Q180_LO40: What does participating preferred stock offer in addition to fixed dividends?
a. No fixed dividends
b. Share of corporate profits
c. Callable feature
d. Convertibility to common stock

HINTS: Understand an additional feature of participating preferred stock.

Correct Answers & Explanations
Individual Securities – ADRs AND PREFERRED STOCK

Q136_LO39: Correct Answer: d EXPLANATIONS: ADRs are designed to simplify foreign investing for U.S. investors.

Q137_LO39: Correct Answer: c EXPLANATIONS: ADRs are created when common shares are purchased in the foreign company's home market.

Q138_LO39: Correct Answer: c EXPLANATIONS: ADRs are typically listed on the NYSE or Nasdaq.

Q139_LO39: Correct Answer: c EXPLANATIONS: ADRs trade and settle (T+2) in the same fashion as traditional U.S. common stocks.

Q140_LO39: Correct Answer: b EXPLANATIONS: ADRs trading in U.S. dollars eliminate the complications of currency conversion for investors.

Q141_LO39: Correct Answer: b EXPLANATIONS: Dividends paid to a U.S. investor may be subject to a withholding tax by the home country of the underlying foreign stock issuer.

Q142_LO39: Correct Answer: c EXPLANATIONS: Changes in currency exchange rates can impact ADR dividends, causing them to fluctuate.

Q143_LO39: Correct Answer: b EXPLANATIONS: ADR dividends are paid in U.S. dollars.

Q144_LO39: Correct Answer: b EXPLANATIONS: ADRs are designed to eliminate currency conversion complications, reducing currency risk for investors.

Q145_LO39: Correct Answer: b EXPLANATIONS: Currency swings can influence the value of ADRs, affecting dividends.

Q146_LO39: Correct Answer: c EXPLANATIONS: Filing reports with the SEC demonstrates regulatory compliance, offering comfort to buyers.

Q147_LO39: Correct Answer: d EXPLANATIONS: Trading ADRs in a familiar, well-regulated setting provides comfort to U.S. investors.

Q148_LO39: Correct Answer: d EXPLANATIONS: Political risk arises if the ADR issuer is based in an unstable country.

Q149_LO39: Correct Answer: a EXPLANATIONS: Trading ADRs over the counter may be associated with lower liquidity.

Q150_LO39: Correct Answer: c EXPLANATIONS: SEC filings provide comfort to U.S. investors and contribute to foreign companies attracting a U.S. investor base through ADRs.

Q151_LO40: Correct Answer: b EXPLANATIONS: The rate of return on preferred stock is fixed.

Q152_LO40: Correct Answer: c EXPLANATIONS: Always assume preferred par value is $100 unless stated differently.

Q153_LO40: Correct Answer: b EXPLANATIONS: Preferred shareholders generally have no voting rights.

Q154_LO40: Correct Answer: c EXPLANATIONS: Owners of preferred shares must be paid before any payment to common shareholders.

Q155_LO40: Correct Answer: c EXPLANATIONS: Purchasing power risk is the potential loss due to inflation.

Q156_LO40: Correct Answer: d EXPLANATIONS: Cumulative preferred stockholders receive accumulated dividends when the company resumes dividend payments.

Q157_LO40: Correct Answer: b EXPLANATIONS: Corporations issue callable preferred stock to replace a high fixed-dividend obligation with a lower one when the cost of money decreases.

Q158_LO40: Correct Answer: b EXPLANATIONS: Dividend payments cease on the call date when a corporation calls a preferred stock.

Q159_LO40: Correct Answer: c EXPLANATIONS: Convertible preferred stock may have a lower stated dividend rate due to the potential for capital gain through conversion to common shares.

Q160_LO40: Correct Answer: b EXPLANATIONS: Adjustable-rate preferred stock has variable dividend rates tied to interest rate benchmarks.

Q161_LO40: Correct Answer: c EXPLANATIONS: Participating preferred stock offers a share of corporate profits.

Q162_LO40: Correct Answer: c EXPLANATIONS: Participating preferred stock allows owners to share in corporate profits.

Q163_LO40: Correct Answer: c EXPLANATIONS: Callable preferred stock allows the corporation to buy back shares.

Q164_LO40: Correct Answer: b EXPLANATIONS: The value of preferred shares declines when interest rates rise, reflecting interest rate sensitivity.

Q165_LO40: Correct Answer: d EXPLANATIONS: Straight (noncumulative) preferred stock does not accrue missed dividends.

Q166_LO40: Correct Answer: b EXPLANATIONS: Preferred stock's fixed annual dividend represents its fixed rate of return, appealing to income-oriented investors.

Q167_LO40: Correct Answer: c EXPLANATIONS: Always assume preferred par value is $100 unless stated differently.

Q168_LO40: Correct Answer: c EXPLANATIONS: Preferred stock generally has no voting rights, unlike debt securities.

Q169_LO40: Correct Answer: b EXPLANATIONS: Preferred stockholders have a priority claim over common stockholders on the assets remaining after creditors have been paid.

Q170_LO40: Correct Answer: c EXPLANATIONS: Purchasing power risk refers to the potential impact of inflation on the fixed income produced.

Q171_LO40: Correct Answer: b EXPLANATIONS: Like fixed-income securities, the value of preferred shares declines when interest rates rise.

Q172_LO40: Correct Answer: c EXPLANATIONS: The decision to pay a dividend for preferred stock rests with the Board of Directors (BOD).

Q173_LO40: Correct Answer: c EXPLANATIONS: Preferred shareholders are paid before common shareholders in case of bankruptcy.

Q174_LO40: Correct Answer: b EXPLANATIONS: Preferred stock provides a fixed income from dividends.

Q175_LO40: Correct Answer: b EXPLANATIONS: Cumulative preferred stock accrues payments due to shareholders if dividends are reduced or suspended.

Q176_LO40: Correct Answer: b EXPLANATIONS: Callable preferred stock allows the company to replace a relatively high fixed-dividend obligation with a lower one.

Q177_LO40: Correct Answer: b EXPLANATIONS: Dividend payments cease when a corporation calls preferred stock.

Q178_LO40: Correct Answer: b EXPLANATIONS: Convertible preferred stock is generally issued with a lower stated dividend rate.

Q179_LO40: Correct Answer: b EXPLANATIONS: Adjustable-rate preferred stock has dividends tied to interest rate benchmarks, making them variable.

Q180_LO40: Correct Answer: b EXPLANATIONS: Participating preferred stock offers its owners a share of corporate profits in addition to fixed dividends.

Individual Securities – Debt

Q181_LO41: What is the par value of most debt securities?
a. $500
b. $1,000
c. $5,000
d. $10,000

HINTS: Recall the typical par value for most debt securities.

Q182_LO41: What is the maturity date of a bond?
a. Date of issuance
b. Date of purchase
c. Date of interest payment
d. Date the investor receives the loan principal back

HINTS: Recognize the definition of the maturity date for a bond.

Q183_LO41: What distinguishes a term bond from a serial bond?
a. Repayment at intervals
b. Entire principal matures at once
c. Scheduled portions mature at intervals
d. Repayment at maturity with a premium

HINTS: Identify the characteristic that distinguishes a term bond.

Q184_LO41: What is a balloon bond's maturity structure?
a. Entire principal matures at once
b. Scheduled portions mature at intervals
c. Repayment at intervals
d. Pays off major portion at maturity

HINTS: Recognize the unique maturity structure of a balloon bond.

Q185_LO41: What does the coupon rate represent for a bond?
a. Market value
b. Principal amount
c. Interest rate
d. Maturity date

HINTS: Identify the definition of the coupon rate for a bond.

Q186_LO41: How is the coupon rate calculated for a bond with a par value of $1,000 and a 6% coupon?
a. $6
b. $60
c. $600
d. $6,000

HINTS: Apply the calculation for the coupon rate.

Q187_LO41: What happens to accrued interest when a bond trades between coupon payments?
a. Buyer pays the full coupon
b. No accrued interest is paid
c. Seller pays the full coupon
d. No impact on accrued interest

HINTS: Understand the transaction involving accrued interest between buyer and seller.

Q188_LO41: How is accrued interest calculated for corporate and municipal bonds?
a. 365-day-year calculation
b. 30-day-month/360-day-year calculation
c. Actual number of days elapsed
d. Weekly calculation

HINTS: Recognize the method used for calculating accrued interest for corporate and municipal bonds.

Q189_LO41: In bond pricing, what does each point represent?
a. 0.01% of face value
b. 0.1% of face value
c. 1% of face value
d. 10% of face value

HINTS: Understand the measure of bond pricing in points.

Q190_LO41: If a bond is trading at 103, what is its dollar value?
a. $1,030
b. $1,300
c. $10,300
d. $103

HINTS: Apply the calculation to determine the dollar value of a bond trading at 103.

Q191_LO41: How do bond prices generally respond to changes in market interest rates?
a. No impact
b. Direct relationship
c. Inverse relationship
d. Linear relationship

HINTS: Understand the relationship between bond prices and market interest rates.

Q192_LO41: When interest rates go up, what happens to bond prices?
a. Rise
b. Fall
c. Remain unchanged
d. Depend on inflation

HINTS: Recognize the impact of rising interest rates on bond prices.

Q193_LO41: What attracts investors to a bond trading at a premium when market interest rates are 6%?
a. Higher coupon rate
b. Lower coupon rate
c. Longer maturity
d. Lower face value

HINTS: Identify the factor that attracts investors to a bond trading at a premium.

Q194_LO41: Why might a bond with a 4% coupon look less attractive when market interest rates are 6%?
a. Lower face value
b. Shorter maturity
c. Higher coupon rate
d. Lower coupon rate

HINTS: Understand why a bond might look less attractive with a 4% coupon when market rates are 6%.

Q195_LO41: Why do bond prices rise when interest rates are falling?
a. Decreased demand
b. Increased supply
c. Inverse relationship
d. Linear relationship

HINTS: Recognize the impact of falling interest rates on bond prices.

Q196_LO41: What is the typical par value assumed for most debt securities?
a. $500
b. $750
c. $1,000
d. $1,500

HINTS: Recall the typical par value for most debt securities.

Q197_LO41: When does an investor receive the loan principal back in a bond investment?
a. At the coupon payment
b. At the maturity date
c. Monthly
d. Annually

HINTS: Recognize the event when the investor receives the loan principal back.

Q198_LO41: What is the structure of a term bond's principal repayment?
a. Matures in portions over a period
b. Repaid at intervals
c. Matures all at once
d. Partial repayment before final maturity

HINTS: Identify the structure of a term bond's principal repayment.

Q199_LO41: How is the principal of a serial bond repaid?
a. Matures all at once
b. Partial repayment before final maturity
c. Repaid at intervals
d. Not repaid

HINTS: Recognize the structure of a serial bond's principal repayment.

Q200_LO41: What is a characteristic of a balloon bond's maturity?
a. Matures all at once
b. Partial repayment before final maturity
c. Repaid at intervals
d. No maturity date

HINTS: Understand the characteristic of a balloon bond's maturity.

Q201_LO41: What does the term "coupon" refer to in bond terminology?
a. Stated yield
b. Face value
c. Principal
d. Maturity date

HINTS: Identify the term that represents the interest rate the issuer has agreed to pay.

Q202_LO41: How is the coupon rate calculated for a bond with a par value of $1,000 and a 6% coupon?
a. $10
b. $60
c. $600
d. $6,000

HINTS: Calculate the coupon rate for a bond with a given par value and coupon rate.

Q203_LO41: What is the calculation method for accrued interest in corporate and municipal trades?
a. Actual days elapsed
b. 30-day-month/360-day-year
c. Weekly average
d. Monthly average
HINTS: Recognize the calculation method for accrued interest in corporate and municipal trades.

Q204_LO41: In bond pricing, what is the significance of each point?
a. 10% of face value
b. 1% of face value
c. 5% of face value
d. 2% of face value

HINTS: Understand the significance of each point in bond pricing.

Q205_LO41: If a bond is trading at 90, what is its dollar worth?
a. $90
b. $900
c. $9,000
d. $900,000

HINTS: Calculate the dollar worth of a bond trading at a given price.

Q206_LO41: How do bond prices generally respond to changes in market interest rates?
a. Direct relationship
b. No relationship
c. Inverse relationship
d. Random relationship

HINTS: Identify the general relationship between bond prices and market interest rates.

Q207_LO41: Why do bond prices rise when interest rates fall?
a. Increased borrowing cost
b. Attraction of higher coupon rates
c. Decreased borrowing cost
d. Stable coupon rates

HINTS: Recognize the reason behind the rise in bond prices when interest rates fall.

Q208_LO41: How are bond prices impacted if interest rates rise?
a. Rise
b. Stay the same
c. Remain unpredictable
d. Fall

HINTS: Understand the impact of rising interest rates on bond prices.

Q209_LO41: What market force has a particular sensitivity to changes in market interest rates for bonds?
a. Supply and demand
b. Political factors
c. Economic indicators
d. Weather conditions

HINTS: Identify the market force with particular sensitivity to changes in market interest rates for bonds.

Q210_LO41: If a bond is trading at a premium of $1,200, what is its dollar worth?
a. $1,200
b. $1,020
c. $12,000
d. $120,000

HINTS: Calculate the dollar worth of a bond trading at a premium.

Q211_LO42: What does a bond's yield express?
a. Coupon rate
b. Cash interest payments in relation to the bond's value
c. Par value
d. Maturity date

HINTS: Recognize the concept expressed by a bond's yield.

Q212_LO42: What is the nominal yield also known as?
a. Face yield
b. Current yield
c. Stated yield
d. Market yield

HINTS: Recall another term used for the nominal yield.

Q213_LO42: How is the current yield calculated?
a. Annual coupon payment × par value
b. Market price ÷ annual coupon payment
c. Annual coupon payment ÷ market price
d. Par value ÷ market price

HINTS: Understand the calculation method for current yield.

Q214_LO42: What does the yield to maturity (YTM) reflect?
a. Annual coupon payment relative to market price
b. Annualized return if held to maturity
c. Coupon rate set at the time of issue
d. Nominal yield

HINTS: Identify what the yield to maturity reflects.

Q215_LO42: How are yields measured in the bond market?
a. Percentage points
b. Basis points
c. Face value points
d. Coupon points

HINTS: Recognize the measurement unit for yields in the bond market.

Q216_LO42: What is the relationship between basis points and percentage points?
a. 1 basis point = 1 percentage point
b. 10 basis points = 1 percentage point
c. 100 basis points = 1 percentage point
d. 1 basis point = 10 percentage points

HINTS: Understand the relationship between basis points and percentage points.

Q217_LO42: What does YTM stand for in bond terminology?
a. Yield to Market
b. Yield to Maturity
c. Yield to Call
d. Yield to Coupon

HINTS: Recognize the abbreviation for YTM in bond terminology.

Q218_LO42: What is the calculation method for yield to call (YTC)?
a. Annualized return if held to maturity
b. Annual coupon payment ÷ market price
c. Early redemption gain or loss calculations
d. Coupon rate set at the time of issue

HINTS: Understand the calculation method for yield to call (YTC).

Q219_LO42: When is a bond with a call feature redeemed?
a. Always at maturity
b. Only when market prices rise
c. At the issuer's option before maturity
d. Never before maturity

HINTS: Recognize the condition for redeeming a bond with a call feature.

Q220_LO42: What does a YTC calculation consider for a callable bond originally purchased at a premium?
a. Early redemption gain
b. Early redemption loss
c. Par value
d. Nominal yield

HINTS: Identify the consideration in YTC calculation for a callable bond at a premium.

Q221_LO42: In the context of bond yields, what remains constant regardless of price changes?
a. Current yield
b. YTM
c. Coupon rate
d. YTC

HINTS: Identify the yield that remains constant regardless of price changes.

Q222_LO42: What factor determines the relationship between CY, YTM, and YTC for a bond trading at a premium?
a. Market demand
b. Bond issuer's credit rating
c. Market price
d. Call feature

HINTS: Recognize the factor determining the relationship between CY, YTM, and YTC for a bond trading at a premium.

Q223_LO42: If a bond is purchased at a discount, what happens at maturity?
a. The investor makes money
b. The investor loses money
c. No impact on return
d. The bond is automatically called

HINTS: Understand the impact of purchasing a bond at a discount on the return at maturity.

Q224_LO42: What is the significance of 5.83 basis in bond trading?
a. YTM of 5.83%
b. Discount of 5.83%
c. Premium of 5.83%
d. Par value of 5.83%

HINTS: Recognize the significance of the term "basis" in bond trading.

Q225_LO42: How is a point defined in bond pricing?
a. 1% of face value
b. 5% of face value
c. 10% of face value
d. 20% of face value

HINTS: Understand the definition of a point in bond pricing.

Q226_LO42: What does a bond's yield express?
a. Principal value
b. Coupon rate
c. Cash interest payments relative to the bond's value
d. Market price
HINTS: Understand the concept expressed by a bond's yield.

Q227_LO42: What is the Nominal Yield also known as?
a. Stated yield
b. Current yield
c. Yield to maturity
d. Yield to call

HINTS: Recall the alternative name for Nominal Yield.

Q228_LO42: How is Current Yield (CY) calculated?
a. Annual coupon payment ÷ Face value
b. Annual coupon payment × Market price
c. Annual coupon payment ÷ Market price
d. Annual coupon payment + Market price

HINTS: Recognize the correct formula for calculating Current Yield.

Q229_LO42: What does Yield to Maturity (YTM) reflect?

a. Short-term return
b. Annualized return if held to maturity
c. Market volatility
d. Current market price

HINTS: Identify the concept reflected by Yield to Maturity.

Q230_LO42: In YTM calculations, what factor influences the return for a bond purchased at a discount?
a. Decreases the return
b. Has no effect
c. Increases the return
d. Stays constant

HINTS: Understand the impact on return for a bond purchased at a discount.

Q231_LO42: What is the measurement unit for Yields?
a. Points
b. Basis points
c. Percentage
d. Fractions

HINTS: Distinguish between the measurement units for Yields.

Q232_LO42: What is a full percentage point equivalent to in basis points?
a. 10 bps
b. 50 bps
c. 100 bps
d. 500 bps

HINTS: Convert a full percentage point to basis points.

Q233_LO42: What is another term for Yield to Call (YTC)?
a. Yield to Redemption
b. Yield to Acceleration
c. Callable Yield
d. Early Redemption Yield

HINTS: Recognize the alternative term for Yield to Call.

Q234_LO42: When a callable bond is called in by the issuer, what happens to the investor's return?
a. Decreases
b. Stays constant
c. Increases
d. Turns negative

HINTS: Understand the impact on the investor's return when a callable bond is called.

Q235_LO42: What is the relationship between Nominal Yield and CY?
a. They are equal
b. Nominal yield is always higher
c. CY is always higher
d. They are unrelated

HINTS: Recognize the relationship between Nominal Yield and CY.

Q236_LO42: What does the YTM reflect in relation to bond pricing?
a. Historical pricing
b. Future pricing
c. Premium or discount at purchase
d. Inflation-adjusted pricing

HINTS: Understand what aspect of bond pricing YTM reflects.

Q237_LO42: How does YTM change if a bond is purchased at a premium?

a. Increases
b. Stays constant
c. Decreases
d. Varies unpredictably

HINTS: Understand the relationship between YTM and bond purchase price.

Q238_LO42: What does a bond's basis represent?
a. Annual interest
b. Face value
c. Yield to maturity
d. YTM measurement

HINTS: Identify the concept represented by a bond's basis.

Q239_LO42: What does a bond trading at a 5.83 basis mean?
a. 5.83% annual interest
b. YTM of 5.83%
c. CY of 5.83%
d. Nominal yield of 5.83%

HINTS: Interpret the meaning of a bond trading at a given basis.

Q240_LO42: How are YTM, CY, and YTC affected by a bond trading at a discount?
a. Increase
b. Stay constant
c. Decrease
d. Vary unpredictably

HINTS: Understand the relationship between YTM, CY, and YTC when a bond is trading at a discount.

Q241_LO43: Which of the following is NOT a major credit rating agency?
a. Fitch Ratings, Inc.
b. Moody's Investors Service, Inc.
c. A.M. Best Co., Inc.
d. Standard and Poor's Rating Service (S&P)

HINTS: Identify the agency not among the "major" credit rating agencies.

Q242_LO43: What is the purpose of a bond rating?
a. Predict future market trends
b. Assess the safety of the bond
c. Determine the bond's current market value
d. Analyze the issuer's marketing strategy

HINTS: Understand the primary purpose of assigning a bond rating.

Q243_LO43: Which organization is historically associated with rating insurance companies?
a. Fitch Ratings, Inc.
b. Moody's Investors Service, Inc.
c. A.M. Best Co., Inc.
d. Standard and Poor's Rating Service (S&P)

HINTS: Recall the organization historically associated with rating insurance companies.

Q244_LO43: What is the highest rating for an investment-grade bond according to Standard & Poor's?
a. A
b. AA
c. AAA
d. BBB

HINTS: Recognize the highest rating for an investment-grade bond by S&P.

Q245_LO43: Which Moody's rating indicates the highest capacity to repay principal and interest for an investment-grade bond?

a. Aa
b. A
c. Aaa
d. Baa

HINTS: Identify the highest Moody's rating for an investment-grade bond.

Q246_LO43: What does a Standard & Poor's rating of "BBB" indicate for an investment-grade bond?
a. Highest rating
b. Adequate capacity to repay, slightly speculative
c. No interest being paid
d. Speculative, significant chance of missing payments

HINTS: Understand the meaning of a "BBB" rating by Standard & Poor's.

Q247_LO43: How does Moody's rate a bond with "Ba" for an investment-grade bond?
a. Adequate capacity to repay
b. Speculative, significant chance of missing payments
c. No interest being paid
d. Highest rating

HINTS: Recognize Moody's rating indicating a significant chance of missing payments.

Q248_LO43: What does a Standard & Poor's rating of "C" imply?
a. Adequate capacity to repay
b. No interest being paid
c. Speculative, missed interest or principal payments
d. Highest rating

HINTS: Understand the meaning of a "C" rating by Standard & Poor's.

Q249_LO43: How is a bond rated by Moody's when it is in default?
a. Baa
b. Aaa
c. D
d. Caa

HINTS: Identify the Moody's rating when a bond is in default.

Q250_LO43: What does a Standard & Poor's rating of "D" imply?
a. Adequate capacity to repay
b. No interest being paid
c. Highest rating
d. Issuer is in default

HINTS: Recognize the meaning of a "D" rating by Standard & Poor's.

Q251_LO43: How does Moody's rate a bond with "Caa"?
a. Adequate capacity to repay
b. No interest being paid
c. Speculative, missed interest or principal payments
d. Highest rating

HINTS: Understand the meaning of a "Caa" rating by Moody's.

Q252_LO43: What type of bond has a Standard & Poor's rating of "BB"?
a. Highest-grade
b. Investment-grade
c. Speculative
d. Defaulted

HINTS: Identify the type of bond with a "BB" rating by Standard & Poor's.

Q253_LO43: According to Moody's, what does a "B" rating indicate?

a. Speculative
b. Default
c. Adequate capacity to repay
d. Highest rating

HINTS: Understand the meaning of a "B" rating by Moody's.

Q254_LO43: How are bond ratings related to safety?
a. Higher ratings indicate lower safety
b. Ratings and safety are unrelated
c. Higher ratings indicate higher safety
d. Safety depends on market conditions

HINTS: Recognize the relationship between bond ratings and safety.

Q255_LO43: Which rating indicates the highest chance of an issuer missing an interest payment, according to S&P?
a. AAA
b. BBB
c. C
d. AA

HINTS: Understand the significance of a "C" rating in terms of missing interest payments.

Q256_LO43: What is the primary factor that enhances the safety of a debt security?
a. Maturity date
b. Strength of the borrower
c. Interest rate
d. Collateral value

HINTS: Recognize the key factor influencing the safety of a debt security.

Q257_LO43: Which organization is historically associated with rating insurance companies?
a. Fitch Ratings
b. Moody's Investors Service
c. A.M. Best Co.
d. Standard and Poor's

HINTS: Identify the credit rating agency historically associated with insurance companies.

Q258_LO43: Which are the three major credit rating agencies by the SEC?
a. Moody's, Fitch, S&P
b. S&P, A.M. Best, Fitch
c. Moody's, A.M. Best, S&P
d. Fitch, A.M. Best, Moody's

HINTS: Recognize the three major credit rating agencies acknowledged by the SEC.

Q259_LO43: What does an AAA rating from Standard & Poor's indicate?
a. Speculative
b. Very strong capacity to repay principal and interest
c. Adequate capacity to repay
d. No interest being paid

HINTS: Understand the significance of an AAA rating from Standard & Poor's.

Q260_LO43: How does Moody's rate a bond with the highest capacity to repay principal and interest?
a. Baa
b. A
c. Aaa
d. Ba

HINTS: Identify Moody's highest rating indicating a high capacity to repay principal and interest.

Q261_LO43: According to Standard & Poor's, what does a BB rating suggest?

a. No interest being paid
b. Adequate capacity to repay
c. Speculative, significant chance of missing an interest payment
d. Very strong capacity to repay

HINTS: Interpret the meaning of a BB rating according to Standard & Poor's.

Q262_LO43: What does a rating of D from Moody's indicate?
a. Adequate capacity to repay
b. No interest being paid
c. Very strong capacity to repay
d. Issuer is in default

HINTS: Understand the implication of a D rating from Moody's.

Q263_LO43: In Moody's rating system, what does a Caa rating signify?
a. Very strong
b. Speculative
c. Adequate
d. No interest being paid

HINTS: Interpret the meaning of a Caa rating in Moody's system.

Q264_LO43: What does a Ba rating from Moody's suggest?
a. Speculative, significant chance of missing an interest payment
b. Adequate capacity to repay
c. Very strong capacity to repay
d. No interest being paid

HINTS: Understand the implication of a Ba rating from Moody's.

Q265_LO43: According to Standard & Poor's, what does a rating of C indicate?
a. Adequate capacity to repay
b. No interest being paid
c. Speculative, significant chance of missing an interest payment
d. Very strong capacity to repay

HINTS: Interpret the meaning of a C rating according to Standard & Poor's.

Q266_LO43: What is the commonality between Fitch, S&P, and Moody's rating scales?
a. They use the same letter ratings
b. They follow the same pattern
c. They have identical criteria
d. They share the same analysts

HINTS: Recognize the commonality among the rating scales of Fitch, S&P, and Moody's.

Q267_LO43: How are bonds rated by Moody's if judged to be slightly more susceptible to adverse economic conditions?
a. Aa
b. A
c. Baa
d. Aaa

HINTS: Identify the rating assigned by Moody's for bonds slightly more susceptible to adverse economic conditions.

Q268_LO43: Which rating by Standard & Poor's suggests a slightly speculative nature with adequate capacity to repay?
a. BBB
b. AA
c. A
d. BB

HINTS: Understand the meaning of a BBB rating by Standard & Poor's.

Q269_LO43: If an issuer has missed one or more interest or principal payments, how would Moody's rate the bond?

a. B
b. D
c. Caa
d. Ba

HINTS: Interpret Moody's rating for a bond with missed interest or principal payments.

Q270_LO43: What does the term "noninvestment-grade" refer to in the context of bond ratings?
a. Bonds with a higher yield
b. Bonds with a lower risk of default
c. Bonds with a speculative nature
d. Bonds with a guaranteed return

HINTS: Understand the meaning of "noninvestment-grade" in the context of bond ratings.

Q271_LO43: What is the term for bonds rated in the top four categories (BBB or Baa and higher)?
a. Nonrated bonds
b. High-yield bonds
c. Investment-grade bonds
d. Volatile bonds

HINTS: Recognize the category of bonds with higher ratings.

Q272_LO43: How is the risk/reward concept related to bond ratings?
a. Higher ratings correspond to higher yields
b. Higher ratings correspond to lower yields
c. Risk and reward are not related
d. All bonds offer the same reward

HINTS: Understand the relationship between bond ratings and the risk/reward concept.

Q273_LO43: What is the primary factor influencing the liquidity of investment-grade bonds?
a. Collateral value
b. Credit rating
c. Maturity date
d. Interest rate

HINTS: Identify the key factor affecting the liquidity of investment-grade bonds.

Q274_LO43: What are lower-grade bonds commonly called in the industry?
a. Investment-grade bonds
b. Nonrated bonds
c. High-yield bonds
d. Volatile bonds

HINTS: Recognize the common term for lower-grade bonds in the industry.

Q275_LO43: What is the primary reason high-yield bonds may experience substantial price erosion?
a. Lower volatility
b. Higher credit ratings
c. Lower risk of default
d. Additional risk of default

HINTS: Identify the factor contributing to potential price erosion in high-yield bonds.

Q276_LO43: Why might high-yield bonds be suitable for sophisticated investors?
a. Lower returns
b. Lower volatility
c. Higher risk and possible capital appreciation
d. Higher liquidity

HINTS: Understand the suitability of high-yield bonds for sophisticated investors.

Q277_LO43: How do lower-rated bonds compensate for the additional risk to lenders?

a. Lower returns
b. Lower volatility
c. Higher returns
d. Lower risk

HINTS: Identify how lower-rated bonds compensate lenders for additional risk.

Q278_LO43: What does "noninvestment-grade" refer to in the context of bond ratings?
a. Bonds with a higher yield
b. Bonds with a lower risk of default
c. Bonds with a speculative nature
d. Bonds with a guaranteed return

HINTS: Understand the meaning of "noninvestment-grade" in bond ratings.

Q279_LO43: How does the rating organizations' evaluation of a bond include collateral?
a. Collateral is the primary factor
b. Collateral is not considered
c. Collateral is the only factor
d. Collateral is considered along with other factors

HINTS: Recognize the role of collateral in the rating organizations' evaluation of a bond.

Q280_LO43: What does the term "volatility" refer to in the context of bonds?
a. Bond's sensitivity to changes in interest rates
b. Bond's credit rating
c. Bond's maturity date
d. Bond's coupon rate

HINTS: Understand the meaning of "volatility" in the context of bonds.

Q281_LO43: Why is a bond with 10 years to maturity generally more volatile than a bond with 5 years to maturity?
a. Longer maturity increases volatility
b. Shorter maturity increases volatility
c. Longer maturity decreases volatility
d. Maturity is unrelated to volatility

HINTS: Recognize the relationship between maturity and a bond's volatility.

Q282_LO43: How does a lower coupon rate affect a bond's volatility?
a. Increases volatility
b. Decreases volatility
c. Has no impact on volatility
d. Depends on the maturity

HINTS: Understand the impact of a lower coupon rate on a bond's volatility.

Q283_LO43: What is used to measure a bond's overall volatility, considering maturity and coupon rate?
a. Volatility index
b. Interest rate index
c. Duration
d. Credit rating

HINTS: Identify the measure used to gauge a bond's overall volatility.

Q284_LO43: How does a higher duration affect a bond's price volatility?
a. Increases volatility
b. Decreases volatility
c. Has no impact on volatility
d. Depends on the coupon rate

HINTS: Understand the impact of a higher duration on a bond's price volatility.

Q285_LO43: When might a bond with 3% coupon rate and 5 years to maturity be more volatile than a 6% bond with the same 5 years left?

a. Never
b. Always
c. When interest rates are low
d. When interest rates are high

HINTS: Recognize the conditions under which a 3% bond might be more volatile than a 6% bond.

Q286_LO44: What does a call feature allow an issuer to do?
a. Extend the bond's maturity
b. Convert the bond into shares
c. Call in the bond before maturity
d. Increase the bond's interest rate

HINTS: Recognize the purpose of a call feature for issuers.

Q287_LO44: When would an issuer typically use a call feature?
a. When interest rates are rising
b. When interest rates are falling
c. When the bond matures
d. When the bondholder requests it

HINTS: Identify the market condition favoring the use of a call feature.

Q288_LO44: What is the benefit of a call feature for the issuer?
a. Higher interest payments
b. Avoiding principal repayment
c. Lowering the bond's interest rate
d. Issuing a new bond at a lower interest rate

HINTS: Understand the advantage of a call feature for the issuer.

Q289_LO44: What is the opposite of a call feature for a bond?
a. Convertible feature
b. Maturity feature
c. Put feature
d. Redemption feature

HINTS: Recognize the opposite of a call feature.

Q290_LO44: When would an investor typically use a put feature?
a. When interest rates are falling
b. When interest rates are rising
c. When the bond matures
d. When the issuer requests it

HINTS: Identify the market condition favoring the use of a put feature.

Q291_LO44: What is the benefit of a put feature for the bondholder?
a. Higher interest payments
b. Avoiding principal repayment
c. Lowering the bond's interest rate
d. Putting the bond back to the issuer at a higher interest rate

HINTS: Understand the advantage of a put feature for the bondholder.

Q292_LO44: What does a convertible feature allow an investor to do?
a. Extend the bond's maturity
b. Convert the bond into shares
c. Call in the bond before maturity
d. Increase the bond's interest rate

HINTS: Recognize the opportunity provided by a convertible feature.

Q293_LO44: What is an arbitrage transaction related to convertible bonds?

a. Buying and selling the bond to manipulate prices
b. Simultaneous buying and selling to capture price differentials
c. Converting the bond into shares at a profit
d. Issuing a new bond at a higher interest rate

HINTS: Understand the nature of an arbitrage transaction related to convertible bonds.

Q294_LO44: How might convertible bonds behave concerning the underlying stock?
a. They have no relationship
b. They track the value of the underlying stock
c. They decrease in value
d. They have higher interest rates

HINTS: Recognize the typical behavior of convertible bonds in relation to the underlying stock.

Q295_LO44: What is the purpose of engaging in arbitrage transactions with convertible bonds?
a. To manipulate bond prices
b. To capture price differentials between securities
c. To increase the bond's interest rate
d. To convert the bond into shares

HINTS: Identify the objective of engaging in arbitrage transactions related to convertible bonds.

Q296_LO44: Which feature allows an investor to exchange a debt instrument for ownership rights?
a. Call feature
b. Put feature
c. Convertible feature
d. Maturity feature

HINTS: Recognize the nature of the feature allowing an exchange for ownership rights.

Q297_LO44: Why might an investor use a put feature for a bond?
a. To increase interest payments
b. To avoid principal repayment
c. To lower the bond's interest rate
d. To put the bond back to the issuer at a higher interest rate

HINTS: Understand the motivation for an investor to use a put feature.

Q298_LO44: In a call feature, why might the (former) bondholder face a dilemma?
a. Due to a decrease in bond value
b. Due to an increase in bond value
c. Due to finding a similar rate of return in a lower interest rate environment
d. Due to a decrease in interest rates

HINTS: Recognize the dilemma faced by a (former) bondholder in a call feature.

Q299_LO44: What is the primary factor influencing the benefit of a put feature for the bondholder?
a. Higher interest payments
b. Avoiding principal repayment
c. Lowering the bond's interest rate
d. Rising interest rates

HINTS: Identify the market condition influencing the benefit of a put feature.

Q300_LO44: What does a put feature allow the investor to do before the bond matures?
a. Convert the bond into shares
b. Call in the bond
c. Put the bond back to the issuer
d. Increase the bond's interest rate

HINTS: Recognize the action facilitated by a put feature before the bond matures.

Q301_LO44: What does a call feature allow an issuer to do?

a. Extend the bond maturity
b. Increase the bond's interest rate
c. Call in the bond before maturity
d. Convert the bond into shares

HINTS: Recognize the purpose of a call feature for an issuer.

Q302_LO44: Why would an issuer prefer to use a call feature on a bond?
a. To increase the interest rate
b. To extend the bond maturity
c. To take advantage of falling interest rates
d. To convert the bond into shares

HINTS: Understand the issuer's motivation for using a call feature.

Q303_LO44: What is the primary benefit of a put feature for a bondholder?
a. Higher interest rate
b. The ability to convert the bond into shares
c. The option to put the bond back to the issuer
d. Extended maturity

HINTS: Identify the primary advantage of a put feature for a bondholder.

Q304_LO44: When would an investor typically use a put feature?
a. When interest rates are falling
b. When interest rates are rising
c. When interest rates are stable
d. When converting the bond into shares

HINTS: Recognize the scenario in which an investor would use a put feature.

Q305_LO44: What is the main benefit of a convertible feature for an investor?
a. Higher interest rate
b. Extended maturity
c. The ability to convert the bond into shares
d. Lower risk of default

HINTS: Identify the advantage of a convertible feature for an investor.

Q306_LO44: How may convertible bonds behave in relation to the underlying stock when the stock rises in value?
a. They decrease in value
b. They remain unchanged
c. They often track the value of the underlying shares
d. They become non-convertible

HINTS: Understand the typical behavior of convertible bonds when the related stock rises in value.

Q307_LO44: What is arbitrage in the context of convertible bonds?
a. Issuing new bonds at lower rates
b. Buying and selling the bond and underlying stock simultaneously
c. Extending the bond maturity
d. Calling in the bond before maturity

HINTS: Recognize the concept of arbitrage in relation to convertible bonds.

Q308_LO44: In what scenario would an investor engage in arbitrage transactions with convertible bonds?
a. Stable market conditions
b. Rising interest rates
c. Falling interest rates
d. Decreasing stock value

HINTS: Identify the market conditions under which an investor might engage in arbitrage transactions.

Q309_LO44: What does a put feature allow an investor to do?

a. Extend the bond maturity
b. Put the bond back to the issuer before maturity
c. Convert the bond into shares
d. Increase the bond's interest rate

HINTS: Recognize the action enabled by a put feature for an investor.

Q310_LO44: Why might an investor use a put feature on a bond?
a. To convert the bond into shares
b. To extend the bond maturity
c. To take advantage of falling interest rates
d. To put the bond back in a rising interest rate environment

HINTS: Understand the investor's motivation for using a put feature.

Q311_LO44: What is the opposite of a call feature for a bond?
a. Put feature
b. Convertible feature
c. Arbitrage feature
d. Duration feature

HINTS: Identify the opposite of a call feature.

Q312_LO44: When might an issuer typically use a call feature?
a. In a rising interest rate environment
b. In a stable interest rate environment
c. In a falling interest rate environment
d. In a volatile market

HINTS: Recognize the scenario in which an issuer would typically use a call feature.

Q313_LO44: What is the primary benefit of a call feature for an issuer?
a. Higher interest rate
b. Extended maturity
c. The ability to convert the bond into shares
d. The option to call in the bond before maturity

HINTS: Identify the primary advantage of a call feature for an issuer.

Q314_LO44: How does a put feature benefit a bondholder in a rising interest rate environment?
a. Higher interest rate
b. Extended maturity
c. The ability to convert the bond into shares
d. The option to put the bond back to the issuer

HINTS: Understand how a put feature benefits a bondholder in a rising interest rate environment.

Q315_LO44: What is the purpose of a convertible feature for a bondholder?
a. To increase the bond's interest rate
b. To extend the bond maturity
c. To put the bond back to the issuer
d. To convert the bond into shares of common stock

HINTS: Recognize the purpose of a convertible feature for a bondholder.

Correct Answers & Explanations
Individual Securities – Debt

Q181_LO41: Correct Answer: b EXPLANATIONS: Most debt securities have a par value of $1,000.

Q182_LO41: Correct Answer: d EXPLANATIONS: The maturity date is when the investor receives the loan principal back.

Q183_LO41: Correct Answer: b EXPLANATIONS: A term bond is structured so that the principal of the whole issue matures at once.

Q184_LO41: Correct Answer: d EXPLANATIONS: A balloon bond pays off the major portion of the bond at maturity, combining elements of both serial and term maturities.

Q185_LO41: Correct Answer: c EXPLANATIONS: The coupon rate represents the interest rate the issuer has agreed to pay the investor.

Q186_LO41: Correct Answer: b EXPLANATIONS: A bond with a 6% coupon is paying $60 in interest per year (6% × $1,000 par value = $60).

Q187_LO41: Correct Answer: a EXPLANATIONS: The buyer must pay the seller the amount of interest earned to date at the time of settlement.

Q188_LO41: Correct Answer: b EXPLANATIONS: Corporate and municipal trades use a 30-day-month/360-day-year calculation for accrued interest.

Q189_LO41: Correct Answer: c EXPLANATIONS: Each point equals 1% of face value, or $10.

Q190_LO41: Correct Answer: a EXPLANATIONS: Multiply the quoted price by 10 to get the dollar amount.

Q191_LO41: Correct Answer: c EXPLANATIONS: Bond prices generally have an inverse relationship to interest rates.

Q192_LO41: Correct Answer: b EXPLANATIONS: Bond prices for those trading in the secondary markets will go down.

Q193_LO41: Correct Answer: a EXPLANATIONS: A premium bond has a higher coupon rate, making it attractive when market interest rates are lower.

Q194_LO41: Correct Answer: d EXPLANATIONS: A bond paying only 4% may look less attractive when compared to the prevailing market interest rate of 6%.

Q195_LO41: Correct Answer: c EXPLANATIONS: Bond prices for those trading in the secondary market will be going up when interest rates are falling.

Q196_LO41: Correct Answer: c EXPLANATIONS: Most debt securities have a par value of $1,000.

Q197_LO41: Correct Answer: b EXPLANATIONS: The maturity date is when the investor receives the loan principal back.

Q198_LO41: Correct Answer: c EXPLANATIONS: A term bond is structured so that the principal matures all at once.

Q199_LO41: Correct Answer: c EXPLANATIONS: A serial bond issue schedules portions of the principal to mature at intervals over a period.

Q200_LO41: Correct Answer: b EXPLANATIONS: A balloon bond repays part of the principal before the final maturity date.

Q201_LO41: Correct Answer: a EXPLANATIONS: The coupon represents the interest rate the issuer has agreed to pay.

Q202_LO41: Correct Answer: b EXPLANATIONS: A bond with a 6% coupon pays $60 in interest per year (6% × $1,000 par value = $60).

Q203_LO41: Correct Answer: b EXPLANATIONS: Corporate and municipal trades use a 30-day-month/360-day-year calculation for accrued interest.

Q204_LO41: Correct Answer: b EXPLANATIONS: Each point in bond pricing is equal to 1% of face value.

Q205_LO41: Correct Answer: b EXPLANATIONS: A bond trading at 90 is worth $900 (90 × $10).

Q206_LO41: Correct Answer: c EXPLANATIONS: Bond prices generally have an inverse relationship to interest rates.

Q207_LO41: Correct Answer: b EXPLANATIONS: Bond prices rise when interest rates fall because higher coupon rates become more attractive.

Q208_LO41: Correct Answer: d EXPLANATIONS: Bond prices fall when interest rates rise due to the less attractive fixed coupon rates.

Q209_LO41: Correct Answer: a EXPLANATIONS: Bond prices can be impacted by the usual market force of supply and demand.

Q210_LO41: Correct Answer: b EXPLANATIONS: A bond trading at $1,200 is worth $1,200 - $1,000 = $200 above face value (premium).

Q211_LO42: Correct Answer: b EXPLANATIONS: A bond's yield expresses the cash interest payments in relation to the bond's value.

Q212_LO42: Correct Answer: c EXPLANATIONS: The nominal yield is also known as the stated yield.

Q213_LO42: Correct Answer: c EXPLANATIONS: Current yield is calculated as annual coupon payment ÷ market price.

Q214_LO42: Correct Answer: b EXPLANATIONS: YTM reflects the annualized return of the bond if held to maturity.

Q215_LO42: Correct Answer: b EXPLANATIONS: Yields are measured in basis points, where 1 basis point is equal to 1/100 of 1%.

Q216_LO42: Correct Answer: c EXPLANATIONS: 100 basis points make up 1 percentage point.

Q217_LO42: Correct Answer: b EXPLANATIONS: YTM stands for Yield to Maturity.

Q218_LO42: Correct Answer: c EXPLANATIONS: YTC calculations reflect early redemption and consequent gain or loss.

Q219_LO42: Correct Answer: c EXPLANATIONS: A bond with a call feature may be redeemed before maturity at the issuer's option.

Q220_LO42: Correct Answer: b EXPLANATIONS: YTC calculations consider the accelerated premium loss for callable bonds originally purchased at a premium.

Q221_LO42: Correct Answer: c EXPLANATIONS: The coupon (nominal or stated) yield never changes regardless of price.

Q222_LO42: Correct Answer: c EXPLANATIONS: The relationship depends on whether a bond is trading at a premium, par, or discount.

Q223_LO42: Correct Answer: a EXPLANATIONS: If a bond is purchased at a discount, the investor makes money at maturity.

Q224_LO42: Correct Answer: a EXPLANATIONS: A bond trading at a 5.83 basis means the bond has a YTM of 5.83%.

Q225_LO42: Correct Answer: a EXPLANATIONS: A point is a measurement of the change in a bond's price, equal to 1% of face value or $10 per bond.

Q226_LO42: Correct Answer: c EXPLANATIONS: A bond's yield expresses the cash interest payments relative to the bond's value.

Q227_LO42: Correct Answer: a EXPLANATIONS: Nominal yield is also known as Stated yield.

Q228_LO42: Correct Answer: c EXPLANATIONS: CY is calculated as annual coupon payment ÷ market price.

Q229_LO42: Correct Answer: b EXPLANATIONS: YTM reflects the annualized return of the bond if held to maturity.

Q230_LO42: Correct Answer: c EXPLANATIONS: If the bond is purchased at a discount, the investor's return increases at maturity.

Q231_LO42: Correct Answer: b EXPLANATIONS: Yields are measured in basis points, where 1% is equal to 100 basis points (bps).

Q232_LO42: Correct Answer: c EXPLANATIONS: A full percentage point is equal to 100 basis points (bps).

Q233_LO42: Correct Answer: c EXPLANATIONS: Yield to Call is sometimes known as Callable Yield.

Q234_LO42: Correct Answer: c EXPLANATIONS: The investor's return increases due to early redemption.

Q235_LO42: Correct Answer: a EXPLANATIONS: Nominal Yield and CY are equal.

Q236_LO42: Correct Answer: c EXPLANATIONS: YTM reflects the premium or discount at the time of purchase.

Q237_LO42: Correct Answer: c EXPLANATIONS: YTM decreases when a bond is purchased at a premium.

Q238_LO42: Correct Answer: c EXPLANATIONS: A bond's basis is sometimes called its YTM measurement.

Q239_LO42: Correct Answer: b EXPLANATIONS: A bond trading at a 5.83 basis means it has a YTM of 5.83%.

Q240_LO42: Correct Answer: a EXPLANATIONS: YTM, CY, and YTC increase when a bond is trading at a discount.

Q241_LO43: Correct Answer: c EXPLANATIONS: A.M. Best Co., Inc. is not one of the "majors" among credit rating agencies.

Q242_LO43: Correct Answer: b EXPLANATIONS: The primary purpose of a bond rating is to assess the safety of the bond.

Q243_LO43: Correct Answer: c EXPLANATIONS: A.M. Best Co., Inc. is historically associated with rating insurance companies.

Q244_LO43: Correct Answer: c EXPLANATIONS: AAA is the highest rating for an investment-grade bond according to Standard & Poor’s.

Q245_LO43: Correct Answer: c EXPLANATIONS: Aaa is the highest Moody's rating for an investment-grade bond.

Q246_LO43: Correct Answer: b EXPLANATIONS: BBB indicates adequate capacity to repay, slightly speculative for an investment-grade bond.

Q247_LO43: Correct Answer: b EXPLANATIONS: Ba by Moody's indicates a speculative bond with a significant chance of missing payments.

Q248_LO43: Correct Answer: c EXPLANATIONS: C indicates no interest being paid, with missed interest or principal payments.

Q249_LO43: Correct Answer: c EXPLANATIONS: D by Moody's indicates that the issuer is in default with payment in arrears.

Q250_LO43: Correct Answer: d EXPLANATIONS: D by S&P indicates that the issuer is in default.

Q251_LO43: Correct Answer: c EXPLANATIONS: Caa by Moody's indicates a speculative bond with missed interest or principal payments.

Q252_LO43: Correct Answer: c EXPLANATIONS: BB by S&P indicates a speculative bond.

Q253_LO43: Correct Answer: a EXPLANATIONS: B by Moody's indicates a speculative bond.

Q254_LO43: Correct Answer: c EXPLANATIONS: Higher ratings indicate higher safety for bonds.

Q255_LO43: Correct Answer: c EXPLANATIONS: C by S&P indicates no interest being paid at the moment.

Q256_LO43: Correct Answer: b EXPLANATIONS: The safety of a debt security is enhanced by the strength of the borrower.

Q257_LO43: Correct Answer: c EXPLANATIONS: A.M. Best Co. is historically associated with rating insurance companies.

Q258_LO43: Correct Answer: a EXPLANATIONS: The three major credit rating agencies are Moody's, Fitch, and Standard and Poor's (S&P).

Q259_LO43: Correct Answer: b EXPLANATIONS: AAA indicates a very strong capacity to repay principal and interest.

Q260_LO43: Correct Answer: c EXPLANATIONS: Moody's highest rating is Aaa, indicating a high capacity to repay principal and interest.

Q261_LO43: Correct Answer: c EXPLANATIONS: A BB rating by Standard & Poor's suggests a speculative nature with a significant chance of missing an interest payment.

Q262_LO43: Correct Answer: d EXPLANATIONS: A D rating from Moody's indicates the issuer is in default, with interest or principal payment in arrears.

Q263_LO43: Correct Answer: b EXPLANATIONS: A Caa rating in Moody's system signifies a speculative nature.

Q264_LO43: Correct Answer: a EXPLANATIONS: A Ba rating from Moody's suggests a speculative nature with a significant chance of missing an interest payment.

Q265_LO43: Correct Answer: b EXPLANATIONS: A C rating by Standard & Poor's indicates that no interest is being paid on the bond at this time.

Q266_LO43: Correct Answer: b EXPLANATIONS: Fitch, S&P, and Moody's follow the same pattern in their rating scales.

Q267_LO43: Correct Answer: b EXPLANATIONS: Moody's rates such bonds as A.

Q268_LO43: Correct Answer: a EXPLANATIONS: A BBB rating by Standard & Poor's suggests a slightly speculative nature with adequate capacity to repay.

Q269_LO43: Correct Answer: b EXPLANATIONS: Moody's would rate such a bond as D, indicating the issuer is in default.

Q270_LO43: Correct Answer: c EXPLANATIONS: Noninvestment-grade refers to bonds with a speculative nature and a higher risk of default.

Q271_LO43: Correct Answer: c EXPLANATIONS: Bonds rated BBB or Baa and higher are termed investment-grade bonds.

Q272_LO43: Correct Answer: b EXPLANATIONS: Higher ratings correspond to lower yields, reflecting lower risk and lower reward.

Q273_LO43: Correct Answer: b EXPLANATIONS: Credit rating, indicated by the bond's creditworthiness, influences liquidity.

Q274_LO43: Correct Answer: c EXPLANATIONS: Lower-grade bonds are commonly called high-yield bonds.

Q275_LO43: Correct Answer: d EXPLANATIONS: High-yield bonds may experience price erosion due to their additional risk of default.

Q276_LO43: Correct Answer: c EXPLANATIONS: High-yield bonds may offer higher returns and possible capital appreciation, making them suitable for sophisticated investors.

Q277_LO43: Correct Answer: c EXPLANATIONS: Lower-rated bonds offer higher returns to compensate for additional risk.
Q278_LO43: Correct Answer: c EXPLANATIONS: Noninvestment-grade refers to bonds with a speculative nature.

Q279_LO43: Correct Answer: d EXPLANATIONS: Collateral is considered along with other factors in the evaluation of a bond.

Q280_LO43: Correct Answer: a EXPLANATIONS: Volatility refers to a bond's sensitivity to changes in interest rates.

Q281_LO43: Correct Answer: a EXPLANATIONS: A bond with 10 years to maturity is generally more volatile due to its longer time left to maturity.

Q282_LO43: Correct Answer: a EXPLANATIONS: A lower coupon rate increases a bond's volatility.

Q283_LO43: Correct Answer: c EXPLANATIONS: Duration is used to measure a bond's overall volatility, considering both maturity and coupon rate.

Q284_LO43: Correct Answer: a EXPLANATIONS: A higher duration increases a bond's price volatility.

Q285_LO43: Correct Answer: a EXPLANATIONS: A 3% bond might be more volatile than a 6% bond, especially when interest rates are low.

Q286_LO44: Correct Answer: c EXPLANATIONS: A call feature allows an issuer to call in a bond before maturity, especially when interest rates are falling.

Q287_LO44: Correct Answer: b EXPLANATIONS: Issuers generally use a call feature when interest rates are falling.

Q288_LO44: Correct Answer: d EXPLANATIONS: A call feature allows the issuer to issue a new bond at a lower current interest rate.
Q289_LO44: Correct Answer: c EXPLANATIONS: The opposite of a call feature is a put feature.

Q290_LO44: Correct Answer: b EXPLANATIONS: Investors typically use a put feature when interest rates are rising.

Q291_LO44: Correct Answer: d EXPLANATIONS: A put feature allows the bondholder to put the bond back to the issuer at a higher interest rate.

Q292_LO44: Correct Answer: b EXPLANATIONS: A convertible feature allows the investor to convert the bond into shares of common stock.

Q293_LO44: Correct Answer: b EXPLANATIONS: Arbitrage transactions involve simultaneous buying and selling to capture price differentials between securities.

Q294_LO44: Correct Answer: b EXPLANATIONS: Convertible bonds may often track the value of the underlying shares they can be converted into.

Q295_LO44: Correct Answer: b EXPLANATIONS: The purpose is to capture price differentials between the convertible bond and the underlying stock.

Q296_LO44: Correct Answer: c EXPLANATIONS: A convertible feature allows the exchange of a debt instrument for shares of common stock, providing ownership rights.

Q297_LO44: Correct Answer: d EXPLANATIONS: An investor might use a put feature to put the bond back to the issuer at a higher interest rate.

Q298_LO44: Correct Answer: c EXPLANATIONS: The dilemma arises when the bondholder needs to find a similar rate of return in a lower interest rate environment.

Q299_LO44: Correct Answer: d EXPLANATIONS: The benefit of a put feature for the bondholder is influenced by rising interest rates.

Q300_LO44: Correct Answer: c EXPLANATIONS: A put feature allows the investor to put the bond back to the issuer before it matures.

Q301_LO44: Correct Answer: c EXPLANATIONS: A call feature allows an issuer to call in a bond before maturity, particularly when interest rates are falling.

Q302_LO44: Correct Answer: c EXPLANATIONS: An issuer would use a call feature to take advantage of falling interest rates and issue new bonds at lower rates.

Q303_LO44: Correct Answer: c EXPLANATIONS: A put feature allows the bondholder to put the bond back to the issuer before maturity.

Q304_LO44: Correct Answer: b EXPLANATIONS: An investor would typically use a put feature when interest rates are rising.

Q305_LO44: Correct Answer: c EXPLANATIONS: A convertible feature allows the investor to convert the bond into shares of common stock.

Q306_LO44: Correct Answer: c EXPLANATIONS: Convertible bonds often track the value of the underlying shares when the stock rises.

Q307_LO44: Correct Answer: b EXPLANATIONS: Arbitrage involves the simultaneous buying and selling of the bond and underlying stock to capture price differentials.

Q308_LO44: Correct Answer: c EXPLANATIONS: Investors often engage in arbitrage transactions with convertible bonds, especially in falling interest rate scenarios.

Q309_LO44: Correct Answer: b EXPLANATIONS: A put feature allows the investor to put the bond back to the issuer before maturity.

Q310_LO44: Correct Answer: d EXPLANATIONS: An investor might use a put feature to put the bond back to the issuer in a rising interest rate environment.

Q311_LO44: Correct Answer: a EXPLANATIONS: The opposite of a call feature is a put feature.

Q312_LO44: Correct Answer: c EXPLANATIONS: An issuer would typically use a call feature in a falling interest rate environment.
Q313_LO44: Correct Answer: d EXPLANATIONS: A call feature allows the issuer to call in the bond before maturity, especially when interest rates are falling.
Q314_LO44: Correct Answer: d EXPLANATIONS: A put feature allows the bondholder to put the bond back to the issuer in a rising interest rate environment.

Q315_LO44: Correct Answer: d EXPLANATIONS: A convertible feature allows the bondholder to convert the bond into shares of common stock.

ZEROS AND TYPES OF CORPORATE DEBT & Benefits / risks of Debt

Q316_LO44: What is a defining feature of zero-coupon bonds?
a. Regular interest payments
b. High coupon rates
c. Issued at face value
d. No regular interest payments

HINTS: Recall the primary characteristic of zero-coupon bonds.

Q317_LO44: How do zero-coupon bonds differ from other bonds regarding interest payments?
a. They have higher interest rates
b. They make regular interest payments
c. They pay interest annually
d. They do not make regular interest payments

HINTS: Recognize the key difference in interest payments for zero-coupon bonds.

Q318_LO44: What is the return mechanism for zero-coupon bonds?
a. Coupon payments
b. Accreted interest
c. Face value appreciation
d. Higher interest rates

HINTS: Understand how investors receive returns from zero-coupon bonds.

Q319_LO44: Why are zero-coupon bonds more volatile than other bonds?
a. They have lower face values
b. They lack face value
c. They have zero coupon rates
d. They have higher interest rates

HINTS: Identify the reason for the increased volatility of zero-coupon bonds.

Q320_LO44: Who issues STRIPS, which are a type of zero-coupon bond?
a. Broker-dealers
b. Municipalities
c. Corporations
d. U.S. Treasury

HINTS: Recognize the issuer of STRIPS, a type of zero-coupon bond.

Q321_LO44: What distinguishes treasury receipts from STRIPS?
a. Credit rating
b. Coupon rate
c. Maturity period
d. Issuer backing

HINTS: Identify the key distinction between treasury receipts and STRIPS.

Q322_LO44: How does the price of a zero-coupon bond behave concerning interest rates?
a. It has no correlation
b. It increases with interest rates
c. It decreases with interest rates
d. It remains constant

HINTS: Understand the relationship between the price of zero-coupon bonds and interest rates.

Q323_LO44: What is the tax implication of owning zero-coupon bonds?
a. No taxes are paid
b. Taxes are paid only at maturity
c. Taxes are paid on the interest annually
d. Taxes are paid on the face value at maturity

HINTS: Recognize the tax treatment for owners of zero-coupon bonds.

Q324_LO44: How is the return on zero-coupon bonds calculated?
a. Face value divided by coupon rate
b. Purchase price minus face value
c. Purchase price plus coupon rate
d. Face value minus purchase price

HINTS: Recall the calculation method for the return on zero-coupon bonds.

Q325_LO44: What is the common term for the tax payment on zero-coupon bonds?
a. Tax refund
b. Accreted tax
c. Phantom income
d. Discount tax

HINTS: Identify the term associated with the annual tax payment on zero-coupon bonds.

Q326_LO44: Which entity may create treasury receipts, a type of zero-coupon bond?
a. U.S. Treasury
b. Broker-dealers
c. Municipalities
d. Corporations

HINTS: Recognize the issuer of treasury receipts, a type of zero-coupon bond.

Q327_LO44: What is the primary characteristic of zero-coupon bonds regarding maturity?
a. They have extended maturity periods
b. They mature at face value
c. They lack maturity
d. They have shorter maturity periods

HINTS: Recall the primary characteristic of zero-coupon bonds at maturity.

Q328_LO44: In an inverse relationship, how does the price of zero-coupon bonds behave concerning interest rates?
a. It increases with interest rates
b. It remains constant
c. It has no correlation
d. It decreases with interest rates

HINTS: Understand the inverse relationship between the price of zero-coupon bonds and interest rates.

Q329_LO44: What distinguishes STRIPS from other zero-coupon bonds?
a. Higher coupon rates
b. Backed by the U.S. Treasury
c. Extended maturity periods
d. Created by broker-dealers

HINTS: Identify the distinguishing feature of STRIPS, a type of zero-coupon bond.

Q330_LO44: What does "annual accretion of the discount" refer to in zero-coupon bonds?
a. The increase in face value
b. The annual tax payment
c. The decrease in purchase price
d. The annual increase in interest

HINTS: Understand the meaning of "annual accretion of the discount" in zero-coupon bonds.

Q331_LO45: What differentiates secured debt securities from unsecured debt securities?
a. Maturity period
b. Interest rate
c. Asset backing
d. Issuer's reputation

HINTS: Recognize the distinguishing factor between secured and unsecured debt securities.

Q332_LO45: What is the settlement cycle for corporate debt securities?
a. T+1
b. T+2
c. T+3
d. T+4

HINTS: Recall the settlement cycle for corporate debt securities.

Q333_LO45: What type of asset backs mortgage bonds?
a. Intellectual property
b. Real estate
c. Equipment
d. Marketable securities

HINTS: Identify the asset that serves as collateral for mortgage bonds.

Q334_LO45: In the case of financial problems, what happens to the real assets pledged as collateral for mortgage bonds?
a. Sold to pay off bondholders
b. Converted to stocks
c. Transferred to a trustee
d. Used for interest payments

HINTS: Understand the fate of real assets pledged as collateral for mortgage bonds during financial problems.

Q335_LO45: What type of corporation issues equipment trust certificates?
a. Pharmaceutical
b. Transportation
c. Technology
d. Energy

HINTS: Recognize the industry that typically issues equipment trust certificates.

Q336_LO45: What is held in trust in the case of equipment trust certificates?
a. Cash
b. Equipment
c. Intellectual property
d. Marketable securities

HINTS: Identify the collateral held in trust for equipment trust certificates.

Q337_LO45: What is the primary backing for collateral trust bonds?
a. Real estate
b. Equipment
c. Marketable securities
d. Intellectual property

HINTS: Recognize the primary backing for collateral trust bonds.

Q338_LO45: What is a debenture backed by?
a. Real estate
b. Intellectual property
c. Reputation and creditworthiness
d. Equipment

HINTS: Identify the backing for a debenture.

Q339_LO45: What distinguishes guaranteed bonds from other corporate debt?
a. Higher interest rates
b. Backed by a parent company
c. Longer maturity periods
d. Secured by real assets

HINTS: Recognize the distinguishing feature of guaranteed bonds.

Q340_LO45: When are income bonds typically used?
a. During bankruptcy
b. During mergers
c. During economic downturns
d. During IPOs

HINTS: Understand the typical situation in which income bonds are used.

Q341_LO45: What triggers the payment of interest for income bonds?
a. Regular intervals
b. Board of directors' declaration
c. Bondholder's request
d. Market conditions

HINTS: Identify the condition that triggers interest payments for income bonds.

Q342_LO45: What is the primary characteristic of subordinated debt?
a. High interest rates
b. Superior claim in liquidation
c. Lower rank in liquidation
d. Shorter maturity periods

HINTS: Recall the primary characteristic of subordinated debt.

Q343_LO45: In the hierarchy of debt, what is subordinated debenture's claim status?
a. Junior to stockholders
b. Superior to all creditors
c. Equal to mortgage bondholders
d. Equal to stockholders

HINTS: Recognize the claim status of subordinated debentures in the hierarchy of debt.

Q344_LO45: What is another term for income bonds?
a. Adjustment bonds
b. Subordinated bonds
c. Convertible bonds
d. Guaranteed bonds

HINTS: Identify the alternative term for income bonds.

Q345_LO45: What does "full faith and credit" refer to in the context of unsecured debt?
a. Backed by marketable securities
b. Backed by reputation and creditworthiness
c. Guaranteed by a parent company
d. Secured by real estate

HINTS: Understand the meaning of "full faith and credit" in the context of unsecured debt.

Q346_LO45: What distinguishes secured debt securities from unsecured debt securities?
a. Payment frequency
b. Backing by assets
c. Settlement period
d. Credit record

HINTS: Identify the key characteristic of secured debt securities.

Q347_LO45: What is the settlement period for corporate debt securities?
a. T+1
b. T+2
c. T+3
d. T+4

HINTS: Recall the settlement period for corporate debt securities.

Q348_LO45: In a secured loan, what happens if a corporation defaults on interest payments for mortgage bonds?
a. Principal is forgiven
b. Real assets are sold to pay bondholders
c. Mortgage bonds are converted to equity
d. Bondholders lose their rights

HINTS: Recognize the consequence of default on interest payments for mortgage bonds.

Q349_LO45: What type of corporations issues equipment trust certificates?
a. Manufacturing companies
b. Transportation companies
c. Technology companies
d. Financial companies

HINTS: Identify the type of corporations that issue equipment trust certificates.

Q350_LO45: How are collateral trust bonds secured?
a. Real estate
b. Equipment
c. Deposited securities
d. Full faith and credit

HINTS: Understand the security mechanism for collateral trust bonds.

Q351_LO45: What backs a debenture issued by a corporation?
a. Real estate
b. Equipment
c. General creditworthiness
d. Deposited securities

HINTS: Recognize the backing for a debenture issued by a corporation.

Q352_LO45: What distinguishes guaranteed bonds from other types of corporate debt?
a. Secured by real assets
b. Backed by a parent company
c. Pay interest only in bankruptcy
d. Subordinated to other debt

HINTS: Identify the characteristic that sets guaranteed bonds apart.

Q353_LO45: When are income bonds typically used?
a. During bankruptcy
b. When issuing equipment
c. Reorganizing after bankruptcy
d. In case of default

HINTS: Recognize the circumstances under which income bonds are used.
Q354_LO45: How do income bonds differ from other debt securities regarding interest payments?
a. Pay interest only if BOD declares
b. Pay interest only in bankruptcy
c. Pay interest annually
d. Pay interest regardless of income

HINTS: Identify the unique characteristic of income bonds concerning interest payments.

Q355_LO45: What is the primary responsibility for debt in the case of guaranteed bonds?
a. Bondholders
b. Guarantor
c. Lender
d. Trustee

HINTS: Recognize the entity primarily responsible for debt in the case of guaranteed bonds.

Q356_LO45: What characterizes subordinated debentures in terms of claims?
a. Senior to all creditors
b. Junior to other creditors
c. Equal to stockholders
d. No claim on assets

HINTS: Understand the hierarchy of claims for subordinated debentures.

Q357_LO45: What does "subordinated" mean in the context of debt securities?
a. Higher rank
b. Lower rank
c. Equal rank
d. Unranked

HINTS: Understand the meaning of the term "subordinated" in the context of debt securities.

Q358_LO45: What is the distinguishing feature of income bonds in terms of interest payments?
a. Guaranteed payments
b. Board of directors approval
c. Interest paid regardless of income
d. Payable only in bankruptcy

HINTS: Identify the factor that distinguishes income bonds in terms of interest payments.

Q359_LO45: What is the primary backing for debentures?
a. Real assets
b. Equipment
c. Full faith and credit
d. Parent company

HINTS: Recognize the primary backing for debentures.

Q360_LO45: In the case of subordinated debentures, what is the claim priority compared to stockholders?
a. Senior to stockholders
b. Equal to stockholders
c. Junior to stockholders
d. No claim on assets

HINTS: Understand the claim priority of subordinated debentures compared to stockholders.

Q361_LO45: In the order of liquidation, who gets paid first?
a. Unsecured debt holders
b. Common stockholders
c. Secured debt holders
d. Subordinated debt holders
HINTS: Recognize the priority in the order of liquidation.

Q362_LO45: What are secured debt holders paid from in the order of liquidation?
a. General creditor payments
b. Preferred stock proceeds
c. Sale of assets that secured the debt
d. Common stock dividends

HINTS: Identify the source from which secured debt holders are paid during liquidation.

Q363_LO45: Who comes second in the order of liquidation after secured debt holders?
a. Subordinated debt holders
b. Common stockholders
c. Unsecured debt holders
d. General creditors

HINTS: Understand the order of liquidation after secured debt holders.

Q364_LO45: What do general creditors include in the context of liquidation?

a. Subordinated debt holders
b. Preferred stockholders
c. Vendors and suppliers
d. Common stockholders

HINTS: Recognize the entities included in the category of general creditors during liquidation.

Q365_LO45: Why do subordinated debt holders have a higher coupon rate?
a. Lower risk
b. Seniority in liquidation
c. Higher risk
d. Tax advantages

HINTS: Identify the reason why subordinated debt holders have a higher coupon rate.

Q366_LO45: After general creditors, who is third in line in the order of liquidation?
a. Subordinated debt holders
b. Preferred stockholders
c. Unsecured debt holders
d. Common stockholders

HINTS: Understand the position of subordinated debt holders in the order of liquidation.

Q367_LO45: What is the equity status of preferred stockholders in the order of liquidation?
a. Senior to common stockholders
b. Junior to common stockholders
c. Equal to common stockholders
d. Junior to secured debt holders

HINTS: Recognize the equity status of preferred stockholders in relation to common stockholders during liquidation.

Q368_LO45: In the order of liquidation, who is last in line to be paid?
a. Unsecured debt holders
b. Common stockholders
c. Preferred stockholders
d. Subordinated debt holders

HINTS: Identify the last group to be paid in the order of liquidation.

Q369_LO45: What is the primary reason for common stockholders being last in the order of liquidation?
a. Higher investment
b. Lower risk
c. Equity ownership
d. Tax advantages

HINTS: Understand the rationale behind common stockholders being the last to be paid.

Q370_LO45: What is the downside of being a common stockholder in a bankruptcy?
a. Lower dividends
b. No voting rights
c. Loss of equity ownership
d. Rare payout at liquidation

HINTS: Recognize the downside of being a common stockholder in a bankruptcy scenario.

Q371_LO45: Why do subordinated debt holders have a claim junior to other creditors?
a. Tax advantages
b. Equity ownership
c. Increased risk
d. Lower coupon rate

HINTS: Identify the reason why subordinated debt holders have a junior claim.

Q372_LO45: What do preferred stockholders receive before common stockholders in the order of liquidation?

a. Higher dividends
b. Voting rights
c. Interest payments
d. Proceeds from asset sales

HINTS: Recognize the priority of preferred stockholders compared to common stockholders in liquidation.

Q373_LO45: In liquidation, from where are secured debt holders paid if the asset sales are insufficient?
a. General creditor level
b. Subordinated debt holders
c. Common stockholders
d. Unsecured debt holders

HINTS: Understand the course of action if asset sales are insufficient to pay secured debt holders.

Q374_LO45: What distinguishes subordinated debt holders from other debt holders in the order of liquidation?
a. Lower risk
b. Higher coupon rate
c. Equity ownership
d. Seniority in liquidation

HINTS: Recognize the distinguishing factor for subordinated debt holders in the order of liquidation.

Q375_LO45: What defines the position of common stockholders in a bankruptcy scenario?
a. Senior to all creditors
b. Equal to secured debt holders
c. Junior to all creditors
d. Equal to preferred stockholders

HINTS: Understand the hierarchical position of common stockholders in a bankruptcy.

Q376_LO46: What is considered the best way to produce current income for an investor?
a. Stocks
b. Bonds
c. Preferred stock
d. Mutual funds

HINTS: Recognize the investment vehicle that is best for producing current income.

Q377_LO46: Why do bonds produce a steady and predictable income for investors?
a. Guaranteed dividends
b. Mandatory interest payments
c. High price volatility
d. Equity ownership

HINTS: Understand the characteristic of debt securities that leads to steady and predictable income.

Q378_LO46: What is the primary risk associated with owning debt securities?
a. Interest rate risk
b. Default risk
c. Purchasing power risk
d. Market risk

HINTS: Identify the main risk related to owning debt securities.

Q379_LO46: Why are bonds generally considered safer than stocks?
a. Guaranteed returns
b. Priority in liquidation
c. Higher price volatility
d. Equity ownership

HINTS: Recognize the factor that contributes to the relative safety of bonds compared to stocks.

Q380_LO46: What is the worst outcome of owning a bond?

a. Decreased market value
b. Default
c. Interest rate fluctuation
d. Inflation risk

HINTS: Identify the severe consequence of owning a bond.

Q381_LO46: How do credit rating agencies contribute to the evaluation of debt securities?
a. Predicting interest rates
b. Assessing market risk
c. Rating financial strength
d. Estimating dividend yields

HINTS: Recognize the role of credit rating agencies in evaluating debt securities.

Q382_LO46: What risk is associated with fixed payments in the context of security holdings?
a. Market risk
b. Purchasing power risk
c. Interest rate risk
d. Credit risk

HINTS: Identify the risk associated with fixed payments in the context of security holdings.

Q383_LO46: What term is used for the risk that debt securities will fluctuate with changes in prevailing interest rates?
a. Default risk
b. Market risk
c. Credit risk
d. Interest rate risk

HINTS: Recognize the specific risk related to fluctuations in interest rates for debt securities.

Q384_LO46: In terms of priority, where do bondholders stand compared to equity securities in liquidation?
a. Equal to equity securities
b. Senior to equity securities
c. Junior to equity securities
d. Concurrent with equity securities

HINTS: Understand the hierarchical position of bondholders compared to equity securities in liquidation.

Q385_LO46: What is the term for the risk that arises from a rise in the price of goods over time?
a. Market risk
b. Interest rate risk
c. Default risk
d. Purchasing power risk

HINTS: Identify the specific risk associated with a rise in the price of goods.

Q386_LO46: What characteristic makes bonds suitable for conservative investors seeking stability?
a. High price volatility
b. Equity ownership
c. Predictable income
d. Default risk

HINTS: Recognize the characteristic of bonds that attracts conservative investors seeking stability.
Q387_LO46: Why are stocks considered riskier than bonds for conservative investors?
a. Lower market risk
b. Guaranteed dividends
c. Lower price volatility
d. Lack of mandatory payments

HINTS: Identify the factor that makes stocks riskier than bonds for conservative investors.

Q388_LO46: What type of payment does preferred stock produce, exposing it to purchasing power risk?
a. Variable dividends

b. Mandatory interest payments
c. Fixed payments
d. Guaranteed returns

HINTS: Recognize the payment characteristic of preferred stock that exposes it to purchasing power risk.

Q389_LO46: What does default risk refer to in the context of debt securities?
a. Fluctuation in interest rates
b. Failure to make interest or principal payments
c. Credit rating changes
d. Market risk

HINTS: Understand the specific risk associated with default in the context of debt securities.
Q390_LO46: How does inflation impact the real value of fixed payments over time?
a. Increases the real value
b. Maintains the real value
c. Decreases the real value
d. Has no impact on the real value

HINTS: Recognize the impact of inflation on the real value of fixed payments.

Correct Answers & Explanations
ZEROS AND TYPES OF CORPORATE DEBT & Benefits / risks of Debt

Q316_LO44: Correct Answer: d EXPLANATIONS: Zero-coupon bonds do not make regular interest payments.

Q317_LO44: Correct Answer: d EXPLANATIONS: Zero-coupon bonds do not make regular interest payments.

Q318_LO44: Correct Answer: b EXPLANATIONS: The return for zero-coupon bonds is the difference between the discounted purchase price and the full face value at maturity, known as accreted interest.

Q319_LO44: Correct Answer: c EXPLANATIONS: Zero-coupon bonds, having a zero coupon rate, tend to be more volatile than other bonds. .

Q320_LO44: Correct Answer: d EXPLANATIONS: STRIPS, or zero-coupon bonds issued by the U.S. Treasury, are issued by the U.S. Treasury.
Q321_LO44: Correct Answer: d EXPLANATIONS: Unlike a STRIP, a treasury receipt is not backed by the full faith and credit of the Treasury.

Q322_LO44: Correct Answer: c EXPLANATIONS: The price of zero-coupon bonds tends to decrease with rising interest rates.

Q323_LO44: Correct Answer: c EXPLANATIONS: Owners of zero-coupon bonds pay taxes on the interest annually.
Q324_LO44: Correct Answer: b EXPLANATIONS: The return is the difference between the discounted purchase price and the full face value at maturity.

Q325_LO44: Correct Answer: c EXPLANATIONS: The annual tax payment on zero-coupon bonds is known as "annual accretion of the discount" or "phantom income."

Q326_LO44: Correct Answer: b EXPLANATIONS: Treasury receipts are created by broker-dealers.

Q327_LO44: Correct Answer: b EXPLANATIONS: Zero-coupon bonds mature at face value.
Q328_LO44: Correct Answer: d EXPLANATIONS: The price of zero-coupon bonds tends to decrease with rising interest rates.

Q329_LO44: Correct Answer: b EXPLANATIONS: STRIPS are zero-coupon bonds backed by the U.S. Treasury.
Q330_LO44: Correct Answer: b EXPLANATIONS: Annual accretion of the discount refers to the annual tax payment on zero-coupon bonds.

Q331_LO45: Correct Answer: c EXPLANATIONS: Secured debt securities are backed by various assets owned by the issuer.
Q332_LO45: Correct Answer: b EXPLANATIONS: Corporate debt securities settle T+2.

Q333_LO45: Correct Answer: b EXPLANATIONS: Mortgage bonds are backed by real estate and physical assets of the corporation.
Q334_LO45: Correct Answer: a EXPLANATIONS: Real assets pledged as collateral for mortgage bonds are generally sold to pay off bondholders.

Q335_LO45: Correct Answer: b EXPLANATIONS: Transportation companies, such as railroads, issue equipment trust certificates.

Q336_LO45: Correct Answer: b EXPLANATIONS: Title to the newly acquired equipment is held in trust until the certificates have been paid in full.
Q337_LO45: Correct Answer: c EXPLANATIONS: Collateral trust bonds are secured by marketable securities deposited into a trust.

Q338_LO45: Correct Answer: c EXPLANATIONS: A debenture is backed only by the corporation's word and general creditworthiness.
Q339_LO45: Correct Answer: b EXPLANATIONS: Guaranteed bonds are backed by a company other than the issuing corporation, such as a parent company.

Q340_LO45: Correct Answer: a EXPLANATIONS: Income bonds are used when a company is reorganizing and coming out of bankruptcy.

Q341_LO45: Correct Answer: b EXPLANATIONS: Interest on income bonds is paid only if the corporation has enough income, and if the board of directors declares the payment.

Q342_LO45: Correct Answer: c EXPLANATIONS: Subordinated debt has a claim that is behind that of any other creditor.

Q343_LO45: Correct Answer: a EXPLANATIONS: Subordinated debentures are junior to any other creditor but senior to stockholders.

Q344_LO45: Correct Answer: a EXPLANATIONS: Income bonds are also known as adjustment bonds.
Q345_LO45: Correct Answer: b EXPLANATIONS: Unsecured debt is backed only by the reputation, credit record, and financial stability of the issuer.

Q346_LO45: Correct Answer: b EXPLANATIONS: Secured debt securities are backed by various kinds of assets owned by the issuer.

Q347_LO45: Correct Answer: b EXPLANATIONS: Corporate debt securities settle T+2.
Q348_LO45: Correct Answer: b EXPLANATIONS: Real assets pledged as collateral are generally sold to pay off mortgage bondholders.

Q349_LO45: Correct Answer: b EXPLANATIONS: Transportation companies, like railroads, issue equipment trust certificates.
Q350_LO45: Correct Answer: c EXPLANATIONS: Collateral trust certificates are secured by the securities deposited into a trust.

Q351_LO45: Correct Answer: c EXPLANATIONS: Debentures are backed only by the general creditworthiness of the corporation.
Q352_LO45: Correct Answer: b EXPLANATIONS: Guaranteed bonds are backed by a company other than the issuing corporation, such as a parent company.

Q353_LO45: Correct Answer: c EXPLANATIONS: Income bonds are used when a company is reorganizing and coming out of bankruptcy.

Q354_LO45: Correct Answer: a EXPLANATIONS: Income bonds pay interest only if the board of directors (BOD) declares the interest payment.
Q355_LO45: Correct Answer: b EXPLANATIONS: The primary responsibility for the debt belongs to the issuer, but the guarantor must make payments if the issuer defaults.

Q356_LO45: Correct Answer: b EXPLANATIONS: Subordinated debentures have a claim that is junior to that of any other creditor.

Q357_LO45: Correct Answer: b EXPLANATIONS: Subordinated means belonging to a lower or inferior class or rank; secondary.

Q358_LO45: Correct Answer: b EXPLANATIONS: Income bonds pay interest only if the board of directors (BOD) declares the interest payment.

Q359_LO45: Correct Answer: c EXPLANATIONS: Debentures are backed only by the general good faith and credit of the company, unsecured.

Q360_LO45: Correct Answer: c EXPLANATIONS: Subordinated debentures have a claim that is senior to any stockholder.

Q361_LO45: Correct Answer: c EXPLANATIONS: Secured debt holders are first in line to be paid during liquidation.

Q362_LO45: Correct Answer: c EXPLANATIONS: Secured debt holders are paid from the sale of assets that secured the debt.
Q363_LO45: Correct Answer: c EXPLANATIONS: Unsecured debt (debentures) and general creditors come second in line for payments.

Q364_LO45: Correct Answer: c EXPLANATIONS: General creditors typically include vendors and other suppliers the company owes money to.
Q365_LO45: Correct Answer: c EXPLANATIONS: Subordinated debt holders have increased risk, leading to a higher coupon rate.

Q366_LO45: Correct Answer: a EXPLANATIONS: Subordinated debt holders are third in line for payments during liquidation.

Q367_LO45: Correct Answer: a EXPLANATIONS: Preferred stockholders are senior to common stockholders in the order of liquidation.

Q368_LO45: Correct Answer: b EXPLANATIONS: Common stockholders are the last in line to be paid during liquidation.

Q369_LO45: Correct Answer: c EXPLANATIONS: Common stockholders are the actual owners of the company and are last in line during liquidation.
Q370_LO45: Correct Answer: d EXPLANATIONS: In a bankruptcy, it is extremely rare for common stockholders to get anything at liquidation.

Q371_LO45: Correct Answer: c EXPLANATIONS: Subordinated debt holders have a claim that is junior to other creditors due to increased risk.

Q372_LO45: Correct Answer: c EXPLANATIONS: Preferred stockholders receive payments before common stockholders in the order of liquidation.
Q373_LO45: Correct Answer: a EXPLANATIONS: If the assets are insufficient, any additional amount is paid at the general creditor level.

Q374_LO45: Correct Answer: b EXPLANATIONS: Subordinated debt holders have a higher coupon rate compared to other debt holders.
Q375_LO45: Correct Answer: c EXPLANATIONS: In a bankruptcy, common stockholders have a junior position compared to all creditors.

Q376_LO46: Correct Answer: b EXPLANATIONS: Bonds are considered the best way to produce current income for an investor.

Q377_LO46: Correct Answer: b EXPLANATIONS: Debt securities, including bonds, require mandatory interest payments, providing a steady income for investors.

Q378_LO46: Correct Answer: b EXPLANATIONS: The primary risk associated with owning debt securities is default risk.

Q379_LO46: Correct Answer: b EXPLANATIONS: Bonds are higher in priority than equity securities, contributing to their general safety.
Q380_LO46: Correct Answer: b EXPLANATIONS: The worst outcome of owning a bond is default, where the issuer fails to pay interest or principal.

Q381_LO46: Correct Answer: c EXPLANATIONS: Credit rating agencies rate the financial strength of an issuer, assisting in assessing default risk.

Q382_LO46: Correct Answer: b EXPLANATIONS: Purchasing power risk, or inflation risk, is associated with fixed payments as it erodes the real value over time.

Q383_LO46: Correct Answer: d EXPLANATIONS: Interest rate risk refers to the fluctuation of debt securities in response to changes in prevailing interest rates.
Q384_LO46: Correct Answer: b EXPLANATIONS: Bondholders are senior to equity securities in liquidation.

Q385_LO46: Correct Answer: d EXPLANATIONS: Purchasing power risk, or inflation risk, arises from a decrease in the real value of fixed payments over time.

Q386_LO46: Correct Answer: c EXPLANATIONS: Bonds, with mandatory interest payments, offer a predictable income, attracting conservative investors.

Q387_LO46: Correct Answer: d EXPLANATIONS: Stocks lack mandatory payments, making them riskier compared to bonds, which have predictable interest payments.

Q388_LO46: Correct Answer: c EXPLANATIONS: Preferred stock, producing fixed payments, is subject to purchasing power risk due to inflation.
Q389_LO46: Correct Answer: b EXPLANATIONS: Default risk refers to the failure of the issuer to make interest or principal payments.

Q390_LO46: Correct Answer: c EXPLANATIONS: Inflation decreases the real value of fixed payments over time, leading to purchasing power risk.

MUNICIPAL BONDS & TREASURIES

Q391_LO47: What are municipal bonds?
a. Corporate securities
b. Issued by state or local governments
c. International bonds
d. Equity securities

HINTS: Identify the correct category for municipal bonds.

Q392_LO47: Which type of municipal bond is backed by the municipality's taxing power?
a. Revenue bonds
b. General obligation bonds
c. Anticipation notes
d. Variable-rate demand notes

HINTS: Recognize the type of municipal bond backed by the taxing power of the municipality.

Q393_LO47: What is the primary source of repayment for general obligation bonds?
a. Project-generated revenues
b. Taxes collected by the municipality
c. Sales of bonds
d. Federal grants

HINTS: Identify the primary source of repayment for general obligation bonds.

Q394_LO47: What makes general obligation bonds known as "full faith and credit issues"?
a. High coupon rates
b. Tax-free status
c. Backing by the municipality's taxing power
d. Guaranteed returns

HINTS: Recognize the characteristic that leads to general obligation bonds being known as "full faith and credit issues."

Q395_LO47: Why do general obligation bonds often require voter approval?
a. High coupon rates
b. Federal regulations
c. Backing by taxing power
d. State statutes

HINTS: Understand the reason general obligation bonds often require voter approval.

Q396_LO47: What type of projects typically benefit from general obligation bonds?
a. Self-supporting projects
b. Income-generating projects
c. Community improvements
d. Industrial development projects

HINTS: Identify the nature of projects that generally benefit from general obligation bonds.

Q397_LO47: In what situations might a public referendum be required for general obligation bonds?
a. To increase tax rates
b. To reduce debt limits
c. To lower coupon rates
d. To extend maturities

HINTS: Recognize the circumstances under which a public referendum might be required for general obligation bonds.

Q398_LO47: What is the characteristic of revenue bonds that distinguishes them from general obligation bonds?
a. Backed by taxing power
b. Self-supporting debt
c. Guaranteed returns
d. Low coupon rates

HINTS: Identify the characteristic that distinguishes revenue bonds from general obligation bonds.

Q399_LO47: What type of projects typically benefit from revenue bonds?
a. Community improvements
b. Non-revenue-generating projects
c. Tax-funded projects
d. Projects with sufficient income

HINTS: Recognize the nature of projects that typically benefit from revenue bonds.

Q400_LO47: Why are revenue bonds not subject to statutory debt limits and voter approval?
a. Lower coupon rates
b. Federal exemptions
c. No backing by taxing power
d. Shorter maturities

HINTS: Understand why revenue bonds are not subject to statutory debt limits and voter approval.

Q401_LO47: What is the primary source of repayment for revenue bonds?
a. Taxes collected by the municipality
b. Project-generated revenues
c. Federal grants
d. Sales of bonds

HINTS: Identify the primary source of repayment for revenue bonds.

Q402_LO47: What distinguishes short-term municipal anticipation notes from long-term bonds?
a. Backing by taxing power
b. Higher coupon rates
c. Shorter maturities
d. Federal exemptions

HINTS: Recognize the characteristic that distinguishes short-term municipal anticipation notes from long-term bonds.

Q403_LO47: What is the purpose of tax anticipation notes (TANs)?
a. Financing current operations
b. Financing long-term projects
c. Financing housing projects
d. Financing transportation projects

HINTS: Identify the purpose of tax anticipation notes (TANs) among the given options.

Q404_LO47: What is the tax status of interest on most municipal bonds?
a. Taxable at the federal level
b. Tax-free at the federal and state levels
c. Taxable at the state level
d. Tax-free at the federal level

HINTS: Understand the tax status of interest on most municipal bonds.

Q405_LO47: How is the tax-equivalent yield calculated for a tax-exempt bond?
a. Divide tax-free yield by the investor's tax rate
b. Multiply tax-free yield by 100%
c. Add the investor's tax rate to the tax-free yield
d. Subtract the investor's tax rate from 100%

HINTS: Understand the calculation method for tax-equivalent yield.

Q406_LO47: What distinguishes municipal bonds from other securities?
a. Corporate backing
b. Government issuance
c. Foreign ownership
d. Volatile market

HINTS: Identify the unique characteristic of municipal bonds.

Q407_LO47: What is the purpose of municipal securities issuance?
a. Stock trading
b. Public works and construction projects
c. Currency exchange
d. Corporate financing

HINTS: Recognize the primary purpose of issuing municipal securities.

Q408_LO47: What is the tax status of interest on most municipal bonds?
a. Taxed at a federal level
b. Tax-free at both federal and state levels
c. Taxed at a state level
d. Exempt from all taxes

HINTS: Understand the tax status of interest on most municipal bonds.

Q409_LO47: How are general obligation bonds (GO) typically backed?
a. Corporate assets
b. Municipality's taxing power
c. Project-generated revenues
d. Federal backing

HINTS: Identify the backing source for general obligation bonds.

Q410_LO47: What limits the amount of debt a municipal government may incur?
a. Federal regulations
b. State or local statutes
c. Bondholders' approval
d. Municipal ordinances

HINTS: Recognize the factor that limits municipal debt and contributes to investor safety.

Q411_LO47: Why are GO bonds associated with requiring voter approval?
a. Lower risk for investors
b. Mandatory regulatory requirement
c. Higher potential returns
d. Protection against excessive borrowing

HINTS: Understand the association of GO bonds with a specific approval process.

Q412_LO47: What makes revenue bonds self-supporting debt?
a. Municipality's taxing power
b. Federal backing
c. Project or facility-generated revenues
d. Bondholders' contributions

HINTS: Recognize the characteristic that makes revenue bonds self-supporting.

Q413_LO47: Why are revenue bonds not subject to statutory debt limits?
a. Federal regulations exempt them
b. Project-specific revenues
c. Voter approval is not required
d. Lower risk for investors

HINTS: Identify the reason revenue bonds are not subject to statutory debt limits.

Q414_LO47: What is the purpose of short-term municipal anticipation notes?
a. Long-term financing
b. Interim financing
c. Tax collection
d. Construction projects

HINTS: Recognize the purpose of short-term municipal anticipation notes.

Q415_LO47: What distinguishes tax and revenue anticipation notes (TRANs)?
a. Interim financing
b. Tax collection
c. Project-generated revenues
d. Long-term funding

HINTS: Identify the specific characteristic of TRANs among short-term municipal notes.

Q416_LO47: How is the tax-equivalent yield calculated for a tax-exempt bond?
a. Divide corporate yield by 100%
b. Divide municipal yield by 100%
c. Divide tax-free yield by (100% minus tax rate)
d. Multiply tax rate by municipal yield

HINTS: Understand the calculation of tax-equivalent yield for a tax-exempt bond.

Q417_LO47: Why is the municipal yield always less than the corporate yield?
a. Lower market risk
b. Higher default risk
c. Tax exemption value
d. Higher interest rates

HINTS: Recognize the relationship between municipal and corporate yields.

Q418_LO47: What type of financing do bond anticipation notes (BANs) represent?
a. Long-term financing
b. Interim financing
c. Tax collection
d. Project-generated revenues

HINTS: Identify the financing purpose of bond anticipation notes.

Q419_LO47: What is the characteristic of variable-rate demand notes?
a. Fixed interest rate
b. Fluctuating interest rate
c. No interest payments
d. Convertible to equity

HINTS: Recognize the interest rate characteristic of variable-rate demand notes.

Q420_LO47: What are grant anticipation notes (GANs) issued in expectation of?
a. Tax collection
b. Project-generated revenues
c. Federal grant money
d. Bondholders' contributions

HINTS: Identify the purpose of issuing grant anticipation notes.

Q421_LO47: What determines the interest rates on U.S. government securities?
a. Market demand
b. Federal Reserve
c. U.S. Treasury Department
d. Congress

HINTS: Identify the key determinant of interest rates on government securities.

Q422_LO47: What is the classification of U.S. Treasury securities based on their term to maturity?
a. Short, medium, long
b. Bills, notes, bonds
c. T-bills, T-notes, T-bonds
d. Direct, indirect, indexed

HINTS: Recognize the classification of U.S. Treasury securities based on their term to maturity.

Q423_LO47: How are government securities issued by the U.S. Treasury backed?
a. Corporate backing
b. Full faith and credit
c. Gold reserves
d. Foreign investments

HINTS: Identify the backing source for government securities issued by the U.S. Treasury.

Q424_LO47: What is the maximum maturity for Treasury bills (T-bills)?
a. 6 months
b. 1 year
c. 2 years
d. Subject to change

HINTS: Recognize the characteristic of T-bills regarding their maximum maturity.

Q425_LO47: How do T-bills pay interest to investors?
a. Semiannually
b. At maturity
c. Quarterly
d. Annually

HINTS: Understand the method through which T-bills pay interest.

Q426_LO47: What distinguishes T-bills from other Treasury securities?
a. Stated interest rate
b. Long-term maturity
c. Semiannual interest payments
d. Issued without interest rate

HINTS: Identify the distinctive feature of T-bills among Treasury securities.

Q427_LO47: Which Treasury security is considered a stereotypical risk-free investment in market analysis?
a. T-notes
b. T-bills
c. T-bonds
d. STRIPS

HINTS: Recognize the Treasury security often considered a stereotypical risk-free investment.

Q428_LO47: What is the maturity range for Treasury notes (T-notes)?
a. Less than 1 year
b. 2–10 years
c. 10–30 years
d. Subject to change

HINTS: Identify the intermediate term maturity range for T-notes.
Q429_LO47: How are T-notes priced?
a. Issued at a discount
b. Priced at a percentage of par
c. Issued with fixed interest
d. Priced at a premium

HINTS: Understand the pricing method for T-notes.

Q430_LO47: What is the common maturity range for Treasury bonds (T-bonds)?
a. Less than 1 year
b. 2–10 years
c. 10–30 years
d. Subject to change

HINTS: Recognize the long-term maturity range for T-bonds.

Q431_LO47: How is accrued interest calculated for Treasury notes (T-notes)?
a. None
b. Based on discount
c. Fixed percentage
d. Actual days elapsed

HINTS: Understand the method used to calculate accrued interest for T-notes.

Q432_LO47: What type of securities are T-bills and STRIPS with respect to issuance?
a. Issued at a premium
b. Issued with fixed interest
c. Issued at a discount
d. Issued with variable rates

HINTS: Identify the common issuance characteristic of T-bills and STRIPS.

Q433_LO47: Why are T-bills highly liquid?
a. Long-term maturity
b. Frequent issuance
c. Fixed interest payments
d. Stated interest rate

HINTS: Recognize the factor contributing to the high liquidity of T-bills.

Q434_LO47: What distinguishes Treasury bonds (T-bonds) from T-notes?
a. Issued at a discount
b. Semiannual interest payments
c. Short-term maturity
d. Priced at a premium

HINTS: Identify the characteristic that distinguishes T-bonds from T-notes.

Q435_LO47: Why are government securities issued by the U.S. Treasury considered high in quality regarding safety of principal?
a. Corporate backing
b. Gold reserves
c. Full faith and credit
d. Market demand

HINTS: Understand the reason for the high quality of U.S. Treasury securities regarding safety of principal.

Q436_LO47: What determines the interest rates on U.S. government securities?
a. Market demand
b. Federal Reserve
c. U.S. Treasury Department
d. Congressional approval

HINTS: Identify the key factor determining interest rates on government securities.

Q437_LO47: How are securities issued by the U.S. government backed?
a. Corporate assets
b. Full faith and credit
c. Foreign investments
d. Stock market

HINTS: Recognize the basis of the backing for U.S. government securities.

Q438_LO47: What classifies government securities as bills, notes, or bonds?
a. Interest rates
b. Maturity term
c. Coupon payments
d. Issuing authority

HINTS: Identify the classification criteria for government securities.

Q439_LO47: What is the settlement cycle for U.S. Treasury securities?
a. T+2
b. T+1
c. T+3
d. T+4

HINTS: Understand the settlement cycle for U.S. Treasury securities.

Q440_LO47: How is accrued interest calculated for U.S. T-bills?
a. Percentage of par
b. Based on calendar days elapsed
c. Semiannually
d. No accrued interest

HINTS: Recognize the specific feature of accrued interest for T-bills.

Q441_LO47: Which U.S. Treasury security is considered a stereotypical risk-free investment in market analysis?
a. T-bonds
b. T-notes
c. 4-week T-bills
d. 26-week T-bills

HINTS: Identify the U.S. Treasury security often used as a stereotypical risk-free investment.

Q442_LO47: How are T-notes priced?
a. Issued at a discount
b. Priced at a percentage of par
c. No stated interest rate
d. Liquid pricing

HINTS: Understand the pricing mechanism for U.S. T-notes.

Q443_LO47: What is the maturity range for U.S. T-notes?
a. Less than 1 year
b. 2–10 years
c. Greater than 10 years
d. 2–30 years

HINTS: Recognize the intermediate-term maturity range for T-notes.

Q444_LO47: Which U.S. Treasury security has maturities greater than 10 years?
a. T-bills
b. T-notes
c. T-bonds
d. 52-week T-bills

HINTS: Identify the U.S. Treasury security with long-term maturities.

Q445_LO47: What type of interest payments do T-bonds make?
a. Annual interest
b. Quarterly interest
c. Semiannual interest
d. Monthly interest

HINTS: Recognize the frequency of interest payments for U.S. T-bonds.

Q446_LO47: Which type of U.S. Treasury securities are issued at a discount?
a. T-notes
b. T-bills
c. T-bonds
d. 52-week T-bills

HINTS: Identify the U.S. Treasury security issued at a discount.

Q447_LO47: Why do T-bills not pay regular interest like other bonds?
a. Issued at a premium
b. Short-term instruments
c. High-interest rates
d. Lack of demand

HINTS: Understand the reason T-bills do not pay regular interest.

Q448_LO47: What is the primary characteristic of T-bills and STRIPS?
a. Stated interest rate
b. No stated interest rate
c. Liquid pricing
d. Long-term maturities

HINTS: Identify the common characteristic of T-bills and STRIPS.

Q449_LO47: Why are T-bills considered highly liquid?
a. Long-term maturity
b. Frequent interest payments
c. Short-term maturity
d. High coupon rates

HINTS: Recognize the factor contributing to the high liquidity of T-bills.

Q450_LO47: What distinguishes U.S. T-bonds from T-notes?
a. Maturity
b. Pricing mechanism
c. Interest payments
d. Settlement cycle

HINTS: Identify the key factor distinguishing U.S. T-bonds from T-notes.

Q451_LO48: What is the purpose of creating Treasury receipts by brokerage firms?
a. Enhance coupon payments
b. Create new securities
c. Increase inflation protection
d. Boost principal payments

HINTS: Recognize the purpose of creating Treasury receipts.

Q452_LO48: How do Treasury receipts differ from Treasury securities?
a. They have higher yields
b. They are backed by the U.S. government
c. They lack inflation protection
d. They are not backed by the U.S. government

HINTS: Identify a key difference between Treasury receipts and Treasury securities.

Q453_LO48: What is the common characteristic of Treasury receipts and STRIPS?
a. Fixed coupon rate
b. Zero-coupon bonds
c. Monthly interest payments
d. U.S. government backing

HINTS: Recognize the common characteristic of both Treasury receipts and STRIPS.

Q454_LO48: Who performs the separation of interest coupon and principal for Treasury STRIPS?
a. Investors
b. Banks and BDs
c. U.S. Treasury Department
d. Brokerage firms

HINTS: Identify the entities responsible for separating interest coupon and principal for Treasury STRIPS.

Q455_LO48: What does STRIPS stand for in the context of Treasury securities?
a. Separate Trading of Registered Interest and Principal of Securities
b. Securities Trading Receipts and Inflation Protection
c. Structured Trading of Interest Payments and Securities
d. STRIPS is not an acronym

HINTS: Recognize the correct expansion of the acronym STRIPS.

Q456_LO48: What is the unique feature of Treasury Inflation Protected Securities (TIPS)?
a. Fixed principal value
b. Quarterly interest payments
c. Adjusted principal value based on inflation
d. Monthly coupon payments

HINTS: Identify the unique feature of TIPS among treasury securities.

Q457_LO48: How often do TIPS pay interest?
a. Annually
b. Semiannually
c. Quarterly
d. Monthly

HINTS: Recognize the frequency of interest payments for TIPS.

Q458_LO48: What is the minimum principal payment at maturity for TIPS?
a. Original $1,000 par
b. Adjusted for inflation
c. Half of the original par value
d. No minimum

HINTS: Identify the minimum principal payment at maturity for TIPS.

Q459_LO48: Which entity designates certain issues suitable for stripping into interest and principal components?
a. Investors
b. U.S. Congress
c. U.S. Treasury Department
d. Brokerage firms

HINTS: Identify the entity responsible for designating issues suitable for stripping into components.

Q460_LO48: What is the term for bonds that have a fixed coupon rate and pay interest every six months?
a. Zero-coupon bonds
b. Treasury receipts
c. STRIPS
d. TIPS

HINTS: Recognize the term for bonds with a fixed coupon rate and semiannual interest payments.

Q461_LO48: How do TIPS interest payments behave during periods of inflation?
a. Increase
b. Decrease
c. Remain constant
d. Suspend

HINTS: Identify the behavior of TIPS interest payments during periods of inflation.

Q462_LO48: What risk do TIPS protect investors against?
a. Credit risk
b. Inflation risk
c. Interest rate risk
d. Market risk

HINTS: Recognize the risk that TIPS are specifically designed to protect investors against.

Q463_LO48: Why do brokerage firms prefer creating treasury receipts rather than selling original Treasury securities outright?
a. Lower risk
b. Higher profit
c. Guaranteed returns
d. Faster settlement

HINTS: Understand the reason brokerage firms create treasury receipts.

Q464_LO48: What is the maturity range for TIPS?
a. 1–5 years
b. 5–10 years
c. 10–20 years
d. 20–30 years

HINTS: Identify the maturity range for TIPS.

Q465_LO48: How does the stripping process benefit brokerage firms?
a. Reduces inflation risk
b. Enhances market liquidity
c. Increases profit
d. Ensures government backing

HINTS: Recognize the benefit that brokerage firms derive from the stripping process.

Correct Answers & Explanations
MUNICIPAL BONDS & TREASURIES

Q391_LO47: Correct Answer: b EXPLANATIONS: Municipal bonds are securities issued by state or local governments.

Q392_LO47: Correct Answer: b EXPLANATIONS: General obligation bonds are backed by the municipality's taxing power.

Q393_LO47: Correct Answer: b EXPLANATIONS: General obligation bonds are repaid by taxes collected by the municipality.

Q394_LO47: Correct Answer: c EXPLANATIONS: General obligation bonds are known as "full faith and credit issues" due to their backing by the municipality's taxing power.

Q395_LO47: Correct Answer: c EXPLANATIONS: Voter approval is often required for general obligation bonds due to their backing by taxing power.

Q396_LO47: Correct Answer: c EXPLANATIONS: General obligation bonds are used for community improvements that benefit the entire community.

Q397_LO47: Correct Answer: a EXPLANATIONS: Public referendums for general obligation bonds may be required to increase tax rates.

Q398_LO47: Correct Answer: b EXPLANATIONS: Revenue bonds are considered self-supporting debt as payments come from project-generated revenues.

Q399_LO47: Correct Answer: d EXPLANATIONS: Revenue bonds finance projects that generate sufficient income, such as utilities, transportation, and housing.

Q400_LO47: Correct Answer: c EXPLANATIONS: Revenue bonds are not backed by the issuers' authority to tax, making them exempt from statutory debt limits and voter approval.

Q401_LO47: Correct Answer: b EXPLANATIONS: Revenue bonds are repaid by revenues generated by the project or facility they finance.

Q402_LO47: Correct Answer: c EXPLANATIONS: Municipal anticipation notes have shorter maturities, often less than 12 months.

Q403_LO47: Correct Answer: a EXPLANATIONS: TANs are issued to finance current operations in anticipation of future tax receipts.

Q404_LO47: Correct Answer: b EXPLANATIONS: Interest on most municipal bonds is tax-free on the federal and state levels.

Q405_LO47: Correct Answer: a EXPLANATIONS: Tax-equivalent yield is calculated by dividing the tax-free yield by 100% less the investor's tax rate.

Q406_LO47: Correct Answer: b EXPLANATIONS: Municipal bonds are securities issued by state or local governments or by U.S. territories, authorities, and special districts.

Q407_LO47: Correct Answer: b EXPLANATIONS: Municipal securities are issued for public works and construction projects, such as roads, hospitals, and civic centers.

Q408_LO47: Correct Answer: b EXPLANATIONS: Interest on most municipal bonds is tax-free on a federal level and tax-free on a state level if the investor lives in the state of issuance.

Q409_LO47: Correct Answer: b EXPLANATIONS: GO bonds are backed by the municipality's taxing power and are known as full faith and credit issues.

Q410_LO47: Correct Answer: b EXPLANATIONS: The amount of debt that a municipal government may incur can be limited by state or local statutes.
Q411_LO47: Correct Answer: d EXPLANATIONS: GO bonds are often associated with requiring voter approval to protect against excessive borrowing.

Q412_LO47: Correct Answer: c EXPLANATIONS: Revenue bonds are considered self-supporting debt because payments come exclusively from project or facility-generated revenues.

Q413_LO47: Correct Answer: b EXPLANATIONS: Revenue bonds are not subject to statutory debt limits as they are backed by project-specific revenues, not the municipality's taxing power.

Q414_LO47: Correct Answer: b EXPLANATIONS: Municipal anticipation notes provide short-term financing for municipalities expecting other revenues soon.

Q415_LO47: Correct Answer: c EXPLANATIONS: TRANs combine the characteristics of both TANs and RANs, involving both tax collection and revenue-producing projects.

Q416_LO47: Correct Answer: c EXPLANATIONS: To calculate the tax equivalent yield, divide the tax-free yield by 100% less the investor's tax rate.

Q417_LO47: Correct Answer: c EXPLANATIONS: The tax savings of the tax-free municipal bond may be more attractive than a taxable corporate bond with a higher interest rate, making the municipal yield lower.

Q418_LO47: Correct Answer: b EXPLANATIONS: BANs represent interim financing that will eventually be converted to long-term funding through a sale of bonds.

Q419_LO47: Correct Answer: b EXPLANATIONS: Variable-rate demand notes have a fluctuating interest rate, often issued with a put option allowing the investor to return the security periodically.

Q420_LO47: Correct Answer: c EXPLANATIONS: GANs are issued with the expectation of receiving grant money from the federal government.

Q421_LO47: Correct Answer: a EXPLANATIONS: The marketplace determines the interest rates on U.S. government securities.

Q422_LO47: Correct Answer: c EXPLANATIONS: U.S. Treasury securities are classified as T-bills, T-notes, and T-bonds based on their term to maturity.

Q423_LO47: Correct Answer: b EXPLANATIONS: Securities issued by the U.S. government are backed by its full faith and credit, based on its power to tax.

Q424_LO47: Correct Answer: d EXPLANATIONS: The maximum maturity for T-bills is subject to change.

Q425_LO47: Correct Answer: b EXPLANATIONS: T-bills are issued at a discount from par value and redeemed at par, paying no regular interest but providing interest income at maturity.

Q426_LO47: Correct Answer: d EXPLANATIONS: T-bills are the only Treasury security issued without a stated interest rate.

Q427_LO47: Correct Answer: b EXPLANATIONS: The 13-week T-bills are used in market analysis as the stereotypical risk-free investment.

Q428_LO47: Correct Answer: b EXPLANATIONS: T-notes have intermediate maturities ranging from 2 to 10 years.

Q429_LO47: Correct Answer: b EXPLANATIONS: T-notes are priced at a percentage of par.

Q430_LO47: Correct Answer: c EXPLANATIONS: T-bonds have long-term maturities, greater than 10 years and up to 30 years.

Q431_LO47: Correct Answer: d EXPLANATIONS: Accrued interest for T-notes is calculated based on actual calendar days elapsed.

Q432_LO47: Correct Answer: c EXPLANATIONS: T-bills and STRIPS are the only Treasury securities issued at a discount.

Q433_LO47: Correct Answer: b EXPLANATIONS: T-bills are highly liquid due to their frequent issuance.

Q434_LO47: Correct Answer: b EXPLANATIONS: T-bonds, like T-notes, have semiannual interest payments, but they have long-term maturities greater than 10 years.

Q435_LO47: Correct Answer: c EXPLANATIONS: U.S. Treasury securities are considered high in quality due to being backed by the full faith and credit of the U.S. government.

Q436_LO47: Correct Answer: a EXPLANATIONS: The marketplace determines the interest rates on U.S. government securities.

Q437_LO47: Correct Answer: b EXPLANATIONS: Securities issued by the U.S. government are backed by its full faith and credit.

Q438_LO47: Correct Answer: b EXPLANATIONS: The term to maturity (short, intermediate, and long term) distinguishes government securities as bills, notes, or bonds.

Q439_LO47: Correct Answer: b EXPLANATIONS: U.S. Treasury securities have a T+1 settlement cycle.

Q440_LO47: Correct Answer: d EXPLANATIONS: T-bills have no accrued interest; they are issued at a discount and redeemed at par.

Q441_LO47: Correct Answer: c EXPLANATIONS: The 13-week (90-day) T-bills are used in market analysis as the stereotypical risk-free investment.

Q442_LO47: Correct Answer: b EXPLANATIONS: T-notes are priced at a percentage of par.

Q443_LO47: Correct Answer: b EXPLANATIONS: T-notes have intermediate maturities ranging from 2 to 10 years.

Q444_LO47: Correct Answer: c EXPLANATIONS: T-bonds have maturities greater than 10 years, up to 30 years.

Q445_LO47: Correct Answer: c EXPLANATIONS: T-bonds pay semiannual interest.

Q446_LO47: Correct Answer: b EXPLANATIONS: T-bills and STRIPS are the only Treasury securities issued at a discount.

Q447_LO47: Correct Answer: b EXPLANATIONS: T-bills are short-term instruments, issued at a discount and redeemed at par.

Q448_LO47: Correct Answer: b EXPLANATIONS: T-bills and STRIPS are the only Treasury securities issued without a stated interest rate.

Q449_LO47: Correct Answer: c EXPLANATIONS: T-bills are highly liquid due to their short-term maturity.

Q450_LO47: Correct Answer: a EXPLANATIONS: U.S. T-bonds have long-term maturities greater than 10 years, while T-notes have intermediate maturities of 2–10 years.

Q451_LO48: Correct Answer: b EXPLANATIONS: Treasury receipts are created by brokerage firms to separate coupon interest payments from the principal, creating new securities.

Q452_LO48: Correct Answer: d EXPLANATIONS: Unlike Treasury securities, Treasury receipts are not backed by the full faith and credit of the U.S. government.

Q453_LO48: Correct Answer: b EXPLANATIONS: Both Treasury receipts and STRIPS are zero-coupon bonds.

Q454_LO48: Correct Answer: b EXPLANATIONS: Banks and BDs perform the actual separation of interest coupon and principal for Treasury STRIPS.

Q455_LO48: Correct Answer: a EXPLANATIONS: STRIPS stands for Separate Trading of Registered Interest and Principal of Securities.

Q456_LO48: Correct Answer: c EXPLANATIONS: The principal value of TIPS is adjusted every six months based on the inflation rate.

Q457_LO48: Correct Answer: b EXPLANATIONS: TIPS pay interest every six months, semiannually.

Q458_LO48: Correct Answer: a EXPLANATIONS: The final principal payment at maturity for TIPS will never be less than the original $1,000 par.

Q459_LO48: Correct Answer: c EXPLANATIONS: The U.S. Treasury Department designates certain issues for stripping into interest and principal components.

Q460_LO48: Correct Answer: d EXPLANATIONS: TIPS (Treasury Inflation Protected Securities) have a fixed coupon rate and pay interest every six months.

Q461_LO48: Correct Answer: a EXPLANATIONS: TIPS interest payments increase during periods of inflation.

Q462_LO48: Correct Answer: b EXPLANATIONS: TIPS protect investors against inflation risk.

Q463_LO48: Correct Answer: b EXPLANATIONS: Creating treasury receipts yields more profit for brokerage firms compared to selling the original Treasury securities outright.

Q464_LO48: Correct Answer: c EXPLANATIONS: TIPS have maturities of 5, 10, or 20 years.

Q465_LO48: Correct Answer: c EXPLANATIONS: The stripping process of creating treasury receipts increases profit for brokerage firms.

AGENCY ISSUES, TAXATION, MONEY MARKETS AND ASSET-BACKED SECURITIES

Q466_LO49: Which of the following entities is a government-owned corporation?
a. Fannie Mae
b. Freddie Mac
c. Ginnie Mae
d. Farm Credit System

HINTS: Recognize the government-owned corporation among the given options.

Q467_LO49: What is the primary role of the Farm Credit System (FCS)?
a. Mortgage financing
b. Agricultural financing
c. Student loans
d. Home mortgages

HINTS: Identify the primary focus of the Farm Credit System.

Q468_LO49: Among the listed agencies, which is a government-sponsored enterprise (GSE)?
a. Freddie Mac
b. Fannie Mae
c. Ginnie Mae
d. Farm Credit Administration

HINTS: Recognize the government-sponsored enterprise among the agencies listed.

Q469_LO49: What is the primary purpose of the Farm Credit Administration (FCA)?
a. Overseeing the Farm Credit System
b. Managing student loans
c. Administering housing programs
d. Promoting urban development

HINTS: Identify the primary function of the Farm Credit Administration.

Q470_LO49: Which agency securities are backed by the full faith and credit of the federal government?
a. Fannie Mae
b. Freddie Mac
c. Ginnie Mae
d. Farm Credit System

HINTS: Recognize the agency securities backed by the full faith and credit of the federal government.

Q471_LO49: What risk is associated with Ginnie Mae securities due to mortgages being retired early?
a. Credit risk
b. Market risk
c. Prepayment risk
d. Interest rate risk

HINTS: Identify the risk associated with Ginnie Mae securities due to early mortgage repayment.

Q472_LO49: What is the taxation frequency for interest from FNMA and FHLMC securities?
a. Monthly
b. Biannually
c. Annually
d. Quarterly

HINTS: Recognize the taxation frequency for interest from FNMA and FHLMC securities.

Q473_LO49: From which agencies does FNMA purchase conventional and insured mortgages?
a. FHA and VA
b. USDA and SBA
c. Ginnie Mae
d. Freddie Mac

HINTS: Identify the agencies from which FNMA purchases conventional and insured mortgages.

Q474_LO49: Which agency was created to promote the development of a nationwide secondary market in mortgages?
a. Ginnie Mae
b. Farm Credit System
c. Freddie Mac
d. Fannie Mae

HINTS: Recognize the agency created to develop a secondary market in mortgages.

Q475_LO49: What does GNMA stand for?
a. Government National Mortgage Association
b. General National Mortgage Authority
c. Guaranteed National Mortgage Agency
d. Governmental National Mortgage Association

HINTS: Identify the correct expansion of the acronym GNMA.

Q476_LO49: In which sectors does the Farm Credit System provide financing?
a. Health and education
b. Housing and development
c. Agriculture and farming
d. Transportation and infrastructure

HINTS: Recognize the sectors for which the Farm Credit System provides financing.

Q477_LO49: What type of corporation is Fannie Mae?
a. Private
b. Public
c. Government-owned
d. Government-sponsored

HINTS: Identify the type of corporation Fannie Mae is.

Q478_LO49: What risk is associated with the early payout of mortgages for Ginnie Mae investors?
a. Credit risk
b. Prepayment risk
c. Interest rate risk
d. Market risk

HINTS: Recognize the risk associated with the early payout of mortgages for Ginnie Mae investors.

Q479_LO49: What is the tax treatment for interest from Treasury securities at the federal level?
a. Tax-free
b. Biannual
c. Monthly
d. Annually

HINTS: Identify the tax treatment for interest from Treasury securities at the federal level.

Q480_LO49: What is the primary function of the Ginnie Mae corporation?
a. Mortgage financing
b. Agricultural financing
c. Student loans
d. Supporting the Department of Housing and Urban Development

HINTS: Recognize the primary function of the Ginnie Mae corporation.

Q481_LO50: What is the primary distinction between the capital market and the money market?
a. Maturity of securities
b. Source of financing
c. Liquidity of instruments
d. Nature of securities

HINTS: Identify the primary difference between the capital market and the money market.

Q482_LO50: How are money market instruments typically issued?
a. At a premium
b. At face value
c. At a discount
d. Through auctions

HINTS: Recognize the typical issuance method of money market instruments.

Q483_LO50: What is the primary return for investors who purchase money market securities?
a. Capital gains
b. Dividends
c. Interest payments
d. The difference between purchase price and face value

HINTS: Identify the primary return for investors in money market securities.

Q484_LO50: Which money market instrument is considered a bank's version of an unsecured promissory note?
a. U.S. Treasury bills
b. Commercial paper
c. Banker's acceptance
d. Certificate of deposit

HINTS: Recognize the money market instrument that acts as a bank's unsecured promise to pay.

Q485_LO50: What purpose do Banker's acceptances (BAs) serve in international trade?
a. Financing seasonal inventory
b. Payment for goods and services
c. Raising cash for accounts receivable
d. Securing loans for corporations

HINTS: Identify the primary purpose of Banker's acceptances in international trade.

Q486_LO50: Which money market instrument is an unsecured promissory note issued by corporations?
a. Commercial paper
b. U.S. Treasury bills
c. Repurchase agreements
d. Federal funds loans

HINTS: Recognize the unsecured promissory note issued by corporations.

Q487_LO50: What is the maturity range for U.S. Treasury bills?
a. 1 to 90 days
b. 1 to 180 days
c. 1 to 270 days
d. 1 to 365 days

HINTS: Identify the maturity range for U.S. Treasury bills.

Q488_LO50: What is the primary purpose of a repurchase agreement (repo)?
a. Raising cash by selling assets
b. Financing international trade
c. Meeting the reserve requirement
d. Providing short-term loans between banks
HINTS: Recognize the primary purpose of a repurchase agreement.

Q489_LO50: What are federal funds loans primarily used for?
a. Financing international trade
b. Meeting the reserve requirement
c. Raising cash by selling assets
d. Providing short-term loans between banks

HINTS: Identify the primary purpose of federal funds loans.

Q490_LO50: What term is used for deposits in excess of the required amount at the Federal Reserve?
a. Surplus funds
b. Excess reserves
c. Federal funds loans
d. Repurchase agreements

HINTS: Recognize the term for deposits exceeding the required amount at the Federal Reserve.

Q491_LO50: What is the taxation frequency for interest from money market securities?
a. Monthly
b. Biannually
c. Annually
d. Quarterly

HINTS: Recognize the taxation frequency for interest from money market securities.

Q492_LO50: Why are money market securities considered suitable for short-term investments?
a. High return
b. Low liquidity
c. Low safety
d. High safety and liquidity

HINTS: Identify the reasons why money market securities are suitable for short-term investments.

Q493_LO50: What risk do investors in money market securities face due to short-term maturities?
a. Market risk
b. Credit risk
c. Inflation risk
d. Interest rate risk

HINTS: Recognize the risk associated with short-term maturities of money market securities.

Q494_LO50: Which money market instrument is issued by the U.S. government?
a. Commercial paper
b. Certificate of deposit
c. Banker's acceptance
d. U.S. Treasury bills

HINTS: Identify the money market instrument issued by the U.S. government.

Q495_LO50: What role does commercial paper play in a corporation's financing strategy?
a. Financing seasonal inventory
b. Providing short-term loans between banks
c. Meeting the reserve requirement
d. Raising cash for accounts receivable

HINTS: Recognize the role of commercial paper in a corporation's financing strategy.

Q496_LO50: What is the primary characteristic that distinguishes money market instruments from capital market securities?
a. Maturity
b. Safety
c. Liquidity
d. Interest payments

HINTS: Identify the key feature that sets money market instruments apart.

Q497_LO50: Which money market instrument is essentially a postdated check or line of credit used for international trade financing?
a. Certificate of Deposit
b. Commercial Paper
c. Banker's Acceptance
d. Treasury Bills

HINTS: Recognize the money market instrument associated with international trade financing.

Q498_LO50: What is the primary purpose of a repurchase agreement (repo)?
a. Long-term financing
b. Raising capital temporarily
c. Financing international trade
d. Investing in equities

HINTS: Identify the primary function of a repurchase agreement (repo).

Q499_LO50: What type of financial institution issues negotiable certificates of deposit (CDs)?
a. Brokerage Firms
b. Banks
c. Credit Unions
d. Federal Reserve Banks

HINTS: Recognize the issuer of negotiable certificates of deposit (CDs).

Q500_LO50: Which money market instrument is a direct short-term debt obligation of the U.S. government?
a. Banker's Acceptance
b. Commercial Paper
c. U.S. Treasury Bills
d. Federal Funds Loans

HINTS: Identify the money market instrument issued by the U.S. government.

Q501_LO50: What is the maturity range for commercial paper?
a. 1 to 30 days
b. 1 to 90 days
c. 1 to 180 days
d. 1 to 270 days

HINTS: Recognize the typical maturity range for commercial paper.

Q502_LO50: In a repurchase agreement, what is the purpose of selling assets temporarily?
a. To finance international trade
b. To raise capital temporarily
c. To invest in equities
d. To meet reserve requirements

HINTS: Identify the purpose of selling assets temporarily in a repurchase agreement.

Q503_LO50: What is the primary reason why money market securities are not suitable for long-term investors?
a. Low liquidity
b. Low safety
c. Fluctuating returns
d. Short-term maturities

HINTS: Recognize the factor that makes money market securities unsuitable for long-term investors.

Q504_LO50: What does the return on money market securities represent?
a. Interest payments
b. Capital gains
c. Difference between purchase price and face value
d. Dividend payments

HINTS: Identify what the return on money market securities represents.

Q505_LO50: Which money market instrument is a time draft drawn on a bank and serves as a postdated check?
a. U.S. Treasury Bills
b. Certificate of Deposit
c. Banker's Acceptance
d. Commercial Paper

HINTS: Recognize the money market instrument that functions as a postdated check.

Q506_LO50: What distinguishes negotiable certificates of deposit (CDs) from traditional CDs?
a. Higher face values
b. Longer maturities
c. Trading in the secondary market
d. Fixed interest rates

HINTS: Identify the distinguishing feature of negotiable certificates of deposit (CDs).

Q507_LO50: What role do federal funds loans play in the money market?
a. Financing international trade
b. Raising capital temporarily
c. Meeting reserve requirements
d. Providing long-term financing

HINTS: Recognize the role of federal funds loans in the money market.

Q508_LO50: What is the typical minimum face value for jumbo certificates of deposit (CDs)?
a. $1,000
b. $10,000
c. $100,000
d. $1 million

HINTS: Identify the typical minimum face value for jumbo certificates of deposit (CDs).

Q509_LO50: What distinguishes negotiable certificates of deposit (CDs) from commercial paper?
a. Maturity
b. Issuer
c. Trading in the secondary market
d. Face value

HINTS: Recognize the distinguishing feature of negotiable certificates of deposit (CDs).

Q510_LO50: What term is used for the excess reserves that banks can loan to each other in the federal funds market?
a. Surplus funds
b. Excess deposits
c. Federal funds
d. Residual reserves

HINTS: Identify the term used for excess reserves loaned between banks in the federal funds market.

Q511_LO51: What is the primary characteristic of asset-backed securities?
a. Backed by equity
b. Derived from specific pools of underlying assets
c. Government-issued
d. Exclusively tied to real estate

HINTS: Identify the key characteristic of asset-backed securities.

Q512_LO51: What is the process called when pools of assets are structured into financial instruments and sold to investors more easily?
a. Securitization
b. Liquidation
c. Consolidation
d. Diversification

HINTS: Recognize the process of structuring pools of assets into financial instruments.

Q513_LO51: In collateralized mortgage obligations (CMOs), what are maturity classes called?
a. Layers
b. Tiers
c. Tranches
d. Sections

HINTS: Identify the term used for maturity classes in collateralized mortgage obligations (CMOs).

Q514_LO51: How are principal payments made in collateralized mortgage obligations (CMOs)?
a. Equal payments to all tranches
b. Randomly selected bonds within a tranche
c. Sequentially to all tranches
d. Proportionally to the total mortgage pool

HINTS: Recognize the method of making principal payments in CMOs.

Q515_LO51: What factor affects the flow of interest payments and principal repayment to the CMO investor in response to changes in interest rates?
a. Credit risk
b. Maturity dates
c. Mortgage prepayments
d. Asset liquidity

HINTS: Identify the factor influencing the flow of payments in response to interest rate changes.

Q516_LO51: What is the primary function of CDOs (Collateralized Debt Obligations)?
a. Backed by government agency securities
b. Specialize in mortgage loans
c. Represent different types of debt and credit risk
d. Pay principal and interest monthly

HINTS: Recognize the primary function of Collateralized Debt Obligations (CDOs).

Q517_LO51: What is the term used for the diverse pool of assets that back CDOs?
a. Bundle
b. Cluster
c. Portfolio
d. Consortium

HINTS: Identify the term used for the diverse pool of assets backing CDOs.

Q518_LO51: What is the common term for the different types of debt and risk categories in CDOs?
a. Slices
b. Layers
c. Divisions
d. Segments

HINTS: Recognize the common term for different types of debt and risk categories in CDOs.

Q519_LO51: How does the risk profile and payout change across different tranches in CDOs?
a. Risk decreases, payout decreases
b. Risk increases, payout increases
c. Risk decreases, payout increases
d. Risk increases, payout decreases

HINTS: Understand how the risk profile and payout typically change across tranches in CDOs.

Q520_LO51: What is the role of securitization in collateralized debt obligations (CDOs)?
a. Increases risk
b. Facilitates sale to individual investors
c. Reduces diversification
d. Encourages asset concentration

HINTS: Identify the role of securitization in collateralized debt obligations (CDOs).

Q521_LO51: What distinguishes CMOs from CDOs in terms of underlying assets?
a. CMOs specialize in mortgage loans
b. CDOs are backed by Ginnie Mae, Fannie Mae, and Freddie Mac pass-through securities
c. CDOs pool auto loans
d. CMOs are exclusively tied to real estate

HINTS: Recognize the distinguishing feature of underlying assets in CMOs.

Q522_LO51: What is the typical method of principal repayment in CMOs?
a. Proportional repayment to all tranches
b. Sequential repayment to all tranches
c. Randomly selected bonds within a tranche
d. Equal payments to all tranches

HINTS: Understand the typical method of principal repayment in CMOs.

Q523_LO51: In CDOs, what allows the risk of investing in underlying assets to be diversified?
a. Tranches
b. Repackaging
c. Derivative products
d. Liquidation

HINTS: Identify the element that enables diversification of risk in CDOs.

Q524_LO51: What backs CMOs and makes them historically highly rated?
a. Auto loans
b. Government agency securities
c. Corporate bonds
d. Derivative products

HINTS: Recognize the backing that historically gives high ratings to CMOs.

Q525_LO51: What is the primary source of income for investors in CMOs?
a. Capital gains
b. Interest payments only
c. Principal repayments only
d. Both interest payments and principal repayments

HINTS: Identify the primary source of income for investors in collateralized mortgage obligations (CMOs).

Correct Answers & Explanations
AGENCY ISSUES, TAXATION, MONEY MARKETS AND ASSET-BACKED SECURITIES

Q466_LO49: Correct Answer: c EXPLANATIONS: Ginnie Mae (GNMA) is a government-owned corporation.

Q467_LO49: Correct Answer: b EXPLANATIONS: The Farm Credit System provides agricultural financing and credit.

Q468_LO49: Correct Answer: a EXPLANATIONS: Freddie Mac (FHLMC) is a government-sponsored enterprise.

Q469_LO49: Correct Answer: a EXPLANATIONS: The Farm Credit Administration oversees the Farm Credit System.

Q470_LO49: Correct Answer: c EXPLANATIONS: Ginnie Mae (GNMA) securities are backed by the full faith and credit of the federal government.

Q471_LO49: Correct Answer: c EXPLANATIONS: Ginnie Mae securities have prepayment risk when mortgages are retired early.

Q472_LO49: Correct Answer: b EXPLANATIONS: Interest from FNMA and FHLMC securities is taxed biannually.

Q473_LO49: Correct Answer: a EXPLANATIONS: FNMA purchases mortgages from agencies such as FHA and VA.

Q474_LO49: Correct Answer: c EXPLANATIONS: Freddie Mac was created for the development of a secondary market in mortgages.

Q475_LO49: Correct Answer: a EXPLANATIONS: GNMA stands for Government National Mortgage Association.

Q476_LO49: Correct Answer: c EXPLANATIONS: The Farm Credit System provides financing for agriculture and farming.

Q477_LO49: Correct Answer: b EXPLANATIONS: Fannie Mae is a publicly held corporation.

Q478_LO49: Correct Answer: b EXPLANATIONS: Ginnie Mae investors face prepayment risk when mortgages are retired early.

Q479_LO49: Correct Answer: a EXPLANATIONS: Interest from Treasury securities is tax-free at the federal level.

Q480_LO49: Correct Answer: d EXPLANATIONS: Ginnie Mae supports the Department of Housing and Urban Development.

Q481_LO50: Correct Answer: b EXPLANATIONS: The capital market provides intermediate- to long-term financing, while the money market offers short-term funds.

Q482_LO50: Correct Answer: c EXPLANATIONS: Money market instruments are typically issued at a discount and mature at face value.

Q483_LO50: Correct Answer: d EXPLANATIONS: The return is the difference between the discounted purchase price and the face value received at maturity.

Q484_LO50: Correct Answer: c EXPLANATIONS: A negotiable CD (Certificate of Deposit) is a bank's version of an unsecured promissory note.

Q485_LO50: Correct Answer: b EXPLANATIONS: BAs typically pay for goods and services in a foreign country in international trade.

Q486_LO50: Correct Answer: a EXPLANATIONS: Commercial paper is a short-term, unsecured promissory note issued by corporations.

Q487_LO50: Correct Answer: c EXPLANATIONS: U.S. Treasury bills have maturities of 4, 13, 26, and 52 weeks.

Q488_LO50: Correct Answer: a EXPLANATIONS: A repo allows a financial institution to raise cash by temporarily selling some of its assets.

Q489_LO50: Correct Answer: b EXPLANATIONS: Federal funds loans are used for banks to meet the reserve requirement.

Q490_LO50: Correct Answer: b EXPLANATIONS: Excess reserves or federal funds refer to deposits in excess of the required amount at the Federal Reserve.

Q491_LO50: Correct Answer: c EXPLANATIONS: Interest from money market securities is typically taxed annually.

Q492_LO50: Correct Answer: d EXPLANATIONS: Money market securities are highly liquid, very safe, and suitable for short-term investments.

Q493_LO50: Correct Answer: a EXPLANATIONS: Principal is potentially reinvested at a different rate each time the instrument matures, leading to market risk.

Q494_LO50: Correct Answer: d EXPLANATIONS: U.S. Treasury bills are direct short-term debt obligations of the U.S. government.

Q495_LO50: Correct Answer: a EXPLANATIONS: Commercial paper is issued to raise cash to finance accounts receivable and seasonal inventory gluts.

Q496_LO50: Correct Answer: c EXPLANATIONS: Money market instruments are highly liquid.

Q497_LO50: Correct Answer: c EXPLANATIONS: A Banker's Acceptance (BA) is used extensively for international trade financing.

Q498_LO50: Correct Answer: b EXPLANATIONS: A repo is used to raise cash temporarily by selling assets with an agreement to repurchase them later.

Q499_LO50: Correct Answer: b EXPLANATIONS: Banks issue negotiable certificates of deposit (CDs).

Q500_LO50: Correct Answer: c EXPLANATIONS: U.S. Treasury Bills are direct short-term debt obligations of the U.S. government.

Q501_LO50: Correct Answer: d EXPLANATIONS: Commercial paper maturities range from 1 to 270 days.

Q502_LO50: Correct Answer: b EXPLANATIONS: The primary purpose is to raise capital temporarily.

Q503_LO50: Correct Answer: c EXPLANATIONS: Fluctuating returns due to short-term maturities are not suitable for long-term investors.

Q504_LO50: Correct Answer: c EXPLANATIONS: The return is the difference between the discounted purchase price and the face value received at maturity.

Q505_LO50: Correct Answer: c EXPLANATIONS: A Banker's Acceptance (BA) serves as a postdated check or line of credit.

Q506_LO50: Correct Answer: c EXPLANATIONS: Negotiable CDs can be traded in the secondary market.

Q507_LO50: Correct Answer: c EXPLANATIONS: Federal funds loans help banks meet reserve requirements by lending excess reserves to other banks.

Q508_LO50: Correct Answer: c EXPLANATIONS: Jumbo CDs typically have minimum face values of $100,000.

Q509_LO50: Correct Answer: c EXPLANATIONS: Negotiable CDs can be traded in the secondary market, unlike commercial paper.

Q510_LO50: Correct Answer: c EXPLANATIONS: Excess reserves loaned between banks in the federal funds market are known as federal funds.

Q511_LO51: Correct Answer: b EXPLANATIONS: Asset-backed securities derive their value from specific pools of underlying assets.

Q512_LO51: Correct Answer: a EXPLANATIONS: Securitization allows the sale of diverse pools of assets to investors more easily.

Q513_LO51: Correct Answer: c EXPLANATIONS: Maturity classes in CMOs are called tranches.

Q514_LO51: Correct Answer: b EXPLANATIONS: Principal payments are made in $1,000 increments to randomly selected bonds within a tranche.

Q515_LO51: Correct Answer: c EXPLANATIONS: Changes in interest rates affect the rate of mortgage prepayments, impacting interest and principal repayments in CMOs.

Q516_LO51: Correct Answer: c EXPLANATIONS: CDOs represent different types of debt and credit risk.

Q517_LO51: Correct Answer: c EXPLANATIONS: The diverse pool of assets backing CDOs is referred to as a portfolio.

Q518_LO51: Correct Answer: a EXPLANATIONS: The different types of debt and risk categories in CDOs are often called tranches or slices.

Q519_LO51: Correct Answer: b EXPLANATIONS: Higher-risk tranches in CDOs generally offer higher payouts.

Q520_LO51: Correct Answer: b EXPLANATIONS: Securitization facilitates the sale of diverse assets to individual investors.

Q521_LO51: Correct Answer: a EXPLANATIONS: CMOs specialize in mortgage loans as underlying assets.

Q522_LO51: Correct Answer: c EXPLANATIONS: Principal payments are made to randomly selected bonds within a tranche.

Q523_LO51: Correct Answer: a EXPLANATIONS: Tranches allow the risk of investing in underlying assets to be diversified.

Q524_LO51: Correct Answer: b EXPLANATIONS: CMOs backed by government agency securities have historically been rated high.

Q525_LO51: Correct Answer: d EXPLANATIONS: Investors in CMOs receive income from both interest payments and principal repayments.

Derivatives

Q526_LO52: What is a derivative?
a. A standalone financial product
b. A contract with underlying assets
c. A tangible asset
d. A government-issued security

HINTS: Recall the definition of a derivative.

Q527_LO52: In a derivative contract, who has the right to exercise the contract to buy or sell the underlying asset?
a. Buyer
b. Seller
c. Both parties
d. Broker

HINTS: Identify the party with the right to exercise the contract.

Q528_LO52: Which asset class is NOT commonly used for derivatives?
a. Commodities
b. Currencies
c. Government-issued securities
d. Stocks

HINTS: Recognize an asset class not typically associated with derivatives.

Q529_LO52: What is the term for the amount paid for the contract when purchased or received when sold?
a. Contract fee
b. Premium
c. Commission
d. Transaction cost

HINTS: Recall the term for the amount associated with option contracts.

Q530_LO52: What happens in the process of an opening purchase followed by a closing sale?
a. Buying and selling the same contract
b. Selling and buying the same contract
c. Buying different contracts
d. Selling different contracts

HINTS: Identify the correct sequence of transactions.

Q531_LO52: Who is obligated to fulfill the terms of the contract in an option agreement?
a. Buyer
b. Seller
c. Broker
d. Exchange

HINTS: Recognize the party obligated to fulfill the terms.

Q532_LO52: What is the primary risk for buyers of option contracts?
a. Market risk
b. Credit risk
c. Premium loss
d. Interest rate risk

HINTS: Identify the primary risk for buyers of option contracts.

Q533_LO52: In option contracts, what is a closing purchase?
a. Selling the option
b. Buying back the option
c. Selling the underlying asset
d. Exercising the option

HINTS: Recognize the correct definition of a closing purchase.

Q534_LO52: What term is used for the party who is short the contract in an option agreement?
a. Owner
b. Holder
c. Writer
d. Long

HINTS: Identify the term for the party who is short the contract.

Q535_LO52: In options trading, what is the role of the party who sells calls?
a. Receives premium
b. Pays premium
c. Exercises the option
d. Buys the underlying asset

HINTS: Recognize the role of the party selling calls.

Q536_LO52: What is the primary function of options?
a. Ensure guaranteed profits
b. Speculate on price movements
c. Eliminate market volatility
d. Act as insurance for the underlying asset

HINTS: Identify the primary purpose of options.

Q537_LO52: What distinguishes equity options from other types of options?
a. Backed by government securities
b. Issued on common stocks
c. Tied to foreign currencies
d. Based on interest rates

HINTS: Recognize the distinguishing feature of equity options.

Q538_LO52: What are the two types of option contracts?
a. Calls and swaps
b. Puts and forwards
c. Calls and puts
d. Futures and options

HINTS: Identify the correct types of option contracts.

Q539_LO52: In options, what allows an investor to profit by the amount of premium received if the option expires as worthless?
a. Market volatility
b. Time decay
c. Dividends
d. Interest rates

HINTS: Recognize the factor that allows a seller to profit in certain scenarios.

Q540_LO52: What is the primary source of income for investors who sell puts?
a. Capital gains
b. Premium received
c. Dividend payments
d. Principal repayments

HINTS: Identify the primary source of income for sellers of puts.
Q541_LO52: What is the definition of "premium" in the context of options?
a. Strike price of the option
b. Cost of the option contract
c. Market value of the underlying asset
d. Expiration date of the option

HINTS: Recall the term associated with the cost of an option.

Q542_LO52: In options trading, what does a long call (purchase) give the investor the right to do?
a. Sell the underlying asset
b. Buy the underlying asset
c. Both buy and sell the underlying asset
d. Hold the option indefinitely

HINTS: Identify the right granted to the investor in a long call.

Q543_LO52: What is the market attitude of a call writer (seller)?
a. Bullish
b. Bearish
c. Neutral
d. Indifferent

HINTS: Recognize the market attitude associated with a call writer.

Q544_LO52: Why would a put buyer exercise the put option?
a. To buy the underlying asset
b. To sell the underlying asset
c. To hold the option indefinitely
d. To receive dividends

HINTS: Identify the objective of a put buyer in exercising the option.

Q545_LO52: What is the obligation of a short put (sale) writer?
a. Buy the underlying asset
b. Sell the underlying asset
c. Both buy and sell the underlying asset
d. Hold the option indefinitely

HINTS: Recognize the obligation of a short put writer.

Q546_LO52: In options, what is the distinguishing feature of equity options?
a. Backed by government securities
b. Issued on common stocks
c. Tied to foreign currencies
d. Based on interest rates

HINTS: Identify the characteristic that distinguishes equity options.

Q547_LO52: What is the primary risk for a long call buyer?
a. Market risk
b. Credit risk
c. Premium loss
d. Interest rate risk

HINTS: Recognize the primary risk associated with a long call buyer.

Q548_LO52: For a short call writer, what happens if the option is unexercised by expiration?
a. Receives the premium
b. Pays the premium
c. Buys the underlying asset
d. Sells the underlying asset

HINTS: Identify the outcome for a short call writer if the option is unexercised.

Q549_LO52: What is the market attitude of a put writer (seller)?
a. Bullish
b. Bearish
c. Neutral
d. Indifferent

HINTS: Recognize the market attitude associated with a put writer.

Q550_LO52: In index options, what is the settlement method if the option is exercised?
a. Delivery of underlying shares
b. Cash payment
c. Exchange of assets
d. Physical delivery of assets

HINTS: Identify the settlement method for index options.

Q551_LO52: What does the VIX Index measure in the U.S. stock market?
a. Expected volatility
b. Stock prices
c. Dividend yields
d. Interest rates

HINTS: Recall the parameter measured by the VIX Index.

Q552_LO52: What is the common term for options based on the S&P 500 Index?
a. Equity options
b. Index options
c. VIX options
d. Fear options

HINTS: Identify the category of options related to the S&P 500 Index.

Q553_LO52: What is the primary role of the buyer of puts?
a. Speculate on rising prices
b. Speculate on falling prices
c. Hold the option indefinitely
d. Receive premium payments

HINTS: Recognize the primary objective of a put buyer.

Q554_LO52: Why might a call buyer choose not to exercise the option?
a. To receive premium
b. To buy the underlying asset
c. To avoid market risk
d. To sell the underlying asset

HINTS: Identify a reason for a call buyer not exercising the option.

Q555_LO52: What does a put writer hope for regarding the market price of the underlying stock?
a. Rise or remain unchanged
b. Fall or remain unchanged
c. Spike upward
d. Fluctuate unpredictably

HINTS: Recognize the desired market movement for a put writer.

Q556_LO52: What is a premium in the context of options?
a. A bonus for early exercise
b. The contract price of an option
c. Interest paid on margin
d. Dividend received by the seller

HINTS: Recall the definition of premium in options trading.

Q557_LO52: In options, what does a long call buyer anticipate?
a. A rise in the market price
b. A fall in the market price
c. Unchanged market conditions
d. A rise in interest rates

HINTS: Identify the market expectation of a long call buyer.

Q558_LO52: What is the market attitude of a short put writer?
a. Bullish
b. Bearish
c. Neutral
d. Unpredictable

HINTS: Recognize the market attitude of a short put writer.

Q559_LO52: Why does a call writer hope the market price stays below the strike price?
a. To maximize premium
b. To minimize premium
c. To exercise the option
d. To incur a loss

HINTS: Understand the motivation of a call writer.

Q560_LO52: What does a long put buyer want the market price to do?
a. Rise
b. Fall
c. Remain unchanged
d. Fluctuate

HINTS: Identify the desired market movement for a long put buyer.

Q561_LO52: What distinguishes equity options from other types of options?
a. Backed by government securities
b. Issued on common stocks
c. Tied to foreign currencies
d. Based on interest rates

HINTS: Recognize the distinguishing feature of equity options.

Q562_LO52: What is the obligation of a short call writer?
a. To sell the underlying asset
b. To buy the underlying asset
c. To exercise the option
d. To pay dividends

HINTS: Identify the obligation of a short call writer.

Q563_LO52: When is a put option exercised by the buyer?
a. Market price rises
b. Market price falls
c. Market price remains unchanged
d. Upon expiration

HINTS: Understand the condition for a put option exercise.
Q564_LO52: What is the primary risk for a long call buyer?
a. Premium loss
b. Market volatility
c. Interest rate risk
d. Dividend risk

HINTS: Identify the primary risk for a long call buyer.

Q565_LO52: What happens if a call option is unexercised by expiration for the buyer?
a. Premium loss
b. Premium refund
c. Premium remains with the seller
d. Dividend payment

HINTS: Understand the outcome if a call option is unexercised.

Q566_LO52: In options, what is the market attitude of a long put buyer?

a. Bullish
b. Bearish
c. Neutral
d. Volatile

HINTS: Recognize the market attitude of a long put buyer.

Q567_LO52: What is the role of a short put writer in the market?
a. To sell the underlying asset
b. To buy the underlying asset
c. To exercise the option
d. To speculate on volatility

HINTS: Identify the role of a short put writer.

Q568_LO52: What distinguishes VIX options from stock options?
a. Settlement in cash
b. Tied to foreign currencies
c. Backed by government securities
d. Exercise of the underlying shares

HINTS: Recognize the distinguishing feature of VIX options.

Q569_LO52: Why might an investor use VIX options?
a. To speculate on interest rates
b. To hedge against currency risk
c. To speculate on market volatility
d. To receive dividend payments

HINTS: Understand the purpose of using VIX options.

Q570_LO52: What happens if an index option is exercised?
a. Delivery of underlying shares
b. Premium refund
c. Cash settlement
d. Dividend payment

HINTS: Identify the outcome of exercising an index option.

Q571_LO53: When is a call considered "in the money"?
a. When the stock price is equal to the strike price
b. When the stock price is higher than the strike price
c. When the stock price is lower than the strike price
d. When the option expires
HINTS: Recall the condition for a call to be "in the money."

Q572_LO53: What is the intrinsic value of an option?
a. Always negative
b. The amount it is in the money
c. The time value component
d. The premium at expiration

HINTS: Identify the definition of intrinsic value.

Q573_LO53: When is a put considered "at the money"?
a. When the stock price is equal to the strike price
b. When the stock price is higher than the strike price
c. When the stock price is lower than the strike price
d. When the option expires

HINTS: Recognize the condition for a put to be "at the money."

Q574_LO53: What is the primary objective of a call buyer?
a. To minimize intrinsic value

b. To maximize time value
c. To have options expire worthless
d. To have options in the money

HINTS: Understand the goal of a call buyer.

Q575_LO53: What is the intrinsic value of an at-the-money call option?
a. Zero
b. The premium
c. The stock price
d. The strike price

HINTS: Recall the intrinsic value of an at-the-money call.

Q576_LO53: When does a put buyer exercise the option?
a. When the option is out of the money
b. When the option is at the money
c. When the option is in the money
d. When the option expires

HINTS: Identify the condition for a put buyer to exercise.

Q577_LO53: What does the term "parity" mean for a call option?
a. Premium equals intrinsic value
b. Premium equals time value
c. Premium is zero
d. Intrinsic value is zero

HINTS: Recognize the definition of parity for a call option.

Q578_LO53: What contributes to the subjective component of an option premium?
a. Intrinsic value
b. Time value
c. Stock price
d. Strike price

HINTS: Identify the subjective component of an option premium.

Q579_LO53: What is the formula for an option premium?
a. IV - TV = Pr
b. TV - IV = Pr
c. IV + TV = Pr
d. Pr - IV = TV

HINTS: Recall the basic formula for an option premium.

Q580_LO53: How does time to expiration affect time value?
a. Increases time value
b. Decreases time value
c. No effect on time value
d. Converts time value to intrinsic value

HINTS: Understand the impact of time to expiration on time value.

Q581_LO53: What factor influences time value besides time to expiration?
a. Strike price
b. Volatility
c. Intrinsic value
d. Stock dividend

HINTS: Recognize the factor influencing time value along with time to expiration.

Q582_LO53: What happens to the premium of an option with no intrinsic value at expiration?
a. Premium is zero

b. Premium is maximum
c. Premium is refunded
d. Premium remains with the seller

HINTS: Identify the outcome for the premium of an option with no intrinsic value.

Q583_LO53: When is a call considered "out of the money"?
a. When the stock price is equal to the strike price
b. When the stock price is higher than the strike price
c. When the stock price is lower than the strike price
d. When the option expires

HINTS: Recall the condition for a call to be "out of the money."

Q584_LO53: What is the intrinsic value of an out-of-the-money put option?
a. Zero
b. The premium
c. The stock price
d. The strike price

HINTS: Recognize the intrinsic value of an out-of-the-money put option.

Q585_LO53: What is the goal of a put seller regarding the option's status?
a. To be in the money
b. To be at parity
c. To be out of the money
d. To maximize intrinsic value

HINTS: Understand the objective of a put seller concerning the option's status.

Q586_LO53: What does it mean when a call option is "in the money"?
a. The stock price is below the strike price
b. The stock price equals the strike price
c. The stock price exceeds the strike price
d. The stock price is irrelevant

HINTS: Recall the definition of an "in the money" call option.

Q587_LO53: When is a put option considered "out of the money"?
a. Stock price is above the strike price
b. Stock price equals the strike price
c. Stock price is below the strike price
d. Stock price is irrelevant

HINTS: Recognize the condition for an "out of the money" put option.

Q588_LO53: What is intrinsic value in options trading?
a. Subjective time value
b. Premium exceeding parity
c. Amount a contract is in the money
d. Premium equal to strike price

HINTS: Understand the concept of intrinsic value.

Q589_LO53: When is a call option at parity?
a. When the premium is zero
b. When the premium equals intrinsic value
c. When the stock price equals the strike price
d. When the option is exercised

HINTS: Identify the condition for a call option to be at parity.

Q590_LO53: What is the primary motivation for a put buyer?
a. Rise in stock price

b. Fall in stock price
c. Unchanged stock price
d. Dividend payments

HINTS: Recognize the desired outcome for a put buyer.

Q591_LO53: In the options formula IV + TV = Pr, what does IV stand for?
a. Intrinsic Value
b. Interest Value
c. Inherent Value
d. Investment Value

HINTS: Recall the meaning of IV in the options premium formula.

Q592_LO53: What is the role of time value in the options premium?
a. Objective calculation
b. Determined by supply and demand
c. Affects intrinsic value
d. Subjective number

HINTS: Distinguish between intrinsic value and time value.

Q593_LO53: How does volatility impact time value?
a. More volatility, less time value
b. Less volatility, more time value
c. No impact on time value
d. Volatility is irrelevant

HINTS: Understand the relationship between volatility and time value.

Q594_LO53: What happens if a put option has no intrinsic value at expiration?
a. It is exercised
b. It is allowed to expire
c. Premium is refunded
d. Stock price is irrelevant
HINTS: Identify the outcome for a put option with no intrinsic value.

Q595_LO53: Why do sellers prefer options to be "out of the money"?
a. Maximize premium
b. Minimize premium
c. Maximize intrinsic value
d. Minimize intrinsic value

HINTS: Recognize the preference of sellers regarding option status.

Q596_LO53: When does a call buyer exercise the option?
a. Stock price falls
b. Stock price rises
c. Stock price remains unchanged
d. At the money

HINTS: Identify the condition for a call buyer to exercise the option.

Q597_LO53: What is the intrinsic value of an at-the-money call option?
a. Positive value
b. Negative value
c. Zero
d. Equal to the premium

HINTS: Understand the intrinsic value of an at-the-money call option.

Q598_LO53: How is parity defined in options trading?
a. Premium equals intrinsic value
b. Premium is zero

c. Option is exercised
d. Option is allowed to expire

HINTS: Recognize the condition for an option to be at parity.

Q599_LO53: What is the primary risk for a put seller?
a. Market volatility
b. Rising interest rates
c. Falling stock prices
d. Premium loss

HINTS: Identify the primary risk for a put seller.

Q600_LO53: How is intrinsic value calculated for a call option?
a. Stock price minus strike price
b. Strike price minus stock price
c. Premium plus time value
d. Intrinsic value is subjective

HINTS: Understand the calculation of intrinsic value for a call option.

Q601_LO54: What distinguishes nonequity options from equity options?
a. Contract size and exercise standards
b. Premium amount
c. Settlement price
d. Exercise time

HINTS: Recall the key differences in nonequity options.

Q602_LO54: Which index reflects the movement of the entire market?
a. S&P 100 (OEX)
b. S&P 500
c. Major Market Index (XMI)
d. VIX (Volatility Index)

HINTS: Identify the broad-based index among the options.

Q603_LO54: What does the VIX Index measure?
a. Stock prices
b. Implied volatility of S&P 500 options
c. Interest rates
d. Market fear

HINTS: Understand the focus and purpose of the VIX Index.

Q604_LO54: How is the settlement price determined for index options?
a. At the time of exercise
b. Closing value of the index on the day of exercise
c. Opening value of the index
d. A fixed value

HINTS: Recognize the basis for determining the settlement price of index options.

Q605_LO54: What is the multiplier for index options?
a. $50
b. $75
c. $100
d. $150

HINTS: Recall the multiplier used for index options.

Q606_LO54: When do index options stop trading?
a. 3:00 pm ET
b. 4:00 pm ET (for narrow-based)

c. 4:15 pm ET (for broad-based)
d. 5:00 pm ET

HINTS: Be aware of the trading hours for index options.

Q607_LO54: What does the strategy of buying index puts aim to achieve?
a. Speculate on market rise
b. Speculate on market fall
c. Hedge against market fall
d. Hedge against market rise

HINTS: Recognize the purpose of buying index puts.

Q608_LO54: What is the primary use of index options for portfolio managers?
a. Speculation
b. Hedging a diverse portfolio
c. Generating income
d. Market timing

HINTS: Identify the primary application of index options for portfolio managers.

Q609_LO54: What is the characteristic of interest rate options?
a. Direct relationship to stock prices
b. Yield-based with a direct relationship to interest rates
c. Settlement in securities
d. Use of a multiplier

HINTS: Understand the nature of interest rate options.

Q610_LO54: How is the premium of a yield-based option calculated?
a. Strike price multiplied by $100
b. Intrinsic value plus time value
c. Cash settlement on expiration
d. Premium multiplied by $100

HINTS: Recall the components of the premium for yield-based options.

Q611_LO54: In which situation would an investor buy calls on interest rate options?
a. Expecting rates to fall
b. Expecting rates to rise
c. Unchanged interest rates
d. Expecting volatility

HINTS: Recognize the appropriate situation for buying calls on interest rate options.

Q612_LO54: Why do importers buy calls in currency options trading?
a. To hedge against rising currency value
b. To hedge against falling currency value
c. Speculation on currency rise
d. Speculation on currency fall

HINTS: Remember the EPIC acronym for currency options.

Q613_LO54: What is the settlement style for exchange-listed foreign currency options?
a. American style
b. European style
c. Asian style
d. Australian style

HINTS: Recognize the settlement style for foreign currency options.

Q614_LO54: How do American-style options differ from European-style options?
a. Settlement on expiration day
b. Exercise anytime before expiration

c. Settlement in cash
d. Multiplier usage

HINTS: Differentiate the exercise rules between American and European styles.

Q615_LO54: Which option is suitable for an exporter to hedge against currency drop?
a. Write puts
b. Buy puts
c. Write calls
d. Buy calls

HINTS: Remember the EPIC acronym for currency options.

Q616_LO54: What is a major difference in settlement between index options and equity options?
a. Both settle next business day
b. Index options settle two business days later
c. Equity options settle next business day, index options two business days later
d. Equity options settle on expiration day

HINTS: Recall the settlement difference between index and equity options.

Q617_LO54: What is the purpose of the VIX Index?
a. Measure of market volume
b. Reflect investor expectations of market volatility
c. Track the performance of technology stocks
d. Measure of market fear
HINTS: Recognize the role of the VIX Index.

Q618_LO54: When do index options expire?
a. Second Friday of the expiration month
b. Third Friday of the expiration month
c. Last business day of the month
d. Monthly, based on market conditions

HINTS: Identify the expiration timing for index options.

Q619_LO54: What is the settlement method for exercised index options?
a. Delivery of the underlying securities
b. Cash settlement
c. Physical delivery of the index
d. In-kind settlement

HINTS: Understand how index options are settled upon exercise.

Q620_LO54: How is the settlement price determined for index options?
a. At the time of exercise
b. Based on the opening value of the index
c. Based on the closing value of the index on the day of exercise
d. A fixed value determined by the SEC

HINTS: Recognize the basis for determining the settlement price of index options.

Q621_LO54: What is the primary use of index options for portfolio managers?
a. Speculation on individual stocks
b. Portfolio insurance against market declines
c. Hedging against currency risk
d. Speculation on interest rate movements

HINTS: Identify the key use of index options for portfolio managers.

Q622_LO54: In interest rate options, what does a call option with a strike price of 35 represent?
a. Interest rate of 35%
b. Intrinsic value of 35
c. Yield of 3.5%

d. Premium of $35

HINTS: Understand the representation of strike prices in interest rate options.

Q623_LO54: When do European-style exercise options allow exercise?
a. Anytime before expiration
b. Only on expiration day
c. Two business days before expiration
d. On the last trading day of the month

HINTS: Distinguish the exercise rules for European-style options.

Q624_LO54: How do currency options settle in comparison to equity options?
a. Next business day
b. Two business days later
c. On expiration day
d. In-kind settlement

HINTS: Recognize the settlement timing for currency options.

Q625_LO54: Which currency option strategy is suitable for an exporter?
a. Buy calls
b. Sell calls
c. Buy puts
d. Sell puts

HINTS: Apply the EPIC rule for exporters.

Q626_LO54: Why do importers buy calls in currency options?
a. To hedge against currency depreciation
b. To speculate on currency appreciation
c. To offset currency risk
d. To maximize premium

HINTS: Understand the rationale for importers buying calls.

Q627_LO54: What type of exercise do yield-based options follow?
a. American style
b. European style
c. Asian style
d. Monthly style

HINTS: Identify the exercise style for yield-based options.

Q628_LO54: When is an American-style option exercisable?
a. Only on expiration day
b. Anytime before expiration
c. Two business days before expiration
d. On the last trading day of the month

HINTS: Distinguish the exercise rules for American-style options.

Q629_LO54: Which type of options is suitable for speculation on interest rate movements?
a. Currency options
b. Index options
c. Equity options
d. Interest rate options

HINTS: Identify the appropriate options for speculating on interest rates.

Q630_LO54: What is the multiplier typically used for index options?
a. $50
b. $75
c. $100

d. $150

HINTS: Recall the typical multiplier for index options.

Q631_LO55: What is the breakeven point for a long call?
a. Strike price - Premium
b. Strike price + Premium
c. Premium - Strike price
d. Premium + Strike price

HINTS: Recall the formula for calculating the breakeven point for a long call.

Q632_LO55: What is the maximum gain for a long call?
a. Unlimited
b. Premium received
c. Strike price - Premium
d. Premium paid

HINTS: Understand the potential maximum gain for a long call position.

Q633_LO55: What is the maximum loss for a long call?
a. Premium paid
b. Unlimited
c. Strike price - Premium
d. Premium received

HINTS: Recognize the maximum loss scenario for a long call.

Q634_LO55: What is the breakeven point for a short call?
a. Premium received - Strike price
b. Premium paid + Strike price
c. Strike price + Premium
d. Premium - Strike price

HINTS: Understand the formula for calculating the breakeven point for a short call.

Q635_LO55: What is the maximum gain for a short call?
a. Premium received
b. Unlimited
c. Premium paid
d. Strike price - Premium

HINTS: Identify the maximum gain for a short call position.

Q636_LO55: What is the maximum loss for a short call?
a. Strike price + Premium
b. Premium received
c. Unlimited
d. Premium paid

HINTS: Recognize the unlimited loss potential for a short call position.

Q637_LO55: How is the breakeven point calculated for a long put?
a. Premium paid - Strike price
b. Strike price - Premium paid
c. Strike price + Premium paid
d. Premium paid + Strike price

HINTS: Recall the formula for calculating the breakeven point for a long put.

Q638_LO55: What is the maximum gain for a long put?
a. Strike price - Premium paid
b. Premium paid
c. Premium received

d. Unlimited

HINTS: Understand the potential maximum gain for a long put position.

Q639_LO55: What is the maximum loss for a long put?
a. Premium paid
b. Premium received
c. Unlimited
d. Strike price - Premium paid

HINTS: Recognize the maximum loss scenario for a long put.

Q640_LO55: How is the breakeven point calculated for a short put?
a. Strike price + Premium received
b. Premium received - Strike price
c. Premium received + Strike price
d. Premium received / Strike price
HINTS: Understand the formula for calculating the breakeven point for a short put.

Q641_LO55: What is the maximum gain for a short put?
a. Unlimited
b. Premium received
c. Premium paid
d. Strike price - Premium received

HINTS: Identify the maximum gain for a short put position.

Q642_LO55: What is the maximum loss for a short put?
a. Strike price - Premium received
b. Premium received
c. Unlimited
d. Premium paid

HINTS: Recognize the maximum loss scenario for a short put.

Q643_LO55: In theory, how far can a stock's price rise for a long call's potential gain to be unlimited?
a. To the strike price
b. To twice the strike price
c. To three times the strike price
d. To infinity

HINTS: Understand the theoretical concept related to the potential gain of a long call.

Q644_LO55: What does the breakeven point represent for an investor?
a. Profitable point
b. Neither profit nor loss
c. Maximum gain
d. Maximum loss

HINTS: Recognize the significance of the breakeven point in options trading.

Q645_LO55: What is the maximum loss for a long call if the stock price is at or below the strike price at expiration?
a. Premium received
b. Premium paid
c. Strike price - Premium
d. Unlimited

HINTS: Understand the maximum loss scenario for a long call.

Q646_LO55: What is the breakeven (BE) point for a long call option?
a. Strike price + Premium
b. Strike price - Premium
c. Premium - Strike price
d. Premium / Strike price

HINTS: Recall the formula for the breakeven point in a long call.

Q647_LO55: What is the maximum gain (MG) for a long call option?
a. Premium paid
b. Unlimited
c. Strike price + Premium
d. Strike price - Premium

HINTS: Understand the potential maximum gain for a long call.

Q648_LO55: What is the maximum loss (ML) for a long call option?
a. Premium paid
b. Unlimited
c. Strike price + Premium
d. Strike price - Premium

HINTS: Recognize the maximum loss scenario for a long call.

Q649_LO55: What is the breakeven (BE) point for a short call option?
a. Premium paid
b. Strike price + Premium
c. Strike price - Premium
d. Unlimited

HINTS: Apply the formula for the breakeven point in a short call.

Q650_LO55: What is the maximum gain (MG) for a short call option?
a. Unlimited
b. Premium received
c. Strike price - Premium
d. Premium paid

HINTS: Understand the maximum gain scenario for a short call.

Q651_LO55: What is the maximum loss (ML) for a short call option?
a. Unlimited
b. Premium received
c. Strike price - Premium
d. Premium paid

HINTS: Identify the potential maximum loss for a short call.

Q652_LO55: How is the breakeven (BE) point calculated for a long put option?
a. Strike price - Premium
b. Strike price + Premium
c. Premium - Strike price
d. Premium / Strike price

HINTS: Recall the formula for the breakeven point in a long put.

Q653_LO55: What is the maximum gain (MG) for a long put option?
a. Unlimited
b. Premium paid
c. Strike price - Premium
d. Premium received

HINTS: Understand the potential maximum gain for a long put.

Q654_LO55: What is the maximum loss (ML) for a long put option?
a. Unlimited
b. Premium received
c. Premium paid
d. Strike price - Premium

HINTS: Recognize the maximum loss scenario for a long put.

Q655_LO55: How is the breakeven (BE) point calculated for a short put option?
a. Premium - Strike price
b. Strike price - Premium
c. Strike price + Premium
d. Premium / Strike price

HINTS: Apply the formula for the breakeven point in a short put.

Q656_LO55: What is the maximum gain (MG) for a short put option?
a. Unlimited
b. Premium paid
c. Premium received
d. Strike price - Premium

HINTS: Understand the maximum gain scenario for a short put.

Q657_LO55: What is the maximum loss (ML) for a short put option?
a. Unlimited
b. Premium received
c. Premium paid
d. Strike price - Premium

HINTS: Identify the potential maximum loss for a short put.

Q658_LO55: What is the BE point for a long call if the strike price is $50 and the premium paid is $5?
a. $55
b. $45
c. $50
d. $5

HINTS: Apply the formula for calculating the breakeven point.

Q659_LO55: What is the MG for a short call if the premium received is $8?
a. $8
b. Unlimited
c. $8 + Strike price
d. Strike price - $8

HINTS: Recognize the formula for the maximum gain in a short call.

Q660_LO55: What is the ML for a long put if the premium paid is $6?
a. Unlimited
b. $6
c. $6 + Strike price
d. Strike price - $6

HINTS: Identify the maximum loss scenario for a long put.

Q661_LO56: What is the purpose of a protective put option?
a. Lock in maximum sales price
b. Hedge against a rising stock
c. Lock in minimum sales price
d. Hedge against a falling stock

HINTS: Recognize the objective of a protective put.

Q662_LO56: How does a protective put benefit an investor with a long stock position?
a. Locks in unlimited gains
b. Locks in minimum sales price
c. Increases short position risk
d. Provides unlimited risk

HINTS: Understand the advantage of a protective put for a long stock position.

Q663_LO56: What is the formula for calculating the breakeven of a protective put?
a. Breakeven = stock price – premium
b. Breakeven = stock price + premium
c. Breakeven = stock price x premium
d. Breakeven = stock price / premium

HINTS: Recall the correct formula for the breakeven of a protective put.

Q664_LO56: When does a protective put investor break even?
a. When the stock price exceeds the premium
b. When the stock price is below the premium
c. When the stock price rises above the total cost
d. When the stock price falls below the total cost

HINTS: Identify the breakeven point for a protective put.

Q665_LO56: Why might an investor use a protective call?
a. To lock in maximum purchase price
b. To hedge against a falling stock
c. To control the risk of selling a stock short
d. To hedge against a rising stock

HINTS: Recognize the purpose of using a protective call.

Q666_LO56: What does a protective call investor benefit from in a short stock position?
a. Locks in maximum gains
b. Locks in maximum losses
c. Locks in minimum purchase price
d. Provides unlimited risk

HINTS: Understand the advantage of a protective call for a short stock position.

Q667_LO56: What is the formula for calculating the breakeven of a protective call?
a. Breakeven = stock price – premium
b. Breakeven = stock price + premium
c. Breakeven = stock price x premium
d. Breakeven = stock price / premium

HINTS: Recall the correct formula for the breakeven of a protective call.

Q668_LO56: When does a protective call investor break even?
a. When the stock price exceeds the premium
b. When the stock price is below the premium
c. When the stock price rises above the total cost
d. When the stock price falls below the total cost

HINTS: Identify the breakeven point for a protective call.

Q669_LO56: Which option hedges a long stock position?
a. Protective call
b. Covered call
c. Protective put
d. Naked put

HINTS: Distinguish between options used for hedging a long stock position.

Q670_LO56: What is the core position for a protective put?
a. Short stock
b. Long call
c. Long stock
d. Short put

HINTS: Identify the core position for a protective put.

Q671_LO56: Which option hedges a short stock position?
a. Protective call
b. Covered call
c. Protective put
d. Naked put

HINTS: Distinguish between options used for hedging a short stock position.

Q672_LO56: What is the core position for a protective call?
a. Short stock
b. Long call
c. Long stock
d. Short put

HINTS: Identify the core position for a protective call.

Q673_LO56: In a protective put, what happens if the stock price is below the strike price at expiration?
a. Maximum gain
b. Breakeven
c. Maximum loss
d. Unlimited loss

HINTS: Recognize the outcome if the stock price is below the strike price for a protective put.

Q674_LO56: In a protective call, what happens if the stock price is above the strike price at expiration?
a. Maximum gain
b. Breakeven
c. Maximum loss
d. Unlimited loss

HINTS: Recognize the outcome if the stock price is above the strike price for a protective call.

Q675_LO56: Why might an investor use a protective put for a long stock position?
a. To lock in unlimited gains
b. To hedge against a falling stock
c. To control the risk of selling a stock short
d. To lock in unlimited losses

HINTS: Understand the purpose of using a protective put for a long stock position.

Q676_LO56: What strategy is employed when an investor is long stock and buys a put option to protect against a potential decline in stock value?
a. Bullish call
b. Protective call
c. Bull put spread
d. Protective put

HINTS: Recognize the strategy used for hedging a long stock position.

Q677_LO56: When calculating the breakeven for a protective put, what formula should be used?
a. Breakeven = Stock price - Premium
b. Breakeven = Premium - Stock price
c. Breakeven = Stock price + Premium
d. Breakeven = Premium / Stock price

HINTS: Recall the correct formula for calculating the breakeven of a protective put.

Q678_LO56: What does a protective call do for an investor who is short stock?
a. Locks in a maximum purchase price
b. Locks in a minimum sales price
c. Increases unlimited risk
d. Decreases maximum loss

HINTS: Identify the purpose of a protective call for an investor who is short stock.

Q679_LO56: When calculating the breakeven for a protective call, what formula should be used?
a. Breakeven = Premium - Stock price
b. Breakeven = Stock price + Premium
c. Breakeven = Stock price - Premium
d. Breakeven = Premium / Stock price

HINTS: Recall the correct formula for calculating the breakeven of a protective call.

Q680_LO56: What is the purpose of a protective put for an investor who is long stock?
a. Locks in a maximum purchase price
b. Locks in a minimum sales price
c. Increases unlimited risk
d. Decreases maximum loss

HINTS: Understand the role of a protective put for an investor who is long stock.

Q681_LO56: In a protective put strategy, what is the relationship between the value of the stock and the breakeven point?
a. Stock value should fall below the breakeven
b. Stock value should rise above the breakeven
c. No relationship
d. Stock value equals the breakeven

HINTS: Understand the relationship between stock value and the breakeven point in a protective put.

Q682_LO56: How does a protective call control the risk of selling a stock short?
a. Locks in a maximum purchase price
b. Locks in a minimum sales price
c. Increases unlimited risk
d. Decreases maximum loss

HINTS: Identify the risk control mechanism of a protective call for a short stock position.

Q683_LO56: In a protective call strategy, what is the relationship between the value of the stock and the breakeven point?
a. Stock value should fall below the breakeven
b. Stock value should rise above the breakeven
c. No relationship
d. Stock value equals the breakeven

HINTS: Understand the relationship between stock value and the breakeven point in a protective call.

Q684_LO56: What is the core position in a strategy involving a protective put?
a. Short stock
b. Long stock
c. Short call
d. Long call

HINTS: Recognize the core position when using a protective put strategy.

Q685_LO56: What is the hedge in a strategy involving a protective call?
a. Short stock
b. Long stock
c. Short call
d. Long call

HINTS: Identify the hedge in a strategy involving a protective call.

Q686_LO56: Which strategy is used by an investor who is short stock and buys a call option as protection?
a. Bullish call
b. Protective call
c. Bearish put
d. Protective put

HINTS: Recognize the strategy used for hedging a short stock position.

Q687_LO56: What is the core position in a strategy involving a protective call?
a. Short stock
b. Long stock
c. Short call
d. Long call

HINTS: Recognize the core position when using a protective call strategy.

Q688_LO56: What is the hedge in a strategy involving a protective put?
a. Short stock
b. Long stock
c. Short call
d. Long call

HINTS: Identify the hedge in a strategy involving a protective put.

Q689_LO56: What is the purpose of a protective put for an investor who is short stock?
a. Locks in a maximum purchase price
b. Locks in a minimum sales price
c. Increases unlimited risk
d. Decreases maximum loss

HINTS: Understand the role of a protective put for an investor who is short stock.

Q690_LO56: In a protective put strategy, what is the relationship between the value of the stock and the breakeven point?
a. Stock value should fall below the breakeven
b. Stock value should rise above the breakeven
c. No relationship
d. Stock value equals the breakeven

HINTS: Understand the relationship between stock value and the breakeven point in a protective put.

Q691_LO57: What does it mean when a call option is referred to as "uncovered" (naked)?
a. The writer owns the underlying security
b. The writer does not own the underlying security
c. The writer has sufficient cash to buy the stock
d. The writer has limited risk

HINTS: Recognize the characteristic of an uncovered call option.

Q692_LO57: In covered call writing, what does the writer already possess?
a. Cash available to buy the stock
b. The underlying security
c. A put option
d. Unlimited risk

HINTS: Identify the feature of a covered call option.

Q693_LO57: What is the risk associated with uncovered (naked) call writing?
a. Limited risk
b. Unlimited risk
c. Cash availability risk
d. Market price risk

HINTS: Understand the risk involved in writing uncovered call options.

Q694_LO57: How does covered put writing differ from uncovered (naked) put writing?
a. Covered put requires owning the underlying security
b. Uncovered put has limited risk
c. Covered put has unlimited risk
d. Uncovered put involves cash availability

HINTS: Differentiate between covered and uncovered put writing.

Q695_LO57: What is the risk in uncovered (naked) put writing?
a. Limited risk
b. Unlimited risk
c. Cash availability risk
d. Market price risk

HINTS: Identify the risk associated with writing uncovered put options.

Q696_LO57: What does a covered put involve?
a. Owning the underlying security
b. Owning a call option
c. Having cash available
d. Uncovered position

HINTS: Understand the characteristic of a covered put.

Q697_LO57: What is the term for a theoretical hedge where a customer is short the stock and writes a put?
a. Covered put
b. Uncovered put
c. Synthetic hedge
d. Cash hedge

HINTS: Recognize the term for a theoretical hedge involving short stock and a put option.

Q698_LO57: What is the main motivation for writers of naked calls?
a. Limited risk
b. Speculative premium income
c. Guaranteed profit
d. Reduced market exposure

HINTS: Understand the primary motivation for writing naked calls.

Q699_LO57: What does it mean if a put option is covered against a short stock?
a. The writer owns the underlying security
b. The writer has sufficient cash
c. The writer has no control over the option
d. The writer has a guaranteed profit

HINTS: Recognize the feature of a covered put against a short stock.

Q700_LO57: In writing a covered put, what does the writer possess?
a. Cash available to buy the stock
b. The underlying security
c. A call option
d. Unlimited risk

HINTS: Identify the feature of a covered put option.

Q701_LO57: Why is writing an uncovered (naked) call considered to have unlimited risk?
a. Cash availability risk
b. Market price risk
c. Speculative premium income
d. The uncertainty of the stock's market price
HINTS: Understand the reason behind the unlimited risk in uncovered call writing.

Q702_LO57: What is the key characteristic of covered call writing?
a. Unlimited risk
b. Speculative premium income
c. Owning the underlying security
d. Cash availability

HINTS: Identify the key feature of covered call writing.

Q703_LO57: What is the risk associated with uncovered (naked) put writing?
a. Limited risk
b. Unlimited risk
c. Cash availability risk
d. Market price risk

HINTS: Recognize the risk involved in writing uncovered put options.

Q704_LO57: In a covered put, what does the writer already have sufficient cash for?
a. Buying the stock
b. Selling the stock
c. Writing more puts
d. Guaranteed profit

HINTS: Understand the purpose of having sufficient cash in a covered put.

Q705_LO57: What is the main risk in writing uncovered (naked) calls?
a. Limited risk
b. Cash availability risk
c. Market price risk
d. Speculative premium income

HINTS: Identify the main risk associated with writing uncovered calls.

Q706_LO57: What is the key difference between a covered call and a naked call option?
a. Ownership of the underlying security
b. Premium income potential
c. Expiration date
d. Exercise price

HINTS: Recognize the primary distinction between covered and naked call options.

Q707_LO57: What risk is associated with writing an uncovered (naked) call option?
a. Limited risk
b. No risk
c. Theoretical risk
d. Predictable risk

HINTS: Identify the risk characteristic of writing an uncovered call option.

Q708_LO57: In covered put writing, what does the writer already possess?
a. Stock ownership
b. Cash to buy the stock
c. Call option
d. Unpredictable risk

HINTS: Understand what the writer of a covered put already has in covered put writing.

Q709_LO57: What is the risk associated with writing an uncovered (naked) put option?
a. Limited risk
b. No risk
c. Predictable risk
d. Unlimited risk

HINTS: Recognize the risk characteristic of writing an uncovered put option.

Q710_LO57: How do writers of naked calls justify the risk they take?
a. Predictable outcomes
b. Unlimited premium income
c. Guaranteed exercise
d. Fixed risk

HINTS: Recognize the motivation behind writers of naked calls despite the associated risk.

Q711_LO57: In covered put writing, what does the writer need to have available?
a. Stock ownership
b. Cash to buy the stock
c. Call option
d. Unpredictable risk

HINTS: Understand what the writer of a covered put needs to have available.

Q712_LO57: What is a covered put against a short stock position considered?
a. Theoretical hedge
b. Guaranteed hedge
c. Limited-risk position
d. Unlimited-risk position

HINTS: Identify the nature of a covered put against a short stock position.

Q713_LO57: Why is an uncovered call option considered riskier than a covered call option?
a. Lack of premium income
b. Fixed risk
c. Predictable outcomes
d. Unlimited risk

HINTS: Understand the risk comparison between uncovered and covered call options.

Q714_LO57: What is the primary purpose of a covered put strategy?
a. Generate unlimited premium
b. Hedge against a decline in stock value
c. Speculate on stock prices
d. Eliminate premium income

HINTS: Recognize the primary objective of a covered put strategy.

Q715_LO57: What does the term "uncovered against a short stock" mean in a put option context?
a. Theoretical hedge
b. Guaranteed hedge
c. Limited-risk position
d. Unlimited-risk position

HINTS: Understand the meaning of "uncovered against a short stock" in put option context.

Q716_LO57: What does the writer of an uncovered (naked) put option need to come up with if the option is exercised?
a. Call option
b. Unlimited premium
c. Cash to buy the stock
d. Predictable outcomes

HINTS: Recognize the obligation of the writer of an uncovered put option if exercised.

Q717_LO57: What is the primary motivation for writers of naked calls despite the risk?
a. Guaranteed exercise
b. Fixed risk
c. Predictable outcomes
d. Unlimited premium income

HINTS: Understand the primary motivation for writers of naked calls.

Q718_LO57: Why is an uncovered put option considered riskier than a covered put option?
a. Lack of premium income
b. Fixed risk
c. Predictable outcomes
d. Unlimited risk

HINTS: Understand the risk comparison between uncovered and covered put options.

Q719_LO57: What does the term "covered against a short stock" mean in a put option context?
a. Theoretical hedge
b. Guaranteed hedge
c. Limited-risk position
d. Unlimited-risk position

HINTS: Understand the meaning of "covered against a short stock" in a put option context.

Q720_LO57: What risk is associated with writing an uncovered (naked) call option?
a. Limited risk
b. No risk
c. Predictable risk
d. Unlimited risk

HINTS: Recognize the risk characteristic of writing an uncovered call option.

Q721_LO57: What is the primary role of the Options Clearing Corporation (OCC) in options trading?
a. Account approval
b. Provide disclosure document
c. Options trading regulation
d. Payment of premiums

HINTS: Identify the primary role of the OCC in options trading.

Q722_LO57: Who must approve an options account before any trading can take place?
a. Registered Representative
b. Customer
c. OCC
d. Registered Options Principal (ROP)

HINTS: Recognize the authority responsible for approving an options account.

Q723_LO57: When must the options disclosure document (ODD) be provided to a customer?
a. After account approval
b. Before account approval
c. During the first trade
d. Upon account funding

HINTS: Understand the timing for providing the options disclosure document to the customer.

Q724_LO57: What document must a customer return within 15 days after account approval?
a. Account funding form
b. Signed options agreement
c. Trade confirmation
d. Financial statements

HINTS: Identify the document that the customer must return within 15 days after account approval.

Q725_LO57: What is the purpose of the options agreement?
a. Approve account funding
b. Confirm executed trades
c. Acknowledge understanding of risks
d. Provide trade recommendations

HINTS: Recognize the purpose of the options agreement.

Q726_LO57: What is the consequence if the signed options agreement is not returned within 15 days?
a. Account closure
b. Only closing transactions allowed
c. Unlimited trading access
d. Premium refund

HINTS: Understand the consequence of not returning the signed options agreement within the specified period.

Q727_LO57: In what sequence do the following steps occur: account approval, providing the ODD, and entering option trades?
a. Account approval, ODD, trades
b. ODD, account approval, trades
c. Trades, ODD, account approval
d. ODD, trades, account approval

HINTS: Understand the sequence of steps for setting up an options account.

Q728_LO57: What is the significance of the customer returning the signed options agreement?
a. Account approval
b. Allows new options positions
c. Acknowledges understanding of risks
d. Fund withdrawal

HINTS: Recognize the significance of the customer returning the signed options agreement.

Q729_LO57: When is the first trade allowed in an options account following approval?
a. Before account approval
b. Immediately after account approval
c. 15 days after account approval
d. After the options agreement is returned

HINTS: Understand when the first trade is allowed in an options account following approval.

Q730_LO57: What role does the Registered Representative play in options account setup?
a. Approves account
b. Provides ODD
c. Determines suitability
d. Approves option trades

HINTS: Identify the role of the Registered Representative in setting up an options account.

Q731_LO57: What is the purpose of the Options Disclosure Document (ODD)?
a. Account approval
b. Explain options strategies, risks, and rewards
c. Provide trade recommendations
d. Confirm executed trades

HINTS: Understand the purpose of the Options Disclosure Document (ODD).

Q732_LO57: What restriction applies if the options agreement is not returned within 15 days?
a. Account closure
b. Only opening transactions allowed
c. Only closing transactions allowed
d. No restriction

HINTS: Identify the restriction if the options agreement is not returned within the specified period.

Q733_LO57: Who is responsible for approving an options account for trading?
a. OCC
b. Customer
c. Registered Representative
d. Registered Options Principal (ROP)

HINTS: Recognize the authority responsible for approving an options account.

Q734_LO57: Why is there a 15-day timeframe for returning the signed options agreement?
a. Regulatory requirement
b. Customer preference
c. Risk management
d. Market volatility

HINTS: Understand the reason for the 15-day timeframe for returning the signed options agreement.

Q735_LO57: What is the primary document that signifies a customer's commitment to understanding options risks?
a. Trade confirmation
b. Financial statements
c. Options agreement
d. Account statement

HINTS: Identify the document that signifies a customer's commitment to understanding options risks.

Q736_LO57: Who are the primary regulators for options trading?
a. SEC and FINRA
b. OCC and CBOE
c. NYSE and NASDAQ
d. FDIC and CFTC

HINTS: Identify the primary regulators for options trading.

Q737_LO57: What document, explaining options strategies, risks, and rewards, must be provided to customers before they begin options trading?
a. SEC Report
b. Options Trading Handbook
c. Options Disclosure Document (ODD)
d. Trading Regulations Manual

HINTS: Recognize the document designed to provide full disclosure before options trading.

Q738_LO57: Who must approve an options account before any trading can take place?
a. Senior Account Executive
b. Risk Management Officer
c. Registered Options Principal (ROP)
d. Compliance Analyst

HINTS: Identify the role responsible for approving options accounts.

Q739_LO57: What must a representative believe before considering options trading for a client?
a. High-risk tolerance
b. Adequate financial resources
c. Interest in day trading
d. Desire for short-term gains
HINTS: Understand the criteria for considering options trading for a client.

Q740_LO57: When should the customer return the signed options agreement after account approval?
a. Within 30 days
b. Within 10 days
c. Within 15 days
d. Within 5 days

HINTS: Recognize the time frame for returning the signed options agreement.

Q741_LO57: What is the purpose of the options agreement?
a. Approving trade specifics
b. Confirming trade execution
c. Acknowledging risk understanding
d. Verifying account balance

HINTS: Identify the primary purpose of the options agreement.

Q742_LO57: What transactions are allowed if the options agreement is not returned within 15 days of account approval?
a. New options positions
b. Closing transactions only
c. Both new and closing transactions
d. No transactions

HINTS: Understand the limitations if the options agreement is not returned within the specified timeframe.

Q743_LO57: What is the chronological conundrum in the options account setup process?
a. Account approval after trading
b. Trading before account approval
c. Options agreement after account approval
d. Customer returning agreement before account approval

HINTS: Identify the chronological challenge in the options account setup process.

Q744_LO57: What happens if the signed options agreement is not returned within 15 days of account approval?
a. Account closure
b. Limited trading access
c. Only new positions allowed
d. Only closing transactions allowed

HINTS: Recognize the trading restrictions if the options agreement is not returned within the specified timeframe.

Q745_LO57: When may the first trade take place in an options account?
a. After options disclosure
b. Immediately following account approval
c. After 30 days
d. Only after the signed agreement is received

HINTS: Understand when the first trade may occur in an options account.

Q746_LO57: What does the Options Disclosure Document (ODD) provide information on?
a. Trade execution procedures
b. Options market trends
c. Options strategies, risks, and rewards
d. Economic indicators

HINTS: Identify the content covered by the Options Disclosure Document (ODD).

Q747_LO57: What is the primary role of a Registered Options Principal (ROP)?
a. Trade execution oversight
b. Options strategy development
c. Approving options accounts
d. Economic analysis

HINTS: Recognize the primary responsibility of a Registered Options Principal (ROP).

Q748_LO57: Why is the Options Disclosure Document (ODD) crucial in the options trading process?
a. Marketing tool
b. Regulatory requirement
c. Trade confirmation
d. Account statement

HINTS: Understand the significance of the Options Disclosure Document (ODD).

Q749_LO57: What role does a representative play in the options account setup process?
a. Executing trades
b. Providing financial advice
c. Determining suitability
d. Monitoring market trends

HINTS: Identify the key role of a representative in the options account setup process.

Q750_LO57: What restriction applies if the customer does not return the signed options agreement within 15 days?
a. No new positions
b. No account access
c. No trading at all
d. Only closing transactions

HINTS: Recognize the specific trading restriction if the agreement is not returned on time.

Q751_LO58: What is the primary role of the Options Clearing Corporation (OCC)?
a. Stock trading
b. Standardizing, guaranteeing, and issuing option contracts
c. Currency exchange
d. Commodity futures

HINTS: Recognize the primary function of the OCC.

Q752_LO58: When do listed options trade during a regular trading day?
a. 8:00 am to 3:30 pm
b. 9:30 am to 4:00 pm
c. 10:00 am to 4:30 pm
d. 9:00 am to 5:00 pm

HINTS: Identify the regular trading hours for listed options.

Q753_LO58: What is the settlement period for listed options?
a. Same day (T+0)
b. Next business day (T+1)
c. Two business days (T+2)
d. End of the week

HINTS: Recognize the settlement period for listed options.

Q754_LO58: When do listed options contracts expire?
a. Second Friday of the expiration month
b. Last business day of the month
c. Third Friday of the expiration month
d. Last Friday of the month

HINTS: Identify the expiration timing for listed options contracts.

Q755_LO58: What is the process for exercising listed options contracts?
a. Notify the broker
b. Notify the OCC
c. Automatic exercise
d. Contact the stock exchange

HINTS: Understand the process of exercising listed options contracts.

Q756_LO58: How does the OCC handle assignment of exercise notices to short BDs?
a. Random basis
b. First-in, first-out (FIFO) basis
c. Last-in, first-out (LIFO) basis
d. Alphabetical basis

HINTS: Recognize the method used by the OCC to assign exercise notices to short BDs.

Q757_LO58: What happens if a call option is in the money at expiration?
a. Automatic exercise
b. Automatic assignment
c. Automatic renewal
d. Automatic expiration

HINTS: Understand the automatic action for call options that are in the money at expiration.

Q758_LO58: How does the OCC ensure fairness in the assignment process?
a. Random basis
b. FIFO basis
c. LIFO basis
d. Customer request basis

HINTS: Recognize the fairness principle applied by the OCC in assignment.

Q759_LO58: What is the proof of ownership for an investor with options contracts?
a. Options certificate
b. Trade confirmation
c. Stock certificate
d. Exercise notice

HINTS: Identify the document serving as proof of ownership for options contracts.

Q760_LO58: When is an options contract considered automatically exercised?
a. In the money by at least 0.05
b. In the money by at least 0.01
c. Out of the money by at least 0.01
d. At the money

HINTS: Understand the criteria for automatic exercise of options contracts.

Q761_LO58: What is the primary role of a Registered Options Principal (ROP)?
a. Trading oversight
b. Approving option contracts
c. Option strategy development
d. Securities regulation

HINTS: Recognize the primary responsibility of a Registered Options Principal (ROP).

Q762_LO58: Who has the right to exercise an options contract?
a. Only buyers (long positions)
b. Only sellers (short positions)
c. Both buyers and sellers
d. Only OCC
HINTS: Identify the party with the right to exercise options contracts.

Q763_LO58: What is the automatic exercise threshold for listed options?
a. In the money by at least 0.10
b. In the money by at least 0.05
c. In the money by at least 0.01
d. At the money

HINTS: Understand the minimum criterion for the automatic exercise of listed options.

Q764_LO58: What is the role of the OCC in the exercise and assignment process?
a. Exercising options
b. Assigning exercise notices
c. Approving trades
d. Issuing options contracts

HINTS: Recognize the specific role of the OCC in the exercise and assignment process.

Q765_LO58: What is the significance of the trade confirmation for options contracts?
a. Proof of exercise
b. Proof of ownership
c. Trading authorization
d. Issuance of new contracts

HINTS: Understand the importance of the trade confirmation in options trading.

Correct Answers & Explanations
Derivatives

Q526_LO52: Correct Answer: b EXPLANATIONS: A derivative is a contract that derives its value from an underlying asset.

Q527_LO52: Correct Answer: a EXPLANATIONS: The buyer has the right to exercise the contract.

Q528_LO52: Correct Answer: c EXPLANATIONS: Derivatives are often used for commodities, currencies, and stocks.

Q529_LO52: Correct Answer: b EXPLANATIONS: The amount paid for the contract is called the premium.

Q530_LO52: Correct Answer: a EXPLANATIONS: An opening purchase is followed by a closing sale in options trading.

Q531_LO52: Correct Answer: b EXPLANATIONS: The seller is obligated to fulfill the terms of the option contract.

Q532_LO52: Correct Answer: c EXPLANATIONS: Buyers risk losing the premium paid if the option expires as worthless.

Q533_LO52: Correct Answer: b EXPLANATIONS: A closing purchase involves buying back the option.

Q534_LO52: Correct Answer: c EXPLANATIONS: The seller is often called the writer in an option agreement.

Q535_LO52: Correct Answer: a EXPLANATIONS: The seller of calls receives the premium.

Q536_LO52: Correct Answer: b EXPLANATIONS: Options offer a means to speculate on the price movement of various instruments.

Q537_LO52: Correct Answer: b EXPLANATIONS: Equity options are issued on common stocks.

Q538_LO52: Correct Answer: c EXPLANATIONS: The two types of option contracts are calls and puts.

Q539_LO52: Correct Answer: b EXPLANATIONS: Time decay allows the seller to profit if the option expires as worthless.

Q540_LO52: Correct Answer: b EXPLANATIONS: Investors who sell puts receive income in the form of the premium.

Q541_LO52: Correct Answer: b EXPLANATIONS: The premium is the cost of the option contract.

Q542_LO52: Correct Answer: b EXPLANATIONS: A long call gives the right to buy the underlying asset.

Q543_LO52: Correct Answer: b EXPLANATIONS: A call writer is bearish, as they want the market to fall or remain unchanged.

Q544_LO52: Correct Answer: b EXPLANATIONS: A put buyer exercises to sell the underlying asset.

Q545_LO52: Correct Answer: a EXPLANATIONS: A short put writer has the obligation to buy the underlying asset.

Q546_LO52: Correct Answer: b EXPLANATIONS: Equity options are issued on common stocks.

Q547_LO52: Correct Answer: c EXPLANATIONS: The primary risk is the potential loss of the premium.

Q548_LO52: Correct Answer: a EXPLANATIONS: The short call writer keeps the premium with no further obligation.

Q549_LO52: Correct Answer: a EXPLANATIONS: A put writer is bullish, as they want the market to rise or remain unchanged.

Q550_LO52: Correct Answer: b EXPLANATIONS: Index options settle in cash.

Q551_LO52: Correct Answer: a EXPLANATIONS: The VIX Index measures expected volatility in the stock market.

Q552_LO52: Correct Answer: c EXPLANATIONS: VIX options are based on the S&P 500 Index.

Q553_LO52: Correct Answer: b EXPLANATIONS: A put buyer speculates on falling prices.

Q554_LO52: Correct Answer: c EXPLANATIONS: A call buyer may choose not to exercise to avoid market risk.

Q555_LO52: Correct Answer: a EXPLANATIONS: A put writer hopes for the market price to rise or remain unchanged.

Q556_LO52: Correct Answer: b EXPLANATIONS: The premium is the contract price of an option.

Q557_LO52: Correct Answer: a EXPLANATIONS: A long call buyer anticipates a rise in the market price.

Q558_LO52: Correct Answer: a EXPLANATIONS: A short put writer is bullish, wanting the market to rise or remain unchanged.

Q559_LO52: Correct Answer: a EXPLANATIONS: A call writer hopes the market price stays below the strike price to maximize premium.

Q560_LO52: Correct Answer: b EXPLANATIONS: A long put buyer wants the market price to fall.

Q561_LO52: Correct Answer: b EXPLANATIONS: Equity options are issued on common stocks.

Q562_LO52: Correct Answer: a EXPLANATIONS: A short call writer has the obligation to sell the underlying asset.

Q563_LO52: Correct Answer: b EXPLANATIONS: A put option is exercised by the buyer when the market price falls.

Q564_LO52: Correct Answer: a EXPLANATIONS: The primary risk for a long call buyer is losing the premium.

Q565_LO52: Correct Answer: c EXPLANATIONS: The premium remains with the seller if the call option is unexercised.

Q566_LO52: Correct Answer: b EXPLANATIONS: A long put buyer is bearish, wanting the market to fall.

Q567_LO52: Correct Answer: a EXPLANATIONS: A short put writer has the obligation to buy the underlying asset.

Q568_LO52: Correct Answer: a EXPLANATIONS: VIX options settle in cash with European exercise provisions.

Q569_LO52: Correct Answer: c EXPLANATIONS: Investors use VIX options to speculate on volatility in the equity markets.

Q570_LO52: Correct Answer: c EXPLANATIONS: An index option results in cash settlement; no delivery of underlying shares is made.

Q571_LO53: Correct Answer: b EXPLANATIONS: A call is in the money when the stock price is higher than the strike price.

Q572_LO53: Correct Answer: b EXPLANATIONS: Intrinsic value is the amount an option is in the money.

Q573_LO53: Correct Answer: a EXPLANATIONS: A put is at the money when the stock price is equal to the strike price.

Q574_LO53: Correct Answer: d EXPLANATIONS: A call buyer wants options to be in the money.

Q575_LO53: Correct Answer: a EXPLANATIONS: At-the-money options have an intrinsic value of zero.

Q576_LO53: Correct Answer: c EXPLANATIONS: A put buyer exercises when the option is in the money.

Q577_LO53: Correct Answer: a EXPLANATIONS: A call option is at parity when the premium equals intrinsic value.

Q578_LO53: Correct Answer: b EXPLANATIONS: Time value is a subjective number determined by supply and demand.

Q579_LO53: Correct Answer: c EXPLANATIONS: Premium = Intrinsic Value + Time Value (IV + TV = Pr).

Q580_LO53: Correct Answer: a EXPLANATIONS: The more time until expiration, the more time value an option will have.

Q581_LO53: Correct Answer: b EXPLANATIONS: Volatility affects time value in the premium.

Q582_LO53: Correct Answer: d EXPLANATIONS: The premium remains with the seller if there is no intrinsic value.

Q583_LO53: Correct Answer: c EXPLANATIONS: A call is out of the money when the stock price is lower than the strike price.

Q584_LO53: Correct Answer: a EXPLANATIONS: Out-of-the-money options have an intrinsic value of zero.

Q585_LO53: Correct Answer: c EXPLANATIONS: A put seller wants the option to be out of the money.

Q586_LO53: Correct Answer: c EXPLANATIONS: A call is in the money when the stock price exceeds the strike price.

Q587_LO53: Correct Answer: a EXPLANATIONS: A put is out of the money when the stock price is higher than the strike price.

Q588_LO53: Correct Answer: c EXPLANATIONS: Intrinsic value is the amount a contract is in the money.

Q589_LO53: Correct Answer: b EXPLANATIONS: A call option is at parity when the premium equals intrinsic value.

Q590_LO53: Correct Answer: b EXPLANATIONS: A put buyer wants the stock price to fall.

Q591_LO53: Correct Answer: a EXPLANATIONS: IV stands for Intrinsic Value.

Q592_LO53: Correct Answer: d EXPLANATIONS: Time value is a subjective number determined by supply and demand.

Q593_LO53: Correct Answer: b EXPLANATIONS: More volatility increases the time value in the premium.

Q594_LO53: Correct Answer: b EXPLANATIONS: A put with no intrinsic value is allowed to expire.

Q595_LO53: Correct Answer: a EXPLANATIONS: Sellers want options to be out of the money to maximize premium.

Q596_LO53: Correct Answer: b EXPLANATIONS: A call buyer exercises when the stock price rises.

Q597_LO53: Correct Answer: c EXPLANATIONS: At-the-money options have an intrinsic value of zero.

Q598_LO53: Correct Answer: a EXPLANATIONS: Parity is when the premium equals intrinsic value.

Q599_LO53: Correct Answer: c EXPLANATIONS: The primary risk for a put seller is falling stock prices.

Q600_LO53: Correct Answer: a EXPLANATIONS: Intrinsic value for a call is the stock price minus the strike price.

Q601_LO54: Correct Answer: a EXPLANATIONS: Nonequity options have different contract sizes and delivery/exercise standards.

Q602_LO54: Correct Answer: b EXPLANATIONS: Broad-based indexes reflect the movement of the entire market, including S&P 500.

Q603_LO54: Correct Answer: b EXPLANATIONS: The VIX measures the implied volatility of S&P 500 options, often associated with market fear.

Q604_LO54: Correct Answer: b EXPLANATIONS: Settlement is based on the closing value of the index on the day of exercise.

Q605_LO54: Correct Answer: c EXPLANATIONS: Index options typically use a multiplier of $100.

Q606_LO54: Correct Answer: c EXPLANATIONS: Broad-based index options stop trading at 4:15 pm ET.

Q607_LO54: Correct Answer: c EXPLANATIONS: Buying index puts is a strategy for hedging against the risk of a market decline.

Q608_LO54: Correct Answer: b EXPLANATIONS: Portfolio managers use index options to hedge a diverse portfolio, known as portfolio insurance.

Q609_LO54: Correct Answer: b EXPLANATIONS: Interest rate options are yield-based, reflecting movements in interest rates.

Q610_LO54: Correct Answer: b EXPLANATIONS: The premium of a yield-based option is calculated as intrinsic value plus time value.

Q611_LO54: Correct Answer: b EXPLANATIONS: Investors buy calls on interest rate options when expecting rates to rise.

Q612_LO54: Correct Answer: b EXPLANATIONS: Importers buy calls to hedge against the rising value of foreign currency.

Q613_LO54: Correct Answer: b EXPLANATIONS: Exchange-listed foreign currency options are European-style exercise only.

Q614_LO54: Correct Answer: b EXPLANATIONS: American-style options allow exercise anytime before expiration.

Q615_LO54: Correct Answer: a EXPLANATIONS: Exporters buy puts to hedge against the dropping value of foreign currency.

Q616_LO54: Correct Answer: c EXPLANATIONS: Index options settle next business day, whereas equity options settle two business days later.

Q617_LO54: Correct Answer: b EXPLANATIONS: The VIX Index reflects investor expectations of market volatility over the next 30 days.

Q618_LO54: Correct Answer: b EXPLANATIONS: Index options expire on the third Friday of the expiration month.

Q619_LO54: Correct Answer: b EXPLANATIONS: Exercised index options settle in cash, not in the delivery of a security.

Q620_LO54: Correct Answer: c EXPLANATIONS: The settlement price is based on the closing value of the index on the day of exercise.

Q621_LO54: Correct Answer: b EXPLANATIONS: Portfolio managers use index options for portfolio insurance against market declines.

Q622_LO54: Correct Answer: c EXPLANATIONS: A yield-based option with a strike price of 35 reflects a yield of 3.5%.

Q623_LO54: Correct Answer: b EXPLANATIONS: European-style options can be exercised only on expiration day.

Q624_LO54: Correct Answer: a EXPLANATIONS: Currency options settle on the next business day, similar to equity options.

Q625_LO54: Correct Answer: c EXPLANATIONS: Exporters buy puts (EPIC - Exporters Puts).

Q626_LO54: Correct Answer: a EXPLANATIONS: Importers buy calls to hedge against the value of the foreign currency rising.

Q627_LO54: Correct Answer: b EXPLANATIONS: Yield-based options are European-style exercise.

Q628_LO54: Correct Answer: b EXPLANATIONS: American-style options can be exercised anytime before expiration.

Q629_LO54: Correct Answer: d EXPLANATIONS: Interest rate options are suitable for speculation on interest rate movements.

Q630_LO54: Correct Answer: c EXPLANATIONS: Index options typically use a multiplier of $100.

Q631_LO55: Correct Answer: b EXPLANATIONS: The breakeven for a long call is found by adding the strike price and the premium.

Q632_LO55: Correct Answer: a EXPLANATIONS: The potential gains for a long call are theoretically unlimited as the stock price can rise to infinity.

Q633_LO55: Correct Answer: a EXPLANATIONS: The most the call buyer can lose is the premium paid.

Q634_LO55: Correct Answer: c EXPLANATIONS: The breakeven for a short call is found by adding the strike price to the premium.

Q635_LO55: Correct Answer: a EXPLANATIONS: A call writer's maximum gain is the premium received.

Q636_LO55: Correct Answer: c EXPLANATIONS: A call writer's maximum loss is unlimited as the writer could be forced to buy the stock at a potentially unlimited price.

Q637_LO55: Correct Answer: b EXPLANATIONS: The breakeven for a long put is found by subtracting the premium from the strike price.

Q638_LO55: Correct Answer: a EXPLANATIONS: The maximum potential gain for put owners is the option's strike price less the amount of the premium paid.

Q639_LO55: Correct Answer: a EXPLANATIONS: The most the put buyer can lose is the premium paid.

Q640_LO55: Correct Answer: a EXPLANATIONS: The breakeven for a short put is found by adding the premium received to the strike price.

Q641_LO55: Correct Answer: b EXPLANATIONS: A put writer's maximum gain is the premium received.

Q642_LO55: Correct Answer: a EXPLANATIONS: A put writer's maximum loss is the put's strike price less the premium received.

Q643_LO55: Correct Answer: d EXPLANATIONS: Theoretically, the potential gains available to call buyers are unlimited as the stock price can rise to infinity.

Q644_LO55: Correct Answer: b EXPLANATIONS: The breakeven point is the point at which the investor neither makes nor loses money.

Q645_LO55: Correct Answer: b EXPLANATIONS: The most the call buyer can lose is the premium paid if the stock price is at or below the strike price at expiration.

Q646_LO55: Correct Answer: a EXPLANATIONS: For long calls, the breakeven point is found by adding the strike price and the premium.

Q647_LO55: Correct Answer: b EXPLANATIONS: Theoretically, the potential gains available to call buyers are unlimited.

Q648_LO55: Correct Answer: a EXPLANATIONS: The most the call buyer can lose is the premium paid.

Q649_LO55: Correct Answer: c EXPLANATIONS: For short calls, the breakeven point is found by adding the strike price to the premium.

Q650_LO55: Correct Answer: b EXPLANATIONS: A call writer's maximum gain is the premium received.

Q651_LO55: Correct Answer: a EXPLANATIONS: A call writer's maximum loss is unlimited.

Q652_LO55: Correct Answer: a EXPLANATIONS: For long puts, the breakeven point is found by subtracting the premium from the strike price.

Q653_LO55: Correct Answer: a EXPLANATIONS: The maximum potential gain available to put owners is the option's strike price.

Q654_LO55: Correct Answer: b EXPLANATIONS: The most the put buyer can lose is the premium paid.

Q655_LO55: Correct Answer: b EXPLANATIONS: For short puts, the breakeven point is found by subtracting the premium from the strike price.

Q656_LO55: Correct Answer: c EXPLANATIONS: A put writer's maximum gain is the premium received.

Q657_LO55: Correct Answer: d EXPLANATIONS: A put writer's maximum loss is the put's strike price less the premium received.

Q658_LO55: Correct Answer: a EXPLANATIONS: BE = Strike price + Premium = $50 + $5 = $55

Q659_LO55: Correct Answer: a EXPLANATIONS: A call writer's maximum gain is the premium received, in this case, $8.

Q660_LO55: Correct Answer: b EXPLANATIONS: The most the put buyer can lose is the premium paid, in this case, $6.

Q661_LO56: Correct Answer: c EXPLANATIONS: A protective put ensures a minimum sales price if the long stock position moves in the wrong direction.

Q662_LO56: Correct Answer: b EXPLANATIONS: A protective put ensures the investor can sell the stock at no less than the option's strike price if the share price declines.

Q663_LO56: Correct Answer: b EXPLANATIONS: Breakeven = stock price + premium (long stock and long put positions)

Q664_LO56: Correct Answer: c EXPLANATIONS: The investor breaks even when the stock price rises above what was paid for the stock by enough to cover the cost of the option position.

Q665_LO56: Correct Answer: c EXPLANATIONS: A protective call controls the risk of selling a stock short by ensuring a maximum purchase price.

Q666_LO56: Correct Answer: c EXPLANATIONS: A protective call ensures the shorted stock's value falls below what was paid for the stock by enough to cover the cost of the option position.

Q667_LO56: Correct Answer: a EXPLANATIONS: Breakeven = stock price – premium (short stock and long call positions)

Q668_LO56: Correct Answer: b EXPLANATIONS: The investor breaks even when the value of the shorted stock falls below what was paid for the stock by enough to cover the cost of the option position.

Q669_LO56: Correct Answer: c EXPLANATIONS: A protective put hedges a long stock position.

Q670_LO56: Correct Answer: c EXPLANATIONS: The core position for a protective put is long stock.

Q671_LO56: Correct Answer: a EXPLANATIONS: A protective call hedges a short stock position.

Q672_LO56: Correct Answer: a EXPLANATIONS: The core position for a protective call is short stock.

Q673_LO56: Correct Answer: c
EXPLANATIONS: The investor experiences the maximum loss, which is the premium paid.

Q674_LO56: Correct Answer: c EXPLANATIONS: The investor experiences the maximum loss, which is the premium paid.

Q675_LO56: Correct Answer: b EXPLANATIONS: A protective put hedges against a falling stock, ensuring a minimum sales price.

Q676_LO56: Correct Answer: d EXPLANATIONS: An investor who is long stock could buy a put option as a hedge, known as a "protective put."

Q677_LO56: Correct Answer: c EXPLANATIONS: The breakeven for a protective put is calculated as Breakeven = Stock price + Premium.

Q678_LO56: Correct Answer: a EXPLANATIONS: A protective call for a short stock position locks in a maximum purchase price.

Q679_LO56: Correct Answer: b EXPLANATIONS: The breakeven for a protective call is calculated as Breakeven = Stock price - Premium.

Q680_LO56: Correct Answer: b EXPLANATIONS: A protective put for a long stock position locks in a minimum sales price.

Q681_LO56: Correct Answer: b EXPLANATIONS: For a protective put, the stock value should rise above the breakeven for the strategy to be profitable.

Q682_LO56: Correct Answer: a EXPLANATIONS: A protective call locks in a maximum purchase price, controlling the risk of selling a stock short.

Q683_LO56: Correct Answer: b EXPLANATIONS: For a protective call, the stock value should fall below the breakeven for the strategy to be profitable.

Q684_LO56: Correct Answer: b EXPLANATIONS: The core position in a protective put strategy is long stock.

Q685_LO56: Correct Answer: c EXPLANATIONS: The hedge in a protective call strategy is a long call.

Q686_LO56: Correct Answer: b EXPLANATIONS: An investor who is short stock could buy a call option as a hedge, known as a "protective call."

Q687_LO56: Correct Answer: a EXPLANATIONS: The core position in a protective call strategy is short stock.

Q688_LO56: Correct Answer: d EXPLANATIONS: The hedge in a protective put strategy is a long call.

Q689_LO56: Correct Answer: a EXPLANATIONS: A protective put for a short stock position locks in a maximum purchase price.

Q690_LO56: Correct Answer: a EXPLANATIONS: For a protective put, the stock value should fall below the breakeven for the strategy to be profitable.

Q691_LO57: Correct Answer: b EXPLANATIONS: An uncovered (naked) call means the writer does not own the underlying security, exposing them to unlimited risk.

Q692_LO57: Correct Answer: b EXPLANATIONS: In a covered call, the writer already owns the underlying security.

Q693_LO57: Correct Answer: b EXPLANATIONS: Uncovered (naked) call writing entails unlimited risk due to the uncertainty of the stock's market price at the time of exercise.

Q694_LO57: Correct Answer: a EXPLANATIONS: Covered put writing involves owning the underlying security, reducing risk.

Q695_LO57: Correct Answer: b EXPLANATIONS: Uncovered (naked) put writing exposes the writer to unlimited risk.

Q696_LO57: Correct Answer: a EXPLANATIONS: Covered put involves owning the underlying security, ensuring the ability to purchase the stock.

Q697_LO57: Correct Answer: c EXPLANATIONS: A covered put where the customer is short the stock and writes the put is a theoretical hedge known as a synthetic hedge.

Q698_LO57: Correct Answer: b EXPLANATIONS: Writers of naked calls are motivated by the speculative premium income in exchange for accepting the risk.

Q699_LO57: Correct Answer: a EXPLANATIONS: Covered put against a short stock means the writer owns the underlying security.

Q700_LO57: Correct Answer: b EXPLANATIONS: In a covered put, the writer already owns the underlying security.

Q701_LO57: Correct Answer: d EXPLANATIONS: Uncovered (naked) calls have unlimited risk due to uncertainty about the stock's market price at the time of exercise.

Q702_LO57: Correct Answer: c EXPLANATIONS: Covered call writing involves owning the underlying security.

Q703_LO57: Correct Answer: b EXPLANATIONS: Uncovered (naked) put writing exposes the writer to unlimited risk.

Q704_LO57: Correct Answer: a EXPLANATIONS: Covered put involves having sufficient cash available to buy the stock.

Q705_LO57: Correct Answer: c EXPLANATIONS: Writing uncovered (naked) calls exposes the writer to market price risk.

Q706_LO57: Correct Answer: a EXPLANATIONS: A covered call involves ownership of the underlying security, providing the ability to deliver if exercised.

Q707_LO57: Correct Answer: c EXPLANATIONS: Uncovered calls have theoretical unlimited risk due to uncertainty in the stock price if exercised.

Q708_LO57: Correct Answer: b EXPLANATIONS: The writer of a covered put already has sufficient cash to buy the stock.

Q709_LO57: Correct Answer: d EXPLANATIONS: Uncovered puts have theoretical unlimited risk as the writer may need to come up with cash if exercised.

Q710_LO57: Correct Answer: b EXPLANATIONS: Writers of naked calls are willing to accept the risk for the opportunity to take in unlimited premium income.

Q711_LO57: Correct Answer: b EXPLANATIONS: The writer of a covered put needs to have sufficient cash available to buy the stock.

Q712_LO57: Correct Answer: a EXPLANATIONS: A covered put against a short stock is a theoretical hedge, not occurring in the real world.

Q713_LO57: Correct Answer: d EXPLANATIONS: Uncovered calls have unlimited risk, making them riskier due to uncertainty in stock price if exercised.

Q714_LO57: Correct Answer: b EXPLANATIONS: The primary purpose of a covered put strategy is to hedge against a decline in stock value.

Q715_LO57: Correct Answer: a EXPLANATIONS: It refers to a theoretical hedge, not occurring in the real world.

Q716_LO57: Correct Answer: c EXPLANATIONS: The writer needs to come up with cash to buy the stock if the put option is exercised.

Q717_LO57: Correct Answer: d EXPLANATIONS: Writers of naked calls are motivated by the opportunity to take in unlimited premium income.

Q718_LO57: Correct Answer: d EXPLANATIONS: Uncovered puts have unlimited risk, making them riskier due to the need for cash if exercised.

Q719_LO57: Correct Answer: c EXPLANATIONS: It refers to a covered put strategy, creating a limited-risk position.

Q720_LO57: Correct Answer: d EXPLANATIONS: Uncovered calls have theoretical unlimited risk due to uncertainty in the stock price if exercised.

Q721_LO57: Correct Answer: b EXPLANATIONS: The OCC provides an options disclosure document (ODD) explaining strategies, risks, and rewards.

Q722_LO57: Correct Answer: d EXPLANATIONS: An options account must be approved by a Registered Options Principal (ROP) before trading.

Q723_LO57: Correct Answer: b EXPLANATIONS: The ODD must be provided at or before the time of account approval.

Q724_LO57: Correct Answer: b EXPLANATIONS: The customer must return the signed options agreement within 15 days of account approval.

Q725_LO57: Correct Answer: c EXPLANATIONS: The options agreement acknowledges understanding of risks and commitment to follow rules and regulations.

Q726_LO57: Correct Answer: b EXPLANATIONS: Only closing transactions are allowed if the options agreement is not returned within 15 days.

Q727_LO57: Correct Answer: a EXPLANATIONS: Account approval precedes providing the ODD and entering option trades.

Q728_LO57: Correct Answer: c EXPLANATIONS: It acknowledges understanding of risks and commitment to follow rules and regulations.

Q729_LO57: Correct Answer: b EXPLANATIONS: The first trade may take place immediately after account approval.

Q730_LO57: Correct Answer: c EXPLANATIONS: The representative determines the suitability of options trading based on the client's circumstances.

Q731_LO57: Correct Answer: b EXPLANATIONS: The ODD explains options strategies, risks, and rewards to customers.

Q732_LO57: Correct Answer: c EXPLANATIONS: Only closing transactions are allowed if the options agreement is not returned within 15 days.

Q733_LO57: Correct Answer: d EXPLANATIONS: An options account must be approved by a Registered Options Principal (ROP) before trading.

Q734_LO57: Correct Answer: a EXPLANATIONS: It is a regulatory requirement for customers to return the signed options agreement within 15 days.

Q735_LO57: Correct Answer: c EXPLANATIONS: The options agreement acknowledges understanding of risks and commitment to follow rules and regulations.

Q736_LO57: Correct Answer: b EXPLANATIONS: The Options Clearing Corporation (OCC) and the Chicago Board Options Exchange (CBOE) are the primary regulators for options.

Q737_LO57: Correct Answer: c EXPLANATIONS: The Options Disclosure Document (ODD) explains options strategies, risks, and rewards.

Q738_LO57: Correct Answer: c EXPLANATIONS: A Registered Options Principal (ROP) must approve an options account before trading.

Q739_LO57: Correct Answer: b EXPLANATIONS: A representative must believe that options are a suitable investment based on the client's circumstances and objectives.

Q740_LO57: Correct Answer: c EXPLANATIONS: The customer must return the signed options agreement within 15 days of account approval.

Q741_LO57: Correct Answer: c EXPLANATIONS: The options agreement acknowledges the customer's understanding of risks and commitment to trading rules.

Q742_LO57: Correct Answer: b EXPLANATIONS: Only closing transactions are allowed if the options agreement is not returned as required.

Q743_LO57: Correct Answer: b EXPLANATIONS: It is possible that the account has been approved, trades occurred, and yet the customer has not returned the signed options agreement within 15 days.

Q744_LO57: Correct Answer: d EXPLANATIONS: If not returned, only closing transactions are allowed.

Q745_LO57: Correct Answer: b EXPLANATIONS: The first trade may take place immediately following account approval.
Q746_LO57: Correct Answer: c EXPLANATIONS: The ODD provides information on options strategies, risks, and rewards.

Q747_LO57: Correct Answer: c EXPLANATIONS: An ROP approves options accounts before trading can occur.

Q748_LO57: Correct Answer: b EXPLANATIONS: It is a regulatory requirement providing full disclosure before options trading.

Q749_LO57: Correct Answer: c EXPLANATIONS: A representative determines the suitability of options trading for a client.
Q750_LO57: Correct Answer: d EXPLANATIONS: Only closing transactions are allowed if the options agreement is not returned within 15 days.

Q751_LO58: Correct Answer: b EXPLANATIONS: The OCC's primary functions are to standardize, guarantee, and issue option contracts.

Q752_LO58: Correct Answer: b EXPLANATIONS: Listed options trade from 9:30 am to 4:00 pm ET.

Q753_LO58: Correct Answer: b EXPLANATIONS: Listed options settle on the next business day after the trade date (T+1).
Q754_LO58: Correct Answer: c EXPLANATIONS: Listed options expire on the third Friday of the expiration month at 11:59 pm.

Q755_LO58: Correct Answer: c EXPLANATIONS: Listed options can be exercised by the owner, and any contract in the money by at least 0.01 will be automatically exercised at expiration.

Q756_LO58: Correct Answer: a EXPLANATIONS: The OCC assigns exercise notices to short BDs on a random basis.

Q757_LO58: Correct Answer: a EXPLANATIONS: Any call option in the money by at least 0.01 will be exercised automatically at expiration.

Q758_LO58: Correct Answer: a EXPLANATIONS: The OCC assigns exercise notices to short BDs on a random basis to ensure fairness.

Q759_LO58: Correct Answer: b EXPLANATIONS: An investor's proof of ownership for options contracts is the trade confirmation.

Q760_LO58: Correct Answer: b EXPLANATIONS: Any contract in the money by at least 0.01 will be exercised automatically at expiration.
Q761_LO58: Correct Answer: b EXPLANATIONS: An ROP approves option contracts before trading can occur.

Q762_LO58: Correct Answer: a EXPLANATIONS: Only owners of options contracts (buyers/long positions) have the right to exercise them.

Q763_LO58: Correct Answer: c EXPLANATIONS: Any contract in the money by at least 0.01 will be exercised automatically at expiration.

Q764_LO58: Correct Answer: b EXPLANATIONS: The OCC assigns exercise notices to short BDs in the exercise and assignment process.

Q765_LO58: Correct Answer: b EXPLANATIONS: The trade confirmation serves as an investor's proof of ownership for options contracts.

Packaged Investments

Q766_LO59: What is the primary function of an investment company?
a. Lending money
b. Pooled investment in securities
c. Real estate development
d. Retailing goods

HINTS: Identify the core function of an investment company.

Q767_LO59: How does pooling funds in an investment company reduce risk for individual investors?
a. By investing in real estate
b. By diversifying investments
c. By holding cash reserves
d. By trading in derivatives

HINTS: Recognize the risk reduction mechanism in pooled investments.

Q768_LO59: Under the Investment Company Act of 1940, what are the three broad types of investment companies?
a. Mutual funds, ETFs, hedge funds
b. Face-amount certificate, unit investment trust, management investment company
c. Stocks, bonds, commodities
d. Real estate investment trusts (REITs), closed-end funds, open-end funds

HINTS: Recall the three broad types of investment companies specified by the Act.

Q769_LO59: What is a characteristic of a fully paid face-amount certificate (FAC)?
a. Periodic installments
b. Lump-sum payment
c. Trading in the secondary market
d. Active management

HINTS: Recognize a characteristic of fully paid face-amount certificates.

Q770_LO59: What is a distinguishing feature of unit investment trusts (UITs)?
a. Active management
b. Board of directors
c. Redeemable units
d. Maturity date for shares

HINTS: Identify a distinguishing feature of UITs.

Q771_LO59: In a nonfixed UIT, what does the trust invest in?
a. Real estate
b. Bonds
c. Underlying mutual fund shares
d. Individual stocks

HINTS: Understand the investment focus of a nonfixed UIT.

Q772_LO59: Why do fixed UITs generally not assess management fees?
a. Low investor interest
b. No need for active management
c. Limited investment objectives
d. High portfolio turnover

HINTS: Recognize the reason for the absence of management fees in fixed UITs.

Q773_LO59: What is a defining characteristic of a closed-end management investment company?
a. Perpetual offering of new shares
b. Limited initial offering of shares
c. Fixed maturity date
d. No board of directors

HINTS: Identify a defining characteristic of closed-end management investment companies.

Q774_LO59: How does an open-end management investment company differ from a closed-end company?
a. Perpetual offering of new shares
b. Fixed maturity date
c. Limited initial offering of shares
d. No board of directors

HINTS: Differentiate between open-end and closed-end companies.

Q775_LO59: Which investment company type may purchase shares of an underlying mutual fund?
a. Closed-end
b. Unit investment trust
c. Face-amount certificate
d. Open-end

HINTS: Identify the investment company type associated with purchasing mutual fund shares.

Q776_LO59: Under what Act are investment companies regulated?
a. Securities Act of 1933
b. Securities Exchange Act of 1934
c. Investment Company Act of 1940
d. Commodity Exchange Act

HINTS: Recognize the regulatory framework for investment companies.

Q777_LO59: What document must investment companies provide to the public, similar to corporate issuers?
a. Annual report
b. Bond prospectus
c. Offering memorandum
d. Prospectus

HINTS: Identify the document required by investment companies for public disclosure.

Q778_LO59: What is the role of boards of directors in unit investment trusts (UITs)?
a. Active management oversight
b. Trustee appointment
c. Securities trading
d. Portfolio creation

HINTS: Understand the role of boards of directors in UITs.

Q779_LO59: Why are face-amount certificate (FAC) companies considered rare today?
a. Lack of investor interest
b. Regulatory restrictions
c. Changes in market dynamics
d. Advances in technology

HINTS: Recognize a reason for the rarity of FAC companies.

Q780_LO59: What is the common minimum investment feature of many investment vehicles?
a. $1,000 or more
b. $500 or more
c. $100 or less
d. $1 million or more

HINTS: Identify a common minimum investment characteristic of investment vehicles.

Q781_LO59: What is the primary purpose of an investment company?
a. Buying individual stocks
b. Pooling investors' money and investing in securities
c. Issuing corporate bonds
d. Establishing venture capital funds

HINTS: Identify the main function of an investment company.

Q782_LO59: How do investment companies reduce overall risk for investors?
a. By investing in a single security
b. By focusing on speculative investments
c. By pooling funds and investing in multiple securities
d. By avoiding securities altogether

HINTS: Recognize the strategy used by investment companies to reduce risk.

Q783_LO59: What legislation imposes registration and prospectus requirements on investment companies?
a. Securities Act of 1933
b. Securities Exchange Act of 1934
c. Investment Company Act of 1940
d. Sarbanes-Oxley Act

HINTS: Identify the legislation regulating the registration and prospectus requirements for investment companies.

Q784_LO59: How are investment companies regulated under the Investment Company Act of 1940?
a. By the SEC
b. By FINRA
c. By the OCC
d. By the NYSE

HINTS: Recognize the regulatory authority for investment companies under the Investment Company Act of 1940.

Q785_LO59: What are the three broad types of investment companies according to the Investment Company Act of 1940?
a. Stock, bond, and commodity companies
b. Growth, income, and balanced companies
c. Face-amount certificate (FAC) companies, unit investment trusts (UITs), and management investment companies
d. Closed-end, open-end, and hybrid companies

HINTS: Identify the three broad types of investment companies classified by the Investment Company Act of 1940.

Q786_LO59: What is a face-amount certificate (FAC)?
a. A fixed-income security
b. A lump-sum payment to an investor
c. A contract guaranteeing future payment
d. A certificate of ownership

HINTS: Recognize the definition of a face-amount certificate (FAC).

Q787_LO59: What is the primary characteristic of a unit investment trust (UIT)?
a. Active management
b. Board of directors
c. Redeemable interests in a portfolio
d. Continuous offering of new shares

HINTS: Identify the key feature of a unit investment trust (UIT).

Q788_LO59: How does a fixed UIT differ from a nonfixed UIT?
a. Portfolio turnover
b. Management fees
c. Maturity of portfolio securities
d. Active management

HINTS: Differentiate between a fixed UIT and a nonfixed UIT.

Q789_LO59: Why do fixed UITs generally not assess management fees?
a. Active portfolio management
b. Low portfolio turnover
c. No need for an investment adviser
d. Continuous offering of new shares

HINTS: Understand the reason for fixed UITs not typically assessing management fees.

Q790_LO59: How do FACs and UITs differ from managed investment companies?
a. They trade in the secondary market
b. They have boards of directors
c. They pool investors' money
d. They are managed and trade actively

HINTS: Differentiate FACs and UITs from managed investment companies.

Q791_LO59: What is the perpetual offering characteristic of an open-end management company?
a. It closes after a specific authorized number of shares have been sold
b. It is continually open to new investors
c. It issues a fixed number of shares
d. It terminates when the bonds mature

HINTS: Recognize the perpetual offering feature of an open-end management company.

Q792_LO59: What is the primary difference between closed-end and open-end management companies?
a. Portfolio management style
b. Continuous offering of new shares
c. Maturity of portfolio securities
d. Initial offering of shares

HINTS: Differentiate between closed-end and open-end management companies.

Q793_LO59: Which investment company type has a predetermined termination date?
a. Open-end management company
b. Closed-end management company
c. Unit investment trust (UIT)
d. Face-amount certificate (FAC)

HINTS: Identify the investment company type with a predetermined termination date.

Q794_LO59: What is the proof of ownership for an investor in an investment company?
a. Options agreement
b. Trade confirmation
c. Share certificate
d. Prospectus

HINTS: Recognize the document serving as proof of ownership for an investor in an investment company.

Q795_LO59: What is the key characteristic of a nonfixed UIT?
a. Maturity of portfolio securities
b. Active management
c. Purchase of bonds
d. Investment in an underlying mutual fund

HINTS: Identify the defining feature of a nonfixed UIT.

Q796_LO60: What is a characteristic of closed-end investment companies?
a. Continuous primary offering
b. Unlimited issuance of shares
c. Redeemable shares
d. Publicly traded in the secondary market

HINTS: Identify the characteristic of closed-end investment companies.

Q797_LO60: How does a closed-end company raise capital for its portfolio?
a. Continuous primary offering
b. Redeeming shares
c. Conducting a common stock offering
d. Issuing bonds and preferred stock

HINTS: Recognize the method used by closed-end companies to raise capital.

Q798_LO60: What is a common nickname for closed-end investment companies?
a. FACs
b. UITs
c. Mutual funds
d. Publicly traded funds

HINTS: Identify the common nickname for closed-end investment companies.

Q799_LO60: When do closed-end fund shares trade at a premium or discount?
a. When NAV is high
b. When the market is volatile
c. When shares are redeemed
d. Depending on supply and demand

HINTS: Recognize the factor determining whether closed-end fund shares trade at a premium or discount.

Q800_LO60: What is the NAV per share formula for closed-end companies?
a. Assets - Liabilities
b. Liabilities - Assets
c. Liabilities / Assets
d. Assets / Outstanding shares

HINTS: Understand the formula for calculating NAV per share for closed-end companies.

Q801_LO60: What type of securities does an open-end investment company issue?
a. Common stock only
b. Preferred stock and bonds
c. Debt securities only
d. Fixed number of shares

HINTS: Identify the types of securities issued by open-end investment companies.

Q802_LO60: How are shares of an open-end company redeemed?
a. In the secondary market
b. By selling on an exchange
c. By the fund itself
d. Through underwriters

HINTS: Recognize the method of redeeming shares in an open-end company.

Q803_LO60: What determines the selling price of open-end investment company shares?
a. Supply and demand
b. NAV + sales charge
c. CMV + commission
d. Fixed offering price

HINTS: Understand the factor determining the selling price of open-end investment company shares.

Q804_LO60: When are mutual funds priced, and when do buyers and sellers receive the next calculated NAV and POP?
a. Priced at the opening bell
b. Priced at the end of each business day
c. Priced weekly
d. Priced at the discretion of the fund manager

HINTS: Recognize when mutual funds are priced and when buyers and sellers receive the next calculated NAV and POP.

Q805_LO60: What is the significance of the 4:00 pm deadline for mutual fund transactions?
a. Determines NAV
b. Sets the ex-date
c. Closes the primary offering
d. Receives the next business day's NAV or POP

HINTS: Identify the significance of the 4:00 pm deadline for mutual fund transactions.

Q806_LO60: How do mutual funds handle share redemptions?
a. Decrease NAV
b. Increase NAV
c. Increase outstanding shares
d. Decrease outstanding shares

HINTS: Recognize the impact of share redemptions on mutual funds.

Q807_LO60: What document serves as proof of ownership for an investor in an open-end investment company?
a. Share certificate
b. Options agreement
c. Trade confirmation
d. Prospectus

HINTS: Identify the document serving as proof of ownership for an investor in an open-end investment company.

Q808_LO60: What is the pricing method for closed-end investment companies?
a. NAV + sales charge
b. CMV + commission
c. Set by BOD
d. Set by the exchange or FINRA

HINTS: Identify the pricing method for closed-end investment companies.

Q809_LO60: What is the primary difference between closed-end and open-end investment companies?
a. Open-end allows trading on an exchange
b. Closed-end continuously offers new shares
c. Open-end issues only common stock
d. Closed-end's initial offering is limited

HINTS: Differentiate between closed-end and open-end investment companies based on their offering approach.

Q810_LO60: What is a primary characteristic of a closed-end investment company?
a. Continuous offering of new shares
b. Common stock offering with a limited time
c. Unlimited offering of shares
d. Redeeming shares at NAV

HINTS: Identify a characteristic of closed-end investment companies.

Q811_LO60: When are closed-end investment companies closed to new investors?
a. After the initial common stock offering
b. After all shares are sold in the secondary market
c. After redeeming shares at NAV
d. After issuing preferred stock

HINTS: Recognize when closed-end companies close to new investors.

Q812_LO60: What are closed-end investment companies often referred to as?
a. Continuous offering funds
b. Publicly traded funds
c. Mutual funds
d. Fixed-end funds

HINTS: Identify a common term used for closed-end investment companies.

Q813_LO60: Where can shares of closed-end funds be bought or sold after the initial offering?
a. Only during the initial offering
b. In the primary market
c. On the secondary market (exchange or OTC)
d. Through fund redemptions

HINTS: Recognize where closed-end fund shares can be traded after the initial offering.

Q814_LO60: How is the bid price determined for closed-end fund shares?
a. By the fund's NAV
b. By supply and demand
c. At the next calculated POP
d. Through fund redemptions

HINTS: Identify the factor determining the bid price for closed-end fund shares.

Q815_LO60: What is the Net Asset Value (NAV) of a closed-end fund?
a. Assets minus liabilities divided by the number of outstanding shares
b. Market value of all assets
c. Offering price for new shares
d. Commission added to the bid price

HINTS: Understand the formula for calculating the Net Asset Value (NAV) of a closed-end fund.

Q816_LO60: In which market can shares of open-end investment companies be bought or sold?
a. Secondary market
b. Initial public offering market
c. Exchange or OTC
d. Fund redemptions

HINTS: Recognize where shares of open-end investment companies can be traded.

Q817_LO60: How are shares of open-end investment companies priced?
a. Net Asset Value (NAV) + sales charge
b. Closing market value (CMV) + commission
c. Net Asset Value (NAV) determined by the fund
d. Offering price determined by supply and demand

HINTS: Identify the pricing method for shares of open-end investment companies.

Q818_LO60: When are open-end investment companies priced?
a. At the end of each business day
b. Continuously throughout the day
c. Only during the initial public offering
d. At the next calculated POP

HINTS: Understand the timing of pricing for open-end investment companies.

Q819_LO60: What happens to the value of each share in a mutual fund after an investor redeems shares?
a. It falls
b. It remains unchanged
c. It rises
d. It depends on the market conditions

HINTS: Recognize the impact on the value of each share in a mutual fund after redemption.

Q820_LO60: How is the price determined for closed-end fund shares?
a. By supply and demand
b. At the next calculated POP
c. Net Asset Value (NAV) + sales charge
d. Through fund redemptions

HINTS: Identify the method of determining the price for closed-end fund shares.

Q821_LO60: What is the primary characteristic of an open-end investment company's offering?
a. Initial common stock offering
b. Continuous primary offering of shares
c. Limited time offering
d. Fixed number of shares offered

HINTS: Recognize a key feature of an open-end investment company's offering.

Q822_LO60: What is the primary difference between open-end and closed-end investment companies regarding the offering of shares?
a. Continuous vs. limited offering
b. Offering common vs. preferred stock
c. Selling vs. redeeming shares
d. Market-determined vs. formula-based pricing

HINTS: Differentiate the primary offering characteristic between open-end and closed-end investment companies.

Q823_LO60: How are open-end investment companies capitalized compared to closed-end ones?
a. Fixed capitalization
b. Unlimited capitalization
c. Limited capitalization
d. Continuous capitalization

HINTS: Understand the capitalization distinction between open-end and closed-end investment companies.

Q824_LO60: Which statement about closed-end investment companies is accurate?
a. Shares always trade at NAV
b. NAV is irrelevant for pricing
c. Shares may trade at a premium or discount to NAV
d. NAV is determined by the exchange

HINTS: Identify a correct statement about closed-end investment companies.

Q825_LO61: What is the primary purpose of an annuity?
a. Providing lump-sum payments
b. Guaranteeing lifetime retirement income
c. Offering short-term investment options
d. Covering medical expenses

HINTS: Recognize the primary purpose of an annuity.

Q826_LO61: What does the term "mortality guarantee" in an annuity contract address?
a. Guaranteeing investment returns
b. Ensuring death benefits
c. Protecting against inflation
d. Fear of outliving income

HINTS: Identify the focus of the mortality guarantee in annuities.

Q827_LO61: Why is a variable annuity considered a security?
a. Guaranteed investment returns
b. Insurance company assumes all investment risk
c. No mortality guarantee
d. Investor assumes investment risk

HINTS: Understand the reason why a variable annuity is classified as a security.

Q828_LO61: What is the role of an investor in a variable annuity concerning investment risk?
a. Assumes no investment risk
b. Assumes all investment risk
c. Insurance company assumes all risk
d. Guarantees investment returns

HINTS: Recognize the investor's role regarding investment risk in a variable annuity.

Q829_LO61: During the accumulation period, where are premium payments for variable annuities invested?
a. Fixed account
b. General account
c. Mutual funds
d. Separate account

HINTS: Identify the location of premium payments in the accumulation period for variable annuities.

Q830_LO61: When is a separate account for variable annuities directly managed?
a. When overseen by an external portfolio manager
b. When insurance company's manager selects securities
c. When registered as a UIT
d. When overseen by the SEC

HINTS: Recognize the condition for a variable annuity separate account to be directly managed.

Q831_LO61: What type of fees must be disclosed to a variable annuity buyer?
a. Marketing fees only
b. Administrative, investment advisory, and custodial fees
c. Surrender charges only
d. Insurance premiums

HINTS: Identify the fees that must be disclosed to a variable annuity buyer.

Q832_LO61: How are the returns in the separate account of a variable annuity determined?
a. Guaranteed returns
b. By SEC regulations
c. By the insurance company's manager
d. Performance of subaccounts

HINTS: Understand the factor influencing returns in the separate account of a variable annuity.

Q833_LO61: What is the limit on annual contributions for commercial (nonqualified) variable annuity contracts?
a. No limit
b. Limited by the insurance company
c. Subject to SEC approval
d. Limited by IRS rules

HINTS: Recognize the annual contribution limit for commercial variable annuity contracts.

Q834_LO61: In qualified variable contracts for employer-sponsored plans, what limits annual contributions?
a. SEC regulations
b. Insurance company policies
c. IRS rules
d. Investment advisory fees

HINTS: Identify the authority limiting annual contributions for qualified variable contracts.

Q835_LO61: What does annuitization involve for an investor in a variable annuity?
a. Liquidating the annuity
b. Surrendering ownership for lifetime income
c. Receiving lump-sum payments
d. Adjusting the investment strategy

HINTS: Recognize the process of annuitization in a variable annuity.

Q836_LO61: How is the income amount determined during annuitization?
a. Fixed rate set by the investor
b. Based on the insurance company's discretion
c. By SEC regulations
d. Consideration of gender, age, account value, and assumed interest rate

HINTS: Understand the factors influencing the income amount during annuitization.

Q837_LO61: What distinguishes a fixed annuity from a variable annuity?
a. Level of investment risk
b. Ownership structure
c. Annuity term length
d. Liquidity features

HINTS: Differentiate a key characteristic between fixed and variable annuities.

Q838_LO61: Why is a fixed annuity not considered a security?
a. It guarantees investment returns
b. It has no mortality guarantee
c. It is regulated by the SEC
d. It assumes investment risk

HINTS: Identify the reason why a fixed annuity is not considered a security.

Q839_LO61: What does the mortality guarantee in an annuity address?
a. Investment risk
b. Outliving income
c. Surrender charges
d. Insurance premiums

HINTS: Recognize the focus of the mortality guarantee in annuities.

Q840_LO61: What is the primary purpose of an annuity?
a. Generate wealth quickly
b. Provide retirement income
c. Accumulate investment returns
d. Speculate on market trends

HINTS: Identify the primary purpose of an annuity.

Q841_LO61: Why are variable annuities considered securities?
a. Guaranteed returns
b. Mortality guarantee
c. Investment risk assumed by the investor
d. Fixed income payments

HINTS: Recognize the characteristic that classifies variable annuities as securities.

Q842_LO61: What is the purpose of the separate account in a variable annuity?
a. Guarantee investment returns
b. Ensure fixed income payments
c. Provide mortality guarantee
d. Invest premium payments in subaccounts

HINTS: Understand the role of the separate account in a variable annuity.

Q843_LO61: How are the subaccounts in a variable annuity managed?
a. Directly by the insurance company
b. Indirectly by a separate investment manager
c. Managed as fixed-income portfolios
d. Without any management

HINTS: Identify the management structure of subaccounts in a variable annuity.

Q844_LO61: When is a separate account in a variable annuity directly managed?
a. When there is no portfolio management
b. When managed by an investment company under the 1940 Act
c. When there is no investment risk
d. When there is a guaranteed return

HINTS: Recognize the condition under which a separate account is directly managed.

Q845_LO61: What determines the investment performance of a variable annuity?
a. Surrender charges
b. Administrative fees
c. Performance of subaccounts
d. Insurance company's rate of return

HINTS: Identify the factor that determines the investment performance of a variable annuity.

Q846_LO61: What must be disclosed to a variable annuity buyer regarding fees?
a. Only surrender charges
b. Only investment advisory fees
c. All product-specific charges
d. Only custodial fees

HINTS: Understand the information that must be disclosed regarding fees to a variable annuity buyer.

Q847_LO61: What is the primary purpose of annuitization?
a. Accumulate wealth
b. Generate a lifetime income
c. Guarantee investment returns
d. Avoid surrender charges

HINTS: Identify the primary purpose of annuitization.

Q848_LO61: What factors determine the amount of income in annuitization?
a. Surrender charges and investment returns
b. Gender, age, account value, payout option, and assumed interest rate
c. Administrative fees and custodial fees
d. Only market conditions

HINTS: Recognize the factors considered in determining the amount of income in annuitization.

Q849_LO61: How is the income in annuitization affected by inflation?
a. Adjusted for inflation
b. Unaffected by inflation
c. Decreases with inflation
d. Increases with inflation

HINTS: Understand the impact of inflation on the income in annuitization.

Q850_LO61: What distinguishes a variable annuity from a fixed annuity?
a. Guarantee of a stated rate of return
b. Mortality guarantee
c. Insurance company at risk for providing returns
d. Product not considered a security

HINTS: Differentiate a variable annuity from a fixed annuity.

Q851_LO61: Why is a fixed annuity not considered a security?
a. It guarantees returns
b. It involves investment risk
c. It provides lifetime income
d. It offers market speculation

HINTS: Recognize the characteristic that excludes fixed annuities from being considered securities.

Q852_LO61: What is the key distinction in investment risk between variable and fixed annuities?
a. Investors assume no risk in both
b. Fixed annuity involves market risk
c. Variable annuity involves investment risk
d. Both have guaranteed returns

HINTS: Differentiate the investment risk involved in variable and fixed annuities.

Q853_LO61: What limits the annual contributions to qualified variable contracts?
a. Surrender charges
b. Regulatory restrictions similar to 401(k) plans
c. Administrative fees
d. Premium payments

HINTS: Identify the factor limiting annual contributions to qualified variable contracts.

Q854_LO61: What is the primary difference between variable and fixed annuities regarding returns?
a. Guaranteed returns in both
b. Market-driven returns in variable
c. Fixed returns in variable
d. Returns determined by the insurance company

HINTS: Recognize the primary difference in returns between variable and fixed annuities.

Q855_LO62: What is a unique characteristic of mutual funds regarding marketability?
a. Limited marketability
b. No marketability
c. Guaranteed marketability
d. Variable marketability

HINTS: Recognize a distinctive feature of mutual funds related to marketability.

Q856_LO62: How are distributions typically done in mutual funds?
a. At a fixed price
b. At net asset value (NAV)
c. At market price
d. At a premium

HINTS: Identify the usual method of handling distributions in mutual funds.

Q857_LO62: What is the conduit theory of taxation in mutual funds?
a. Taxation only on dividends
b. Tax events flow down to shareholders each year
c. Tax exemption for all shareholders
d. Taxation only on capital gains

HINTS: Understand the taxation principle applied to mutual funds.

Q858_LO62: How does an investor's account value fluctuate in mutual funds?
a. Unrelated to the fund's portfolio value
b. Proportionately with the portfolio's value
c. Inversely with the portfolio's value
d. Constant and fixed

HINTS: Recognize the relationship between an investor's account value and the fund's portfolio value in mutual funds.

Q859_LO62: What allows an investor to think in terms of dollars rather than shares in mutual funds?
a. Full share purchases only
b. Fractional share purchases
c. Fixed share purchases
d. Limited share purchases

HINTS: Identify the characteristic that allows investors to think in terms of dollars.

Q860_LO62: What is a key characteristic of the investment adviser in mutual funds?
a. Shareholder voting rights
b. Portfolio diversification
c. Professional management of the portfolio
d. Tax event disclosure

HINTS: Identify a significant role of the investment adviser in mutual funds.

Q861_LO62: What is the maximum sales charge allowed under the Investment Company Act of 1940?
a. 5% of the POP
b. 7% of the POP
c. 8½% of the POP
d. 10% of the POP

HINTS: Recognize the maximum sales charge permitted under the Investment Company Act of 1940.

Q862_LO62: What distinguishes Class A shares from other mutual fund classes?
a. Front-end load
b. Back-end load
c. Level-load
d. No-load

HINTS: Differentiate Class A shares based on their sales charge structure.

Q863_LO62: What is a characteristic feature of Class B shares?
a. Front-end load
b. Back-end load
c. Level-load
d. No-load

HINTS: Identify a characteristic of Class B shares related to sales charges.

Q864_LO62: How do Class C shares typically impose sales charges?
a. Front-end load
b. Back-end load
c. Level-load
d. No-load

HINTS: Recognize the common sales charge structure for Class C shares.

Q865_LO62: Which share class may have a contingent deferred sales charge (CDSC)?
a. Class A
b. Class B
c. Class C
d. No-load

HINTS: Identify the share class that commonly employs a contingent deferred sales charge (CDSC).

Q866_LO62: In what way do Class B shares often convert over time?
a. To Class A shares
b. To Class C shares
c. To no-load shares
d. To Class D shares

HINTS: Understand the common conversion pattern of Class B shares.

Q867_LO62: What is a key characteristic of no-load funds?
a. No sales charges
b. Front-end load
c. Back-end load
d. Level-load

HINTS: Recognize a defining feature of no-load funds.

Q868_LO62: How are sales charges typically paid in no-load funds?
a. By the investor
b. By the underwriter
c. By the investment adviser
d. By the portfolio manager

HINTS: Understand the payment structure of sales charges in no-load funds.

Q869_LO62: What tax implication is associated with reinvestments in mutual funds?
a. Taxable
b. Tax-exempt
c. Tax-deductible
d. Tax-deferred

HINTS: Identify the tax implication related to reinvestments in mutual funds.

Q870_LO62: What is a unique characteristic of mutual funds in terms of marketability?
a. Traded on secondary markets
b. Issued preferred stock
c. Guaranteed marketability
d. Non-redeemable securities

HINTS: Identify the distinctive feature related to marketability in mutual funds.

Q871_LO62: What theory of taxation do mutual funds operate under?
a. Capital gains theory
b. Compounding theory
c. Conduit theory
d. Tax-exempt theory

HINTS: Recognize the taxation theory under which mutual funds operate.

Q872_LO62: How are distributions typically done in mutual funds?
a. At a premium to NAV
b. At a discount to NAV
c. At net asset value (NAV)
d. Without any distribution

HINTS: Understand the common method of distributing in mutual funds.

Q873_LO62: What is the effect of reinvesting distributions in mutual funds on the investor's cost basis?
a. Decreases the cost basis
b. Increases the cost basis
c. No impact on the cost basis
d. Resets the cost basis

HINTS: Identify the impact of reinvesting distributions on the investor's cost basis.

Q874_LO62: How does an investor's participation in a mutual fund's performance depend on?
a. Number of shares owned
b. Market conditions
c. Portfolio value
d. All of the above

HINTS: Recognize the factor that determines an investor's participation in a mutual fund's performance.

Q875_LO62: What is the key distinction between mutual funds and corporate stock regarding share purchase?
a. Mutual funds allow fractional shares
b. Corporate stock allows fractional shares
c. Mutual funds have fixed share prices
d. Corporate stock has guaranteed marketability

HINTS: Differentiate mutual funds from corporate stock in terms of share purchase.

Q876_LO62: Under the Investment Company Act of 1940, what is the maximum sales charge allowed?
a. 5% of the POP
b. 8½% of the POP
c. 10% of the NAV
d. No sales charges allowed

HINTS: Identify the maximum sales charge allowed under the Investment Company Act of 1940.

Q877_LO62: What is a unique feature of no-load funds?
a. High sales charges
b. No sales charges
c. Only offered through underwriters
d. Exclusively marketed to institutions

HINTS: Recognize the characteristic that distinguishes no-load funds.

Q878_LO62: What is the primary difference among Class A, B, and C shares of mutual funds?
a. Investment objectives
b. Portfolio management
c. Sales charges and expenses
d. Dividend distribution

HINTS: Differentiate Class A, B, and C shares based on the primary difference.

Q879_LO62: When are Class A shares most suitable for investors?
a. Long-term investors
b. Short-term investors
c. Risk-averse investors
d. Speculative investors

HINTS: Identify the type of investors for whom Class A shares are most suitable.

Q880_LO62: What characterizes Class B shares in terms of sales charges?
a. Front-end load
b. Back-end load
c. Level load
d. No load

HINTS: Recognize the sales charge characteristic of Class B shares.

Q881_LO62: How are Class C shares distinguished in terms of sales charges?
a. Front-end load
b. Back-end load
c. Level load
d. No load

HINTS: Identify the sales charge characteristic of Class C shares.

Q882_LO62: What is the main consideration for investors when choosing between Class A and Class B shares?
a. Dividend distribution
b. Portfolio management
c. Sales charge structure
d. Investment objective

HINTS: Recognize the key consideration for investors when choosing between Class A and Class B shares.

Q883_LO62: When might Class C shares be advantageous for investors?
a. Short-term investment horizon
b. Long-term investment horizon
c. Risk-averse investors
d. Speculative investors

HINTS: Identify the investment horizon for which Class C shares might be advantageous.

Q884_LO62: What feature makes Class C shares less suitable for long-term investors?
a. No sales charges
b. Front-end load
c. Level load
d. Contingent deferred sales charge (CDSC)

HINTS: Recognize the feature that makes Class C shares less suitable for long-term investors.

Q885_LO62: How are sales charges applied to Class A shares?
a. At redemption
b. Annually
c. At the time of purchase
d. Never applied

HINTS: Identify when sales charges are applied to Class A shares.

Q886_LO62: What characterizes the sales load structure of Class B shares?
a. Front-end load
b. Back-end load
c. Level load
d. No load

HINTS: Recognize the sales load structure associated with Class B shares.

Q887_LO62: When is the back-end load of Class B shares usually reduced to zero?
a. After one year
b. After three years
c. After five years
d. After ten years

HINTS: Identify the typical duration after which the back-end load of Class B shares reduces to zero.

Q888_LO62: What happens to the sales charge in Class B shares at the time of purchase?
a. Applied and deducted
b. Deferred to the time of redemption
c. Waived for the first year
d. Doubled for the first year

HINTS: Recognize what happens to the sales charge in Class B shares at the time of purchase.

Q889_LO62: Why might the sales charges in Class B shares become costly over time?
a. They are fixed regardless of the holding period
b. They increase annually
c. They are based on the initial investment amount
d. They are not applied to redeemed shares

HINTS: Identify the factor that can make sales charges in Class B shares costly over time.

Q890_LO62: What is a distinctive feature of Class C shares in terms of fees?
a. Front-end load
b. Back-end load
c. Level load
d. No load

HINTS: Recognize the fee structure that is distinctive to Class C shares.

Q891_LO62: Why are Class C shares considered appropriate for investors with short time horizons?
a. Lower annual charges
b. Longer CDSC period
c. Higher 12b-1 fees
d. No shareholder services fee

HINTS: Identify the characteristic that makes Class C shares suitable for investors with short time horizons.

Q892_LO62: What characterizes the sales charge of no-load funds?
a. Front-end load
b. Back-end load
c. Level load
d. No sales charge

HINTS: Recognize the characteristic related to sales charges in no-load funds.

Q893_LO62: What fees are permitted in no-load funds that are not considered sales charges?
a. Purchase fees
b. Redemption fees
c. Front-end load
d. CDSC

HINTS: Identify the fees that can be charged in no-load funds without being considered sales charges.

Q894_LO62: How is the sales charge deducted in Class B shares when redeemed?
a. Fixed dollar amount
b. Percentage of NAV
c. Percentage of the initial investment
d. Percentage of the redemption proceeds

HINTS: Recognize how the sales charge is deducted in Class B shares when redeemed.

Q895_LO62: What is the primary consideration for investors when choosing between Class A and Class B shares?
a. Investment objective
b. Portfolio management
c. Sales charge structure
d. CDSC duration

HINTS: Identify the key consideration for investors when choosing between Class A and Class B shares.

Q896_LO62: What distinguishes Class C shares in terms of the CDSC duration?
a. Long-term CDSC
b. Short-term CDSC
c. No CDSC
d. CDSC applied annually

HINTS: Recognize the characteristic that distinguishes Class C shares regarding the CDSC duration.

Q897_LO62: What happens to Class B shares after an extended holding period?
a. Converted to Class A shares
b. Converted to Class C shares
c. Converted to no-load shares
d. No conversion takes place

HINTS: Identify what happens to Class B shares after an extended holding period.

Q898_LO62: Why might Class C shares be expensive to own for more than four to five years?
a. Increasing annual charges
b. Decreasing 12b-1 fees
c. Fixed CDSC
d. No shareholder services fee

HINTS: Recognize the factor that can make Class C shares expensive to own for a longer duration.

Q899_LO62: What makes no-load funds distinct in terms of sales charges?
a. No sales charges applied
b. Fixed sales charges
c. Waived sales charges
d. Sales charges based on NAV

HINTS: Identify the characteristic that makes no-load funds distinct in terms of sales charges.

Q900_LO63: What are breakpoints in the context of mutual funds?
a. Sales below NAV
b. Quantity discounts
c. Initial transaction fees
d. Escrowed shares

HINTS: Identify the correct definition of breakpoints.

Q901_LO63: How can investors qualify for reduced sales charges through letters of intent (LOI)?
a. Completing the LOI within 12 months
b. Informing the fund of share appreciation
c. Holding escrowed shares for 13 months
d. Reinvesting dividends

HINTS: Recognize the key factor that allows investors to qualify for reduced sales charges through LOI.

Q902_LO63: What happens if a customer does not complete the investment within 13 months of signing an LOI?
a. Escrowed shares are forfeited
b. Reduced sales charges are maintained
c. Customer receives a refund
d. Choice to pay the difference or cash in escrowed shares

HINTS: Identify the consequence if a customer does not complete the investment within the specified time frame.

Q903_LO63: How do rights of accumulation (ROA) differ from breakpoints?
a. Apply only to initial transactions
b. Impose time limits
c. Allow use of prior share appreciation
d. Are not available for subsequent investments

HINTS: Recognize the key differences between rights of accumulation and breakpoints.

Q904_LO63: What does the total value for rights of accumulation include for qualifying investors?
a. Initial transaction amount
b. Current NAV
c. Total purchases made to date
d. Escrowed shares

HINTS: Identify what the mutual fund bases the quantity of securities owned on for rights of accumulation.

Q905_LO63: At what point does an investor qualify for the lowest sales charge under rights of accumulation?
a. $25,000 total investment
b. $50,000 total investment
c. $75,000 total investment
d. $100,000 total investment

HINTS: Recognize the threshold at which an investor qualifies for the lowest sales charge under rights of accumulation.

Q906_LO63: What privilege allows an investor to combine separate investments in two or more funds within the same family to reach a breakpoint?
a. Exchange privilege
b. Combination privilege
c. Rights of accumulation
d. Letters of intent

HINTS: Identify the privilege that allows the combination of separate investments to reach a breakpoint.

Q907_LO63: What is a taxable event associated with exchange privileges?
a. Dividend reinvestment
b. Share appreciation
c. Fund conversion
d. Breakpoint sale

HINTS: Recognize the taxable event associated with exchange privileges.

Q908_LO63: How does a breakpoint sale differ from a normal sale?
a. Occurs above NAV
b. Involves escrowed shares
c. Just below the breakpoint
d. Results in higher sales charges

HINTS: Identify the characteristic that differentiates a breakpoint sale from a normal sale.

Q909_LO63: Why does FINRA have rules against breakpoint sales?
a. Increases concession dollars
b. Encourages share appreciation
c. Supports escrowed shares
d. Aligns with just and equitable principles

HINTS: Recognize the reason FINRA has rules against breakpoint sales.

Q910_LO63: How does an LOI affect the overall sales charges for investors?
a. Increases sales charges
b. Decreases sales charges
c. Maintains constant sales charges
d. Converts sales charges to dividends

HINTS: Recognize the impact of an LOI on the overall sales charges for investors.

Q911_LO63: What must a customer do to qualify for reduced sales charges through an LOI?
a. Complete the LOI within 12 months
b. Pay upfront sales charges
c. Hold escrowed shares for 13 months
d. Purchase additional shares

HINTS: Identify the requirement for a customer to qualify for reduced sales charges through an LOI.

Q912_LO63: How do rights of accumulation benefit investors over time?
a. By reducing sales charges for initial transactions
b. By allowing use of prior share appreciation
c. By providing an extended CDSC period
d. By applying time limits

HINTS: Recognize the benefit that rights of accumulation provide to investors over time.

Q913_LO63: What is the consequence of not completing an LOI investment within 13 months?
a. Forfeiture of escrowed shares
b. Increased sales charges
c. Automatic conversion to Class A shares
d. No consequence

HINTS: Identify the consequence if an LOI investment is not completed within the specified time frame.

Q914_LO63: When do breakpoints apply to mutual fund shares?
a. Only for initial transactions
b. Only for subsequent investments
c. For initial and subsequent investments
d. For dividend reinvestments

HINTS: Recognize when breakpoints apply to mutual fund shares.

Q915_LO63: What is a breakpoint in the context of mutual funds?
a. Quantity discounts
b. Sales charge waiver
c. Fund's total assets
d. Management fee

HINTS: Identify the concept associated with breakpoints in mutual funds.

Q916_LO63: How can an investor reduce overall sales charges through a letter of intent (LOI)?
a. Immediate sales charge reduction
b. Escrow of extra shares
c. Fund's total assets
d. Rights of accumulation

HINTS: Recognize the mechanism through which an LOI helps in reducing sales charges.

Q917_LO63: What happens if a customer fails to complete the investment within 13 months of signing an LOI?
a. Sales charges remain reduced
b. Escrowed shares are forfeited
c. LOI is extended
d. No consequences

HINTS: Understand the outcome if a customer does not fulfill the LOI within the specified timeframe.

Q918_LO63: How do rights of accumulation differ from breakpoints?
a. Apply to initial transactions
b. Have time limits
c. Include prior share appreciation
d. Are industry standardized

HINTS: Identify a major difference between rights of accumulation and breakpoints.

Q919_LO63: When do rights of accumulation not impose time limits?
a. Initial transactions
b. Subsequent investments
c. LOI completion
d. Combination privilege

HINTS: Recognize the circumstance under which rights of accumulation do not have time limits.

Q920_LO63: How is the quantity of securities owned calculated for rights of accumulation?
a. Based on current NAV
b. Based on initial purchase amount
c. Based on LOI completion
d. Based on fund's total assets

HINTS: Identify the basis for calculating the quantity of securities owned for rights of accumulation.

Q921_LO63: What does the combination privilege allow an investor to do?
a. Combine different fund families
b. Combine separate investments to reach a breakpoint
c. Combine different share classes
d. Combine mutual funds and stocks

HINTS: Recognize the purpose of the combination privilege.

Q922_LO63: What is an exchange privilege in the context of mutual funds?
a. Convert funds to cash
b. Convert shares between different fund families
c. Exchange stocks for mutual funds
d. Exchange one fund for another within the same family

HINTS: Identify the nature of an exchange privilege in mutual funds.

Q923_LO63: What tax consideration is associated with exchange privileges?
a. Tax-deductible exchanges
b. Tax-free exchanges
c. Taxable event
d. Tax credits

HINTS: Recognize the tax implications of using exchange privileges.

Q924_LO63: Define breakpoint sales in the securities industry.
a. Sales just above the breakpoint
b. Sales just below the breakpoint
c. Sales exceeding the breakpoint
d. Sales without breakpoints

HINTS: Understand the meaning of breakpoint sales in the securities industry.

Q925_LO63: Why does FINRA regulate breakpoint sales closely?
a. To discourage large investments
b. To ensure fairness and equity
c. To limit overall sales
d. To standardize breakpoint schedules
HINTS: Recognize the regulatory intent behind the close regulation of breakpoint sales.

Q926_LO63: How does the industry define "near" or "just below" a breakpoint?
a. Based on percentage difference
b. Based on fund's total assets
c. It is not defined
d. As a fixed dollar amount

HINTS: Recognize the industry's stance on defining "near" or "just below" a breakpoint.

Q927_LO63: Why is allowing sales just below a breakpoint considered inconsistent with trade principles?
a. It benefits investors
b. It encourages large investments
c. It may earn higher sales charges
d. It standardizes sales practices

HINTS: Identify the reason why allowing sales just below a breakpoint is viewed as inconsistent with trade principles.

Q928_LO63: How does FINRA address the potential issue of breakpoint sales?
a. By setting standardized schedules
b. By defining specific percentages
c. By regulating and ensuring disclosure
d. By eliminating breakpoints

HINTS: Understand how FINRA addresses the issue of breakpoint sales.

Q929_LO63: Why might a representative prefer breakpoint sales?
a. To discourage large investments
b. To earn higher sales charges
c. To benefit investors
d. To standardize sales practices

HINTS: Recognize a potential motivation for representatives to prefer breakpoint sales.

Q930_LO64: What is the NAV of a fund share?
a. Net Assets Value
b. Next Available Value
c. Number of Assets Value
d. Net Asset Variation

HINTS: Recall the acronym and meaning of NAV.

Q931_LO64: When is the NAV of a fund calculated?
a. Weekly
b. Monthly
c. Quarterly
d. Daily

HINTS: Identify the frequency of NAV calculation for a typical fund.

Q932_LO64: What is the price the customer receives in forward pricing?
a. Previous NAV
b. Latest NAV
c. Average NAV
d. Future NAV

HINTS: Recognize the NAV used in forward pricing.

Q933_LO64: How is the purchase price (POP) calculated for front-end loaded shares?
a. NAV - Sales Charge
b. NAV + Sales Charge
c. NAV * Sales Charge
d. NAV / Sales Charge

HINTS: Calculate the public offering price (POP) for front-end loaded shares.

Q934_LO64: Why do sales charges exist in mutual funds?
a. To reduce NAV
b. To compensate underwriters
c. To increase expense ratio
d. To encourage redemptions

HINTS: Understand the purpose of sales charges in mutual funds.

Q935_LO64: How does the NAV change daily?
a. Due to supply and demand
b. Due to changes in market value
c. Due to redemptions only
d. Due to fund's total assets

HINTS: Identify the reason for daily changes in NAV.

Q936_LO64: What is the formula to calculate NAV per share?
a. Total NAV / Shares Outstanding
b. Total Assets - Total Liabilities
c. Average Net Assets / Expense Ratio
d. Sales Charge / NAV

HINTS: Recall the formula for NAV per share.

Q937_LO64: Define the expense ratio of a mutual fund.
a. Marketing costs
b. Total Assets / Total Liabilities
c. Management fees and operating expenses
d. Sales charge percentage

HINTS: Understand what the expense ratio includes.

Q938_LO64: What typically constitutes a stock fund's expense ratio?
a. 0.1% to 0.5%
b. 1% to 1.5%
c. 2% to 2.5%
d. 3% to 3.5%

HINTS: Identify the range of expense ratios for stock funds.

Q939_LO64: Which funds usually have higher expense ratios?
a. Conservative funds
b. Aggressive funds
c. Balanced funds
d. Index funds

HINTS: Recognize the correlation between fund type and expense ratios.

Q940_LO64: What does a higher expense ratio imply for fund returns?
a. Higher returns
b. Lower returns
c. No impact on returns
d. Fixed returns

HINTS: Understand the relationship between expense ratios and fund returns.

Q941_LO64: In the expense ratio, what are 12b-1 fees used for?
a. Manager's fee
b. Administrative fees
c. Marketing and distribution
d. Board of directors' costs

HINTS: Identify the purpose of 12b-1 fees in the expense ratio.

Q942_LO64: How is the expense ratio calculated?
a. Average Net Assets / Total Expenses
b. Total Expenses / Average Net Assets
c. NAV per share / Total Liabilities
d. Total Assets - Sales Charge

HINTS: Recall the correct formula for calculating the expense ratio.

Q943_LO64: What is a direct impact of higher expenses on a fund?
a. Increased returns
b. Decreased returns
c. No impact on returns
d. Fixed expense returns

HINTS: Understand the direct impact of higher expenses on fund returns.

Q944_LO64: Why is it important for investors to consider expense ratios?
a. To increase returns
b. To reduce returns
c. To compare fund costs
d. To ignore fund costs

HINTS: Recognize the significance of considering expense ratios for investors.

Q945_LO64: What does NAV stand for in the context of mutual funds?
a. Net Asset Volatility
b. New Asset Valuation
c. Net Asset Value
d. Non-Asset Variability

HINTS: Identify the correct expansion of NAV in mutual funds.

Q946_LO64: When is the NAV of a mutual fund typically calculated?
a. Once a week
b. Monthly
c. Daily
d. Annually

HINTS: Recognize the frequency at which NAV is calculated for a mutual fund.

Q947_LO64: What is forward pricing in the context of mutual funds?
a. Pricing in advance
b. Real-time pricing
c. Historical pricing
d. Pricing at redemption

HINTS: Understand the meaning of forward pricing in mutual funds.

Q948_LO64: How is the public offering price (POP) calculated for front-end loaded shares?
a. NAV + Market Value
b. NAV - Sales Charge
c. NAV + Sales Charge
d. NAV * Sales Charge

HINTS: Calculate the POP for front-end loaded shares.

Q949_LO64: Why does the NAV of a mutual fund change daily?
a. Due to changes in ownership
b. Due to changes in liabilities
c. Due to changes in market value of securities
d. Due to changes in fund expenses

HINTS: Identify the primary reason for daily changes in the NAV of a mutual fund.

Q950_LO64: How is the NAV per share calculated?
a. Total assets - Total liabilities
b. NAV of the fund / Shares outstanding
c. Total liabilities - Total assets
d. Shares outstanding / NAV of the fund

HINTS: Calculate the NAV per share for a mutual fund.

Q951_LO64: What does the term "expense ratio" in mutual funds compare?
a. Sales charges and NAV
b. Fund's assets and liabilities
c. Management fees and operating expenses
d. Redemption fees and NAV

HINTS: Identify the components compared in a mutual fund's expense ratio.

Q952_LO64: In general, what do higher expense ratios in mutual funds indicate?
a. Higher returns
b. Lower returns
c. No impact on returns
d. Consistent returns

HINTS: Understand the impact of higher expense ratios on mutual fund returns.

Q953_LO64: What is included in a fund's expense ratio?
a. Only manager's fee
b. Administrative fees
c. 12b-1 fees
d. All of the above
HINTS: Recognize the components included in a mutual fund's expense ratio.

Q954_LO64: What typically comprises a fund's expense ratio in the context of bond funds?
a. 0.5% - 1%
b. 1% - 1.5%
c. 2% - 2.5%
d. 3% - 3.5%
HINTS: Identify the typical range of expense ratios for bond funds.

Q955_LO64: What is the purpose of 12b-1 fees included in a fund's expense ratio?
a. Manager's bonus
b. Administrative costs
c. Marketing and distribution
d. Legal fees

HINTS: Recognize the purpose of 12b-1 fees in a mutual fund's expense ratio.

Q956_LO64: How are a fund's expenses treated in relation to its returns?
a. A boost to returns
b. A drag on returns
c. No impact on returns
d. A guarantee of returns
HINTS: Understand the effect of a fund's expenses on its returns.

Q957_LO64: What is the significance of the term "forward pricing" for investors?
a. Immediate pricing
b. Delayed pricing
c. Real-time pricing
d. Future pricing
HINTS: Recognize the timing implication associated with forward pricing for investors.

Q958_LO64: How is the purchase price of a front-end loaded fund share calculated?
a. NAV - Sales Charge
b. NAV + Sales Charge
c. NAV * Sales Charge

d. NAV / Sales Charge

HINTS: Calculate the purchase price (POP) for front-end loaded fund shares.

Q959_LO64: What is the primary purpose of forward pricing in mutual funds?
a. To benefit underwriters
b. To standardize sales charges
c. To determine current share value
d. To calculate future NAV

HINTS: Identify the primary purpose of forward pricing in mutual funds.

Q960_LO65: What is the primary purpose of a full or statutory prospectus in a mutual fund?
a. Marketing material
b. Fair disclosure document
c. Sales application
d. Performance history report
HINTS: Identify the main purpose of a full or statutory prospectus.

Q961_LO65: When must a full or statutory prospectus be distributed to an investor?
a. After the sale
b. During the solicitation
c. Before or during the solicitation
d. Only upon request

HINTS: Recognize the correct timing for distributing a full or statutory prospectus.

Q962_LO65: What is a summary prospectus in mutual funds?
a. Detailed fund history
b. Abbreviated prospectus
c. Legal document
d. Marketing brochure

HINTS: Understand the nature of a summary prospectus.

Q963_LO65: What is required to be included on the cover page of a summary prospectus?
a. Fund's name and class
b. Marketing slogans
c. Stock ticker symbols
d. Toll-free number for complaints

HINTS: Identify the mandatory elements on the cover page of a summary prospectus.

Q964_LO65: What option does an investor have after receiving a summary prospectus?
a. Request a discount
b. Request a full prospectus
c. Request a performance report
d. Request a tax statement

HINTS: Recognize the investor's option after receiving a summary prospectus.

Q965_LO65: What is the purpose of a Statement of Additional Information (SAI) in mutual funds?
a. Mandatory for investment decisions
b. Detailed fund history
c. Additional information not in the prospectus
d. Marketing material

HINTS: Understand the purpose of a Statement of Additional Information (SAI).

Q966_LO65: When must an SAI be available for delivery to an investor?
a. Within one business day
b. Within two business days
c. Within three business days
d. Within five business days

HINTS: Identify the timeframe for delivering an SAI to an investor upon request.

Q967_LO65: What does the term "omitting prospectus" refer to in mutual funds?
a. Comprehensive disclosure document
b. Fund advertisement
c. Legal document
d. Marketing brochure
HINTS: Recognize the nature of an omitting prospectus in mutual funds.

Q968_LO65: What is Rule 482 related to mutual fund advertising?
a. Full disclosure requirement
b. Summary prospectus requirement
c. Omitting prospectus requirement
d. Disclosure exemption

HINTS: Understand the significance of Rule 482 in mutual fund advertising.

Q969_LO65: What does the pipeline theory aim to avoid in mutual fund taxation?
a. Double taxation
b. Triple taxation
c. Single taxation
d. No taxation

HINTS: Identify the taxation scenario that the pipeline theory aims to avoid.

Q970_LO65: How does a mutual fund qualify for taxation benefits under Subchapter M?
a. By retaining 90% of investment income
b. By distributing 100% of investment income
c. By avoiding any distribution
d. By paying taxes on all investment income

HINTS: Recognize the condition for a mutual fund to qualify for taxation benefits.

Q971_LO65: What happens if a mutual fund distributes only 89% of its net investment income?
a. Pays taxes on 0% of investment income
b. Pays taxes on 89% of investment income
c. Pays taxes on 100% of investment income
d. Qualifies for tax exemption

HINTS: Understand the tax consequences if a mutual fund distributes only 89% of net investment income.

Q972_LO65: What does the term "forward pricing" refer to in mutual funds?
a. Real-time pricing
b. Pricing at redemption
c. Future pricing
d. Delayed pricing
HINTS: Recognize the meaning of forward pricing in mutual funds.

Q973_LO65: In which situation is a full or statutory prospectus necessary for the sale of mutual fund shares?
a. Always required
b. When using a summary prospectus
c. When using an SAI
d. When using an omitting prospectus

HINTS: Identify the situation requiring a full or statutory prospectus for the sale of mutual fund shares.

Q974_LO65: What is the key purpose of the summary prospectus in mutual funds?
a. Full disclosure of all material facts
b. Providing detailed historical data
c. Simplifying complex legal language
d. Attracting new investors

HINTS: Understand the primary purpose of a summary prospectus in mutual funds.

Correct Answers & Explanations
Packaged Investments

Q766_LO59: Correct Answer: b EXPLANATIONS: An investment company pools investors' money and invests it in securities on their behalf.

Q767_LO59: Correct Answer: b EXPLANATIONS: Pooling allows investment in various securities, reducing the risk associated with investing in a single security.

Q768_LO59: Correct Answer: b EXPLANATIONS: The Act classifies investment companies into FACs, UITs, and management investment companies.

Q769_LO59: Correct Answer: b EXPLANATIONS: A fully paid FAC involves a lump-sum payment by the investor.

Q770_LO59: Correct Answer: c EXPLANATIONS: UITs issue redeemable units, providing investors with the option to redeem their shares.

Q771_LO59: Correct Answer: c EXPLANATIONS: A nonfixed UIT invests in shares of an underlying mutual fund.

Q772_LO59: Correct Answer: b EXPLANATIONS: Fixed UITs have static portfolios with little or no need for active management.

Q773_LO59: Correct Answer: b EXPLANATIONS: Closed-end companies have a limited initial offering of shares.
Q774_LO59: Correct Answer: a EXPLANATIONS: Open-end companies continually offer new shares to the public.

Q775_LO59: Correct Answer: b EXPLANATIONS: A nonfixed UIT may purchase shares of an underlying mutual fund.

Q776_LO59: Correct Answer: c EXPLANATIONS: Investment companies are regulated by the Investment Company Act of 1940.

Q777_LO59: Correct Answer: d EXPLANATIONS: Investment companies must provide a prospectus, similar to corporate issuers.

Q778_LO59: Correct Answer: b EXPLANATIONS: UITs do not have boards of directors; they have trustees.

Q779_LO59: Correct Answer: c EXPLANATIONS: Very few FAC companies operate today due to changes in market dynamics.
Q780_LO59: Correct Answer: c EXPLANATIONS: Investment companies commonly allow minimum investments of perhaps only $100 or even less.

Q781_LO59: Correct Answer: b EXPLANATIONS: An investment company pools investors' money and invests it in securities on their behalf.

Q782_LO59: Correct Answer: c EXPLANATIONS: Investment companies reduce risk by pooling funds and investing in many different securities.

Q783_LO59: Correct Answer: a EXPLANATIONS: Investment companies must abide by the Securities Act of 1933.
Q784_LO59: Correct Answer: a EXPLANATIONS: Investment companies are regulated by the Securities and Exchange Commission (SEC) under the Investment Company Act of 1940.

Q785_LO59: Correct Answer: c EXPLANATIONS: The three types are FAC companies, UITs, and management investment companies.

Q786_LO59: Correct Answer: c EXPLANATIONS: A FAC is a contract guaranteeing payment of a stated sum to the investor at a future date.

Q787_LO59: Correct Answer: c EXPLANATIONS: UITs sell redeemable interests in their portfolio of securities.

Q788_LO59: Correct Answer: c EXPLANATIONS: A fixed UIT terminates when its portfolio securities mature, while a nonfixed UIT may invest in an underlying mutual fund.

Q789_LO59: Correct Answer: c EXPLANATIONS: Fixed UITs don't usually assess management fees as there's no need for active management or hiring an investment adviser.

Q790_LO59: Correct Answer: b EXPLANATIONS: FACs and UITs are not managed or actively traded; they do not have boards of directors.
Q791_LO59: Correct Answer: b EXPLANATIONS: An open-end company is continually open to new investors.

Q792_LO59: Correct Answer: b EXPLANATIONS: Closed-end companies have a limited initial offering of shares, while open-end companies continually offer new shares.

Q793_LO59: Correct Answer: c EXPLANATIONS: A UIT may have a predetermined termination date, especially in the case of a fixed UIT.

Q794_LO59: Correct Answer: c EXPLANATIONS: The proof of ownership is the share certificate.

Q795_LO59: Correct Answer: d EXPLANATIONS: A nonfixed UIT typically purchases shares of an underlying mutual fund.
Q796_LO60: Correct Answer: d EXPLANATIONS: Closed-end companies are publicly traded in the secondary market.

Q797_LO60: Correct Answer: c EXPLANATIONS: Closed-end companies raise capital by conducting a common stock offering.

Q798_LO60: Correct Answer: d EXPLANATIONS: Closed-end investment companies are often called publicly traded funds.

Q799_LO60: Correct Answer: d EXPLANATIONS: Closed-end fund shares may trade at a premium or discount based on supply and demand.

Q800_LO60: Correct Answer: a EXPLANATIONS: NAV per share = (Assets - Liabilities) / Outstanding shares

Q801_LO60: Correct Answer: a EXPLANATIONS: Open-end companies issue common stock only.

Q802_LO60: Correct Answer: c EXPLANATIONS: Shares of an open-end company are redeemed by the fund itself.

Q803_LO60: Correct Answer: b EXPLANATIONS: The selling price is determined by NAV + sales charge.

Q804_LO60: Correct Answer: b EXPLANATIONS: Mutual funds are priced at the end of each business day, with buyers and sellers receiving the next calculated NAV and POP.

Q805_LO60: Correct Answer: d EXPLANATIONS: Transactions after 4:00 pm receive the next business day's NAV or POP.
Q806_LO60: Correct Answer: d EXPLANATIONS: Share redemptions decrease the number of outstanding shares.

Q807_LO60: Correct Answer: a EXPLANATIONS: The share certificate serves as proof of ownership.

Q808_LO60: Correct Answer: b EXPLANATIONS: Closed-end investment companies are priced at CMV + commission.

Q809_LO60: Correct Answer: b EXPLANATIONS: Closed-end companies have an initial offering that is limited, closing after a specific authorized number of shares have been sold, while open-end companies continuously offer new shares.

Q810_LO60: Correct Answer: b EXPLANATIONS: Closed-end companies conduct a common stock offering with a limited time.

Q811_LO60: Correct Answer: a EXPLANATIONS: Closed-end companies close after the initial common stock offering.
Q812_LO60: Correct Answer: b EXPLANATIONS: Closed-end investment companies are often called publicly traded funds.

Q813_LO60: Correct Answer: c EXPLANATIONS: Closed-end fund shares can be bought or sold on the secondary market, such as an exchange or OTC.

Q814_LO60: Correct Answer: b EXPLANATIONS: The bid price is determined by supply and demand.

Q815_LO60: Correct Answer: a EXPLANATIONS: NAV is assets minus liabilities divided by the number of outstanding shares.

Q816_LO60: Correct Answer: a EXPLANATIONS: Open-end funds are not traded in the secondary market; they are sold and redeemed by the fund.

Q817_LO60: Correct Answer: a EXPLANATIONS: Open-end funds are priced at NAV + sales charge.

Q818_LO60: Correct Answer: a EXPLANATIONS: Open-end funds are priced at the end of each business day.

Q819_LO60: Correct Answer: b EXPLANATIONS: The value of each share does not fall as a result of redemption; it remains unchanged.

Q820_LO60: Correct Answer: a EXPLANATIONS: The price is determined by supply and demand in the secondary market.
Q821_LO60: Correct Answer: b EXPLANATIONS: Open-end companies conduct a continuous primary offering of shares.

Q822_LO60: Correct Answer: a EXPLANATIONS: Open-end companies have a continuous offering, while closed-end companies have a limited offering.

Q823_LO60: Correct Answer: b EXPLANATIONS: Open-end companies have unlimited capitalization through continuous offering.

Q824_LO60: Correct Answer: c EXPLANATIONS: Closed-end fund shares may trade at a premium or discount to NAV.

Q825_LO61: Correct Answer: b EXPLANATIONS: An annuity is designed to provide retirement income, guaranteeing a stream of payments, typically for the life of the annuitant.

Q826_LO61: Correct Answer: d EXPLANATIONS: The mortality guarantee addresses the fear of outliving income, providing a stream of payments for life.

Q827_LO61: Correct Answer: d EXPLANATIONS: In a variable annuity, the investor assumes the investment risk, making it a security.
Q828_LO61: Correct Answer: b EXPLANATIONS: In a variable annuity, the investor assumes the investment risk.

Q829_LO61: Correct Answer: d EXPLANATIONS: Premium payments for variable annuities are invested in the separate account.

Q830_LO61: Correct Answer: b EXPLANATIONS: It is directly managed when the insurance company's manager selects securities.
Q831_LO61: Correct Answer: b EXPLANATIONS: Buyers must be informed of administrative, investment advisory, and custodial fees.

Q832_LO61: Correct Answer: d EXPLANATIONS: Returns are determined by the performance of subaccounts within the separate account.

Q833_LO61: Correct Answer: a EXPLANATIONS: There is no limit to the annual contribution amounts on commercial (nonqualified) contracts.

Q834_LO61: Correct Answer: c EXPLANATIONS: Annual contributions in qualified variable contracts are limited by IRS rules, similar to 401(k) plans.

Q835_LO61: Correct Answer: b EXPLANATIONS: Annuitization involves surrendering ownership for a lifetime income guaranteed by the insurance company.

Q836_LO61: Correct Answer: d EXPLANATIONS: The income amount is determined by factors like gender, age, account value, payout option, and assumed interest rate.

Q837_LO61: Correct Answer: a EXPLANATIONS: A fixed annuity promises a stated rate of return, with no investment risk for the investor.

Q838_LO61: Correct Answer: a EXPLANATIONS: A fixed annuity guarantees a stated rate of return, and the insurance company bears the investment risk.

Q839_LO61: Correct Answer: b EXPLANATIONS: The mortality guarantee addresses the fear of outliving income, providing a stream of payments for life

Q840_LO61: Correct Answer: b EXPLANATIONS: An annuity is designed to provide retirement income.

Q841_LO61: Correct Answer: c EXPLANATIONS: Variable annuities involve investment risk assumed by the investor.
Q842_LO61: Correct Answer: d EXPLANATIONS: Premium payments are invested in subaccounts within the separate account.

Q843_LO61: Correct Answer: b EXPLANATIONS: Subaccounts may be directly or indirectly managed, depending on portfolio management responsibility.

Q844_LO61: Correct Answer: b EXPLANATIONS: It is directly managed when handled by an investment company under the 1940 Act.

Q845_LO61: Correct Answer: c EXPLANATIONS: The performance of subaccounts within the separate account determines the annuity's investment performance.

Q846_LO61: Correct Answer: c EXPLANATIONS: Buyers must be informed of all product-specific charges, including administrative, investment advisory, and custodial fees.

Q847_LO61: Correct Answer: b EXPLANATIONS: Annuitization involves giving up ownership for a lifetime income guaranteed by the insurance company.

Q848_LO61: Correct Answer: b EXPLANATIONS: Factors include gender, age, account value, payout option, and assumed interest rate.

Q849_LO61: Correct Answer: b EXPLANATIONS: The initial calculation does not include adjustments for inflation.

Q850_LO61: Correct Answer: c EXPLANATIONS: Variable annuities involve the investor assuming investment risk, unlike fixed annuities.
Q851_LO61: Correct Answer: a EXPLANATIONS: Fixed annuities guarantee a stated rate of return, and the investor assumes no investment risk.

Q852_LO61: Correct Answer: c EXPLANATIONS: Variable annuities involve investment risk assumed by the investor.

Q853_LO61: Correct Answer: b EXPLANATIONS: Regulatory restrictions limit contributions to qualified variable contracts.

Q854_LO61: Correct Answer: b EXPLANATIONS: Variable annuities have market-driven returns, unlike fixed annuities that provide guaranteed returns.

Q855_LO62: Correct Answer: c EXPLANATIONS: Mutual funds offer guaranteed marketability; the fund stands ready to buy back shares.

Q856_LO62: Correct Answer: b EXPLANATIONS: Distributions are typically done at net asset value (NAV).

Q857_LO62: Correct Answer: b EXPLANATIONS: The conduit theory means tax events flow down to shareholders each year.
Q858_LO62: Correct Answer: b EXPLANATIONS: The investor's account value fluctuates proportionately with the mutual fund portfolio's value.

Q859_LO62: Correct Answer: b EXPLANATIONS: Mutual fund shares can be fractional, enabling thinking in terms of dollars.

Q860_LO62: Correct Answer: c EXPLANATIONS: The investment adviser professionally manages the portfolio for investors.

Q861_LO62: Correct Answer: c EXPLANATIONS: The maximum sales charge allowed is 8½% of the POP.

Q862_LO62: Correct Answer: a EXPLANATIONS: Class A shares often have a front-end load.
Q863_LO62: Correct Answer: b EXPLANATIONS: Class B shares often have a back-end load.

Q864_LO62: Correct Answer: b EXPLANATIONS: Class C shares often have a back-end load.

Q865_LO62: Correct Answer: c EXPLANATIONS: Class C shares often have a contingent deferred sales charge (CDSC).
Q866_LO62: Correct Answer: a EXPLANATIONS: Class B shares often convert to Class A shares over time.

Q867_LO62: Correct Answer: a EXPLANATIONS: No-load funds do not impose sales charges.

Q868_LO62: Correct Answer: a EXPLANATIONS: Sales charges in no-load funds are typically paid by the investor directly.

Q869_LO62: Correct Answer: a EXPLANATIONS: Reinvestments, whether taken or reinvested, are taxable.

Q870_LO62: Correct Answer: c EXPLANATIONS: Mutual funds offer guaranteed marketability; they are redeemable securities.

Q871_LO62: Correct Answer: c EXPLANATIONS: Mutual funds operate under the conduit theory of taxation.

Q872_LO62: Correct Answer: c EXPLANATIONS: Distributions are typically done at net asset value (NAV).

Q873_LO62: Correct Answer: b EXPLANATIONS: Reinvestments increase the investor's cost basis in the fund.

Q874_LO62: Correct Answer: a EXPLANATIONS: It depends on the number of shares owned.

Q875_LO62: Correct Answer: a EXPLANATIONS: Mutual fund shares can be fractional, allowing investors to think in terms of dollars.

Q876_LO62: Correct Answer: b EXPLANATIONS: The maximum sales charge allowed is 8½% of the POP.

Q877_LO62: Correct Answer: b EXPLANATIONS: No-load funds are funds with no sales charges.
Q878_LO62: Correct Answer: c EXPLANATIONS: The differences lie in how much and in what way investors will pay sales charges and related expenses.

Q879_LO62: Correct Answer: a EXPLANATIONS: Class A shares are typically suitable for long-term investors.

Q880_LO62: Correct Answer: b EXPLANATIONS: Class B shares often have a back-end load or contingent deferred sales charge (CDSC).

Q881_LO62: Correct Answer: c EXPLANATIONS: Class C shares typically have a level load or a contingent deferred sales charge (CDSC).

Q882_LO62: Correct Answer: c EXPLANATIONS: The sales charge structure is a crucial consideration.

Q883_LO62: Correct Answer: a EXPLANATIONS: Class C shares can be advantageous for short-term investors.

Q884_LO62: Correct Answer: d EXPLANATIONS: Class C shares typically have a contingent deferred sales charge (CDSC), making them less suitable for long-term investors.
Q885_LO62: Correct Answer: c EXPLANATIONS: Sales charges for Class A shares are applied at the time of purchase.

Q886_LO62: Correct Answer: b EXPLANATIONS: Class B shares have a back-end sales load or contingent deferred sales charge (CDSC).

Q887_LO62: Correct Answer: c EXPLANATIONS: The back-end load of Class B shares usually drops to zero after an extended holding period, often no longer than five years.

Q888_LO62: Correct Answer: b EXPLANATIONS: The sales charge in Class B shares is deferred to the time of redemption.

Q889_LO62: Correct Answer: c EXPLANATIONS: Sales charges in Class B shares are applied to amounts greater than the initial investment if the shares grow in value.

Q890_LO62: Correct Answer: c EXPLANATIONS: Class C shares typically have a level load, including a 1% CDSC and 0.75% 12b-1 fee.

Q891_LO62: Correct Answer: a EXPLANATIONS: Class C shares are appropriate for short-term investors due to lower annual charges.
Q892_LO62: Correct Answer: d EXPLANATIONS: No-load funds do not charge any type of sales charge; shares are purchased at NAV.

Q893_LO62: Correct Answer: a EXPLANATIONS: No-load funds are permitted to charge purchase fees, among other fees, that are not considered sales charges.

Q894_LO62: Correct Answer: d EXPLANATIONS: The sales charge in Class B shares is a percentage of the redemption proceeds.

Q895_LO62: Correct Answer: c EXPLANATIONS: The sales charge structure is a crucial consideration.

Q896_LO62: Correct Answer: b EXPLANATIONS: Class C shares typically have a one-year, 1% CDSC.

Q897_LO62: Correct Answer: a EXPLANATIONS: Class B shares are usually converted to Class A shares after an extended holding period.

Q898_LO62: Correct Answer: a EXPLANATIONS: Class C shares have annual charges that make them expensive to own if investing for more than four to five years.
Q899_LO62: Correct Answer: a EXPLANATIONS: No-load funds do not apply any type of sales charge; shares are purchased at NAV.

Q900_LO63: Correct Answer: b EXPLANATIONS: Breakpoints are quantity discounts on mutual fund shares based on the dollar amount of a purchase.

Q901_LO63: Correct Answer: b EXPLANATIONS: LOI allows investors to inform the fund of their intention to invest additional funds within 13 months.

Q902_LO63: Correct Answer: d EXPLANATIONS: The customer has the choice to pay the difference in sales charges or cash in escrowed shares.

Q903_LO63: Correct Answer: c EXPLANATIONS: ROA allows investors to use prior share appreciation to qualify for reduced sales charges and is not subject to time limits.

Q904_LO63: Correct Answer: c EXPLANATIONS: The total value for rights of accumulation includes the total purchases made to date.

Q905_LO63: Correct Answer: b EXPLANATIONS: Once an investor accumulates $50,000 in the fund, each additional investment qualifies for the lowest sales charge.

Q906_LO63: Correct Answer: b EXPLANATIONS: The combination privilege allows investors to combine investments in different funds within the same family.

Q907_LO63: Correct Answer: c EXPLANATIONS: The conversion of an investment in one fund for an equal investment in another fund is considered a taxable event.

Q908_LO63: Correct Answer: c EXPLANATIONS: A breakpoint sale occurs just below the breakpoint, potentially resulting in higher sales charges.

Q909_LO63: Correct Answer: d EXPLANATIONS: FINRA prohibits breakpoint sales to align with just and equitable principles in trade.

Q910_LO63: Correct Answer: b EXPLANATIONS: An LOI can decrease the overall sales charges for investors.

Q911_LO63: Correct Answer: a EXPLANATIONS: The customer must complete the LOI within 13 months to qualify for reduced sales charges.

Q912_LO63: Correct Answer: b EXPLANATIONS: ROA allows investors to use prior share appreciation to qualify for reduced sales charges over time.

Q913_LO63: Correct Answer: a EXPLANATIONS: The consequence is the forfeiture of escrowed shares if the investment is not completed within 13 months.

Q914_LO63: Correct Answer: c EXPLANATIONS: Breakpoints can apply to both initial and subsequent investments.

Q915_LO63: Correct Answer: a EXPLANATIONS: Breakpoints refer to quantity discounts on mutual fund shares.

Q916_LO63: Correct Answer: b EXPLANATIONS: An LOI involves the escrow of extra shares purchased at the reduced sales charge.

Q917_LO63: Correct Answer: b EXPLANATIONS: Escrowed shares may be forfeited, and the customer has options for paying the difference.

Q918_LO63: Correct Answer: c EXPLANATIONS: Rights of accumulation allow the use of prior share appreciation to qualify for reduced sales charges.
Q919_LO63: Correct Answer: b EXPLANATIONS: Rights of accumulation apply to subsequent investments and do not impose time limits.
Q920_LO63: Correct Answer: a EXPLANATIONS: The quantity is based on the higher of the current NAV or the total of purchases made to date.

Q921_LO63: Correct Answer: b EXPLANATIONS: It allows combining separate investments in two or more funds within the same family to reach a breakpoint.

Q922_LO63: Correct Answer: d EXPLANATIONS: It allows converting an investment in one fund for an equal investment in another fund within the same family.

Q923_LO63: Correct Answer: c EXPLANATIONS: Exchanging funds within the same family is considered a taxable event with potential tax consequences.

Q924_LO63: Correct Answer: b EXPLANATIONS: Breakpoint sales refer to sales just below the breakpoint.

Q925_LO63: Correct Answer: b EXPLANATIONS: FINRA regulates to ensure fairness and equity in sales practices related to breakpoints.

Q926_LO63: Correct Answer: c EXPLANATIONS: The industry does not provide a specific definition for "near" or "just below" a breakpoint.

Q927_LO63: Correct Answer: c EXPLANATIONS: Allowing sales just below a breakpoint may be seen as an effort to earn higher sales charges.

Q928_LO63: Correct Answer: c EXPLANATIONS: FINRA regulates and ensures disclosure to prevent inconsistent sales practices related to breakpoints.

Q929_LO63: Correct Answer: b EXPLANATIONS: Representatives could earn more concession dollars on smaller customer investments with higher sales charges.

Q930_LO64: Correct Answer: a EXPLANATIONS: NAV stands for Net Asset Value, representing the amount an investor receives upon redemption.

Q931_LO64: Correct Answer: d EXPLANATIONS: NAV is calculated at least once per business day, typically at the end of each business day.
Q932_LO64: Correct Answer: b EXPLANATIONS: The customer receives the next NAV calculated after the redemption request.

Q933_LO64: Correct Answer: b EXPLANATIONS: POP = NAV + Sales Charge

Q934_LO64: Correct Answer: b EXPLANATIONS: Sales charges compensate underwriters for marketing or bringing shares to the public.

Q935_LO64: Correct Answer: b EXPLANATIONS: NAV changes because of changes in the market value of the securities in the fund's portfolio.
Q936_LO64: Correct Answer: a EXPLANATIONS: NAV of the fund / Shares outstanding = NAV per share

Q937_LO64: Correct Answer: c EXPLANATIONS: Expense ratio compares management fees, operating expenses, and 12b-1 fees with a fund's net assets.

Q938_LO64: Correct Answer: b EXPLANATIONS: Stock funds generally have expense ratios between 1% and 1.5% of a fund's average net assets.

Q939_LO64: Correct Answer: b EXPLANATIONS: Typically, more aggressive funds have higher expense ratios.

Q940_LO64: Correct Answer: b EXPLANATIONS: Higher expenses generally result in lower returns for a fund.

Q941_LO64: Correct Answer: c EXPLANATIONS: 12b-1 fees are used for marketing and distribution.

Q942_LO64: Correct Answer: b EXPLANATIONS: Expense ratio = Total Expenses / Average Net Assets

Q943_LO64: Correct Answer: b EXPLANATIONS: Higher expenses are a drag on the fund's returns, leading to lower returns.

Q944_LO64: Correct Answer: c EXPLANATIONS: Expense ratios help investors compare the costs of different funds, impacting potential returns.
Q945_LO64: Correct Answer: c EXPLANATIONS: NAV stands for Net Asset Value, representing the value of each share in a mutual fund.

Q946_LO64: Correct Answer: c EXPLANATIONS: NAV is typically calculated at least once per business day.

Q947_LO64: Correct Answer: a EXPLANATIONS: Forward pricing involves determining the value of shares at the next NAV calculation after a transaction.

Q948_LO64: Correct Answer: c EXPLANATIONS: The POP for front-end loaded shares is calculated as NAV + Sales Charge.

Q949_LO64: Correct Answer: c EXPLANATIONS: The NAV changes daily due to changes in the market value of securities in the fund's portfolio.

Q950_LO64: Correct Answer: b EXPLANATIONS: NAV per share is calculated as NAV of the fund divided by the number of shares outstanding.

Q951_LO64: Correct Answer: c EXPLANATIONS: The expense ratio compares management fees, operating expenses, and 12b-1 fees with the fund's net assets.

Q952_LO64: Correct Answer: b EXPLANATIONS: Higher expenses generally lead to lower returns for mutual fund investors.

Q953_LO64: Correct Answer: d EXPLANATIONS: A fund's expense ratio includes manager's fee, administrative fees, 12b-1 fees, and more.
Q954_LO64: Correct Answer: a EXPLANATIONS: Expense ratios for bond funds are typically between 0.5% and 1% of average net assets.

Q955_LO64: Correct Answer: c EXPLANATIONS: 12b-1 fees cover marketing and distribution costs within a fund's expense ratio.

Q956_LO64: Correct Answer: b EXPLANATIONS: Fund expenses act as a drag on returns, reducing the overall returns for investors.
Q957_LO64: Correct Answer: b EXPLANATIONS: Forward pricing means waiting until the next NAV calculation to determine transaction values.

Q958_LO64: Correct Answer: b EXPLANATIONS: The purchase price (POP) for front-end loaded shares is calculated as NAV + Sales Charge.
Q959_LO64: Correct Answer: c EXPLANATIONS: Forward pricing helps determine the value of shares at the next NAV calculation after a transaction.

Q960_LO65: Correct Answer: b EXPLANATIONS: The full or statutory prospectus serves as a fair disclosure document for making informed investment decisions.

Q961_LO65: Correct Answer: c EXPLANATIONS: A full or statutory prospectus must be distributed before or during the solicitation.

Q962_LO65: Correct Answer: b EXPLANATIONS: A summary prospectus is an abbreviated version providing key information from the full prospectus.

Q963_LO65: Correct Answer: a EXPLANATIONS: The cover page must include the fund's name and class, among other details.

Q964_LO65: Correct Answer: b EXPLANATIONS: An investor can choose to request a full prospectus after receiving a summary prospectus.

Q965_LO65: Correct Answer: c EXPLANATIONS: The SAI provides additional information not mandatory for investment decisions but useful to investors.

Q966_LO65: Correct Answer: c EXPLANATIONS: An SAI must be available within three business days of an investor's request.
Q967_LO65: Correct Answer: b EXPLANATIONS: Omitting prospectus is another term for a fund advertisement.

Q968_LO65: Correct Answer: c EXPLANATIONS: Rule 482 pertains to the use of omitting prospectus, which is a form of fund advertisement.

Q969_LO65: Correct Answer: b EXPLANATIONS: The pipeline theory aims to avoid triple taxation of investment income.

Q970_LO65: Correct Answer: a EXPLANATIONS: A mutual fund must distribute at least 90% of its net investment income to qualify for Subchapter M taxation benefits.

Q971_LO65: Correct Answer: c EXPLANATIONS: If a fund distributes less than 90%, it pays taxes on 100% of net investment income.

Q972_LO65: Correct Answer: c EXPLANATIONS: Forward pricing refers to determining the value of shares at the next NAV calculation after a transaction.

Q973_LO65: Correct Answer: a EXPLANATIONS: A full or statutory prospectus is always required for the sale of mutual fund shares.

Q974_LO65: Correct Answer: c EXPLANATIONS: The key purpose of a summary prospectus is to provide key information in simplified and standardized form.

Types of Risk

Q1125_LO75: What is systematic risk?
a. Company-specific risk
b. Changes in overall economy
c. Market volatility
d. Interest rate fluctuations

HINTS: Identify the type of risk associated with changes in the overall economy.

Q1126_LO75: What is the primary cause of systematic risk?
a. Company performance
b. Global security threats
c. Individual circumstances
d. Inflation

HINTS: Recognize a factor contributing to systematic risk.

Q1127_LO75: How does market risk affect a portfolio during a market decline?
a. Portfolio value increases
b. No impact on portfolio
c. Portfolio value decreases
d. Portfolio becomes risk-free

HINTS: Identify the impact of market risk on a portfolio during a market decline.

Q1128_LO75: What is interest rate risk?
a. Bond default risk
b. Market volatility
c. Fluctuation in bond prices due to interest rate changes
d. Credit risk

HINTS: Define the risk associated with changes in bond prices due to market interest rate changes.

Q1129_LO75: How are existing bonds priced in the market if interest rates rise?
a. At a discount
b. At par value
c. At a premium
d. At face value

HINTS: Recognize the pricing impact on existing bonds when interest rates rise.

Q1130_LO75: What is the relationship between interest rate movements and bond duration?
a. No relationship
b. Inverse relationship
c. Direct relationship
d. Positive relationship

HINTS: Understand the relationship between interest rate movements and bond duration.

Q1131_LO75: Why is interest rate risk considered systematic for fixed-income securities?
a. Market conditions impact interest rates
b. Fixed-income securities have no risk
c. Interest rates do not affect bond prices
d. Only credit risk affects bond prices

HINTS: Recognize a characteristic of interest rate risk as systematic for fixed-income securities.

Q1132_LO75: What is reinvestment risk?
a. Risk of bond default
b. Difficulty reinvesting proceeds at the same income level
c. Market risk for bonds
d. Risk of rising inflation

HINTS: Define the risk associated with difficulty reinvesting proceeds at the same income level.

Q1133_LO75: In what scenario is reinvestment risk most pronounced?
a. Rising interest rates
b. Falling interest rates
c. Stable interest rates
d. No correlation with interest rates

HINTS: Identify a scenario where reinvestment risk is most pronounced.

Q1134_LO75: What is another term for inflation risk?
a. Market risk
b. Purchasing power risk
c. Interest rate risk
d. Reinvestment risk

HINTS: Recognize an alternative term for inflation risk.

Q1135_LO75: How does inflation risk impact investment returns?
a. Increases returns
b. Maintains returns
c. Diminishes purchasing power
d. Eliminates risk

HINTS: Identify the effect of inflation risk on investment returns.

Q1136_LO75: What is deflation?
a. Prolonged period of falling prices
b. Sudden increase in prices
c. Stable prices
d. Inflationary pressure

HINTS: Define the economic condition associated with falling prices.

Q1137_LO75: How does deflation impact fixed-income payments?
a. Reduces their value
b. Increases their value
c. No impact
d. Converts them to equity

HINTS: Recognize the impact of deflation on fixed-income payments.

Q1138_LO75: Why is inflation risk considered systematic?
a. Unrelated to overall economy
b. Affects only individual securities
c. Affects all businesses
d. Limited to bond markets

HINTS: Identify a characteristic of inflation risk as systematic.

Q1139_LO75: How is inflation risk related to purchasing power?
a. Increases purchasing power
b. Maintains purchasing power
c. Diminishes purchasing power
d. No correlation with purchasing power

HINTS: Recognize the impact of inflation risk on purchasing power.

Q1140_LO76: What is nonsystematic risk?
a. Diversifiable risk
b. Market risk
c. Interest rate risk
d. Currency risk

HINTS: Recognize the type of risk that can be reduced through diversification.

Q1141_LO76: How is beta related to the volatility of an asset?
a. Measures credit risk
b. Measures liquidity risk
c. Measures asset volatility
d. Measures legislative risk

HINTS: Understand the role of beta in measuring the volatility of an asset.

Q1142_LO76: What does a beta greater than 1.00 indicate?
a. Less volatile than the market
b. Stable compared to the market
c. More volatile than the market
d. No volatility

HINTS: Interpret the meaning of a beta greater than 1.00.

Q1143_LO76: What is default risk?
a. Risk of business failure
b. Risk of losing invested capital due to an issuer's financial strength
c. Risk of interest rate fluctuations
d. Risk of currency devaluation

HINTS: Identify the risk associated with losing invested capital due to an issuer's financial strength.

Q1144_LO76: What is business risk primarily caused by?
a. Interest rate changes
b. Poor management decisions
c. Currency fluctuations
d. Legislative changes

HINTS: Recognize the cause of business risk.

Q1145_LO76: What is financial risk related to?
a. Market volatility
b. Business operations
c. Debt financing (leverage)
d. Interest rate movements

HINTS: Identify the primary factor related to financial risk.

Q1146_LO76: What is call risk associated with?
a. Currency exchange rates
b. Bond redemptions before maturity
c. Interest rate fluctuations
d. Marketability risk

HINTS: Recognize the risk associated with bonds being called before maturity.

Q1147_LO76: What can lead to reinvestment risk?
a. Rising interest rates
b. Stable interest rates
c. Falling interest rates
d. Regulatory changes
HINTS: Identify the condition that can lead to reinvestment risk.

Q1148_LO76: What is prepayment risk associated with?
a. Borrower repaying principal before maturity
b. Marketability of securities
c. Interest rate fluctuations
d. Currency exchange rates

HINTS: Recognize the risk associated with borrowers repaying principal before maturity.

Q1149_LO76: What is currency risk related to?
a. Interest rate changes
b. Marketability of securities
c. Political instability
d. Exchange rate fluctuations

HINTS: Identify the risk associated with changes in exchange rates.

Q1150_LO76: What is liquidity risk also known as?
a. Default risk
b. Marketability risk
c. Credit risk
d. Legislative risk

HINTS: Recognize another term for liquidity risk.

Q1151_LO76: What does regulatory risk result from?
a. Change in law
b. Change in regulations
c. Political instability
d. Business failure

HINTS: Differentiate between regulatory risk and legislative risk.

Q1152_LO76: What is legislative risk associated with?
a. Business failure
b. Change in law
c. Change in regulations
d. Political instability

HINTS: Identify the risk resulting from a change in law.

Q1153_LO76: What does political risk specifically relate to?
a. Currency exchange rates
b. Legislative changes
c. Business failure
d. Political instability

HINTS: Recognize the specific aspect of risk related to political risk.

Q1154_LO76: What does sovereign risk capture?
a. Risk of bond default
b. Risk of business failure
c. Risk of currency devaluation
d. Risk of a country defaulting on its commercial debt obligations

HINTS: Identify the type of risk captured by sovereign risk ratings.

Q1155_LO76: What is nonsystematic risk?
a. Diversifiable risk
b. Market risk
c. Interest rate risk
d. Legislative risk

HINTS: Identify the type of risk that can be reduced through diversification.

Q1156_LO76: What does beta measure?
a. Market volatility
b. Default risk
c. Interest rate changes
d. Legislative changes

HINTS: Recognize the parameter measured by beta.

Q1157_LO76: How is a high beta security perceived in terms of risk?
a. Less volatile
b. Market-neutral
c. More stable
d. Riskier

HINTS: Identify the perception of risk associated with a high beta security.

Q1158_LO76: What does default risk entail?
a. Market fluctuations
b. Loss of invested capital
c. Business failure
d. Interest payment delays

HINTS: Define the risk associated with potential loss of invested capital.

Q1159_LO76: What is business risk primarily caused by?
a. Interest rate changes
b. Poor management decisions
c. Market fluctuations
d. Legislative changes

HINTS: Identify the primary cause of business risk.

Q1160_LO76: What is financial risk related to?
a. Market conditions
b. Interest rate movements
c. Debt financing (leverage)
d. Business operations

HINTS: Recognize the aspect of financial risk related to debt financing.

Q1161_LO76: What is call risk associated with?
a. Bond defaults
b. Reinvestment risk
c. Interest rate fluctuations
d. Business decisions

HINTS: Identify the risk associated with the inability to reinvest principal at a comparable rate.

Q1162_LO76: What is prepayment risk related to?
a. Interest rate movements
b. Business failures
c. Bond defaults
d. Repayment of principal before maturity

HINTS: Define the risk associated with the borrower repaying principal before maturity.

Q1163_LO76: When is prepayment risk more likely in securities like GNMAs?
a. Rising interest rates
b. Falling interest rates
c. Stable interest rates
d. No correlation with interest rates

HINTS: Identify the scenario where prepayment risk is more likely.

Q1164_LO76: What is currency risk associated with?
a. Business decisions
b. Interest rate movements
c. Exchange rate fluctuations
d. Legislative changes

HINTS: Recognize the risk associated with the decline in the value of a currency.

Q1165_LO76: What is liquidity risk also known as?
a. Marketability risk
b. Default risk
c. Interest rate risk
d. Currency risk

HINTS: Identify the alternative term for liquidity risk.

Q1166_LO76: What does regulatory risk result from?
a. Business decisions
b. Legislative changes
c. Interest rate fluctuations
d. Market conditions

HINTS: Differentiate regulatory risk from legislative risk.

Q1167_LO76: What does political risk primarily relate to?
a. Interest rate changes
b. Business operations
c. Legislative decisions
d. Political instability

HINTS: Identify the primary concern of political risk.

Q1168_LO76: What do sovereign risk ratings capture?
a. Market fluctuations
b. Interest rate movements
c. Risk of business failure
d. Risk of a country defaulting on commercial debt

HINTS: Recognize the focus of sovereign risk ratings.

Q1169_LO76: How is nonsystematic risk different from systematic risk in terms of diversification?
a. Both can be diversified
b. Only nonsystematic risk can be diversified
c. Only systematic risk can be diversified
d. Neither can be diversified

HINTS: Understand the diversifiability of nonsystematic risk.

Q1170_LO77: How can systematic risk be mitigated or hedged?
a. Diversification
b. Use of derivative securities
c. Building a portfolio
d. Issuing new securities
HINTS: Identify the method used to hedge systematic risk.

Q1171_LO77: What is the primary characteristic of systematic risk?
a. Unique to a specific security
b. Can be diversified away
c. Built into the system
d. Influenced by management decisions

HINTS: Recognize the defining characteristic of systematic risk.

Q1172_LO77: How do portfolio managers typically hedge against systematic risk?
a. Increasing investment in high-beta securities
b. Reducing diversification
c. Using derivative securities
d. Ignoring systematic risk

HINTS: Identify the common approach for portfolio managers to hedge systematic risk.

Q1173_LO77: What is the term for reducing risks associated with a specific security by holding securities of different issuers?
a. Concentration
b. Specialization
c. Diversification
d. Hedging

HINTS: Recognize the strategy used to reduce nonsystematic risk.

Q1174_LO77: Which type of risk can be diversified away?
a. Systematic risk
b. Interest rate risk
c. Default risk
d. Market risk

HINTS: Identify the risk that can be mitigated through diversification.

Q1175_LO77: What is the main method to hedge nonsystematic risk?
a. Using options and futures
b. Increasing concentration
c. Reducing diversification
d. Building a diversified portfolio

HINTS: Recognize the primary strategy for mitigating nonsystematic risk.

Q1176_LO77: In the context of systematic risk, what does a portfolio manager seek in an asset?
a. High correlation with the market
b. Low correlation with the market
c. Stability in market movements
d. Consistency in dividend payouts

HINTS: Understand the characteristic sought in an asset to hedge systematic risk.

Q1177_LO77: What is the rationale behind diversification to mitigate nonsystematic risk?
a. To increase concentration
b. To reduce the impact of specific security risks
c. To eliminate all risks
d. To increase volatility

HINTS: Understand the purpose of diversification in managing nonsystematic risk.

Q1178_LO77: Which risk is often referred to as market risk?
a. Nonsystematic risk
b. Credit risk
c. Systematic risk
d. Interest rate risk

HINTS: Identify the risk often synonymous with systematic risk.

Q1179_LO77: What is the key characteristic of a security used to hedge systematic risk?
a. High beta
b. Low beta
c. Consistent dividends
d. Long maturity

HINTS: Recognize the characteristic sought in a security to hedge systematic risk.

Q1180_LO77: How does diversification contribute to risk management?
a. By increasing risk exposure
b. By reducing specific security risks
c. By concentrating risk
d. By ignoring market conditions

HINTS: Understand the risk management aspect of diversification.

Q1181_LO77: What is the primary goal of holding securities of different issuers in a portfolio?
a. To increase risk
b. To decrease liquidity
c. To diversify and reduce risk
d. To concentrate risk

HINTS: Identify the primary goal of holding securities of different issuers.

Q1182_LO77: Which risk is more controllable through individual company decisions?
a. Systematic risk
b. Interest rate risk
c. Nonsystematic risk
d. Market risk

HINTS: Recognize the risk that can be influenced by company-specific decisions.

Q1183_LO77: In what way does diversification impact the correlation of assets in a portfolio?
a. Increases correlation
b. Decreases correlation
c. Has no impact on correlation
d. Changes the beta values

HINTS: Understand the impact of diversification on the correlation of assets.

Q1184_LO77: What is the primary reason for using derivative securities in hedging systematic risk?
a. To increase volatility
b. To eliminate risk
c. To hedge against market movements
d. To speculate on interest rates

HINTS: Identify the primary purpose of using derivative securities in hedging systematic risk.

Correct Answers & Explanations
Types of Risk

Q1125_LO75: Correct Answer: b EXPLANATIONS: Systematic risk is the risk that changes in the overall economy will impact individual securities.

Q1126_LO75: Correct Answer: b EXPLANATIONS: Systematic risk is generally caused by factors affecting all businesses, such as global security threats.

Q1127_LO75: Correct Answer: c EXPLANATIONS: Market risk results in a decline in the value of a portfolio when the overall market declines.

Q1128_LO75: Correct Answer: c EXPLANATIONS: Interest rate risk is the potential change in bond prices caused by market interest rate fluctuations.

Q1129_LO75: Correct Answer: a EXPLANATIONS: Existing bonds are viewed as less attractive and priced at a discount when interest rates rise.

Q1130_LO75: Correct Answer: b EXPLANATIONS: Bonds with longer maturities fluctuate more than those with shorter maturities when interest rates change.

Q1131_LO75: Correct Answer: a EXPLANATIONS: Market conditions impact interest rates, affecting the market price of bonds.

Q1132_LO75: Correct Answer: b EXPLANATIONS: Reinvestment risk is the challenge of maintaining the same income level when reinvesting proceeds.

Q1133_LO75: Correct Answer: b EXPLANATIONS: Reinvestment risk is challenging when interest rates decline.

Q1134_LO75: Correct Answer: b EXPLANATIONS: Inflation risk is sometimes called purchasing power risk.

Q1135_LO75: Correct Answer: c EXPLANATIONS: If an investment's yield is lower than the inflation rate, the purchasing power diminishes over time.

Q1136_LO75: Correct Answer: a EXPLANATIONS: Deflation is a prolonged period of falling prices.

Q1137_LO75: Correct Answer: b EXPLANATIONS: Falling prices make fixed-income payments more valuable as investors can buy more goods and services.

Q1138_LO75: Correct Answer: c EXPLANATIONS: Inflation risk is the effect of rising prices on investment returns and affects all businesses.

Q1139_LO75: Correct Answer: c EXPLANATIONS: If an investment's yield is lower than the inflation rate, the purchasing power diminishes over time.

Q1140_LO76: Correct Answer: a EXPLANATIONS: Nonsystematic risks are diversifiable risks unique to a specific industry, business, or investment type.

Q1141_LO76: Correct Answer: c EXPLANATIONS: Beta measures the volatility of an asset.

Q1142_LO76: Correct Answer: c EXPLANATIONS: A beta greater than 1.00 indicates that the security is more volatile than the market.

Q1143_LO76: Correct Answer: b EXPLANATIONS: Default risk is the potential for an investor to lose money under circumstances related to an issuer's financial strength.

Q1144_LO76: Correct Answer: b EXPLANATIONS: Business risk is caused by poor management decisions.

Q1145_LO76: Correct Answer: c EXPLANATIONS: Financial risk relates primarily to companies using debt financing (leverage).

Q1146_LO76: Correct Answer: b EXPLANATIONS: Call risk is the risk that a bond might be called before maturity.

Q1147_LO76: Correct Answer: a EXPLANATIONS: Reinvestment risk occurs when interest rates are rising.

Q1148_LO76: Correct Answer: a EXPLANATIONS: Prepayment risk is the risk of a borrower repaying principal on a loan or debt instrument before maturity.

Q1149_LO76: Correct Answer: d EXPLANATIONS: Currency risk is the possibility of an investment declining if the value of the currency in which it is denominated declines.

Q1150_LO76: Correct Answer: b EXPLANATIONS: Liquidity risk is also known as marketability risk.

Q1151_LO76: Correct Answer: b EXPLANATIONS: Regulatory risk results from changes in regulations.

Q1152_LO76: Correct Answer: b EXPLANATIONS: Legislative risk results from a change in the law.

Q1153_LO76: Correct Answer: d EXPLANATIONS: Political risk is specifically related to potential instability in the political underpinnings of a country.

Q1154_LO76: Correct Answer: d EXPLANATIONS: Sovereign risk captures the risk of a country defaulting on its commercial debt obligations.

Q1155_LO76: Correct Answer: a EXPLANATIONS: Nonsystematic risks are unique to specific industries, businesses, or investments and can be diversified away.

Q1156_LO76: Correct Answer: a EXPLANATIONS: Beta measures the volatility of an asset, indicating its sensitivity to market movements.

Q1157_LO76: Correct Answer: d EXPLANATIONS: A high beta security is considered riskier and more volatile than the market.

Q1158_LO76: Correct Answer: b EXPLANATIONS: Default risk involves the potential for an investor to lose some or all of their invested capital.

Q1159_LO76: Correct Answer: b EXPLANATIONS: Business risk is caused by poor management decisions.

Q1160_LO76: Correct Answer: c EXPLANATIONS: Financial risk is related to companies using debt financing, leading to credit or default risk.

Q1161_LO76: Correct Answer: b EXPLANATIONS: Call risk is associated with the risk that a bond might be called, leading to reinvestment risk.

Q1162_LO76: Correct Answer: d EXPLANATIONS: Prepayment risk is the risk of early repayment of principal on a loan or debt instrument.

Q1163_LO76: Correct Answer: b EXPLANATIONS: Prepayment risk is associated with falling interest rates, leading to refinancing.

Q1164_LO76: Correct Answer: c EXPLANATIONS: Currency risk is the possibility that an investment could decline due to a drop in its currency's exchange rate.

Q1165_LO76: Correct Answer: a EXPLANATIONS: Liquidity risk is also known as marketability risk.

Q1166_LO76: Correct Answer: b EXPLANATIONS: Regulatory risk results from changes to regulations, while legislative risk results from changes in the law.

Q1167_LO76: Correct Answer: d EXPLANATIONS: Political risk is specifically attributed to potential instability in the political underpinnings of a country.

Q1168_LO76: Correct Answer: d EXPLANATIONS: Sovereign risk ratings capture the risk of a country defaulting on its commercial debt obligations.

Q1169_LO76: Correct Answer: b EXPLANATIONS: Nonsystematic risk, unlike systematic risk, can be reduced through diversification.

Q1170_LO77: Correct Answer: b EXPLANATIONS: Systematic risk can be mitigated by finding an asset that moves in the opposite direction of the market, often achieved using derivative securities.

Q1171_LO77: Correct Answer: c EXPLANATIONS: Systematic risk is inherent in the system, affecting all securities.

Q1172_LO77: Correct Answer: c EXPLANATIONS: Portfolio managers often use derivative securities to hedge against systematic risk.

Q1173_LO77: Correct Answer: c EXPLANATIONS: Diversification involves holding securities of different issuers to reduce the impact of specific security risks.

Q1174_LO77: Correct Answer: c EXPLANATIONS: Nonsystematic risk, such as default risk, can be reduced through diversification.

Q1175_LO77: Correct Answer: d EXPLANATIONS: The most common way to hedge nonsystematic risk is by building a diversified portfolio.

Q1176_LO77: Correct Answer: b EXPLANATIONS: Portfolio managers seek assets with low correlation to the market to hedge systematic risk effectively.

Q1177_LO77: Correct Answer: b EXPLANATIONS: Diversification aims to reduce the impact of specific security risks.

Q1178_LO77: Correct Answer: c EXPLANATIONS: Systematic risk is commonly referred to as market risk, affecting the entire market.

Q1179_LO77: Correct Answer: b EXPLANATIONS: Securities with low beta, moving opposite to the market, are often used to hedge systematic risk.

Q1180_LO77: Correct Answer: b EXPLANATIONS: Diversification reduces the impact of specific security risks, contributing to risk management.

Q1181_LO77: Correct Answer: c EXPLANATIONS: Holding securities of different issuers aims to diversify and reduce risk.

Q1182_LO77: Correct Answer: c EXPLANATIONS: Nonsystematic risk is specific to individual companies and can be influenced by company decisions.

Q1183_LO77: Correct Answer: b EXPLANATIONS: Diversification tends to decrease the correlation of assets in a portfolio.

Q1184_LO77: Correct Answer: c EXPLANATIONS: Derivative securities are often used to hedge against market movements and mitigate systematic risk.

UNIT 3: Understanding Trading, Customer Accounts, and Prohibited Activities

Trade & Quotes

Q1_LO78: What does it mean when an investor is described as "bullish" in the securities market?
a. Expecting a market or stock to go down
b. Expecting a market or stock to go up
c. Holding a short position
d. Having a neutral market stance

HINTS: Recognize the meaning of the term "bullish" in market language.

Q2_LO78: In a hybrid position like a covered call, how is the market attitude determined for the investor?
a. Based on the covered call leg
b. Based on the option leg
c. Based on the short position
d. Based on the long position

HINTS: Identify the factor determining market attitude in a covered call position.

Q3_LO78: If an investor holds a long stock position, what is their market attitude?
a. Bullish
b. Bearish
c. Neutral
d. Hedged

HINTS: Recognize the market attitude associated with a long stock position.

Q4_LO78: What term describes an investor who believes a market or stock is likely to go down in value?
a. Bullish
b. Bearish
c. Neutral
d. Hedged

HINTS: Identify the term for an investor with a negative outlook on market or stock movement.

Q5_LO78: In a hedge involving a short stock position and a long call, what determines the market attitude?
a. Long call leg
b. Short stock leg
c. Both legs equally
d. Market conditions

HINTS: Recognize the factor determining market attitude in a hedge involving a short stock position.

Q6_LO78: If an investor is short a stock, what is their market attitude?
a. Bullish
b. Bearish
c. Neutral
d. Hedged

HINTS: Identify the market attitude associated with a short stock position.

Q7_LO78: How is the market attitude determined in a hedge involving a long put and a short call?
a. Long put leg
b. Short call leg
c. Both legs equally
d. Market conditions

HINTS: Recognize the factor determining market attitude in a hedge involving a short call position.

Q8_LO78: If an investor is bearish, what do they expect regarding market or stock movement?
a. Upward movement
b. Downward movement
c. Sideways movement

d. Random movement

HINTS: Identify the expected market or stock movement for a bearish investor.

Q9_LO78: What is the primary characteristic of a bullish investor's outlook on a market or stock?
a. Positive outlook
b. Negative outlook
c. Neutral outlook
d. Diversified outlook

HINTS: Recognize the key characteristic of a bullish investor's outlook.

Q10_LO78: In a covered call position, what is the investor's market attitude if the covered call leg represents the larger position?
a. Bullish
b. Bearish
c. Neutral
d. Market conditions determine

HINTS: Identify the market attitude when the covered call leg represents the larger position.

Q11_LO78: What does a bearish investor believe about a given market or stock?
a. It will remain stable
b. It will go up in value
c. It will go down in value
d. It is unpredictable

HINTS: Understand the belief of a bearish investor regarding market or stock movement.

Q12_LO78: If an investor is long a call option, what is their market attitude?
a. Bullish
b. Bearish
c. Neutral
d. Hedged

HINTS: Recognize the market attitude associated with being long a call option.

Q13_LO78: What term is used for a hybrid position that involves a long put and a short call?
a. Bullish position
b. Bearish position
c. Straddle
d. Strangle

HINTS: Identify the term for a hybrid position involving a long put and a short call.

Q14_LO78: In a straddle position, what determines the market attitude?
a. Long put leg
b. Short call leg
c. Both legs equally
d. Market conditions

HINTS: Recognize the factor determining market attitude in a straddle position.

Q15_LO78: What is the primary characteristic of a bearish investor's outlook on a market or stock?
a. Positive outlook
b. Negative outlook
c. Neutral outlook
d. Diversified outlook

HINTS: Recognize the key characteristic of a bearish investor's outlook.

Q16_LO79: What is a market order?
a. Executed at a specified limit price
b. Executed immediately at the best available market price
c. Placed with a time priority

d. Requires manual intervention for execution

HINTS: Recall the nature of a market order.

Q17_LO79: In a limit order to buy, what does the limit price represent?
a. Maximum purchase price
b. Minimum selling price
c. Average market price
d. Current market price

HINTS: Understand the significance of the limit price in a limit order to buy.

Q18_LO79: How are market orders prioritized compared to limit orders?
a. Market orders have no priority
b. Market orders always have priority
c. Market and limit orders have equal priority
d. Priority depends on the order size

HINTS: Recognize the priority of market orders over limit orders.

Q19_LO79: What is the key characteristic of a market order?
a. Executes at a specified limit
b. Executes at a specific time
c. Executes immediately at the best available market price
d. Requires manual confirmation

HINTS: Identify the primary characteristic of a market order.

Q20_LO79: For a sell limit order, what does "or better" mean?
a. At the limit price or higher
b. At the limit price or lower
c. At the average market price
d. At the current market price

HINTS: Understand the meaning of "or better" in a sell limit order.

Q21_LO79: In a buy limit order, what does "or better" mean?
a. At the limit price or higher
b. At the limit price or lower
c. At the average market price
d. At the current market price

HINTS: Understand the meaning of "or better" in a buy limit order.

Q22_LO79: What takes precedence when prioritizing market and limit orders?
a. Larger order size
b. Time priority
c. Price priority
d. Market conditions

HINTS: Recognize the factor determining priority between market and limit orders.

Q23_LO79: In the execution of orders, what does time priority refer to?
a. Order size
b. Order entry time
c. Priority based on order type
d. Priority based on market conditions

HINTS: Understand the concept of time priority in order execution.

Q24_LO79: How is the priority of limit orders determined when multiple orders exist at the same price?
a. By order size
b. By order type
c. By alphabetical order

d. By random selection

HINTS: Recognize the factor determining priority among limit orders at the same price.

Q25_LO79: What must be true for a limit order to be executed?
a. It must be a market order
b. It must have a specific time frame
c. It must be entered with time priority
d. The market must reach the limit price

HINTS: Identify the condition for the execution of a limit order.

Q26_LO79: What happens to market orders when entered in time priority?
a. They are prioritized based on order size
b. They are prioritized based on order type
c. They are executed immediately
d. They are delayed for manual confirmation

HINTS: Recognize the outcome of market orders entered in time priority.

Q27_LO79: What does a sell limit order aim to achieve?
a. Purchase securities at the lowest price
b. Sell securities at the highest price
c. Sell securities immediately
d. Execute at the market price

HINTS: Understand the objective of a sell limit order.

Q28_LO79: In a buy limit order, what is the condition for execution?
a. Market conditions must be favorable
b. The order size must be large
c. The market must reach the limit price
d. It must be a market order

HINTS: Identify the condition that triggers the execution of a buy limit order.

Q29_LO79: Why do market orders always take precedence over limit orders?
a. Market orders have higher priority
b. Limit orders are manually processed
c. Market orders are faster to execute
d. Priority is determined by market conditions

HINTS: Recognize the reason for the priority of market orders over limit orders.

Q30_LO79: What defines the limit price in a limit order?
a. Average market price
b. Maximum purchase price
c. Minimum selling price
d. Current market price

HINTS: Understand the significance of the limit price in a limit order.

Q31_LO80: What is a stop order in trading?
a. A live working order
b. A trigger price for an order
c. A market order
d. A standing time priority

HINTS: Recall the definition of a stop order.

Q32_LO80: When does a stop order become a live working order?
a. When the order is triggered
b. When the market is favorable
c. At the time of order placement

d. After the market closes

HINTS: Recognize the condition under which a stop order becomes active.

Q33_LO80: What happens when a stop order is triggered?
a. It becomes a market order
b. It becomes a limit order
c. It is canceled
d. It becomes a standing order
HINTS: Understand the outcome of a stop order being triggered.

Q34_LO80: How is a stop limit order different from a stop order?
a. A stop limit order is executed immediately
b. A stop limit order has no limit price
c. A stop limit order becomes a limit order after triggering
d. A stop limit order has no trigger price

HINTS: Differentiate between a stop order and a stop limit order.

Q35_LO80: In a stop order, what is the specified trigger price called?
a. Market price
b. Stop price
c. Limit price
d. Execution price

HINTS: Identify the term for the specified trigger price in a stop order.

Q36_LO80: When does a stop limit order become a live working order?
a. After the market closes
b. When the order is triggered
c. When the limit price is reached
d. At the time of order placement

HINTS: Recognize the condition for a stop limit order to become active.

Q37_LO80: What does a stop limit order transform into after being triggered?
a. A market order
b. A limit order
c. A stop order
d. An immediate execution order

HINTS: Understand the transformation of a stop limit order after triggering.

Q38_LO80: What type of order is a stop limit order after triggering?
a. Market order
b. Immediate execution order
c. Limit order
d. Stop order
HINTS: Identify the order type that a stop limit order becomes after triggering.

Q39_LO80: What is the primary function of a stop order?
a. To initiate immediate execution
b. To trigger a limit order
c. To specify the execution price
d. To become a live working order
HINTS: Recognize the primary purpose of a stop order.

Q40_LO80: How does a stop order differ from a market order?
a. Stop orders have time priority
b. Market orders have no trigger price
c. Market orders have limit prices
d. Stop orders are executed immediately

HINTS: Differentiate between stop orders and market orders.

Q41_LO80: When is a stop limit order canceled?
a. When the market is favorable
b. When the limit price is reached
c. When the stop price is reached
d. When the order is placed

HINTS: Understand the condition under which a stop limit order is canceled.

Q42_LO80: What is the unique characteristic of a stop order's trigger price?
a. It is set at the market price
b. It is set at the execution price
c. It is determined by market conditions
d. It is specified by the investor
HINTS: Recognize the unique feature of a stop order's trigger price.

Q43_LO80: In a stop order, when does the order become a market order?
a. After the order placement
b. When the trigger price is reached
c. When the market is favorable
d. After the market closes

HINTS: Identify the condition under which a stop order becomes a market order.

Q44_LO80: What role does a stop limit order play after being triggered?
a. It becomes a standing order
b. It becomes a market order
c. It becomes a limit order
d. It becomes an immediate execution order

HINTS: Understand the role of a stop limit order after being triggered.

Q45_LO80: What is the status of a stop order in terms of time priority?
a. Stop orders have no standing time priority
b. Stop orders are always prioritized
c. Stop orders have equal priority with market orders
d. Priority depends on market conditions

HINTS: Recognize the time priority status of stop orders.

Q46_LO81: What is the default time limit for a day order?
a. Until executed
b. Until the last business day of October
c. Until the close of trading on the day it is entered
d. Until the last business day of April

HINTS: Recall the default time limit for a day order.

Q47_LO81: When are GTC orders automatically canceled if unexecuted?
a. Every last business day of October
b. Every last business day of April
c. Every last business day of the month
d. Every last business day of the year
HINTS: Identify the conditions under which GTC orders are canceled.

Q48_LO81: What does a day order become if not filled by the end of the trading day?
a. Automatically renewed
b. Partially executed
c. Automatically canceled
d. Extended to the next day

HINTS: Understand the outcome of a day order if not fully filled.

Q49_LO81: What is the primary characteristic of a fill-or-kill (FOK) order?

a. Partial execution allowed
b. Order must be filled immediately or canceled
c. Order can be canceled at any time
d. Order must be executed at the opening or closing price

HINTS: Identify the primary feature of a fill-or-kill (FOK) order.

Q50_LO81: What is the key distinction between an immediate-or-cancel (IOC) order and a fill-or-kill (FOK) order?
a. Acceptance of partial execution
b. Execution at the opening or closing price
c. Order's duration
d. Order type applicability

HINTS: Differentiate between an IOC order and a FOK order.

Q51_LO81: What is the primary characteristic of an all-or-none (AON) order?
a. Order must be filled immediately
b. Order must be canceled immediately
c. Order must be executed in entirety or not at all
d. Order must be executed at the best available price

HINTS: Recognize the primary feature of an all-or-none (AON) order.

Q52_LO81: When does a GTC order remain working beyond specific days?
a. When requested by the broker
b. When automatically renewed
c. When specified by the customer
d. When filled on the last business day

HINTS: Identify the condition for a GTC order to continue beyond specific days.

Q53_LO81: What happens to a market-on-open order?
a. Immediate execution at the opening price
b. Execution throughout the trading day
c. Guaranteed execution at the closing price
d. Delayed execution at the opening price
HINTS: Understand the outcome of a market-on-open order.

Q54_LO81: Which type of order stands in time priority behind market orders?
a. All-or-none (AON) order
b. Immediate-or-cancel (IOC) order
c. Fill-or-kill (FOK) order
d. Limit order

HINTS: Differentiate between order types in terms of time priority.

Q55_LO81: What is the primary purpose of a good 'til canceled (GTC) order?
a. To ensure immediate execution
b. To allow partial execution
c. To remain valid until executed or canceled
d. To be executed at the closing price

HINTS: Recognize the primary function of a GTC order.

Q56_LO81: Which time restriction applies to market-on-close orders?
a. GTC
b. Day order
c. Market-at-open
d. Immediate-or-cancel

HINTS: Identify the time restriction applicable to market-on-close orders.

Q57_LO81: What is the primary purpose of a fill-or-kill (FOK) order?
a. Immediate execution or complete cancellation

b. Partial execution is acceptable
c. Execution at the closing price
d. Execution at the opening price
HINTS: Recognize the primary objective of a fill-or-kill (FOK) order.

Q58_LO81: When can an all-or-none (AON) order be held until the end of the day?
a. For GTC orders
b. For day orders
c. For IOC orders
d. For market orders

HINTS: Identify the scenario in which an AON order can be held.

Q59_LO81: What does an immediate-or-cancel (IOC) order accept?
a. Partial execution
b. Immediate cancellation
c. Execution at the closing price
d. Execution at the opening price

HINTS: Understand the acceptance criteria of an immediate-or-cancel (IOC) order.

Q60_LO81: What is the primary characteristic of a market-at-open or market-on-close order?
a. Guaranteed execution at the opening or closing price
b. Immediate execution at the market price
c. Acceptance of partial execution
d. Execution at the best available price

HINTS: Recognize the primary feature of market-at-open or market-on-close orders.

Q61_LO82: What is the bid price in a securities quote?
a. The lowest selling price
b. The highest buying price
c. The average market price
d. The closing price
HINTS: Understand the concept of the bid price.

Q62_LO82: How is the bid size expressed for a stock quote?
a. In decimals
b. In odd lots
c. In even lots
d. In round lots

HINTS: Recall the unit of measurement for bid size.

Q63_LO82: What does the ask price represent in a securities quote?
a. The highest buying price
b. The lowest selling price
c. The average market price
d. The closing price
HINTS: Identify the nature of the ask price in a quote.

Q64_LO82: How is the ask size expressed for a stock quote?
a. In decimals
b. In odd lots
c. In even lots
d. In round lots
HINTS: Recall the unit of measurement for ask size.

Q65_LO82: In a securities quote, what does the bid size indicate?
a. The number of shares someone is willing to sell
b. The number of shares someone is willing to buy
c. The average market size
d. The closing size

HINTS: Understand the significance of bid size.

Q66_LO82: What does the ask size indicate in a securities quote?
a. The number of shares someone is willing to sell
b. The number of shares someone is willing to buy
c. The average market size
d. The closing size
HINTS: Recognize the significance of ask size.

Q67_LO82: If an investor wants to sell a security, what price does she receive?
a. Bid price
b. Ask price
c. Closing price
d. Average market price

HINTS: Identify the price received when selling a security.

Q68_LO82: If an investor wants to buy a security, what price does she pay?
a. Bid price
b. Ask price
c. Closing price
d. Average market price

HINTS: Identify the price paid when buying a security.

Q69_LO82: How is the bid established for listed stocks on an exchange?
a. Highest sell limit
b. Highest buy limit
c. Lowest sell limit
d. Lowest buy limit
HINTS: Understand how the bid is determined on an exchange.

Q70_LO82: What establishes the ask for listed stocks on an exchange?
a. Highest sell limit
b. Highest buy limit
c. Lowest sell limit
d. Lowest buy limit

HINTS: Recognize the factor determining the ask on an exchange.

Q71_LO82: In the context of OTC stocks and bonds, what is the bid?
a. The highest buying price from a dealer
b. The lowest selling price from a dealer
c. The average market price
d. The closing price
HINTS: Identify the nature of the bid in OTC markets.

Q72_LO82: In the context of OTC stocks and bonds, what is the ask?
a. The highest buying price from a dealer
b. The lowest selling price from a dealer
c. The average market price
d. The closing price
HINTS: Recognize the nature of the ask in OTC markets.

Q73_LO82: What is the trading relationship between a customer and a dealer in OTC markets?
a. Customer sells at the bid, buys at the ask
b. Customer sells at the ask, buys at the bid
c. Customer sells at the average market price
d. Customer buys at the average market price

HINTS: Understand the trading dynamics in OTC markets.

Q74_LO82: In a securities quote, what does the bid represent?
a. The highest buying price

b. The lowest selling price
c. The average market price
d. The closing price

HINTS: Identify the characteristic of the bid in a quote.

Q75_LO82: In a securities quote, what does the ask represent?
a. The highest buying price
b. The lowest selling price
c. The average market price
d. The closing price
HINTS: Recognize the characteristic of the ask in a quote.

Q76_LO82: What does the bid price represent in a stock quote?
a. The lowest amount someone is willing to sell
b. The highest amount someone is willing to buy
c. The average price of the stock
d. The closing price of the stock
HINTS: Identify the role of the bid price in a stock quote.

Q77_LO82: How is size expressed in a stock quote?
a. In decimals
b. In percentage
c. In round lots (units of 100 shares)
d. In whole numbers

HINTS: Recall the unit of measurement for size in a stock quote.

Q78_LO82: What is the ask price in a stock quote?
a. The highest amount someone is willing to buy
b. The lowest amount someone is willing to sell
c. The average price of the stock
d. The closing price of the stock

HINTS: Recognize the purpose of the ask price in a stock quote.

Q79_LO82: What does the size represent in a stock quote?
a. The number of outstanding shares
b. The market capitalization
c. The number of shares available at the bid and ask
d. The average trading volume

HINTS: Identify the content of the size in a stock quote.

Q80_LO82: In a stock quote, what does the ask size indicate?
a. The number of shares someone is willing to buy
b. The number of shares someone is willing to sell
c. The total trading volume for the day
d. The number of outstanding shares

HINTS: Understand the meaning of the ask size in a stock quote.

Q81_LO82: What establishes the bid in quotes for listed stocks on an exchange?
a. Highest buy limit
b. Lowest sell limit
c. Average trading price
d. Opening price

HINTS: Recall the factor determining the bid in exchange quotes.

Q82_LO82: How is the ask established in quotes for listed stocks on an exchange?
a. Lowest buy limit
b. Highest sell limit
c. Average trading price

d. Opening price

HINTS: Recognize the factor determining the ask in exchange quotes.

Q83_LO82: What do market makers act as in the OTC market?
a. Buyers
b. Sellers
c. Both buyers and sellers
d. Intermediaries
HINTS: Identify the role of market makers in the OTC market.

Q84_LO82: In the OTC market, what does the bid represent?
a. The lowest bid from a market maker
b. The highest bid from a market maker
c. The average bid from all market makers
d. The closing bid from the previous day
HINTS: Understand the meaning of the bid in the OTC market.

Q85_LO82: How is the ask determined in the OTC market?
a. Lowest ask from a market maker
b. Highest ask from a market maker
c. Average ask from all market makers
d. Closing ask from the previous day

HINTS: Recognize the factor determining the ask in the OTC market.

Q86_LO82: Where does a customer sell to or buy from in the OTC market?
a. Other customers
b. Dealers
c. Brokers
d. Exchange floor traders

HINTS: Identify the counterparties in OTC market transactions.

Q87_LO82: What is the bid size in OTC market quotes?
a. The number of shares someone is willing to buy
b. The number of shares someone is willing to sell
c. The average trading volume
d. The number of market makers
HINTS: Recognize the content of the bid size in OTC market quotes.

Q88_LO82: What does the ask size indicate in OTC market quotes?
a. The number of shares someone is willing to buy
b. The number of shares someone is willing to sell
c. The total trading volume for the day
d. The number of market makers

HINTS: Understand the meaning of the ask size in OTC market quotes.

Q89_LO82: How is size determined in quotes for listed stocks on an exchange?
a. Highest buy limit
b. Lowest sell limit
c. Average trading volume
d. Opening price

HINTS: Recall the factor determining the size in exchange quotes for listed stocks.

Q90_LO82: In a stock quote, what does the ask represent?
a. The highest amount someone is willing to buy
b. The lowest amount someone is willing to sell
c. The average price of the stock
d. The closing price of the stock
HINTS: Recognize the purpose of the ask in a stock quote.

Correct Answers & Explanations
Trade & Quotes

Q1_LO78: Correct Answer: b EXPLANATIONS: A "bullish" investor expects the market or stock to go up in value.

Q2_LO78: Correct Answer: a EXPLANATIONS: The larger position in a hybrid, like a covered call, determines the market attitude.

Q3_LO78: Correct Answer: a EXPLANATIONS: An investor with a long stock position is considered bullish, expecting the stock to go up.

Q4_LO78: Correct Answer: b EXPLANATIONS: A "bearish" investor expects the market or stock to go down in value.

Q5_LO78: Correct Answer: b EXPLANATIONS: The larger position, which is the short stock position, determines the market attitude in this hedge.

Q6_LO78: Correct Answer: b EXPLANATIONS: An investor with a short stock position is considered bearish, expecting the stock to go down.

Q7_LO78: Correct Answer: b EXPLANATIONS: The larger position, which is the short call position, determines the market attitude in this hedge.

Q8_LO78: Correct Answer: b EXPLANATIONS: A bearish investor expects the market or stock to go down in value.

Q9_LO78: Correct Answer: a EXPLANATIONS: A bullish investor has a positive outlook, expecting the market or stock to go up.

Q10_LO78: Correct Answer: a EXPLANATIONS: The market attitude is determined by the larger position, which is the covered call leg in this scenario.

Q11_LO78: Correct Answer: c EXPLANATIONS: A bearish investor believes that the market or stock will go down in value.

Q12_LO78: Correct Answer: a EXPLANATIONS: An investor with a long call option is considered bullish, expecting the underlying stock to go up.

Q13_LO78: Correct Answer: c EXPLANATIONS: A position involving a long put and a short call is known as a straddle.

Q14_LO78: Correct Answer: c EXPLANATIONS: In a straddle position, the market attitude is determined by both legs of the position equally.

Q15_LO78: Correct Answer: b EXPLANATIONS: A bearish investor has a negative outlook, expecting the market or stock to go down.

Q16_LO79: Correct Answer: b EXPLANATIONS: A market order is executed immediately at the best available market price.

Q17_LO79: Correct Answer: a EXPLANATIONS: The limit price in a buy limit order represents the maximum purchase price.

Q18_LO79: Correct Answer: b EXPLANATIONS: Market orders always take precedence over limit orders.

Q19_LO79: Correct Answer: c EXPLANATIONS: A market order executes immediately at the best available market price.

Q20_LO79: Correct Answer: a EXPLANATIONS: Or better for a sell limit order means at the limit price or higher.

Q21_LO79: Correct Answer: b EXPLANATIONS: Or better for a buy limit order means at the limit price or lower.

Q22_LO79: Correct Answer: b EXPLANATIONS: Time priority takes precedence when prioritizing market and limit orders.

Q23_LO79: Correct Answer: b EXPLANATIONS: Time priority refers to the order entry time in the execution of orders.

Q24_LO79: Correct Answer: a EXPLANATIONS: The priority of limit orders at the same price is determined by their order size.

Q25_LO79: Correct Answer: d EXPLANATIONS: A limit order is executed when the market reaches the specified limit price.

Q26_LO79: Correct Answer: c EXPLANATIONS: Market orders entered in time priority are executed immediately.

Q27_LO79: Correct Answer: b EXPLANATIONS: A sell limit order aims to sell securities at the highest possible price.

Q28_LO79: Correct Answer: c EXPLANATIONS: A buy limit order is executed when the market reaches the specified limit price.

Q29_LO79: Correct Answer: c EXPLANATIONS: Market orders are prioritized over limit orders because they are faster to execute.

Q30_LO79: Correct Answer: c EXPLANATIONS: The limit price in a sell limit order represents the minimum selling price.

Q31_LO80: Correct Answer: b EXPLANATIONS: A stop order is a trigger price that, when reached, initiates an order.

Q32_LO80: Correct Answer: a EXPLANATIONS: A stop order becomes a live working order when the stock trades at or through the specified stop price.

Q33_LO80: Correct Answer: a EXPLANATIONS: When triggered, a stop order becomes a market order.

Q34_LO80: Correct Answer: c EXPLANATIONS: A stop limit order becomes a limit order after triggering, with a specified limit price.

Q35_LO80: Correct Answer: b EXPLANATIONS: The specified trigger price in a stop order is called the stop price.

Q36_LO80: Correct Answer: b EXPLANATIONS: A stop limit order becomes a live working order when the stock trades at or through the specified stop price.

Q37_LO80: Correct Answer: b EXPLANATIONS: A stop limit order becomes a limit order after being triggered.

Q38_LO80: Correct Answer: c EXPLANATIONS: A stop limit order becomes a limit order after being triggered.

Q39_LO80: Correct Answer: d EXPLANATIONS: The primary function of a stop order is to become a live working order when the trigger price is reached.

Q40_LO80: Correct Answer: b EXPLANATIONS: Unlike market orders, stop orders have a specified trigger price.

Q41_LO80: Correct Answer: b EXPLANATIONS: A stop limit order is canceled if the limit price is not reached after the stop price is triggered.

Q42_LO80: Correct Answer: d EXPLANATIONS: The trigger price in a stop order is specified by the investor.

Q43_LO80: Correct Answer: b EXPLANATIONS: A stop order becomes a market order when the stock trades at or through the specified stop price.

Q44_LO80: Correct Answer: c EXPLANATIONS: A stop limit order becomes a limit order with a specified limit price after being triggered.

Q45_LO80: Correct Answer: a EXPLANATIONS: Stop orders have no standing time priority and are triggered based on the specified price.

Q46_LO81: Correct Answer: c EXPLANATIONS: A day order is valid only until the close of trading on the day it is entered.

Q47_LO81: Correct Answer: b EXPLANATIONS: GTC orders are automatically canceled if unexecuted on the last business day of April and the last business day of October.

Q48_LO81: Correct Answer: c EXPLANATIONS: If a day order is not filled, it is canceled at the close of the day's trading.

Q49_LO81: Correct Answer: b EXPLANATIONS: A FOK order instructs to fill the order immediately or cancel it completely.

Q50_LO81: Correct Answer: a EXPLANATIONS: Unlike FOK orders, IOC orders accept partial execution.

Q51_LO81: Correct Answer: c EXPLANATIONS: An AON order must be executed in its entirety or not at all.

Q52_LO81: Correct Answer: c EXPLANATIONS: The customer must request that the GTC order continue for the next cycle.

Q53_LO81: Correct Answer: a EXPLANATIONS: A market-on-open order is designated to be executed at the opening of the day.

Q54_LO81: Correct Answer: d EXPLANATIONS: Market orders always take precedence over limit orders and are executed when entered in time priority.

Q55_LO81: Correct Answer: c EXPLANATIONS: GTC orders are valid until executed or canceled.

Q56_LO81: Correct Answer: b EXPLANATIONS: Market-on-close orders are designated to be executed at the close of the day.

Q57_LO81: Correct Answer: a EXPLANATIONS: FOK orders instruct to fill the order immediately or cancel it completely.

Q58_LO81: Correct Answer: b EXPLANATIONS: AON orders can be held until the end of the day for day orders.

Q59_LO81: Correct Answer: a EXPLANATIONS: IOC orders accept partial execution if the entire order cannot be filled.

Q60_LO81: Correct Answer: a EXPLANATIONS: These orders are designated to be executed at the opening or closing of the day, but the exact price is not guaranteed.

Q61_LO82: Correct Answer: b EXPLANATIONS: The bid price is the highest amount someone is currently willing to pay for the security.

Q62_LO82: Correct Answer: d EXPLANATIONS: Size for a stock quote is expressed in round lots (units of 100 shares).

Q63_LO82: Correct Answer: b EXPLANATIONS: The ask price is the lowest amount someone is currently willing to sell the security for.

Q64_LO82: Correct Answer: d EXPLANATIONS: Size for a stock quote is expressed in round lots (units of 100 shares).

Q65_LO82: Correct Answer: b EXPLANATIONS: Bid size is the number of shares that someone is willing to buy at the bid.

Q66_LO82: Correct Answer: a EXPLANATIONS: Ask size is the number of shares that someone is willing to sell at the ask.

Q67_LO82: Correct Answer: a EXPLANATIONS: When selling, the investor receives the bid price.

Q68_LO82: Correct Answer: b EXPLANATIONS: When buying, the investor pays the ask price.

Q69_LO82: Correct Answer: b EXPLANATIONS: The highest buy limit establishes the bid.

Q70_LO82: Correct Answer: c EXPLANATIONS: The lowest sell limit establishes the ask.

Q71_LO82: Correct Answer: a EXPLANATIONS: The bid is the highest bid from a market maker (dealer) in OTC markets.

Q72_LO82: Correct Answer: b EXPLANATIONS: The ask is the lowest ask from a market maker (dealer) in OTC markets.

Q73_LO82: Correct Answer: a EXPLANATIONS: A customer will sell to the dealer at the bid and buy from the dealer at the ask.

Q74_LO82: Correct Answer: a EXPLANATIONS: The bid represents the highest amount someone is willing to pay for the security.

Q75_LO82: Correct Answer: b EXPLANATIONS: The ask represents the lowest amount someone is willing to sell the security for.

Q76_LO82: Correct Answer: b EXPLANATIONS: The bid price is the highest amount someone is currently willing to pay for the security.

Q77_LO82: Correct Answer: c EXPLANATIONS: Size for a stock quote is expressed in round lots (units of 100 shares).

Q78_LO82: Correct Answer: b EXPLANATIONS: The ask price is the lowest amount someone is currently willing to sell the security for.

Q79_LO82: Correct Answer: c EXPLANATIONS: Size for a stock quote is the number of shares available at the bid and ask.

Q80_LO82: Correct Answer: b EXPLANATIONS: The ask size is the number of shares that someone is willing to sell at the ask.

Q81_LO82: Correct Answer: a EXPLANATIONS: The highest buy limit establishes the bid in quotes for listed stocks on an exchange.

Q82_LO82: Correct Answer: b EXPLANATIONS: The lowest sell limit establishes the ask in quotes for listed stocks on an exchange.

Q83_LO82: Correct Answer: c EXPLANATIONS: Market makers in the OTC market act as both buyers and sellers.

Q84_LO82: Correct Answer: b EXPLANATIONS: In the OTC market, the bid is the highest bid from a market maker.

Q85_LO82: Correct Answer: a EXPLANATIONS: In the OTC market, the ask is the lowest ask from a market maker.

Q86_LO82: Correct Answer: b EXPLANATIONS: Customers sell to dealers at the bid or buy from dealers at the ask in the OTC market.

Q87_LO82: Correct Answer: a EXPLANATIONS: The bid size in OTC market quotes is the number of shares someone is willing to buy.

Q88_LO82: Correct Answer: b EXPLANATIONS: The ask size in OTC market quotes is the number of shares that someone is willing to sell.

Q89_LO82: Correct Answer: c EXPLANATIONS: Size in exchange quotes is determined by the number of shares available at the bid and ask.

Q90_LO82: Correct Answer: b EXPLANATIONS: The ask is the lowest amount someone is currently willing to sell the security for.

Q91_LO83: What is the outcome of an investor taking a long position in a security?
a. A bearish position
b. Anticipating a rise in value
c. Maximum loss potential
d. Selling at a loss

HINTS: Recognize the result of taking a long position.

Q92_LO83: When does an investor incur the maximum loss in a long position?
a. When selling the security
b. If the security becomes worthless
c. At the time of purchase
d. When buying more shares

HINTS: Understand the risk associated with a long position.

Q93_LO83: What is the term for the amount an investor paid for a long position?
a. Cost basis
b. Sales proceeds
c. Market value
d. Capital gain

HINTS: Recall the terminology for the amount paid for a long position.

Q94_LO83: How does an investor open a long position?
a. By selling the security
b. By shorting the security
c. By buying the security
d. By borrowing the security

HINTS: Identify the action taken by an investor to open a long position.

Q95_LO83: What is the primary expectation of an investor in a long position?
a. The security will decline in value
b. The security will become worthless
c. The security will rise in value
d. The security will have a constant price

HINTS: Recognize the investor's expectation in a long position.

Q96_LO83: In a short sale, what does a short customer anticipate?
a. The security will rise in value
b. The security will become worthless
c. The security will have a constant price
d. The security will decline in value

HINTS: Understand the expectation of a short customer in a short sale.

Q97_LO83: What is the risk to a short seller in a short sale?
a. Maximum loss potential
b. The security becoming worthless
c. Limited loss potential
d. The security's price increasing

HINTS: Recognize the risk faced by a short seller in a short sale.

Q98_LO83: What is the profit in a short sale calculated by?
a. Selling price minus cost basis
b. Buying price minus selling price
c. Selling price minus buying price
d. Cost basis minus sales proceeds

HINTS: Understand the calculation for profit in a short sale.

Q99_LO83: How does an investor open a short position in a security?
a. By selling the security
b. By shorting the security
c. By buying the security
d. By borrowing the security

HINTS: Identify the action taken by an investor to open a short position.

Q100_LO83: What does it mean to "cover" a short position?
a. To sell the borrowed shares
b. To buy back the borrowed shares
c. To hold the short position indefinitely
d. To increase the short position

HINTS: Recognize the meaning of "covering" a short position.

Q101_LO83: What is the term for selling a stock short that one owns?
a. Selling short
b. Covering the box
c. Short against the box
d. Short covering

HINTS: Recall the term for selling a stock short that one owns.

Q102_LO83: Why was "short against the box" historically done by investors?
a. To profit from declining prices
b. To delay the realization of a capital gain
c. To avoid Regulation SHO violations
d. To achieve unlimited loss potential

HINTS: Understand the historical purpose of "short against the box."

Q103_LO83: What was the impact of the Taxpayer Relief Act on "short against the box"?
a. Increased its popularity
b. Eliminated its use for delaying capital gains
c. Limited the loss potential
d. Encouraged short selling

HINTS: Recognize the impact of the Taxpayer Relief Act on "short against the box."

Q104_LO83: What does the locate requirement in short sales involve?
a. Locating the broker-dealer
b. Locating the shares to be borrowed
c. Locating the market price
d. Locating the short seller

HINTS: Understand the purpose of the locate requirement in short sales.

Q105_LO83: What violation does executing a short sale before locating shares result in?
a. Violation of Regulation T
b. Violation of Regulation SHO
c. Violation of SEC Rule 10b-5
d. Violation of FDIC regulations

HINTS: Recognize the regulatory violation associated with not locating shares before a short sale.

Q106_LO83: What is the primary motive of an investor taking a long position in a security?
a. To borrow the security
b. To profit from a price decline
c. To own the security and profit from a price rise
d. To return borrowed shares

HINTS: Recognize the purpose of taking a long position.

Q107_LO83: What is the maximum loss potential for an investor in a long position?
a. Unlimited
b. The cost basis
c. The sales proceeds
d. The price of the security

HINTS: Identify the measure of maximum loss in a long position.

Q108_LO83: How is a long position opened and closed by an investor?
a. Selling the security
b. Borrowing the security
c. Buying and then selling the security
d. Owning and then selling the security

HINTS: Understand the process of opening and closing a long position.

Q109_LO83: What is the term for selling a security one does not own, anticipating a price decline?
a. Long position
b. Short position
c. Cost basis
d. Sales proceeds

HINTS: Recognize the concept of selling short.

Q110_LO83: What is the risk to a short seller?
a. Maximum loss is the sales proceeds
b. Limited to the cost basis
c. Unlimited loss potential
d. Tied to the price of the security

HINTS: Identify the risk associated with being a short seller.

Q111_LO83: What does "covering" a short position involve?
a. Selling the security
b. Buying back the security
c. Borrowing the security
d. Owning the security

HINTS: Understand the action of covering a short position.

Q112_LO83: What is the term for selling short a stock that an investor already owns?
a. Short against the box
b. Short sale
c. Covered short
d. Uncovered short

HINTS: Recall the term for selling short against stock already owned.

Q113_LO83: Why was "short against the box" historically used by investors?
a. To profit from a price rise
b. To delay the realization of capital gains
c. To avoid a short sale
d. To maximize losses

HINTS: Recognize the historical purpose of "short against the box."

Q114_LO83: What changed the usage of "short against the box" in 1997?
a. Taxpayer Relief Act
b. Regulation SHO
c. Stock Lending Rule
d. Short Sale Act

HINTS: Identify the regulatory change affecting "short against the box" in 1997.

Q115_LO83: What is the locate requirement associated with short sales?
a. The need to locate the broker's office
b. The need to locate the stock lender
c. The need to locate and secure shares for borrowing
d. The need to locate the investor's account

HINTS: Understand the purpose of the locate requirement.

Q116_LO83: What does "uncovered short" refer to in Regulation SHO?
a. A short sale executed without borrowing shares
b. A short sale executed with borrowed shares
c. A short sale with limited loss potential
d. A short sale with guaranteed profits

HINTS: Recognize the violation referred to as "uncovered short."

Q117_LO83: What is the primary goal of an investor in a short sale?
a. To borrow shares
b. To own the security
c. To profit from a price rise
d. To profit from a price decline

HINTS: Identify the objective of an investor in a short sale.

Q118_LO83: What is the risk to an investor in a short sale?
a. Limited to the sales proceeds
b. Unlimited loss potential
c. Tied to the cost basis
d. Equal to the size of the short position

HINTS: Understand the risk associated with being a short seller.

Q119_LO83: How is profit calculated in a short sale?
a. Short sale price minus cost basis
b. Cost basis minus short sale price
c. Sales proceeds minus cost basis
d. Cost basis plus sales proceeds

HINTS: Recognize the calculation for profit in a short sale.

Q120_LO83: What is the term for buying back borrowed shares in a short sale?
a. Closing the position
b. Opening the position
c. Initiating the position
d. Covering the position

HINTS: Understand the action of buying back borrowed shares in a short sale.

Q121_LO84: What characterizes a solicited trade?
a. Customer's unsolicited action
b. Introduction by a BD or representative
c. No trade ticket marking
d. Regulatory violation

HINTS: Recognize the key feature of a solicited trade.

Q122_LO84: How should solicited trades be marked on the trade ticket?
a. Marked "unsolicited"
b. No marking required
c. Marked "solicited"
d. Marked "discretionary"

HINTS: Identify the correct marking for solicited trades.

Q123_LO84: What distinguishes an unsolicited trade?
a. Customer's action suggested by BD
b. Introduced by BD or representative
c. Marked "unsolicited" on the trade ticket
d. Regulatory violation

HINTS: Recognize the defining characteristic of an unsolicited trade.

Q124_LO84: In discretionary trades, what are the three key elements known as?
a. Three Ds
b. Three Bs
c. Three As
d. Three Cs

HINTS: Identify the terminology for the three key elements in discretionary trades.

Q125_LO84: What constitutes a discretionary trade?
a. Customer's preauthorization
b. Customer's written approval
c. Representative's independent choice
d. Principal's authorization

HINTS: Recognize the defining factor of a discretionary trade.

Q126_LO84: How can discretionary trading authority be granted?
a. Verbally
b. Through actions
c. In writing
d. By email

HINTS: Identify the correct method for granting discretionary trading authority.

Q127_LO84: What is required for a discretionary trade to be properly entered?
a. Customer's verbal agreement
b. Principal's verbal approval
c. Principal's written approval
d. Representative's email approval

HINTS: Identify the necessary approvals for a discretionary trade.

Q128_LO84: How can a client revoke discretionary trading authority?
a. Verbally
b. In writing
c. Through actions
d. By email

HINTS: Recognize the correct method for revoking discretionary trading authority.

Q129_LO84: Why are accounts allowing discretionary trades closely supervised?
a. To limit profits
b. To ensure compliance with regulations
c. To increase risks
d. To encourage discretionary trading

HINTS: Understand the reason for close supervision of accounts allowing discretionary trades.

Q130_LO84: What features does a wrap account typically provide?
a. Asset allocation, portfolio management, and executions
b. Brokerage services only
c. Unlimited free trades
d. Fixed monthly fee

HINTS: Identify the services typically provided in a wrap account.

Q131_LO84: What is the fee structure for wrap accounts?
a. Fixed monthly or quarterly amount
b. Per-trade basis
c. Percentage of assets under management (AUM)
d. A and B

HINTS: Recognize the common fee structure for wrap accounts.

Q132_LO84: What regulatory requirements must a BD meet for wrap accounts?
a. Fiduciary requirements under the Investment Advisers Act
b. No specific requirements
c. Exempt from regulations
d. Self-regulation

HINTS: Identify the regulatory obligations for BDs with wrap accounts.

Q133_LO84: What must be disclosed in wrap account agreements?
a. Customer's personal details
b. Ability to get services separately for less cost
c. Brokerage fees only
d. Earnings projections

HINTS: Recognize a required disclosure in wrap account agreements.

Q134_LO84: What term describes a discretionary trade without proper authorizations?
a. Unauthorized trade
b. Uncovered trade
c. Unapproved trade
d. Unsupervised trade

HINTS: Identify the term for a discretionary trade without proper authorizations.

Q135_LO84: What additional elements are considered in discretionary trades, besides the three As?
a. Four Ps
b. Two Ts
c. Time and price
d. Size and color

HINTS: Recognize the additional elements considered in discretionary trades.

Q136_LO84: How is a solicited trade defined in the securities industry?
a. A trade suggested by a customer
b. A trade introduced by a BD or representative
c. An unsolicited trade with specific authorization
d. A trade marked as unsolicited

HINTS: Recognize the definition of a solicited trade.

Q137_LO84: What action is required for a trade to be marked as solicited?
a. Customer's approval
b. BD's approval
c. Representative's approval
d. Market's approval

HINTS: Identify the necessary approval for marking a trade as solicited.

Q138_LO84: What is the consequence of marking a solicited trade as unsolicited?
a. Regulatory violation
b. Enhanced supervision
c. Reduced fees
d. Increased disclosure

HINTS: Recognize the consequence of marking a solicited trade incorrectly.

Q139_LO84: How is an unsolicited trade defined in the securities industry?
a. A trade suggested by a customer
b. A trade introduced by a BD or representative
c. A trade without specific authorization
d. A trade marked as unsolicited

HINTS: Understand the definition of an unsolicited trade.

Q140_LO84: What is a discretionary trade?
a. A trade suggested by a customer
b. A trade initiated by a representative
c. A trade without preauthorization
d. A trade approved by a principal

HINTS: Recognize the definition of a discretionary trade.

Q141_LO84: What are the three key elements of all trades, including discretionary trades?
a. Action, amount, and asset
b. Authorization, amount, and asset
c. Action, authorization, and asset
d. Action, amount, and authorization

HINTS: Identify the three key elements of all trades.

Q142_LO84: In a discretionary trade, what is the significance of the three As?
a. Affordability, availability, and asset
b. Authorization, action, and asset
c. Action, amount, and affordability
d. Authorization, amount, and availability

HINTS: Understand the significance of the three As in discretionary trades.

Q143_LO84: What authorizations are required for discretionary trading?
a. Customer approval only
b. Representative's approval only
c. Principal and customer approvals
d. Market and customer approvals

HINTS: Identify the necessary authorizations for discretionary trading.

Q144_LO84: How can a client revoke discretionary trading authority?
a. Verbally
b. In writing
c. By phone call
d. Through email

HINTS: Understand the correct method for revoking discretionary trading authority.

Q145_LO84: What additional supervision is applied to accounts allowing discretionary trades?
a. Reduced fees
b. Enhanced supervision
c. Increased disclosure
d. Decreased monitoring

HINTS: Recognize the additional supervision applied to accounts with discretionary trades.

Q146_LO84: What characterizes a wrap account?
a. Fixed monthly fee
b. Variable quarterly fee
c. Percentage of assets under management
d. Flat transaction fee

HINTS: Identify a characteristic of wrap accounts.

Q147_LO84: What regulatory requirements do wrap accounts have to meet?
a. Securities Act of 1933
b. Securities Exchange Act of 1934
c. Investment Advisers Act of 1940
d. Securities Investor Protection Act

HINTS: Recognize the regulatory requirements for wrap accounts.

Q148_LO84: What does AUM stand for in the context of wrap accounts?
a. Assets Under Market
b. Assets Under Management
c. Account Under Management
d. Asset Utilization Measure

HINTS: Understand the acronym AUM in the context of wrap accounts.

Q149_LO84: What disclosure is required for clients with wrap accounts?
a. Fee reduction notice
b. Increased trading frequency
c. Availability of services at lower cost
d. Asset diversification notice

HINTS: Identify a required disclosure for clients with wrap accounts.

Q150_LO84: How are wrap accounts generally categorized?
a. Brokerage accounts
b. Investment advisory accounts
c. Savings accounts
d. Retirement accounts

HINTS: Recognize the typical categorization of wrap accounts.

Q151_LO85: What is regular way settlement expressed as for trades that settle the next business day?
a. T+1
b. T+2
c. T+3
d. T+4

HINTS: Recall the expression for trades settling the next business day.

Q152_LO85: When do settlements occur for trades expressed as "T+2"?
a. Same day
b. One business day after the trade
c. Two business days after the trade
d. Three business days after the trade

HINTS: Understand the settlement timing for trades expressed as "T+2".

Q153_LO85: What must happen by the end of the settlement day in a securities trade?
a. Buyer receives cash
b. Seller receives cash
c. Both buyer and seller receive cash
d. Buyer receives securities, and seller receives cash

HINTS: Recognize the key actions by the end of the settlement day.

Q154_LO85: What characterizes a cash settlement trade?
a. Settlement on the trade date
b. Settlement one day after the trade
c. Settlement two days after the trade
d. Settlement without cash involvement

HINTS: Understand the characteristic of a cash settlement trade.

Q155_LO85: In a cash settlement, when must both parties agree for the trade to occur?
a. After the trade date
b. Before the trade date
c. On the trade date
d. During settlement

HINTS: Recognize the requirement for both parties to agree in a cash settlement.

Q156_LO85: What is the difference between a cash settlement trade and a cash trade?
a. Settlement timing
b. Involvement of cash
c. Trade date
d. Margin borrowing

HINTS: Differentiate between a cash settlement trade and a cash trade.

Q157_LO85: When does settlement occur for option trades?
a. T+1
b. T+2
c. T+3
d. T+4

HINTS: Recall the settlement timing for option trades.

Q158_LO85: What is the required completion time for equity option exercises?
a. T+1
b. T+2
c. T+3
d. T+4

HINTS: Understand the required time for completing equity option exercises.

Q159_LO85: In the exercise of an index option, when is the payment made?
a. T+1
b. T+2
c. T+3
d. T+4

HINTS: Recognize the settlement timing for the exercise of an index option.

Q160_LO85: Define "good delivery" in the context of physical stock and bond certificates.
a. On-time delivery
b. Proper endorsement and signature
c. Fast delivery
d. Electronic delivery

HINTS: Understand the requirements for good delivery of physical certificates.

Q161_LO85: What does "exactly" mean in the context of good delivery rules?
a. Precisely
b. Approximately
c. Timely
d. Verbally

HINTS: Interpret the meaning of "exactly" in good delivery rules.

Q162_LO85: When is a stock power commonly used in the delivery of certificates?
a. For fast delivery
b. For electronic delivery
c. When certificates will be mailed
d. For physical endorsement

HINTS: Recognize the common use of a stock power in certificate delivery.

Q163_LO85: How is good delivery different for electronic holdings in street name?
a. No physical signatures required
b. Faster delivery
c. No endorsement required
d. No need for good delivery

HINTS: Differentiate the requirements for good delivery in electronic holdings.

Q164_LO85: What must happen for a certificate to be considered good delivery in electronic form?
a. Proper endorsement
b. Physical delivery
c. Electronic filing
d. Record keeping

HINTS: Understand the conditions for good delivery in electronic form.

Q165_LO85: In the context of wrap accounts, what is the meaning of "street name"?
a. BD's trading name
b. Physical address of the client
c. Holding securities in electronic form
d. Client's legal name

HINTS: Recognize the meaning of "street name" in the context of wrap accounts.

Q166_LO85: What does "T+1" and "T+2" refer to in regular way settlement?
a. Trade approval times
b. Transaction types
c. Settlement dates
d. Trading platforms

HINTS: Recall the meaning of "T+1" and "T+2" in regular way settlement.

Q167_LO85: When is cash settlement, or same-day settlement, typically required?
a. For stocks only
b. For bonds only
c. For option trades
d. For trades executed on the spot

HINTS: Identify the scenario where cash settlement is required.

Q168_LO85: What is a key requirement for a cash settlement trade to occur?
a. BD approval
b. Market approval
c. Agreement from both parties
d. Regulatory approval

HINTS: Recognize a key requirement for cash settlement trades.

Q169_LO85: When does settlement occur for option trades?
a. T+1
b. T+2
c. T+3
d. T+4

HINTS: Recall the settlement timeline for option trades.

Q170_LO85: For equity option exercises, when must the transaction be completed?
a. T+1
b. T+2
c. T+3
d. T+4

HINTS: Identify the timeframe for completing an equity option exercise.

Q171_LO85: What happens in the exercise of an index option?
a. Stock delivery
b. Cash payment
c. Bond issuance
d. T+1 settlement

HINTS: Recognize the outcome of exercising an index option.

Q172_LO85: What is the purpose of good delivery rules in the securities industry?
a. Transaction approval
b. Trade negotiation
c. Delivery of physical certificates
d. Electronic filing

HINTS: Understand the purpose of good delivery rules.

Q173_LO85: How must a certificate be endorsed for good delivery?
a. Signed by the issuer only
b. Signed by all owners
c. Unsigned
d. Signed by the buyer only

HINTS: Identify the correct endorsement for good delivery.

Q174_LO85: What does "exactly" mean in the context of good delivery rules?
a. Similar signature style
b. Matching initials
c. Verified signature
d. Different signature style

HINTS: Understand the meaning of "exactly" in good delivery rules.

Q175_LO85: When might a customer use a stock power in the delivery process?
a. To endorse the certificate
b. To replace a certificate
c. When mailing a certificate
d. To transfer ownership

HINTS: Recognize when a customer might use a stock power in the delivery process.

Q176_LO85: How is the delivery process different for electronic holdings in street name?
a. No requirement for physical signatures
b. Requires physical certificates
c. Lengthy delivery timelines
d. Separate delivery for each certificate

HINTS: Differentiate delivery for electronic holdings in street name.

Q177_LO85: In the context of settlement, what does AUM stand for?
a. Assets Under Market
b. Assets Under Management
c. Account Under Management
d. Asset Utilization Measure

HINTS: Understand the acronym AUM in the context of settlement.

Q178_LO85: What is the disclosure regarding wrap accounts and separate services?
a. Increased fees
b. Lower fees
c. Higher trading frequency
d. Availability of services at lower cost

HINTS: Identify the disclosure related to wrap accounts and separate services.

Q179_LO85: What category do wrap accounts typically fall under?
a. Brokerage accounts
b. Investment advisory accounts
c. Savings accounts
d. Retirement accounts

HINTS: Recognize the typical categorization of wrap accounts.

Q180_LO85: What regulatory requirements do wrap accounts have to meet?
a. Securities Act of 1933
b. Securities Exchange Act of 1934
c. Investment Advisers Act of 1940
d. Securities Investor Protection Act

HINTS: Identify the regulatory requirements for wrap accounts.

Correct Answers & Explanations
Position, Strategies, Trade Authority & Settlement

Q91_LO83: Correct Answer: b EXPLANATIONS: An investor taking a long position hopes that the security will rise in value.

Q92_LO83: Correct Answer: b EXPLANATIONS: The maximum loss for an investor in a long position occurs if the security becomes worthless.

Q93_LO83: Correct Answer: a EXPLANATIONS: The amount an investor paid for a long position is called the "cost basis."

Q94_LO83: Correct Answer: c EXPLANATIONS: An investor opens a long position by buying the security.

Q95_LO83: Correct Answer: c EXPLANATIONS: An investor in a long position anticipates that the security will rise in value.

Q96_LO83: Correct Answer: d EXPLANATIONS: A short customer in a short sale anticipates that the security will decline in value.

Q97_LO83: Correct Answer: d EXPLANATIONS: The risk to a short seller is that the price of the borrowed shares increases.

Q98_LO83: Correct Answer: c EXPLANATIONS: The profit in a short sale is calculated by the difference between the short sale price and the price at which the shares are bought back.

Q99_LO83: Correct Answer: b EXPLANATIONS: An investor opens a short position by selling (shorting) a security.

Q100_LO83: Correct Answer: b EXPLANATIONS: To "cover" a short position means to buy back the borrowed shares.

Q101_LO83: Correct Answer: c EXPLANATIONS: Selling a stock short that one owns is known as "short against the box."

Q102_LO83: Correct Answer: b EXPLANATIONS: Historically, it was used to delay the realization of a capital gain until a later time.

Q103_LO83: Correct Answer: b EXPLANATIONS: The Taxpayer Relief Act eliminated the use of "short against the box" for delaying capital gains.

Q104_LO83: Correct Answer: b EXPLANATIONS: The locate requirement involves locating the shares that will be borrowed for the short sale.

Q105_LO83: Correct Answer: b EXPLANATIONS: Executing a short sale before locating the shares is a violation of Regulation SHO.

Q106_LO83: Correct Answer: c EXPLANATIONS: When an investor takes a long position, they aim to own the security and profit from a rise in its value.

Q107_LO83: Correct Answer: b EXPLANATIONS: The maximum loss for an investor in a long position is the cost basis.

Q108_LO83: Correct Answer: c EXPLANATIONS: Investors open a long position by buying a security and close it by selling the security.

Q109_LO83: Correct Answer: b EXPLANATIONS: Selling a security one does not own, anticipating a price decline, is known as having a short position.

Q110_LO83: Correct Answer: c EXPLANATIONS: The risk to a short seller is that the price of the borrowed shares increases, leading to unlimited loss potential.

Q111_LO83: Correct Answer: b EXPLANATIONS: Covering a short position involves buying back the security.

Q112_LO83: Correct Answer: a EXPLANATIONS: Selling short against stock already owned is known as "short against the box."

Q113_LO83: Correct Answer: b EXPLANATIONS: It was used to delay the realization of a capital gain until a later time.

Q114_LO83: Correct Answer: a EXPLANATIONS: The Taxpayer Relief Act changed the rules related to "short against the box" in 1997.

Q115_LO83: Correct Answer: c EXPLANATIONS: Before executing a short sale, the broker must locate and secure shares for borrowing.

Q116_LO83: Correct Answer: a EXPLANATIONS: An "uncovered short" is a short sale executed before locating and securing the shares, violating Regulation SHO.

Q117_LO83: Correct Answer: d EXPLANATIONS: The primary goal of an investor in a short sale is to profit from a price decline.

Q118_LO83: Correct Answer: b EXPLANATIONS: The risk to an investor in a short sale is unlimited loss potential.

Q119_LO83: Correct Answer: a EXPLANATIONS: Profit in a short sale is calculated as the short sale price minus the cost basis.

Q120_LO83: Correct Answer: d EXPLANATIONS: Buying back borrowed shares in a short sale is known as "covering" the position.

Q121_LO84: Correct Answer: b EXPLANATIONS: A solicited trade is introduced by a BD or representative to a customer.

Q122_LO84: Correct Answer: c EXPLANATIONS: Solicited trades must be marked as "solicited" on the trade ticket.

Q123_LO84: Correct Answer: a EXPLANATIONS: An unsolicited trade is initiated by the customer without BD suggestion.

Q124_LO84: Correct Answer: c EXPLANATIONS: The three key elements in discretionary trades are known as the three As: Action, Amount, and Asset.

Q125_LO84: Correct Answer: c EXPLANATIONS: A discretionary trade is one where the representative independently chooses one or more of the three As.

Q126_LO84: Correct Answer: c EXPLANATIONS: Discretionary trading authority must be granted in writing by the client.

Q127_LO84: Correct Answer: c EXPLANATIONS: Properly entering a discretionary trade requires the client's written agreement and the principal's written approval.

Q128_LO84: Correct Answer: b EXPLANATIONS: A client must revoke discretionary trading authority in writing.

Q129_LO84: Correct Answer: b EXPLANATIONS: Supervision ensures compliance with regulations regarding discretionary trades.

Q130_LO84: Correct Answer: a EXPLANATIONS: Wrap accounts offer services like asset allocation, portfolio management, and executions for a fee.

Q131_LO84: Correct Answer: c EXPLANATIONS: Wrap account fees are often a percentage of assets under management (AUM).

Q132_LO84: Correct Answer: a EXPLANATIONS: BDs with wrap accounts must meet fiduciary requirements under the Investment Advisers Act.

Q133_LO84: Correct Answer: b EXPLANATIONS: Clients must be informed that they could get services separately for less cost.

Q134_LO84: Correct Answer: a EXPLANATIONS: An unauthorized discretionary trade lacks proper authorizations.

Q135_LO84: Correct Answer: c EXPLANATIONS: Besides the three As, discretionary trades also consider elements of time and price.

Q136_LO84: Correct Answer: b EXPLANATIONS: A solicited trade is introduced by a BD or representative to a customer.

Q137_LO84: Correct Answer: a EXPLANATIONS: Customer's approval is required to mark a trade as solicited.

Q138_LO84: Correct Answer: a EXPLANATIONS: Marking a solicited trade as unsolicited is a regulatory violation.

Q139_LO84: Correct Answer: a EXPLANATIONS: An unsolicited trade is initiated by the customer without BD or representative suggestion.

Q140_LO84: Correct Answer: c EXPLANATIONS: A discretionary trade is placed in the customer's account without preauthorization.

Q141_LO84: Correct Answer: d EXPLANATIONS: The three key elements of all trades are action, amount, and asset.

Q142_LO84: Correct Answer: b EXPLANATIONS: The three As of discretion are Authorization, Action, and Asset.

Q143_LO84: Correct Answer: c EXPLANATIONS: Both customer and principal approvals are required for discretionary trading.

Q144_LO84: Correct Answer: b EXPLANATIONS: Discretionary trading authority must be revoked in writing by the client.

Q145_LO84: Correct Answer: b EXPLANATIONS: Accounts allowing discretionary trades are supervised more closely.

Q146_LO84: Correct Answer: c EXPLANATIONS: Wrap accounts typically charge a percentage of assets under management.

Q147_LO84: Correct Answer: c EXPLANATIONS: Wrap accounts must meet the fiduciary requirements under the Investment Advisers Act of 1940.

Q148_LO84: Correct Answer: b EXPLANATIONS: AUM stands for Assets Under Management in wrap accounts.

Q149_LO84: Correct Answer: c EXPLANATIONS: Clients must be informed that they may get the same services for less cost on a separate basis.

Q150_LO84: Correct Answer: b EXPLANATIONS: Wrap accounts are generally considered investment advisory accounts.

Q151_LO85: Correct Answer: a EXPLANATIONS: Regular way settlement expressed as T+1 means settling on the next business day.

Q152_LO85: Correct Answer: c EXPLANATIONS: Settlement occurs two business days after the trade for T+2 expressions.

Q153_LO85: Correct Answer: d EXPLANATIONS: By the end of the settlement day, the buyer receives securities, and the seller receives cash.

Q154_LO85: Correct Answer: a EXPLANATIONS: A cash settlement trade settles on the trade date itself.

Q155_LO85: Correct Answer: b EXPLANATIONS: Both parties must agree before the trade takes place in a cash settlement.

Q156_LO85: Correct Answer: a EXPLANATIONS: A cash settlement trade settles on the trade date, while a cash trade doesn't involve margin borrowing.

Q157_LO85: Correct Answer: a EXPLANATIONS: Settlement for option trades is typically T+1.

Q158_LO85: Correct Answer: b EXPLANATIONS: Equity option exercises must be completed by T+2.

Q159_LO85: Correct Answer: a EXPLANATIONS: Payment in the exercise of an index option is made on T+1.

Q160_LO85: Correct Answer: b EXPLANATIONS: Good delivery involves proper endorsement and signature on physical certificates.

Q161_LO85: Correct Answer: a EXPLANATIONS: Exactly in good delivery rules means precisely matching the signature on the certificate.

Q162_LO85: Correct Answer: c EXPLANATIONS: A stock power is commonly used when certificates will be mailed.

Q163_LO85: Correct Answer: a EXPLANATIONS: In street name, no physical signatures are required for good delivery.

Q164_LO85: Correct Answer: d EXPLANATIONS: In electronic form, good delivery involves proper record keeping without physical certificates.

Q165_LO85: Correct Answer: c EXPLANATIONS: Street name refers to holding securities in electronic form on behalf of a customer.

Q166_LO85: Correct Answer: c EXPLANATIONS: T+1 refers to settlement on the next business day, and "T+2" refers to settlement in two business days.

Q167_LO85: Correct Answer: d EXPLANATIONS: Cash settlement requires delivery of securities and payment on the same day a trade is executed.

Q168_LO85: Correct Answer: c EXPLANATIONS: Both buyer and seller must agree before a cash settlement trade takes place.

Q169_LO85: Correct Answer: a EXPLANATIONS: Settlement for option trades is typically on the next business day (T+1).

Q170_LO85: Correct Answer: b EXPLANATIONS: Equity option exercises must be completed by the second business day (T+2) after the exercise.

Q171_LO85: Correct Answer: b EXPLANATIONS: In the exercise of an index option, the writer pays the owner cash, typically on the next business day (T+1).

Q172_LO85: Correct Answer: c EXPLANATIONS: Good delivery rules govern the delivery of physical stock and bond certificates.

Q173_LO85: Correct Answer: b EXPLANATIONS: A certificate must be endorsed (signed) by all owners whose name appears on the face of the certificate.

Q174_LO85: Correct Answer: a EXPLANATIONS: Exactly means the signature must match the name on the certificate.

Q175_LO85: Correct Answer: c EXPLANATIONS: A stock power is used when mailing a certificate for easier negotiation.

Q176_LO85: Correct Answer: a EXPLANATIONS: Electronic holdings in street name do not require physical signatures for good delivery.

Q177_LO85: Correct Answer: b EXPLANATIONS: AUM stands for Assets Under Management in the context of settlement.

Q178_LO85: Correct Answer: d EXPLANATIONS: Clients must be informed that they may get the same services for less cost on a separate basis.

Q179_LO85: Correct Answer: b EXPLANATIONS: Wrap accounts are generally considered investment advisory accounts.

Q180_LO85: Correct Answer: c EXPLANATIONS: Wrap accounts must meet the fiduciary requirements under the Investment Advisers Act of 1940.

Investment Returns & Corporate Actions

Q181_LO86: What are the dates involved in a cash dividend from a stock in the DERP order?
a. Distribution, Execution, Record, Payable
b. Declaration, Execution, Record, Payable
c. Declaration, Execution, Record, Purchase
d. Distribution, Execution, Redemption, Payable

HINTS: Recall the dates involved in a cash dividend from a stock in DERP order.

Q182_LO86: What is the primary difference in the distribution process of dividends between stocks and mutual funds?
a. Settlement delay for mutual funds
b. Trading on secondary markets for stocks
c. DERP order for mutual funds
d. Ex-dividend date for stocks

HINTS: Identify the key difference in the distribution process of dividends between stocks and mutual funds.

Q183_LO86: When does the ex-dividend date for a mutual fund occur?
a. Same day as the record date
b. Day before the record date
c. Day after the record date
d. Two days after the record date

HINTS: Recognize when the ex-dividend date for a mutual fund occurs.

Q184_LO86: What is the formula for calculating current yield?
a. Annual income / (Current market value)^2
b. Annual income / Current market value
c. Current market value / Annual income
d. Annual income * Current market value

HINTS: Remember the formula for calculating current yield.

Q185_LO86: What must be considered when calculating current yield from a quarterly dividend?
a. Use the quarterly dividend directly
b. Multiply quarterly dividend by 4
c. Convert quarterly dividend to monthly
d. Convert quarterly dividend to annual

HINTS: Pay attention to the frequency of the dividend when calculating current yield.

Q186_LO86: What is the formula for calculating capital gains or losses?
a. Sales proceeds * Adjusted cost basis
b. Sales proceeds / Adjusted cost basis
c. Sales proceeds + Adjusted cost basis
d. Sales proceeds - Adjusted cost basis

HINTS: Recall the formula for calculating capital gains or losses.

Q187_LO86: When is a position considered to have long-term gains?
a. Held for less than one year
b. Held exactly for one year
c. Held for more than one year
d. Held for exactly two years

HINTS: Understand the holding period for a position to be considered long-term gains.

Q188_LO86: How are long-term gains taxed compared to short-term gains?
a. Taxed at a higher rate
b. Taxed at a lower rate
c. Taxed at the same rate
d. Taxed only on income

HINTS: Identify the tax treatment difference between long-term and short-term gains.

Q189_LO86: What is the formula for calculating total return?
a. [Income received + Gains] / Cost basis
b. [Income received - Gains] / Cost basis
c. [Income received + Losses] / Cost basis
d. [Income received - Losses] / Cost basis

HINTS: Recall the formula for calculating total return.

Q190_LO86: Why is it essential to determine the holding period for tax purposes?
a. To delay the tax payment
b. To determine the tax rate
c. To identify the security type
d. To decide the sale timing

HINTS: Understand the significance of determining the holding period for tax purposes.

Q191_LO86: What is the primary difference in the distribution of dividends between stocks and mutual funds?
a. Record date
b. DERP order
c. Settlement date
d. Ex-dividend date

HINTS: Recognize the key difference in dividend distribution.

Q192_LO86: For mutual funds, what is the order of dates in the dividend distribution process?
a. Ex-dividend date - (record and payable date) - declaration date
b. Declaration date - (record and payable date) - ex-dividend date
c. Record date - (declaration and payable date) - ex-dividend date
d. Declaration date - (ex-dividend and payable date) - record date

HINTS: Recall the correct order of dates for mutual fund dividends.

Q193_LO86: What determines the ex-dividend date for a mutual fund?
a. FINRA
b. Exchange
c. SEC
d. Fund's board of directors

HINTS: Identify the authority responsible for setting the ex-dividend date for mutual funds.

Q194_LO86: How is current yield calculated for both stocks and bonds?
a. Dividend income / market value
b. Annual income / cost basis
c. Annual income / market value
d. Quarterly income / market value

HINTS: Calculate the current yield correctly.

Q195_LO86: When calculating current yield, what is essential if the question provides a quarterly dividend?
a. Multiply by 4
b. Divide by 4
c. Multiply by 12
d. Divide by 12

HINTS: Recognize the adjustment needed when dealing with a quarterly dividend.

Q196_LO86: What formula is used to calculate capital gains or losses?
a. Sales proceeds - cost basis
b. Sales proceeds + cost basis
c. Adjusted cost basis - sales proceeds
d. Sales proceeds - adjusted cost basis

HINTS: Identify the correct formula for calculating capital gains or losses.

Q197_LO86: How is adjusted cost basis determined?
a. Initial purchase price
b. Closing market value
c. Amount paid modified by adjustments
d. Dividend income

HINTS: Recognize the factors involved in determining adjusted cost basis.

Q198_LO86: What is the key factor in determining whether a gain is long-term or short-term?
a. Holding period
b. Type of investment
c. Dividend frequency
d. Trading frequency

HINTS: Identify the primary factor for distinguishing between long-term and short-term gains.

Q199_LO86: Why is the determination of long-term gains important?
a. It affects trading fees
b. It influences dividend payments
c. It impacts how gains are taxed
d. It determines settlement timelines

HINTS: Understand the significance of distinguishing long-term gains.

Q200_LO86: What is the formula for calculating total return?
a. [Gains - losses] / cost basis
b. [Income + gains] / market value
c. [Income received + gains] / cost basis
d. [Income - losses] / adjusted cost basis

HINTS: Calculate total return using the correct formula.

Q201_LO86: In the context of total return, what does "cost basis" represent?
a. Initial investment
b. Market value
c. Adjusted cost basis
d. Dividend income

HINTS: Recognize the meaning of "cost basis" in the total return formula.

Q202_LO86: If a position yields $500 in dividends and incurs a $200 loss upon closing, what is the total return if the cost basis is $10,000?
a. 2.0%
b. 3.0%
c. 5.0%
d. 7.0%

HINTS: Apply the total return formula to calculate the percentage.

Q203_LO86: When is the dividend no longer available to new owners of a mutual fund?
a. Record date
b. Ex-dividend date
c. Payable date
d. Declaration date

HINTS: Recognize the point at which the dividend is no longer available to new owners.

Q204_LO86: In the DERP order for stock dividends, what does "R" stand for?
a. Record date
b. Redemption date
c. Reinvestment date
d. Regulatory approval date

HINTS: Recall the meaning of "R" in the DERP order for stock dividends.

Q205_LO86: What is the primary purpose of the ex-dividend date in the dividend distribution process?
a. To determine the market value
b. To calculate the cost basis
c. To identify the day the customer becomes an owner of record
d. To establish when the dividend is no longer available to new owners

HINTS: Understand the primary purpose of the ex-dividend date.

Q206_LO87: What does ordinary income consist of?
a. Only earned income
b. Only investment income
c. Only passive income
d. A combination of earned, investment, and passive income

HINTS: Recognize the components of ordinary income.

Q207_LO87: Which type of income is derived from active participation in a trade or business?
a. Investment income
b. Passive income
c. Earned income
d. Portfolio income

HINTS: Identify the type of income derived from active participation.

Q208_LO87: What is the basis for eligibility for IRA contributions?
a. Ordinary income
b. Earned income
c. Investment income
d. Passive income

HINTS: Understand the basis for IRA contribution eligibility.

Q209_LO87: What is the taxation rate for long-term capital gains compared to ordinary income tax rates?
a. Always higher
b. Always lower
c. Always the same
d. It varies, but usually lower

HINTS: Recognize the general taxation advantage of long-term capital gains.

Q210_LO87: How are short-term capital gains taxed?
a. As ordinary income
b. At a fixed rate
c. Exempt from taxation
d. With a penalty tax

HINTS: Identify the taxation treatment of short-term capital gains.

Q211_LO87: What is the primary advantage of long-term capital gains taxation?
a. Fixed taxation rate
b. Lower tax rate compared to short-term gains
c. Exemption from taxation
d. Immediate tax credits

HINTS: Understand the primary advantage of long-term capital gains taxation.

Q212_LO87: How are capital losses used to offset gains for tax purposes?
a. On a percentage basis
b. Dollar-for-dollar
c. With a penalty
d. Exclusively against short-term gains

HINTS: Recognize the manner in which capital losses offset gains.

Q213_LO87: If an investor has losses exceeding gains, how much of those losses can be used to reduce ordinary income?
a. Up to $1,000
b. Up to $2,000
c. Up to $3,000
d. Up to $5,000

HINTS: Identify the limit for using losses to reduce ordinary income.

Q214_LO87: What is the term for losses carried forward to the next tax year with no time limit?
a. Rolling losses
b. Forward losses
c. Carried losses
d. Carryforward losses

HINTS: Recognize the term for losses carried forward indefinitely.

Q215_LO87: What is the purpose of a wash sale?
a. To evade taxes
b. To create a loss for tax purposes while maintaining ownership
c. To maximize capital gains
d. To generate passive income

HINTS: Understand the purpose of a wash sale.

Q216_LO87: Is a wash sale illegal?
a. Always
b. Never
c. Only in certain circumstances
d. It depends on the intent

HINTS: Recognize the legality of a wash sale.

Q217_LO87: To what types of positions do wash sale rules apply?
a. Only long positions
b. Only short positions
c. Both long and short positions
d. Only stock positions

HINTS: Identify the types of positions to which wash sale rules apply.

Q218_LO87: Besides the exact same security, what else is considered "substantially identical" in wash sale rules?
a. Any stock from the same issuer
b. Convertible bonds or preferred stock from the same issuer
c. Only options or rights
d. Stocks with similar dividends

HINTS: Understand the concept of "substantially identical" in wash sale rules.

Q219_LO87: How long is the time limit for carrying forward losses?
a. 1 year
b. 5 years
c. 10 years
d. Indefinitely

HINTS: Recognize the time limit for carrying forward losses.

Q220_LO87: What is the consequence of repurchasing the same security within 30 days in a wash sale?
a. Legal penalty
b. Tax exemption
c. Disallowance of the established loss
d. Capital gains tax reduction

HINTS: Identify the consequence of repurchasing the same security within 30 days in a wash sale.

Q221_LO87: What is ordinary income used for in determining an investor's tax rate?
a. Calculating deductions
b. Determining capital gains
c. Establishing tax credits
d. Setting income tax rate

HINTS: Recognize the purpose of ordinary income in tax rate determination.

Q222_LO87: Which of the following is NOT considered earned income?
a. Salary
b. Dividends
c. Bonuses
d. Tips

HINTS: Identify the type of income that is NOT considered earned income.

Q223_LO87: What is the primary factor that determines eligibility for IRA contributions?
a. Ordinary income
b. Adjusted gross income
c. Net investment income
d. Earned income

HINTS: Recognize the key factor for IRA contribution eligibility.

Q224_LO87: Which type of income is derived from active participation in a trade or business?
a. Passive income
b. Investment income
c. Earned income
d. Portfolio income

HINTS: Identify the type of income derived from active participation in a trade or business.

Q225_LO87: What is another term for investment income?
a. Active income
b. Passive income
c. Portfolio income
d. Ordinary income

HINTS: Recognize the alternative term for investment income.

Q226_LO87: In taxation, what is the distinguishing feature of long-term capital gains?
a. Taxed at a higher rate
b. Taxed as ordinary income
c. Tax rate changes frequently
d. Taxed at an advantageous rate

HINTS: Identify the distinguishing feature of long-term capital gains in taxation.

Q227_LO87: When are short-term capital gains taxed as ordinary income?
a. Held for more than one year
b. Held for less than one year
c. Held for exactly one year
d. Held for at least five years

HINTS: Recognize the holding period for short-term capital gains taxation.

Q228_LO87: How are capital losses used to offset capital gains for tax purposes?
a. On a percentage basis
b. On a dollar-for-dollar basis
c. As a tax credit
d. In a lump sum

HINTS: Understand how capital losses are used to offset capital gains.

Q229_LO87: If an investor has $2,000 in capital losses and $1,000 in capital gains, how much can be used to offset ordinary income?
a. $500
b. $1,000
c. $2,000
d. $3,000

HINTS: Apply the rule for using capital losses to offset ordinary income.

Q230_LO87: What happens to excess capital losses that are not used to offset gains or ordinary income?
a. They are forfeited
b. They can be carried forward indefinitely
c. They can only be carried forward for one year
d. They are converted to tax credits

HINTS: Recognize the treatment of excess capital losses.

Q231_LO87: What is the purpose of a wash sale in taxation?
a. To avoid taxes
b. To create a loss for tax purposes
c. To establish ownership of securities
d. To generate capital gains

HINTS: Identify the purpose of a wash sale in taxation.

Q232_LO87: Is a wash sale illegal?
a. Yes
b. No
-
-

HINTS: Confirm the legal status of a wash sale.

Q233_LO87: In a wash sale, what type of positions does the rule apply to?
a. Only long positions
b. Only short positions
c. Both long and short positions
d. Neither long nor short positions

HINTS: Recognize the application of wash sale rules to positions.

Q234_LO87: What does the wash sale rule consider as "substantially identical" to the sold security?
a. Securities of the same issuer
b. Securities with similar prices
c. Securities of different classes
d. Securities with different maturities

HINTS: Understand the concept of "substantially identical" in the wash sale rule.

Q235_LO87: How does the wash sale rule treat substantially identical securities in different forms?
a. They are not considered substantially identical
b. They are considered substantially identical
c. Only applies to long positions
d. Only applies to short positions

HINTS: Recognize the treatment of substantially identical securities in different forms.

Q236_LO88: What is the primary purpose of understanding broader market performance for investors?
a. Predicting individual stock prices
b. Setting reasonable return expectations
c. Timing market fluctuations
d. Identifying short-term trends

HINTS: Recognize the key purpose of understanding broader market performance.

Q237_LO88: Which index is considered the benchmark most professionals use when discussing overall market performance?
a. Russell 2000 Index
b. DJIA
c. S&P 500 Index
d. Wilshire 5000

HINTS: Identify the widely used benchmark for overall market performance.

Q238_LO88: What does the Russell 2000 Index primarily track?
a. Large U.S. companies
b. Small-company stocks
c. International equities
d. Bond market

HINTS: Recognize the primary focus of the Russell 2000 Index.

Q239_LO88: How many stocks does the Wilshire 5000 actually track, despite its name?
a. 500
b. 3,000
c. 5,000
d. 2,000

HINTS: Be aware of the number of components in the Wilshire 5000, despite its name.

Q240_LO88: What type of companies does the MSCI EAFE Index measure the equity market performance of?
a. Large U.S. companies
b. Developed markets outside the U.S. and Canada
c. Small-company stocks
d. Emerging market companies

HINTS: Identify the type of companies covered by the MSCI EAFE Index.

Q241_LO88: Which index is often cited as a measure of the market's performance in the popular press?
a. S&P 500 Index
b. Wilshire 5000
c. Russell 2000 Index
d. DJIA

HINTS: Recognize the index widely cited in the popular press for market performance.

Q242_LO88: In terms of market breadth, which index is considered the broadest measure of overall stock market performance?
a. S&P 500 Index
b. DJIA
c. Wilshire 5000
d. MSCI EAFE Index

HINTS: Identify the index considered the broadest measure of overall stock market performance.

Q243_LO88: Which composite index combines several bond indexes to represent the entire bond market?
a. DJIA
b. S&P 500 Index
c. Russell 2000 Index
d. Barclays Capital U.S. Aggregate Bond Index

HINTS: Recognize the composite index representing the entire bond market.

Q244_LO88: What does the acronym EAFE stand for in the MSCI EAFE Index?
a. Europe, Africa, and Far East
b. Europe, Australasia, and Far East
c. Emerging Asia and Far East
d. Eastern Asia, Far East, and Europe

HINTS: Understand the meaning of the acronym EAFE in the MSCI EAFE Index.

Q245_LO88: If an investor wants to focus on smaller companies in the overall market, which index would be most relevant?
a. DJIA
b. S&P 500 Index
c. Wilshire 5000
d. Russell 2000 Index

HINTS: Identify the index relevant for focusing on smaller companies.

Q246_LO88: Which index tracks slightly more than 500 stocks of large U.S. companies?
a. DJIA
b. S&P 500 Index
c. Russell 2000 Index
d. Wilshire 5000

HINTS: Recognize the index tracking slightly more than 500 stocks of large U.S. companies.

Q247_LO88: In setting reasonable return expectations, why is it important to judge an investment within the context of the portfolio's strategy?
a. To time market fluctuations
b. To identify short-term trends
c. To avoid broader market risks
d. To consider the portfolio's objectives

HINTS: Understand the importance of considering the portfolio's strategy in judging an investment.

Q248_LO88: Which index is designed to measure the equity market performance of developed markets outside of the U.S. and Canada?
a. DJIA
b. S&P 500 Index
c. Wilshire 5000
d. MSCI EAFE Index

HINTS: Identify the index designed for measuring the equity market performance outside the U.S. and Canada.

Q249_LO88: What does the acronym DJIA stand for?
a. Dow Jones Industry Average
b. Dow Jones Investment Assessment
c. Dow Jones Industrial Assessment
d. Dow Jones Industrial Average

HINTS: Understand the meaning of the acronym DJIA.

Q250_LO88: Which index is often used as the basis for several index mutual funds and ETFs?
a. DJIA
b. S&P 500 Index
c. Russell 2000 Index
d. Wilshire 5000

HINTS: Recognize the index used as the basis for several index mutual funds and ETFs.

Q251_LO88: Which index is often considered the benchmark for overall market performance by professionals?
a. Dow Jones Industrial Average
b. Russell 2000 Index
c. Wilshire 5000
d. MSCI EAFE Index

HINTS: Considered the broadest measure of overall stock market performance.

Q252_LO88: How many stocks does the Dow Jones Industrial Average (DJIA) track?
a. 100
b. 200
c. 500
d. 30

HINTS: Identify the number of stocks tracked by the DJIA.

Q253_LO88: What does the MSCI EAFE Index measure?
a. U.S. equity market
b. Global bond market
c. Developed markets outside the U.S. and Canada
d. Small-company stocks

HINTS: Recognize the focus of the MSCI EAFE Index.

Q254_LO88: Which index serves as the benchmark for smaller companies in the overall market?
a. Wilshire 5000
b. S&P 500 Index
c. Dow Jones Industrial Average
d. Russell 2000 Index

HINTS: Identify the index that tracks approximately 2,000 small-company stocks.

Q255_LO88: What is the basis for several index mutual funds and exchange-traded funds (ETFs)?
a. DJIA
b. S&P 500 Index
c. Wilshire 5000
d. MSCI EAFE Index

HINTS: Recognize the index that forms the basis for many index mutual funds and ETFs.

Q256_LO88: Which index is often cited in the popular press and tracks 30 large, well-known companies?
a. Russell 2000 Index
b. DJIA
c. Wilshire 5000
d. Barclays Capital U.S. Aggregate Bond Index

HINTS: Identify the index widely cited in the popular press.

Q257_LO88: What is the purpose of the Barclays Capital U.S. Aggregate Bond Index?
a. Measure overall market performance
b. Track small-company stocks
c. Combine several bond indexes
d. Measure foreign equities

HINTS: Understand the purpose of the Barclays Capital U.S. Aggregate Bond Index.

Q258_LO88: How many components does the Wilshire 5000 actually have, despite its name?
a. 4,000
b. 5,000
c. 3,500
d. 2,000

HINTS: Recognize the approximate number of components in the Wilshire 5000.

Q259_LO88: What does EAFE stand for in the MSCI EAFE Index?
a. Europe, Asia, and Far East
b. Eastern Asia and Far East
c. Europe, Australasia, and Far East
d. Euro-Asian Foreign Entities

HINTS: Identify the correct expansion of the acronym EAFE.

Q260_LO88: Which index is designed to measure the equity market performance of developed markets outside the U.S. and Canada?
a. S&P 500 Index
b. Russell 2000 Index
c. Wilshire 5000
d. MSCI EAFE Index

HINTS: Recognize the focus of the MSCI EAFE Index.

Q261_LO88: If a security is in a bear market but still outperforming the market as a whole, what does this suggest?
a. The security is overvalued
b. The market is strongly bullish
c. The security has a negative return
d. Context is important in evaluating performance

HINTS: Consider the significance of a security outperforming in a bear market.

Q262_LO88: How can an investment be judged within the context of a portfolio's strategy?
a. By comparing it to other individual securities
b. By assessing its absolute return
c. By comparing it to an appropriate benchmark
d. By considering its risk alone

HINTS: Understand how to judge an investment within the context of a portfolio's strategy.

Q263_LO88: Why is it essential for investors to understand how the broader market is performing?
a. To maximize returns
b. To minimize risk
c. To set reasonable return expectations
d. To avoid market fluctuations

HINTS: Recognize the importance of understanding broader market performance for investors.

Q264_LO88: What is the role of a benchmark in evaluating investment performance?
a. To provide absolute return
b. To compare performance against a standard
c. To predict market trends
d. To eliminate market risk

HINTS: Understand the role of a benchmark in evaluating investment performance.

Q265_LO88: What does the term "benchmark" mean in the context of investments?
a. A guaranteed return
b. A standard for comparison
c. A risk-free investment
d. A speculative investment

HINTS: Identify the meaning of the term "benchmark" in the context of investments.

Q266_LO89: What is the primary reason for a company to declare a stock dividend?
a. Attracting new investors
b. Paying cash dividends
c. Reinvesting profits for business purposes
d. Reducing the number of outstanding shares

HINTS: Consider the purpose of a stock dividend.

Q267_LO89: How does a stock dividend impact the cost per share for shareholders?
a. It remains unchanged
b. It increases
c. It decreases
d. It fluctuates

HINTS: Recognize the effect of a stock dividend on the cost per share.

Q268_LO89: What is the tax implication at the time of a stock split?
a. Tax event with immediate consequences
b. No tax event, no implications
c. Taxable event for shareholders
d. Tax-free event for the company

HINTS: Understand the tax implications during a stock split.

Q269_LO89: In a forward stock split, what happens to the number of shares and the price per share?
a. Both increase
b. Both decrease
c. Number increases, price decreases
d. Number decreases, price increases

HINTS: Identify the impact of a forward stock split on shares and price.

Q270_LO89: How is a forward stock split characterized in terms of share distribution?
a. Even split only
b. Uneven split only
c. Both even and uneven splits
d. No specific ratio

HINTS: Recognize the types of share distribution in a forward split.

Q271_LO89: When does the total market value of shares remain unchanged in a forward split?
a. Before and after the split
b. Only after the split
c. Only before the split
d. Depends on the stock price

HINTS: Understand when the total market value remains constant.

Q272_LO89: What effect does a reverse stock split have on the number and price of shares?
a. Both increase
b. Both decrease
c. Number increases, price decreases
d. Number decreases, price increases

HINTS: Identify the impact of a reverse stock split on shares and price.

Q273_LO89: How is a reverse stock split characterized in terms of share distribution?
a. Even split only
b. Uneven split only
c. Both even and uneven splits
d. No specific ratio

HINTS: Recognize the types of share distribution in a reverse split.

Q274_LO89: What is the primary reason for a company to declare a reverse stock split?
a. Attracting new investors
b. Reducing the stock price
c. Complying with listing criteria
d. Issuing additional shares

HINTS: Consider the purpose of a reverse stock split.

Q275_LO89: In a reverse split, what happens to the cost basis per share?
a. It remains unchanged
b. It increases
c. It decreases
d. It depends on market conditions

HINTS: Identify the impact of a reverse split on the cost basis per share.

Q276_LO89: How is the total value of an investor's position affected in a reverse split?
a. It increases
b. It decreases
c. It remains unchanged
d. It fluctuates

HINTS: Understand the impact on the total value of an investor's position.

Q277_LO89: What is the mathematical relationship between the number of shares and the price per share in a stock split?
a. Directly proportional
b. Inversely proportional
c. No relationship
d. Exponential relationship

HINTS: Understand the mathematical relationship in a stock split.

Q278_LO89: When might a company consider a forward stock split?
a. To reduce the number of shares
b. To increase the stock price
c. To make the stock price attractive
d. To issue additional shares

HINTS: Identify the circumstances for considering a forward stock split.

Q279_LO89: What is the purpose of calculating cost basis adjustments for stock dividends and stock splits?
a. To maximize shareholder profits
b. To comply with tax regulations
c. To determine total market value
d. To adjust share ownership

HINTS: Recognize the purpose of calculating cost basis adjustments.

Q280_LO89: Why might a company opt for a reverse stock split?
a. To attract new investors
b. To increase the number of outstanding shares
c. To comply with stock exchange listing criteria
d. To issue dividends

HINTS: Consider the reasons for a company to choose a reverse stock split.

Q281_LO89: What is the primary reason for a company to declare a stock dividend instead of paying cash dividends?
a. Tax benefits for shareholders
b. To attract more investors
c. To reinvest profits for business purposes
d. To increase the market value of shares

HINTS: Consider the purpose of a stock dividend.

Q282_LO89: How is the cost per share adjusted in the case of a stock dividend?
a. Adjusted upward
b. Remains unchanged
c. Adjusted downward
d. Doubled

HINTS: Recognize the impact on the cost per share in a stock dividend.

Q283_LO89: What is the tax status of the stock dividend itself?
a. Tax-deductible for the company
b. Taxable for shareholders
c. Non-taxable
d. Subject to capital gains tax

HINTS: Identify the tax status of the stock dividend.

Q284_LO89: In a forward stock split, what happens to the number of shares and the price per share?
a. Both increase
b. Both decrease
c. Number increases, price decreases
d. Number decreases, price increases

HINTS: Understand the impact of a forward stock split.

Q285_LO89: How is a forward stock split characterized in terms of the number of shares received by investors?
a. Even split only
b. Uneven split only
c. Both even and uneven split
d. No specific pattern

HINTS: Recognize the types of splits in a forward split.

Q286_LO89: What happens to the cost basis per share in a forward split?
a. Remains unchanged
b. Adjusted upward
c. Adjusted downward
d. Doubled

HINTS: Identify the impact on the cost basis per share in a forward split.

Q287_LO89: When might a corporation decide to do a reverse stock split?
a. To attract more investors
b. To increase the market value of shares
c. When the stock price is too low
d. To reinvest profits

HINTS: Recognize the circumstances leading to a reverse stock split.

Q288_LO89: In a reverse stock split, what happens to the number of shares and the price per share?
a. Both increase
b. Both decrease
c. Number increases, price decreases
d. Number decreases, price increases

HINTS: Understand the impact of a reverse stock split.

Q289_LO89: How is a reverse stock split characterized in terms of the number of shares received by investors?
a. Even split only
b. Uneven split only
c. Both even and uneven split
d. No specific pattern

HINTS: Recognize the types of splits in a reverse split.

Q290_LO89: What happens to the cost basis per share in a reverse split?
a. Remains unchanged
b. Adjusted upward
c. Adjusted downward
d. Doubled

HINTS: Identify the impact on the cost basis per share in a reverse split.

Q291_LO89: At the time of a stock split, what are the tax implications?
a. Tax event occurs
b. Tax implications for shareholders
c. No tax event
d. Only taxable for the company

HINTS: Consider the tax implications at the time of a stock split.

Q292_LO89: When may the adjusted cost per share have tax consequences for shareholders?
a. At the time of the split
b. When the shares are sold
c. Only in the case of a reverse split
d. Only in the case of a forward split

HINTS: Understand when the adjusted cost per share may have tax consequences.

Q293_LO89: What is the total market value of the ownership interest after a forward split?
a. Decreases
b. Increases
c. Remains unchanged
d. Cannot be determined

HINTS: Recognize the impact on the total market value after a forward split.

Q294_LO89: Why might a company declare a reverse stock split?
a. To decrease the market value of shares
b. To combat delisting due to a low stock price
c. To attract fewer investors
d. To reinvest profits

HINTS: Identify the reason for declaring a reverse stock split.

Q295_LO89: In a forward stock split, what happens to the total market value of the ownership interest?
a. Decreases
b. Increases
c. Remains unchanged
d. Doubles

HINTS: Understand the impact on the total market value after a forward split.

Q296_LO90: What happens to the shareholders' old shares in a typical merger?
a. They are sold in the open market
b. They are canceled
c. They are converted to cash
d. They remain unchanged

HINTS: Consider the outcome for shareholders in a merger.

Q297_LO90: How do shareholders of the acquired company benefit in a typical acquisition?
a. Receive cash only
b. Receive shares of the acquiring company
c. Keep their old shares
d. Receive a discount on new shares

HINTS: Identify the benefit for shareholders in a typical acquisition.

Q298_LO90: What is the key outcome for shareholders in a spin-off?
a. Their shares are canceled
b. They receive shares of the new subsidiary
c. They receive cash
d. They keep their old shares

HINTS: Recognize the key outcome for shareholders in a spin-off.

Q299_LO90: Why might a company choose to engage in a share buyback?
a. To increase the number of available shares
b. To reduce the value of existing shares
c. To decrease shareholder value
d. To increase shareholder value

HINTS: Understand the purpose of a share buyback.

Q300_LO90: What impact does a buyback have on the number of shares available in the market?
a. Increases
b. Decreases
c. Remains unchanged
d. Doubles

HINTS: Recognize the impact of a buyback on the number of available shares.

Q301_LO90: What is a tender offer in the context of corporate actions?
a. A discount on share purchases
b. An offer to buy a security from owners directly
c. A public offering of new shares
d. A share repurchase program

HINTS: Identify the definition of a tender offer.

Q302_LO90: How is a tender offer different from buying shares in the open market?
a. Tender offers are always hostile
b. Tender offers involve buying shares from owners directly
c. Tender offers are only for debt securities
d. Tender offers are less common

HINTS: Distinguish the unique aspect of a tender offer.

Q303_LO90: When might a corporation make a tender offer on its own debt?
a. To increase debt outstanding
b. To retire debt early
c. To reduce shareholder value
d. To issue more convertible securities

HINTS: Recognize a scenario for a corporation making a tender offer on its own debt.

Q304_LO90: What is the primary reason for a corporation to engage in a spin-off?
a. To increase shareholder value
b. To form a subsidiary
c. To attract more investors
d. To retire outstanding debt

HINTS: Identify the primary reason for a corporation to undertake a spin-off.

Q305_LO90: In a share buyback, what effect does it have on the value of existing shares?
a. Increases
b. Decreases
c. Remains unchanged
d. Doubles

HINTS: Understand the impact of a share buyback on the value of existing shares.

Q306_LO90: What is a key advantage of a share buyback for a company?
a. Increases the number of outstanding shares
b. Decreases shareholder value
c. Reduces the number of outstanding shares
d. Increases dividend payments

HINTS: Recognize a key advantage of a share buyback.

Q307_LO90: What type of action is a spin-off in terms of corporate restructuring?
a. Consolidation
b. Expansion
c. Separation
d. Merger

HINTS: Understand the nature of a spin-off in corporate restructuring.

Q308_LO90: How are tender offers related to acquisitions?
a. Tender offers are only for hostile takeovers
b. Tender offers are never used in acquisitions
c. Tender offers can be used in acquisitions to buy target company shares
d. Tender offers are only for buying debt securities

HINTS: Recognize the relationship between tender offers and acquisitions.

Q309_LO90: What happens to the market value of a company's shares in a buyback?
a. Increases
b. Decreases
c. Remains unchanged
d. Doubles

HINTS: Understand the impact of a buyback on the market value of shares.

Q310_LO90: How are shareholders' old shares treated in an acquisition?
a. Converted to cash
b. Canceled
c. Remain unchanged
d. Exchanged for new shares

HINTS: Identify the treatment of shareholders' old shares in an acquisition.

Q311_LO90: What occurs in a merger?
a. Shareholders receive new shares of the acquiring company
b. Shareholders of both companies receive new shares of the combined company
c. Shareholders receive cash payments
d. Shareholders retain their old shares

HINTS: Consider the outcome of a typical merger.

Q312_LO90: What is the primary result of an acquisition?
a. Issuance of new shares to shareholders of the acquiring company
b. Shareholders of the acquired company receive shares of the acquiring company
c. Cancellation of all shares involved
d. Shareholders retain their old shares

HINTS: Identify the key outcome of a typical acquisition.

Q313_LO90: How is a spin-off different from a merger or acquisition?
a. Shareholders receive cash payments
b. Formation of a subsidiary company
c. Shareholders retain their old shares
d. Shareholders receive shares of the acquiring company

HINTS: Recognize the distinctive feature of a spin-off.

Q314_LO90: What is a buyback, and why might a company engage in it?
a. Selling shares to external investors
b. Buying shares of another company
c. Companies buy their own outstanding shares
d. Issuing new shares to the public

HINTS: Understand the concept and purpose of a buyback.

Q315_LO90: Why do companies prefer share buybacks over paying dividends?
a. Dividends are tax-deductible
b. Share buybacks increase the number of available shares
c. Buybacks decrease the value of shares
d. Reduces the number of shares available and increases share value

HINTS: Consider the rationale behind companies choosing buybacks.

Q316_LO90: What is a tender offer in the context of corporate actions?
a. Offering new shares to the public
b. A direct purchase of securities from owners
c. Issuing debt to retire outstanding debt
d. Offering shares at a discounted price

HINTS: Understand the nature of a tender offer.

Q317_LO90: When might a company make a tender offer on its own debt?
a. To increase the company's debt
b. To retire the debt early
c. To issue more convertible securities
d. To acquire another company

HINTS: Identify the purpose of a tender offer on a company's own debt.

Q318_LO90: In a spin-off, what happens to the newly formed corporation's shares?
a. Distributed to the acquiring company
b. Retained by the original corporation
c. Issued to the shareholders of the original company
d. Sold to external investors

HINTS: Recognize the distribution of shares in a spin-off.

Q319_LO90: What is the effect of a buyback on the number of available shares?
a. Increases the number of available shares
b. Decreases the number of available shares
c. Has no impact on available shares
d. Depends on the market conditions

HINTS: Understand the impact of a buyback on the number of available shares.

Q320_LO90: What motivates companies to engage in share buybacks?
a. To issue more shares
b. To decrease shareholder value
c. To increase the value of remaining shares
d. To increase the number of outstanding shares

HINTS: Recognize the motivation behind companies opting for share buybacks.

Q321_LO90: How does a tender offer relate to the acquisition of another company?
a. Unrelated to acquisitions
b. A way to acquire the target company's shares
c. Used only for acquiring debt
d. An alternative to issuing new shares

HINTS: Understand the role of a tender offer in acquiring another company.

Q322_LO90: What distinguishes a spin-off from a merger or acquisition in terms of shares?
a. No shares are exchanged
b. New shares are issued to shareholders
c. Old shares are canceled
d. Original company retains all shares

HINTS: Identify the share-related characteristic of a spin-off.

Q323_LO90: In a buyback, what impact does it have on the value of remaining shares?
a. Decreases the value
b. Increases the value
c. No impact on the value
d. Doubles the value

HINTS: Recognize the effect of a buyback on the value of remaining shares.

Q324_LO90: What is the primary focus of a tender offer on convertible securities in an acquisition?
a. To increase the number of convertible securities
b. To retire convertible securities early
c. To issue new convertible securities
d. To decrease the market value of convertible securities

HINTS: Identify the objective of a tender offer on convertible securities in an acquisition.

Q325_LO90: When might a company consider a buyback as a strategic move?
a. To issue more shares
b. To increase shareholder dilution
c. To combat market volatility
d. To adjust the capital structure and increase value

HINTS: Understand the strategic considerations behind a buyback.

Q326_LO91: What is the tax treatment for shareholders receiving additional shares through a stock split?
a. Taxable event
b. Tax-free event
c. Capital gain event
d. Capital loss event

HINTS: Consider the tax consequences of stock splits.

Q327_LO91: In a merger, when may a tax event occur for shareholders?
a. When receiving stock
b. When receiving cash
c. Always a tax-free event
d. Only for stockholders

HINTS: Recognize the tax implications in a merger.

Q328_LO91: What makes buybacks and tender offers different in terms of tax treatment?
a. Both are tax-free events
b. Buybacks result in capital gains, tender offers result in losses
c. Buybacks are taxable, tender offers are tax-free
d. Both are taxable events

HINTS: Distinguish between the tax treatment of buybacks and tender offers.

Q329_LO91: When are cash dividends generally considered a tax event for shareholders?
a. Always
b. Only for certain shareholders
c. When they exceed a specific amount
d. Only when paid to institutional investors

HINTS: Understand the tax treatment of cash dividends.

Q330_LO91: For notification requirements, what details should be included in a notice for stock dividends?
a. Title, date of declaration, and rate of the dividend
b. Title, date of record, and date of payment
c. Title, date of payment, and amount to be paid
d. Title, date of declaration, and amount to be paid

HINTS: Identify the essential details for notifying stock dividends.

Q331_LO91: What is the primary reason for the SEC's requirement of notice for corporate actions?
a. To increase administrative burden
b. To inform shareholders about market conditions
c. To ensure timely and accurate information for shareholders
d. To control corporate actions

HINTS: Recognize the purpose behind the SEC's notification requirements.

Q332_LO91: Why are stock splits and stock dividends generally not taxable events?
a. They result in capital gains
b. They involve the receipt of additional shares
c. They always involve cash payments
d. They are considered gifts

HINTS: Understand the tax treatment of stock splits and stock dividends.

Q333_LO91: In a tender offer, what is the predominant form of consideration offered to shareholders?
a. Additional shares
b. Cash
c. Stocks of the acquiring company
d. Warrants

HINTS: Identify the common form of consideration in tender offers.

Q334_LO91: When should notification of corporate actions be given, according to the SEC?
a. No specific timeline
b. At least 10 days after the record date
c. On or before the record date
d. At least 10 days before the record date

HINTS: Recognize the SEC's timeline for notification of corporate actions.

Q335_LO91: What is the tax treatment for shareholders receiving cash in a spin-off?
a. Tax-free event
b. Taxable as ordinary income
c. Taxable as a capital loss
d. Taxable as a gift

HINTS: Understand the tax implications of cash received in a spin-off.

Q336_LO91: How do mergers and acquisitions differ in terms of tax treatment for shareholders?
a. Both are tax-free
b. Mergers are taxable, acquisitions are tax-free
c. Mergers are tax-free, acquisitions are taxable
d. Both are taxable

HINTS: Differentiate between the tax treatment of mergers and acquisitions.

Q337_LO91: In a buyback, what type of offer is commonly made to shareholders?
a. All stock offer
b. Mix of stocks and cash
c. All-cash offer
d. Mix of stocks and bonds

HINTS: Identify the common form of offer in buybacks.

Q338_LO91: What is the significance of the date of record in notification requirements?
a. It determines the tax implications
b. It identifies the date of payment
c. It establishes the entitlement of shareholders
d. It is optional information

HINTS: Understand the importance of the date of record in notification requirements.

Q339_LO91: Why might a company choose to issue a stock dividend instead of a cash dividend?
a. To increase shareholder taxes
b. To decrease shareholder value
c. To conserve cash for business purposes
d. To avoid SEC regulations

HINTS: Recognize a potential motive behind issuing stock dividends.

Q340_LO91: In which scenario may a shareholder face a capital gain or loss in a corporate action?
a. Receiving additional shares through a stock split
b. Receiving cash in a tender offer
c. Receiving stock in a merger
d. Receiving stock dividends

HINTS: Identify the scenario where a shareholder may face a capital gain or loss.

Q341_LO92: What is a proxy in the context of corporate actions?
a. Corporate decision
b. Absentee ballot
c. Stock certificate
d. Annual report

HINTS: Think about the role of a proxy in voting.

Q342_LO92: When is a proxy automatically revoked?
a. If the proxy solicitation fails
b. If the stockholder attends the meeting
c. If the proxy is not registered
d. If the stockholder receives multiple proxies

HINTS: Consider the circumstances under which a proxy is no longer valid.

Q343_LO92: What is the purpose of proxy solicitation in the context of corporate actions?
a. To buy and sell proxies
b. To provide unsolicited advice
c. To register with the SEC
d. To offer third-party voting options

HINTS: Understand the purpose of proxy solicitation.

Q344_LO92: In a proxy contest, who must register with the SEC?
a. Only direct participants
b. Anyone providing unsolicited advice
c. Both direct participants and advisors
d. SEC is not involved in proxy contests

HINTS: Recognize the registration requirements in a proxy contest.

Q345_LO92: When can a proxy be replaced by another proxy?
a. Anytime before the shareholder meeting
b. Only if the stockholder attends the meeting
c. Only if the proxy is solicited
d. Only if the SEC approves

HINTS: Consider the conditions under which a proxy can be replaced.

Q346_LO92: What role do member BD firms play in forwarding proxies?
a. Proxy sponsors
b. Forwarding agents
c. Direct participants
d. Proxy advisors

HINTS: Identify the role of member BD firms in proxy forwarding.

Q347_LO92: How do member BD firms vote street name stock in the absence of customer instructions?
a. As recommended by the issuer's management
b. As recommended by the SEC
c. In accordance with BD's interests
d. Based on BD's discretion

HINTS: Understand the voting procedure for street name stock in the absence of instructions.

Q348_LO92: What happens if a customer fails to return the proxy by the 10th day before the annual meeting for major matters?
a. BD must vote the shares as it sees fit
b. SEC determines the vote
c. Shares are automatically voted against the proposal
d. BD is not allowed to vote the shares

HINTS: Consider the consequences if a customer does not return the proxy for major matters.

Q349_LO92: What costs are reimbursed to member BD firms for proxy forwarding?
a. Registration fees
b. Legal expenses
c. Postage and clerical expenses
d. SEC filing fees

HINTS: Identify the costs reimbursed to BD firms for proxy forwarding.

Q350_LO92: What is the primary purpose of proxy voting?
a. To elect corporate executives
b. To decide on dividend payments
c. To approve or disapprove decisions requiring shareholder approval
d. To determine the stock price

HINTS: Recognize the primary purpose of proxy voting.

Q351_LO92: Why might a stockholder choose to vote by proxy instead of attending a shareholder meeting?
a. To avoid registration with the SEC
b. To exercise voting rights personally
c. To revoke the proxy
d. To replace the proxy

HINTS: Understand the reasons for stockholders to choose proxy voting.

Q352_LO92: In proxy voting, what does a stockholder transfer to another person?
a. Ownership of the shares
b. Right to attend the meeting
c. Right to vote on the stockholder's behalf
d. Right to receive dividends

HINTS: Identify the right transferred to another person in proxy voting.

Q353_LO92: What is the significance of the 10th day before the annual shareholder meeting?
a. SEC filing deadline
b. Last day for proxy solicitation
c. Deadline for customer instructions
d. Voting day

HINTS: Understand the significance of the 10th day before the annual meeting.

Q354_LO92: When is a proxy automatically revoked according to SEC regulations?
a. If the proxy is not registered
b. If the proxy is replaced
c. If the stockholder attends the meeting
d. If SEC does not approve

HINTS: Recognize the SEC's regulations on automatic proxy revocation.

Q355_LO92: What is the purpose of SEC review in proxy solicitation?
a. To approve proxies
b. To prevent proxy contests
c. To ensure accurate information for stockholders
d. To determine the voting outcomes

HINTS: Understand the purpose of SEC review in proxy solicitation.

Correct Answers & Explanations
Investment Returns & Corporate Actions

Q181_LO86: Correct Answer: b EXPLANATIONS: DERP stands for Declaration, Execution, Record, and Payable.

Q182_LO86: Correct Answer: a EXPLANATIONS: Mutual funds settle transactions the same day they are executed, eliminating the settlement delay.

Q183_LO86: Correct Answer: c EXPLANATIONS: The ex-dividend date for a mutual fund is the day after the record date.

Q184_LO86: Correct Answer: b EXPLANATIONS: Current yield = Annual income / Current market value

Q185_LO86: Correct Answer: b EXPLANATIONS: Convert a quarterly dividend to an annual amount by multiplying it by 4.

Q186_LO86: Correct Answer: d EXPLANATIONS: Capital gains/losses = Sales proceeds - Adjusted cost basis

Q187_LO86: Correct Answer: c EXPLANATIONS: A position must be held for more than one year to have long-term gains.

Q188_LO86: Correct Answer: b EXPLANATIONS: Long-term gains are generally taxed at a lower rate compared to short-term gains.

Q189_LO86: Correct Answer: a EXPLANATIONS: Total return = [Income received + Gains] / Cost basis

Q190_LO86: Correct Answer: b EXPLANATIONS: The holding period determines the tax rate for gains.

Q191_LO86: Correct Answer: d EXPLANATIONS: The ex-dividend date for mutual funds is set by the fund's board of directors, occurring the day after the record date.

Q192_LO86: Correct Answer: b EXPLANATIONS: Declaration date - (record and payable date) - ex-dividend date.

Q193_LO86: Correct Answer: d EXPLANATIONS: The ex-dividend date for a mutual fund is set by the fund's board of directors.

Q194_LO86: Correct Answer: c EXPLANATIONS: Current yield = Annual income (in dollars) / Current market value.

Q195_LO86: Correct Answer: a EXPLANATIONS: If the question provides a quarterly dividend, multiply it by 4 to get the annual amount.

Q196_LO86: Correct Answer: d EXPLANATIONS: Sales proceeds - adjusted cost basis = (capital gains if positive, capital losses if negative).

Q197_LO86: Correct Answer: c EXPLANATIONS: Adjusted cost basis is the amount paid for a position modified by any adjustments.

Q198_LO86: Correct Answer: a EXPLANATIONS: A position held for more than one year qualifies for long-term gains treatment.

Q199_LO86: Correct Answer: c EXPLANATIONS: Long-term gains are taxed differently than short-term gains.

Q200_LO86: Correct Answer: c EXPLANATIONS: [Income received + gains] / cost basis = total return.

Q201_LO86: Correct Answer: a EXPLANATIONS: Cost basis refers to the initial investment in the context of total return.

Q202_LO86: Correct Answer: c EXPLANATIONS: ($500 - $200) / $10,000 * 100 = 3.0%

Q203_LO86: Correct Answer: b EXPLANATIONS: The ex-dividend date for a mutual fund is the day after the record date.

Q204_LO86: Correct Answer: a EXPLANATIONS: R stands for the record date in the DERP order.

Q205_LO86: Correct Answer: d EXPLANATIONS: The ex-dividend date marks the day after which the dividend is no longer available to new owners.

Q206_LO87: Correct Answer: d EXPLANATIONS: Ordinary income consists of earned, investment, and passive income.

Q207_LO87: Correct Answer: c EXPLANATIONS: Earned income includes salary, wages, bonuses, tips, and other income from active participation.

Q208_LO87: Correct Answer: b EXPLANATIONS: Eligibility for IRA contributions is based on earned income.

Q209_LO87: Correct Answer: b EXPLANATIONS: Long-term capital gains are taxed at a generally lower rate than ordinary income.

Q210_LO87: Correct Answer: a EXPLANATIONS: Short-term capital gains are taxed as ordinary income.

Q211_LO87: Correct Answer: b EXPLANATIONS: Long-term capital gains are usually taxed at a lower rate than short-term gains.

Q212_LO87: Correct Answer: b EXPLANATIONS: Capital losses may be used to offset capital gains on a dollar-for-dollar basis.

Q213_LO87: Correct Answer: c EXPLANATIONS: An investor can use up to $3,000 of losses exceeding gains to reduce ordinary income.

Q214_LO87: Correct Answer: d EXPLANATIONS: Losses carried forward to the next tax year with no time limit are called carryforward losses.

Q215_LO87: Correct Answer: b EXPLANATIONS: A wash sale is an attempt to create a loss for tax purposes while maintaining ownership.

Q216_LO87: Correct Answer: b EXPLANATIONS: A wash sale is not illegal; however, using losses from it to reduce taxes is illegal.

Q217_LO87: Correct Answer: c EXPLANATIONS: Wash sale rules apply to both re-creating long and short positions.

Q218_LO87: Correct Answer: b EXPLANATIONS: Besides the exact same security, convertible bonds or preferred stock from the same issuer are considered "substantially identical."

Q219_LO87: Correct Answer: d EXPLANATIONS: Losses may be carried forward indefinitely with no time limit.

Q220_LO87: Correct Answer: c EXPLANATIONS: Repurchasing the same security within 30 days disallows the established loss in a wash sale.

Q221_LO87: Correct Answer: d EXPLANATIONS: Ordinary income is used to determine the income tax rate an investor will pay.

Q222_LO87: Correct Answer: b EXPLANATIONS: Earned income includes salary, wages, bonuses, and tips but excludes dividends.

Q223_LO87: Correct Answer: d EXPLANATIONS: Eligibility for IRA contributions is based on earned income.

Q224_LO87: Correct Answer: c EXPLANATIONS: Earned income includes salary, wages, and other income from active participation.

Q225_LO87: Correct Answer: c EXPLANATIONS: Investment income is also referred to as portfolio income.

Q226_LO87: Correct Answer: d EXPLANATIONS: Long-term capital gains are taxed at an advantageous rate.

Q227_LO87: Correct Answer: b EXPLANATIONS: Short-term capital gains from assets held for one year or less are taxed as ordinary income.

Q228_LO87: Correct Answer: b EXPLANATIONS: Capital losses may be used to offset capital gains on a dollar-for-dollar basis.

Q229_LO87: Correct Answer: b EXPLANATIONS: Up to $3,000 of capital losses can be used to reduce ordinary income.

Q230_LO87: Correct Answer: b EXPLANATIONS: Excess capital losses may be carried forward indefinitely for future use.

Q231_LO87: Correct Answer: b EXPLANATIONS: A wash sale is an attempt to create a loss for tax purposes when maintaining ownership.

Q232_LO87: Correct Answer: b EXPLANATIONS: A wash sale is not illegal, but attempting to use losses to reduce taxes is illegal.

Q233_LO87: Correct Answer: c EXPLANATIONS: The rule applies to both long and short positions.

Q234_LO87: Correct Answer: a EXPLANATIONS: The rule considers securities of the same issuer as "substantially identical."

Q235_LO87: Correct Answer: b EXPLANATIONS: The wash sale rule applies to substantially identical securities, even if in different forms (e.g., stock and call options).

Q236_LO88: Correct Answer: b EXPLANATIONS: Understanding broader market performance helps investors set reasonable return expectations.

Q237_LO88: Correct Answer: c EXPLANATIONS: The S&P 500 Index is the benchmark most professionals use when discussing overall market performance.

Q238_LO88: Correct Answer: b EXPLANATIONS: The Russell 2000 Index primarily tracks approximately 2,000 small-company stocks.

Q239_LO88: Correct Answer: b EXPLANATIONS: The Wilshire 5000 has closer to 3,500 components, not 5,000 as its name suggests.

Q240_LO88: Correct Answer: b EXPLANATIONS: The MSCI EAFE Index measures the equity market performance of developed markets outside the U.S. and Canada.

Q241_LO88: Correct Answer: d EXPLANATIONS: The DJIA (Dow Jones Industrial Average) is the most widely cited measure of the market's performance in the popular press.

Q242_LO88: Correct Answer: c EXPLANATIONS: The Wilshire 5000 is considered the broadest measure of overall stock market performance.

Q243_LO88: Correct Answer: d EXPLANATIONS: The Barclays Capital U.S. Aggregate Bond Index combines several bond indexes.

Q244_LO88: Correct Answer: b EXPLANATIONS: EAFE stands for Europe, Australasia, and Far East.

Q245_LO88: Correct Answer: d EXPLANATIONS: The Russell 2000 Index is the benchmark for smaller companies in the overall market.

Q246_LO88: Correct Answer: b EXPLANATIONS: The S&P 500 Index tracks slightly more than 500 stocks of large U.S. companies.

Q247_LO88: Correct Answer: d EXPLANATIONS: Judging an investment within the context of the portfolio's strategy is essential to consider the portfolio's objectives.

Q248_LO88: Correct Answer: d EXPLANATIONS: The MSCI EAFE Index is designed to measure the equity market performance of developed markets outside of the U.S. and Canada.

Q249_LO88: Correct Answer: d EXPLANATIONS: DJIA stands for Dow Jones Industrial Average.

Q250_LO88: Correct Answer: b EXPLANATIONS: The S&P 500 Index is often used as the basis for several index mutual funds and ETFs.

Q251_LO88: Correct Answer: c EXPLANATIONS: The Wilshire 5000 is often considered the benchmark for overall market performance.

Q252_LO88: Correct Answer: d EXPLANATIONS: The DJIA tracks the performance of 30 stocks of large, well-known companies.

Q253_LO88: Correct Answer: c EXPLANATIONS: The MSCI EAFE Index measures the equity market performance of developed markets outside the U.S. and Canada.

Q254_LO88: Correct Answer: d EXPLANATIONS: The Russell 2000 Index serves as the benchmark for smaller companies in the overall market.

Q255_LO88: Correct Answer: b EXPLANATIONS: The S&P 500 Index is the basis for several index mutual funds and ETFs.

Q256_LO88: Correct Answer: b EXPLANATIONS: The DJIA is often cited in the popular press and tracks 30 large, well-known companies.

Q257_LO88: Correct Answer: c EXPLANATIONS: It combines several bond indexes to provide a picture of the entire bond market.

Q258_LO88: Correct Answer: c EXPLANATIONS: Despite its name, the Wilshire 5000 has closer to 3,500 components.

Q259_LO88: Correct Answer: c EXPLANATIONS: EAFE stands for Europe, Australasia, and Far East.

Q260_LO88: Correct Answer: d EXPLANATIONS: It is designed to measure the equity market performance of developed markets outside the U.S. and Canada.

Q261_LO88: Correct Answer: d EXPLANATIONS: It suggests that context is important in evaluating performance.

Q262_LO88: Correct Answer: c EXPLANATIONS: Judging an investment involves comparing its performance against an appropriate benchmark.

Q263_LO88: Correct Answer: c EXPLANATIONS: It is essential for setting reasonable return expectations.

Q264_LO88: Correct Answer: b EXPLANATIONS: A benchmark is used to compare investment performance against a standard.

Q265_LO88: Correct Answer: b EXPLANATIONS: A benchmark serves as a standard for comparison in evaluating investment performance.

Q266_LO89: Correct Answer: c EXPLANATIONS: A stock dividend is declared to reinvest profits for business purposes.

Q267_LO89: Correct Answer: c EXPLANATIONS: A stock dividend results in a downward adjustment of the cost per share.

Q268_LO89: Correct Answer: b EXPLANATIONS: At the time of a stock split, there is no tax event; no tax implications.

Q269_LO89: Correct Answer: c EXPLANATIONS: In a forward split, the number of shares increases, and the price per share decreases.

Q270_LO89: Correct Answer: c EXPLANATIONS: A forward split can be characterized as either an even split or an uneven split.

Q271_LO89: Correct Answer: a EXPLANATIONS: The total market value of shares remains unchanged before and after a forward split.

Q272_LO89: Correct Answer: d EXPLANATIONS: In a reverse split, the number of shares decreases, and the price per share increases.

Q273_LO89: Correct Answer: c EXPLANATIONS: A reverse split can be characterized as either an even split or an uneven split.

Q274_LO89: Correct Answer: c EXPLANATIONS: A reverse stock split is often done to comply with listing criteria.

Q275_LO89: Correct Answer: b EXPLANATIONS: In a reverse split, the cost basis per share increases.

Q276_LO89: Correct Answer: c EXPLANATIONS: The total value of an investor's position remains unchanged after a reverse split.

Q277_LO89: Correct Answer: a EXPLANATIONS: The number of shares and the price per share are directly proportional in a stock split.

Q278_LO89: Correct Answer: c EXPLANATIONS: A forward stock split is often done to make the stock price attractive to a wider base of investors.

Q279_LO89: Correct Answer: b EXPLANATIONS: Calculating cost basis adjustments is essential for determining tax consequences when shares are sold.

Q280_LO89: Correct Answer: c EXPLANATIONS: A reverse stock split is often done to comply with stock exchange listing criteria.

Q281_LO89: Correct Answer: c EXPLANATIONS: A stock dividend is declared to reinvest profits for business purposes.

Q282_LO89: Correct Answer: c EXPLANATIONS: The cost per share is adjusted downward in the case of a stock dividend.

Q283_LO89: Correct Answer: c EXPLANATIONS: The stock dividend itself is non-taxable.

Q284_LO89: Correct Answer: c EXPLANATIONS: In a forward split, the number of shares increases, and the price per share decreases.

Q285_LO89: Correct Answer: c EXPLANATIONS: A forward split can be characterized as either an even or uneven split.

Q286_LO89: Correct Answer: c EXPLANATIONS: The cost basis per share is adjusted downward in a forward split.

Q287_LO89: Correct Answer: c EXPLANATIONS: A reverse split is done when the stock price is too low.

Q288_LO89: Correct Answer: d EXPLANATIONS: In a reverse split, the number of shares decreases, and the price per share increases.

Q289_LO89: Correct Answer: a EXPLANATIONS: A reverse split can be characterized as either an even or uneven split.

Q290_LO89: Correct Answer: b EXPLANATIONS: The cost basis per share is adjusted upward in a reverse split.

Q291_LO89: Correct Answer: c EXPLANATIONS: There is no tax event at the time of a stock split.

Q292_LO89: Correct Answer: b EXPLANATIONS: Tax consequences arise when the shares are sold, not at the time of the split.

Q293_LO89: Correct Answer: c EXPLANATIONS: The total market value remains unchanged after a forward split.

Q294_LO89: Correct Answer: b EXPLANATIONS: A reverse split is done to combat delisting due to a low stock price.

Q295_LO89: Correct Answer: c EXPLANATIONS: The total market value remains unchanged after a forward split.
Q296_LO90: Correct Answer: b EXPLANATIONS: In a typical merger, shareholders' old shares are canceled.

Q297_LO90: Correct Answer: b EXPLANATIONS: Shareholders of the acquired company receive shares of the acquiring company.

Q298_LO90: Correct Answer: b EXPLANATIONS: In a spin-off, shareholders receive shares of the newly formed subsidiary.

Q299_LO90: Correct Answer: d EXPLANATIONS: A share buyback is typically done to increase shareholder value.
Q300_LO90: Correct Answer: b EXPLANATIONS: A buyback reduces the number of shares available in the market.

Q301_LO90: Correct Answer: b EXPLANATIONS: A tender offer is an offer to buy a security directly from owners.

Q302_LO90: Correct Answer: b EXPLANATIONS: Tender offers involve buying shares directly from owners, not through secondary markets.

Q303_LO90: Correct Answer: b EXPLANATIONS: A corporation may make a tender offer on its own debt to retire the debt early.

Q304_LO90: Correct Answer: a EXPLANATIONS: A spin-off is typically done to increase shareholder value.

Q305_LO90: Correct Answer: a EXPLANATIONS: A share buyback is often done to increase the value of existing shares.

Q306_LO90: Correct Answer: c EXPLANATIONS: A share buyback reduces the number of outstanding shares.

Q307_LO90: Correct Answer: c EXPLANATIONS: A spin-off involves the separation of assets to form a new subsidiary.

Q308_LO90: Correct Answer: c EXPLANATIONS: Tender offers can be used in acquisitions to buy shares of the target company.

Q309_LO90: Correct Answer: a EXPLANATIONS: A buyback can increase the market value of a company's shares.

Q310_LO90: Correct Answer: b EXPLANATIONS: In an acquisition, shareholders' old shares are typically canceled.
Q311_LO90: Correct Answer: b EXPLANATIONS: In a merger, shareholders of both companies receive new shares of the combined company.

Q312_LO90: Correct Answer: b EXPLANATIONS: In an acquisition, shareholders of the acquired company receive shares of the acquiring company.

Q313_LO90: Correct Answer: b EXPLANATIONS: In a spin-off, a subsidiary company is formed from the corporation's assets and operations.
Q314_LO90: Correct Answer: c EXPLANATIONS: A buyback involves a company purchasing its own outstanding shares, often to increase shareholder value.

Q315_LO90: Correct Answer: d EXPLANATIONS: Share buybacks reduce the number of shares available, potentially increasing share value.

Q316_LO90: Correct Answer: b EXPLANATIONS: A tender offer is a direct purchase of securities from the owners, not through secondary markets.

Q317_LO90: Correct Answer: b EXPLANATIONS: A company may make a tender offer on its own debt to retire the debt early.

Q318_LO90: Correct Answer: c EXPLANATIONS: Shares of the newly formed corporation are issued to the shareholders of the original company.

Q319_LO90: Correct Answer: b EXPLANATIONS: A buyback decreases the number of available shares.

Q320_LO90: Correct Answer: c EXPLANATIONS: Companies engage in buybacks to increase the value of remaining shares.

Q321_LO90: Correct Answer: b EXPLANATIONS: A tender offer is a method used to acquire the target company's shares, either friendly or hostile.

Q322_LO90: Correct Answer: b EXPLANATIONS: In a spin-off, new shares are issued to shareholders of the original company.
Q323_LO90: Correct Answer: b EXPLANATIONS: A buyback often increases the value of remaining shares.

Q324_LO90: Correct Answer: b EXPLANATIONS: A tender offer on convertible securities may be made to retire the convertible securities early.

Q325_LO90: Correct Answer: d EXPLANATIONS: Companies consider buybacks to adjust the capital structure and potentially increase shareholder value.

Q326_LO91: Correct Answer: b EXPLANATIONS: Stock splits result in the receipt of additional shares and are tax-free events.

Q327_LO91: Correct Answer: b EXPLANATIONS: Cash received in a merger is generally taxable as a capital gain or loss.

Q328_LO91: Correct Answer: c EXPLANATIONS: Buybacks are treated as sales, resulting in a capital gain or loss, while tender offers may be tax-free.

Q329_LO91: Correct Answer: a EXPLANATIONS: Cash dividends are generally considered tax events as they involve a sale of the security.

Q330_LO91: Correct Answer: a EXPLANATIONS: Notice for stock dividends should include the title, date of declaration, and rate of the dividend.

Q331_LO91: Correct Answer: c EXPLANATIONS: SEC requires notice to ensure timely and accurate information for shareholders.

Q332_LO91: Correct Answer: b EXPLANATIONS: These events result in the receipt of additional shares and are not taxable.

Q333_LO91: Correct Answer: b EXPLANATIONS: Tender offers are usually all-cash offers.
Q334_LO91: Correct Answer: d EXPLANATIONS: Notice should be given no later than 10 days before the record date.

Q335_LO91: Correct Answer: b EXPLANATIONS: Cash received in a spin-off is generally taxable as ordinary income.

Q336_LO91: Correct Answer: c EXPLANATIONS: Mergers are generally tax-free, while acquisitions may involve taxable cash portions.

Q337_LO91: Correct Answer: c EXPLANATIONS: Buybacks are almost always all-cash offers.

Q338_LO91: Correct Answer: c EXPLANATIONS: The date of record determines the entitlement of shareholders for the distribution.
Q339_LO91: Correct Answer: c EXPLANATIONS: Issuing stock dividends can help conserve cash for business purposes.

Q340_LO91: Correct Answer: b EXPLANATIONS: Cash received in a tender offer is generally taxable, resulting in a capital gain or loss.

Q341_LO92: Correct Answer: b EXPLANATIONS: A proxy is like an absentee ballot used by stockholders to vote on their behalf.

Q342_LO92: Correct Answer: b EXPLANATIONS: A proxy is automatically revoked if the stockholder attends the shareholder meeting.

Q343_LO92: Correct Answer: d EXPLANATIONS: Proxy solicitation involves offers to let a third party vote the shares on behalf of stockholders.
Q344_LO92: Correct Answer: c EXPLANATIONS: Everyone participating, including advisors, must register with the SEC.

Q345_LO92: Correct Answer: a EXPLANATIONS: A proxy can be replaced by another proxy executed at a later date by the stockholder.

Q346_LO92: Correct Answer: b EXPLANATIONS: BD firms act as forwarding agents for proxies received from issuers for street name stock.

Q347_LO92: Correct Answer: a EXPLANATIONS: BD firms vote street name stock as recommended by the issuer's management if customer instructions are not provided.

Q348_LO92: Correct Answer: d EXPLANATIONS: BD may never vote the shares as it sees fit for major matters if the proxy is not returned.

Q349_LO92: Correct Answer: c EXPLANATIONS: Member BD firms are reimbursed for postage and related clerical expenses.

Q350_LO92: Correct Answer: c EXPLANATIONS: Proxy voting is used to approve or disapprove decisions requiring shareholder approval.

Q351_LO92: Correct Answer: b EXPLANATIONS: Stockholders may vote by proxy to avoid attending the meeting in person and still exercise their voting rights.

Q352_LO92: Correct Answer: c EXPLANATIONS: A stockholder transfers the right to vote on their behalf through a proxy.

Q353_LO92: Correct Answer: c EXPLANATIONS: This is the deadline for customer instructions for BDs to vote shares as they see fit.

Q354_LO92: Correct Answer: c EXPLANATIONS: A proxy is automatically revoked if the stockholder attends the shareholder meeting.

Q355_LO92: Correct Answer: c EXPLANATIONS: SEC reviews information to ensure accurate details before proxies are sent to stockholders.

Nonqualifified Accounts, Trust, Custodial, & Education Accounts

Q356_LO93: What characterizes an individual account?
a. Multiple owners
b. One beneficial owner
c. Joint control
d. Estate distribution

HINTS: Think about the defining feature of an individual account.

Q357_LO93: Who can control investments and request distributions in an individual account?
a. Co-owners
b. Appointed traders
c. Authorized family members
d. The account holder

HINTS: Identify the sole controller in an individual account.

Q358_LO93: What happens to the assets in an individual account when the owner dies?
a. Assets are frozen
b. Distribution through the estate
c. Transfer to a joint account
d. Liquidation of assets

HINTS: Consider the fate of assets in an individual account upon the owner's death.

Q359_LO93: How many owners does a joint account have?
a. One
b. Two or more
c. Three
d. Unlimited

HINTS: Recall the number of owners in a joint account.

Q360_LO93: What is required for transactions in a joint account?
a. Single signature
b. Signatures of all owners
c. Signature of the primary owner
d. Joint endorsement

HINTS: Consider the signature requirements for transactions in a joint account.

Q361_LO93: In a joint account, how are checks endorsed for deposit?
a. Single endorsement
b. Endorsement by the primary owner
c. Joint endorsement
d. No endorsement required

HINTS: Understand the endorsement process for checks in a joint account.

Q362_LO93: What determines the handling of account ownership in a joint account if one party dies?
a. Signature requirements
b. Designation as TIC or JTWROS
c. Number of co-owners
d. Account balance

HINTS: Identify the factor that determines account ownership handling in case of death.

Q363_LO93: What does JTWROS stand for in joint account registration?
a. Joint Trading with Right of Shareholders
b. Just Two Winners in a Row
c. Joint Tenants with Right of Survivorship
d. Joint Trust with Respect to Shares

HINTS: Recognize the abbreviation for a specific joint account registration.

Q364_LO93: In JTWROS ownership, what happens to a deceased tenant's interest in the account?
a. Transferred to surviving tenant(s)
b. Retained by the estate
c. Liquidated
d. Frozen

HINTS: Understand the fate of a deceased tenant's interest in JTWROS ownership.

Q365_LO93: What is the common scenario for JTWROS ownership?
a. Business partners
b. Siblings
c. Married couples
d. Friends

HINTS: Identify the common scenario for JTWROS ownership.

Q366_LO93: What is the key characteristic of Tenants in Common (TIC) ownership?
a. All tenants own the account equally
b. Fractional interest retained by the estate
c. Undivided interest in the account
d. Account remains frozen

HINTS: Recognize the defining feature of TIC ownership.

Q367_LO93: What must tenants in a TIC agree upon regarding the account?
a. Joint control
b. Percentage ownership
c. Trading strategy
d. Distribution frequency

HINTS: Consider the agreement required in TIC ownership.

Q368_LO93: What happens to a TIC account when a tenant dies?
a. Account is liquidated
b. Assets are transferred to surviving tenants
c. Account remains frozen
d. Decedent's portion distributed through the estate

HINTS: Understand the fate of a TIC account upon the death of a tenant.

Q369_LO93: What does BD stand for in the context of forwarding proxies?
a. Bond Distribution
b. Broker Dealer
c. Business Development
d. Bond Depository

HINTS: Recognize the abbreviation related to proxy forwarding.

Q370_LO93: What must be included in the notice for corporate actions related to shareholder meetings?
a. Names of the CEOs
b. Percentage of ownership
c. Date of record and payment
d. SEC registration number

HINTS: Identify the essential details in the notice for corporate actions.

Q371_LO93: What characterizes an individual account in terms of ownership?
a. Multiple owners
b. One beneficial owner
c. Joint control
d. Court-appointed ownership

HINTS: Consider the description of an individual account.

Q372_LO93: In an individual account, who can control investments and request distributions?
a. Co-owners
b. Beneficiaries
c. Authorized traders
d. Court-appointed representatives

HINTS: Identify the party with control in an individual account.

Q373_LO93: What happens to the assets in an individual account when the owner dies?
a. Assets are distributed to co-owners
b. Assets are frozen
c. Assets pass to the owner's estate
d. Assets are sold immediately

HINTS: Consider the fate of assets in an individual account upon the owner's death.

Q374_LO93: How many adults are named as co-owners in a joint account?
a. One
b. Two
c. Three
d. Unlimited

HINTS: Understand the number of co-owners in a joint account.

Q375_LO93: What signatures are required for joint account transactions?
a. Signature of any co-owner
b. Signature of the primary owner
c. Signatures of all owners
d. Signature of the account manager

HINTS: Identify the signing requirements for joint account transactions.

Q376_LO93: What designation determines account ownership handling in a joint account?
a. Registration form
b. Account type
c. Ownership agreement
d. Tenants in common (TIC) or JTWROS

HINTS: Recognize the key designation for joint account ownership.

Q377_LO93: In JTWROS, what happens to a deceased tenant's interest in the account?
a. Passed to the surviving tenant(s)
b. Retained by the estate
c. Sold in the open market
d. Frozen until further notice

HINTS: Understand the handling of a deceased tenant's interest in JTWROS.

Q378_LO93: What is the characteristic of JTWROS account ownership?
a. Equal ownership
b. Divided ownership
c. Sequential ownership
d. Rotational ownership

HINTS: Identify the nature of ownership in JTWROS.

Q379_LO93: In TIC ownership, what happens to a deceased tenant's fractional interest?
a. Passed to the surviving tenant(s)
b. Retained by the estate
c. Sold in the open market
d. Automatically transferred to the surviving tenant

HINTS: Understand the handling of a deceased tenant's interest in TIC.

Q380_LO93: What must tenants in common (TIC) specify regarding account ownership?
a. Percentage interest
b. Primary owner
c. Account manager
d. Trading preferences

HINTS: Recognize the requirement for specifying ownership details in TIC.

Q381_LO93: What is the primary reason for choosing JTWROS for married couples?
a. Tax advantages
b. Simplifies account management
c. Avoids estate taxes
d. Ensures equal ownership

HINTS: Identify a key reason for choosing JTWROS in specific situations.

Q382_LO93: In a joint account, who can transact business according to joint account agreements?
a. Primary owner only
b. Any or all tenants
c. Co-owners with majority votes
d. Authorized traders

HINTS: Recognize the authority granted by joint account agreements.

Q383_LO93: What occurs to a joint account when a tenant dies in JTWROS?
a. Assets are frozen
b. Account is closed
c. Assets pass to surviving tenants
d. Assets are sold immediately

HINTS: Understand the outcome of a tenant's death in JTWROS.

Q384_LO93: Why might a TIC account be frozen upon a tenant's death?
a. Legal requirement
b. Tax implications
c. Trading restrictions
d. Estate paperwork processing

HINTS: Consider the reason for potential freezing of a TIC account.

Q385_LO93: What information is crucial for handling TIC account ownership?
a. Ownership agreement
b. Trading preferences
c. Account type
d. Court appointment

HINTS: Recognize the key information needed for handling TIC account ownership.

Q386_LO94: What is the primary purpose of a Transfer on Death (TOD) designation?
a. Avoiding estate tax
b. Bypassing probate
c. Gifting assets
d. Facilitating withdrawals

HINTS: Consider the key feature of TOD.

Q387_LO94: In which types of accounts can a Transfer on Death (TOD) be added?
a. Only individual accounts
b. Only joint accounts
c. Both individual and JTWROS accounts
d. Only corporate accounts

HINTS: Recognize the eligible account types for TOD.

Q388_LO94: When does a TOD become effective in a joint account?
a. Upon account creation
b. After the death of the first tenant
c. After the death of the account owner
d. After the death of any tenant

HINTS: Identify the triggering event for TOD in a joint account.

Q389_LO94: What is the purpose of a Power of Attorney (POA) in financial accounts?
a. Withdrawal of assets
b. Bypassing taxes
c. Granting trading authorization
d. Naming beneficiaries

HINTS: Understand the primary function of a Power of Attorney.

Q390_LO94: Which document specifies the level of access granted in a Limited Power of Attorney (LPOA)?
a. Account agreement
b. Trading authorization
c. Will and testament
d. Power of Attorney document

HINTS: Identify the document specifying the level of access in LPOA.

Q391_LO94: What does a Full Power of Attorney (FPOA) grant to the appointed person?
a. Withdrawal of assets
b. Full control over the account
c. Naming beneficiaries
d. Tax exemptions

HINTS: Recognize the extensive authority granted by FPOA.

Q392_LO94: Why is a Registered Representative (RR) having FPOA on a customer account unusual?
a. Legal restrictions
b. Ethical concerns
c. Tax implications
d. Regulatory requirements

HINTS: Consider the typical stance of firms regarding FPOA for RRs.

Q393_LO94: What is the key distinction between Full Power of Attorney (FPOA) and Limited Power of Attorney (LPOA)?
a. Authorization duration
b. Tax implications
c. Level of control granted
d. Withdrawal limitations

HINTS: Identify the primary difference between FPOA and LPOA.

Q394_LO94: When is a Power of Attorney (POA) canceled?
a. After a year
b. Upon the death of either party
c. Upon account creation
d. After the grantor's incapacitation

HINTS: Understand the circumstances leading to the cancellation of a POA.

Q395_LO94: What is the significance of a Durable Power of Attorney?
a. Continues after death
b. Facilitates withdrawals
c. Increases tax benefits
d. Allows account creation

HINTS: Recognize the distinctive feature of a Durable Power of Attorney.

Q396_LO94: In a Limited Power of Attorney (LPOA), what can the appointed person do?
a. Withdraw assets
b. Enter buy and sell orders
c. Deposit cash or securities
d. Make investment decisions

HINTS: Identify the actions permitted under LPOA.

Q397_LO94: What is the primary duty of persons appointed under Power of Attorney (POA)?
a. Tax planning
b. Account management
c. Fiduciary duty to the owners
d. Asset distribution

HINTS: Recognize the responsibility of appointed persons under POA.

Q398_LO94: How does a Transfer on Death (TOD) account handle estate tax?
a. Assets are exempt from estate tax
b. Assets increase estate tax
c. Assets reduce estate tax
d. Assets are not affected by estate tax

HINTS: Understand the impact of TOD on estate tax.

Q399_LO94: What role does a Power of Attorney (POA) play after the death of either party?
a. Continues indefinitely
b. Passes to the estate
c. Ends immediately
d. Depends on the account type

HINTS: Recognize the outcome of a POA after the death of either party.

Q400_LO94: Why might a customer grant Limited Power of Attorney (LPOA) for an IRA account?
a. Estate planning
b. Tax exemptions
c. Trading flexibility
d. Asset withdrawal

HINTS: Identify a common reason for granting LPOA for an IRA account.

Q401_LO95: What distinguishes a sole proprietor account from other business accounts?
a. Requires a partnership agreement
b. Involves multiple owners
c. Has a business owner as the sole proprietor
d. Excludes corporate resolutions

HINTS: Recognize the defining characteristic of a sole proprietor account.

Q402_LO95: What is the purpose of a fictitious business name associated with a sole proprietor account?
a. Exempt from taxes
b. Enhances business reputation
c. Required by regulatory bodies
d. Indicates multiple owners

HINTS: Consider the additional name associated with a sole proprietor account.

Q403_LO95: In a partnership account, what is required for the partnership to open a margin account?
a. Annual partnership agreement
b. Written partnership agreement
c. Corporate charter
d. Authorization from stockholders

HINTS: Identify the necessary document for opening a margin account in a partnership.

Q404_LO95: What is the role of an amended partnership agreement in a partnership account?
a. Annual renewal
b. Authorizes account transactions
c. Appoints officers
d. Permits margin trading

HINTS: Recognize the purpose of an amended partnership agreement.

Q405_LO95: When opening a corporate account, what document proves the existence of the corporation?
a. Corporate resolution
b. Amended charter
c. Business registration
d. Corporate charter

HINTS: Identify the document establishing the existence of a corporation.

Q406_LO95: What information must be included in a corporate resolution for opening a brokerage account?
a. Business limitations
b. Investment preferences
c. Legal right to open an account
d. Margin account approval

HINTS: Recognize the essential components of a corporate resolution.

Q407_LO95: In a corporate resolution, what does the term "limitations" refer to?
a. Trading restrictions
b. Investment strategies
c. Margin account terms
d. Corporate officer details

HINTS: Understand the meaning of "limitations" in a corporate resolution.

Q408_LO95: Why must a corporation's charter not prohibit margin trading for a margin account?
a. Regulatory requirement
b. Enhances profitability
c. Legal preference
d. Investor protection

HINTS: Recognize the regulatory aspect related to margin trading in a corporate account.

Q409_LO95: What is the common term for a business account that is "doing business as"?
a. Doing Business Name (DBN)
b. Account Alias
c. Fictitious Business Name (d/b/a)
d. Business Trading Name

HINTS: Identify the common term for a business account with an additional name.

Q410_LO95: How does a sole proprietor account handle checks made payable to the business name?
a. Requires additional endorsement
b. Rejects the checks
c. Deposits as usual
d. Requires a court order

HINTS: Understand the handling of checks in a sole proprietor account.

Q411_LO95: What is the legal status of a partnership in terms of incorporation?
a. Incorporated
b. Unincorporated
c. Limited liability
d. LLC status

HINTS: Recognize the legal status of a partnership.

Q412_LO95: What document must a corporation provide when opening a brokerage account?
a. Partnership agreement
b. Corporate charter
c. LLC operating agreement
d. Individual tax returns

HINTS: Identify the necessary document for a corporation to open a brokerage account.

Q413_LO95: What entity must issue an amended partnership agreement for changes?
a. Stockholders
b. Regulatory authorities
c. Board of directors
d. SEC

HINTS: Recognize the authority responsible for issuing an amended partnership agreement.

Q414_LO95: What happens if a corporate resolution lacks the designation of an individual to represent the business?
a. No impact on the account
b. Prohibits account transactions
c. Requires court approval
d. Violates SEC rules

HINTS: Understand the consequence of missing information in a corporate resolution.

Q415_LO95: In a partnership account, what must be obtained annually for margin account approval?
a. Corporate charter
b. Written partnership agreement
c. SEC approval
d. Amended partnership agreement

HINTS: Identify the document needed annually for margin account approval in a partnership.

Q416_LO95: What is the primary purpose of a trust in terms of ownership?
a. Legal possession
b. Financial gain
c. Flexibility in ownership
d. Asset liquidation

HINTS: Identify the primary purpose of a trust in relation to ownership.

Q417_LO95: When is a living trust created and funded?
a. After the grantor's death
b. During the grantor's lifetime
c. Upon the beneficiary's request
d. At the trustee's discretion

HINTS: Recognize the timing of the creation and funding of a living trust.

Q418_LO95: What is another term for a trust funded by a will or estate process after the owner's death?
a. Living trust
b. Revocable trust
c. Irrevocable trust
d. Decedent’s trust

HINTS: Identify the term for a trust funded posthumously through a will or estate process.

Q419_LO95: Which type of trust allows the grantor to modify or revoke it during their lifetime?
a. Irrevocable trust
b. Decedent’s trust
c. Living trust
d. Testamentary trust

HINTS: Recognize the characteristic of a trust that can be modified or revoked during the grantor's lifetime.

Q420_LO95: What is common in a revocable living trust regarding the roles of grantor, trustee, and beneficiary?
a. They are always separate individuals
b. The grantor is always the beneficiary
c. The trustee is the grantor's estate executor
d. The grantor may hold all three roles

HINTS: Understand the common arrangement in a revocable living trust.

Q421_LO95: What happens to assets placed in an irrevocable trust in terms of the grantor's estate?
a. They remain part of the estate
b. They are exempt from estate taxes
c. They are removed from the estate
d. They pass to the grantor's heirs

HINTS: Understand the impact of placing assets in an irrevocable trust on the grantor's estate.

Q422_LO95: In an irrevocable life insurance trust, what problem does it aim to address?
a. Asset consolidation
b. Estate liquidity
c. Tax planning
d. Family business management

HINTS: Recognize the specific issue addressed by an irrevocable life insurance trust.

Q423_LO95: Who typically serves as the trustee in a revocable living trust?
a. Court-appointed individual
b. Financial institution
c. Grantor
d. Beneficiary

HINTS: Identify the usual trustee in a revocable living trust.

Q424_LO95: What power does a grantor retain in an irrevocable trust?
a. Power to modify beneficiaries
b. Power to change trustees
c. Complete control over assets
d. Power to remove assets from the estate

HINTS: Recognize the power retained by the grantor in an irrevocable trust.

Q425_LO95: What role does the beneficiary play in a trust arrangement?
a. Legal owner
b. Asset manager
c. Asset owner
d. Trustee

HINTS: Identify the role of the beneficiary in a trust.

Q426_LO95: What duty does the trustee have in managing a trust?
a. Legal representation
b. Fiduciary duty
c. Tax assessment
d. Beneficiary advocacy

HINTS: Recognize the primary duty of a trustee in managing a trust.

Q427_LO95: What does the term "revocable" imply about the nature of a trust?
a. Cannot be modified
b. Cannot be revoked
c. Can be modified or revoked
d. Permanent and unchangeable

HINTS: Understand the meaning of the term "revocable" in the context of a trust.

Q428_LO95: In a decedent's trust, when are assets placed into the trust?
a. During the grantor's lifetime
b. After the grantor's death
c. At the beneficiary's request
d. At the trustee's discretion

HINTS: Identify the timing of placing assets into a decedent's trust.

Q429_LO95: What does "JTWROS" stand for in a trust context?
a. Joint Trust with Rights of Survivorship
b. Joint Trust with Rightful Ownership Stipulation
c. Joint Tenants with Rights of Survivorship
d. Joint Tenancy with Rightful Ownership Stipulation

HINTS: Understand the acronym "JTWROS" in a trust context.

Q430_LO95: Why might a grantor choose to establish an irrevocable life insurance trust?
a. Estate asset consolidation
b. Avoiding probate
c. Funding a family business
d. Addressing estate tax obligations

HINTS: Recognize a common reason for establishing an irrevocable life insurance trust.

Q431_LO96: Who acts as the custodian in a custodial account?
a. Minor
b. Parent
c. Legal guardian
d. Adult

HINTS: Identify the role of the custodian in a custodial account.

Q432_LO96: What does UGMA stand for in custodial accounts?
a. Uniform Gifts to Minors Act
b. Unified Guardianship Management Act
c. Uniform Grants for Minors Authorization
d. United Guardian Minor Accounts

HINTS: Understand the acronym UGMA in the context of custodial accounts.

Q433_LO96: What is the primary responsibility of the custodian in managing a custodial account?
a. Maximize profits
b. Ensure tax efficiency
c. Act in the minor's best interest
d. Generate income for the parent

HINTS: Recognize the primary duty of the custodian in managing a custodial account.

Q434_LO96: When can a custodian use the property in the custodial account for the minor's benefit?
a. Only for education expenses
b. Only for support and maintenance
c. In any way deemed proper for the minor's benefit
d. Only for general use

HINTS: Understand the flexibility in using the property for the minor's benefit.

Q435_LO96: What is the tax liability associated with a custodial account?
a. Parent's liability
b. Minor's liability
c. Custodian's liability
d. Shared liability

HINTS: Identify the party responsible for tax liability in a custodial account.

Q436_LO96: What is the consequence if the beneficiary (minor) of a custodial account dies?
a. Securities pass to the parents' estate
b. Securities pass to the custodian's estate
c. Securities pass to the minor's estate
d. Securities are liquidated and distributed to parents

HINTS: Understand the outcome in case of the beneficiary's death in a custodial account.

Q437_LO96: What action is required in the event of the custodian's death or resignation?
a. Automatic transfer to a new custodian
b. Court appointment of a new custodian
c. Transfer to the parent's custody
d. Liquidation of the account

HINTS: Recognize the necessary step in case of the custodian's death or resignation.

Q438_LO96: Which accounts allow for real estate to be titled in custodial name?
a. UGMA accounts
b. UTMA accounts
c. Both UGMA and UTMA accounts
d. Neither UGMA nor UTMA accounts

HINTS: Differentiate between UGMA and UTMA accounts in terms of real estate titling.

Q439_LO96: What must be included in the account application when opening a custodial account?
a. Court certification
b. Trust agreement
c. Custodian's birth certificate
d. Custodian's name, minor's name, and SSN

HINTS: Identify the essential information needed when opening a custodial account.

Q440_LO96: What is the main difference between UTMA and UGMA accounts?
a. Age of majority for the minor
b. Taxation rules
c. Custodial rights documentation
d. Availability in certain states

HINTS: Recognize a key difference between UTMA and UGMA accounts.

Q441_LO96: When is a custodian allowed to loan money to a custodial account?
a. Only for educational purposes
b. At any time
c. Only with donor's permission
d. Never

HINTS: Understand the circumstances under which a custodian may loan money to the account.

Q442_LO96: What restriction is placed on investment decisions in custodial accounts?
a. No speculative transactions
b. No cash transactions
c. No dividend reinvestment
d. No investment in stocks

HINTS: Identify a restriction on investment decisions in custodial accounts.

Q443_LO96: What does the term "JTWROS" stand for in custodial accounts?
a. Joint Trust with Rights of Survivorship
b. Joint Trust with Rightful Ownership Stipulation
c. Joint Tenants with Rights of Survivorship
d. Joint Tenancy with Rightful Ownership Stipulation

HINTS: Understand the acronym "JTWROS" in the context of custodial accounts.

Q444_LO96: What is the fiduciary's role in a custodial account?
a. Maximize profits
b. Ensure tax efficiency
c. Act in the minor's best interest
d. All of the above

HINTS: Recognize the responsibilities of a fiduciary in managing a custodial account.

Q445_LO96: What is required for opening a fiduciary account?
a. Birth certificate of the fiduciary
b. Court certification of authority
c. Custodian's approval
d. Parent's consent

HINTS: Identify the necessary document for opening a fiduciary account.

Q446_LO96: Who acts as the custodian in a custodial account established under the Uniform Gift to Minors Act (UGMA) or the Uniform Transfers to Minors Act (UTMA)?
a. The minor
b. The parent
c. The donor
d. An adult

HINTS: Identify the role of the custodian in custodial accounts.

Q447_LO96: When does the custodian's control over a minor's account end in UGMA or UTMA accounts?
a. At age 18
b. When the minor reaches the age of majority
c. When the donor decides
d. At age 21

HINTS: Recognize the termination point of the custodian's control in custodial accounts.

Q448_LO96: How are securities in a custodial account registered?
a. In the donor's name
b. In the minor's name
c. In custodial name for the minor
d. In the custodian's name

HINTS: Understand the registration of securities in a custodial account.

Q449_LO96: What responsibility does the custodian have regarding cash proceeds, dividends, and interest in a custodial account?
a. Hold them indefinitely
b. Invest them in high-risk securities
c. Reinvest within a reasonable time
d. Distribute them to the donor

HINTS: Recognize the proper handling of cash proceeds, dividends, and interest by the custodian.

Q450_LO96: What is the tax liability for a custodial account, and who is responsible for paying the taxes?
a. No tax liability
b. Minor's tax liability, paid by the custodian
c. Donor's tax liability, paid by the minor
d. Minor's tax liability, paid by the minor

HINTS: Identify the tax liability for a custodial account and the responsible party.

Q451_LO96: In the event of the beneficiary's death, where do the securities in a custodial account pass?
a. Custodian's estate
b. Donor's estate
c. Minor's estate
d. Donor's heirs

HINTS: Recognize the destination of securities in a custodial account if the beneficiary (minor) dies.

Q452_LO96: What must happen in the event of the custodian's death or resignation?
a. Automatic transfer to the donor
b. Court appointment of a new custodian
c. Securities liquidation
d. Beneficiary decides

HINTS: Understand the process in the event of the custodian's death or resignation.

Q453_LO96: What is a key difference between UTMA and UGMA accounts?
a. Availability in different states
b. Age until the beneficiary can access UTMA accounts
c. Permissible investments
d. Treatment of real estate

HINTS: Identify a specific difference between UTMA and UGMA accounts.

Q454_LO96: What is the significance of the fiduciary in financial contexts?
a. Asset owner
b. Legal representative
c. Tax advisor
d. Financial planner

HINTS: Recognize the role of a fiduciary in financial contexts.

Q455_LO96: What is the prudent investor rule as it relates to fiduciaries?
a. Seek maximum profits at any cost
b. Make safe and wise investments
c. Invest in speculative securities
d. Favor high-risk options

HINTS: Understand the guiding principle for fiduciaries under the prudent investor rule.

Q456_LO96: In fiduciary accounts, what must be filed with and verified by the BD to ensure proper authorization?
a. Tax returns
b. Court documents
c. Donor's consent
d. Custodian's approval

HINTS: Recognize the documentation needed for proper authorization in fiduciary accounts.

Q457_LO96: What is the primary restriction on speculative transactions in fiduciary accounts?
a. Speculative transactions are generally permitted
b. Speculative transactions are allowed with donor approval
c. Speculative transactions are not permitted
d. Speculative transactions require custodian approval

HINTS: Identify the primary restriction on speculative transactions in fiduciary accounts.

Q458_LO96: When is the opening of margin accounts in fiduciary accounts permitted?
a. Always permitted
b. Only with donor approval
c. If authorized by legal documents
d. Never permitted

HINTS: Understand the conditions under which margin accounts can be opened in fiduciary accounts.

Q459_LO96: What may a fiduciary charge for services in managing an account?
a. A percentage of profits
b. A flat fee only
c. Only reimbursement of expenses
d. No compensation allowed

HINTS: Identify the permissible compensation for a fiduciary managing an account.

Q460_LO96: How are custodial accounts taxed, and at whose tax rate?
a. At the donor's tax rate
b. At the custodian's tax rate
c. At the minor's tax rate
d. Split between custodian and minor

HINTS: Recognize the tax treatment of custodial accounts and the applicable tax rate.

Q461_LO96: Who is the beneficial owner in a custodial account established under UGMA or UTMA?
a. Custodian
b. Minor
c. Parent
d. Fiduciary

HINTS: Identify the individual who is considered the beneficial owner in custodial accounts for minors.

Q462_LO96: What is the role of the custodian in a custodial account?
a. Make investment decisions
b. Exercise trading authority
c. Manage the account until the minor reaches majority
d. All of the above

HINTS: Recognize the responsibilities of a custodian in a custodial account.

Q463_LO96: How are securities in a custodial account taxed?
a. At the parent's tax rate
b. At the custodian's tax rate
c. At the minor's tax rate
d. Split between custodian and minor

HINTS: Understand the tax implications for securities in a custodial account.

Q464_LO96: In a custodial account, who can be reimbursed for managing the account?
a. Custodian
b. Parent
c. Minor
d. Fiduciary

HINTS: Identify the individual eligible for reimbursement in managing a custodial account.

Q465_LO96: What is the fate of securities in a custodial account if the minor beneficiary dies?
a. Pass to the custodian
b. Pass to the parent
c. Pass to the minor's estate
d. Remain in the custodial account

HINTS: Recognize the outcome for securities in a custodial account if the minor beneficiary dies.

Q466_LO96: What is required for court certification when opening a fiduciary account for a trustee?
a. Trust agreement
b. Custodian's authorization
c. Court documents verifying appointment
d. Minor's Social Security number

HINTS: Identify the necessary documentation for court certification when opening a fiduciary account for a trustee.

Q467_LO96: Which type of custodial account allows real estate to be titled in custodial name?
a. UGMA
b. UTMA
c. Both UGMA and UTMA
d. Neither UGMA nor UTMA

HINTS: Distinguish between UGMA and UTMA in terms of real estate titling.

Q468_LO96: When can a UTMA account be held in custodial name until the beneficiary turns 25?
a. Always
b. In some states
c. Only with court approval
d. Never

HINTS: Identify the conditions under which a UTMA account can be held in custodial name until a later age.

Q469_LO96: What is the primary responsibility of a fiduciary in a custodial account?
a. Generate profits
b. Ensure speculative transactions
c. Make wise and safe investments
d. Share in the account's profits

HINTS: Recognize the primary responsibility of a fiduciary in managing a custodial account.

Q470_LO96: What is the fiduciary's role in speculative transactions within a custodial account?
a. Encourage speculative transactions
b. Permit speculative transactions
c. Generally not permitted
d. Share in speculative profits

HINTS: Understand the approach to speculative transactions in custodial accounts managed by fiduciaries.

Q471_LO96: When are margin accounts permitted for fiduciary accounts?
a. Always
b. Only with court approval
c. If authorized by legal documents
d. Never

HINTS: Identify the conditions under which margin accounts are permitted for fiduciary accounts.

Q472_LO96: According to the prudent investor rule, what is required of fiduciaries?
a. Generate maximum profits
b. Make safe investments
c. Follow market trends
d. Invest in high-risk securities

HINTS: Understand the requirement imposed by the prudent investor rule on fiduciaries.

Q473_LO96: What may a fiduciary charge for services in a custodial account?
a. Share in account profits
b. Only reimbursement of expenses
c. Compensation for services
d. Both reimbursement and compensation

HINTS: Identify the type of charges a fiduciary may impose for services in a custodial account.

Q474_LO96: What happens to securities in a custodial account if the custodian resigns?
a. Pass to the minor
b. Pass to the parent
c. Pass to the custodian's estate
d. Requires court appointment of a new custodian

HINTS: Recognize the procedure when the custodian resigns in a custodial account.

Q475_LO96: How are custodial accounts taxed?
a. At the custodian's tax rate
b. At the parent's tax rate
c. At the minor's tax rate
d. A combination of custodian and minor's tax rates

HINTS: Understand the taxation of custodial accounts.

Q476_LO97: What is a key difference between a Coverdell ESA and a 529 plan?
a. Contribution limits
b. Tax deduction for contributions
c. Qualified education expenses
d. Age restriction on beneficiaries

HINTS: Identify a distinguishing feature between Coverdell ESA and 529 plans.

Q477_LO97: How much can be contributed annually per student to a Coverdell ESA?
a. $5,000
b. $2,000
c. $10,000
d. No limit

HINTS: Recall the annual contribution limit for a student in a Coverdell ESA.

Q478_LO97: What happens if nonqualified distributions are made from a Coverdell ESA?
a. Tax deduction for contributions
b. Tax-free distributions
c. Penalty plus income tax
d. No consequences

HINTS: Recognize the consequences of nonqualified distributions from a Coverdell ESA.

Q479_LO97: Why is the Coverdell ESA not as popular as 529 plans?
a. Lower contribution limits
b. Higher contribution limits
c. Tax deduction for contributions
d. No penalty for nonqualified distributions

HINTS: Understand a factor contributing to the lower popularity of Coverdell ESA.

Q480_LO97: What is a defining feature of 529 plans regarding state sponsorship?
a. Federal sponsorship
b. Municipal fund security
c. Private sponsorship
d. No sponsorship required

HINTS: Identify the characteristic related to state sponsorship in 529 plans.

Q481_LO97: Which type of 529 plan allows donors to lock in current tuition rates?
a. Savings plan
b. Prepaid tuition plan
c. College savings plan
d. Municipal savings plan

HINTS: Identify the type of 529 plan that provides protection against inflation in education costs.

Q482_LO97: Who can open a 529 plan for a future college student?
a. Parents only
b. Adults only
c. Any adult
d. Donors related to the student

HINTS: Recognize the eligibility to open a 529 plan for a future college student.

Q483_LO97: How are contributions to a 529 plan treated for federal tax purposes?
a. Deductible from federal taxes
b. Tax-free
c. Taxed as income
d. Tax-free with conditions

HINTS: Understand the federal tax treatment of contributions to a 529 plan.

Q484_LO97: What is the consequence if a beneficiary doesn't need 529 plan funds for school?
a. Tax deduction for contributions
b. Penalty for nonqualified distributions
c. Tax consequences for the donor
d. Tax-free rollover to another family member

HINTS: Recognize the outcome if a beneficiary doesn't need 529 plan funds for school.

Q485_LO97: How often can rollovers be performed from one state's 529 plan to another?
a. Once every 6 months
b. Once every 12 months
c. No limitations
d. Once every 24 months

HINTS: Identify the frequency of permitted rollovers from one state's 529 plan to another.

Q486_LO97: What is a feature of 529 plans regarding control over assets?
a. Assets transferred to the beneficiary at legal age
b. Limited control for donors
c. Full control for donors
d. Assets transferred to the state

HINTS: Recognize the level of control donors have over assets in 529 plans.

Q487_LO97: Are there income limitations on making contributions to a 529 plan?
a. Yes, for all contributors
b. Yes, for high-income contributors
c. No income limitations
d. Yes, for out-of-state contributors

HINTS: Identify the status of income limitations for contributors to a 529 plan.

Q488_LO97: What can be transferred if account balances in a 529 plan are left unused?
a. Tax deductions
b. Assets to another state
c. Balances to a related beneficiary
d. Contributions to another account

HINTS: Recognize the options for transferring unused account balances in a 529 plan.

Q489_LO97: What is the distribution limit for qualified expenses in a 529 plan for K-12 education?
a. $5,000
b. $10,000
c. $15,000
d. No limit

HINTS: Recall the distribution limit for qualified expenses in a 529 plan for K-12 education.

Q490_LO97: What type of securities sale requires an official statement for 529 plans?
a. Municipal securities
b. Corporate securities
c. Federal securities
d. Municipal fund securities

HINTS: Identify the type of securities sale that requires an official statement for 529 plans.

Q491_LO97: What is the primary purpose of both Coverdell Education Savings Accounts (ESA) and 529 plans?
a. Retirement savings
b. Health savings
c. Education savings
d. Homeownership savings

HINTS: Identify the main objective of both ESAs and 529 plans.

Q492_LO97: What is the annual contribution limit for a Coverdell ESA per student?
a. $1,000
b. $2,000
c. $5,000
d. $10,000

HINTS: Recognize the annual contribution limit for a Coverdell ESA.

Q493_LO97: How are contributions to a Coverdell ESA taxed?
a. Tax-deductible
b. Tax-free
c. Tax-deferred
d. After-tax

HINTS: Understand the tax treatment of contributions to a Coverdell ESA.

Q494_LO97: What is the consequence of nonqualified distributions from a Coverdell ESA?
a. No consequence
b. Income tax only
c. Penalty only
d. Income tax plus a 10% penalty

HINTS: Recognize the consequence of nonqualified distributions from a Coverdell ESA.

Q495_LO97: What happens if a student's Coverdell ESA is not depleted by age 30?
a. Tax-free rollover
b. Mandatory distribution
c. Penalty waiver
d. Funds distributed subject to tax and penalty

HINTS: Identify the outcome if a student's Coverdell ESA is not depleted by age 30.

Q496_LO97: Why is the Coverdell ESA less popular than 529 plans?
a. Lower contribution limits
b. Higher tax deductions
c. More investment options
d. Unlimited distribution options

HINTS: Recognize a factor contributing to the lesser popularity of Coverdell ESAs.

Q497_LO97: What type of expenses do qualified distributions from a Coverdell ESA cover?
a. Medical expenses
b. Housing expenses
c. Qualified education expenses
d. Entertainment expenses

HINTS: Identify the type of expenses covered by qualified distributions from a Coverdell ESA.

Q498_LO97: How are 529 plans categorized, considering their state sponsorship?
a. Federal funds
b. Corporate funds
c. Municipal fund securities
d. Private funds

HINTS: Understand the categorization of 529 plans based on state sponsorship.

Q499_LO97: What is the distribution limit for K-12 tuition expenses in a 529 plan?
a. $5,000
b. $7,500
c. $10,000
d. No limit

HINTS: Recognize the distribution limit for K-12 tuition expenses in a 529 plan.

Q500_LO97: Which 529 plan option allows donors to save for future education costs?
a. Prepaid tuition plan
b. College savings plan
c. Postsecondary plan
d. Secondary education plan

HINTS: Identify the option that allows donors to save for future education costs in a 529 plan.

Q501_LO97: What is the main advantage of a prepaid tuition plan in a 529 plan?
a. Tax-free withdrawals
b. Protection against inflation
c. Higher contribution limits
d. Unlimited investment options

HINTS: Recognize the primary advantage of a prepaid tuition plan in a 529 plan.

Q502_LO97: Who can open a 529 plan for a future college student?
a. Only parents
b. Only related individuals
c. Any adult
d. Only grandparents

HINTS: Identify the eligibility to open a 529 plan for a future college student.

Q503_LO97: What are the tax implications of contributions to a 529 plan?
a. Tax-deductible
b. Tax-free
c. Tax-deferred
d. After-tax

HINTS: Understand the tax treatment of contributions to a 529 plan.

Q504_LO97: What happens if a beneficiary does not need 529 plan funds for school?
a. Penalty on withdrawals
b. Tax consequences for the donor
c. Tax-free rollover to another beneficiary
d. Account closure

HINTS: Recognize the consequence if a beneficiary does not need 529 plan funds for school.

Q505_LO97: What is a key characteristic of 529 plan contributions?
a. Annual contribution limits
b. Limited control by donors
c. Age restrictions
d. Restricted to in-state donors

HINTS: Identify a key characteristic of 529 plan contributions.

Correct Answers & Explanations
Nonqualifified Accounts, Trust, Custodial, & Education Accounts

Q356_LO93: Correct Answer: b EXPLANATIONS: An individual account has one beneficial owner.

Q357_LO93: Correct Answer: d EXPLANATIONS: The account holder is the only person who can control investments and request distributions.

Q358_LO93: Correct Answer: b EXPLANATIONS: Assets are distributed through the owner's estate.

Q359_LO93: Correct Answer: b EXPLANATIONS: A joint account has two or more owners.

Q360_LO93: Correct Answer: b EXPLANATIONS: Joint accounts require the signatures of all owners for transactions.

Q361_LO93: Correct Answer: c EXPLANATIONS: Checks must be endorsed for deposit by all tenants in a joint account.

Q362_LO93: Correct Answer: b EXPLANATIONS: The designation as TIC or JTWROS determines account ownership handling.

Q363_LO93: Correct Answer: c EXPLANATIONS: JTWROS stands for Joint Tenants with Right of Survivorship.

Q364_LO93: Correct Answer: a EXPLANATIONS: The interest is transferred to the surviving tenant(s).

Q365_LO93: Correct Answer: c EXPLANATIONS: JTWROS ownership is common for married couples.

Q366_LO93: Correct Answer: b EXPLANATIONS: In TIC ownership, a deceased tenant's fractional interest is retained by the estate.

Q367_LO93: Correct Answer: b EXPLANATIONS: Tenants in a TIC should agree on the percentage of ownership.

Q368_LO93: Correct Answer: d EXPLANATIONS: The decedent's portion is distributed through the estate.

Q369_LO93: Correct Answer: b EXPLANATIONS: BD stands for Broker Dealer in this context.

Q370_LO93: Correct Answer: c EXPLANATIONS: The notice should include the date of record and payment for corporate actions.

Q371_LO93: Correct Answer: b EXPLANATIONS: An individual account has one beneficial owner.

Q372_LO93: Correct Answer: c EXPLANATIONS: The account holder is the only person who can control investments and request distributions.

Q373_LO93: Correct Answer: c EXPLANATIONS: The account assets are distributed through the owner's estate.

Q374_LO93: Correct Answer: b EXPLANATIONS: In a joint account, two or more adults are named as co-owners.

Q375_LO93: Correct Answer: c EXPLANATIONS: Joint account agreements require the signatures of all owners for transactions.

Q376_LO93: Correct Answer: d EXPLANATIONS: The joint account must be designated as either TIC or JTWROS.

Q377_LO93: Correct Answer: a EXPLANATIONS: The deceased tenant's interest passes to the surviving tenant(s).

Q378_LO93: Correct Answer: a EXPLANATIONS: All tenants in the account have an undivided interest in the account, effectively owning it equally.

Q379_LO93: Correct Answer: b EXPLANATIONS: The deceased tenant's fractional interest is retained by the estate.

Q380_LO93: Correct Answer: a EXPLANATIONS: Each party in TIC must specify a percentage interest in the account.

Q381_LO93: Correct Answer: b EXPLANATIONS: JTWROS simplifies account management for married couples.

Q382_LO93: Correct Answer: b EXPLANATIONS: Joint account agreements provide that any or all tenants may transact business in the account.

Q383_LO93: Correct Answer: c EXPLANATIONS: Assets pass to the surviving tenants in JTWROS.

Q384_LO93: Correct Answer: d EXPLANATIONS: The account will remain frozen until required estate paperwork has been received and processed.

Q385_LO93: Correct Answer: a EXPLANATIONS: TIC requires an agreement specifying the percentage ownership of each tenant.

Q386_LO94: Correct Answer: b EXPLANATIONS: TOD allows the owner to pass the account to a named beneficiary, bypassing probate.

Q387_LO94: Correct Answer: c EXPLANATIONS: TOD may be added to individual accounts and JTWROS accounts.

Q388_LO94: Correct Answer: b EXPLANATIONS: In a joint account, the TOD becomes effective after the death of the last surviving tenant.

Q389_LO94: Correct Answer: c EXPLANATIONS: A POA grants trading authorization to a person other than the owner.

Q390_LO94: Correct Answer: d EXPLANATIONS: The document is the Limited Power of Attorney (LPOA) itself.

Q391_LO94: Correct Answer: b EXPLANATIONS: An FPOA grants the appointed person full control over the account.

Q392_LO94: Correct Answer: b EXPLANATIONS: Most firms would not approve the appointment of an RR with FPOA on a customer account, especially if not a family member.

Q393_LO94: Correct Answer: c EXPLANATIONS: FPOA grants extensive control, while LPOA provides limited control over an account.

Q394_LO94: Correct Answer: b EXPLANATIONS: All POAs are canceled upon the death of either party.

Q395_LO94: Correct Answer: a EXPLANATIONS: A durable POA continues even if the account owner is incapacitated.

Q396_LO94: Correct Answer: b EXPLANATIONS: LPOA allows the entering of buy and sell orders but no withdrawal of assets.

Q397_LO94: Correct Answer: c EXPLANATIONS: All persons so appointed have a fiduciary duty to the account's owners.

Q398_LO94: Correct Answer: a EXPLANATIONS: TOD avoids probate but does not exempt assets from estate tax.

Q399_LO94: Correct Answer: c EXPLANATIONS: All POAs are canceled upon the death of either party.

Q400_LO94: Correct Answer: c EXPLANATIONS: LPOA allows trading flexibility, which may be useful for managing an IRA account.

Q401_LO95: Correct Answer: c EXPLANATIONS: A sole proprietor account is owned by a single business owner.

Q402_LO95: Correct Answer: b EXPLANATIONS: A fictitious business name, or d/b/a, can enhance the business's reputation.

Q403_LO95: Correct Answer: b EXPLANATIONS: A written partnership agreement is required for a partnership to open a margin account.

Q404_LO95: Correct Answer: a EXPLANATIONS: It is needed annually for any changes in a partnership agreement.

Q405_LO95: Correct Answer: d EXPLANATIONS: The corporate charter is proof that the corporation exists.

Q406_LO95: Correct Answer: c EXPLANATIONS: It includes the legal right to open an investment account.

Q407_LO95: Correct Answer: a EXPLANATIONS: It indicates any restrictions on the securities in which the business can invest.

Q408_LO95: Correct Answer: a EXPLANATIONS: The charter must not prohibit margin if a corporation desires a margin account.

Q409_LO95: Correct Answer: c EXPLANATIONS: It is referred to as a fictitious business name or d/b/a.

Q410_LO95: Correct Answer: c EXPLANATIONS: Checks can be made payable to the account owner or the business name.

Q411_LO95: Correct Answer: b EXPLANATIONS: A partnership is an unincorporated association.

Q412_LO95: Correct Answer: b EXPLANATIONS: A corporation must provide a copy of the corporate charter.

Q413_LO95: Correct Answer: c EXPLANATIONS: Changes require authorization from the partners or board of directors.

Q414_LO95: Correct Answer: b EXPLANATIONS: A corporate resolution must designate the individual representing the business.

Q415_LO95: Correct Answer: d EXPLANATIONS: An amended partnership agreement, similar to a corporate resolution, is required annually.

Q416_LO95: Correct Answer: c EXPLANATIONS: A trust allows for flexibility in assigning different aspects of ownership.

Q417_LO95: Correct Answer: b EXPLANATIONS: A living trust is created and funded by the grantor during their lifetime.

Q418_LO95: Correct Answer: d EXPLANATIONS: It is known as a decedent's trust.

Q419_LO95: Correct Answer: c EXPLANATIONS: A living trust is revocable during the grantor's lifetime.

Q420_LO95: Correct Answer: d EXPLANATIONS: The grantor may be the trustee and beneficiary in a revocable living trust.

Q421_LO95: Correct Answer: c EXPLANATIONS: Assets are removed from the grantor's estate in an irrevocable trust.

Q422_LO95: Correct Answer: c EXPLANATIONS: It helps pay estate taxes in the case of a large illiquid asset.

Q423_LO95: Correct Answer: c EXPLANATIONS: The grantor is often the trustee in a revocable living trust.

Q424_LO95: Correct Answer: b EXPLANATIONS: The grantor retains the power to change trustees.

Q425_LO95: Correct Answer: a EXPLANATIONS: The beneficiary is the individual for whom the trust is managed.

Q426_LO95: Correct Answer: b EXPLANATIONS: The trustee has a fiduciary duty to manage the trust for the benefit of the beneficiary.

Q427_LO95: Correct Answer: c EXPLANATIONS: It implies that the trust can be modified or revoked by the grantor.

Q428_LO95: Correct Answer: b EXPLANATIONS: Assets are placed after the grantor's death.

Q429_LO95: Correct Answer: c EXPLANATIONS: It stands for Joint Tenants with Rights of Survivorship.

Q430_LO95: Correct Answer: d EXPLANATIONS: It is often used to help pay estate taxes.

Q431_LO96: Correct Answer: d EXPLANATIONS: The custodian is an adult who manages the account for the minor.

Q432_LO96: Correct Answer: a EXPLANATIONS: It stands for Uniform Gift to Minors Act.

Q433_LO96: Correct Answer: c EXPLANATIONS: The custodian must act in the minor's best interest.

Q434_LO96: Correct Answer: c EXPLANATIONS: The custodian can use the property in any way deemed proper for the minor's benefit.

Q435_LO96: Correct Answer: b EXPLANATIONS: The minor is responsible for any tax liability in the account.

Q436_LO96: Correct Answer: c EXPLANATIONS: Securities pass to the minor's estate.

Q437_LO96: Correct Answer: b EXPLANATIONS: A new custodian must be appointed by a court or the donor.

Q438_LO96: Correct Answer: b EXPLANATIONS: UTMA accounts allow for real estate to be titled in custodial name.

Q439_LO96: Correct Answer: d EXPLANATIONS: The application must contain the custodian's name, minor's name, and SSN.

Q440_LO96: Correct Answer: a EXPLANATIONS: UTMA accounts may be held until the beneficiary turns 25 (21 in some states).

Q441_LO96: Correct Answer: b EXPLANATIONS: A custodian may loan money to an account.

Q442_LO96: Correct Answer: a EXPLANATIONS: Speculative transactions are generally not permitted.

Q443_LO96: Correct Answer: c EXPLANATIONS: It stands for Joint Tenants with Rights of Survivorship.

Q444_LO96: Correct Answer: d EXPLANATIONS: The fiduciary must act in the minor's best interest and ensure tax efficiency.

Q445_LO96: Correct Answer: b EXPLANATIONS: Opening a fiduciary account may require a court certification of the individual's appointment and authority.

Q446_LO96: Correct Answer: d EXPLANATIONS: An adult acts as the custodian for a minor.

Q447_LO96: Correct Answer: b EXPLANATIONS: The custodian's control ends when the minor reaches the age of majority.

Q448_LO96: Correct Answer: c EXPLANATIONS: Securities are registered in custodial name for the benefit of the minor.

Q449_LO96: Correct Answer: c EXPLANATIONS: The custodian must reinvest within a reasonable time.

Q450_LO96: Correct Answer: d EXPLANATIONS: The minor is responsible for taxes on the account, paid by the minor or legal guardian.

Q451_LO96: Correct Answer: c EXPLANATIONS: Securities pass to the minor's estate.

Q452_LO96: Correct Answer: b EXPLANATIONS: A new custodian must be appointed by a court or the donor.

Q453_LO96: Correct Answer: b EXPLANATIONS: UTMA accounts may be held in custodial name until the beneficiary turns 25 (21 in some states).

Q454_LO96: Correct Answer: b EXPLANATIONS: A fiduciary is legally appointed to represent another person and make decisions on their behalf.

Q455_LO96: Correct Answer: b EXPLANATIONS: Fiduciaries are required to make safe and wise investments.

Q456_LO96: Correct Answer: b EXPLANATIONS: Court documents must be filed and verified by the BD.

Q457_LO96: Correct Answer: c EXPLANATIONS: Generally, speculative transactions are not permitted.

Q458_LO96: Correct Answer: c EXPLANATIONS: Margin accounts are permitted if authorized by legal documents.

Q459_LO96: Correct Answer: c EXPLANATIONS: A fiduciary may charge reasonable fees for services and reimbursement of expenses.

Q460_LO96: Correct Answer: c EXPLANATIONS: Custodial accounts are taxed at the minor's tax rate.

Q461_LO96: Correct Answer: b EXPLANATIONS: The minor is the beneficial owner in UGMA or UTMA custodial accounts.

Q462_LO96: Correct Answer: d EXPLANATIONS: The custodian has various responsibilities, including investment decisions and managing the account until the minor reaches majority.

Q463_LO96: Correct Answer: c EXPLANATIONS: Securities in a custodial account are taxed at the minor's tax rate.

Q464_LO96: Correct Answer: a EXPLANATIONS: The custodian may be reimbursed for reasonable expenses and, if not the donor, not compensated.

Q465_LO96: Correct Answer: c EXPLANATIONS: Securities pass to the minor's estate in the event of the minor's death.

Q466_LO96: Correct Answer: c EXPLANATIONS: Court documents verifying the appointment and authority of the fiduciary are required.

Q467_LO96: Correct Answer: b EXPLANATIONS: UTMA accounts allow real estate to be titled in custodial name.

Q468_LO96: Correct Answer: b EXPLANATIONS: UTMA accounts may be held in custodial name until the beneficiary turns 25 in some states.

Q469_LO96: Correct Answer: c EXPLANATIONS: Fiduciaries are required to make wise and safe investments.

Q470_LO96: Correct Answer: c EXPLANATIONS: Speculative transactions are generally not permitted.

Q471_LO96: Correct Answer: c EXPLANATIONS: Margin accounts are permitted if authorized by legal documents establishing the fiduciary account.

Q472_LO96: Correct Answer: b EXPLANATIONS: Fiduciaries are required to make wise and safe investments.

Q473_LO96: Correct Answer: b EXPLANATIONS: A fiduciary may charge only reimbursement of expenses, not compensation.

Q474_LO96: Correct Answer: d EXPLANATIONS: A new custodian must be appointed by either a court or the donor of the securities.

Q475_LO96: Correct Answer: c EXPLANATIONS: Custodial accounts are taxed at the minor's tax rate since the minor is the beneficial owner.

Q476_LO97: Correct Answer: a EXPLANATIONS: Coverdell ESA has a smaller contribution limit compared to 529 plans.

Q477_LO97: Correct Answer: b EXPLANATIONS: Coverdell ESA allows after-tax contributions of up to $2,000 per student per year.

Q478_LO97: Correct Answer: c EXPLANATIONS: Nonqualified distributions are subject to income tax plus a 10% penalty.

Q479_LO97: Correct Answer: a EXPLANATIONS: Coverdell ESA has a lower contribution limit compared to 529 plans.

Q480_LO97: Correct Answer: b EXPLANATIONS: 529 plans are defined as municipal fund securities due to state sponsorship.

Q481_LO97: Correct Answer: b EXPLANATIONS: Prepaid tuition plans allow residents to lock in current tuition rates.

Q482_LO97: Correct Answer: c EXPLANATIONS: Any adult can open a 529 plan for a future college student.

Q483_LO97: Correct Answer: b EXPLANATIONS: Contributions are made with after-tax dollars, and earnings accumulate on a tax-deferred basis.

Q484_LO97: Correct Answer: d EXPLANATIONS: Unused funds can be rolled over to another family member without tax consequences.

Q485_LO97: Correct Answer: b EXPLANATIONS: Rollovers are permitted, but no more than once every 12 months.

Q486_LO97: Correct Answer: c EXPLANATIONS: Donors retain control over assets even after the student reaches legal age.

Q487_LO97: Correct Answer: c EXPLANATIONS: There are no income limitations on making contributions to a 529 plan.

Q488_LO97: Correct Answer: c EXPLANATIONS: Unused balances may be transferred to a related beneficiary.

Q489_LO97: Correct Answer: b EXPLANATIONS: The distribution limit for K-12 education is up to $10,000 per year.

Q490_LO97: Correct Answer: a EXPLANATIONS: 529 plans are considered municipal securities, requiring an official statement.

Q491_LO97: Correct Answer: c EXPLANATIONS: Both ESAs and 529 plans are designed for education savings.

Q492_LO97: Correct Answer: b EXPLANATIONS: The annual contribution limit for a Coverdell ESA is $2,000 per student.

Q493_LO97: Correct Answer: d EXPLANATIONS: Contributions to a Coverdell ESA are made with after-tax dollars.

Q494_LO97: Correct Answer: d EXPLANATIONS: Nonqualified distributions are subject to income tax plus a 10% penalty.

Q495_LO97: Correct Answer: d EXPLANATIONS: Funds must be distributed to the individual subject to income tax and a 10% penalty or rolled into another ESA.

Q496_LO97: Correct Answer: a EXPLANATIONS: The Coverdell ESA has a relatively small contribution limit.

Q497_LO97: Correct Answer: c EXPLANATIONS: Qualified distributions cover expenses for college, secondary, or elementary school.

Q498_LO97: Correct Answer: c EXPLANATIONS: 529 plans are considered municipal fund securities due to state sponsorship.

Q499_LO97: Correct Answer: c EXPLANATIONS: The distribution limit for K-12 tuition is up to $10,000 per year.

Q500_LO97: Correct Answer: b EXPLANATIONS: The college savings plan allows donors to save for future education expenses.

Q501_LO97: Correct Answer: b EXPLANATIONS: A prepaid plan provides protection against inflation in education costs.

Q502_LO97: Correct Answer: c EXPLANATIONS: Any adult can open a 529 plan for a future college student.

Q503_LO97: Correct Answer: d EXPLANATIONS: Contributions are made with after-tax dollars in a 529 plan.

Q504_LO97: Correct Answer: c EXPLANATIONS: Unused funds may be rolled over to a related beneficiary without tax consequences.

Q505_LO97: Correct Answer: a EXPLANATIONS: There are no annual contribution limits for 529 plans.

Qualifified Plans & Account Features

Q506_LO98: What is the primary purpose of Individual Retirement Accounts (IRAs)?
a. Tax-free income
b. Encourage retirement savings
c. Health savings
d. Education savings

HINTS: Identify the main purpose of IRAs as stated in the passage.

Q507_LO98: Why are IRAs not considered qualified plans by the IRS?
a. Lack of tax benefits
b. No employer sponsorship
c. Limited investment options
d. Lower contribution limits

HINTS: Recognize the reason IRAs are not classified as qualified plans.

Q508_LO98: In a Traditional IRA, what determines the deductibility of contributions for an individual actively participating in another qualified plan?
a. Investment returns
b. Age of the individual
c. Income level
d. Account balance

HINTS: Identify the factor determining the deductibility of contributions in a Traditional IRA.

Q509_LO98: What is the catch-up contribution amount for individuals aged 50 and older in a Traditional IRA?
a. $500
b. $1,000
c. $2,000
d. $5,000

HINTS: Recognize the additional contribution allowed for individuals aged 50 and older.

Q510_LO98: What is the maximum time limit for completing a rollover of IRA assets?
a. 30 calendar days
b. 45 calendar days
c. 60 calendar days
d. 90 calendar days

HINTS: Identify the time limit for completing a rollover of IRA assets.

Q511_LO98: Which investment is generally considered inappropriate for an IRA?
a. Stocks
b. Bonds
c. Mutual funds
d. Collectibles

HINTS: Recognize the type of investment generally considered inappropriate for an IRA.

Q512_LO98: What is the penalty for failing to take a required minimum distribution (RMD) from an IRA by the required date?
a. 25%
b. 35%
c. 50%
d. 75%

HINTS: Identify the penalty for failing to take an RMD by the required date.

Q513_LO98: When do required minimum distributions (RMDs) from an IRA begin?
a. Age 59½
b. Age 65
c. Age 70½
d. Age 72

HINTS: Recognize the age when RMDs from an IRA begin.

Q514_LO98: What is a key characteristic of Roth IRA contributions?
a. Tax-deductible
b. Tax-free
c. Income-dependent
d. Employer-sponsored

HINTS: Identify a key characteristic of Roth IRA contributions.

Q515_LO98: What is the eligibility limitation for contributing to a Roth IRA?
a. Age limit
b. Income limit
c. Employment status
d. Investment portfolio

HINTS: Recognize the limitation for contributing to a Roth IRA.

Q516_LO98: What distinguishes qualified distributions from nonqualified distributions in a Roth IRA?
a. Account age
b. Cost basis
c. Tax-free status
d. Distribution age and purpose

HINTS: Understand the distinction between qualified and nonqualified distributions in a Roth IRA.

Q517_LO98: What is the primary advantage of Roth IRAs regarding withdrawals?
a. Penalty-free withdrawals
b. Tax-free withdrawals
c. Unlimited withdrawals
d. Higher contribution limits

HINTS: Identify the main advantage of Roth IRAs related to withdrawals.

Q518_LO98: What is the required holding period for a Roth IRA to qualify for tax-free withdrawals?
a. 2 years
b. 3 years
c. 5 years
d. 10 years

HINTS: Recognize the holding period required for tax-free withdrawals in a Roth IRA.

Q519_LO98: What age is significant for avoiding the 10% penalty on nonqualified Roth IRA distributions?
a. 55
b. 59½
c. 62
d. 65

HINTS: Identify the age significant for avoiding the 10% penalty on nonqualified distributions.

Q520_LO98: What is the key difference between Traditional and Roth IRAs regarding required minimum distributions (RMDs)?
a. Roth IRAs have higher RMDs
b. Traditional IRAs have higher RMDs
c. Roth IRAs have no RMDs
d. Traditional IRAs have no RMDs

HINTS: Understand the key difference between RMDs in Traditional and Roth IRAs.

Q521_LO98: What is the primary purpose of Individual Retirement Accounts (IRAs)?
a. Homeownership
b. Education savings
c. Retirement savings
d. Health savings

HINTS: Identify the primary purpose of IRAs.

Q522_LO98: What is a key difference between qualified plans and IRAs?
a. Employer sponsorship
b. Tax deductions
c. Investment options
d. Age requirements

HINTS: Recognize a distinguishing feature between qualified plans and IRAs.

Q523_LO98: When is the full amount of an IRA contribution tax-deductible?
a. Always
b. If covered by another qualified plan
c. If not actively participating in other qualified plans
d. If over 60 years old

HINTS: Identify the conditions for the full tax deduction of an IRA contribution.

Q524_LO98: What is the catch-up amount for IRA contributions for individuals age 50 and older?
a. $500
b. $750
c. $1,000
d. $1,500

HINTS: Recognize the catch-up amount for IRA contributions for individuals aged 50 and older.

Q525_LO98: Which investment is NOT considered eligible for an IRA?
a. Stocks
b. Mutual funds
c. Collectibles
d. Government securities

HINTS: Identify the ineligible investment for an IRA.

Q526_LO98: What is a permissible investment practice within an IRA?
a. Short sales of stock
b. Speculative option strategies
c. Covered call writing
d. Margin account trading

HINTS: Identify the permissible investment practice within an IRA.

Q527_LO98: How is a rollover different from a transfer in the context of IRAs?
a. Time limit
b. Tax implications
c. Number of times allowed
d. Type of assets involved

HINTS: Recognize a difference between rollovers and transfers in IRAs.

Q528_LO98: At what age can distributions from a traditional IRA begin without a penalty?
a. 55
b. 59½
c. 62
d. 65

HINTS: Identify the age at which distributions from a traditional IRA can begin without a penalty.

Q529_LO98: What is a required minimum distribution (RMD) for traditional IRAs?
a. Required at age 65
b. Required at age 70½
c. Required at age 72
d. Not required

HINTS: Recognize the age at which RMDs are required for traditional IRAs.

Q530_LO98: What is the penalty for failing to take the RMD by the required date?
a. 25%
b. 50%
c. 75%
d. 100%

HINTS: Identify the penalty for failing to take the RMD by the required date.

Q531_LO98: What is a distinguishing feature of Roth IRA distributions?
a. Always taxed
b. Tax-free cost basis distributions
c. Tax-free qualified distributions
d. Subject to 20% penalty

HINTS: Recognize a key feature of Roth IRA distributions.

Q532_LO98: What is a qualification for a distribution from a Roth IRA to be tax-free?
a. At least 5 years of account holding
b. Age 50 or older
c. Employment status
d. Monthly contributions

HINTS: Identify the qualification for a tax-free distribution from a Roth IRA.

Q533_LO98: What is an exception to the age limit for tax-free Roth IRA distributions?
a. Death
b. Disability
c. First-time home purchase
d. All of the above

HINTS: Recognize exceptions to the age limit for tax-free Roth IRA distributions.

Q534_LO98: Why are Roth IRAs considered suitable for those in lower income tax brackets?
a. Higher contribution limits
b. Tax deductions
c. Tax-free distributions
d. No contribution limits

HINTS: Identify a reason why Roth IRAs are considered suitable for those in lower income tax brackets.

Q535_LO98: What is a major advantage of Roth IRAs regarding required minimum distributions?
a. No RMDs required
b. Lower RMD amounts
c. Delayed RMDs until age 75
d. RMDs based on account values

HINTS: Recognize a major advantage of Roth IRAs concerning required minimum distributions.

Q536_LO99: What is the primary characteristic of a defined benefit plan?
a. Employee contributions
b. Employer-defined retirement benefit
c. Individual investment choices
d. Portable assets

HINTS: Recognize the key feature of defined benefit plans.

Q537_LO99: In a defined benefit plan, how is the retirement benefit determined?
a. Employee's investment choices
b. Years of service, age, and salary
c. Employer contributions
d. Portable asset value

HINTS: Identify the factors used to determine the retirement benefit in a defined benefit plan.

Q538_LO99: Who bears the investment risk in a defined benefit plan?
a. Employees
b. Employers
c. Outside firms
d. Government

HINTS: Recognize which party bears the investment risk in a defined benefit plan.

Q539_LO99: What is a common alternative name for defined benefit plans?
a. 401(k) plans
b. Pension plans
c. Profit-sharing plans
d. SIMPLE plans

HINTS: Identify an alternative name often used for defined benefit plans.

Q540_LO99: What distinguishes defined contribution plans from defined benefit plans?
a. Employer-defined retirement benefit
b. Individual investment choices
c. Portable assets
d. Fixed employer contributions

HINTS: Differentiate the defining characteristic of defined contribution plans.

Q541_LO99: Which party typically carries the investment risk in defined contribution plans?
a. Employees
b. Employers
c. Outside firms
d. Government

HINTS: Recognize the party usually bearing the investment risk in defined contribution plans.

Q542_LO99: What is a characteristic feature of assets in defined contribution plans?
a. Fixed employer contributions
b. Portable between employer plans
c. Employer-defined retirement benefit
d. Outside firm management

HINTS: Identify a key characteristic of assets in defined contribution plans.

Q543_LO99: Which plan type is more popular today due to lower employer liability?
a. 401(k) plans
b. Defined benefit plans
c. Profit-sharing plans
d. 403(b) plans

HINTS: Recognize the plan type more popular today for its lower employer liability.

Q544_LO99: What is a significant advantage of defined contribution plans for a mobile workforce?
a. Fixed employer contributions
b. Employee investment choices
c. Employer-defined retirement benefit
d. Outside firm management

HINTS: Identify an advantage of defined contribution plans for a mobile workforce.

Q545_LO99: In which plan type do employees often transfer assets to an IRA at retirement?
a. 401(k) plans
b. Defined benefit plans
c. Profit-sharing plans
d. 403(b) plans

HINTS: Recognize the plan type where employees often transfer assets to an IRA at retirement.

Q546_LO99: What defines the contribution amount in defined contribution plans?
a. Employee's age
b. Employer's discretion
c. Employee's investment choices
d. Plan document

HINTS: Identify the defining factor for the contribution amount in defined contribution plans.

Q547_LO99: What is a characteristic feature of employee balances in defined contribution plans?
a. Fixed retirement benefit
b. Determined by employer contributions
c. Portable and invested by employees
d. Defined by government regulations

HINTS: Identify a characteristic feature of employee balances in defined contribution plans.

Q548_LO99: What role do outside firms play in defined contribution plans?
a. Determine retirement benefits
b. Manage employee investments
c. Contribute to the plan
d. Carry investment risk

HINTS: Recognize the role of outside firms in defined contribution plans.

Q549_LO99: What is a common feature of both defined benefit and defined contribution plans?
a. Employee investment choices
b. Portable assets
c. Retirement benefits determined by employers
d. Individual contribution limits

HINTS: Identify a common feature shared by both defined benefit and defined contribution plans.

Q550_LO99: Why are many companies moving away from defined benefit plans?
a. Higher employee contributions
b. Lower employer liability
c. Fixed retirement benefits
d. Greater employee control

HINTS: Recognize a reason many companies are moving away from defined benefit plans.

Q551_LO99: What is the key characteristic of a defined benefit plan?
a. Employees define contributions
b. Retirement benefit is predefined
c. Employer investment risk
d. Portable assets

HINTS: Identify the defining feature of a defined benefit plan.

Q552_LO99: How is the retirement benefit determined in a defined benefit plan?
a. Employee contributions
b. Years of service, age, and salary
c. Employer-defined investments
d. IRA distributions

HINTS: Recognize the factors that determine the retirement benefit in a defined benefit plan.

Q553_LO99: What is the primary responsibility of the employer in a defined benefit plan?
a. Employee contributions
b. Investment decisions
c. Making predefined benefit payments
d. Portable asset management

HINTS: Identify the primary responsibility of the employer in a defined benefit plan.

Q554_LO99: Why are many companies moving away from defined benefit plans?
a. Employee preference
b. Lower investment risk for employers
c. Increased portability
d. Flexibility in contributions

HINTS: Recognize a reason why companies are shifting away from defined benefit plans.

Q555_LO99: What defines the contribution amount in a defined contribution plan?
a. Employee-defined benefits
b. Employer investment risk
c. Plan document
d. IRS regulations

HINTS: Identify what determines the contribution amount in a defined contribution plan.

Q556_LO99: In which type of plan does the investing risk primarily lie with the employee?
a. Defined benefit plan
b. 401(k) plan
c. Traditional pension plan
d. Profit-sharing plan

HINTS: Recognize the type of plan where the investing risk is carried by the employee.

Q557_LO99: What happens to the assets in a defined contribution plan at retirement?
a. Returned to the employer
b. Transferred to an IRA
c. Converted to annuities
d. Donated to charity

HINTS: Identify the typical outcome for assets in a defined contribution plan at retirement.

Q558_LO99: Which of the following is a defined contribution plan?
a. Traditional pension plan
b. 403(b) plan
c. Money purchase plan
d. Simplified Employee Pension (SEP)

HINTS: Recognize a defined contribution plan from the given options.

Q559_LO99: What is a characteristic of defined contribution plans that makes them attractive for a mobile workforce?
a. Higher investment risk
b. Fixed employer liability
c. Non-portable assets
d. Limited employee choices

HINTS: Identify a feature that makes defined contribution plans suitable for a mobile workforce.

Q560_LO99: Which plan requires employers to make contributions based on a fixed percentage of employees' compensation?
a. Profit-sharing plan
b. Money purchase plan
c. 401(k) plan
d. SIMPLE plan

HINTS: Recognize the type of plan where employers contribute a fixed percentage of employees' compensation.

Q561_LO99: What is the primary advantage of defined contribution plans for employers?
a. Lower employee turnover
b. Greater investment control
c. Predefined benefit payments
d. Reduced portability

HINTS: Identify a benefit that makes defined contribution plans advantageous for employers.

Q562_LO99: Which plan type is more popular today due to the lower liability for employers?
a. Traditional pension plan
b. Defined benefit plan
c. Profit-sharing plan
d. 401(k) plan

HINTS: Recognize the plan type that is more popular today due to lower liability for employers.

Q563_LO99: What distinguishes a defined contribution plan from a defined benefit plan regarding employee choices?
a. Limited investment options
b. Fixed employer contributions
c. Employer-defined benefits
d. Employee-defined benefits

HINTS: Identify a distinguishing feature of defined contribution plans regarding employee choices.

Q564_LO99: In which plan does the plan document play a crucial role in determining benefits?
a. Defined contribution plan
b. Traditional pension plan
c. Profit-sharing plan
d. Simplified Employee Pension (SEP)

HINTS: Recognize the plan type where the plan document is crucial for determining benefits.

Q565_LO99: What feature makes defined contribution plans more flexible for employees?
a. Fixed employer contributions
b. Predefined benefit payments
c. Portable assets
d. Limited investment choices

HINTS: Identify a feature that makes defined contribution plans flexible for employees.

Q566_LO100: When must payment be made in a cash account for most corporate and municipal securities?
a. T+1
b. T+2
c. T+3
d. T+4

HINTS: Identify the standard settlement period for most corporate and municipal securities.

Q567_LO100: What does Regulation T require regarding payment in cash accounts?
a. Payment within 1 business day
b. Payment within 2 business days
c. Payment within 3 business days
d. Payment within 4 business days

HINTS: Recognize the regulatory requirement for payment under Regulation T.

Q568_LO100: In which type of account must certain accounts, such as IRAs, be opened due to contribution limits?
a. Fee-based accounts
b. Margin accounts
c. Cash accounts
d. Custodial accounts

HINTS: Identify the account type where contribution limits, like those for IRAs, require opening.

Q569_LO100: What is the primary advantage for customers trading on margin in a long margin account?
a. Higher initial cash outlay
b. Lower interest payments
c. Increased trading capital
d. Reduced trading risks

HINTS: Recognize an advantage for customers trading on margin in a long margin account.

Q570_LO100: In a short margin account, what enables the customer to profit if the stock value declines?
a. Borrowing cash
b. Paying interest
c. Borrowing stock and selling short
d. Purchasing options

HINTS: Identify the action that allows customers to profit in a short margin account.

Q571_LO100: What is a common source for stock borrowing in short sales in a margin account?
a. Government agencies
b. Stock lending firms
c. Insurance companies
d. Retail investors

HINTS: Recognize a common source for stock borrowing in short sales in a margin account.

Q572_LO100: What advantage do margin accounts offer for customers in terms of leveraging?
a. Lower initial cash outlay
b. Reduced trading risks
c. Fixed interest rates
d. Decreased rate of return

HINTS: Identify an advantage for customers in margin accounts related to leveraging.

Q573_LO100: What is a disadvantage for customers leveraging in margin accounts during adverse market conditions?
a. Lower interest payments
b. Magnified rate of return
c. Increased rate of loss
d. Reduced trading risks

HINTS: Recognize a disadvantage for customers leveraging in margin accounts during adverse market conditions.

Q574_LO100: What generates interest income for brokerage firms in margin accounts?
a. Customer deposits
b. Margin account loans
c. Fixed-rate securities
d. Leverage ratio

HINTS: Identify a source of interest income for brokerage firms in margin accounts.

Q575_LO100: What is the term for the pledging of customer securities as collateral for margin loans?
a. Repossession
b. Leverage
c. Hypothecation
d. Liquidation

HINTS: Recognize the term for pledging customer securities as collateral for margin loans.

Q576_LO100: What agreement must be signed by a customer to allow the pledging of securities for margin loans?
a. Margin agreement
b. Pledge agreement
c. Hypothecation agreement
d. Collateral agreement

HINTS: Identify the agreement required for customers to allow the pledging of securities for margin loans.

Q577_LO100: Where does a BD typically borrow money from for margin purchases?
a. Other BDs
b. Stock lending firms
c. The Federal Reserve
d. The bank

HINTS: Recognize the typical source of borrowed money for margin purchases in a BD.

Q578_LO100: What oversees the process of a bank lending money to BDs based on customer securities as collateral?
a. SEC
b. FINRA
c. Federal Reserve Regulation U
d. FDIC

HINTS: Identify the regulatory oversight for a bank lending money to BDs based on customer securities as collateral.

Q579_LO100: What is NOT allowed regarding the commingling of customer securities in margin accounts?
a. Commingle with securities owned by the firm
b. Commingle between different customers
c. Commingle for rehypothecation
d. Commingle with fixed-rate securities

HINTS: Recognize a restriction on commingling customer securities in margin accounts.

Q580_LO100: What type of accounts may not be margin accounts?
a. Corporate accounts
b. Trust and other fiduciary accounts
c. Joint accounts
d. Individual accounts

HINTS: Identify the account type that may not have a margin feature.

Q581_LO100: What is the expected payment period for settlement in a cash account for most corporate and municipal securities?
a. T+1
b. T+2
c. T+3
d. T+4

HINTS: Identify the standard settlement period for most corporate and municipal securities.

Q582_LO100: Under Federal Reserve Regulation T, when must payment for securities occur in a cash account?
a. Within 1 business day
b. Within 2 business days
c. Within 3 business days
d. Within 4 business days

HINTS: Recognize the payment expectation under Federal Reserve Regulation T.

Q583_LO100: Which type of accounts must be opened as cash accounts due to contribution limits and custodial arrangements?
a. Corporate accounts
b. Margin accounts
c. Retirement plans and custodial accounts
d. Fee-based accounts

HINTS: Identify the accounts that must be opened as cash accounts.

Q584_LO100: What is the primary advantage of trading on margin in a long margin account?
a. Reduced trading capital
b. Tax deductions
c. Increased trading capital
d. Fixed interest rates

HINTS: Recognize the advantage for customers in a long margin account.

Q585_LO100: In a short margin account, what is the customer's potential profit scenario?
a. Stock value increase
b. Stock value decrease
c. No impact on stock value
d. Fixed interest earnings

HINTS: Identify the scenario where a customer profits in a short margin account.

Q586_LO100: What does leveraging in a margin account primarily do for a customer?
a. Increases trading costs
b. Reduces rate of return
c. Magnifies rate of return or loss
d. Stabilizes investments

HINTS: Identify the primary impact of leveraging in a margin account for a customer.

Q587_LO100: What advantage do margin accounts offer for customers in terms of initial cash outlay?
a. Higher initial cash outlay
b. Lower initial cash outlay
c. Fixed initial cash outlay
d. No initial cash outlay

HINTS: Recognize the advantage for customers in terms of initial cash outlay in margin accounts.

Q588_LO100: What generates interest income for a brokerage firm in margin accounts?
a. Customer deposits
b. Margin account loans
c. Dividend payments
d. Stock appreciation

HINTS: Identify the source of interest income for brokerage firms in margin accounts.

Q589_LO100: What is the primary advantage of margin accounts for brokerage firms?
a. Fixed interest rates
b. Increased customer turnover
c. Higher commissions
d. Reduced risk

HINTS: Recognize the primary benefit for brokerage firms in offering margin accounts.

Q590_LO100: What is hypothecation in the context of margin accounts?
a. Selling borrowed stock
b. Pledging customer securities as collateral
c. Withdrawing cash from margin accounts
d. Investing in high-risk securities

HINTS: Identify the action associated with hypothecation in margin accounts.

Q591_LO100: When does rehypothecation occur in the margin account process?
a. Before margin approval
b. After the margin agreement is signed
c. During regular way settlement
d. When customers withdraw funds

HINTS: Recognize the timing of rehypothecation in the margin account process.

Q592_LO100: What regulation oversees the process of banks lending money to broker-dealers based on customer securities as collateral?
a. Federal Reserve Regulation T
b. Federal Reserve Regulation U
c. FINRA Regulation M
d. SEC Regulation SHO

HINTS: Identify the regulation overseeing bank loans to broker-dealers based on customer securities.

Q593_LO100: In margin accounts, can a brokerage firm commingle customer securities with its own securities?
a. Yes, without restrictions
b. Yes, with restrictions
c. No, never
d. Only with SEC approval

HINTS: Recognize the rule regarding commingling of customer and firm securities in margin accounts.

Q594_LO100: Which account type requires checking the corporate charter or bylaws for margin eligibility?
a. Trust accounts
b. Individual accounts
c. Corporate accounts
d. Joint accounts

HINTS: Identify the account type where corporate charter or bylaws must be checked for margin eligibility.

Q595_LO100: What is the requirement for margin account approval in trust and fiduciary accounts?
a. Trust document approval
b. Principal approval
c. SEC approval
d. Regulatory approval

HINTS: Recognize the requirement for margin account approval in trust and fiduciary accounts.

Q596_LO101: What does the credit agreement associated with a margin account disclose?
a. Investment strategy
b. Credit extended terms
c. Account balance
d. Trading commissions

HINTS: Identify the information disclosed in the credit agreement.

Q597_LO101: What is the purpose of the hypothecation agreement in a margin account?
a. Settling trades
b. Pledging securities for a loan
c. Authorizing fund transfers
d. Updating account information

HINTS: Recognize the primary purpose of the hypothecation agreement.

Q598_LO101: When customer securities are held in street name, what is the customer's status?
a. Beneficial owner
b. Nominal owner
c. Joint owner
d. Margin owner

HINTS: Identify the customer's status when securities are held in street name.

Q599_LO101: What does the consent to loan agreement permit the firm to do in a margin account?
a. Execute trades
b. Borrow securities
c. Change interest rates
d. Facilitate short sales

HINTS: Recognize the action permitted by the consent to loan agreement.

Q600_LO101: Before opening a margin account, what must be provided to customers?
a. Risk disclosure document
b. Trading strategy guide
c. Fee schedule
d. Market research report

HINTS: Identify the document that must be provided to customers before opening a margin account.

Q601_LO101: According to the risk disclosure document, what risk do customers face if a maintenance call is not met?
a. Loss of trading privileges
b. Limited securities selection
c. Loss of more money than deposited
d. Extension of time for margin call

HINTS: Recognize a risk associated with maintenance calls in the risk disclosure document.

Q602_LO101: What is a key risk associated with margin trading, as per the risk disclosure document?
a. Guaranteed profits
b. Extension of margin calls
c. Unrestricted securities selection
d. Increased in-house margin requirements

HINTS: Identify a risk in the risk disclosure document related to margin trading.

Q603_LO101: Which of the following securities cannot be purchased on margin or used as collateral for a margin loan?
a. Exchange-listed stocks
b. Warrants
c. Rights
d. Options

HINTS: Recognize securities that cannot be purchased on margin or used as collateral.

Q604_LO101: After being held for 30 days, which securities can be used as collateral in a margin account?
a. Exchange-listed stocks
b. Options
c. Mutual funds
d. OTC issues

HINTS: Identify securities that can be used as collateral after a 30-day holding period.

Q605_LO101: What is the minimum requirement for exempt securities from Regulation T in a margin account?
a. Initial deposit requirement
b. 10% maintenance margin
c. 30% maintenance margin
d. No minimum requirement

HINTS: Recognize the minimum requirement for exempt securities from Regulation T.

Q606_LO101: Which securities are exempt from Regulation T margin requirements?
a. Exchange-listed stocks
b. U.S. Treasury bills
c. Mutual funds
d. Options

HINTS: Identify securities exempt from Regulation T margin requirements.

Q607_LO101: What can firms impose on exempt securities bought or sold in a margin account?
a. Increased trading limits
b. Stricter requirements
c. Lower maintenance margins
d. No additional requirements

HINTS: Recognize the actions firms can take with exempt securities in a margin account.

Q608_LO101: Which form associated with a margin account gives permission for repledging securities?
a. Credit agreement
b. Hypothecation agreement
c. Consent to loan agreement
d. Risk disclosure document

HINTS: Identify the form that provides permission for repledging securities in a margin account.

Q609_LO101: What does Regulation T identify regarding securities eligible for margin borrowing?
a. Eligible ETFs
b. Eligible mutual funds
c. Eligible OTC issues
d. Eligible exchange-listed stocks

HINTS: Recognize the securities identified by Regulation T as eligible for margin borrowing.

Q610_LO101: How often must risk disclosure information be provided to margin customers?
a. Semi-annually
b. Annually
c. Quarterly
d. Biennially

HINTS: Identify the frequency of providing risk disclosure information to margin customers.

Q611_LO101: What is the purpose of the credit agreement in a margin account?
a. Disclose securities eligibility
b. Outline margin trading risks
c. Disclose credit terms
d. Determine initial deposit

HINTS: Identify the primary purpose of the credit agreement.

Q612_LO101: Which agreement allows securities to be pledged for a loan and permits repledging of customer margin securities as collateral?
a. Risk disclosure agreement
b. Credit agreement
c. Hypothecation agreement
d. Consent to loan agreement

HINTS: Recognize the agreement associated with pledging securities for a loan.

Q613_LO101: What permission does the consent to loan agreement grant to the firm in a margin account?
a. Change interest rates
b. Repledge customer securities
c. Execute short sales
d. Determine maintenance requirements

HINTS: Identify the action permitted by the consent to loan agreement.

Q614_LO101: What must customers be provided with before opening a margin account?
a. Credit agreement
b. Hypothecation agreement
c. Risk disclosure document
d. Consent to loan agreement

HINTS: Recognize the document required to be provided to customers before opening a margin account.

Q615_LO101: In street name registration, who is the nominal owner of customer securities?
a. Customer
b. Bank
c. Broker-dealer
d. Regulatory authority

HINTS: Identify the nominal owner in street name registration.

Q616_LO101: What risks are discussed in the risk disclosure document for margin trading?
a. Securities eligibility risks
b. Market volatility risks
c. Customer withdrawal risks
d. Brokerage commission risks

HINTS: Recognize the types of risks discussed in the risk disclosure document.

Q617_LO101: According to Regulation T, what securities can be purchased on margin and used as collateral?
a. Options and rights
b. Mutual funds and new issues
c. Exchange-listed stocks and bonds
d. Non-NMS OTC issues

HINTS: Identify securities eligible for purchase on margin and as collateral.

Q618_LO101: What cannot be purchased on margin or used as collateral for a margin loan?
a. Mutual funds
b. Options
c. New issues
d. U.S. Treasury bills

HINTS: Identify the securities that cannot be purchased on margin or used as collateral.

Q619_LO101: What is the holding period required for mutual funds to be used as collateral after purchase?
a. 15 days
b. 30 days
c. 45 days
d. 60 days

HINTS: Recognize the holding period for mutual funds to be used as collateral.

Q620_LO101: Which securities are exempt from Regulation T margin requirements?
a. Exchange-listed stocks
b. U.S. Treasury bills
c. Rights
d. Non-NMS OTC issues

HINTS: Identify the securities exempt from Regulation T.

Q621_LO101: If exempt securities are bought or sold in a margin account, what determines the initial deposit requirement?
a. Broker's discretion
b. Regulatory approval
c. Customer's preference
d. Firm's determination

HINTS: Recognize the factor determining the initial deposit requirement for exempt securities.

Q622_LO101: What minimum requirements must firms follow for exempt securities under FINRA regulations?
a. SEC requirements
b. Maintenance requirements
c. Customer preferences
d. Industry standards

HINTS: Identify the regulatory requirements for exempt securities.

Q623_LO101: What is the primary purpose of the risk disclosure document in a margin account?
a. Outline margin trading benefits
b. Disclose credit agreement terms
c. Discuss risks associated with margin trading
d. Determine customer eligibility

HINTS: Recognize the main purpose of the risk disclosure document.

Q624_LO101: What agreement allows the firm to loan customer margin securities to others?
a. Credit agreement
b. Hypothecation agreement
c. Consent to loan agreement
d. Risk disclosure agreement

HINTS: Identify the agreement associated with loaning customer securities.

Q625_LO101: Why are customer securities held in street name in margin accounts?
a. To facilitate short sales
b. To expedite customer withdrawals
c. To avoid maintenance requirements
d. To reduce credit risks

HINTS: Recognize the purpose of holding customer securities in street name.

Q626_LO102: What is the Regulation T requirement for the initial deposit in a margin account?
a. 25%
b. 50%
c. $2,000
d. 100%

HINTS: Remember the Regulation T requirement for the first purchase.

Q627_LO102: According to FINRA, what is the minimum initial requirement for a margin account?
a. $1,000
b. $2,000
c. $4,000
d. 50% of the purchase

HINTS: Identify the minimum initial requirement set by FINRA.

Q628_LO102: How should the initial deposit be calculated for a customer's first purchase exceeding $4,000 in a margin account?
a. 25%
b. 50%
c. $2,000
d. 100%

HINTS: Recognize the calculation for a first purchase exceeding $4,000.

Q629_LO102: If a customer's first purchase is between $2,000 and $4,000, what is the FINRA minimum initial deposit requirement?
a. $1,000
b. $2,000
c. $4,000
d. 100% of the purchase

HINTS: Identify the FINRA minimum for a purchase between $2,000 and $4,000.

Q630_LO102: When should a maintenance call be triggered in a margin account?
a. When equity drops below 50%
b. When equity drops below 25%
c. When the account value increases
d. At the customer's discretion

HINTS: Recognize the condition for triggering a maintenance call.

Q631_LO102: What is the customer required to do upon receiving a maintenance call?
a. Withdraw all funds
b. Make additional deposits
c. Close the account
d. Ignore the call

HINTS: Identify the required action upon receiving a maintenance call.

Q632_LO102: What is the FINRA minimum maintenance equity for a short margin account?
a. 20%
b. 30%
c. $1,000
d. $2,000

HINTS: Recognize the FINRA minimum maintenance equity for a short margin account.

Q633_LO102: What is the purpose of a house call in a margin account?
a. Request for additional documents
b. Higher minimum maintenance requirements
c. Withdrawal of assets
d. Margin trading approval

HINTS: Identify the purpose of a house call.

Q634_LO102: Is the calculation of a maintenance call expected to be on the SIE Exam?
a. Yes
b. No
c. Depends on the account type
d. Only for short positions

HINTS: Determine the exam expectation regarding the calculation of maintenance calls.

Q635_LO102: What is a fee-based account's primary characteristic?
a. Higher transaction costs
b. Quarterly trading fees
c. Set fee for all trading
d. Commission-based trading

HINTS: Recognize the primary characteristic of a fee-based account.

Q636_LO102: When is a fee-based account most appropriate for a customer?
a. Frequent trading
b. Buy-and-hold strategy
c. High-risk tolerance
d. Large initial deposit

HINTS: Identify the scenario where a fee-based account is most appropriate.

Q637_LO102: What is the common fee structure in a fee-based account?
a. Fixed fee per transaction
b. Percentage of account value
c. No fees
d. Varied fees for different assets

HINTS: Recognize the common fee structure in a fee-based account.

Q638_LO102: What trading strategy is least suitable for a fee-based account?
a. Day trading
b. Swing trading
c. Long-term investing
d. Options trading

HINTS: Identify the trading strategy least suitable for a fee-based account.

Q639_LO102: If a customer's first purchase in a margin account is $1,500, what is the required initial deposit?
a. $1,500
b. $2,000
c. $750
d. $1,000

HINTS: Calculate the required initial deposit for a purchase less than $2,000.

Q640_LO102: What is the primary purpose of calculating the initial deposit in a margin account?
a. Determine trading frequency
b. Cover brokerage commissions
c. Meet regulatory requirements
d. Assess customer risk tolerance

HINTS: Recognize the primary purpose of calculating the initial deposit.

Correct Answers & Explanations
Qualified Plans & Account Features

Q506_LO98: Correct Answer: b EXPLANATIONS: IRAs were created to encourage people to save for retirement.

Q507_LO98: Correct Answer: b EXPLANATIONS: IRAs do not require employer sponsorship, a key characteristic of qualified plans.

Q508_LO98: Correct Answer: c EXPLANATIONS: Deductibility is determined by the individual's income level.

Q509_LO98: Correct Answer: b EXPLANATIONS: The catch-up amount is currently $1,000.

Q510_LO98: Correct Answer: c EXPLANATIONS: Rollovers must be completed within 60 calendar days.

Q511_LO98: Correct Answer: d EXPLANATIONS: Collectibles, such as antiques and rare coins, are not acceptable IRA investments.

Q512_LO98: Correct Answer: c EXPLANATIONS: The penalty is 50% of the shortfall.

Q513_LO98: Correct Answer: d EXPLANATIONS: RMDs begin in the year the account owner turns 72.

Q514_LO98: Correct Answer: a EXPLANATIONS: Contributions to Roth IRAs are not tax-deductible.

Q515_LO98: Correct Answer: b EXPLANATIONS: Eligibility is phased out at higher income limits.

Q516_LO98: Correct Answer: d EXPLANATIONS: Qualified distributions require both account age and specific purposes.

Q517_LO98: Correct Answer: b EXPLANATIONS: Distributions of income or gains are tax-free in qualified Roth IRA withdrawals.

Q518_LO98: Correct Answer: c EXPLANATIONS: The account holder must have held a Roth IRA for at least five years.

Q519_LO98: Correct Answer: b EXPLANATIONS: Age 59½ allows for penalty-free nonqualified distributions.

Q520_LO98: Correct Answer: c EXPLANATIONS: Roth IRAs do not have required minimum distributions (RMDs).

Q521_LO98: Correct Answer: c EXPLANATIONS: IRAs were created as a way of encouraging people to save for retirement.

Q522_LO98: Correct Answer: a EXPLANATIONS: Qualified plans require an employer sponsor, while IRAs are self-sponsored.

Q523_LO98: Correct Answer: c EXPLANATIONS: The full amount is deductible if not actively participating in other qualified plans.

Q524_LO98: Correct Answer: c EXPLANATIONS: The catch-up amount is currently $1,000.

Q525_LO98: Correct Answer: c EXPLANATIONS: Collectibles, such as antiques and gems, are not acceptable IRA investments.

Q526_LO98: Correct Answer: c EXPLANATIONS: Covered call writing is a conservative way to generate investment income.

Q527_LO98: Correct Answer: a EXPLANATIONS: Rollovers have a time limit of 60 calendar days.

Q528_LO98: Correct Answer: b EXPLANATIONS: Distributions can begin without a penalty after age 59½.

Q529_LO98: Correct Answer: c EXPLANATIONS: RMDs are required starting in the year the account owner turns 72.

Q530_LO98: Correct Answer: b EXPLANATIONS: The penalty is 50% of the shortfall.

Q531_LO98: Correct Answer: c EXPLANATIONS: Qualified distributions from a Roth IRA are tax-free.

Q532_LO98: Correct Answer: a EXPLANATIONS: A tax-free distribution requires at least five years of account holding.

Q533_LO98: Correct Answer: d EXPLANATIONS: Exceptions include death, disability, and a first-time home purchase.

Q534_LO98: Correct Answer: c EXPLANATIONS: Roth IRAs offer tax-free distributions, which are valuable for those in lower tax brackets.

Q535_LO98: Correct Answer: a EXPLANATIONS: Roth IRAs do not have a required minimum distribution rule.

Q536_LO99: Correct Answer: b EXPLANATIONS: Defined benefit plans define the retirement benefit provided by the employer.

Q537_LO99: Correct Answer: b EXPLANATIONS: The benefit is determined based on years of service, age, and salary.

Q538_LO99: Correct Answer: b EXPLANATIONS: The investment risk is on the employer in a defined benefit plan.

Q539_LO99: Correct Answer: b EXPLANATIONS: Defined benefit plans are often referred to as pension plans.

Q540_LO99: Correct Answer: b EXPLANATIONS: In defined contribution plans, individuals make investment choices for their contributions.

Q541_LO99: Correct Answer: a EXPLANATIONS: The investment risk is often carried by employees in defined contribution plans.

Q542_LO99: Correct Answer: b EXPLANATIONS: Assets in these plans are transportable between employer plans.

Q543_LO99: Correct Answer: a EXPLANATIONS: Defined contribution plans, like 401(k) plans, are more popular due to lower employer liability.

Q544_LO99: Correct Answer: b EXPLANATIONS: Employees can carry their assets between employers in defined contribution plans.

Q545_LO99: Correct Answer: a EXPLANATIONS: Employees often transfer assets from 401(k) plans to an IRA.

Q546_LO99: Correct Answer: d EXPLANATIONS: The contribution amount is defined by the plan document.

Q547_LO99: Correct Answer: c EXPLANATIONS: Employee balances are portable and invested by employees in defined contribution plans.

Q548_LO99: Correct Answer: b EXPLANATIONS: Outside firms often do not manage employee investments in defined contribution plans.

Q549_LO99: Correct Answer: b EXPLANATIONS: Portable assets are a common feature in both types of plans.

Q550_LO99: Correct Answer: b EXPLANATIONS: Companies are moving away due to the higher investment risk and liability associated with defined benefit plans.

Q551_LO99: Correct Answer: b EXPLANATIONS: Defined benefit plans define the retirement benefit paid to retirees.

Q552_LO99: Correct Answer: b EXPLANATIONS: The benefit is based on years of service, age, and salary.

Q553_LO99: Correct Answer: c EXPLANATIONS: Employers must make predefined benefit payments.

Q554_LO99: Correct Answer: b EXPLANATIONS: These plans place the investment risk on the company.

Q555_LO99: Correct Answer: c EXPLANATIONS: The plan document defines the contribution amount.

Q556_LO99: Correct Answer: b EXPLANATIONS: Defined contribution plans, like 401(k), place the investing risk on the employee.

Q557_LO99: Correct Answer: b EXPLANATIONS: Employees often transfer assets to an IRA for distribution during retirement.

Q558_LO99: Correct Answer: b EXPLANATIONS: 403(b) plans are a type of defined contribution plan.

Q559_LO99: Correct Answer: b EXPLANATIONS: The liability for the employer is smaller, and assets are portable between plans.

Q560_LO99: Correct Answer: b EXPLANATIONS: Money purchase plans involve fixed employer contributions.

Q561_LO99: Correct Answer: b EXPLANATIONS: Employers have greater control over investments in defined contribution plans.

Q562_LO99: Correct Answer: d EXPLANATIONS: Defined contribution plans like 401(k) are more popular due to lower employer liability.

Q563_LO99: Correct Answer: d EXPLANATIONS: Employees have more control over their investments in defined contribution plans.

Q564_LO99: Correct Answer: b EXPLANATIONS: Defined benefit plans rely on the plan document to define benefits.

Q565_LO99: Correct Answer: c EXPLANATIONS: Assets in defined contribution plans are often portable between employers.

Q566_LO100: Correct Answer: b EXPLANATIONS: Regular way settlement is typically T+2.

Q567_LO100: Correct Answer: b EXPLANATIONS: Regulation T requires payment within 2 business days after the standard settlement period.

Q568_LO100: Correct Answer: c EXPLANATIONS: Cash accounts have contribution limits for certain accounts.

Q569_LO100: Correct Answer: c EXPLANATIONS: Trading on margin allows customers to leverage their investment and increase trading capital.

Q570_LO100: Correct Answer: c EXPLANATIONS: In a short margin account, stock is borrowed and sold short.

Q571_LO100: Correct Answer: b EXPLANATIONS: Stock lending firms are one source for borrowed stock in margin accounts.

Q572_LO100: Correct Answer: a EXPLANATIONS: Customers can purchase more securities with a lower initial cash outlay.

Q573_LO100: Correct Answer: c EXPLANATIONS: Leveraging magnifies the rate of loss in adverse market conditions.

Q574_LO100: Correct Answer: b EXPLANATIONS: Margin account loans generate interest income for the firm.

Q575_LO100: Correct Answer: c EXPLANATIONS: Hypothecation involves using customer securities as collateral for margin loans.

Q576_LO100: Correct Answer: c EXPLANATIONS: A hypothecation agreement is generally contained within the margin agreement.

Q577_LO100: Correct Answer: d EXPLANATIONS: BDs often borrow money from the bank for margin purchases.

Q578_LO100: Correct Answer: c EXPLANATIONS: Federal Reserve Regulation U oversees this process.

Q579_LO100: Correct Answer: a EXPLANATIONS: Firms cannot commingle customer securities with securities owned by the firm.

Q580_LO100: Correct Answer: b EXPLANATIONS: Trust and other fiduciary accounts may not have a margin feature unless the document allows it.

Q581_LO100: Correct Answer: b EXPLANATIONS: Regular way settlement is typically on the second business day (T+2).

Q582_LO100: Correct Answer: b EXPLANATIONS: Payment must occur within two business days after the standard settlement period.

Q583_LO100: Correct Answer: c EXPLANATIONS: Contribution-limited accounts and custodial accounts fall under cash accounts.

Q584_LO100: Correct Answer: c EXPLANATIONS: Customers can leverage their investment with increased trading capital.

Q585_LO100: Correct Answer: b EXPLANATIONS: Customers profit if the value of the borrowed stock decreases.

Q586_LO100: Correct Answer: c EXPLANATIONS: Leverage magnifies the rate of return or loss.

Q587_LO100: Correct Answer: b EXPLANATIONS: Customers can purchase more securities with a lower initial cash outlay.

Q588_LO100: Correct Answer: b EXPLANATIONS: Interest income is generated from margin account loans.

Q589_LO100: Correct Answer: c EXPLANATIONS: Margin customers typically trade larger positions, generating higher commissions.

Q590_LO100: Correct Answer: b EXPLANATIONS: Hypothecation is pledging customer securities as collateral for margin loans.

Q591_LO100: Correct Answer: b EXPLANATIONS: Rehypothecation occurs after customers pledge securities by signing the margin agreement.

Q592_LO100: Correct Answer: b EXPLANATIONS: Federal Reserve Regulation U oversees this process.

Q593_LO100: Correct Answer: c EXPLANATIONS: Firms cannot commingle customer securities with securities owned by the firm.

Q594_LO100: Correct Answer: c EXPLANATIONS: Corporate accounts require checking for margin eligibility in the corporate charter or bylaws.

Q595_LO100: Correct Answer: a EXPLANATIONS: The trust or similar document must specifically allow margin for approval.

Q596_LO101: Correct Answer: b EXPLANATIONS: The credit agreement discloses the terms of the credit extended by the BD.

Q597_LO101: Correct Answer: b EXPLANATIONS: It allows securities to be pledged for a loan and gives permission for repledging.

Q598_LO101: Correct Answer: a EXPLANATIONS: The customer is the beneficial owner, retaining all rights of ownership.

Q599_LO101: Correct Answer: b EXPLANATIONS: It gives permission to loan customer margin securities, often for short sales.

Q600_LO101: Correct Answer: a EXPLANATIONS: A risk disclosure document discussing associated risks.

Q601_LO101: Correct Answer: c EXPLANATIONS: Customers can lose more money than initially deposited.

Q602_LO101: Correct Answer: d EXPLANATIONS: Firms can increase in-house margin requirements without notice.

Q603_LO101: Correct Answer: d EXPLANATIONS: Options cannot be purchased on margin or used as collateral for a margin loan.

Q604_LO101: Correct Answer: c EXPLANATIONS: Mutual funds can be used as collateral after being held for 30 days.

Q605_LO101: Correct Answer: a EXPLANATIONS: Firms must determine an initial deposit requirement for exempt securities.

Q606_LO101: Correct Answer: b EXPLANATIONS: U.S. Treasury bills are exempt from Regulation T margin requirements.

Q607_LO101: Correct Answer: b EXPLANATIONS: Firms may impose stricter requirements on exempt securities.

Q608_LO101: Correct Answer: c EXPLANATIONS: The consent to loan agreement gives permission for loaning customer securities to others.

Q609_LO101: Correct Answer: d EXPLANATIONS: Exchange-listed stocks are eligible for margin borrowing.

Q610_LO101: Correct Answer: b EXPLANATIONS: Risk disclosure information must be provided annually to margin customers.

Q611_LO101: Correct Answer: c EXPLANATIONS: The credit agreement discloses the terms of credit extended by the BD.

Q612_LO101: Correct Answer: c EXPLANATIONS: The hypothecation agreement allows securities to be pledged and repledged as collateral.

Q613_LO101: Correct Answer: b EXPLANATIONS: The consent to loan agreement allows the firm to repledge customer securities.

Q614_LO101: Correct Answer: c EXPLANATIONS: Customers must receive a risk disclosure document.

Q615_LO101: Correct Answer: c EXPLANATIONS: In street name, the BD is the nominal owner.

Q616_LO101: Correct Answer: b EXPLANATIONS: The document discusses risks, including market volatility and potential losses.

Q617_LO101: Correct Answer: c EXPLANATIONS: Regulation T allows exchange-listed stocks, bonds, Nasdaq stocks, and warrants.

Q618_LO101: Correct Answer: b EXPLANATIONS: Options cannot be bought on margin or used as collateral.

Q619_LO101: Correct Answer: b EXPLANATIONS: Mutual funds can be used after being held for 30 days.

Q620_LO101: Correct Answer: b EXPLANATIONS: U.S. Treasury bills are exempt from Regulation T margin requirements.

Q621_LO101: Correct Answer: d EXPLANATIONS: Firms determine the initial deposit requirement for exempt securities.

Q622_LO101: Correct Answer: b EXPLANATIONS: Firms must follow maintenance requirements established by FINRA.

Q623_LO101: Correct Answer: c EXPLANATIONS: The document discusses risks associated with margin trading.

Q624_LO101: Correct Answer: c EXPLANATIONS: The consent to loan agreement permits the firm to loan customer securities.

Q625_LO101: Correct Answer: a EXPLANATIONS: Holding securities in street name facilitates repledging for loans and short sales.

Q626_LO102: Correct Answer: b EXPLANATIONS: Regulation T requires a 50% deposit of the market value.

Q627_LO102: Correct Answer: b EXPLANATIONS: FINRA has an initial requirement of $2,000 or 100%, whichever is less.

Q628_LO102: Correct Answer: b EXPLANATIONS: Deposit 50% for a purchase exceeding $4,000 (Regulation T).

Q629_LO102: Correct Answer: b EXPLANATIONS: The FINRA minimum is $2,000.

Q630_LO102: Correct Answer: b EXPLANATIONS: A maintenance call is triggered when equity drops below 25%.

Q631_LO102: Correct Answer: b EXPLANATIONS: The customer must make additional deposits to meet the 25% minimum.

Q632_LO102: Correct Answer: b EXPLANATIONS: The FINRA minimum for a short margin account is the higher of 30% or $2,000.

Q633_LO102: Correct Answer: b EXPLANATIONS: A house call refers to higher minimum maintenance requirements set by the BD.

Q634_LO102: Correct Answer: b EXPLANATIONS: The calculation of a maintenance call is not expected on the SIE Exam.

Q635_LO102: Correct Answer: c EXPLANATIONS: In a fee-based account, customers pay a set fee for all trading.

Q636_LO102: Correct Answer: a EXPLANATIONS: Fee-based accounts are suitable for customers who trade frequently.

Q637_LO102: Correct Answer: b EXPLANATIONS: The fee is commonly based on a percentage of the account's value.

Q638_LO102: Correct Answer: c EXPLANATIONS: Fee-based accounts are less suitable for customers who buy and hold securities.

Q639_LO102: Correct Answer: c EXPLANATIONS: For a purchase less than $2,000, deposit 100% of the purchase price (FINRA minimum).

Q640_LO102: Correct Answer: c EXPLANATIONS: Calculating the initial deposit ensures compliance with regulatory requirements.

Q641_LO103: What is the primary focus of money laundering rules before September 11, 2001?
a. Destination of funds
b. Origin of cash
c. Types of transactions
d. Financial institutions

HINTS: Recall the primary concern before 9/11.

Q642_LO103: According to the USA PATRIOT Act, what aspect of money laundering became a significant concern post-9/11?
a. Placement
b. Integration
c. Layering
d. Funds' destination

HINTS: Identify the focus after the USA PATRIOT Act.

Q643_LO103: What is the first stage of money laundering, where funds are moved into the laundering system?
a. Layering
b. Integration
c. Placement
d. Concealment

HINTS: Recognize the initial stage of money laundering.

Q644_LO103: During the layering stage, what is the goal of money launderers?
a. Increase funds
b. Conceal the source
c. Integrate funds
d. Generate interest

HINTS: Identify the objective during the layering stage.

Q645_LO103: In the integration stage of money laundering, illegal funds are mixed with legitimate funds in what type of businesses?
a. Sole proprietorships
b. Front companies
c. Publicly traded companies
d. Non-profit organizations

HINTS: Recognize the businesses used in the integration stage.

Q646_LO103: What is the primary purpose of FinCEN?
a. Enforce money laundering laws
b. Analyze financial transactions
c. Collect taxes
d. Investigate terrorism

HINTS: Identify the main function of FinCEN.

Q647_LO103: When should Currency Transaction Reports (CTRs) be filed by broker-dealers?
a. For all transactions
b. Only for cash transactions
c. When the amount exceeds $5,000
d. When the amount exceeds $10,000

HINTS: Recognize the triggering condition for CTRs.

Q648_LO103: What is the prohibited activity known as when deposits are designed to fall under the $10,000 radar?
a. Money laundering
b. Structuring
c. Concealing
d. Layering

HINTS: Identify the term for designing deposits to avoid reporting.

Q649_LO103: According to the USA PATRIOT Act, when must firms file a Suspicious Activity Report (SAR)?
a. Within 15 days
b. Within 30 days
c. Within 10 days
d. Immediately

HINTS: Recognize the timeframe for filing a SAR.

Q650_LO103: Which of the following is a condition for filing a Suspicious Activity Report (SAR)?
a. Legitimate business purpose
b. Transparent financial transactions
c. Facilitating criminal activity
d. Routine customer transactions

HINTS: Identify a condition warranting a SAR.

Q651_LO103: How long must firms retain copies of Suspicious Activity Report (SAR) filings and related documentation?
a. 2 years
b. 5 years
c. 10 years
d. 7 years

HINTS: Recognize the retention period for SAR filings.

Q652_LO103: According to the USA PATRIOT Act, when should a firm notify FinCEN about a SAR request?
a. Immediately
b. Within 30 days
c. Only if subpoenaed
d. At the firm's discretion

HINTS: Identify the timing for notifying FinCEN about a SAR request.

Q653_LO103: What is the minimum amount specified by the USA PATRIOT Act for wire transfers to trigger record-keeping?
a. $1,000
b. $2,000
c. $3,000
d. $5,000

HINTS: Recognize the threshold for wire transfers triggering record-keeping.

Q654_LO103: If a transaction involves funds derived from illegal activity, when must a Suspicious Activity Report (SAR) be filed?
a. Immediately
b. Within 10 days
c. Within 30 days
d. Within 60 days

HINTS: Recognize the urgency for filing a SAR in specific cases.

Q655_LO103: What is the main purpose of Currency Transaction Reports (CTRs) and Suspicious Activity Reports (SARs)?
a. Generate revenue
b. Combat money laundering
c. Facilitate international trade
d. Monitor stock market trends

HINTS: Identify the primary purpose of CTRs and SARs.

Q656_LO103: What is the primary focus of money laundering rules after the USA PATRIOT Act of 2001?
a. Origin of the cash
b. Destination of the funds
c. Source of the funds
d. Legitimate business concerns

HINTS: Identify the focus of money laundering rules post-USA PATRIOT Act.

Q657_LO103: Which stage of money laundering involves moving funds into the laundering system?
a. Placement
b. Layering
c. Integration
d. Concealment

HINTS: Recognize the stage where funds are introduced into the laundering system.

Q658_LO103: What is the goal of the layering stage in money laundering?
a. Conceal the source of funds
b. Integrate funds with legitimate business
c. Move funds into the system
d. Detect illegal activity

HINTS: Identify the goal of the layering stage in money laundering.

Q659_LO103: In the integration stage of money laundering, illegal funds are mixed with what?
a. Clean funds
b. Government funds
c. Charitable funds
d. International funds

HINTS: Recognize what illegal funds are combined with in the integration stage.

Q660_LO103: What is the primary purpose of the Financial Crimes Enforcement Network (FinCEN)?
a. Enforce money laundering rules
b. Collect and analyze financial transaction information
c. Investigate criminal activities
d. Approve currency transactions

HINTS: Identify the main purpose of FinCEN.

Q661_LO103: When should Currency Transaction Reports (CTRs) be filed by Broker-Dealers?
a. Within 30 days of receipt
b. Within 10 days of receipt
c. Within 15 days of receipt
d. Within 5 days of receipt

HINTS: Recognize the timeframe for filing Currency Transaction Reports.

Q662_LO103: What is structuring in the context of money laundering?
a. Legal financial planning
b. Designing deposits to avoid reporting
c. Integrating funds in business
d. Reporting suspicious transactions

HINTS: Identify the prohibited activity known as structuring.

Q663_LO103: What is the purpose of Suspicious Activities Reports (SARs)?
a. Report legal financial activities
b. Monitor customer transactions
c. Report questionable transactions
d. Track financial trends

HINTS: Recognize the purpose of Suspicious Activities Reports.

Q664_LO103: How long must copies of Suspicious Activity Reports (SARs) be retained by firms?
a. 1 year
b. 2 years
c. 3 years
d. 5 years

HINTS: Identify the retention period for copies of SAR filings.

Q665_LO103: Under the USA PATRIOT Act, what transactions must be reported as suspicious activities?
a. Any transaction involving $1,000 or more
b. Any transaction involving $10,000 or more
c. Transactions with unknown sources
d. Transactions involving at least $5,000

HINTS: Recognize the threshold for reporting transactions as suspicious activities.

Q666_LO103: What class of suspicious activity involves funds derived from illegal activity?
a. Class 1
b. Class 2
c. Class 3
d. Class 4

HINTS: Identify the class involving funds from illegal activity.

Q667_LO103: What is the confidentiality requirement for Suspicious Activity Reports (SARs)?
a. Disclose to the person involved
b. Share with regulatory authorities
c. Notify the media
d. Keep the report confidential

HINTS: Recognize the confidentiality requirement for SARs.

Q668_LO103: What information is required for wire transfers of $3,000 or more under the USA PATRIOT Act?
a. Sender's name and address only
b. Amount of the transfer only
c. Name and address of both sender and recipient
d. Account number of the recipient only

HINTS: Identify the information required for wire transfers of $3,000 or more.

Q669_LO103: What is the penalty for failing to report currency transactions as required by the Bank Secrecy Act?
a. Fine of up to $100,000
b. Fine of up to $250,000
c. Fine of up to $500,000
d. Imprisonment for up to 5 years

HINTS: Recognize the potential penalty for failing to report currency transactions.

Q670_LO103: In which stage of money laundering are illegal funds the most susceptible to detection?
a. Placement
b. Layering
c. Integration
d. Concealment

HINTS: Identify the stage where illegal funds are most susceptible to detection.

Q671_LO104: Who is responsible for establishing internal compliance procedures to detect abuses related to money laundering?
a. Chief Financial Officer
b. Chief Compliance Officer
c. Chief Marketing Officer
d. Chief AML Officer

HINTS: Identify the role responsible for establishing procedures to detect money laundering abuses.

Q672_LO104: What action should be taken if a customer exhibits a lack of concern regarding risks, commissions, or transaction costs?
a. No action needed
b. Report to the designated principal
c. Advise the customer
d. Conduct more transactions

HINTS: Recognize the appropriate action when a red flag is detected.

Q673_LO104: Which practice involves designing currency deposits or withdrawals to fall under the $10,000 CTR filing threshold?
a. Legal financial planning
b. Currency structuring
c. Account structuring
d. Transaction structuring

HINTS: Identify the practice associated with attempting to avoid the $10,000 CTR filing threshold.

Q674_LO104: What is the primary purpose of maintaining customer identification programs (CIPs) under the USA PATRIOT Act?
a. Preventing money laundering only
b. Preventing terrorist financing only
c. Preventing both money laundering and terrorist financing
d. Verifying customer income

HINTS: Recognize the main purpose of maintaining CIPs under the USA PATRIOT Act.

Q675_LO104: What list does financial institutions, including BDs, check customer names against under the USA PATRIOT Act?
a. CIA Watchlist
b. Interpol List
c. SDN List maintained by OFAC
d. FBI Most Wanted List

HINTS: Identify the list used for checking customer names under the USA PATRIOT Act.

Q676_LO104: When must new customers be advised about the firm's request for information to verify their identities?
a. After the account is opened
b. During the first transaction
c. Before the account is opened
d. Only if requested by the customer

HINTS: Recognize the timing for advising new customers about identity verification.

Q677_LO104: What does OFAC stand for?
a. Office of Financial Assets Control
b. Office of Foreign Access Control
c. Office of Foreign Assets Control
d. Office of Financial Activities Control

HINTS: Identify the correct expansion of the abbreviation OFAC.

Q678_LO104: What does the OFAC SDN list primarily target?
a. U.S. citizens
b. Specially Designated Nationals (SDNs)
c. Foreign entities
d. Financial institutions

HINTS: Recognize the primary targets of the OFAC SDN list.

Q679_LO104: What happens when individuals or groups appear on the OFAC SDN list?
a. Their assets are blocked
b. They are arrested immediately
c. They are fined
d. They are warned

HINTS: Identify the consequence when individuals or groups appear on the SDN list.

Q680_LO104: What does checking the SDN list help prevent?
a. Fraud
b. Money laundering
c. Financing of terrorist operations
d. All of the above

HINTS: Recognize the purpose of checking the SDN list.

Q681_LO104: Who is prohibited from doing business with anyone on the OFAC SDN list?
a. U.S. citizens only
b. U.S. persons only
c. Foreign entities only
d. Non-U.S. citizens only

HINTS: Identify the category prohibited from doing business with those on the SDN list.

Q682_LO104: What is the notification requirement for new customers regarding identity verification?
a. Must be delivered verbally
b. Must be placed on the firm's website
c. Must be included in the new account form
d. All of the above

HINTS: Recognize the methods for notifying new customers about identity verification.

Q683_LO104: How frequently should businesses check the SDN list concerning their relationships with individuals or entities?
a. Once a year
b. Periodically throughout the relationship
c. Only during the onboarding process
d. Only if suspicious activity is detected

HINTS: Identify the recommended frequency for checking the SDN list in relationships.

Q684_LO104: What is the penalty for conducting transactions with individuals on the OFAC SDN list?
a. Fine only
b. Imprisonment only
c. Both fine and imprisonment
d. No penalty

HINTS: Recognize the potential penalty for conducting transactions with those on the SDN list.

Q685_LO104: What is the primary responsibility of the AML officer in a firm?
a. Conducting transactions
b. Handling customer complaints
c. Establishing internal compliance procedures
d. Marketing financial products

HINTS: Identify the main responsibility of the AML officer.

Q686_LO104: What is the primary responsibility of a chief anti-money laundering (AML) officer in a financial firm?
a. Trade execution
b. Establishing compliance procedures
c. Sales promotion
d. Marketing strategies

HINTS: Identify the primary role of an AML officer in a financial firm.

Q687_LO104: When a red flag suggesting money laundering is detected, what action should be taken?
a. Ignore it unless significant
b. Report to the designated principal immediately
c. Document and analyze internally
d. Inform the customer discreetly

HINTS: Recognize the appropriate action when a red flag is detected.

Q688_LO104: What is an example of a red flag for potential money laundering?
a. Customer expressing concern about risks
b. Customer making regular deposits
c. Customer attempting large currency withdrawals
d. Customer inquiring about investment options

HINTS: Identify an example of a red flag for potential money laundering.

Q689_LO104: What does structuring, in the context of money laundering, involve?
a. Legal financial planning
b. Designing transactions to evade detection
c. Reporting suspicious activities
d. Internal compliance procedures

HINTS: Recognize the definition of structuring in money laundering.

Q690_LO104: Under the USA PATRIOT Act, what is the purpose of maintaining customer identification programs (CIPs)?
a. Enhance customer satisfaction
b. Prevent financing of terrorist operations and money laundering
c. Increase trade volumes
d. Boost marketing efforts

HINTS: Recall the purpose of maintaining customer identification programs (CIPs).

Q691_LO104: What does the Office of Foreign Assets Control (OFAC) maintain to prevent dealings with targeted individuals and entities?
a. Customer identification programs
b. Red flag reports
c. Specially Designated Nationals (SDN) list
d. Compliance manuals

HINTS: Identify what the OFAC maintains to prevent dealings with targeted individuals.

Q692_LO104: What happens when individuals or groups appear on the SDN list maintained by OFAC?
a. They are fined
b. Their assets are blocked
c. They receive a warning
d. They are exempt from regulations

HINTS: Recognize the consequence when individuals appear on the SDN list.

Q693_LO104: When must new customers be advised about the firm's request for identity verification information?
a. After the account is opened
b. During the first transaction
c. Before the account is opened
d. Within 30 days of account opening

HINTS: Identify the correct timing for advising new customers about identity verification.

Q694_LO104: What is the purpose of checking the SDN list for businesses dealing with individuals or entities?
a. Boost customer relations
b. Verify business legitimacy
c. Prevent violations of the law
d. Enhance business reputation

HINTS: Recognize the purpose of checking the SDN list for businesses.

Q695_LO104: Who is prohibited from doing business with anyone on the OFAC SDN list?
a. Only U.S. citizens
b. Only U.S. businesses
c. Only U.S. permanent resident aliens
d. U.S. persons

HINTS: Identify who is prohibited from doing business with individuals on the SDN list.

Q696_LO104: When should businesses consult the SDN list in relation to transactions?
a. After completing transactions
b. Before establishing a relationship
c. Periodically throughout the relationship
d. Only in case of suspicion

HINTS: Recognize when businesses should consult the SDN list in relation to transactions.

Q697_LO104: What type of list is the SDN list maintained by OFAC?
a. Country-specific list
b. Customer blacklist
c. National database
d. Searchable list

HINTS: Identify the nature of the SDN list maintained by OFAC.

Q698_LO104: What is the consequence of breaching the confidentiality of Suspicious Activity Reports (SARs)?
a. Fine and imprisonment
b. Warning letter
c. Temporary suspension
d. Financial reward

HINTS: Recognize the consequence of breaching the confidentiality of SARs.

Q699_LO104: Which government agency maintains the SDN list in a searchable format?
a. Securities and Exchange Commission (SEC)
b. Financial Crimes Enforcement Network (FinCEN)
c. Federal Reserve
d. Office of Foreign Assets Control (OFAC)

HINTS: Identify the government agency maintaining the SDN list in a searchable format.

Q700_LO104: What is the primary purpose of the Specially Designated Nationals (SDN) list?
a. Enhance financial performance
b. Block targeted individuals and entities
c. Facilitate international trade
d. Promote regulatory compliance

HINTS: Recognize the primary purpose of the SDN list.

Correct Answers & Explanations
AML/BSA

Q641_LO103: Correct Answer: b EXPLANATIONS: Money laundering rules were primarily concerned with the origin of cash.

Q642_LO103: Correct Answer: d EXPLANATIONS: Post-9/11, regulators became concerned with where the funds are going.

Q643_LO103: Correct Answer: c EXPLANATIONS: Placement involves moving funds into the laundering system.

Q644_LO103: Correct Answer: b EXPLANATIONS: Money launderers aim to conceal the source of funds during layering.

Q645_LO103: Correct Answer: b EXPLANATIONS: Front companies operating on a cash basis are common in the integration stage.

Q646_LO103: Correct Answer: b EXPLANATIONS: FinCEN collects and analyzes information about financial transactions.

Q647_LO103: Correct Answer: d EXPLANATIONS: CTRs must be filed for currency received in excess of $10,000 on a single day.

Q648_LO103: Correct Answer: b EXPLANATIONS: Structuring involves designing deposits to evade reporting requirements.

Q649_LO103: Correct Answer: b EXPLANATIONS: Firms must file a SAR within 30 days of becoming aware of a suspicious transaction.

Q650_LO103: Correct Answer: c EXPLANATIONS: A SAR must be filed if a transaction involves facilitating criminal activity.

Q651_LO103: Correct Answer: b EXPLANATIONS: Copies of each SAR filing must be retained for five years.

Q652_LO103: Correct Answer: a EXPLANATIONS: Immediate notification is required unless prohibited by FinCEN, the SEC, or law enforcement.

Q653_LO103: Correct Answer: c EXPLANATIONS: The USA PATRIOT Act requires record-keeping for wire transfers of $3,000 or more.

Q654_LO103: Correct Answer: a EXPLANATIONS: A SAR must be filed immediately for transactions involving funds from illegal activity.

Q655_LO103: Correct Answer: b EXPLANATIONS: CTRs and SARs are tools to combat money laundering and financial crimes.

Q656_LO103: Correct Answer: b EXPLANATIONS: Regulations are now concerned with both the origin and destination of funds.

Q657_LO103: Correct Answer: a EXPLANATIONS: Placement is the first stage of money laundering.

Q658_LO103: Correct Answer: a EXPLANATIONS: Layering aims to conceal the source of funds through complex transactions.

Q659_LO103: Correct Answer: a EXPLANATIONS: Illegal funds are commingled with legitimate funds, creating the appearance of legality.

Q660_LO103: Correct Answer: b EXPLANATIONS: FinCEN collects and analyzes financial transaction information.

Q661_LO103: Correct Answer: c EXPLANATIONS: CTRs must be filed within 15 days of receiving currency over $10,000.

Q662_LO103: Correct Answer: b EXPLANATIONS: Structuring involves designing deposits to fall below the $10,000 reporting threshold.

Q663_LO103: Correct Answer: c EXPLANATIONS: SARs are filed to report transactions that appear questionable.

Q664_LO103: Correct Answer: d EXPLANATIONS: Copies of SAR filings must be retained for 5 years.

Q665_LO103: Correct Answer: d EXPLANATIONS: Transactions involving at least $5,000 must be reported.

Q666_LO103: Correct Answer: a EXPLANATIONS: Class 1 involves funds derived from illegal activity.

Q667_LO103: Correct Answer: d EXPLANATIONS: The person involved should not be notified; SARs must remain confidential.

Q668_LO103: Correct Answer: c EXPLANATIONS: The USA PATRIOT Act requires collecting various details, including sender and recipient information.

Q669_LO103: Correct Answer: c EXPLANATIONS: Failure to report can result in fines of up to $500,000 or imprisonment.

Q670_LO103: Correct Answer: a EXPLANATIONS: Placement is the stage when illegal funds are most vulnerable to detection.

Q671_LO104: Correct Answer: d EXPLANATIONS: The Chief AML Officer is designated to establish internal compliance procedures.

Q672_LO104: Correct Answer: b EXPLANATIONS: Red flags should be reported to the designated principal immediately.

Q673_LO104: Correct Answer: b EXPLANATIONS: Structuring involves designing transactions to fall below reporting thresholds.

Q674_LO104: Correct Answer: c EXPLANATIONS: CIPs aim to prevent both money laundering and terrorist financing.

Q675_LO104: Correct Answer: c EXPLANATIONS: Customer names are checked against the SDN List maintained by OFAC.

Q676_LO104: Correct Answer: c EXPLANATIONS: Customers must be advised before the account is opened.

Q677_LO104: Correct Answer: c EXPLANATIONS: OFAC stands for the Office of Foreign Assets Control.

Q678_LO104: Correct Answer: b EXPLANATIONS: The SDN list primarily targets Specially Designated Nationals.

Q679_LO104: Correct Answer: a EXPLANATIONS: Assets are blocked, and dealings with them are generally prohibited.

Q680_LO104: Correct Answer: d EXPLANATIONS: Checking the SDN list helps prevent fraud, money laundering, and terrorist financing.

Q681_LO104: Correct Answer: b EXPLANATIONS: U.S. persons, including citizens and entities, are prohibited.

Q682_LO104: Correct Answer: d EXPLANATIONS: Notification can be verbal, on the website, or in the new account form.

Q683_LO104: Correct Answer: b EXPLANATIONS: Periodic checks are recommended throughout the relationship.

Q684_LO104: Correct Answer: c EXPLANATIONS: Both fine and imprisonment are potential penalties.

Q685_LO104: Correct Answer: c EXPLANATIONS: The AML officer is primarily responsible for establishing internal compliance procedures.

Q686_LO104: Correct Answer: b EXPLANATIONS: The AML officer is responsible for establishing internal compliance procedures to detect abuses.

Q687_LO104: Correct Answer: b EXPLANATIONS: Red flags should be reported immediately to the designated principal.

Q688_LO104: Correct Answer: c EXPLANATIONS: Large currency withdrawals can be a red flag for potential money laundering.

Q689_LO104: Correct Answer: b EXPLANATIONS: Structuring involves designing transactions to fall under reporting thresholds and evade detection.

Q690_LO104: Correct Answer: b EXPLANATIONS: CIPs aim to prevent financing of terrorist operations and money laundering.

Q691_LO104: Correct Answer: c EXPLANATIONS: OFAC maintains the Specially Designated Nationals (SDN) list.

Q692_LO104: Correct Answer: b EXPLANATIONS: Assets are blocked for those on the SDN list, and dealings with them are generally prohibited.

Q693_LO104: Correct Answer: c EXPLANATIONS: New customers must be advised before the account is opened.

Q694_LO104: Correct Answer: c EXPLANATIONS: Checking the list helps prevent violations of the law by ensuring compliance with OFAC regulations.

Q695_LO104: Correct Answer: d EXPLANATIONS: U.S. persons, including citizens and businesses, are prohibited from dealing with those on the SDN list.

Q696_LO104: Correct Answer: b EXPLANATIONS: Businesses should check the list before establishing a relationship and periodically thereafter.

Q697_LO104: Correct Answer: d EXPLANATIONS: The SDN list is searchable and includes individuals and entities from various targeted categories.

Q698_LO104: Correct Answer: a EXPLANATIONS: Breaching confidentiality can result in fines and imprisonment.

Q699_LO104: Correct Answer: d EXPLANATIONS: OFAC maintains the searchable SDN list.

Q700_LO104: Correct Answer: b EXPLANATIONS: The SDN list is designed to block targeted individuals and entities to ensure regulatory compliance.

Q701_LO105: What is the primary responsibility of brokers regarding the "Know Your Customer" (KYC) rule?
a. Maximizing profits
b. Performing due diligence
c. Generating leads
d. Market forecasting

HINTS: Identify the primary responsibility of brokers related to the KYC rule.

Q702_LO105: According to FINRA, who is excluded from the definition of a customer?
a. Other brokers
b. Family members
c. Potential investors
d. Colleagues

HINTS: Recognize the exclusions from the definition of a customer according to FINRA.

Q703_LO105: What is an example of a financial circumstance that may influence a customer's investment suitability?
a. Marital status
b. Employment status
c. Investment experience
d. Risk tolerance

HINTS: Identify an example of a financial circumstance affecting investment suitability.

Q704_LO105: Which of the following is considered a nonfinancial consideration under the KYC rule?
a. Liquid net worth
b. Total debt
c. Age
d. Income

HINTS: Recognize a nonfinancial consideration under the KYC rule.

Q705_LO105: In the context of KYC, what does an RR or an investment adviser need to know about a customer?
a. Investment strategies only
b. Marital status and age
c. Both financial and nonfinancial considerations
d. Customer's hobbies

HINTS: Understand the information that an RR or an investment adviser needs to know about a customer.

Q706_LO105: Which of the following is a financial circumstance?
a. Employment status
b. Number of dependents
c. Investment goals
d. Tax considerations

HINTS: Identify a financial circumstance among the options.

Q707_LO105: What is the significance of a customer's risk tolerance in shaping their investment portfolio?
a. It determines their age
b. It influences the choice of investment alternatives
c. It affects their employment status
d. It is unrelated to investment goals

HINTS: Recognize the significance of risk tolerance in shaping an investment portfolio.

Q708_LO105: Which question helps understand a customer's investment time horizon?
a. What risks can you afford to take?
b. How liquid must your investments be?
c. Are you seeking long-term or short-term investments?
d. What types of investments do you currently hold?

HINTS: Identify the question related to understanding a customer's investment time horizon.

Q709_LO105: Why is it important for an RR to ask about a customer's tax considerations?
a. To provide tax advice
b. To maximize profits
c. To comply with KYC regulations
d. To assess employment status

HINTS: Recognize the importance of asking about a customer's tax considerations.

Q710_LO105: What does the KYC rule aim to ensure regarding customer recommendations?
a. Maximize profits
b. Ensure risk-free investments
c. Suitability of recommendations
d. Predict market trends

HINTS: Identify the goal of the KYC rule regarding customer recommendations.

Q711_LO105: In KYC, what is the significance of a customer's liquid net worth?
a. It determines employment status
b. It affects the number of dependents
c. It influences risk tolerance
d. It indicates financial capability

HINTS: Recognize the significance of a customer's liquid net worth in KYC.

Q712_LO105: According to FINRA, what should RRs have a reasonable basis to believe in making recommendations?
a. Customer's age only
b. Validity of customer's information
c. Specific market trends
d. Immediate family employment status

HINTS: Identify what RRs should have a reasonable basis to believe when making recommendations.

Q713_LO105: What is the consequence of not performing due diligence under the KYC rule?
a. Increased profits
b. Regulatory fines and penalties
c. Enhanced customer satisfaction
d. Expedited account openings

HINTS: Recognize the consequence of not performing due diligence under the KYC rule.

Q714_LO105: Why does the KYC rule exclude certain potential investors from the definition of a customer?
a. They are not interested in investments
b. They are not part of the financial system
c. They are not currently clients
d. They are exempt from regulations

HINTS: Identify the reason for excluding certain potential investors from the definition of a customer.

Q715_LO105: What does the KYC rule require regarding recommended transactions or investment strategies?
a. Maximize customer's net income
b. Ensure market trends are predicted
c. Have a reasonable basis to believe in suitability
d. Prioritize the firm's interests

HINTS: Recognize the requirement of the KYC rule regarding recommended transactions.

Q716_LO105: What is the primary responsibility of brokers under the KYC rule?
a. Marketing strategies
b. Knowing their customers
c. Sales promotion
d. Trade execution

HINTS: Identify the primary responsibility of brokers under the KYC rule.

Q717_LO105: What is the basis for brokers to believe a recommended transaction is suitable for the customer?
a. Customer preference
b. Financial circumstances
c. Market trends
d. Broker's intuition

HINTS: Recognize the basis for deeming a recommended transaction suitable.

Q718_LO105: According to FINRA, who is excluded from the definition of a customer?
a. Other brokers
b. Potential investors
c. Immediate family members
d. Current clients

HINTS: Identify who is excluded from the definition of a customer according to FINRA.

Q719_LO105: What is considered a financial circumstance in KYC?
a. Marital status
b. Age of dependents
c. Risk tolerance
d. Total debt

HINTS: Recognize an example of a financial circumstance.

Q720_LO105: Which of the following is a nonfinancial consideration in KYC?
a. Liquid net worth
b. Employment status
c. Debt payments
d. Value of home

HINTS: Identify a nonfinancial consideration in KYC.

Q721_LO105: Why is knowing the customer's age relevant in KYC?
a. Marketing purposes
b. Employment opportunities
c. Nonfinancial considerations
d. Determining risk tolerance

HINTS: Recognize the relevance of knowing the customer's age.

Q722_LO105: What is an essential component in shaping a customer's portfolio under KYC?
a. Liquid assets
b. Investment experience
c. Tax considerations
d. Market trends

HINTS: Identify an important factor in shaping a customer's portfolio.

Q723_LO105: In KYC, what does risk tolerance refer to?
a. Willingness to take market risks
b. Willingness to invest in risky assets
c. Acceptance of potential losses
d. All of the above

HINTS: Recognize the components of risk tolerance in KYC.

Q724_LO105: What question helps assess a customer's investment time horizon in KYC?
a. How liquid must your investments be?
b. What is your investment experience?
c. Are you seeking long-term or short-term investments?
d. What types of investments do you currently hold?

HINTS: Identify the question related to assessing investment time horizon.

Q725_LO105: Which factor is NOT part of KYC considerations?
a. Marital status
b. Customer's favorite color
c. Number and ages of dependents
d. Employment status

HINTS: Recognize a factor that is not part of KYC considerations.

Q726_LO105: What is the importance of knowing how liquid a customer's investments must be?
a. Regulatory compliance
b. Marketing strategy
c. Assessing risk tolerance
d. Tax considerations

HINTS: Recognize the importance of knowing the liquidity requirement in KYC.

Q727_LO105: When must new customers be advised about the firm's request for identity verification information in KYC?
a. After the account is opened
b. Before the account is opened
c. During the first transaction
d. Within 30 days of account opening

HINTS: Identify the correct timing for advising new customers about identity verification.

Q728_LO105: What does the KYC rule aim to prevent?
a. High-risk investments
b. Money laundering
c. Market volatility
d. Insider trading

HINTS: Recognize the primary goal of the KYC rule.

Q729_LO105: What does the term "Suitability" mean under KYC?
a. Customer preference
b. Financial circumstances
c. Making recommendations aligning with the customer's profile
d. Market trends

HINTS: Identify the meaning of "Suitability" in the context of KYC.

Q730_LO105: What information is checked against the Specially Designated Nationals (SDN) list under KYC?
a. Employment history
b. Customer identification
c. Financial statements
d. Names of individuals and entities

HINTS: Recognize the information checked against the SDN list in KYC.

Q731_LO106: What constitutes making a recommendation in the financial industry?
a. Offering general information
b. Providing specific investment advice
c. Sharing market news
d. Conducting market research

HINTS: Identify the action that qualifies as making a recommendation.

Q732_LO106: When making a recommendation, what factors should a person consider?
a. Personal opinions
b. Recipient's financial status only
c. Circumstances, recipient's knowledge, and sophistication
d. Market trends

HINTS: Recognize the factors to consider when making a recommendation.

Q733_LO106: What does lack of intent to provide a recommendation prevent?
a. Legal consequences
b. Communication from being considered a recommendation
c. Regulatory scrutiny
d. Transparency in communication

HINTS: Identify the consequence of lacking intent to provide a recommendation.

Q734_LO106: In relating customer objectives with investment characteristics, what is the first rule?
a. Consider the customer's risk tolerance
b. Align the investment's purpose with the customer's primary objective
c. Assess the time frame for investment
d. Evaluate the customer's financial status

HINTS: Recognize the primary rule in aligning customer objectives with investment characteristics.

Q735_LO106: What should be considered in the next step after aligning the investment's purpose with the customer's primary objective?
a. Customer's financial status
b. Customer's risk tolerance
c. Market trends
d. Regulatory compliance

HINTS: Identify the factor to consider in the next step after aligning the investment's purpose.

Q736_LO106: Which investment is suitable for an investor seeking preservation of capital/safety?
a. Common stock
b. CDs, money market mutual funds
c. Municipal bonds
d. Blue-chip stocks

HINTS: Identify the suitable investment for an investor seeking preservation of capital.

Q737_LO106: What is recommended for an investor seeking growth (Aggressive growth)?
a. Municipal bonds
b. Common stock, common stock mutual funds
c. Bonds (but not zero coupons), REITs
d. Utility stocks

HINTS: Recognize the recommendation for an investor seeking aggressive growth.

Q738_LO106: Which investment is appropriate for an investor seeking income (Tax-free income)?
a. Municipal bonds, municipal bond funds, Roth IRAs
b. Common stock, common stock mutual funds
c. Option contracts
d. Technology stocks

HINTS: Identify the appropriate investment for an investor seeking tax-free income.

Q739_LO106: What is recommended for an investor seeking liquidity?
a. Common stock
b. Securities listed on an exchange, unlisted Nasdaq stocks
c. CMOs
d. Defensive stocks

HINTS: Recognize the recommendation for an investor seeking liquidity.

Q740_LO106: What is recommended for an investor seeking portfolio diversification?
a. Option contracts
b. Mutual funds, asset allocation funds
c. Precious metals
d. High-yield bonds

HINTS: Identify the recommendation for an investor seeking portfolio diversification.

Q741_LO106: Which investment is suitable for an investor with a speculation objective?
a. Government securities
b. Option contracts, DPPs
c. Blue-chip stocks
d. Fixed annuities

HINTS: Recognize the suitable investment for an investor with a speculation objective.

Q742_LO106: In customer recommendations, what is the significance of considering the time frame?
a. Regulatory compliance
b. Aligning with the customer's risk tolerance
c. Assessing liquidity requirements
d. Impact on the investment decision

HINTS: Recognize the significance of considering the time frame in customer recommendations.

Q743_LO106: What is the primary purpose of considering the customer's risk tolerance in investment recommendations?
a. Compliance with market trends
b. Aligning with the customer's primary objective
c. Assessing liquidity
d. Regulatory scrutiny

HINTS: Identify the primary purpose of considering the customer's risk tolerance.

Q744_LO106: Why is understanding the customer's financial status crucial in making suitable recommendations?
a. To offer marketing incentives
b. To determine regulatory compliance
c. To assess risk tolerance
d. To align with the customer's objectives

HINTS: Recognize the importance of understanding the customer's financial status.

Q745_LO106: What is the role of the registered representative in the investment recommendation process?
a. Provide personal opinions
b. Make recommendations based on intuition
c. Assess customer circumstances and knowledge
d. Follow market trends

HINTS: Identify the role of the registered representative in the recommendation process.

Q746_LO106: When is a person considered to be making an investment recommendation?
a. When discussing market trends
b. When providing general information
c. When suggesting a course of action regarding a security
d. When sharing financial news

HINTS: Consider the criteria for making an investment recommendation.

Q747_LO106: What should be considered when making a recommendation?
a. Intent to provide a recommendation
b. Knowledge of market trends
c. Sophistication of the recipient
d. Frequency of communication

HINTS: Identify a key consideration when making an investment recommendation.

Q748_LO106: Which rule aligns an investment's primary purpose with the customer's primary objective?
a. Rule of Aggressiveness
b. Rule of Preservation
c. Rule of Liquidity
d. Rule of Alignment

HINTS: Recognize the rule that aligns investment purpose with customer objectives.

Q749_LO106: What is the next step after aligning the investment's purpose with the customer's objective?
a. Consider market trends
b. Assess the investment's historical performance
c. Evaluate the customer's risk tolerance
d. Analyze global economic factors

HINTS: Identify the next step after aligning investment purpose with customer objectives.

Q750_LO106: What should be more appropriate for investors with a low tolerance for risk?
a. Conservative investments
b. Aggressive investments
c. Speculative investments
d. Leveraged investments

HINTS: Identify the type of investments suitable for those with a low tolerance for risk.

Q751_LO106: What impacts the investment decision besides aligning with customer objectives and risk tolerance?
a. Market trends
b. Economic forecasts
c. Time frame
d. Interest rates

HINTS: Recognize a factor that impacts the investment decision.

Q752_LO106: For the objective of "Preservation of capital/safety," what is a suitable recommendation?
a. Common stock
b. Municipal bonds
c. Sector funds
d. CDs, money market mutual funds

HINTS: Identify a suitable recommendation for the preservation of capital.

Q753_LO106: What is suitable for the objective of "Growth (Aggressive growth)"?
a. Defensive stocks
b. Municipal bonds
c. Technology stocks
d. REITs

HINTS: Identify a suitable recommendation for aggressive growth.

Q754_LO106: What is recommended for the objective of "Income (High-yield income)"?
a. Bonds (but not zero coupons)
b. Common stock
c. Municipal bonds
d. Option contracts

HINTS: Recognize a suitable recommendation for high-yield income.

Q755_LO106: What is recommended for the objective of "Liquidity"?
a. Unlisted Nasdaq stocks
b. Mutual funds
c. Blue-chip stocks
d. Defensive stocks

HINTS: Identify a recommendation for the objective of liquidity.

Q756_LO106: What is recommended for the objective of "Portfolio diversification"?
a. High-yield bonds
b. Asset allocation funds
c. Utility stocks
d. Precious metals

HINTS: Recognize a recommendation for portfolio diversification.

Q757_LO106: What is recommended for the objective of "Speculation"?
a. Corporate bond funds
b. Option contracts
c. Municipal bonds
d. Blue-chip stocks

HINTS: Identify a recommendation for speculative objectives.

Q758_LO106: What is the primary purpose of the rule of alignment in investment recommendations?
a. Ensure tax considerations
b. Align customer objectives with investment purpose
c. Evaluate market trends
d. Assess liquidity requirements

HINTS: Recognize the primary purpose of aligning customer objectives with investment purpose.

Q759_LO106: Why is assessing risk tolerance important in making suitable recommendations?
a. To follow regulatory compliance
b. To identify market trends
c. To determine investment time horizon
d. To match investments with the investor's risk appetite

HINTS: Identify the importance of assessing risk tolerance in making recommendations.

Q760_LO106: What is the significance of considering the circumstances of the communication in making recommendations?
a. To determine economic forecasts
b. To assess market trends
c. To tailor recommendations to the recipient's situation
d. To analyze historical performance

HINTS: Recognize the significance of considering the circumstances of the communication.

Q761_LO107: What are the general standards FINRA holds member firms to in communication with the public?
a. Deceptive statements
b. Fair dealing and good faith
c. Exaggerated claims
d. Omission of material facts

HINTS: Identify the general standards for communication with the public.

Q762_LO107: Which of the following is NOT permitted in member communications?
a. Exaggerated statements
b. Fair and balanced information
c. Clear and misleading statements
d. Omission of material facts

HINTS: Identify the practice that is not permitted in member communications.

Q763_LO107: What is mandated by FINRA regarding past performance in communications?
a. It should be highlighted
b. It should be omitted
c. It should be repeated
d. It should not imply future results

HINTS: Recognize the mandate regarding past performance in communications.

Q764_LO107: How should members consider the nature of the audience in communication?
a. By providing complex details
b. By providing appropriate details and explanations
c. By excluding details
d. By using technical language

HINTS: Identify how members should consider the audience in communication.

Q765_LO107: What are the three categories of communications according to FINRA?
a. Public, private, internal
b. Retail, wholesale, institutional
c. Institutional, retail, correspondence
d. Corporate, individual, social

HINTS: Classify the three categories of communications according to FINRA.

Q766_LO107: Which of the following is an example of an institutional investor?
a. Individual investor
b. Registered investment company
c. Retail investor
d. Social media platform

HINTS: Identify an example of an institutional investor.

Q767_LO107: How does FINRA define a retail investor?
a. Any person with an account
b. Any person other than an institutional investor
c. Any person with social media presence
d. Any person in the financial industry

HINTS: Recognize the definition of a retail investor according to FINRA.

Q768_LO107: What must happen before using or filing retail communication with FINRA?
a. Post-use approval
b. Prior principal approval
c. Social media monitoring
d. Internal memos

HINTS: Identify the requirement for retail communication before use or filing.

Q769_LO107: What is the filing requirement for established member firms with retail communication?
a. 15 days before use
b. 10 days after first use
c. 10 days before use
d. 5 days after first use

HINTS: Identify the filing requirement for established member firms with retail communication.

Q770_LO107: What is the filing requirement for new member firms with retail communication?
a. 5 days after first use
b. 10 days before use
c. 20 days after first use
d. 15 days before use

HINTS: Identify the filing requirement for new member firms with retail communication.

Q771_LO107: What defines correspondence in communication with the public?
a. More than 25 retail investors
b. Institutional investors only
c. 25 or fewer retail investors
d. Social media posts

HINTS: Identify the definition of correspondence.

Q772_LO107: What must each firm establish regarding correspondence?
a. Principal approval after use
b. No approval required
c. Prior principal approval or post-use approval
d. Approval by external regulators

HINTS: Recognize what each firm must establish regarding correspondence.

Q773_LO107: What is required for the use of static content like a website or blog on social media?
a. Social media monitoring
b. Approval by FINRA
c. No approval required
d. Approval by a registered principal

HINTS: Identify the requirement for the use of static content on social media.

Q774_LO107: What is the requirement for preapproving individual posts in interactive online forums?
a. Approval by FINRA
b. Approval by external regulators
c. No requirement for preapproval
d. Approval by a registered principal

HINTS: Recognize the requirement for preapproving individual posts in interactive forums.

Q775_LO107: What is required for the use of social media by representatives?
a. Monitoring by external regulators
b. Approval of all posts by FINRA
c. Policies and procedures in written supervisory procedures
d. Daily reporting to FINRA

HINTS: Identify the requirement for the use of social media by representatives.

Q776_LO107: What is a general standard that FINRA holds member firm communications to?
a. Maximum exaggeration
b. Principles of fair dealing and good faith
c. Exclusive promotion
d. Vague statements

HINTS: Recognize the general standard for member firm communications.

Q777_LO107: Which of the following is not permitted in member firm communications?
a. Omission of material facts
b. Making false statements
c. Ambiguous statements
d. Clear and balanced statements

HINTS: Identify what is not permitted in member firm communications.

Q778_LO107: When classifying communications, which category includes written communication to institutional investors?
a. Institutional communications
b. Retail communications
c. Correspondence
d. Retail and correspondence

HINTS: Identify the category that includes communication to institutional investors.

Q779_LO107: What is a requirement for treating a communication as directed to an institutional investor?
a. It must be forwarded to a retail investor
b. It must be available to another member firm
c. It must be distributed internally
d. It must not be forwarded to any retail investor

HINTS: Recognize the requirement for treating a communication as institutional.

Q780_LO107: For institutional communication, when is principal approval required?
a. Always required
b. Never required
c. Required after use
d. Required before use or allowed post-use approval

HINTS: Identify the requirement for principal approval in institutional communication.

Q781_LO107: What is the definition of a retail investor?
a. Any person with an account with the member
b. Any institutional investor
c. Any person other than an institutional investor
d. Any person with $50 million or more in total assets

HINTS: Recognize the definition of a retail investor.

Q782_LO107: How many days before use must a copy of new retail communication be filed for a new member firm?
a. 5 days
b. 10 days
c. 15 days
d. 20 days

HINTS: Identify the filing requirement for new member firms with retail communication.

Q783_LO107: When must a copy of retail communication be filed for established member firms?
a. Within 5 days of first use
b. Within 10 days of first use
c. Within 15 days of first use
d. Within 20 days of first use

HINTS: Recognize the filing requirement for established member firms with retail communication.

Q784_LO107: What is the threshold for the number of retail investors in retail communication?
a. More than 10 investors
b. More than 15 investors
c. More than 20 investors
d. More than 25 investors

HINTS: Identify the threshold for the number of retail investors in retail communication.

Q785_LO107: What is the definition of correspondence?
a. Written communication to institutional investors
b. Written communication to 25 or fewer retail investors
c. Electronic communication to retail investors
d. Internal memos

HINTS: Recognize the definition of correspondence.

Q786_LO107: When is principal approval required for correspondence?
a. Always required
b. Never required
c. Required after use
d. Required before use or allowed post-use approval

HINTS: Identify the requirement for principal approval in correspondence.

Q787_LO107: What is the requirement for the use of social media and online activities?
a. Preapprove individual posts
b. No need for monitoring
c. No policies and procedures required
d. No engagement with prospective clients

HINTS: Recognize the requirement for social media use.

Q788_LO107: What is the purpose of monitoring the business-related social media presence of representatives?
a. Ensure maximum promotion
b. Enhance online engagement
c. Ensure compliance
d. Increase post frequency

HINTS: Identify the purpose of monitoring social media presence.

Q789_LO107: What does FINRA mandate regarding the nature of the audience in communications?
a. Provide vague details
b. Provide details appropriate to the audience
c. Provide maximum information
d. Provide generic information

HINTS: Recognize what FINRA mandates regarding the nature of the audience.

Q790_LO107: What is not permitted in communications regarding past performance?
a. Implication of future performance
b. Guarantees of future performance
c. Historical references
d. Analysis of historical trends

HINTS: Identify what is not permitted in communications regarding past performance.

Q791_LO108: What is the purpose of the Telephone Consumer Protection Act of 1991 (TCPA)?
a. Encouraging telemarketing
b. Protecting consumers from unwanted telephone solicitations
c. Promoting automated calls
d. Regulating fax advertisements

HINTS: Recognize the primary purpose of the TCPA.

Q792_LO108: What is the definition of a telephone solicitation under the TCPA?
a. Any call to a friend
b. A call initiated to encourage the purchase of property, goods, or services
c. Any recorded message
d. A call for social purposes

HINTS: Identify the definition of a telephone solicitation.

Q793_LO108: When can a solicitation occur under TCPA rules?
a. Anytime during the day
b. Between 9:00 am and 9:00 pm based on the prospect's time zone
c. Between 8:00 am and 10:00 pm based on the prospect's time zone
d. Between 8:00 am and 9:00 pm based on the prospect's time zone

HINTS: Recognize the time frame for permissible solicitation.

Q794_LO108: What is a crucial requirement during cold calls under TCPA rules?
a. Ambiguity in identifying the company
b. Ensuring calls only to numbers on the federal do-not-call list
c. Providing prospect information on demand
d. Informing prospects of name, company, and contact details

HINTS: Identify a crucial requirement during cold calls.

Q795_LO108: According to TCPA, when can calls be made to numbers on the company or federal do-not-call list?
a. Always allowed
b. Only with prior permission
c. If offering discounts
d. Prohibited

HINTS: Recognize the rule regarding calls to do-not-call lists.

Q796_LO108: What exemption does TCPA provide for telemarketing calls?
a. Calls made to parties with prior express permission
b. Calls made during lunch hours
c. Calls made for commercial purposes
d. Calls made without any permission

HINTS: Identify the exemption provided by TCPA for telemarketing calls.

Q797_LO108: What is the National Do Not Call Registry, and when should telemarketers check it?
a. A company's internal list
b. A list maintained by FINRA
c. A list maintained by the FCC
d. The Federal Trade Commission's list

HINTS: Recognize the National Do Not Call Registry and when telemarketers should check it.

Q798_LO108: What is the maximum age allowed for a firm's do-not-call list as per TCPA rules?
a. 15 days
b. 20 days
c. 25 days
d. 30 days

HINTS: Identify the maximum age allowed for a firm's do-not-call list.

Q799_LO108: What is a requirement for holding customer mail as per FINRA rules?
a. Unlimited holding period
b. Written instructions with a specified time period
c. No need to inform customers of alternate methods
d. Verification not required

HINTS: Recognize the requirement for holding customer mail.

Q800_LO108: What does a firm need to do during the time it holds mail for a customer?
a. No need for communication
b. Verify customer's instructions monthly
c. Tampering is allowed
d. Confirm customer inconvenience

HINTS: Identify the actions required during the time a firm holds mail for a customer.

Q801_LO108: What does holding mail for a customer imply according to FINRA rules?
a. Required by the rule
b. Courtesy that firms are permitted to extend
c. Mandatory for all firms
d. Violates FINRA rules

HINTS: Recognize the implication of holding mail for a customer.

Q802_LO108: What is a key requirement for telemarketers regarding the do-not-call list?
a. Monthly acknowledgment of prospects
b. Quarterly update of the list
c. Train representatives on using the list
d. No requirement for verification

HINTS: Identify a key requirement for telemarketers regarding the do-not-call list.

Q803_LO108: What is the purpose of maintaining a do-not-call list by organizations doing telemarketing?
a. Enhance telemarketing efficiency
b. Ensure quick responses to prospects
c. Ensure compliance with do-not-call requests
d. Optional for organizations

HINTS: Recognize the purpose of maintaining a do-not-call list.

Q804_LO108: What does the TCPA require regarding the frequency of checking the National Do Not Call Registry?
a. Weekly check
b. Monthly check
c. Quarterly check
d. No requirement for checking

HINTS: Identify the TCPA requirement regarding the frequency of checking the National Do Not Call Registry.

Q805_LO108: What is a permissible reason for holding mail for a customer for periods longer than three months?
a. Convenience for the customer
b. Safety or security concerns
c. Marketing strategy
d. No specific reason required

HINTS: Recognize a permissible reason for holding mail for a customer for periods longer than three months.

Q806_LO108: What does the TCPA of 1991 primarily aim to protect consumers from?
a. Unwanted emails
b. Unwanted door-to-door sales
c. Unwanted telephone solicitations
d. Unwanted social media messages

HINTS: Identify the primary focus of the TCPA of 1991.

Q807_LO108: When making cold calls, what information must the caller provide to prospects, according to the TCPA?
a. Only the company's name
b. Only the caller's name
c. The company's name and telephone number or address
d. No information is required

HINTS: Recognize the information that must be provided during cold calls.

Q808_LO108: During what time frame is solicitation allowed under the TCPA?
a. 6:00 am to 10:00 pm
b. 8:00 am to 9:00 pm
c. 10:00 am to 12:00 pm
d. 9:00 am to 5:00 pm

HINTS: Identify the permissible time frame for solicitation under the TCPA.

Q809_LO108: According to the TCPA, when should cold calls not be made?
a. On weekends
b. To numbers on the company or federal do-not-call list
c. During lunch hours
d. Without prior express permission

HINTS: Identify the restriction on making cold calls according to the TCPA.

Q810_LO108: Which type of calls is exempted from the TCPA rules?
a. Calls made for a commercial purpose
b. Calls made on behalf of a tax-exempt nonprofit organization
c. Calls made for legitimate debt collection purposes
d. Calls made to unknown prospects

HINTS: Recognize the types of calls exempted from the TCPA rules.

Q811_LO108: What is a requirement for maintaining a do-not-call list according to the TCPA?
a. Remove names on prospect request
b. Keep names for a maximum of 60 days
c. Names should be more than 30 days old
d. Train representatives but no acknowledgment required

HINTS: Identify a requirement for maintaining a do-not-call list according to the TCPA.

Q812_LO108: Who maintains the National Do Not Call Registry?
a. FINRA
b. SEC
c. FCC
d. Federal Trade Commission

HINTS: Recognize the organization maintaining the National Do Not Call Registry.

Q813_LO108: What is the maximum age allowed for a company's do-not-call list, according to the TCPA?
a. 10 days
b. 20 days
c. 30 days
d. 40 days

HINTS: Identify the maximum age allowed for a company's do-not-call list.

Q814_LO108: What conditions must be met for a firm to hold mail for a customer?
a. No written instructions required
b. Written instructions with no time period specified
c. Written instructions with a specified time period up to three months
d. Written instructions for any time period

HINTS: Recognize the conditions for a firm to hold mail for a customer.

Q815_LO108: What is required if a firm is holding mail for a customer during a specified period?
a. No verification needed
b. Timely communication with the customer
c. No need to provide alternate methods
d. No need for customer confirmation

HINTS: Identify a requirement when a firm is holding mail for a customer during a specified period.

Q816_LO108: Is holding mail for a customer a mandatory requirement for firms?
a. Yes
b. No
c. Only for certain types of accounts
d. Depends on customer preference

HINTS: Recognize whether holding mail for a customer is a mandatory requirement for firms.

Q817_LO108: If a customer requests to be removed from the do-not-call list, what should the firm do?
a. Ignore the request
b. Remove immediately without verification
c. Verify at reasonable intervals
d. Keep the name for a maximum of 10 days

HINTS: Identify the appropriate action if a customer requests removal from the do-not-call list.

Q818_LO108: When is a new retail communication filing required for an established member firm?
a. Before first use
b. Within 5 days of first use
c. Within 10 days of first use
d. Within 15 days of first use

HINTS: Recognize when a new retail communication filing is required for an established member firm.

Q819_LO108: What is the primary purpose of the TCPA of 1991?
a. Regulate online advertisements
b. Protect consumers from unwanted telemarketing
c. Ensure timely mail delivery
d. Govern email solicitations

HINTS: Identify the primary purpose of the TCPA of 1991.

Q820_LO108: What is the consequence of making calls to numbers on the do-not-call list?
a. Fine imposed by FINRA
b. Warning issued by the SEC
c. Violation of TCPA rules
d. Mandatory training for representatives

HINTS: Recognize the consequence of making calls to numbers on the do-not-call list.

Q821_LO109: What is the primary focus of Regulation S-P?
a. Securities trading
b. Customer privacy protection
c. Business continuity planning
d. Insider trading prevention

HINTS: Identify the primary focus of Regulation S-P.

Q822_LO109: Which of the following is an example of nonpublic personal information under Regulation SP?
a. Publicly available financial statements
b. Customer's name and address
c. Stock market indices
d. Economic forecasts

HINTS: Recognize examples of nonpublic personal information under Regulation SP.

Q823_LO109: What is required if a firm reserves the right to disclose nonpublic personal information to unaffiliated third parties?
a. Opt-in consent
b. No action required
c. Provide a reasonable means to opt out
d. Notify the SEC

HINTS: Identify the requirement if a firm reserves the right to disclose nonpublic personal information.

Q824_LO109: What is considered a reasonable opt-out means under Regulation SP?
a. Verbal consent
b. Sending a letter
c. Providing a toll-free telephone number
d. Not providing any opt-out option

HINTS: Recognize what constitutes a reasonable opt-out means under Regulation SP.

Q825_LO109: When must a firm initially provide a privacy notice to a customer under Regulation SP?
a. Annually
b. At any time
c. When a significant event occurs
d. At the time the relationship is first established

HINTS: Identify when a firm must initially provide a privacy notice to a customer.

Q826_LO109: What does Regulation SP require regarding a firm's business continuity plan (BCP)?
a. Annual submission to SEC
b. Approval, update, and annual review by senior management
c. Public disclosure on the firm's website
d. Submission to FINRA only

HINTS: Recognize the requirements related to a firm's business continuity plan under Regulation SP.

Q827_LO109: How frequently must a firm update the emergency contact information under the business continuity plan?
a. Annually
b. Every two years
c. Quarterly
d. No specific requirement

HINTS: Identify the frequency of updating emergency contact information under the business continuity plan.

Q828_LO109: What is the role of the designated contact persons for significant business disruptions?
a. Both must be non-principals
b. At least one must be a principal and part of senior management
c. Only one is required, and they must be a non-principal
d. No specific requirement for their roles

HINTS: Recognize the role requirements for the designated emergency contact persons.

Q829_LO109: What must a firm disclose to customers regarding significant events?
a. Communication plan with regulators
b. Response plan with competitors
c. How it will respond to significant events
d. Internal contingency plans

HINTS: Identify what a firm must disclose to customers regarding significant events.

Q830_LO109: How soon must a firm update emergency contact information following any change?
a. 15 days
b. 30 days
c. 45 days
d. 60 days

HINTS: Recognize the timeframe for updating emergency contact information following any change.

Q831_LO109: What is NOT a safeguard requirement under Regulation SP?
a. Securing desktop and laptop computers
b. Encrypting email
c. Regularly updating employee job roles
d. Safeguarding customer information

HINTS: Identify the safeguard requirements under Regulation SP.

Q832_LO109: When does Regulation SP consider a person a "consumer" instead of a "customer"?
a. One-time limited relationship
b. Ongoing relationship
c. Relationship with multiple accounts
d. Relationship with high net worth

HINTS: Recognize the conditions for a person to be considered a "consumer" under Regulation SP.

Q833_LO109: What is the consequence of not providing a reasonable means to opt out under Regulation SP?
a. Warning from FINRA
b. SEC fine
c. Violation of Regulation SP
d. Mandatory training for employees

HINTS: Identify the consequence of not providing a reasonable means to opt out.

Q834_LO109: Which of the following is NOT an example of nonpublic personal information under Regulation SP?
a. Social Security number
b. Transaction history
c. Stock market indices
d. Account balances

HINTS: Recognize examples of nonpublic personal information.

Q835_LO109: What must a firm provide to customers annually under Regulation SP?
a. Privacy notice
b. Business continuity plan
c. Emergency contact information
d. Safeguard requirements

HINTS: Identify what Regulation SP requires firms to provide to customers annually.

Q836_LO109: What is the primary focus of Regulation S-P enacted by the SEC?
a. Protecting against fraud
b. Safeguarding customer information privacy
c. Ensuring fair trading practices
d. Monitoring market volatility

HINTS: Identify the primary objective of Regulation S-P.

Q837_LO109: Which of the following is considered nonpublic personal information under Regulation S-P?
a. Publicly available financial reports
b. Customer's name and address
c. General market trends
d. Economic indicators

HINTS: Recognize examples of nonpublic personal information under Regulation S-P.

Q838_LO109: What is required if a firm reserves the right to disclose nonpublic personal information to third parties under Regulation S-P?
a. No action required
b. Provide a reasonable means to opt out
c. Obtain customer consent once a year
d. Disclose information only to affiliated third parties

HINTS: Identify the action required if a firm intends to disclose nonpublic personal information under Regulation S-P.

Q839_LO109: What is considered a reasonable opt-out means under Regulation S-P?
a. Asking customers to write a letter
b. Providing a toll-free telephone number
c. Sending an email
d. Offering no opt-out option

HINTS: Recognize examples of reasonable opt-out means under Regulation S-P.

Q840_LO109: When must a firm provide an updated version of the privacy notice under Regulation S-P?
a. Every 6 months
b. Annually
c. Biennially
d. Only at the establishment of the relationship

HINTS: Recognize the frequency of providing an updated privacy notice under Regulation S-P.

Q841_LO109: What does Regulation S-P require firms to describe in their privacy notice?
a. Investment strategies
b. Types of personal information collected
c. Market predictions
d. Current economic conditions

HINTS: Identify the information that must be described in a firm's privacy notice under Regulation S-P.

Q842_LO109: What does Regulation S-P require regarding the safeguarding of customer information?
a. No specific requirements
b. Safeguarding only electronic information
c. Safeguarding all forms of customer information
d. Safeguarding information only from cyber threats

HINTS: Recognize the requirement of Regulation S-P regarding the safeguarding of customer information.

Q843_LO109: When does a firm need to provide a privacy notice under Regulation S-P?
a. Every month
b. Once at the establishment of the relationship
c. Biennially
d. Annually

HINTS: Identify when a firm needs to provide a privacy notice under Regulation S-P.

Q844_LO109: Under Regulation S-P, what is the consequence of making an annual notification to a consumer instead of a customer?
a. No consequence
b. Annual notification is not required
c. Violation of Regulation S-P
d. Fine imposed by FINRA

HINTS: Recognize the consequence of making an annual notification to a consumer instead of a customer under Regulation S-P.

Q845_LO109: What are the key points that a business continuity plan (BCP) must address, as per FINRA requirements?
a. Investment strategies
b. Data backup and recovery, alternate communications, prompt customer access, etc.
c. Annual financial reports
d. Employee training programs

HINTS: Identify the key points that a BCP must address according to FINRA requirements.

Q846_LO109: Who must approve, update, and conduct an annual review of a firm's business continuity plan (BCP)?
a. Any employee
b. Outside consultant
c. Member of senior management who is also a principal
d. Customer representative

HINTS: Recognize who is responsible for approving, updating, and conducting an annual review of a firm's BCP.

Q847_LO109: According to FINRA, who are the emergency contact persons for a firm in the event of a significant business disruption?
a. Any firm employee
b. Outside contacts familiar with the firm's operations
c. Two random employees
d. Senior management personnel and at least one principal

HINTS: Identify the requirements for emergency contact persons according to FINRA.

Q848_LO109: What action must a firm take if there is a change in the information of emergency contact persons?
a. Update within 60 days
b. Update within 30 days
c. Update within 90 days
d. No requirement for updating

HINTS: Recognize the timeframe for updating information on emergency contact persons according to FINRA.

Q849_LO109: How should a firm communicate its business continuity plan (BCP) information to customers?
a. Through phone calls only
b. In writing at the time of account opening, posted on the website, and mailed to customers on request
c. Only through the firm's website
d. Through social media platforms

HINTS: Identify the channels through which a firm must communicate BCP information to customers.

Q850_LO109: What is the consequence if a firm fails to disclose how it will respond to significant events to customers?
a. Fine imposed by SEC
b. Warning issued by FINRA
c. Violation of FINRA rules
d. No consequence

HINTS: Recognize the consequence of failing to disclose how a firm will respond to significant events to customers.

Correct Answers & Explanations
General Suitability & Communications With the Public

Q701_LO105: Correct Answer: b EXPLANATIONS: Brokers are responsible for performing due diligence to know their customers.

Q702_LO105: Correct Answer: c EXPLANATIONS: FINRA excludes other brokers and certain potential investors from the definition of a customer.

Q703_LO105: Correct Answer: b EXPLANATIONS: Employment status is a financial circumstance that may influence investment suitability.

Q704_LO105: Correct Answer: c EXPLANATIONS: Age is a nonfinancial consideration that is important under the KYC rule.

Q705_LO105: Correct Answer: c EXPLANATIONS: They need to know both financial and nonfinancial considerations to make suitable recommendations.

Q706_LO105: Correct Answer: a EXPLANATIONS: Employment status is considered a financial circumstance.

Q707_LO105: Correct Answer: b EXPLANATIONS: Risk tolerance influences the choice of investment alternatives.

Q708_LO105: Correct Answer: c EXPLANATIONS: Are you seeking long-term or short-term investments? helps understand the time horizon.

Q709_LO105: Correct Answer: c EXPLANATIONS: It is important for KYC compliance and understanding the customer's financial situation.

Q710_LO105: Correct Answer: c EXPLANATIONS: The KYC rule aims to ensure the suitability of recommendations for customers.

Q711_LO105: Correct Answer: d EXPLANATIONS: Liquid net worth indicates financial capability, influencing investment decisions.

Q712_LO105: Correct Answer: b EXPLANATIONS: RRs should have a reasonable basis to believe in the validity of customer information.

Q713_LO105: Correct Answer: b EXPLANATIONS: Failing to perform due diligence may lead to regulatory fines and penalties.

Q714_LO105: Correct Answer: c EXPLANATIONS: The rule does not apply if the recipient of the advice is not currently a client.

Q715_LO105: Correct Answer: c EXPLANATIONS: RRs must have a reasonable basis to believe in the suitability of recommended transactions.

Q716_LO105: Correct Answer: b EXPLANATIONS: Brokers are required to know their customers, including financial status and investment objectives.

Q717_LO105: Correct Answer: b EXPLANATIONS: Brokers must have a reasonable basis to believe a recommendation is suitable based on the customer's financial circumstances.

Q718_LO105: Correct Answer: b EXPLANATIONS: The rule does not apply if the advice recipient is not currently a client and doesn't receive compensation.

Q719_LO105: Correct Answer: d EXPLANATIONS: Total debt is a quantifiable financial circumstance.

Q720_LO105: Correct Answer: b EXPLANATIONS: Employment status is a nonfinancial factor.

Q721_LO105: Correct Answer: c EXPLANATIONS: Age is a nonfinancial consideration in understanding the customer.

Q722_LO105: Correct Answer: b EXPLANATIONS: Investment experience is crucial in shaping a customer's portfolio.

Q723_LO105: Correct Answer: d EXPLANATIONS: Risk tolerance involves the willingness to take risks, invest in risky assets, and accept potential losses.

Q724_LO105: Correct Answer: c EXPLANATIONS: Asking about seeking long-term or short-term investments helps assess the time horizon.

Q725_LO105: Correct Answer: b EXPLANATIONS: The customer's favorite color is not relevant to KYC.

Q726_LO105: Correct Answer: c EXPLANATIONS: It helps assess the customer's risk tolerance.

Q727_LO105: Correct Answer: b EXPLANATIONS: New customers must be advised before the account is opened.

Q728_LO105: Correct Answer: b EXPLANATIONS: The KYC rule aims to prevent money laundering and ensure suitable recommendations.

Q729_LO105: Correct Answer: c EXPLANATIONS: Suitability involves making recommendations aligned with the customer's profile.

Q730_LO105: Correct Answer: d EXPLANATIONS: The SDN list includes names of individuals and entities to prevent dealings with targeted parties.

Q731_LO106: Correct Answer: b EXPLANATIONS: A recommendation involves suggesting a course of action regarding a security or investment strategy.

Q732_LO106: Correct Answer: c EXPLANATIONS: Consider the circumstances, recipient's knowledge, and their circumstances.

Q733_LO106: Correct Answer: b EXPLANATIONS: Lack of intent doesn't prevent a communication from being considered a recommendation if it meets certain criteria.

Q734_LO106: Correct Answer: b EXPLANATIONS: The investment's primary purpose should align with the customer's primary objective.

Q735_LO106: Correct Answer: b EXPLANATIONS: Consider the customer's tolerance for risk, matching conservative or aggressive investments accordingly.

Q736_LO106: Correct Answer: b EXPLANATIONS: CDs, money market mutual funds, and other low-risk options align with this objective.

Q737_LO106: Correct Answer: b EXPLANATIONS: Common stock, especially in aggressive growth sectors, aligns with this objective.

Q738_LO106: Correct Answer: a EXPLANATIONS: Municipal bonds, municipal bond funds, and Roth IRAs provide tax advantages for income investors.

Q739_LO106: Correct Answer: b EXPLANATIONS: Securities listed on an exchange, unlisted Nasdaq stocks, and mutual funds are more liquid.

Q740_LO106: Correct Answer: b EXPLANATIONS: Mutual funds, especially asset allocation and balanced funds, aid in diversifying portfolios.

Q741_LO106: Correct Answer: b EXPLANATIONS: Option contracts, DPPs, and other high-risk options align with a speculation objective.

Q742_LO106: Correct Answer: d EXPLANATIONS: Time frame is another circumstance impacting the investment decision.

Q743_LO106: Correct Answer: b EXPLANATIONS: It ensures that the investment aligns with the customer's primary objective.

Q744_LO106: Correct Answer: d EXPLANATIONS: It is crucial to align recommendations with the customer's objectives.

Q745_LO106: Correct Answer: c EXPLANATIONS: The representative should assess customer circumstances and knowledge in making recommendations.

Q746_LO106: Correct Answer: c EXPLANATIONS: Making an investment recommendation involves suggesting a course of action regarding a security.

Q747_LO106: Correct Answer: c EXPLANATIONS: Consider the knowledge and sophistication of the recipient.

Q748_LO106: Correct Answer: b EXPLANATIONS: The primary purpose of an investment should align with the customer's primary objective.

Q749_LO106: Correct Answer: c EXPLANATIONS: Consider the customer's tolerance for risk.

Q750_LO106: Correct Answer: a EXPLANATIONS: Conservative investments are more appropriate for those with a low risk tolerance.

Q751_LO106: Correct Answer: c EXPLANATIONS: Consider any other circumstance, such as the time frame, that impacts the investment decision.

Q752_LO106: Correct Answer: d EXPLANATIONS: CDs, money market mutual funds, and fixed annuities are suitable for capital preservation.

Q753_LO106: Correct Answer: c EXPLANATIONS: Technology stocks and sector funds are suitable for aggressive growth.

Q754_LO106: Correct Answer: a EXPLANATIONS: Bonds (but not zero coupons) are suitable for high-yield income.

Q755_LO106: Correct Answer: b EXPLANATIONS: Mutual funds, listed securities, and publicly traded REITs provide liquidity.

Q756_LO106: Correct Answer: b EXPLANATIONS: Asset allocation funds and balanced funds contribute to portfolio diversification.

Q757_LO106: Correct Answer: b EXPLANATIONS: Option contracts are suitable for speculation.

Q758_LO106: Correct Answer: b EXPLANATIONS: The rule of alignment ensures the alignment of customer objectives with investment purpose.

Q759_LO106: Correct Answer: d EXPLANATIONS: Assessing risk tolerance helps match investments with the investor's risk appetite.

Q760_LO106: Correct Answer: c EXPLANATIONS: Considering the circumstances helps tailor recommendations to the recipient's situation.

Q761_LO107: Correct Answer: b EXPLANATIONS: Member communications must be based on principles of fair dealing and good faith.

Q762_LO107: Correct Answer: a EXPLANATIONS: Exaggerated statements are not permitted.

Q763_LO107: Correct Answer: d EXPLANATIONS: Past performance should not imply future results.

Q764_LO107: Correct Answer: b EXPLANATIONS: Members should provide appropriate details and explanations for the audience.

Q765_LO107: Correct Answer: c EXPLANATIONS: Institutional, retail, and correspondence are the three categories.

Q766_LO107: Correct Answer: b EXPLANATIONS: A registered investment company is an example of an institutional investor.

Q767_LO107: Correct Answer: b EXPLANATIONS: A retail investor is any person other than an institutional investor.

Q768_LO107: Correct Answer: b EXPLANATIONS: Prior principal approval is required for retail communication.

Q769_LO107: Correct Answer: b EXPLANATIONS: Filing must occur within 10 days of first use for established member firms.

Q770_LO107: Correct Answer: b EXPLANATIONS: Filing must occur at least 10 days before use for new member firms.

Q771_LO107: Correct Answer: c EXPLANATIONS: Correspondence involves 25 or fewer retail investors.

Q772_LO107: Correct Answer: c EXPLANATIONS: Firms must establish if they require prior principal approval or allow post-use approval.

Q773_LO107: Correct Answer: d EXPLANATIONS: Approval by a registered principal is required.

Q774_LO107: Correct Answer: c EXPLANATIONS: There is no requirement for preapproval of individual posts in interactive forums.

Q775_LO107: Correct Answer: c EXPLANATIONS: Firms must have policies and procedures concerning social media activities.

Q776_LO107: Correct Answer: b EXPLANATIONS: Communications must be based on principles of fair dealing and good faith.

Q777_LO107: Correct Answer: c EXPLANATIONS: Ambiguous statements are not permitted; clarity is required.

Q778_LO107: Correct Answer: a EXPLANATIONS: Institutional communications are directed to institutional investors.

Q779_LO107: Correct Answer: d EXPLANATIONS: It should not be forwarded or made available to any retail investor.

Q780_LO107: Correct Answer: d EXPLANATIONS: Principal approval is required before use or allowed post-use approval.

Q781_LO107: Correct Answer: c EXPLANATIONS: A retail investor is any person other than an institutional investor.

Q782_LO107: Correct Answer: b EXPLANATIONS: For new member firms, the filing must occur at least 10 days before use.

Q783_LO107: Correct Answer: b EXPLANATIONS: The filing must happen within 10 days of first use.

Q784_LO107: Correct Answer: d EXPLANATIONS: Retail communication involves more than 25 retail investors.

Q785_LO107: Correct Answer: b EXPLANATIONS: Correspondence involves 25 or fewer retail investors.

Q786_LO107: Correct Answer: a EXPLANATIONS: Principal approval is always required for correspondence.

Q787_LO107: Correct Answer: a EXPLANATIONS: Individual posts in interactive forums do not require preapproval.

Q788_LO107: Correct Answer: c EXPLANATIONS: Monitoring ensures compliance with regulations.

Q789_LO107: Correct Answer: b EXPLANATIONS: Details and explanations should be appropriate to the audience.

Q790_LO107: Correct Answer: a EXPLANATIONS: Communications should not imply that past performance will be repeated.

Q791_LO108: Correct Answer: b EXPLANATIONS: The TCPA was enacted to protect consumers from unwanted telephone solicitations.

Q792_LO108: Correct Answer: b EXPLANATIONS: It is a call initiated to encourage the purchase of or investment in property, goods, or services.

Q793_LO108: Correct Answer: d EXPLANATIONS: Solicitation should occur only between 8:00 am and 9:00 pm based on the prospect's time zone.

Q794_LO108: Correct Answer: d EXPLANATIONS: Informing prospects of name, company, and contact details is essential.

Q795_LO108: Correct Answer: d EXPLANATIONS: Calls to numbers on the do-not-call list are prohibited.

Q796_LO108: Correct Answer: a EXPLANATIONS: Calls made to parties with prior express permission are exempt.

Q797_LO108: Correct Answer: d EXPLANATIONS: It is maintained by the Federal Trade Commission, and telemarketers should check numbers against this list.

Q798_LO108: Correct Answer: d EXPLANATIONS: The do-not-call list should be no more than 30 days old.

Q799_LO108: Correct Answer: b EXPLANATIONS: Written instructions with a specified time period are required.

Q800_LO108: Correct Answer: b EXPLANATIONS: The firm must verify at reasonable intervals that the customer's instructions still apply.

Q801_LO108: Correct Answer: b EXPLANATIONS: Holding mail is a courtesy that firms are permitted to extend.

Q802_LO108: Correct Answer: c EXPLANATIONS: Representatives must be trained on using the do-not-call list.

Q803_LO108: Correct Answer: c EXPLANATIONS: It ensures compliance with do-not-call requests from prospects.

Q804_LO108: Correct Answer: c EXPLANATIONS: Telemarketers are required to check numbers against this list at reasonable intervals.

Q805_LO108: Correct Answer: b EXPLANATIONS: Safety or security concerns are valid reasons.

Q806_LO108: Correct Answer: c EXPLANATIONS: The TCPA aims to protect consumers from unwanted telephone solicitations.

Q807_LO108: Correct Answer: c EXPLANATIONS: The caller must provide the company's name and telephone number or address.

Q808_LO108: Correct Answer: b EXPLANATIONS: Solicitation is allowed only between 8:00 am and 9:00 pm based on the prospect's time zone.

Q809_LO108: Correct Answer: b EXPLANATIONS: No calls should be made to numbers on the company or federal do-not-call list.

Q810_LO108: Correct Answer: b EXPLANATIONS: Calls made on behalf of a tax-exempt nonprofit organization are exempted.

Q811_LO108: Correct Answer: a EXPLANATIONS: Names should be kept on the list until the prospect requests removal.

Q812_LO108: Correct Answer: d EXPLANATIONS: The Federal Trade Commission (FTC) maintains the registry.

Q813_LO108: Correct Answer: c EXPLANATIONS: The company's do-not-call list must not be more than 30 days old.

Q814_LO108: Correct Answer: c EXPLANATIONS: Written instructions must include the time period, up to three months.

Q815_LO108: Correct Answer: b EXPLANATIONS: Timely communication with the customer is required.

Q816_LO108: Correct Answer: b EXPLANATIONS: It is a courtesy, and firms are not required to hold mail.

Q817_LO108: Correct Answer: c EXPLANATIONS: Verification at reasonable intervals is required.

Q818_LO108: Correct Answer: c EXPLANATIONS: The filing must happen within 10 days of first use for established member firms.

Q819_LO108: Correct Answer: b EXPLANATIONS: The TCPA aims to protect consumers from unwanted telephone solicitations (telemarketing).

Q820_LO108: Correct Answer: c EXPLANATIONS: It is a violation of TCPA rules.

Q821_LO109: Correct Answer: b EXPLANATIONS: Regulation S-P is enacted to protect the privacy of customer information.

Q822_LO109: Correct Answer: b EXPLANATIONS: Customer's name and address are examples of nonpublic personal information.

Q823_LO109: Correct Answer: c EXPLANATIONS: A reasonable means to opt out must be provided.

Q824_LO109: Correct Answer: c EXPLANATIONS: Providing a toll-free telephone number is considered a reasonable opt-out means.

Q825_LO109: Correct Answer: d EXPLANATIONS: The notice must be provided at the time the relationship is first established.

Q826_LO109: Correct Answer: b EXPLANATIONS: Senior management must approve, update, and conduct an annual review of the plan.

Q827_LO109: Correct Answer: a EXPLANATIONS: Firms must update the information promptly, annually.

Q828_LO109: Correct Answer: b EXPLANATIONS: At least one must be a principal and part of senior management.

Q829_LO109: Correct Answer: c EXPLANATIONS: Disclosure must be made on how the firm will respond to significant events.

Q830_LO109: Correct Answer: b EXPLANATIONS: The update must be done promptly, in no case later than 30 days following any change.

Q831_LO109: Correct Answer: c EXPLANATIONS: Regularly updating employee job roles is not explicitly as a safeguard requirement.

Q832_LO109: Correct Answer: a EXPLANATIONS: If the relationship is one time and limited, they are referred to as consumers.

Q833_LO109: Correct Answer: c EXPLANATIONS: It constitutes a violation of Regulation SP.

Q834_LO109: Correct Answer: c EXPLANATIONS: Stock market indices are not considered nonpublic personal information.

Q835_LO109: Correct Answer: a EXPLANATIONS: Firms must provide an updated privacy notice annually.

Q836_LO109: Correct Answer: b EXPLANATIONS: Regulation S-P is enacted to safeguard customer information privacy.

Q837_LO109: Correct Answer: b EXPLANATIONS: Customer's name and address are examples of nonpublic personal information.

Q838_LO109: Correct Answer: b EXPLANATIONS: A reasonable means to opt out must be provided.

Q839_LO109: Correct Answer: b EXPLANATIONS: Providing a toll-free telephone number is considered reasonable.

Q840_LO109: Correct Answer: b EXPLANATIONS: An updated version must be provided annually.

Q841_LO109: Correct Answer: b EXPLANATIONS: The notice must state the types of personal information that the firm collects.

Q842_LO109: Correct Answer: c EXPLANATIONS: Firms must safeguard customer information in all forms, including electronic.

Q843_LO109: Correct Answer: b EXPLANATIONS: The firm must provide a privacy notice at the time the relationship is first established.

Q844_LO109: Correct Answer: a EXPLANATIONS: No annual notification is required for consumers; the consequence is that they are not customers.

Q845_LO109: Correct Answer: b EXPLANATIONS: FINRA requires BCPs to address data backup, alternate communications, prompt customer access, and more.

Q846_LO109: Correct Answer: c EXPLANATIONS: A member of senior management who is also a principal must fulfill this responsibility.

Q847_LO109: Correct Answer: d EXPLANATIONS: Two emergency contacts, with at least one being a principal and part of senior management.

Q848_LO109: Correct Answer: b EXPLANATIONS: Information must be updated promptly, in no case later than 30 days following any change.

Q849_LO109: Correct Answer: b EXPLANATIONS: It should be communicated in writing at the time of account opening, posted on the website, and mailed to customers on request.

Q850_LO109: Correct Answer: c EXPLANATIONS: It is a violation of FINRA rules.

Prohibited Activities & Record Keeping Requirements

Q851_LO110: What records are considered part of the life of the firm and retained indefinitely?
a. Customer ledgers
b. Blotters
c. Partnership agreement
d. General ledger

HINTS: Identify records that are kept for the life of the firm.

Q852_LO110: Which document serves as the foundational document of a corporation and must be retained for the life of the firm?
a. Stock certificate books
b. Corporate charter
c. Amendments
d. Minutes

HINTS: Recognize the foundational document of a corporation.

Q853_LO110: What is the purpose of stock certificate books for closely held corporations?
a. Recording general ledger entries
b. Issuing stock certificates
c. Maintaining customer ledgers
d. Documenting customer account records

HINTS: Understand the purpose of stock certificate books for closely held corporations.

Q854_LO110: What records are considered organizational records related to the foundations of the firm?
a. Customer ledgers
b. Designation of principals
c. Minutes
d. Form BD

HINTS: Identify records related to the foundations of the firm.

Q855_LO110: Which records are maintained for six years from the last use and relate to the purchase and sale of securities?
a. Customer account records
b. Blotters
c. Customer ledgers
d. Amendments

HINTS: Recognize records maintained for six years related to the purchase and sale of securities.

Q856_LO110: What is the general ledger's function in a brokerage firm?
a. Issuing stock certificates
b. Preparing financial statements
c. Posting customer ledgers
d. Documenting customer account records

HINTS: Understand the function of the general ledger in a brokerage firm.

Q857_LO110: When must blotters be prepared according to regulatory requirements?
a. Quarterly
b. Annually
c. No specific requirement
d. No later than the following business day

HINTS: Recognize the regulatory requirement for preparing blotters.

Q858_LO110: What is the purpose of a stock record in a brokerage firm?
a. Issuing stock certificates
b. Recording ownership of securities
c. Maintaining customer ledgers
d. Documenting customer account records

HINTS: Understand the purpose of a stock record in a brokerage firm.

Q859_LO110: What must be posted no later than the business day after the settlement date?
a. General ledger
b. Customer ledgers
c. Stock record
d. Designation of principals

HINTS: Identify records that must be posted promptly after the settlement date.

Q860_LO110: What do customer ledgers in a brokerage firm represent?
a. Record of original entry
b. Customer statements
c. Accounting records
d. Ownership of securities

HINTS: Recognize the nature of customer ledgers in a brokerage firm.

Q861_LO110: What is the purpose of customer account records in a brokerage firm?
a. Recording general ledger entries
b. Issuing stock certificates
c. Customer statements
d. Designating principals

HINTS: Understand the purpose of customer account records in a brokerage firm.

Q862_LO110: What is the significance of designating principals in a brokerage firm?
a. Recording general ledger entries
b. Issuing stock certificates
c. Overseeing specific areas
d. Documenting customer account records

HINTS: Recognize the significance of designating principals in a brokerage firm.

Q863_LO110: For how long are records that are part of the life of the firm retained?
a. One year
b. Indefinitely
c. Three years
d. Five years

HINTS: Identify the retention period for records that are part of the life of the firm.

Q864_LO110: What type of records must a brokerage firm maintain for six years from last use?
a. Customer account records
b. Organizational records
c. Six-year retention records
d. General ledger

HINTS: Recognize the type of records maintained for six years from last use.

Q865_LO110: What is the purpose of organizational records in a brokerage firm?
a. Issuing stock certificates
b. Recording ownership of securities
c. Documenting the foundations of the firm
d. Overseeing specific areas

HINTS: Understand the purpose of organizational records in a brokerage firm.

Q866_LO110: What is the term often used to describe records retained for as long as the firm exists?
a. Temporarily
b. Occasionally
c. Indefinitely
d. Periodically

HINTS: Recognize the term used for records kept for the life of the firm.

Q867_LO110: Which of the following is considered part of the life of the firm and retained indefinitely?
a. Customer account records
b. Blotters
c. Stock certificate books
d. General ledger

HINTS: Identify records considered part of the life of the firm and retained indefinitely.

Q868_LO110: What does a partnership lack if there is no written agreement?
a. Assets
b. Partnership status
c. General ledger
d. Blotters

HINTS: Recognize the significance of a written partnership agreement.

Q869_LO110: What records are related to the foundational document of a corporation?
a. Blotters
b. General ledger
c. Minutes
d. Corporate charter or articles of incorporation

HINTS: Identify records related to the foundational document of a corporation.

Q870_LO110: What are the records kept for the meetings of the board of directors or partners?
a. Stock certificate books
b. General ledger
c. Minutes
d. Customer ledgers

HINTS: Identify the records related to the meetings of the board of directors or partners.

Q871_LO110: In what format are closely held corporations' stock certificates held until they are issued?
a. Digital format
b. Online database
c. Physical book
d. Electronic spreadsheet

HINTS: Recognize the format for holding stock certificates in closely held corporations.

Q872_LO110: Which of the following records are generally retained for six years from the last use?
a. Minutes
b. Stock certificate books
c. General ledger
d. Organizational records

HINTS: Identify records generally retained for six years from the last use.

Q873_LO110: What is a blotter in the context of record-keeping for broker-dealers?
a. Record of original entry
b. Financial statement summary
c. Transaction log
d. Customer ledger

HINTS: Recognize the definition of a blotter in the context of record-keeping.

Q874_LO110: What does the general ledger contain?
a. Customer statements
b. Records of securities transactions
c. Accounting records of assets, liabilities, and net worth
d. Minutes of meetings

HINTS: Identify the content of the general ledger.

Q875_LO110: When must blotters be prepared as per SEC requirements?
a. At the end of the month
b. No later than the following business day
c. Quarterly
d. Once a year

HINTS: Recognize the SEC requirement for preparing blotters.

Q876_LO110: What does a stock record show?
a. Customer statements
b. Ownership of securities, where they are held, and all securities held by the firm
c. Accounting records
d. Minutes of meetings

HINTS: Identify the content of a stock record.

Q877_LO110: What is a customer ledger in the context of record-keeping for broker-dealers?
a. Customer statements
b. Records of securities transactions
c. Accounting records of assets, liabilities, and net worth
d. Transaction log

HINTS: Recognize the definition of a customer ledger in the context of record-keeping for broker-dealers.

Q878_LO110: What records might be included in customer account records?
a. New account form and margin agreement
b. General ledger
c. Minutes
d. Stock certificate books

HINTS: Identify the records that might be included in customer account records.

Q879_LO110: What is the responsibility of an associate appointed to a principal position in a firm?
a. Issue stock certificates
b. Maintain blotters
c. Oversee specific areas
d. Prepare general ledger

HINTS: Recognize the responsibility of an associate appointed to a principal position.

Q880_LO110: What is the consequence if a firm fails to disclose its business continuity plan to customers?
a. Fine imposed by SEC
b. Warning issued by FINRA
c. Violation of FINRA rules
d. No consequence

HINTS: Recognize the consequence of failing to disclose a business continuity plan to customers.

Q881_LO111: Which records must be retained for four years after resolution?
a. Trial balances
b. Order tickets
c. Written complaints
d. Advertising

HINTS: Recognize the type of records retained for four years after resolution.

Q882_LO111: What is the typical location for maintaining records of written complaints?
a. Headquarters
b. Offsite location
c. Branch office
d. Office of supervisory jurisdiction

HINTS: Identify the typical location for maintaining records of written complaints.

Q883_LO111: Which type of complaints has regulatory standing according to FINRA and SEC?
a. Verbal complaints
b. Written complaints
c. Email complaints
d. Social media complaints

HINTS: Recognize the type of complaints with regulatory standing.

Q884_LO111: What records must be retained for three years after last use?
a. Customer confirmations
b. Securities borrowed and loaned ledgers
c. Form U-4 and U-5
d. All of the above

HINTS: Identify records retained for three years after last use.

Q885_LO111: According to SEC regulations, what does "written" extend to in the context of complaints?
a. Paper only
b. Emails only
c. Any communication with letters organized into words
d. Social media posts only

HINTS: Understand the extension of "written" in the context of complaints.

Q886_LO111: What must be kept "readily accessible" for the most recent two years among three- and six-year records?
a. Trial balances
b. Order tickets
c. Securities borrowed and loaned ledgers
d. Customer confirmations

HINTS: Identify records that must be kept "readily accessible" for the most recent two years.

Q887_LO111: Where can three- and six-year records be stored after two years?
a. Offsite location
b. Branch office
c. OSJ
d. Headquarters

HINTS: Recognize the permissible storage location for three- and six-year records after two years.

Q888_LO111: What is the purpose of retaining Form U-4 and U-5 for terminated personnel?
a. Compliance manual
b. Advertising
c. Compensation records
d. Employment history records

HINTS: Identify the purpose of retaining Form U-4 and U-5 for terminated personnel.

Q889_LO111: Which type of ledgers must be retained for three years after last use?
a. Customer ledgers
b. Securities borrowed and loaned ledgers
c. General ledger
d. Trial balances

HINTS: Recognize the type of ledgers retained for three years after last use.

Q890_LO111: What records must be maintained at the branch office, OSJ, or headquarters for the most recent two years among three- and six-year records?
a. Compensation records
b. Customer confirmations
c. Compliance manual
d. Order tickets

HINTS: Identify records that must be maintained at specified locations for the most recent two years.

Q891_LO111: What is the retention period for the firm's compliance and procedures manual?
a. Four years
b. Three years
c. Six years
d. One year

HINTS: Recognize the retention period for the firm's compliance and procedures manual.

Q892_LO111: What must be retained for four years after resolution as per regulatory requirements?
a. Trial balances
b. Order tickets
c. Written complaints
d. Advertising

HINTS: Identify records retained for four years after resolution as per regulatory requirements.

Q893_LO111: What records are included in the category of "almost everything else" with a retention period of three years after last use?
a. Customer confirmations
b. Trial balances
c. Advertising
d. All of the above

HINTS: Recognize records included in the category of "almost everything else" with a three-year retention period.

Q894_LO111: What does the term "readily accessible" mean in the context of record retention?
a. Kept at the branch office
b. Easily retrievable
c. Stored at an offsite location
d. Kept at the headquarters

HINTS: Understand the meaning of the term "readily accessible" in the context of record retention.

Q895_LO111: Which records must be maintained for six years?
a. Compensation records
b. Customer confirmations
c. Securities borrowed and loaned ledgers
d. Written complaints

HINTS: Identify records maintained for six years.

Q896_LO112: What is the primary focus of the Insider Trading and Securities Fraud Enforcement Act of 1988?
a. Prohibiting all stock trading
b. Enhancing penalties for insider trading
c. Encouraging insider trading
d. Regulating stock exchanges

HINTS: Identify the primary focus of the Insider Trading and Securities Fraud Enforcement Act of 1988.

Q897_LO112: How does the Insider Trading Act define an insider?
a. Any person involved in stock trading
b. Any person with access to material nonpublic information about a company
c. Any person holding stock options
d. Any person owning publicly traded stocks

HINTS: Recognize the definition of an insider under the Insider Trading Act.

Q898_LO112: What is the purpose of a firewall or an information barrier in the context of insider trading?
a. Encouraging the free flow of sensitive information
b. Restricting the passing of potentially material nonpublic information between a firm's departments
c. Prohibiting all communication within a firm
d. Regulating stock exchanges

HINTS: Understand the purpose of a firewall or an information barrier.

Q899_LO112: According to the Insider Trading Act, what constitutes insider trading?
a. Possession of inside information
b. Use of inside information to make a gain or avoid a loss
c. Communication of inside information
d. All of the above

HINTS: Identify the action that constitutes insider trading according to the Insider Trading Act.

Q900_LO112: Who is liable under the Insider Trading Act for trading on or communicating nonpublic information?
a. Only the tipper
b. Only the tippee
c. Both the tipper and the tippee
d. Neither the tipper nor the tippee

HINTS: Recognize the parties liable for trading on or communicating nonpublic information under the Insider Trading Act.

Q901_LO112: What is one of the key elements of tipper and tippee liability under insider trading rules?
a. Possession of inside information
b. Personal benefits test
c. Length of time the information is held
d. Number of trades executed

HINTS: Identify a key element of tipper and tippee liability under insider trading rules.

Q902_LO112: Under the Insider Trading Act, what penalties may be levied by the SEC for a violation?
a. Criminal penalties only
b. Civil penalties only
c. Both civil and criminal penalties
d. No penalties

HINTS: Understand the penalties that may be levied by the SEC for a violation under the Insider Trading Act.

Q903_LO112: What determines the amount of civil penalties under the Insider Trading Act?
a. A fixed amount
b. Up to three times the profits made or losses avoided
c. A percentage of the violator's income
d. Determined by the court

HINTS: Identify the factor that determines the amount of civil penalties under the Insider Trading Act.

Q904_LO112: What is the maximum criminal penalty for insider trading under the Insider Trading Act?
a. $1 million
b. $5 million
c. $10 million
d. $20 million

HINTS: Recognize the maximum criminal penalty for insider trading under the Insider Trading Act.

Q905_LO112: What is the maximum penalty for a controlling person, such as an RR or BD, under the Insider Trading Act?
a. $1 million
b. $5 million
c. $10 million
d. Three times the profit made or loss avoided, whichever is greater

HINTS: Identify the maximum penalty for a controlling person under the Insider Trading Act.

Q906_LO112: What is the time limit for initiating suits by contemporaneous traders against violators of insider trading regulations?
a. One year
b. Three years
c. Five years
d. Ten years

HINTS: Recognize the time limit for initiating suits by contemporaneous traders.

Q907_LO112: What did the Dodd-Frank legislation amend regarding informers and awards?
a. Abolished payment to informers
b. Increased the bounty range
c. Limited awards to specific violations
d. Prohibited informers from receiving awards

HINTS: Identify the amendment made by the Dodd-Frank legislation regarding informers and awards.

Q908_LO112: What range can the information bounty or award be under the Dodd-Frank legislation?
a. 1% to 10%
b. 10% to 20%
c. 20% to 30%
d. 30% to 40%

HINTS: Recognize the range of the information bounty or award under the Dodd-Frank legislation.

Q909_LO112: What is the purpose of awards under the Dodd-Frank legislation?
a. Encourage insider trading
b. Compensate informers for their efforts
c. Penalize informers for disclosing information
d. Discourage informers from reporting violations

HINTS: Understand the purpose of awards under the Dodd-Frank legislation.

Q910_LO112: What type of information may qualify for an award under the Dodd-Frank legislation?
a. Information related to any violation of securities law
b. Information limited to insider trading violations
c. Only criminal violations
d. Information related to a specific company

HINTS: Recognize the scope of information that may qualify for an award under the Dodd-Frank legislation.

Q911_LO112: What did the Insider Trading and Securities Fraud Enforcement Act of 1988 specify regarding penalties for insider trading and securities fraud?
a. Up to $5,000 in fines
b. No specified penalties
c. Significant penalties
d. Community service

HINTS: Recognize the impact of the 1988 Act on penalties for insider trading.

Q912_LO112: What is the purpose of a firewall or an information barrier in a brokerage firm?
a. Promoting free flow of information
b. Restricting nonpublic information flow
c. Enhancing communication
d. Encouraging insider trading

HINTS: Identify the purpose of a firewall or information barrier in a brokerage firm.

Q913_LO112: How does the Insider Trading Act define an insider?
a. Any shareholder
b. Any employee of a company
c. Any person with access to material nonpublic information
d. Any person with stock options

HINTS: Recognize the definition of an insider under the Insider Trading Act.

Q914_LO112: According to the Insider Trading Act, what constitutes insider trading?
a. Possession of inside information
b. Use of inside information for gain or loss avoidance
c. Communication of nonpublic information
d. All of the above

HINTS: Identify what constitutes insider trading according to the Insider Trading Act.

Q915_LO112: What is the key element of tipper and tippee liability under insider trading rules?
a. Materiality of information
b. Existence of a fiduciary duty
c. Personal benefits test
d. All of the above

HINTS: Recognize key elements of tipper and tippee liability under insider trading rules.

Q916_LO112: When can the SEC investigate a person suspected of violating the provisions of the Insider Trading Act?
a. Only if criminal penalties are involved
b. Only with a court order
c. Anytime
d. Only during market hours

HINTS: Understand the circumstances under which the SEC can investigate suspected violations.

Q917_LO112: What penalties may a controlling person, such as an RR or BD, face for insider trading violations?
a. Up to $5 million
b. Up to 20 years in jail
c. $1 million or three times the profit/loss, whichever is greater
d. All of the above

HINTS: Identify potential penalties for a controlling person involved in insider trading violations.

Q918_LO112: What is the role of contemporaneous traders in insider trading regulations?
a. Informers
b. Violators
c. Witnesses
d. Suits initiators

HINTS: Recognize the role of contemporaneous traders in insider trading regulations.

Q919_LO112: What is the time limit for initiating suits by contemporaneous traders after an insider trading violation?
a. 1 year
b. 2 years
c. 3 years
d. 5 years

HINTS: Identify the time limit for initiating suits by contemporaneous traders after an insider trading violation.

Q920_LO112: What did the Dodd-Frank legislation amend regarding informers' payments in connection with securities law violations?
a. Disallowed payments
b. Limited payments to 10%
c. Allowed payments in connection with any violation
d. Reduced payments to 5%

HINTS: Recognize the impact of the Dodd-Frank legislation on informers' payments.

Q921_LO112: What is the range of information bounty or award for informers under the Dodd-Frank legislation?
a. 5% to 10%
b. 10% to 20%
c. 15% to 25%
d. 10% to 30%

HINTS: Identify the range of information bounty or award for informers under Dodd-Frank.

Q922_LO112: What is the primary focus of the Securities Exchange Act of 1934 regarding insider trading?
a. Imposing fines
b. Prohibiting the use of insider information
c. Encouraging insider trading
d. Promoting transparency

HINTS: Recognize the primary focus of the Securities Exchange Act of 1934 regarding insider trading.

Q923_LO112: What information is considered material under insider trading regulations?
a. Any information
b. Information about competitors
c. Information that influences stock price
d. Publicly available information

HINTS: Identify the type of information considered material under insider trading regulations.

Q924_LO112: What is the primary distinction between legal and illegal possession of inside information?
a. Timing of possession
b. Purpose of possession
c. Type of information
d. Public or private possession

HINTS: Recognize the primary distinction between legal and illegal possession of inside information.

Q925_LO112: What type of information does the Insider Trading Act prohibit insiders from trading on or communicating?
a. Material and nonpublic information
b. Public information
c. Historical information
d. Speculative information

HINTS: Identify the type of information prohibited for trading or communication by insiders under the Insider Trading Act.

Q926_LO113: What is the primary purpose of pump and dump, a form of securities fraud?
a. Inflating stock prices
b. Stabilizing stock prices
c. Enhancing market liquidity
d. Promoting investor education

HINTS: Recognize the primary purpose of the pump and dump scheme.

Q927_LO113: What practice involves placing orders for one's own account ahead of other known orders to gain from likely price movement?
a. Churning
b. Marking the close
c. Freeriding
d. Front running

HINTS: Identify the practice described where orders are placed ahead to gain from expected price movement.

Q928_LO113: How does freeriding impact an account if securities are purchased and sold before making payment?
a. Account closure
b. 90-day freeze
c. Increased trading limits
d. Margin call

HINTS: Understand the consequence of freeriding in both cash and margin accounts.

Q929_LO113: What is the term for the manipulation involving selling stock with the agreement to repurchase it later at the same or similar price?
a. Churning
b. Front running
c. Freeriding
d. Matched Orders

HINTS: Identify the manipulation involving selling and repurchasing stock to create false activity.

Q930_LO113: What is the key feature of excessive trading, also known as churning, in a customer's account?
a. Large transactions
b. Frequent trading for commission

c. Intraday trading
d. Low trading frequency

HINTS: Recognize the key feature of excessive trading (churning) in a customer's account.

Q931_LO113: Which prohibited practice involves entering trades before the opening to manipulate the reported price of a stock?
a. Marking the open
b. Front running
c. Pump and dump
d. Freeriding

HINTS: Identify the practice of entering trades before the opening to influence the reported price.

Q932_LO113: What is the penalty for entering trades at or near the close to influence the closing price of a stock?
a. Account closure
b. 90-day freeze
c. Fines
d. Market ban

HINTS: Understand the penalty for marking the close involving trades at or near the closing of a stock.

Q933_LO113: What is the term for the act of manipulating reported stock prices to create a false impression of market activity?
a. Matched Orders
b. Market rumors
c. Churning
d. Marking the tape

HINTS: Recognize the term for the manipulation involving creating a false impression of market activity.

Q934_LO113: How can social media be misused for market manipulation?
a. Enhancing investor education
b. Spreading false information
c. Encouraging transparency
d. Facilitating regulatory communication

HINTS: Recognize the misuse of social media in the context of market manipulation.

Q935_LO113: What is the regulatory stance on freeriding in both cash and margin accounts?
a. Encouraged
b. Generally prohibited
c. Permitted with a warning
d. Allowed with certain conditions

HINTS: Understand the regulatory stance on freeriding in both cash and margin accounts.

Q936_LO113: What are the key elements regulators consider in determining excessive trading (churning) in a customer's account?
a. Large transactions
b. Trading frequency and size inconsistent with client's history
c. Low account balance
d. Intraday trading only

HINTS: Identify the key elements regulators consider in determining churning in a customer's account.

Q937_LO113: How does the pump and dump scheme operate to profit fraudsters?
a. Selling overvalued shares before the price rises
b. Buying undervalued shares before the price drops
c. Accumulating shares after spreading rumors
d. Manipulating dividends to attract investors

HINTS: Understand the operation of the pump and dump scheme in generating profits for fraudsters.

Q938_LO113: What is the consequence of marking the close for investors who purchased based on the manipulated closing price?
a. Account closure
b. Frozen accounts

c. Loss of trading privileges
d. Financial compensation

HINTS: Recognize the consequence for investors who purchased based on the manipulated closing price.

Q939_LO113: What is the primary goal of matched orders, also known as painting the tape?
a. Enhancing market liquidity
b. Creating false market activity
c. Facilitating fair trading
d. Improving price discovery

HINTS: Identify the primary goal of matched orders in the context of painting the tape.

Q940_LO113: In what scenario is front running considered to be occurring?
a. Placing orders for one's account ahead of other known orders
b. Trading ahead of market opening
c. Executing large transactions during market hours
d. Selling stock before making payment

HINTS: Identify the scenario that describes front running in the context of placing orders ahead of others.

Q941_LO113: What is the primary purpose of pump and dump in securities fraud?
a. Enhancing stock liquidity
b. Reducing market volatility
c. Inflating stock prices
d. Encouraging long-term investment

HINTS: Recognize the primary purpose of the pump and dump scheme.

Q942_LO113: What is the act of placing orders for one's own account ahead of known market orders called?
a. Churning
b. Freeriding
c. Front running
d. Marking the close

HINTS: Identify the trading practice involving placing orders ahead of other known orders.

Q943_LO113: What is the primary purpose of excessive trading (churning) in a customer's account?
a. Achieving customer's investment objectives
b. Generating commissions
c. Reducing market risk
d. Enhancing portfolio diversification

HINTS: Recognize the primary motive behind excessive trading (churning) in a customer's account.

Q944_LO113: What is the primary goal of marking the close in market manipulation?
a. Influencing the opening price
b. Influencing the closing price
c. Maximizing share volume
d. Reducing volatility

HINTS: Identify the primary goal of the market manipulation practice of marking the close.

Q945_LO113: What term describes the prohibited practice of purchasing securities and selling them before making payment?
a. Pump and dump
b. Freeriding
c. Front running
d. Matched orders

HINTS: Recognize the term for the prohibited practice of buying and selling without making payment.

Q946_LO113: What is the primary purpose of matching orders in market manipulation?
a. Reducing trading volume
b. Enhancing liquidity

c. Creating artificial activity
d. Minimizing price fluctuations

HINTS: Identify the primary purpose of the manipulation involving matching orders.

Q947_LO113: In what way does social media present opportunities for fraudsters in market manipulation?
a. Enhancing transparency
b. Facilitating accurate information
c. Spreading false information
d. Encouraging long-term investment

HINTS: Recognize the role of social media in market manipulation opportunities.

Q948_LO113: What is the consequence of freeriding in a securities account?
a. Account closure
b. 90-day account freeze
c. Increased buying power
d. Lower transaction fees

HINTS: Understand the consequence of engaging in freeriding in a securities account.

Q949_LO113: What is the penalty for a controlling person involved in insider trading violations?
a. Up to $5 million
b. Up to 20 years in jail
c. $1 million or three times the profit/loss, whichever is greater
d. All of the above

HINTS: Identify potential penalties for a controlling person involved in insider trading violations.

Q950_LO113: Which manipulation practice involves entering trades before the opening to influence the reported opening price?
a. Marking the open
b. Pump and dump
c. Front running
d. Freeriding

HINTS: Recognize the manipulation practice involving trades before the market opening.

Q951_LO113: What is the primary focus of the Securities Exchange Act of 1934 regarding market manipulation?
a. Imposing fines
b. Prohibiting market rumors
c. Regulating social media
d. Ensuring transparency

HINTS: Recognize the primary focus of the Securities Exchange Act of 1934 regarding market manipulation.

Q952_LO113: How does excessive trading (churning) differ from appropriate trading practices?
a. Higher frequency of transactions
b. Alignment with customer's objectives
c. Lower commissions
d. Larger transaction sizes

HINTS: Differentiate excessive trading (churning) from appropriate trading practices.

Q953_LO113: What does the term "freeriding" imply in securities trading?
a. Risk-free trading
b. Trading without ownership
c. Delayed trade settlement
d. Unauthorized trading

HINTS: Understand the implication of the term "freeriding" in securities trading.

Q954_LO113: What is the primary intention behind the manipulation practice of matched orders?
a. Reducing trading costs
b. Enhancing liquidity

c. Creating a false appearance of trading activity
d. Minimizing order execution time

HINTS: Identify the primary intention behind the manipulation practice of matched orders.

Q955_LO113: What is the primary objective of marking the close in market manipulation?
a. Influencing opening prices
b. Influencing closing prices
c. Facilitating after-hours trading
d. Reducing market speculation

HINTS: Recognize the primary objective of the market manipulation practice of marking the close.

Q956_LO114: Who is considered a restricted person under Rule 5130 in the context of IPOs?
a. Individual owning 8% of a member firm
b. Portfolio manager for an investment company
c. Immediate family member of an uncle
d. Attorney representing the issuing company

HINTS: Identify the category of individuals considered restricted in IPOs under Rule 5130.

Q957_LO114: What is the primary objective of Rule 5130 in the context of public offerings?
a. Ensure maximum profits for member firms
b. Protect the integrity of the public offering process
c. Encourage withholding of securities for future benefits
d. Facilitate insider trading for industry insiders

HINTS: Recognize the main purpose of Rule 5130 related to public offerings.

Q958_LO114: Which family members are considered immediate family under Rule 5130?
a. Aunts and uncles
b. Grandparents
c. Siblings
d. In-laws

HINTS: Identify the family members considered immediate family under Rule 5130.

Q959_LO114: In the context of Rule 5130, what is the de minimis exemption?
a. All restricted persons are exempt
b. Exemption for immediate family members
c. Beneficial interests not exceeding 10%
d. Exemption for attorney representation

HINTS: Understand the de minimis exemption under Rule 5130.

Q960_LO114: Who is restricted from purchasing a new issue at the public offering price (POP) according to Rule 5130?
a. All employees of member firms
b. Finders and fiduciaries acting for the issuing company
c. Any person owning 5% or more of a member firm
d. Aunts and uncles of industry insiders

HINTS: Identify the category of individuals restricted from purchasing a new issue at POP.

Q961_LO114: What representation is required from the account owner before selling an IPO to an account under Rule 5130?
a. Proof of citizenship
b. Confirmation of creditworthiness
c. A written representation of eligibility
d. Legal opinion on securities law compliance

HINTS: Recognize the required representation from the account owner in the context of Rule 5130.

Q962_LO114: Who qualifies for the de minimis exemption under Rule 5130?
a. All restricted persons
b. Portfolio managers

c. Immediate family members
d. Beneficial owners with less than 5% interest

HINTS: Identify the qualifying individuals for the de minimis exemption.

Q963_LO114: What is the consequence of exceeding the 10% threshold for beneficial owners under Rule 5130?
a. Account closure
b. De minimis exemption loss
c. No consequence
d. Mandatory IPO participation

HINTS: Understand the consequence of exceeding the 10% threshold under Rule 5130.

Q964_LO114: Who is responsible for obtaining a written representation of eligibility under Rule 5130?
a. SEC
b. Account custodian
c. Registered representatives
d. Stock exchange

HINTS: Identify the party responsible for obtaining the written representation under Rule 5130.

Q965_LO114: Which category of individuals is NOT considered immediate family under Rule 5130?
a. Siblings
b. Grandparents
c. Spouses
d. Children

HINTS: Identify the category of family members not considered immediate family under Rule 5130.

Q966_LO114: What is the primary reason for restricting industry insiders from taking advantage of their status under Rule 5130?
a. Encourage insider trading
b. Protect public customers
c. Enhance market volatility
d. Facilitate IPO underpricing

HINTS: Recognize the primary reason for restricting industry insiders under Rule 5130.

Q967_LO114: Who falls under the category of finders and fiduciaries acting on behalf of the managing underwriter under Rule 5130?
a. Accountants
b. Retail investors
c. Securities analysts
d. Investment bankers

HINTS: Identify individuals considered finders and fiduciaries under Rule 5130.

Q968_LO114: What is the significance of the de minimis exemption in Rule 5130?
a. Allows unrestricted IPO participation
b. Permits restricted persons to own up to 50% of an account
c. Provides an exemption for family members
d. Allows a limited interest for restricted persons

HINTS: Understand the significance of the de minimis exemption under Rule 5130.

Q969_LO114: Why are aunts and uncles not considered immediate family under Rule 5130?
a. Legal definition
b. Regulatory exemption
c. Industry tradition
d. Specific rule exclusion

HINTS: Recognize the reason why aunts and uncles are not considered immediate family.

Q970_LO114: What is the primary focus of Rule 5130 regarding the public offering process?
a. Maximizing industry profits
b. Ensuring IPO underpricing

c. Protecting public investors
d. Facilitating market manipulation

HINTS: Identify the primary focus of Rule 5130 related to the public offering process.

Q971_LO115: What constitutes improper use of customer assets according to FINRA?
a. Any use of funds for the firm's benefit
b. Any use not intended by the customer
c. Authorized borrowing by the representative
d. Legal investments with customer consent

HINTS: Identify the definition of improper use of customer assets.

Q972_LO115: How does FINRA expect member firms to address improper use of customer funds?
a. By encouraging red flags
b. By implementing reasonable systems and controls
c. By avoiding supervisory review
d. By relying solely on exception reports

HINTS: Recognize the expectations of member firms in addressing improper use.

Q973_LO115: What might be considered a "red flag" indicating improper use of customer funds?
a. Customer satisfaction surveys
b. Activity in a deceased person's account
c. Routine account withdrawals
d. Frequent account balance inquiries

HINTS: Identify a potential red flag related to improper use.

Q974_LO115: When is borrowing from a customer without consent considered indistinguishable from stealing?
a. Always
b. Only on weekdays
c. When the market is volatile
d. During market hours

HINTS: Recognize the circumstances when borrowing without consent is equivalent to stealing.

Q975_LO115: Under what conditions can borrowing and lending arrangements be permitted between representatives and customers?
a. Without any prior notice
b. With verbal approval
c. Under specific written procedures
d. With customer's verbal consent

HINTS: Identify the conditions under which borrowing and lending arrangements can be permitted.

Q976_LO115: In which scenario is firm approval NOT required for a borrowing arrangement?
a. Immediate family relationship
b. Both customer and representative registered with the same firm
c. Personal relationship outside the broker-customer relationship
d. Business relationship outside the broker-customer relationship

HINTS: Recognize the scenario where firm approval is not required for borrowing.

Q977_LO115: What is the primary purpose of the Conduct Rules regarding lending arrangements?
a. Encourage frequent borrowing
b. Discourage borrowing altogether
c. Ensure fair lending practices
d. Protect customers from potential abuses

HINTS: Identify the primary goal of the Conduct Rules related to lending arrangements.

Q978_LO115: According to FINRA, what is prohibited regarding guarantees in customer accounts?
a. Guaranteeing against a gain
b. Guaranteeing against a loss

c. Offering legal guarantees
d. Guaranteeing specific investment outcomes

HINTS: Recognize the prohibited activity regarding guarantees in customer accounts.

Q979_LO115: When can a member firm share in profits and losses in a joint customer account?
a. If the loss is due to a firm error
b. If the customer requests it
c. If the RR has significant knowledge
d. If the firm initiates the sharing

HINTS: Identify the condition under which a firm can share in profits and losses in a joint account.

Q980_LO115: What exception is made to the proportion rule when sharing in a joint account with immediate family members?
a. No exceptions
b. Proportionate sharing mandatory
c. Directly proportionate sharing not mandatory
d. Exceptions only for losses

HINTS: Recognize the exception to the proportion rule for sharing with immediate family members.

Q981_LO115: Why is joint accounts between firms and customers not allowed according to the note?
a. To prevent misuse
b. To avoid paperwork
c. Regulatory requirement
d. Industry tradition

HINTS: Understand the reason for prohibiting joint accounts between firms and customers.

Q982_LO115: What defines immediate family members for the purpose of profit and loss sharing?
a. Anyone living in the same city
b. Parents and children only
c. Individuals providing material support
d. Siblings and spouses only

HINTS: Identify the definition of immediate family members for profit and loss sharing.

Q983_LO115: What role does the joint account's financial contribution play in profit and loss sharing?
a. Measured in knowledge or expertise
b. Must be greater than the customer's contribution
c. Measured only in dollars
d. Not considered in profit and loss sharing

HINTS: Recognize the measure used in determining profit and loss sharing in joint accounts.

Q984_LO115: What is the de minimis exemption related to restricted persons and new equity issues?
a. Prohibits restricted persons from investing
b. Allows restricted persons up to 10% interest
c. Exempts restricted persons from IPOs
d. Limits IPO investment to 5%

HINTS: Understand the de minimis exemption regarding restricted persons and new equity issues.

Q985_LO115: What is the primary focus of Rule 5130 regarding the public offering process?
a. Maximizing industry profits
b. Ensuring IPO underpricing
c. Protecting public investors
d. Facilitating market manipulation

HINTS: Identify the primary focus of Rule 5130 related to the public offering process.

Q986_LO115: What is considered improper use of customer assets?
a. Authorized borrowing
b. Any use not intended by the customer

c. Ethical investing
d. Routine fund transfers

HINTS: Recognize the definition of improper use of customer assets.

Q987_LO115: How does FINRA expect member firms to address improper use of customer funds?
a. Ignore red flags
b. Implement reasonable systems and controls
c. Encourage unethical practices
d. Avoid investigation of suspicious transfers

HINTS: Identify the expectation of member firms in addressing improper use.

Q988_LO115: What might trigger an exception report as a red flag for improper use?
a. Consistent account activity
b. Routine customer complaints
c. Conflicting information in new account applications
d. Approved lending arrangements

HINTS: Recognize red flags that might trigger an exception report for improper use.

Q989_LO115: When is borrowing from or lending to customers considered permissible without prior approval?
a. Any situation involving borrowing
b. Immediate family relationship
c. Personal relationship with the firm's CEO
d. Borrowing for the firm's use

HINTS: Identify situations where borrowing from or lending to customers is permitted without prior approval.

Q990_LO115: What is the consequence of borrowing without consent from a customer?
a. Ethical practice
b. Indistinguishable from stealing
c. Acceptable under certain circumstances
d. Encouraged by regulatory bodies

HINTS: Recognize the consequence of borrowing without consent from a customer.

Q991_LO115: Under what circumstances are lending arrangements between representatives and customers permitted?
a. Without any notice or approval
b. Only with the firm's written approval
c. When it benefits the firm
d. When knowledge or expertise is shared

HINTS: Identify the circumstances under which lending arrangements are permitted.

Q992_LO115: Which situation allows sharing in profits or losses in a customer's account without violating rules?
a. Joint account with a friend
b. Immediate family joint account
c. Account with a business relationship
d. Personal relationship with the firm's CEO

HINTS: Recognize the situation allowing sharing in profits or losses without violating rules.

Q993_LO115: What is the primary prohibition regarding guarantees in customer accounts?
a. Guarantees against gains
b. Guarantees against losses
c. Guarantees by registered persons
d. Guarantees by investment advisers

HINTS: Identify the primary prohibition related to guarantees in customer accounts.

Q994_LO115: What exception is made for sharing in losses in a customer's account by a member firm?
a. Loss due to a firm error
b. Loss in a joint account

c. Loss caused by industry volatility
d. Loss in an account with a personal relationship

HINTS: Recognize the exception allowing a member firm to share in losses.

Q995_LO115: When does sharing in a joint account with immediate family members not require direct proportionate sharing?
a. When profits exceed losses
b. When the firm approves
c. When living in the same residence
d. When knowledge is a significant contribution

HINTS: Identify the condition under which direct proportionate sharing is not mandatory in a joint account with immediate family members.

Q996_LO115: What is the broad definition of immediate family members for joint accounts?
a. Parents and siblings
b. Spouses and children
c. Aunts and uncles
d. Individuals providing material support

HINTS: Recognize the broad definition of immediate family members for joint accounts.

Q997_LO115: Why can't firms have joint accounts with customers?
a. Regulatory prohibition
b. Industry tradition
c. Risk management
d. Customer preference

HINTS: Understand the reason why firms cannot have joint accounts with customers.

Q998_LO115: What is the purpose of exception reports in detecting improper use?
a. Encourage improper use
b. Trigger red flags
c. Promote routine transfers
d. Facilitate unethical practices

HINTS: Recognize the purpose of exception reports in detecting improper use.

Q999_LO115: Which of the following is a red flag for improper use?
a. Routine customer complaints
b. Consistent account activity
c. Address matching on new account applications
d. Conflicting information in new account applications

HINTS: Identify a red flag indicating potential improper use.

Q1000_LO115: What is the primary focus of Rule 5130 regarding the public offering process?
a. Maximizing industry profits
b. Ensuring IPO underpricing
c. Protecting public investors
d. Facilitating market manipulation

HINTS: Identify the primary focus of Rule 5130 related to the public offering process.

Q1001_LO115: What does FINRA consider as financial exploitation of seniors and specified adults?
a. Authorized transactions
b. Wrongful or unauthorized acts
c. Routine account maintenance
d. Legal power of attorney

HINTS: Recognize the definition of financial exploitation as per FINRA.

Q1002_LO115: Which accounts does FINRA specify as impacted by financial exploitation rules?
a. Age 50 and older
b. Age 65 and older

c. Age 18 and older with impairments
d. Age 21 and older

HINTS: Identify the criteria for accounts impacted by financial exploitation rules.

Q1003_LO115: What is the primary responsibility of member firms regarding senior clients?
a. Maximize profits
b. Report all transactions
c. Make reasonable efforts to obtain a trusted contact person
d. Limit services for senior clients

HINTS: Identify the primary responsibility of member firms when serving senior clients.

Q1004_LO115: When should a member firm make a reasonable effort to obtain a trusted contact person?
a. Every month
b. Only for new accounts
c. Only for high net worth clients
d. When opening a customer's account or updating account information

HINTS: Recognize when a member firm should make a reasonable effort to obtain a trusted contact person.

Q1005_LO115: What action can member firms take regarding disbursements if financial exploitation is suspected?
a. Mandatory disbursement
b. Permanent hold
c. Temporary hold
d. Unlimited transactions

HINTS: Identify the action member firms can take if financial exploitation is suspected.

Q1006_LO115: How long can a temporary hold on disbursements last under FINRA rules?
a. 30 business days
b. 15 business days
c. 10 business days
d. No time limit

HINTS: Recognize the duration of a temporary hold on disbursements under FINRA rules.

Q1007_LO115: What does a member firm need to do if a temporary hold on disbursements is initiated?
a. Notify only the affected customer
b. Initiate an internal review
c. Terminate the account
d. Contact the SEC

HINTS: Understand the requirements when a member firm initiates a temporary hold on disbursements.

Q1008_LO115: In what circumstances is a member firm not required to notify the trusted contact person of a hold?
a. If the trusted contact person is unavailable
b. If the trusted contact person is the perpetrator
c. If the hold is less than 5 business days
d. If the member firm decides not to

HINTS: Identify the circumstances where notification to the trusted contact person is not required.

Q1009_LO115: What is the purpose of obtaining the name and contact information for a trusted contact person?
a. Promoting sales
b. Providing investment advice
c. Assisting in account administration and protection
d. Marketing financial products

HINTS: Recognize the purpose of obtaining the name and contact information for a trusted contact person.

Q1010_LO115: How does FINRA define a trusted contact person?
a. A financial advisor
b. A relative of the customer

c. A person who can provide information about the customer
d. A legal guardian

HINTS: Understand the definition of a trusted contact person according to FINRA.

Q1011_LO115: What action can a member firm take if a state regulator terminates a temporary hold?
a. Extend the hold further
b. Challenge the decision
c. Must release the hold immediately
d. Notify the SEC

HINTS: Identify the appropriate action when a state regulator terminates a temporary hold.

Q1012_LO115: What is the purpose of the trusted contact person according to FINRA?
a. Maximize profits
b. Assist in account administration and protection
c. Encourage risky investments
d. Expedite withdrawals

HINTS: Recognize the intended purpose of the trusted contact person.

Q1013_LO115: What criteria qualify individuals for impacted accounts under financial exploitation rules?
a. Age 60 and older
b. Age 18 and older with impairments
c. Age 21 and older
d. Age 50 and older

HINTS: Identify the criteria for individuals with impacted accounts under financial exploitation rules.

Q1014_LO115: What does FINRA expect member firms to detect or investigate regarding senior clients?
a. Routine account maintenance
b. Red flags indicating improper use of customer funds
c. Maximizing profits
d. Providing preferential treatment

HINTS: Understand what FINRA expects member firms to detect or investigate regarding senior clients.

Q1015_LO115: What is the consequence of improper use of customer funds?
a. Mandatory training
b. Account closure
c. Legal action
d. Account freezing

HINTS: Recognize the consequence of improper use of customer funds.

Q1016_LO115: Who is considered a "specified adult" according to FINRA rules?
a. Age 55 and older
b. Age 60 and older
c. Age 65 and older
d. Age 70 and older

HINTS: Identify the age range for individuals considered "specified adults" under FINRA rules.

Q1017_LO115: What does financial exploitation of seniors involve?
a. Authorized use of funds
b. Wrongful or unauthorized taking of funds
c. Routine account withdrawals
d. Legal power of attorney

HINTS: Recognize the definition of financial exploitation of seniors.

Q1018_LO115: What are the two key actions required to prevent potential exploitation of senior clients?
a. Place permanent holds and obtain contact information
b. Obtain trusted contact information and place temporary holds

c. Report to authorities and conduct internal reviews
d. Educate clients and restrict account access

HINTS: Identify the key actions required to prevent potential exploitation of senior clients.

Q1019_LO115: When must a member firm make reasonable efforts to obtain a trusted contact person?
a. Only when there is suspicion of financial exploitation
b. When opening a customer's account or updating account information
c. During routine account reviews
d. At the discretion of the member firm

HINTS: Recognize when member firms are required to obtain a trusted contact person.

Q1020_LO115: What happens if a customer refuses to provide trusted contact information?
a. Account opening is prohibited
b. No action is required
c. Member firms can proceed if they made reasonable efforts
d. Trusted contact information is not essential

HINTS: Understand the outcome if a customer refuses to provide trusted contact information.

Q1021_LO115: What disclosure must be made when a customer provides trusted contact information?
a. No disclosure is required
b. Disclosure of account balances only
c. Disclosure about contacting the trusted person
d. Disclosure of the member firm's profits

HINTS: Identify the required disclosure when a customer provides trusted contact information.

Q1022_LO115: What is the purpose of the trusted contact person?
a. Financial advisor
b. Asset protection
c. Resource for the member firm
d. Legal representative

HINTS: Recognize the role of the trusted contact person.

Q1023_LO115: How long can a temporary hold on disbursements last under FINRA rules?
a. 10 business days
b. 15 business days
c. 20 business days
d. 30 business days

HINTS: Identify the maximum duration of a temporary hold on disbursements under FINRA rules.

Q1024_LO115: Who can terminate a temporary hold on disbursements?
a. SEC
b. FINRA
c. State regulator or agency of jurisdiction
d. Member firm

HINTS: Recognize the authority to terminate a temporary hold on disbursements.

Q1025_LO115: What action must a member firm take if a temporary hold is initiated?
a. Provide a public announcement
b. Conduct an internal review
c. Notify only the trusted contact person
d. Initiate legal proceedings

HINTS: Understand the required action when a member firm initiates a temporary hold.

Q1026_LO115: When should notification of a temporary hold be provided to authorized parties?
a. Within 24 hours
b. No notification is required

c. Within 2 business days
d. At the discretion of the member firm

HINTS: Identify the timeframe for notifying authorized parties of a temporary hold.

Q1027_LO115: Is notification required if the trusted contact person is believed to be the perpetrator?
a. Yes, always
b. No, never
c. Only if requested by the customer
d. At the discretion of the member firm

HINTS: Understand the circumstances under which notification to the trusted contact person is not required.

Q1028_LO115: What is the primary focus of Rule 5130 regarding the public offering process?
a. Maximizing industry profits
b. Ensuring IPO underpricing
c. Protecting public investors
d. Facilitating market manipulation

HINTS: Identify the primary focus of Rule 5130 related to the public offering process.

Q1029_LO115: Which of the following is a red flag for improper use?
a. Routine customer complaints
b. Consistent account activity
c. Address matching on new account applications
d. Conflicting information in new account applications

HINTS: Identify a red flag indicating potential improper use.

Q1030_LO115: What is the primary purpose of obtaining a trusted contact person?
a. Marketing purposes
b. Administering the customer's account
c. Facilitating joint account creation
d. Enhancing customer privacy

HINTS: Recognize the primary purpose of obtaining a trusted contact person.

Q1031_LO116: What is the maximum duration for a temporary hold on disbursements under FINRA rules?
a. 10 business days
b. 15 business days
c. 20 business days
d. 30 business days

HINTS: Consider the timeframe allowed for a temporary hold on disbursements.

Q1032_LO116: When is a member firm required to provide notification of a temporary hold on disbursements?
a. Within 24 hours
b. No notification is required
c. Within 2 business days
d. At the discretion of the member firm

HINTS: Identify the timeframe for notifying authorized parties of a temporary hold.

Q1033_LO116: In what situations is notification to the trusted contact person not required?
a. Yes, always
b. No, never
c. Only if requested by the customer
d. At the discretion of the member firm

HINTS: Understand the circumstances under which notification to the trusted contact person is not required.

Q1034_LO116: What is the primary purpose of obtaining a trusted contact person?
a. Marketing purposes
b. Administering the customer's account

c. Facilitating joint account creation
d. Enhancing customer privacy

HINTS: Recognize the primary purpose of obtaining a trusted contact person.

Q1035_LO116: According to FINRA rules, who can terminate a temporary hold on disbursements?
a. SEC
b. FINRA
c. State regulator or agency of jurisdiction
d. Member firm

HINTS: Recognize the authority to terminate a temporary hold on disbursements.

Q1036_LO116: What disclosure must be made when a customer provides trusted contact information?
a. No disclosure is required
b. Disclosure of account balances only
c. Disclosure about contacting the trusted person
d. Disclosure of the member firm's profits

HINTS: Identify the required disclosure when a customer provides trusted contact information.

Q1037_LO116: How long can a temporary hold on disbursements last under FINRA rules?
a. 10 business days
b. 15 business days
c. 20 business days
d. 30 business days

HINTS: Identify the maximum duration of a temporary hold on disbursements under FINRA rules.

Q1038_LO116: What action must a member firm take if a temporary hold is initiated?
a. Provide a public announcement
b. Conduct an internal review
c. Notify only the trusted contact person
d. Initiate legal proceedings

HINTS: Understand the required action when a member firm initiates a temporary hold.

Q1039_LO116: When should notification of a temporary hold be provided to authorized parties?
a. Within 24 hours
b. No notification is required
c. Within 2 business days
d. At the discretion of the member firm

HINTS: Identify the timeframe for notifying authorized parties of a temporary hold.

Q1040_LO116: Is notification required if the trusted contact person is believed to be the perpetrator?
a. Yes, always
b. No, never
c. Only if requested by the customer
d. At the discretion of the member firm

HINTS: Understand the circumstances under which notification to the trusted contact person is not required.

Q1041_LO116: What is the primary focus of Rule 5130 regarding the public offering process?
a. Maximizing industry profits
b. Ensuring IPO underpricing
c. Protecting public investors
d. Facilitating market manipulation

HINTS: Identify the primary focus of Rule 5130 related to the public offering process.

Q1042_LO116: Which of the following is a red flag for improper use?
a. Routine customer complaints
b. Consistent account activity

c. Address matching on new account applications
d. Conflicting information in new account applications

HINTS: Identify a red flag indicating potential improper use.

Q1043_LO116: What is the maximum duration for a temporary hold on disbursements under FINRA rules?
a. 10 business days
b. 15 business days
c. 20 business days
d. 30 business days

HINTS: Consider the timeframe allowed for a temporary hold on disbursements.

Q1044_LO116: When is a member firm required to provide notification of a temporary hold on disbursements?
a. Within 24 hours
b. No notification is required
c. Within 2 business days
d. At the discretion of the member firm

HINTS: Identify the timeframe for notifying authorized parties of a temporary hold.

Q1045_LO116: In what situations is notification to the trusted contact person not required?
a. Yes, always
b. No, never
c. Only if requested by the customer
d. At the discretion of the member firm

HINTS: Understand the circumstances under which notification to the trusted contact person is not required.

Q1046_LO116: What condition must be met for a firm to electronically send documents to customers?
a. No conditions required
b. Secure personal information
c. Daily delivery requirement
d. Verbal consent

HINTS: Identify the condition that must be met for electronic document delivery.

Q1047_LO116: How often must account records be furnished to a new customer for review?
a. Quarterly
b. Annually
c. Within 30 days of account opening
d. Every 36 months

HINTS: Recall the timeframe for furnishing account records to a new customer.

Q1048_LO116: In electronic delivery, when must customers be provided with information in paper form?
a. Never
b. Within 24 hours
c. Upon request
d. Biannually

HINTS: Recognize the requirement for providing information in paper form in electronic delivery.

Q1049_LO116: What is the primary purpose of updating customer account records?
a. Marketing analysis
b. Recordkeeping convenience
c. Ensuring accurate information
d. Regulatory compliance

HINTS: Identify the primary purpose of updating customer account records.

Q1050_LO116: How frequently must account updating occur after the initial 30 days?
a. Quarterly
b. Biannually

c. Annually
d. At least every 36 months

HINTS: Recognize the frequency of required account updating after the initial 30 days.

Q1051_LO116: According to FINRA rules, how often must statements be sent to customers?
a. Monthly
b. Quarterly
c. Biannually
d. Annually

HINTS: Recall the frequency of statements required by FINRA rules.

Q1052_LO116: What does the term "activity" encompass in the context of account statements?
a. Account balance changes
b. Routine customer inquiries
c. Any interaction with the firm
d. Defined as purchases, sales, interest, or dividends

HINTS: Understand the definition of "activity" in the context of account statements.

Q1053_LO116: In nontrade confirmations, what is the purpose of sending notices of third-party activity?
a. Legal requirement
b. Customer convenience
c. Regulatory reporting
d. Transparency for customer awareness

HINTS: Recognize the purpose of sending notices of third-party activity in nontrade confirmations.

Q1054_LO116: What is the primary focus of a trade confirmation?
a. Account balances
b. Settlement date
c. Customer contact information
d. Marketing promotions

HINTS: Identify the primary focus of a trade confirmation.

Q1055_LO116: What information is NOT typically included in a trade confirmation?
a. Account number
b. Price per share
c. Branch office number
d. Customer's date of birth

HINTS: Recognize the type of information not typically included in a trade confirmation.

Q1056_LO116: When is interest added in bond transactions on trade confirmations?
a. Always
b. Never
c. Only for callable bonds
d. Upon customer request

HINTS: Understand when interest is added in bond transactions on trade confirmations.

Q1057_LO116: What is the maximum duration of a temporary hold on disbursements under FINRA rules?
a. 10 business days
b. 15 business days
c. 20 business days
d. 30 business days

HINTS: Recall the maximum duration of a temporary hold on disbursements under FINRA rules.

Q1058_LO116: In what capacity must a BD disclose its actions on a trade confirmation?
a. Principal only
b. Agent only

c. Both principal and agent
d. No disclosure required

HINTS: Identify the capacity in which a BD must disclose its actions on a trade confirmation.

Q1059_LO116: What must a customer do if there is a discrepancy in the account statement?
a. Notify FINRA
b. Notify the SEC
c. Promptly report to the brokerage firm
d. Wait for the next statement

HINTS: Recognize the correct action for a customer in case of a discrepancy in the account statement.

Q1060_LO116: What is the purpose of a temporary hold on disbursements?
a. To prevent account closure
b. To facilitate trading activities
c. To deter customers from withdrawing funds
d. To prevent financial exploitation

HINTS: Understand the purpose of a temporary hold on disbursements.

Correct Answers & Explanations
Record Keeping Requirements & Prohibited Activities

Q851_LO110: Correct Answer: c EXPLANATIONS: Records such as partnership agreements and corporate charters are kept indefinitely.

Q852_LO110: Correct Answer: b EXPLANATIONS: The corporate charter or articles of incorporation is the foundational document of a corporation.

Q853_LO110: Correct Answer: b EXPLANATIONS: Stock certificate books hold certificates until they are issued, and they also record to whom the certificates are issued.

Q854_LO110: Correct Answer: d EXPLANATIONS: Form BD, the registration application for a broker-dealer, is an example of an organizational record.

Q855_LO110: Correct Answer: b EXPLANATIONS: Blotters are records of original entry for securities transactions.

Q856_LO110: Correct Answer: b EXPLANATIONS: The general ledger contains accounting records and is used to prepare financial statements.

Q857_LO110: Correct Answer: d EXPLANATIONS: Blotters must be prepared no later than the following business day.

Q858_LO110: Correct Answer: b EXPLANATIONS: A stock record shows all securities held, ownership, and location.

Q859_LO110: Correct Answer: c EXPLANATIONS: The stock record must be posted no later than the business day after the settlement date.

Q860_LO110: Correct Answer: b EXPLANATIONS: Customer ledgers are customer statements.

Q861_LO110: Correct Answer: c EXPLANATIONS: Customer account records may include new account forms and margin agreements.

Q862_LO110: Correct Answer: c EXPLANATIONS: Designated principals oversee specific areas within the firm.

Q863_LO110: Correct Answer: b EXPLANATIONS: Records that are part of the life of the firm are retained indefinitely.

Q864_LO110: Correct Answer: c EXPLANATIONS: Six-year retention records include blotters and financial records.

Q865_LO110: Correct Answer: c EXPLANATIONS: Organizational records, such as Form BD, document the foundations of the firm.

Q866_LO110: Correct Answer: c EXPLANATIONS: Records that are part of the life of the firm are retained indefinitely.

Q867_LO110: Correct Answer: c EXPLANATIONS: Stock certificate books are part of the life of the firm and retained indefinitely.

Q868_LO110: Correct Answer: b EXPLANATIONS: If there is no written partnership agreement, there is no partnership.

Q869_LO110: Correct Answer: d EXPLANATIONS: Corporate charter or articles of incorporation are foundational documents of a corporation.

Q870_LO110: Correct Answer: c EXPLANATIONS: Minutes are records of the meetings of the board of directors (corporation) or the partners (partnership).

Q871_LO110: Correct Answer: c EXPLANATIONS: For closely held corporations, stock certificates are held in an actual book until they are issued.

Q872_LO110: Correct Answer: b EXPLANATIONS: Stock certificate books are generally retained for six years from the last use.

Q873_LO110: Correct Answer: a EXPLANATIONS: A blotter is a record of original entry in the context of record-keeping for broker-dealers.

Q874_LO110: Correct Answer: c EXPLANATIONS: The general ledger contains accounting records of the firm's assets, liabilities, and net worth.

Q875_LO110: Correct Answer: b EXPLANATIONS: Blotters must be prepared no later than the following business day.

Q876_LO110: Correct Answer: b EXPLANATIONS: A stock record shows ownership of securities, where they are held, and all securities held by the firm.

Q877_LO110: Correct Answer: a EXPLANATIONS: Customer ledgers are customer statements in the context of record-keeping for broker-dealers.

Q878_LO110: Correct Answer: a EXPLANATIONS: Customer account records might include the new account form and margin agreement.

Q879_LO110: Correct Answer: c EXPLANATIONS: An associate appointed to a principal position oversees specific areas in the firm.

Q880_LO110: Correct Answer: c EXPLANATIONS: It is a violation of FINRA rules.

Q881_LO111: Correct Answer: c EXPLANATIONS: Written complaints must be retained for four years after resolution.

Q882_LO111: Correct Answer: d EXPLANATIONS: Records of written complaints are normally maintained at the office of supervisory jurisdiction (OSJ) for the office where the complaint originated.

Q883_LO111: Correct Answer: b EXPLANATIONS: Only written complaints have regulatory standing according to FINRA and SEC.

Q884_LO111: Correct Answer: d EXPLANATIONS: Customer confirmations, securities borrowed and loaned ledgers, and Form U-4 and U-5 must be retained for three years after last use.

Q885_LO111: Correct Answer: c EXPLANATIONS: Written extends to almost any communication with letters organized into words, including paper, email, text, instant message, tweet, and social media posts.

Q886_LO111: Correct Answer: d EXPLANATIONS: Among three- and six-year records, the most recent two years must be kept "readily accessible," including customer confirmations.

Q887_LO111: Correct Answer: a EXPLANATIONS: After two years, they may be stored at an offsite location.

Q888_LO111: Correct Answer: d EXPLANATIONS: Form U-4 and U-5 for terminated personnel serve as employment history records.

Q889_LO111: Correct Answer: b EXPLANATIONS: Securities borrowed and loaned ledgers must be retained for three years after last use.

Q890_LO111: Correct Answer: b EXPLANATIONS: Among three- and six-year records, the most recent two years must be kept "readily accessible," including customer confirmations.

Q891_LO111: Correct Answer: b EXPLANATIONS: The firm's compliance and procedures manual must be retained for three years after last use.

Q892_LO111: Correct Answer: c EXPLANATIONS: Written complaints must be retained for four years after resolution.

Q893_LO111: Correct Answer: d EXPLANATIONS: Customer confirmations, trial balances, and advertising are included in the category of "almost everything else" with a three-year retention period.

Q894_LO111: Correct Answer: b EXPLANATIONS: Readily accessible means easily retrievable, typically kept at the branch office, OSJ, or headquarters where the document would normally be stored.

Q895_LO111: Correct Answer: c EXPLANATIONS: Securities borrowed and loaned ledgers must be maintained for six years.

Q896_LO112: Correct Answer: b EXPLANATIONS: The act enhanced penalties for insider trading.

Q897_LO112: Correct Answer: b EXPLANATIONS: An insider is defined as any person with access to material nonpublic information about a company.

Q898_LO112: Correct Answer: b EXPLANATIONS: It restricts the passing of potentially material nonpublic information between a firm's departments.

Q899_LO112: Correct Answer: b EXPLANATIONS: Insider trading is the use of inside information to make a gain or avoid a loss.

Q900_LO112: Correct Answer: c EXPLANATIONS: Both the tipper and the tippee are liable.

Q901_LO112: Correct Answer: b EXPLANATIONS: The personal benefits test is one of the key elements.

Q902_LO112: Correct Answer: c EXPLANATIONS: Both civil and criminal penalties may be levied by the SEC.

Q903_LO112: Correct Answer: b EXPLANATIONS: Civil penalties can be up to three times the profits made or losses avoided.

Q904_LO112: Correct Answer: b EXPLANATIONS: The maximum criminal penalty is up to $5 million.

Q905_LO112: Correct Answer: d EXPLANATIONS: The maximum penalty is three times the profit made or loss avoided, whichever is greater.

Q906_LO112: Correct Answer: c EXPLANATIONS: Suits may be initiated up to five years after the violation has occurred.

Q907_LO112: Correct Answer: b EXPLANATIONS: The Dodd-Frank legislation increased the bounty range.

Q908_LO112: Correct Answer: c EXPLANATIONS: The information bounty or award can range from 10% to 30% of amounts recovered.

Q909_LO112: Correct Answer: b EXPLANATIONS: Awards aim to compensate informers for providing original information concerning violations of securities law.

Q910_LO112: Correct Answer: a EXPLANATIONS: Awards may be paid in connection with original information concerning any violation of securities law, including insider trading.

Q911_LO112: Correct Answer: c EXPLANATIONS: The 1988 Act specified significant penalties for insider trading and securities fraud.

Q912_LO112: Correct Answer: b EXPLANATIONS: A firewall or information barrier restricts the passing of potentially material nonpublic information between a firm's departments.

Q913_LO112: Correct Answer: c EXPLANATIONS: An insider is defined as any person who has access to material nonpublic information about a company.

Q914_LO112: Correct Answer: b EXPLANATIONS: Insider trading involves the use of inside information for gain or to avoid a loss.

Q915_LO112: Correct Answer: d EXPLANATIONS: Key elements include material and nonpublic information, a fiduciary duty, and the personal benefits test.

Q916_LO112: Correct Answer: c EXPLANATIONS: The SEC can investigate any person suspected of violating the provisions of the Insider Trading Act.

Q917_LO112: Correct Answer: d EXPLANATIONS: A controlling person may face fines of $1 million or three times the profit/loss, and criminal penalties of up to $5 million and up to 20 years in jail.

Q918_LO112: Correct Answer: d EXPLANATIONS: Contemporaneous traders may initiate suits against persons violating insider trading regulations.

Q919_LO112: Correct Answer: d EXPLANATIONS: Suits may be initiated up to five years after the violation by contemporaneous traders.

Q920_LO112: Correct Answer: c EXPLANATIONS: Dodd-Frank allowed payments in connection with any violation of securities law, including insider trading.

Q921_LO112: Correct Answer: d EXPLANATIONS: The information bounty or award can range from 10% to 30% of amounts recovered.

Q922_LO112: Correct Answer: b EXPLANATIONS: The Act prohibits the use of insider information in making trades.

Q923_LO112: Correct Answer: c EXPLANATIONS: Material information is information that would most likely influence the price of the company's stock.

Q924_LO112: Correct Answer: b EXPLANATIONS: The primary distinction is the purpose of possession – use for gain or loss avoidance constitutes insider trading.

Q925_LO112: Correct Answer: a EXPLANATIONS: The Act prohibits insiders from trading on or communicating material and nonpublic information.

Q926_LO113: Correct Answer: a EXPLANATIONS: Pump and dump involves inflating stock prices through false and misleading positive rumors.

Q927_LO113: Correct Answer: d EXPLANATIONS: Front running is the act of placing orders for one's own account ahead of known orders.

Q928_LO113: Correct Answer: b EXPLANATIONS: Freeriding results in a 90-day account freeze as a penalty.

Q929_LO113: Correct Answer: d EXPLANATIONS: Matching orders involve selling stock with the understanding of repurchasing it later, creating false activity.

Q930_LO113: Correct Answer: b EXPLANATIONS: Churning involves excessive trading to generate commissions, not to achieve the customer's investment objectives.

Q931_LO113: Correct Answer: a EXPLANATIONS: Marking the open involves entering orders before the opening to manipulate the reported price.

Q932_LO113: Correct Answer: b EXPLANATIONS: Marking the close results in a 90-day account freeze.

Q933_LO113: Correct Answer: d EXPLANATIONS: Painting the tape is the act of manipulating reported prices to create a false impression of market activity.

Q934_LO113: Correct Answer: b EXPLANATIONS: Social media can be misused by spreading false or misleading information about a stock.

Q935_LO113: Correct Answer: b EXPLANATIONS: Freeriding is generally prohibited in both cash and margin accounts.

Q936_LO113: Correct Answer: b EXPLANATIONS: Churning involves excessive frequency or size of transactions inconsistent with the client's trading history.

Q937_LO113: Correct Answer: a EXPLANATIONS: Fraudsters profit by selling overvalued shares after inflating the price through false rumors.

Q938_LO113: Correct Answer: c EXPLANATIONS: Marking the close involves manipulating the closing price, potentially causing losses for investors.

Q939_LO113: Correct Answer: b EXPLANATIONS: The primary goal is to create false market activity by making it appear that more activity exists than actually does.

Q940_LO113: Correct Answer: a EXPLANATIONS: Front running occurs when orders are placed for one's own account ahead of other known orders.

Q941_LO113: Correct Answer: c EXPLANATIONS: Pump and dump involves inflating the price of a stock through false rumors to sell at a higher price later.

Q942_LO113: Correct Answer: c EXPLANATIONS: Front running is placing orders for one's own account ahead of known market orders.

Q943_LO113: Correct Answer: b EXPLANATIONS: Churning is the abuse of fiduciary responsibility to generate commissions.

Q944_LO113: Correct Answer: b EXPLANATIONS: Marking the close involves influencing the closing price of a stock.

Q945_LO113: Correct Answer: b EXPLANATIONS: Freeriding is purchasing and selling securities without making payment.

Q946_LO113: Correct Answer: c EXPLANATIONS: Matching orders create artificial activity to inflate perceived trading volume.

Q947_LO113: Correct Answer: c EXPLANATIONS: Fraudsters can use social media to spread false information about stocks.

Q948_LO113: Correct Answer: b EXPLANATIONS: Freeriding results in a 90-day account freeze as a penalty.

Q949_LO113: Correct Answer: d EXPLANATIONS: A controlling person may face fines and criminal penalties for insider trading violations.

Q950_LO113: Correct Answer: a EXPLANATIONS: Marking the open involves entering trades before the opening to influence the reported opening price.

Q951_LO113: Correct Answer: d EXPLANATIONS: The Act focuses on ensuring transparency in securities trading.

Q952_LO113: Correct Answer: a EXPLANATIONS: Excessive trading involves a higher frequency of transactions, unrelated to the customer's objectives.

Q953_LO113: Correct Answer: b EXPLANATIONS: Freeriding involves trading without making payment for the purchase.

Q954_LO113: Correct Answer: c EXPLANATIONS: Matched orders create a false appearance of trading activity.

Q955_LO113: Correct Answer: b EXPLANATIONS: Marking the close involves influencing the closing price of a stock.

Q956_LO114: Correct Answer: b EXPLANATIONS: Restricted persons include portfolio managers for investment companies.

Q957_LO114: Correct Answer: b EXPLANATIONS: Rule 5130 aims to protect the integrity of the public offering process.

Q958_LO114: Correct Answer: c EXPLANATIONS: Immediate family includes parents, in-laws, spouses, siblings, and children.

Q959_LO114: Correct Answer: c EXPLANATIONS: The de minimis exemption allows accounts to purchase new equity issues if the beneficial interests of restricted persons do not exceed 10%.

Q960_LO114: Correct Answer: c EXPLANATIONS: Rule 5130 restricts any person owning 10% or more of a member firm.

Q961_LO114: Correct Answer: c EXPLANATIONS: Representatives need a written representation of eligibility to sell an IPO.

Q962_LO114: Correct Answer: d EXPLANATIONS: The de minimis exemption applies to beneficial interests not exceeding 10%.

Q963_LO114: Correct Answer: b EXPLANATIONS: Exceeding the threshold results in the loss of the de minimis exemption.

Q964_LO114: Correct Answer: c EXPLANATIONS: Registered representatives are required to obtain the written representation.

Q965_LO114: Correct Answer: b EXPLANATIONS: Grandparents are not considered immediate family under Rule 5130.

Q966_LO114: Correct Answer: b EXPLANATIONS: The rule aims to protect public customers from insider advantage.

Q967_LO114: Correct Answer: a EXPLANATIONS: Accountants are considered finders and fiduciaries acting on behalf of the managing underwriter.

Q968_LO114: Correct Answer: d EXPLANATIONS: The exemption allows a limited interest (up to 10%) for restricted persons in an account.

Q969_LO114: Correct Answer: a EXPLANATIONS: The exclusion is based on the legal definition of immediate family under Rule 5130.

Q970_LO114: Correct Answer: c EXPLANATIONS: Rule 5130 focuses on protecting the integrity of the public offering process for public investors.

Q971_LO115: Correct Answer: b EXPLANATIONS: Improper use occurs when customer funds or securities are used in any way other than intended by the customer.

Q972_LO115: Correct Answer: b EXPLANATIONS: FINRA expects firms to implement reasonable systems and controls for supervisory review to prevent improper use of customer funds.

Q973_LO115: Correct Answer: b EXPLANATIONS: Activity in the account of a deceased person is a red flag for improper use.

Q974_LO115: Correct Answer: a EXPLANATIONS: Borrowing without consent is indistinguishable from stealing.

Q975_LO115: Correct Answer: c EXPLANATIONS: Firms must have written procedures, and representatives need prior written notice and firm approval.

Q976_LO115: Correct Answer: a EXPLANATIONS: An immediate family relationship does not require firm approval for borrowing.

Q977_LO115: Correct Answer: d EXPLANATIONS: The rules aim to protect customers from potential abuses in lending arrangements.

Q978_LO115: Correct Answer: b EXPLANATIONS: BDs, investment advisers, and RRs may not guarantee against a loss.

Q979_LO115: Correct Answer: a EXPLANATIONS: The firm may share in a loss if it was due to an error made by the firm.

Q980_LO115: Correct Answer: c EXPLANATIONS: Directly proportionate sharing is not mandatory in joint accounts with immediate family members.

Q981_LO115: Correct Answer: a EXPLANATIONS: The note indicates that firms cannot have joint accounts with customers to prevent misuse.

Q982_LO115: Correct Answer: c EXPLANATIONS: Immediate family includes those to whom the person provides material support, living in the same residence.

Q983_LO115: Correct Answer: c EXPLANATIONS: Contribution to the account is measured only in dollars.

Q984_LO115: Correct Answer: b EXPLANATIONS: Restricted persons can have an interest if it does not exceed 10% of an account.

Q985_LO115: Correct Answer: c EXPLANATIONS: Rule 5130 focuses on protecting the integrity of the public offering process for public investors.

Q986_LO115: Correct Answer: b EXPLANATIONS: Improper use occurs when customer funds or securities are used in ways not intended by the customer.

Q987_LO115: Correct Answer: b EXPLANATIONS: Firms are expected to implement reasonable systems and controls to detect or investigate red flags indicating improper use of customer funds.

Q988_LO115: Correct Answer: c EXPLANATIONS: Conflicting information in new account applications can be a red flag for improper use.

Q989_LO115: Correct Answer: b EXPLANATIONS: An immediate family relationship allows borrowing or lending without notice or approval.

Q990_LO115: Correct Answer: b EXPLANATIONS: Borrowing without consent is considered indistinguishable from stealing.

Q991_LO115: Correct Answer: b EXPLANATIONS: Lending arrangements require the firm's written approval in most cases.

Q992_LO115: Correct Answer: b EXPLANATIONS: Sharing in a joint account with immediate family members allows proportional sharing without violating rules.

Q993_LO115: Correct Answer: a EXPLANATIONS: BDs, investment advisers, and RRs are prohibited from guaranteeing gains in customer accounts.

Q994_LO115: Correct Answer: a EXPLANATIONS: A firm may share in a loss if the loss was due to an error made by the firm.

Q995_LO115: Correct Answer: c EXPLANATIONS: Living in the same residence exempts direct proportionate sharing.

Q996_LO115: Correct Answer: d EXPLANATIONS: Immediate family members include those providing material support, living in the same residence.

Q997_LO115: Correct Answer: a EXPLANATIONS: Regulatory prohibitions prevent firms from having joint accounts with customers.

Q998_LO115: Correct Answer: b EXPLANATIONS: Exception reports trigger red flags that alert firms to potential improper use.

Q999_LO115: Correct Answer: d EXPLANATIONS: Conflicting information in new account applications is a red flag for improper use.

Q1000_LO115: Correct Answer: c EXPLANATIONS: Rule 5130 focuses on protecting the integrity of the public offering process for public investors.

Q1001_LO115: Correct Answer: b EXPLANATIONS: Financial exploitation includes wrongful or unauthorized taking, withholding, or use of funds or securities.

Q1002_LO115: Correct Answer: c EXPLANATIONS: FINRA considers individuals age 65 and older or age 18 and older with mental or physical impairments.

Q1003_LO115: Correct Answer: c EXPLANATIONS: Member firms must make reasonable efforts to obtain a trusted contact person.

Q1004_LO115: Correct Answer: d EXPLANATIONS: It should be done when opening a customer's account or updating existing account information.

Q1005_LO115: Correct Answer: c EXPLANATIONS: Member firms can place a temporary hold on disbursements if financial exploitation is suspected.

Q1006_LO115: Correct Answer: b EXPLANATIONS: It can last no longer than 15 business days.

Q1007_LO115: Correct Answer: b EXPLANATIONS: An internal review of the facts and circumstances must be initiated by the member firm.

Q1008_LO115: Correct Answer: b EXPLANATIONS: Notification is not required if the trusted contact person is the perpetrator or unavailable.

Q1009_LO115: Correct Answer: c EXPLANATIONS: The trusted contact person assists in account administration and protection.

Q1010_LO115: Correct Answer: c EXPLANATIONS: A trusted contact person is someone who can provide information about the customer.

Q1011_LO115: Correct Answer: c EXPLANATIONS: The member firm must release the hold immediately.

Q1012_LO115: Correct Answer: b EXPLANATIONS: The trusted contact person is intended to assist in account administration and protection.

Q1013_LO115: Correct Answer: b EXPLANATIONS: Individuals age 18 and older with impairments are included.

Q1014_LO115: Correct Answer: b EXPLANATIONS: Member firms are expected to detect red flags indicating improper use of customer funds.

Q1015_LO115: Correct Answer: c EXPLANATIONS: Improper use of customer funds may lead to legal action against the responsible party.

Q1016_LO115: Correct Answer: c EXPLANATIONS: FINRA considers individuals aged 65 and older as "specified adults."

Q1017_LO115: Correct Answer: b EXPLANATIONS: Financial exploitation involves the wrongful or unauthorized taking of funds or securities from seniors.

Q1018_LO115: Correct Answer: b EXPLANATIONS: Member firms must obtain trusted contact information and may place temporary holds on accounts.

Q1019_LO115: Correct Answer: b EXPLANATIONS: Reasonable efforts must be made when opening an account or updating account information.

Q1020_LO115: Correct Answer: c EXPLANATIONS: Member firms can proceed if reasonable efforts were made to obtain such information.

Q1021_LO115: Correct Answer: c EXPLANATIONS: The member firm must disclose that it is authorized to contact the trusted person and disclose certain information about the customer's account.

Q1022_LO115: Correct Answer: c EXPLANATIONS: The trusted contact person serves as a resource for the member firm in administering the customer's account and protecting assets.

Q1023_LO115: Correct Answer: b EXPLANATIONS: A temporary hold can last no longer than 15 business days.

Q1024_LO115: Correct Answer: c EXPLANATIONS: A state regulator or agency of jurisdiction can terminate the hold sooner or extend it longer.

Q1025_LO115: Correct Answer: b EXPLANATIONS: The firm must conduct an internal review of the facts and circumstances.

Q1026_LO115: Correct Answer: c EXPLANATIONS: Notification must be provided within 2 business days after the hold is initiated.

Q1027_LO115: Correct Answer: b EXPLANATIONS: Notification is not required if the trusted contact person is believed to be the perpetrator.

Q1028_LO115: Correct Answer: c EXPLANATIONS: Rule 5130 focuses on protecting the integrity of the public offering process for public investors.

Q1029_LO115: Correct Answer: d EXPLANATIONS: Conflicting information in new account applications is a red flag for improper use.

Q1030_LO115: Correct Answer: b EXPLANATIONS: The trusted contact person is intended to be a resource for the member firm in administering the customer's account and protecting assets.

Q1031_LO116: Correct Answer: b EXPLANATIONS: A temporary hold can last no longer than 15 business days under FINRA rules.

Q1032_LO116: Correct Answer: c EXPLANATIONS: Notification must be provided within 2 business days after the hold is initiated.

Q1033_LO116: Correct Answer: b EXPLANATIONS: Notification is not required if the trusted contact person is believed to be the perpetrator.

Q1034_LO116: Correct Answer: b EXPLANATIONS: The trusted contact person is intended to be a resource for the member firm in administering the customer's account and protecting assets.

Q1035_LO116: Correct Answer: c EXPLANATIONS: A state regulator or agency of jurisdiction can terminate the hold sooner or extend it longer.

Q1036_LO116: Correct Answer: c EXPLANATIONS: The member firm must disclose that it is authorized to contact the trusted person and disclose certain information about the customer's account.

Q1037_LO116: Correct Answer: b EXPLANATIONS: A temporary hold can last no longer than 15 business days.

Q1038_LO116: Correct Answer: b EXPLANATIONS: The firm must conduct an internal review of the facts and circumstances.

Q1039_LO116: Correct Answer: c EXPLANATIONS: Notification must be provided within 2 business days after the hold is initiated.

Q1040_LO116: Correct Answer: b EXPLANATIONS: Notification is not required if the trusted contact person is believed to be the perpetrator.

Q1041_LO116: Correct Answer: c EXPLANATIONS: Rule 5130 focuses on protecting the integrity of the public offering process for public investors.

Q1042_LO116: Correct Answer: d EXPLANATIONS: Conflicting information in new account applications is a red flag for improper use.

Q1043_LO116: Correct Answer: b EXPLANATIONS: A temporary hold can last no longer than 15 business days under FINRA rules.

Q1044_LO116: Correct Answer: c EXPLANATIONS: Notification must be provided within 2 business days after the hold is initiated.

Q1045_LO116: Correct Answer: b EXPLANATIONS: Notification is not required if the trusted contact person is believed to be the perpetrator.

Q1046_LO116: Correct Answer: b EXPLANATIONS: FINRA requires firms to have procedures ensuring the security of personal information for electronic delivery.

Q1047_LO116: Correct Answer: c EXPLANATIONS: Account records must be furnished within 30 days of opening the account.

Q1048_LO116: Correct Answer: c EXPLANATIONS: Customers must be provided with information in paper form upon request.

Q1049_LO116: Correct Answer: c EXPLANATIONS: Updating is necessary to ensure accurate and current records.

Q1050_LO116: Correct Answer: d EXPLANATIONS: Account updating must occur at least every 36 months thereafter.

Q1051_LO116: Correct Answer: b EXPLANATIONS: Statements must be sent to customers at least quarterly.

Q1052_LO116: Correct Answer: d EXPLANATIONS: Activity includes purchases, sales, interest, or dividends received.

Q1053_LO116: Correct Answer: d EXPLANATIONS: Notices provide transparency and awareness of third-party activity in accounts.

Q1054_LO116: Correct Answer: b EXPLANATIONS: A trade confirmation primarily focuses on the settlement date of a trade.

Q1055_LO116: Correct Answer: d EXPLANATIONS: Personal information like the customer's date of birth is not included in a trade confirmation.

Q1056_LO116: Correct Answer: a EXPLANATIONS: Interest is always added for bonds traded with accrued interest.

Q1057_LO116: Correct Answer: b EXPLANATIONS: A temporary hold can last no longer than 15 business days.

Q1058_LO116: Correct Answer: c EXPLANATIONS: The BD must disclose whether the transaction is a purchase or sale and whether it acts as principal or agent.

Q1059_LO116: Correct Answer: c EXPLANATIONS: Customers should promptly report any discrepancy to their brokerage firms.

Q1060_LO116: Correct Answer: d EXPLANATIONS: Temporary holds are used to prevent or address financial exploitation concerns.

UNIT 4: Overview of the Regulatory Framework

Overview of the Regulatory Framework

Q1_LO117: How long must elapse before a person can make a second attempt at a qualification exam after failing?
a. 15 days
b. 30 days
c. 60 days
d. 180 days

HINTS: Recall the waiting period for a second attempt after failing an exam.

Q2_LO117: What information is required on the Disclosure Reporting Pages (DRP) of Form U-4 regarding charges, arrests, or convictions?
a. Simple yes or no
b. Detailed explanation
c. Reference to legal counsel
d. No information required

HINTS: Identify the information required on the DRP regarding charges, arrests, or convictions.

Q3_LO117: When must a Form U-4 be filed if an associated person changes employment?
a. Within 15 days
b. Within 30 days
c. Within 60 days
d. Within 90 days

HINTS: Recognize the timeframe for filing a Form U-4 after a change in employment.

Q4_LO117: What does the U-4 filing window allow for when requesting an exam?
a. Unlimited attempts
b. 90 days for exam completion
c. 120 days for exam completion
d. 180 days for exam completion

HINTS: Understand the purpose of the U-4 filing window when requesting an exam.

Q5_LO117: What is the responsibility of an associated person in informing the employer about changes to U-4 information?
a. No responsibility
b. Within 15 days
c. Within 30 days
d. Within 60 days

HINTS: Identify the timeframe for an associated person to inform the employer of U-4 changes.

Q6_LO117: What is exempt from fingerprinting requirements?
a. All registered persons
b. Clerical persons
c. Salespersons
d. Partners

HINTS: Recognize the category exempt from fingerprinting requirements.

Q7_LO117: Who must submit fingerprint cards to the U.S. attorney general for identification?
a. All employees
b. Directors, officers, and partners
c. Clerical persons
d. Registered representatives

HINTS: Identify the individuals required to submit fingerprint cards for identification.

Q8_LO117: When must an amended Form U-4 be filed for standard events, such as moving or new certifications?
a. Within 5 business days
b. Within 10 business days
c. Within 20 business days
d. Within 30 business days

HINTS: Recognize the timeframe for filing an amended Form U-4 for standard events.

Q9_LO117: What is the maximum duration of a temporary hold on disbursements under FINRA rules?
a. 10 business days
b. 15 business days
c. 20 business days
d. 30 business days

HINTS: Recall the maximum duration of a temporary hold on disbursements under FINRA rules.

Q10_LO117: What event requires an amended Form U-4 filing within 10 business days?
a. Change of address
b. New certification
c. Bankruptcy
d. Change of employment

HINTS: Identify the event requiring an amended Form U-4 filing within 10 business days.

Q11_LO117: What can automatically disqualify an applicant for registration?
a. Change of employment
b. Misstatements on the application
c. Change in marital status
d. Change in educational background

HINTS: Recognize the factors that can automatically disqualify an applicant.

Q12_LO117: What is the purpose of the Central Registration Depository (CRD)?
a. Maintain education records
b. Track disciplinary history
c. Conduct background checks
d. Process fingerprint cards

HINTS: Understand the purpose of the CRD in the registration process.

Q13_LO117: What does a bankruptcy or unsatisfied lien not disqualify someone from?
a. Registering as an associated person
b. Registering as an investment adviser
c. Registering as a broker-dealer
d. All of the above

HINTS: Identify what a bankruptcy or unsatisfied lien does not disqualify someone from.

Q14_LO117: What is the timeframe for filing an amended Form U-4 for statutory disqualification involving an expulsion or suspension?
a. 5 business days
b. 10 business days
c. 15 business days
d. 30 business days

HINTS: Recognize the timeframe for filing an amended Form U-4 for statutory disqualification.

Q15_LO117: What must a person do if found to be the cause of another BD or associated person being expelled or suspended?
a. Retire immediately
b. Notify FINRA
c. Submit an appeal
d. File an amended Form U-4

HINTS: Identify the action required if found to be the cause of another BD or associated person being expelled or suspended.

Q16_LO117: What is the primary purpose of Form U-4?
a. Requesting qualification exams
b. Providing 10-year residency history
c. Disclosing financial information
d. Registering an associated person with FINRA

HINTS: Identify the primary purpose of Form U-4.

Q17_LO117: How long must a person wait before making a fourth attempt at an exam if they fail three straight times?
a. 30 days
b. 90 days
c. 180 days
d. 365 days

HINTS: Recall the waiting period after failing an exam three straight times.

Q18_LO117: Which information is NOT required on Form U-4?
a. 5-year residency history
b. 10-year employment history
c. Marital status
d. Disclosure of charges, arrests, or convictions

HINTS: Identify the information not required on Form U-4.

Q19_LO117: When filing Form U-4 requesting an exam, what is the window for completing the exam?
a. 60 days
b. 90 days
c. 120 days
d. 180 days

HINTS: Understand the time window for completing exams after filing Form U-4.

Q20_LO117: What must be filed within 10 business days if an amendment involves a statutory disqualification?
a. New Form U-4
b. Amended Form U-4
c. Form U-5
d. Form ADV

HINTS: Recognize the filing requirement for statutory disqualification amendments.

Q21_LO117: What must a registered person do if there are changes to the information on Form U-4?
a. Notify FINRA
b. Inform the employer within 30 days
c. Update Form U-4 within 10 days
d. Wait for the next annual review

HINTS: Understand the responsibility of a registered person for changes to Form U-4 information.

Q22_LO117: Who is exempt from fingerprinting requirements?
a. All associated persons
b. Those involved in sales and handling cash
c. Directors, officers, and partners
d. Clerical persons

HINTS: Recognize the exemption from fingerprinting requirements.

Q23_LO117: What does the U.S. attorney general use fingerprint records for?
a. Regulatory audits
b. Identification and processing
c. Marketing purposes
d. Employment background checks

HINTS: Identify the purpose of submitting fingerprint records to the U.S. attorney general.

Q24_LO117: Which events can automatically disqualify an applicant for registration?
a. Change in residence
b. Willful misstatements in an application
c. Routine employment changes
d. New certifications

HINTS: Recognize events that can automatically disqualify an applicant.

Q25_LO117: What does a customer have access to through the CRD's BrokerCheck?
a. Exam scores
b. Disciplinary history
c. Personal information
d. Educational background

HINTS: Understand what information customers can access through BrokerCheck.

Q26_LO117: What does a bankruptcy or unsatisfied lien affect regarding registration?
a. Disqualifies from registration
b. Requires additional exams
c. Triggers a background check
d. No impact on registration

HINTS: Recognize the impact of bankruptcy or an unsatisfied lien on registration.

Q27_LO117: What must a person do if expelled or suspended from another SRO?
a. Wait for the suspension to end
b. Appeal the decision
c. Reapply for FINRA registration
d. Automatic rejection of FINRA registration

HINTS: Identify the action required if expelled or suspended from another SRO.

Q28_LO117: How often must fingerprint records be submitted for individuals involved in sales or handling cash?
a. Annually
b. Biannually
c. Every two years
d. Not required

HINTS: Recall the frequency of fingerprint record submissions for individuals involved in sales or handling cash.

Q29_LO117: What disqualifies an individual from acting as an RR or principal?
a. Poor business reputation
b. SEC order against the individual
c. Failure to update Form U-4
d. Involvement in a routine audit

HINTS: Identify factors that disqualify an individual from acting as an RR or principal.

Q30_LO117: When must an amended Form U-4 be filed for standard events?
a. Within 5 business days
b. Within 10 business days
c. Within 15 business days
d. Within 30 business days

HINTS: Recognize the timeframe for filing an amended Form U-4 for standard events.

Q31_LO118: What activities are permitted for nonregistered employees of a broker-dealer?
a. Soliciting trades
b. Responding to general, noninvestment questions
c. Managing investment accounts
d. Engaging in investment banking

HINTS: Identify the permitted activities for nonregistered BD employees.

Q32_LO118: Which of the following is a duty of a principal in a member firm?
a. Handling customer complaints
b. Providing investment advice
c. Engaging in investment banking
d. Managing employee schedules

HINTS: Recognize the duties of a principal in a member firm.

Q33_LO118: How many registered principals must a member firm employ?
a. One
b. Two
c. Three
d. No specific requirement

HINTS: Recall the number of registered principals required in a member firm.

Q34_LO118: What must a registered representative do before being appointed as a principal?
a. Obtain U.S. citizenship
b. Pass a principal's exam
c. Manage investment accounts
d. Engage in investment banking

HINTS: Identify the requirement for a registered representative to become a principal.

Q35_LO118: What is a principal's role in accepting new accounts?
a. Reviewing trading activity
b. Approving accounts for margin or options trading
c. Responding to general inquiries
d. Approving new accounts

HINTS: Recognize a duty of a principal in accepting new accounts.

Q36_LO118: What is a potential consequence of a willful misstatement on Form U-4?
a. Fine by the SEC
b. Suspension for 30 days
c. Bar from the industry for life
d. Mandatory retraining

HINTS: Understand the potential consequence of a willful misstatement on Form U-4.

Q37_LO118: What is the educational requirement for filling out Form U-4?
a. U.S. citizenship
b. Sponsorship by a member firm
c. Passing a principal's exam
d. No specific education requirement

HINTS: Recognize the educational requirement for Form U-4.

Q38_LO118: What is the role of nonregistered personnel in investment banking?
a. Managing investment accounts
b. Opening new accounts
c. Soliciting trades
d. Not permitted to engage in investment banking

HINTS: Identify the role of nonregistered personnel in investment banking.

Q39_LO118: How many principal's exams cover specific areas of securities and investment banking?
a. One
b. Two
c. Three
d. Several

HINTS: Recall the number of principal's exams covering specific areas.

Q40_LO118: What is the consequence of lying on Form U-4?
a. Fine by FINRA
b. Suspension for 90 days
c. Mandatory retraining
d. A good way to end a career before it starts

HINTS: Recognize the consequence of lying on Form U-4.

Q41_LO118: What disclosure is required on Form U-4?
a. Educational background
b. Citizenship status
c. Investment strategies
d. Complete and truthful disclosure

HINTS: Identify the required disclosure on Form U-4.

Q42_LO118: What type of questions can nonregistered personnel respond to?
a. Investment advice questions
b. General, noninvestment questions
c. Margin trading inquiries
d. Complex financial planning queries

HINTS: Recognize the type of questions nonregistered personnel can respond to.

Q43_LO118: How many days must elapse before a person can make a second attempt at an exam if they fail it?
a. 15 days
b. 30 days
c. 60 days
d. 90 days

HINTS: Recall the waiting period for a second attempt at an exam.

Q44_LO118: What is the primary purpose of a principal's review of trading activity?
a. Approving accounts for margin trading
b. Identifying market trends
c. Ensuring compliance with regulations
d. Reviewing customer complaints

HINTS: Understand the primary purpose of a principal's review of trading activity.

Q45_LO118: What is the role of nonregistered personnel in investment banking?
a. Managing investment accounts
b. Opening new accounts
c. Soliciting trades
d. Not permitted to engage in investment banking

HINTS: Identify the role of nonregistered personnel in investment banking.

Q46_LO118: What is a permitted activity for a nonregistered employee of a BD?
a. Soliciting trades
b. Responding to general, noninvestment questions
c. Opening new accounts
d. Managing investment portfolios

HINTS: Identify the permitted activity for nonregistered BD employees.

Q47_LO118: Which activity is NOT allowed for nonregistered persons?
a. Setting appointments
b. Providing literature on request
c. Engaging in investment banking
d. Inviting prospects to a seminar

HINTS: Recognize the prohibited activity for nonregistered persons.

Q48_LO118: What is a responsibility of a principal in a BD?
a. Handling customer complaints
b. Responding to general questions
c. Setting appointments
d. Providing literature on request

HINTS: Understand the duties of a principal in a BD.

Q49_LO118: How many registered principals must a member firm employ, at a minimum?
a. One
b. Two
c. Three
d. It varies by firm size

HINTS: Recall the minimum number of registered principals required for a member firm.

Q50_LO118: What is a duty of a principal regarding accounts?
a. Handling general inquiries
b. Approving new accounts
c. Responding to customer complaints
d. Providing investment advice

HINTS: Recognize the duty of a principal related to accounts.

Q51_LO118: Before becoming a principal, what must a registered representative pass?
a. Series 7 exam
b. Series 63 exam
c. Principal's exam
d. Series 24 exam

HINTS: Identify the exam a registered representative must pass to become a principal.

Q52_LO118: What are the testing requirements for filling out Form U-4?
a. U.S. citizenship
b. Sponsorship by a broker-dealer
c. Completion of a principal's exam
d. Truthful disclosure on required forms

HINTS: Recognize the testing requirements for filling out Form U-4.

Q53_LO118: What consequence may result from a willful misstatement on Form U-4?
a. Suspension for 90 days
b. Bar from the industry for life
c. Fine of $1,000
d. Written warning

HINTS: Understand the potential consequence of a willful misstatement on Form U-4.

Q54_LO118: How many registered principals must a member firm employ, at a minimum?
a. One
b. Two
c. Three
d. It varies by firm size

HINTS: Recall the minimum number of registered principals required for a member firm.

Q55_LO118: What is a duty of a principal regarding accounts?
a. Handling general inquiries
b. Approving new accounts
c. Responding to customer complaints
d. Providing investment advice

HINTS: Recognize the duty of a principal related to accounts.

Q56_LO118: Before becoming a principal, what must a registered representative pass?
a. Series 7 exam
b. Series 63 exam
c. Principal's exam
d. Series 24 exam

HINTS: Identify the exam a registered representative must pass to become a principal.

Q57_LO118: What are the testing requirements for filling out Form U-4?
a. U.S. citizenship
b. Sponsorship by a broker-dealer
c. Completion of a principal's exam
d. Truthful disclosure on required forms

HINTS: Recognize the testing requirements for filling out Form U-4.

Q58_LO118: What consequence may result from a willful misstatement on Form U-4?
a. Suspension for 90 days
b. Bar from the industry for life
c. Fine of $1,000
d. Written warning

HINTS: Understand the potential consequence of a willful misstatement on Form U-4.

Q59_LO118: How often must fingerprint records be submitted for individuals involved in sales or handling cash?
a. Annually
b. Biannually
c. Every two years
d. Not required

HINTS: Recall the frequency of fingerprint record submissions for individuals involved in sales or handling cash.

Q60_LO118: What disqualifies an individual from acting as an RR or principal?
a. Poor business reputation
b. SEC order against the individual
c. Failure to update Form U-4
d. Involvement in a routine audit

HINTS: Identify factors that disqualify an individual from acting as an RR or principal.

Q61_LO119: When must a member file Form U-5 with the CRD after termination?
a. 15 days
b. 30 days
c. 45 days
d. 60 days

HINTS: Identify the correct filing timeframe for Form U-5 after termination.

Q62_LO119: What happens if a member fails to file Form U-5 within the specified time frame?
a. No consequence
b. Fine imposed
c. Warning issued
d. Extended filing period

HINTS: Recognize the consequence of failing to file Form U-5 on time.

Q63_LO119: How many reasons for termination are listed on Form U-5?
a. Two
b. Three
c. Four
d. Five

HINTS: Recall the number of reasons for termination listed on Form U-5.

Q64_LO119: What is the assumed impact of a voluntary resignation on future eligibility for employment?
a. Positive impact
b. Negative impact
c. No impact
d. Depends on the circumstances

HINTS: Understand the assumed impact of a voluntary resignation on future eligibility.

Q65_LO119: When is an amendment to Form U-5 required for a statutory disqualification?
a. Within 5 days
b. Within 10 business days
c. Within 15 days
d. Within 20 days

HINTS: Identify the timeframe for filing an amendment to Form U-5 for a statutory disqualification.

Q66_LO119: What is the time limit before retesting is required after a full termination?
a. One year
b. Two years
c. Three years
d. Four years

HINTS: Recognize the time limit before retesting is required after a full termination.

Q67_LO119: How long does the jurisdiction of regulators last after a full termination?
a. One year
b. Two years
c. Three years
d. Four years

HINTS: Recall the duration of regulators' jurisdiction after a full termination.

Q68_LO119: How long can a person associate with another member firm without requalifying after a full termination?
a. One year
b. Two years
c. Three years
d. Four years

HINTS: Identify the duration a person can associate with another member firm without requalifying after a full termination.

Q69_LO119: What exam allows a person to affiliate for up to four years without retaking the SIE?
a. Series 7
b. Series 63
c. Top-off exam
d. Series 24

HINTS: Understand which exam allows affiliation without retaking the SIE for up to four years.

Q70_LO119: After how many years does a former registered representative need to retake the SIE if not affiliating within that period?
a. Two years
b. Three years
c. Four years
d. Five years

HINTS: Recognize the timeframe for a former representative to retake the SIE if not affiliating within that period.

Q71_LO119: What is the special inactive status for a representative entering regular military service?
a. 30 days
b. 60 days
c. 90 days
d. 120 days

HINTS: Identify the duration of the special inactive status for a representative entering military service.

Q72_LO119: When does the two-year time frame begin for a representative entering regular military service?
a. Immediately
b. After 30 days
c. After 60 days
d. After 90 days

HINTS: Understand when the two-year time frame begins for a representative entering military service.

Q73_LO119: What happens to commissions for representatives after termination?
a. They continue indefinitely
b. No commissions are allowed
c. They continue for one year
d. They continue for two years

HINTS: Recognize the status of commissions for representatives after termination.

Q74_LO119: Under what circumstances are continuing commissions allowed after termination?
a. For new business relationships
b. For retirees
c. For all terminated representatives
d. For non-retirees

HINTS: Identify the circumstances under which continuing commissions are allowed after termination.

Q75_LO119: What is the purpose of Form U-5?
a. Request for retesting
b. Resignation notification
c. Termination notification
d. Military service notification

HINTS: Recognize the purpose of Form U-5.

Q76_LO119: What is the time frame for filing Form U-5 after a termination?
a. 15 days
b. 30 days
c. 45 days
d. 60 days

HINTS: Recall the filing time frame for Form U-5 after termination.

Q77_LO119: What penalty may be assessed if a member fails to file Form U-5 within the specified time?
a. Written warning
b. Termination of membership
c. Late filing fee
d. Suspension of registration

HINTS: Recognize the potential penalty for late filing of Form U-5.

Q78_LO119: How many reasons for termination are listed on Form U-5?
a. Two
b. Three
c. Four
d. Five

HINTS: Identify the number of reasons for termination listed on Form U-5.

Q79_LO119: What is assumed about a voluntary resignation on Form U-5?
a. Future ineligibility for employment
b. Involvement in securities fraud
c. Normal circumstances for future employment
d. Statutory disqualification

HINTS: Understand the assumption about a voluntary resignation on Form U-5.

Q80_LO119: What must be disclosed if the "discharged," "other," or "permitted to resign" box is checked on Form U-5?
a. Only the date of termination
b. All details surrounding the termination
c. Names of other terminated employees
d. None of the above

HINTS: Recognize the disclosure requirements for specific termination reasons on Form U-5.

Q81_LO119: When must an amendment to Form U-5 be filed for statutory disqualification?
a. Within 30 days
b. Within 10 business days
c. Within 60 days
d. Within 90 days

HINTS: Identify the time frame for filing an amendment to Form U-5 for statutory disqualification.

Q82_LO119: How long do FINRA and regulators retain jurisdiction after a full termination?
a. One year
b. Two years
c. Three years
d. Four years

HINTS: Recall the duration of jurisdiction retention after a full termination.

Q83_LO119: What allows a person to affiliate with a member firm without requalifying for up to four years?
a. Passing a top-off exam
b. Passing the Series 7 exam
c. Completing a specialized training
d. Retaking the SIE

HINTS: Recognize the condition allowing affiliation without requalifying for up to four years.

Q84_LO119: If more than four years elapse after taking the SIE, what is required for affiliation?
a. Retaking the SIE
b. Passing the Series 7 exam
c. Completing continuing education
d. Passing a top-off exam

HINTS: Identify the requirement for affiliation if more than four years elapse after taking the SIE.

Q85_LO119: What is the status of a license during regular military service?
a. Revoked
b. Active
c. Inactive
d. Suspended

HINTS: Understand the license status during regular military service.

Q86_LO119: When does the two-year jurisdiction period begin after a full termination?
a. Immediately
b. 30 days after termination
c. 90 days after termination
d. 180 days after termination

HINTS: Recognize when the two-year jurisdiction period begins after a full termination.

Q87_LO119: What is the time frame for continuing commissions after termination?
a. One year
b. Two years
c. Three years
d. Indefinite

HINTS: Understand the time frame for continuing commissions after termination.

Q88_LO119: What is the primary purpose of Form U-5?
a. Requesting requalification
b. Terminating a member firm
c. Reporting financial changes
d. Updating personal information

HINTS: Identify the primary purpose of Form U-5.

Q89_LO119: What does a voluntary resignation on Form U-5 assume about future eligibility?
a. Ineligibility for life
b. Under statutory disqualification
c. Normal circumstances for future employment
d. Involvement in securities fraud

HINTS: Understand the assumption about future eligibility in a voluntary resignation on Form U-5.

Q90_LO119: What must a member provide to a former employee within 30 days of termination?
a. Written warning
b. Final paycheck
c. Copy of Form U-5
d. Termination certificate

HINTS: Recognize the requirement for providing information to a former employee within 30 days of termination.

Q91_LO120: What does the Firm Element Continuing Education (CE) require member firms to do annually?
a. Conduct regulatory audits
b. Prepare an annual training plan
c. Submit financial reports
d. Update compliance manuals

HINTS: Recall the purpose of Firm Element CE for member firms.

Q92_LO120: When must the Firm Element CE requirements be completed?
a. March 31
b. June 30
c. December 31
d. October 31

HINTS: Recall the deadline for completing Firm Element CE requirements.

Q93_LO120: What is the consequence of failing to complete the Firm Element CE requirements?
a. Fine imposition
b. License suspension
c. Written warning
d. Educational credit

HINTS: Recognize the consequence of failing to complete Firm Element CE.

Q94_LO120: What should a significant portion of the Firm Element CE be related to?
a. Personal development
b. Regulatory audits
c. Firm's normal business activities
d. Financial planning

HINTS: Identify the focus of a significant portion of the Firm Element CE.

Q95_LO120: In the Regulatory Element, when must a registered person complete a computer-based training session?
a. Within 60 days of registration
b. Within 90 days of registration
c. Within 120 days of the second registration anniversary
d. Within 180 days of the second registration anniversary

HINTS: Recall the time frame for completing the Regulatory Element.

Q96_LO120: What happens if a person fails to complete the Regulatory Element within the prescribed period?
a. License termination
b. Fine imposition
c. Registration deactivation
d. Continuing education exemption

HINTS: Understand the consequence of failing to complete the Regulatory Element.

Q97_LO120: What is considered a complaint in the securities industry?
a. Oral expression of dissatisfaction
b. Customer dissatisfaction with services
c. Written statement alleging a grievance
d. General market volatility

HINTS: Recognize the definition of a complaint in the securities industry.

Q98_LO120: When should a report listing all written complaints be filed with FINRA?
a. Within 30 days of complaint resolution
b. At the end of each calendar quarter
c. Within 15 days of identifying a complaint
d. Annually on the registration anniversary

HINTS: Identify the timing for filing a report with FINRA on written complaints.

Q99_LO120: What is required if a complaint is resolved to the satisfaction of both the member firm and the customer?
a. Legal action
b. No further action
c. Reporting to regulatory authorities
d. License suspension

HINTS: Understand the action required if a complaint is satisfactorily resolved.

Q100_LO120: What is the primary purpose of the notice required for outside business activities?
a. Gaining regulatory approval
b. Member firm's permission
c. Regulatory reporting
d. Providing employment history

HINTS: Recognize the primary purpose of providing notice for outside business activities.

Q101_LO120: Can an associated person work independently without notifying the employing BD?
a. Yes, if regulatory approval is obtained
b. Yes, with the employing BD's permission
c. No, it is not allowed
d. Only for non-securities-related businesses

HINTS: Identify the requirement for working independently as an associated person.

Q102_LO120: What is considered a passive investment in the context of outside business activities?
a. Active involvement in management
b. Serving as an officer
c. Limited partnership unit purchase
d. Owning interest in a financial services company

HINTS: Recognize the characteristic of a passive investment in outside business activities.

Q103_LO120: Can a registered person make a passive investment without providing notice to the employing BD?
a. Yes, always
b. Yes, if it's a substantial investment
c. No, notice is required
d. Only if it involves real estate

HINTS: Identify the condition for making a passive investment without notice.

Q104_LO120: What right does a member firm have regarding an associated person's outside affiliation?
a. Mandatory approval
b. Right to reject or restrict
c. Regulatory authorization
d. Power to terminate

HINTS: Understand the rights of a member firm regarding outside affiliations.

Q105_LO120: What is the purpose of the Regulatory Element Continuing Education?
a. In-house training
b. Supervisory needs
c. Updating compliance manuals
d. Enhancing regulatory knowledge

HINTS: Recognize the purpose of the Regulatory Element Continuing Education.

Q106_LO120: What is the primary purpose of the firm element continuing education?
a. Individual development
b. Regulatory compliance
c. Enhancing firm profitability
d. Personal enrichment

HINTS: Recall the primary purpose of the firm element continuing education.

Q107_LO120: When must firm element CE requirements be completed?
a. October 31
b. November 15
c. December 31
d. January 15

HINTS: Recognize the deadline for completing firm element CE requirements.

Q108_LO120: What may happen if a representative fails to complete the firm element?
a. Salary reduction
b. Promotion opportunity
c. License suspension
d. Bonus award

HINTS: Understand the consequence of failing to complete the firm element.

Q109_LO120: What factors are considered in preparing the firm's annual training plan?
a. Employee preferences
b. Recent regulatory developments
c. Personal interests of employees
d. External market trends

HINTS: Identify the relevant factors in preparing the firm's annual training plan.

Q110_LO120: How often must registered persons complete the regulatory element continuing education?
a. Every year
b. Every two years
c. Every three years
d. Every five years

HINTS: Recall the frequency of completing the regulatory element CE.

Q111_LO120: What happens if a person fails to complete the regulatory element within the prescribed period?
a. License termination
b. FINRA fine
c. Registration deactivation
d. Mandatory requalification

HINTS: Recognize the consequence of failing to complete the regulatory element.

Q112_LO120: When must a registered person complete the regulatory element after the second registration anniversary?
a. Within 30 days
b. Within 60 days
c. Within 90 days
d. Within 120 days

HINTS: Understand the time frame for completing the regulatory element after the second registration anniversary.

Q113_LO120: What is the content of the regulatory element based on?
a. Personal preferences
b. Industry best practices
c. FINRA's determination
d. Firm-specific requirements

HINTS: Recognize the basis for determining the content of the regulatory element.

Q114_LO120: How should written complaints be handled when identified?
a. Disclose them publicly
b. Notify proper personnel
c. Ignore them
d. Resolve them privately

HINTS: Recognize the appropriate action when written complaints are identified.

Q115_LO120: What defines a complaint in the context of handling written complaints?
a. Oral statement by a customer
b. Written statement by a customer
c. Verbal expression of dissatisfaction
d. Negative online review

HINTS: Identify the definition of a complaint in the context of handling written complaints.

Q116_LO120: When must a report listing all written complaints be filed with FINRA?
a. Within 30 days of identification
b. Within 45 days of resolution
c. Within 60 days of filing
d. Within 15 days of the end of each calendar quarter

HINTS: Recognize the timeline for filing a report listing written complaints with FINRA.

Q117_LO120: What is NOT considered an outside business activity?
a. Serving as an officer
b. Making a passive investment
c. Owning an interest in a financial services company
d. Accepting compensation from another entity

HINTS: Identify the activity not considered an outside business activity.

Q118_LO120: What is required if an associated person wants to be employed by an entity other than the member firm?
a. Prior written notice to the member
b. Regulatory approval
c. Customer consent
d. No requirement

HINTS: Understand the requirement if an associated person wants employment outside the member firm.

Q119_LO120: What right does the firm have regarding outside affiliations of associated persons?
a. Regulate compensation
b. Reject or restrict affiliations
c. Dictate working hours
d. Mandate training programs

HINTS: Recognize the firm's right regarding outside affiliations of associated persons.

Q120_LO120: What is a passive investment in the context of outside business activities?
a. Acquiring ownership in a startup
b. Accepting a consultancy role
c. Purchasing limited partnership units
d. Serving as an officer

HINTS: Identify the definition of a passive investment in the context of outside business activities.

Q121_LO121: What is a private securities transaction also known as?
a. In-house sale
b. Personal investment
c. Outside business activity
d. Selling away

HINTS: Recall the alternative term for a private securities transaction.

Q122_LO121: What is the primary requirement for an associated person entering into a private securities transaction?
a. Obtain regulatory approval
b. Seek customer consent
c. Provide prior written notice to the employer
d. Consult with legal counsel

HINTS: Identify the crucial step an associated person must take before engaging in a private securities transaction.

Q123_LO121: What information must be included in the notice for a private securities transaction?
a. Only the transaction details
b. Only the associated person's role
c. Transaction details and proposed role
d. Only compensation details

HINTS: Recognize the comprehensive details required in the notice for a private securities transaction.

Q124_LO121: What action can the employing member take if the private securities transaction involves compensation?
a. Provide personal supervision
b. Approve or disapprove participation
c. Delegate supervision to the BD accommodating the transaction
d. Ignore the transaction

HINTS: Understand the options available to the employing member when a private securities transaction involves compensation.

Q125_LO121: In a non-compensated private securities transaction, who assumes responsibility for supervision?
a. Employing member firm
b. BD accommodating the transaction
c. Both firms jointly
d. Associated person

HINTS: Recognize the party responsible for supervision in a non-compensated private securities transaction.

Q126_LO121: Which transactions are excluded from the definition of private securities transactions?
a. Transactions with compensation
b. Transactions on behalf of family members
c. Both compensated and non-compensated transactions
d. Non-compensated transactions

HINTS: Identify the excluded transactions from the definition of private securities transactions.

Q127_LO121: What restrictions can an employer BD impose on an associate's participation in a non-compensated private securities transaction?
a. No restrictions allowed
b. Limited to monetary value
c. Prohibit participation entirely
d. Must provide written consent

HINTS: Understand the range of restrictions an employer BD can impose on non-compensated private securities transactions.

Q128_LO121: Who is responsible for supervision in a private securities transaction?
a. Accommodating BD
b. Associated person
c. Both parties jointly
d. Employing member firm

HINTS: Recognize the entity responsible for supervision in a private securities transaction.

Q129_LO121: What is the annual limit for business-related compensation to employees of other member firms?
a. $50
b. $75
c. $100
d. $125

HINTS: Recall the annual limit for business-related compensation to employees of other member firms.

Q130_LO121: Under what conditions may the $100 limit for business-related compensation be exceeded?
a. Occasional noncash expenditures
b. Monthly cash gifts
c. Without prior approval
d. Any form of compensation

HINTS: Identify the conditions under which the $100 limit for business-related compensation may be exceeded.

Q131_LO121: What must accompany the compensation to exceed the $100 limit?
a. Written approval
b. Regulatory exemption
c. Accompanying representative from the providing firm
d. Customer consent

HINTS: Recognize the requirement for exceeding the $100 limit for business-related compensation.

Q132_LO121: What is excluded from the definition of business-related compensation?
a. Cash gifts
b. Dinner invitations
c. Advertising items with logos
d. Wedding gifts

HINTS: Identify the item excluded from the definition of business-related compensation.

Q133_LO121: What is a reminder advertising item?
a. A promotional video
b. A logo-bearing item
c. A discount coupon
d. A press release

HINTS: Understand the definition of a reminder advertising item.

Q134_LO121: When must a report listing all written complaints be filed with FINRA?
a. Within 30 days of identification
b. Within 45 days of resolution
c. Within 60 days of filing
d. Within 15 days of the end of each calendar quarter

HINTS: Recognize the timeline for filing a report listing written complaints with FINRA.

Q135_LO121: What is the main responsibility of the employing member in a private securities transaction?
a. Direct participation in the transaction
b. Complete paperwork for the associated person
c. Treat the transaction as if done on its own behalf
d. Seek regulatory approval

HINTS: Understand the primary responsibility of the employing member in a private securities transaction.

Q136_LO122: What is the primary purpose of industry rules regarding political contributions?
a. Secure business deals
b. Preserve investor confidence and market integrity
c. Encourage political affiliations
d. Facilitate pay-to-play practices

HINTS: Recognize the overarching goal of industry rules related to political contributions.

Q137_LO122: Which organization enforces MSRB Rule G-37 related to political contributions?
a. MSRB
b. SEC
c. FINRA
d. SRO

HINTS: Identify the organization responsible for enforcing MSRB Rule G-37.

Q138_LO122: What does MSRB Rule G-37 specifically address in the municipal securities business?
a. All underwritings
b. Negotiated underwritings and financial advisory work
c. Underwritings with bidding
d. Secondary market transactions

HINTS: Understand the focus of MSRB Rule G-37 within the municipal securities business.

Q139_LO122: How long is a municipal firm prohibited from engaging in municipal securities business after a political contribution?
a. One year
b. Two years
c. Three years
d. Four years

HINTS: Recognize the duration of the prohibition on engaging in municipal securities business after a political contribution.

Q140_LO122: Who is included in the prohibition of engaging in municipal securities business after a contribution, according to Rule G-37?
a. Only the municipal firm
b. Municipal finance professionals (MFPs)
c. Any individual associated with the municipal firm
d. All of the above

HINTS: Identify the parties covered by the prohibition in Rule G-37.

Q141_LO122: What is a Municipal Finance Professional (MFP)?
a. A registered representative
b. Any individual in the financial industry
c. A person engaged in municipal securities activities
d. Clerical or ministerial personnel

HINTS: Recognize the definition of a Municipal Finance Professional (MFP).

Q142_LO122: What is the de minimis exemption for contributions by MFPs?
a. $100
b. $200
c. $250
d. $500

HINTS: Recall the de minimis exemption limit for contributions by MFPs.

Q143_LO122: Who is eligible for the $250 de minimis exemption?
a. Municipal firms
b. MFPs
c. Political action committees
d. All registered persons

HINTS: Identify the individuals eligible for the $250 de minimis exemption.

Q144_LO122: What does the $250 de minimis exemption NOT apply to?
a. Contributions made by municipal firms
b. Contributions made by clerical personnel
c. Contributions made by MFPs
d. Contributions to political action committees

HINTS: Recognize the context in which the $250 de minimis exemption does not apply.

Q145_LO122: What is the purpose of Rule G-37's prohibition on political contributions?
a. To encourage political affiliations
b. To prevent pay-to-play practices
c. To establish a minimum contribution limit
d. To facilitate underwriting negotiations

HINTS: Understand the underlying purpose of Rule G-37's prohibition on political contributions.

Q146_LO122: What is the approval requirement for home-based offices?
a. Regulatory approval
b. Customer consent
c. Member firm's SRO approval
d. Municipal issuer approval

HINTS: Recognize the specific approval required for home-based offices.

Q147_LO122: What activities are permitted at a home office for registered representatives?
a. Limited to clerical functions
b. Restricted to customer orders
c. All normal business activities
d. No customer orders allowed

HINTS: Identify the range of activities permitted at a home office for registered representatives.

Q148_LO122: What is subject to a premise visit and review for home-based offices?
a. Only clerical functions
b. Only customer orders
c. Any normal business activity
d. Advertising materials

HINTS: Recognize the components subject to a premise visit and review for home-based offices.

Q149_LO122: What is the advertising allowance for home office addresses and telephone numbers?
a. No advertising allowed
b. Restricted to newspapers
c. Permitted on business cards and public media
d. Limited to the firm's website

HINTS: Identify the advertising allowance for home office addresses and telephone numbers.

Q150_LO122: Who can conduct visits, inspections, and audits of a home office in a residence?
a. Principals and compliance officers only
b. Regulators only
c. Member firm's SRO, principals, and regulators
d. Homeowners only

HINTS: Recognize the entities authorized to conduct visits, inspections, and audits of a home office in a residence.

Q151_LO122: What is the primary objective of industry rules regarding political contributions?
a. Increase political influence
b. Preserve investor confidence and market integrity
c. Facilitate pay-to-play practices
d. Encourage favoritism

HINTS: Recognize the main goal of industry rules related to political contributions.

Q152_LO122: Which organization enforces MSRB Rule G-37?
a. SEC
b. MSRB
c. FINRA
d. Municipal issuers

HINTS: Identify the organization responsible for enforcing MSRB Rule G-37.

Q153_LO122: What does MSRB Rule G-37 primarily address?
a. Investment advisory practices
b. Pay-to-play practices
c. Securities underwriting procedures
d. Market manipulation

HINTS: Understand the main focus of MSRB Rule G-37.

Q154_LO122: When does Rule G-37 prohibit municipal firms from engaging in municipal securities business with an issuer?
a. One year after a contribution
b. Two years after a contribution
c. Six months after a contribution
d. Three years after a contribution

HINTS: Identify the timeframe during which municipal firms are prohibited from engaging in business after a contribution.

Q155_LO122: Who are considered municipal finance professionals (MFPs) under Rule G-37?
a. All employees of a municipal firm
b. Only registered persons of a municipal firm
c. Any individual associated with a municipal firm
d. Solely salespersons with no advisory functions

HINTS: Recognize the definition of municipal finance professionals (MFPs) under Rule G-37.

Q156_LO122: What activities exclude an associated person from being considered an MFP under Rule G-37?
a. Clerical or ministerial functions
b. Investment advisory services
c. Market research activities
d. Administrative duties

HINTS: Identify the activities that exclude an associated person from being considered an MFP.

Q157_LO122: What is the de minimis exemption for contributions made by MFPs?
a. $100 per election
b. $200 per election
c. $250 per election
d. $300 per election

HINTS: Recall the de minimis exemption for contributions made by MFPs.

Q158_LO122: To whom does the $250 de minimis exemption not apply?
a. Registered persons
b. Municipal finance professionals
c. Municipal firms
d. Political action committees

HINTS: Recognize the entities to which the $250 de minimis exemption does not apply.

Q159_LO122: What does the term "selling away" primarily refer to?
a. Unauthorized securities trading
b. Private securities transactions outside regular business
c. Insider trading practices
d. Fraudulent marketing techniques

HINTS: Understand the primary meaning of the term "selling away."

Q160_LO122: What is the key requirement for an associated person entering into a private securities transaction?
a. Regulatory approval
b. Customer consent
c. Prior written notice to the employer
d. Legal counsel consultation

HINTS: Identify the crucial requirement for an associated person entering into a private securities transaction.

Q161_LO122: What responsibility does the employing member have if a private securities transaction involves compensation?
a. Provide personal supervision
b. Approve or disapprove participation
c. Ignore the transaction
d. Report to regulatory bodies

HINTS: Understand the employing member's responsibility when a private securities transaction involves compensation.

Q162_LO122: In a non-compensated private securities transaction, who assumes supervision responsibility?
a. Employing member firm
b. BD accommodating the transaction
c. Both firms jointly
d. Associated person

HINTS: Recognize the entity responsible for supervision in a non-compensated private securities transaction.

Q163_LO122: What restrictions can an employer BD impose on an associate's participation in a non-compensated private securities transaction?
a. No restrictions allowed
b. Limited to monetary value
c. Prohibit participation entirely
d. Must provide written consent

HINTS: Understand the range of restrictions an employer BD can impose on non-compensated private securities transactions.

Q164_LO122: What is excluded from the definition of business-related compensation?
a. Cash gifts
b. Dinner invitations
c. Advertising items with logos
d. Wedding gifts

HINTS: Identify the item excluded from the definition of business-related compensation.

Q165_LO122: What is the main responsibility of the employing member in a private securities transaction?
a. Direct participation in the transaction
b. Complete paperwork for the associated person
c. Treat the transaction as if done on its own behalf
d. Seek regulatory approval

HINTS: Understand the primary responsibility of the employing member in a private securities transaction.

Correct Answers & Explanations
Overview of the Regulatory Framework

Q1_LO117: Correct Answer: b
EXPLANATIONS: If a person fails the exam, 30 days must elapse before a second attempt.

Q2_LO117: Correct Answer: b
EXPLANATIONS: A detailed explanation is required for an affirmative answer on charges, arrests, or convictions.

Q3_LO117: Correct Answer: b
EXPLANATIONS: The U-4 must be filed within 30 days after the member becomes aware of changes.

Q4_LO117: Correct Answer: c
EXPLANATIONS: The U-4 filing window allows 120 days for exam completion.

Q5_LO117: Correct Answer: c
EXPLANATIONS: Changes to U-4 information must be filed within 30 days after the member becomes aware.

Q6_LO117: Correct Answer: b
EXPLANATIONS: Clerical persons need not be fingerprinted.

Q7_LO117: Correct Answer: b
EXPLANATIONS: Directors, officers, and partners must submit fingerprint cards.

Q8_LO117: Correct Answer: d
EXPLANATIONS: Amendments for standard events must be filed within 30 days.

Q9_LO117: Correct Answer: b
EXPLANATIONS: A temporary hold can last no longer than 15 business days.

Q10_LO117: Correct Answer: c
EXPLANATIONS: Bankruptcy requires an amended filing within 10 business days.

Q11_LO117: Correct Answer: b
EXPLANATIONS: Misstatements on the application can lead to automatic disqualification.

Q12_LO117: Correct Answer: b
EXPLANATIONS: The CRD maintains information on the disciplinary history of registered persons.

Q13_LO117: Correct Answer: a
EXPLANATIONS: A bankruptcy or unsatisfied lien does not disqualify one from registering.

Q14_LO117: Correct Answer: b
EXPLANATIONS: An amended Form U-4 must be filed within 10 business days for statutory disqualification.

Q15_LO117: Correct Answer: d
EXPLANATIONS: An amended Form U-4 must be filed in such a case.

Q16_LO117: Correct Answer: d
EXPLANATIONS: Form U-4 is used to register an associated person with FINRA.

Q17_LO117: Correct Answer: c
EXPLANATIONS: A person must wait six months (180 days) before making a fourth attempt.

Q18_LO117: Correct Answer: c
EXPLANATIONS: Marital status is not required on Form U-4.

Q19_LO117: Correct Answer: c
EXPLANATIONS: Filing a U-4 for an exam opens a window of 120 days for exam completion.

Q20_LO117: Correct Answer: b
EXPLANATIONS: An amended Form U-4 must be filed within 10 business days for statutory disqualifications.

Q21_LO117: Correct Answer: b
EXPLANATIONS: Changes must be reported by filing an amended Form U-4 within 30 days.

Q22_LO117: Correct Answer: d
EXPLANATIONS: Clerical persons are exempt from fingerprinting unless they handle cash or securities.

Q23_LO117: Correct Answer: b
EXPLANATIONS: Fingerprint records are submitted for identification and processing by the U.S. attorney general.

Q24_LO117: Correct Answer: b
EXPLANATIONS: Willful misstatements in an application can lead to automatic disqualification.

Q25_LO117: Correct Answer: b
EXPLANATIONS: Customers can access disciplinary history information through BrokerCheck.

Q26_LO117: Correct Answer: d
EXPLANATIONS: While they don't disqualify, failure to disclose bankruptcy or an unsatisfied lien affects registration.

Q27_LO117: Correct Answer: c
EXPLANATIONS: An individual must reapply for FINRA registration if expelled or suspended from another SRO.

Q28_LO117: Correct Answer: a
EXPLANATIONS: Fingerprint records must be submitted annually for such individuals.

Q29_LO117: Correct Answer: b
EXPLANATIONS: An SEC order against the individual is a disqualifying factor.

Q30_LO117: Correct Answer: d
EXPLANATIONS: An amended form must be filed within 30 days after the member becomes aware of standard events.

Q31_LO118: Correct Answer: b
EXPLANATIONS: Nonregistered employees can respond to general, noninvestment questions.

Q32_LO118: Correct Answer: a
EXPLANATIONS: Principals are responsible for responding to written complaints among other duties.

Q33_LO118: Correct Answer: b
EXPLANATIONS: A member firm must employ at least two registered principals.

Q34_LO118: Correct Answer: b
EXPLANATIONS: Passing a principal's exam is required before being appointed as a principal.

Q35_LO118: Correct Answer: d
EXPLANATIONS: Principals are responsible for approving new accounts.

Q36_LO118: Correct Answer: c
EXPLANATIONS: A willful misstatement may result in being barred from the industry for life.

Q37_LO118: Correct Answer: d
EXPLANATIONS: There is no specific education requirement for filling out Form U-4.

Q38_LO118: Correct Answer: d
EXPLANATIONS: Nonregistered personnel are not permitted to engage in investment banking.

Q39_LO118: Correct Answer: d
EXPLANATIONS: There are several principal's exams covering specific areas of securities and investment banking.

Q40_LO118: Correct Answer: d
EXPLANATIONS: Lying on Form U-4 is a good way to end a career before it starts.

Q41_LO118: Correct Answer: d
EXPLANATIONS: Complete and truthful disclosure is required on Form U-4.

Q42_LO118: Correct Answer: b
EXPLANATIONS: Nonregistered personnel can respond to general, noninvestment questions.

Q43_LO118: Correct Answer: b
EXPLANATIONS: A person must wait 30 days before making a second attempt at an exam.

Q44_LO118: Correct Answer: c
EXPLANATIONS: Principals review trading activity to ensure compliance with regulations.

Q45_LO118: Correct Answer: d
EXPLANATIONS: Nonregistered personnel are not permitted to engage in investment banking.

Q46_LO118: Correct Answer: b
EXPLANATIONS: Nonregistered employees can respond to general, noninvestment questions.

Q47_LO118: Correct Answer: c
EXPLANATIONS: Nonregistered persons may not engage in investment banking.

Q48_LO118: Correct Answer: a
EXPLANATIONS: Principals are responsible for handling written complaints.

Q49_LO118: Correct Answer: b
EXPLANATIONS: A member firm must employ at least two registered principals.

Q50_LO118: Correct Answer: b
EXPLANATIONS: Principals approve new accounts.

Q51_LO118: Correct Answer: c
EXPLANATIONS: A registered representative must pass one of the principal's exams.

Q52_LO118: Correct Answer: b
EXPLANATIONS: Sponsorship by a broker-dealer is a requirement.

Q53_LO118: Correct Answer: b
EXPLANATIONS: A willful misstatement may result in being barred from the industry for life.

Q54_LO118: Correct Answer: b
EXPLANATIONS: A member firm must employ at least two registered principals.

Q55_LO118: Correct Answer: b
EXPLANATIONS: Principals approve new accounts.

Q56_LO118: Correct Answer: c
EXPLANATIONS: A registered representative must pass one of the principal's exams.

Q57_LO118: Correct Answer: b
EXPLANATIONS: Sponsorship by a broker-dealer is a requirement.

Q58_LO118: Correct Answer: b
EXPLANATIONS: A willful misstatement may result in being barred from the industry for life.

Q59_LO118: Correct Answer: a
EXPLANATIONS: Fingerprint records must be submitted annually for such individuals.

Q60_LO118: Correct Answer: b
EXPLANATIONS: An SEC order against the individual is a disqualifying factor.

Q61_LO119: Correct Answer: b
EXPLANATIONS: Form U-5 must be filed within 30 days of termination.

Q62_LO119: Correct Answer: b
EXPLANATIONS: Failure to file on time results in a late filing fee being assessed.

Q63_LO119: Correct Answer: d
EXPLANATIONS: There are five reasons for termination listed on the form.

Q64_LO119: Correct Answer: c
EXPLANATIONS: A voluntary resignation is assumed to have no impact on future eligibility.

Q65_LO119: Correct Answer: b
EXPLANATIONS: An amendment must be filed within 10 business days of discovery.

Q66_LO119: Correct Answer: b
EXPLANATIONS: Regulators retain jurisdiction for two years, and retesting may be required after that period.

Q67_LO119: Correct Answer: b
EXPLANATIONS: Regulators retain jurisdiction for two years after a full termination.

Q68_LO119: Correct Answer: b
EXPLANATIONS: Within two years, a person may affiliate without requalifying.

Q69_LO119: Correct Answer: c
EXPLANATIONS: Passing the SIE allows for a person to take a top-off exam.

Q70_LO119: Correct Answer: c
EXPLANATIONS: If more than four years elapse, the SIE must be retaken.

Q71_LO119: Correct Answer: c
EXPLANATIONS: The special inactive status lasts for 90 days after leaving military service.

Q72_LO119: Correct Answer: d
EXPLANATIONS: The two-year time frame begins after 90 days from leaving military service.

Q73_LO119: Correct Answer: a
EXPLANATIONS: Continuing commissions may be allowed for existing business relationships.

Q74_LO119: Correct Answer: b
EXPLANATIONS: Continuing commissions are typically allowed for retirees.

Q75_LO119: Correct Answer: c
EXPLANATIONS: Form U-5 is a termination notification filed with the CRD.

Q76_LO119: Correct Answer: b
EXPLANATIONS: Form U-5 must be filed within 30 calendar days of termination.

Q77_LO119: Correct Answer: c
EXPLANATIONS: A late filing fee will be assessed against the member.

Q78_LO119: Correct Answer: d
EXPLANATIONS: There are five reasons listed: Discharged, Permitted to resign, Deceased, Voluntary, Other.

Q79_LO119: Correct Answer: c
EXPLANATIONS: A voluntary resignation is assumed to be under circumstances that will not affect future eligibility for employment within the industry.

Q80_LO119: Correct Answer: b
EXPLANATIONS: Details surrounding the termination must be disclosed.

Q81_LO119: Correct Answer: b
EXPLANATIONS: An amendment must be filed within 10 business days of discovery.

Q82_LO119: Correct Answer: b
EXPLANATIONS: Regulators retain jurisdiction for two years after a full termination.

Q83_LO119: Correct Answer: a
EXPLANATIONS: Passing a top-off exam after the SIE allows for affiliation without requalifying.

Q84_LO119: Correct Answer: a
EXPLANATIONS: Retaking the SIE is required.

Q85_LO119: Correct Answer: c
EXPLANATIONS: The license is placed in a special inactive status during regular military service.

Q86_LO119: Correct Answer: c
EXPLANATIONS: It begins 90 days after termination.

Q87_LO119: Correct Answer: d
EXPLANATIONS: Continuing commissions may be allowed indefinitely for existing business relationships.

Q88_LO119: Correct Answer: b
EXPLANATIONS: Form U-5 is filed when a person resigns or is terminated from a member firm.

Q89_LO119: Correct Answer: c
EXPLANATIONS: It assumes normal circumstances for future employment.

Q90_LO119: Correct Answer: c
EXPLANATIONS: A copy of Form U-5 must be provided.

Q91_LO120: Correct Answer: b
EXPLANATIONS: The Firm Element requires member firms to prepare an annual training plan.

Q92_LO120: Correct Answer: c
EXPLANATIONS: Firm Element CE must be completed by December 31, unless the member firm specifies an earlier date.

Q93_LO120: Correct Answer: b
EXPLANATIONS: Failure may result in the suspension of a representative's license.

Q94_LO120: Correct Answer: c
EXPLANATIONS: It should be related to the firm's normal business activities.

Q95_LO120: Correct Answer: c
EXPLANATIONS: It should be done within 120 days of the second registration anniversary.

Q96_LO120: Correct Answer: c
EXPLANATIONS: FINRA will deactivate the person's registration until the requirements are met.

Q97_LO120: Correct Answer: c
EXPLANATIONS: A complaint is a written statement alleging a grievance arising out of a securities transaction.

Q98_LO120: Correct Answer: b
EXPLANATIONS: It should be done within 15 days of the end of each calendar quarter.

Q99_LO120: Correct Answer: b
EXPLANATIONS: No further action is needed.

Q100_LO120: Correct Answer: b
EXPLANATIONS: It is to inform the employing BD, not to seek regulatory approval.

Q101_LO120: Correct Answer: c
EXPLANATIONS: It is not allowed without the employing BD's knowledge.

Q102_LO120: Correct Answer: c
EXPLANATIONS: Passive investments include limited partnership units or investment company shares.

Q103_LO120: Correct Answer: a
EXPLANATIONS: A passive investment for the person's own account does not require notice.

Q104_LO120: Correct Answer: b
EXPLANATIONS: The firm has the right to reject or restrict any outside affiliation if a conflict of interest is perceived.

Q105_LO120: Correct Answer: d
EXPLANATIONS: It is designed to enhance regulatory knowledge of registered persons.

Q106_LO120: Correct Answer: b
EXPLANATIONS: The firm element aims at regulatory compliance.

Q107_LO120: Correct Answer: c
EXPLANATIONS: The firm element must be completed by December 31.

Q108_LO120: Correct Answer: c
EXPLANATIONS: Failure may result in the suspension of a representative's license.

Q109_LO120: Correct Answer: b
EXPLANATIONS: Recent regulatory developments are a key consideration.

Q110_LO120: Correct Answer: c
EXPLANATIONS: It must be completed every three years.

Q111_LO120: Correct Answer: c
EXPLANATIONS: Registration will be deactivated until the requirements are met.

Q112_LO120: Correct Answer: d
EXPLANATIONS: It must be completed within 120 days.

Q113_LO120: Correct Answer: c
EXPLANATIONS: The content is determined by FINRA.

Q114_LO120: Correct Answer: b
EXPLANATIONS: Proper personnel should be notified.

Q115_LO120: Correct Answer: b
EXPLANATIONS: It is a written statement by a customer alleging a grievance.

Q116_LO120: Correct Answer: d
EXPLANATIONS: It must be filed within 15 days of the end of each calendar quarter.

Q117_LO120: Correct Answer: b
EXPLANATIONS: Passive investments, such as purchasing limited partnership units, are not considered outside business activities.

Q118_LO120: Correct Answer: a
EXPLANATIONS: Prior written notice to the member is required.

Q119_LO120: Correct Answer: b
EXPLANATIONS: The firm has the right to reject or restrict affiliations if a conflict of interest exists.

Q120_LO120: Correct Answer: c
EXPLANATIONS: Purchasing limited partnership units is considered a passive investment.

Q121_LO121: Correct Answer: d
EXPLANATIONS: Private securities transactions are also known as selling away.

Q122_LO121: Correct Answer: c
EXPLANATIONS: Prior written notice to the employer is required.

Q123_LO121: Correct Answer: c
EXPLANATIONS: The notice must include transaction details and the associated person's proposed role.

Q124_LO121: Correct Answer: b
EXPLANATIONS: The member can approve or disapprove the associated person's participation.

Q125_LO121: Correct Answer: a
EXPLANATIONS: The employing member firm is responsible for supervision.

Q126_LO121: Correct Answer: b
EXPLANATIONS: Transactions on behalf of immediate family members with no compensation are excluded.

Q127_LO121: Correct Answer: c
EXPLANATIONS: An employer BD may prohibit participation.

Q128_LO121: Correct Answer: d
EXPLANATIONS: The employing member firm is responsible for supervision.

Q129_LO121: Correct Answer: c
EXPLANATIONS: The limit is currently $100 per year.

Q130_LO121: Correct Answer: a
EXPLANATIONS: Occasional noncash expenditures are exceptions.

Q131_LO121: Correct Answer: c
EXPLANATIONS: If a representative accompanies the recipient, it is allowed as normal business entertainment.

Q132_LO121: Correct Answer: c
EXPLANATIONS: Advertising items with logos are excluded.

Q133_LO121: Correct Answer: b
EXPLANATIONS: Items like pens, mouse pads, etc., carrying the firm's logo are considered reminder advertising.

Q134_LO121: Correct Answer: d
EXPLANATIONS: It must be filed within 15 days of the end of each calendar quarter.

Q135_LO121: Correct Answer: c
EXPLANATIONS: The employing member must treat the transaction as if it is being done on its own behalf.

Q136_LO122: Correct Answer: b
EXPLANATIONS: The rules aim to preserve investor confidence and market integrity.

Q137_LO122: Correct Answer: c
EXPLANATIONS: FINRA enforces MSRB Rule G-37 because the MSRB has no enforcement capability.

Q138_LO122: Correct Answer: b
EXPLANATIONS: It addresses negotiated underwritings and financial advisory work.

Q139_LO122: Correct Answer: b
EXPLANATIONS: The prohibition is for two years.

Q140_LO122: Correct Answer: d
EXPLANATIONS: The prohibition includes the municipal firm, MFPs, and any individual associated with the firm.

Q141_LO122: Correct Answer: c
EXPLANATIONS: An MFP is a person engaged in municipal securities activities.

Q142_LO122: Correct Answer: c
EXPLANATIONS: MFPs can make contributions of up to $250 per election.

Q143_LO122: Correct Answer: b
EXPLANATIONS: The $250 exemption applies to MFPs.

Q144_LO122: Correct Answer: a
EXPLANATIONS: The exemption does not apply to contributions made by municipal firms.

Q145_LO122: Correct Answer: b
EXPLANATIONS: It aims to prevent pay-to-play practices.

Q146_LO122: Correct Answer: c
EXPLANATIONS: Member firm's SRO approval is required for home-based offices.

Q147_LO122: Correct Answer: c
EXPLANATIONS: All normal business activities, including customer orders, are permitted.

Q148_LO122: Correct Answer: c
EXPLANATIONS: Any normal business activity is subject to review.

Q149_LO122: Correct Answer: c
EXPLANATIONS: They may be advertised in any normal manner, including business cards and public media.

Q150_LO122: Correct Answer: c
EXPLANATIONS: Principals, compliance officers, and regulators may conduct such visits.

Q151_LO122: Correct Answer: b
EXPLANATIONS: The primary goal is to preserve investor confidence and market integrity.

Q152_LO122: Correct Answer: c
EXPLANATIONS: MSRB rules, including Rule G-37, are enforced by FINRA.

Q153_LO122: Correct Answer: b
EXPLANATIONS: The rule primarily addresses pay-to-play practices in municipal securities business.

Q154_LO122: Correct Answer: b
EXPLANATIONS: Rule G-37 prohibits engagement for two years after a contribution.

Q155_LO122: Correct Answer: c
EXPLANATIONS: MFPs are associated persons engaged in various activities related to municipal securities.

Q156_LO122: Correct Answer: a
EXPLANATIONS: Clerical or ministerial functions exclude an associated person from being an MFP.

Q157_LO122: Correct Answer: c
EXPLANATIONS: MFPs are permitted contributions of up to $250 per election.

Q158_LO122: Correct Answer: c
EXPLANATIONS: Municipal firms are not eligible for the de minimis exemption.

Q159_LO122: Correct Answer: b
EXPLANATIONS: Selling away refers to private securities transactions outside regular business.

Q160_LO122: Correct Answer: c
EXPLANATIONS: Prior written notice to the employer is required.

Q161_LO122: Correct Answer: b
EXPLANATIONS: The member can approve or disapprove the associated person's participation.
Q162_LO122: Correct Answer: a
EXPLANATIONS: The employing member firm is responsible for supervision.
Q163_LO122: Correct Answer: c
EXPLANATIONS: An employer BD may prohibit participation.

Q164_LO122: Correct Answer: c
EXPLANATIONS: Advertising items with logos are excluded.

Q165_LO122: Correct Answer: c
EXPLANATIONS: The employing member must treat the transaction as if it is being done on its own behalf.

:

********End of All Tests ********

www.ingramcontent.com/pod-product-compliance
Lightning Source LLC
LaVergne TN
LVHW070906210926
848482LV00017B/1005
* 9 7 9 8 8 9 2 3 3 1 3 7 1 *